THE PARANORMAL
AN ILLUSTRATED ENCYCLOPEDIA

Also by Stuart Gordon

Smile on the Void
Fire in the Abyss
Archon
The Hidden World
The Mask
Down the Drain

THE PARANORMAL AN ILLUSTRATED ENCYCLOPEDIA

Stuart Gordon

BCA
LONDON · NEW YORK · SYDNEY · TORONTO

This edition published 1992
by BCA
by arrangement with
HEADLINE BOOK PUBLISHING, PLC

CN 2847

First published in 1992
by HEADLINE BOOK PUBLISHING PLC

10 9 8 7 6 5 4 3 2 1

Phototypeset by Intype, London
Printed and bound in Great Britain by
Butler and Tanner Ltd, Frome

This book is for my father,
George Gordon of Cairnfield –
for your help and patience over many years.

Acknowledgements

Particular thanks are due to Constance Marcham of the Findhorn Foundation Library for the long-term loan of source material; also to Alan Senior of Rafford for letting me plunder his library.

Thanks are also due to the many writers, explorers, and encyclopedists who have been this way before, the debt to whom will be obvious from the text.

And only Pam, my wife, knows how much she had to put up with during the time it took to compile this book.

Contents

Introduction: the Mystery

> Man's perceptions are not bounded by organs of perception; he perceives more than sense (tho' ever so acute) can discover.
>
> William Blake, *There is No Natural Religion* (1788)

Hands up anyone who doesn't *secretly* believe in ghosts! Is there anyone alive who has never, lying awake and alone in bed on a dark night, sensed the presence of *something else* hovering invisibly nearby? Is there anyone who has never eyed the stars with wonder, or who has deliberately walked under a ladder without a tingle of fear, or who has thought *Friday the 13th* just another day? Who has never suddenly thought about someone then unexpectedly met them, heard of premonitions that came true, or been tempted to have their fortune told by the palmist at a fair? Who never thrilled as a child to fairy tales, or to tales of ancient haunted sites? Who can claim *absolute certainty* that all U F O reports are hoaxes; that all ouija-board messages are fraudulent; or that psychokinetic spoon-bending on TV is just stage-magicianship?

If you are such a person, are you being wholly honest with yourself? Perhaps you just don't want to admit that the universe is not only odd, but odder than we realise. Perhaps you need to believe that life holds no mystery at all, and that already we know everything that needs to be known.

Such an attitude is understandable. For we are born, live and die alongside a mystery which, preoccupied as we are with the trials of everyday life, we forget or deny. We are encouraged to do so not only out of our fear of the unknown but by social and moral pressures including a prevalent scientific contempt for whatever cannot be weighed and measured in *material* terms.

Yet despite our supposed advances as a civilisation the truth of things remains as obscure to us as once it was to Neanderthal Man. The Mystery remains so vast that most of the terms we use to describe phenomena beyond scientific recognition only outline our persistent ignorance and confusion.

Such terms – occult, supernatural, paranormal – suggest phenomena, experiences and events, real or imagined, beyond the reach of consensus reality or hope of scientific validation. To some they warn of madness, delusion or spiritual danger. To others they speak of essential truths we must face if we are to progress (and survive) individually or as a species.

To those holding this latter view it seems especially important now, as we charge headlong through one of the most critical and tumultuous eras in recorded human history, that we enter regions impossible to penetrate with purely material transport. If not, the physical walls we have built about ourselves will collapse on us, as in the myths of the Flood or the Tower of Babel.

We pay a high price for 'civilisation'. To gain it, we reject natural contact with life's root forces. The culprit is rational consciousness.

There is nothing wrong as such with this useful faculty. The problem is that, since it gained power, increasingly it interprets the world in its own manipulative image, denying or demonising any other processes that fail to fit its cold definitions – such as our common intuition of the world as Gaia: a living being and mystery of which we are but a (responsible?) part.

Yet no one paradigm endures forever. Today, despite or because of our spoliation of the planet, increasingly people seek knowledge of the realms sometimes called 'paranormal'. The uneasy sensation grows in many that for a mess of mortgage and Porsche we have sold ourselves short, denying all truths that fail to fit materialist dogma.

We have gone dangerously far down the road opened up centuries ago when Faust first struck his rational deal with Mephistopheles.

For these truths have not gone away. They knock in us all the time. The longer we ignore them, the louder they get. Can you hear what they say? *'We've been here all along! We are part of you, and you of us!'*

For what we call 'paranormal' is not only *more* 'normal' than we admit; it *is* normal. The *para*normality lies in our refusal to admit it.

Habitually we erect false barriers between the phenomena we choose to accept and those we do not. Usually we fail even to acknowledge that the choice exists. We practise a spiritual apartheid in our common conspiracy (called 'society') to agree upon a mutually convenient, fixed worldview.

This *material* worldview is one that helps trains to run on time, but it lacks deeper logic. It is a convention that too easily becomes tyrannical and blinding. Its lack of logic is seen in the variance between cultures as to what is 'normal'. Reincarnation is part and parcel of the ordinary Hindu worldview; to the Christian, rebirth is held to occur, but not in this world; to others, reincarnation is but a 'paranormal' or superstitious theory, like a belief in ghosts.

Yet again: who doesn't *secretly* believe in ghosts?

Today the forward frontiers of what was once seemingly solid material science dissolve into new yet curiously familiar patterns. Chaos Theory, quantum mechanics, quarks called 'Strangeness' and 'Charm', particles that arrive before they begin, reports of UFO entities behaving oddly like the beings once called fairies? It begins to seem as if our universe is, as our ancestors always thought, shared by intelligences identified under many names – before we denied them. And what do they say? *'We've been here all along! We are part of you, and you of us!'* Exploring the 'paranormal' is about exploring ourselves.

Yet before entering this world of apparently strange concepts, events, folk and experiences, it must be said that there is no real conflict between science – *true* science – and those phenomena called 'paranormal'.

Newton and Kepler knew that. Newton sought angelic contact as well as discovering the Law of Gravity. And Kepler's Laws of Planetary motion were virtually an accidental byproduct of his search to prove that the planets danced according to Pythagorean harmony – the Song of the Spheres.

Perhaps not one or the other but *both* approaches are fruitful: angels and gravity; mathematical law and the singing harmony of a living, vibrant, intelligent universe; reason and intuition; and 'normal' and 'paranormal'.

For calling something 'paranormal' describes not the phenomenon but the point of view of the witness. Where this is preconceived and rigid, then conflict, rejection and denial arise. If the mind is open to strangeness and charm, and willing to learn, then unfamiliar sensations and confusions vie with awe, terror, delight, doubt and wonder – all experiences we knew as children . . . only to forget.

Now why did we ever do that?

Maybe, before it's too late, we can rediscover ourselves. For we've been here all along, strangers to ourselves, dwellers not only on the threshold of, but within the very heart of, the Mystery. So read on . . .

Note on sources and usage

Little of the conceptual material in this encyclopedia is original. For the most part I have drawn on easily available, widely published sources. Where relevant or useful for further study, these are referred to directly following each entry. Publication dates and publishers given for the works thus cited may not always be of the original edition, but of the edition used in research. Other useful texts are listed under those referred to by numbers in the entry.

Given the A–Z format and the interconnection of many subjects detailed under particular headings, repetition is inevitable. Where possible this has been reduced by extensive cross-referencing. So **Ley lines** cross-refers to **black dogs, dowsing, dragon, earth-spirit, geomancy, Lethbridge, megalithic mysteries, U F Os**, etc. Where such references are not headlined, they are **highlighted** in the text via the terms set in bold face.

A

ABDUCTIONS (*See* **ANCIENT ASTRONAUTS, FAIRIES, UFOs**) Tales of humans abducted by alien beings are as old as that of the prophet **Enoch** who 'walked with God and was not' and as new as the celebrated case of Betty and Barney Hill – a case typifying many of the increasing numbers of 'UFO'-abductions reported. Driving through the bleak White Mountains of New Hampshire one night in September 1961, this couple saw a bright light descending erratically towards them, and stopped. The light resolved into a hovering pancake-like object ringed with windows through which Barney saw **humanoid** figures in 'shiny black uniform'. Shocked, he drove on. They got home to Portsmouth on the Atlantic coast at dawn. Soon Betty began dreaming they had been seized by the UFO's humanoid crew, taken on board, separated, and medically examined. Reporting the encounter to UFO investigators, they realised they'd 'lost' two hours – at the speed Barney usually drove they should have got home at least two hours earlier. Meanwhile Barney's ulcer got worse; he became exhausted and depressed. His doctor suggested **hypnosis** to learn what, if anything, had happened during the 'lost' two hours. Under hypnosis (at their own cost) they both told a tale matching Betty's dream-'memory'. They recalled being taken on board the circular craft by the UFO **entities** and placed in separate rooms. Betty's 'examination' involved the removal of her dress. Samples of her hair, skin, ear-wax and fingernails were taken; a 'pregnancy test' involved the jabbing of a needle into her navel. Recollecting seeing a star map showing the aliens' 'home port', Betty drew it from memory. Later schoolteacher Marjorie Fish suggested it showed the stars zeta–1 and zeta–2 Reticuli, thirty-seven light years from Earth.

Key aspects of their tale recur again and again in such reports. These are: (1) amnesia after the abduction; (2) sexual/medical examination forced on abductees; (3) the bald heads, slit mouths, almond eyes and pointed chins of the abductors; (4) the circular nature of the craft or realm into which abductees are seized; and (5) nervous breakdown. Paradoxical sensations of horror, yearning, familiarity and strangeness are often reported. 'They swarmed at me, climbing up out of my unconscious,' writes Whitley **Streiber** of his 'visitors' in his account (*see below*) of such an abduction.[1]

Another well-known account concerns Brazilian farmer Antonio Villas-Boas. Late one night in October 1957 he was ploughing alone on his tractor when a red star above him grew into an egg-like object that landed softly. His tractor engine died (electrical failures in such encounters are often reported); he was caught by four 'men', taken on board the UFO, stripped, washed and left alone in a room. A small naked blonde thin-lipped blue-eyed woman entered. After they made love a man entered. The woman smiled, pointed at her belly then at the sky and followed the man out. Allowed to dress, Villas-Boas was taken to another room where crew members sat 'growling' at each other. Seeing what looked like a clock, he tried to steal it as evidence of the event . . . much as Betty Hill had tried to get her captors to let her take a 'book' she saw inside their craft. Failing, he was released with no evidence other than his own memory.[2]

Streiber's account of abduction by 'visitors' in rural upstate New York in December 1985 compares with older abduction tales of a sort once blamed on **fairies, demons** or **angels**. He points out that the experience is not new, and that the entities responsible have long been known under a variety of guises. Under hypnosis he recalled being enticed out of his house into a 'black iron cot' which levitated him into a little round room. Here he underwent medical examination including sexual interference. He reports four types of entity: the first robot-like; the second, short, stocky beings in blue coveralls (the 'good army'); the third, delicate beings with vestigial mouth, nose and mesmerising black slanted eyes; the fourth, likewise bald and small but with round black button-like eyes. His 'examination' was overseen by a third-category female with yellow-brown leathery skin. She seemd old, wise and insect-like: later he associated her big slanted eyes with images of the Sumerian goddess Ishtar.

Streiber implies that these entities are physically 'real' yet also in some way rooted in the human unconscious. They can enter the mind, affect perception, and draw the **soul** from the body; they communicate mostly by means of **symbol** and demonstration. He felt they have occupied Earth for a long time and may be involved with human evolution. They said this world 'is a school' and that they 'recycle souls'. Though terrified of them, he felt they are equally scared of us: his fear was mixed with yearning for communion. Rejecting the extraterrestrial hypothesis he examines several theories: that they are: (1) a modern manifestation of the 'fairy' race; (2) **spirits** of the dead; (3) creations of the collective unconscious; (4) from other **dimensions**; and (5) an archaic, group-minded, insectile species sharing planet Earth with us – more ancient, in some ways superior, yet afraid of human unpredictability. It may be that they seek to transform us – or that through them we seek unconsciously to transform ourselves. Streiber tells how shaken he was to realise such events had affected him since childhood, but that his fear had imposed amnesia on him, the events remaining hidden behind '**screen memories**' until his memory was released under hypnosis.

Whatever the truth of his account, it strikes a deep chord. The sense of contact with or proximity to alien species, fearful yet glamorous, runs through all recorded human folklore. Certain beliefs are common to every age and culture. One is that the abducting species desires sexual union with humanity: (1) to create a superior hybrid race; or (2) to ensure racial survival by interbreeding. A third category involves tales of (typically) poets (True Thomas), magicians (**Merlin**), or sacred leaders (King **Arthur**) being removed into another realm or dimension, where they are not dead, but will return when required by racial need or if released by correct **ritual**.

Belief in hybridism dates back to Genesis vi where: 'the sons of God saw the daughters of men, that they were fair; and they took them wives', so that 'there were giants in the earth in those days' The apocryphal Book of **Enoch**, excluded from the Bible for telling how **angels** called the **Watchers** mated with humanity, describes what looks like extraterrestrial teachers or colonists 'going native'. The biological compatibility thus assumed begs more complex questions.[3]

The 'survival' hypothesis is seen in Celtic tales of fairies stealing human babies and leaving changelings. This may represent the guerrilla tactics of a defeated older race stealing human infants – or seed – to survive by breeding themselves into the conquering stock. Thus perhaps the sexual aspect of abduction cases as reported above.

The third category relates to modern tales of UFO abductions. Celtic myth is rich in tales of people kidnapped by fairies. The fate of Robert Kirk, a seventeenth-century Scots minister, author of *The Secret Commonwealth* – an account of the faery realm, its organisation and the intelligences that control it – illustrates this theme. Found dead on a fairy knowe, Kirk was (due to his reputation as one in contact with fairies) said to be not dead, but merely translated into the fairy realm, from which he'd return alive were the proper rites undertaken immediately. Of course, they were not.

Likewise the tale of True Thomas (Thomas the Rhymer, medieval Scots poet and prophet). Lying one day on 'Huntlie bank', he saw a lady riding down 'by the Eildon Tree'. Greeted by him as the 'Queen of Heaven', she says she is only 'the queen of fair Elfland'. Warned not to kiss her, of course he does. 'Now, ye maun go wi' me,' she said, 'And ye maun serve me seven years.' Taking him up on her milk-white steed, she carries him away from 'living land' over rushing rivers of blood, through desert and 'mirk mirk night' to 'fair Elfland', warning him, 'if you speak word in Elflyn land, Ye'll never get back to your ain countrie.' He protests, 'My tongue is mine ain,' – but she tells him to hold his peace. Subsequently:

> He has gotten a coat of the elven cloth,
> And a pair of shoes of velvet green,
> And till seven years were gane and past,
> True Thomas on earth was never seen.[12]

Note the 'seven years'. Common to such tales is the relativity of time. The abductee experiences his visit to the UFO or otherworld as lasting but hours, yet on return to the human world he finds 'seven years' have passed, or perhaps 'a hundred years and a day'. The amnesia reported by Betty and Barney Hill – their 'lost two hours' – is a modern description of the same experience. Old Irish tales of magical sea voyages are also apt. Back from one such journey the mariners are warned not to set foot on the land which, to them, they left only months earlier, for over a century has passed. One sailor, ignoring the warning, wades ashore, and crumbles into dust. This description of a **relativity** time effect dates from the eighth century.

Abductions, as reported by Streiber, the Hills and others, are but the modern perception, clad in terms of space-travel, UFOs, etc., of an age-old phenomenon which, whether seen as objectively factual or as arising from a collective subconscious perception of a universe more mysterious than daily sense acknowledges, remains *consistent* . . . but with *what*? The events occur at night to people alone at the time. Phantom steeds are replaced by UFOs. The abductions lead to time lapses, confusion, and encounter with entities who, whatever their purpose, *are never as unfamiliar as we might wish*.

It seems they want to tell us something about ourselves that we need to know. Also, they seem scared to reveal themselves too clearly. They treat us with kid gloves, as if somehow we *endanger* them.

1. *Communion*, Whitley Streiber, Arrow Books, London 1988, p. 95
2. *Dimensions*, Jacques Vallée, Sphere Books, London 1990, pp. 139–40
3. *Forbidden Mysteries of Enoch*, ed. Elizabeth Clare Prophet, Summit University Press, USA 1984 (Laurence translation of *Enoch*)
4. *The Ballad of Thomas the Rhymer* (anon.), as in *The Edinburgh Book of Scottish Verse*, ed. W. MacNeile Dixon, Meiklejohn and Holden, London 1910

ABOMINABLE SNOWMAN (*See* **ALIEN ANIMALS**) The Abominable Snowman, or yeti, is the best-known of many hairy men-apes said to survive in remote mountain or jungle regions. Evidence for the yeti depends on folk-tales and on sightings by mountaineers or folk living by Himalayan snowfields said to be the creature's habitat.

Local tales are legion. At Thyangboche monastery by Mount Everest the abbot matter-of-factly tells how yeti visit the monastery gardens.[1] In 1974 a Sherpa girl, Lakhpa Domani, met a yeti while tending yaks at Pheriche in Nepal. It was a huge apelike creature with black and red-brown hair, large eyes and prominent cheekbones. It carried her off, but dropped her as she struggled, then attacked the yaks, killing two before making off. In January 1987 a youth in northern Kashmir was attacked by a two-legged four-foot tall hairy creature. It ran away, squealing, after he hit it with his fire-pot. Two other villagers witnessed its flight: it jumped a ditch in a man-like way. The Nepalese say there are different types of yeti: the small *yeh-teh*, the larger *meh-teh* and the giant *dzu-teh*.[2]

The first report to the West came in 1832. The UK Resident Officer in Nepal described how his porters fled a hairy beast they called the *rakshas*, 'demon', later telling him that similar wild men had been known and feared for centuries.[3] Westerners saw footprints in 1887, as did a British army officer 21,000 feet up Everest in 1921. F. S. Smythe's photographs of yeti prints were taken at 16,500 feet in 1937. In 1951, crossing the Menlung glacier, UK climber Eric Shipton found tracks in the snow. His photographs show a print as long as his ice-axe, with definite toe formation – *too* definite, some say. Maybe his account began as a joke maintained once it was taken seriously. Yet his partner, surgeon Michael Ward, insisted that the spoor was authentic. Still the reports came in. In 1970 climber Don Whillans one night on Annapurna found footprints in the snow. Later he sensed the creature was still about and looked out of his tent. In bright moonlight he saw a shape bounding into a snow-covered clump of trees. Through binoculars he saw a black ape-like beast. 'Then, quite suddenly, it was almost as if it realised it was being watched, it shot across the whole slope of the mountain.[4]

In 1972 a US expedition found footprints so clear they took plastercasts; in 1973 Lord Hunt (who led the 1953 Everest expedition, and who had previously heard 'high-pitched yelping cries' high in the mountains) found prints: his 1978 pictures show footprints fourteen inches long and seven inches wide. He believes in, 'an unidentified creature still to be discovered'.

No yeti bodies have been found. 'Yeti scalps' held in some Himalayan monasteries are probably made of goatskin, made up to *represent* the yeti in ritual dances. Yet lack of evidence does not prove lack of yeti. Gorilla or orang-utan are not regarded as mythical: they have been shot, captured and so on. The yeti, if real, is a shy creature living amid a wilderness at great height. There is nothing unbelievable about the yeti save in the lack of firm evidence. The local reports of several different species suggests ape-like creatures long ago adapted to living in regions beyond the easy reach of (and extermination by) *homo sapiens*. Given the fate of other wild species, is it odd that the yeti remains secretive?

1. *Arthur Clarke's Mysterious World*, Simon Welfare and John Fairley, Fontana, London 1982, p. 19
2. *Modern Mysteries of the World*, Janet and Colin Bord, Grafton, London 1989
3. *The Directory of Possibilities*, eds Wilson and Grant, Corgi, London 1982
4. *op. cit.* ref. 2, p. 199

ABORIGINES (*See* **NEANDERTHAL MAN**) Isolated on Australia over 30,000 years ago, uninfluenced by the outside world prior to the eighteenth century, Aboriginal culture is too easily dismissed as 'primitive'. In their mythic attitude to the world the Aborigines retain much forgotten elswhere, including powers now dismissed by or atrophied in 'civilised' humankind. Certainly, the implicit religiosity of their relationship with the natural world embodies beliefs once universal, the echoes of which linger on elsewhere. Like the ancient Egyptians (and **Goethe**), they say Man has two souls. The 'real' one is the eternal soul of the *Dreamtime* (**collective unconscious**); the other appears 'in **dreams**, (and) may take up its abode within another person after its owner's death, or may lie in the bush and play tricks'.[1] They claim the Dreamtime spirits were men who did not vanish but married into humanity. They say that once a tree joined Earth to Heaven, as in the Norse World-Tree, Yggdrasil, or in the **Tree of Life** of the **Qabalists**. Nomadic, they hold material goods to be potentially malign, harming their possessors unless always in motion.

Such goods were once continually traded in a vast continent-wide game, the land itself the gaming-board, all its inhabitants players. The value of the goods exchanged was not in material gain but in token of intent – to trade again, meet again, sing, dance, fix frontiers and share ideas.

What to the Westerner is trackless desert ('Outback') is still to the Aborigine a land crisscrossed by the 'Songlines' – psychic highways that men travel singing the songs of their ancestors, thus reaffirming the energies of the past in the ever-living present.[2] As in **Arthurian** psychomyth, Land and King and People are One.

Earlier than any other known culture they knew how to smelt yellow hydrated iron oxide to produce red ochre (haematite: 'blood of the earth'). This, a form of magnetite (lodestone), involved in the migratory sense of **birds** and beasts, was used by Neanderthal Man to pack the bodies of the dead before burial. The Outback's sacred red ochre sites, they claim, were laid down in the Dreamtime: only old men may approach them, crawling on all fours. Does their respect for red ochre involve their capacity to navigate trackless desert (via the Songlines) and find water in it? Certainly they **dowse** without need of a 'dowsing rod', and maintain other connections with the natural world lost to the rest of us. Coastal Aborigines say that the **dolphin** has always helped Man. Some still ask the dolphin to help them catch fish. They beat the water with bits of wood; the dolphins respond by driving fish in from the sea.

Anthropologist A. P. Elkin found them often aware of events at their homes, even if far away. Their assurance is absolute. 'A man will suddenly announce that his father is dead, that his wife had given birth to a child, or that there is some trouble in his country. He is so sure of his facts that he would return at once if he could.'[3] Such **telepathy** reminds one of the **second sight** of the Highland Gael – a faculty now largely lost to urbanised Man.

Aboriginal respect for the Dreamtime exemplifies a world-view once universal. Modern **Freudian** or **Jungian** dream-analysis restates techniques known to the Aborigines, the **Senoi** of Malaysia, and many other 'primitive' folk who remember much we've forgotten.

Take the *Wondjina*. These sacred anthropomorphic figures are found in the Outback, painted on exposed rock, faces and shoulders white, eyes and nose shown in black. A red band always circles their heads like a halo or helmet. This halo bears marks like writing – marks also found on rock carvings in South America.

The Aborigines say the Wondjina were folk who once came to Australia to establish civilisation. The artists long ago returned to the sky, now to be seen at night as lights moving amid the heavens. These rock-paintings are over 10,000 years old. Aborigines don't find the Wondjina mysterious. Mystery arises only when simple truth is denied or confused by new cultural demands. To a man in the desert (of time as well as space) the Wondjina are as real as kangaroos, or 4-wheel-drive Datsuns. One reality does not deny another. Aboriginal Time is not serial, but more a kind of lake allowing movement in any direction.

Einstein, Heisenberg, Planck and their **quantum** successors agree.

1. *The Secret Life of Humans*, Stan Gooch, Dent, London 1981, p. 29
2. *The Songlines*, Bruce Chatwin, Pan, London 1988, p. 63
3. *Beyond Supernature*, Lyall Watson, Hodder and Stoughton, London 1986; *see The Australian Aborigines*, A. P. Elkin, Angus and Robertson, Sydney 1942

ABRAHAMSEN, Aron (1921–) (*See* **POLE SHIFT, PSYCHIC ARCHAEOLOGY**) This Norwegian **psychic** emigrated to the USA in 1939 and settled in Everett, Washington State. In 1970 he abandoned his engineering work and took up esoteric ministry. His *Readings on Earth Changes* predicted California Bay Area earthquakes for 1977. These failed to occur. Yet he succesfully predicted discovery of what may be North America's oldest human culture.

In 1972 Jeffrey **Goodman**, a graduate in archaeology and geology at the University of Arizona, Flagstaff, sought advice as to where to dig for such evidence. Abrahamsen (he had never been to Arizona) told him where to dig, giving details of what would be found down to a depth of fifty feet; including type and age of artefacts to be found, and soil types and rock formation to be met at exact depths down to twenty-three feet. Before starting to dig, Goodman had the reading evaluated by professional archaeologists and geologists. All said it was nonsense. Goodman went ahead with the dig at the location described by Abrahamsen. Their communication was by letter or phone alone.

Of fifty-eight statements made by Abrahamsen (about the geology, chronology and artefacts to be found) fifty-two proved correct. Goodman concluded that people settled North America over 100,000 years ago (70,000 years before currently acceptable dating), but remained cautious about Abrahamsen's claim that **Atlanteans** and **Lemurians** had reached Arizona *c.* 500,000 BC.[1]

In his 1972–3 readings, Abrahmsen predicted a **pole shift** for the year 1999–2000, involving a full 180° 'flip' of the poles. The sun would move rapidly through the sky, stand still, then move again. By 1985 the Earth's axis would begin to tilt, north pole moving west, south pole east. Initial motion would be small. When the axis attained a 30° angle of inclination, the shift would lead to reversal of east and west, north and south, causing long night in the USA, long day in Africa, and violent hurricanes. Alaska would become tropical. The cause would be negative human **thought-forms**.

However in a later reading (No. 3081: 1977) Abrahamsen claims that the shift is not inevitable, given sufficient improvement in human behaviour.

1. *Psychic Archaeology*, Jeffrey Goodman, Berkeley Books, New York 1977
2. *Pole Shift*, John White, W. H. Allen, London 1980

ABRAMELIN THE MAGE (*See* **ANGELS, DEMONS, MAGIC, QABALAH**) A century ago Macgregor **Mathers**, contentious head of the **Golden Dawn**, translated *The Book of the Sacred Magic of Abramelin, the Mage*. This *grimoire* was allegedly written in 1458 (in three books) by 'Abraham the Jew'. Mathers claims that Abraham must have been, 'somewhat broad in his religious views; for [he insists] that this sacred system of magic may be attained by anyone, whether Jew, Christian, Mohometan [*sic*] or Pagan'.

First the author tells how, instructed in Qabalah, he travelled Europe seeking wisdom. Eventually in Egypt he met a hermit, Abramelin, who took him as a student. The second and third books describe the rites required to invoke one's Holy Guardian Angel (or Higher Self). This sacred magic requires six months preparatory purification and prayer, in solitude. The system requires disciplined self-denial if one is to employ the Fallen or Evil Spirits as servants in the undertaking without falling foul of them. It demands recognition that the Good Spirits and Angelic Powers of Light are more potent than the Fallen Spirits of Darkness; that the latter must serve initiates of the Magic of Light; that in consequence all material projects arise from the labour of Evil Spirits commanded by the Good.

Such command is won only by extreme self-control and self-denial, gained only by sure knowledge of the Higher Self, the Guardian Angel.[1,2]

Dealing with demons is dangerous in any age! Yet this publication by Mathers marked a transition in magical practice, publicising mysteries formerly held secret among Western occult groups.

1. *Don Juan, Mescalito and Modern Magic*, Neville Drury, Arkana, London 1985
2. *The Roots of Consciousness*, Jeffrey Mishlove, Random House, New York, 1975

ACUPUNCTURE (*See* **CH'I, GEOMANCY, HEALING**) This ancient Chinese healing art is based on the manipulation of the body's *ch'i* (subtle) energy. A pragmatic discipline, there is nothing **paranormal** about it, yet orthodox Western medicine, dealing with the physical body alone, often denies it as such. Thus it is included here to highlight the typically Western confusion between what is 'magic' and what is 'science'.

During the Chinese Stone Age it was learned that puncturing or burning certain points on the human body aids treatment of sickness. At first the puncturing was done with stone needles and only a few points were known.

Today some 722 points – symmetrically distributed over both halves of the human body – have been identified. In *The Yellow Emperor's Classic of Internal Medicine* (*c.* AD 26) it was noted that many widely separated points on the body affect the health of any specific organ. These interconnected points were called *Ching*, or *meridians*. At first there were twelve meridians: two have since been added. Another list was made of points affecting the skin and muscles, forming *twelve extra meridians*.

All such meridians possess specific characteristics relating to their effect on organs, muscles or skin, in human or animal bodies. Traditional Chinese medicine divides the internal organs into two groups; the 'storage' (passive: ***Yin***) and 'working' (active: ***Yang***). The former group includes: lung, spleen, heart, kidneys and liver; the latter; large and small intestine, stomach, urinary and gall bladder.

Both traditional and modern systems link all these organs in terms of function. *Yin* and *Yang* organs coordinate in pairs. Thus a diseased organ may best be treated by stimulating the preceding or succeeding organ. No part of the body exists in isolation; every part connects with every other part; no illness is purely that of the organ that manifests it obviously.

Mind and body are thus united in a pragmatic system barely understood as such by specialist modern medicine. Acupuncture survives today because it is a holistic method that often succeeds where orthodox medicine fails.

1. *The Chinese Art of Healing*, Stephan Pálos, Bantam Books, New York 1972

ADAMSKI, George (1891–1965) (*See* **UFOs**) In 1952 Californian mystic George Adamski claimed the first contact with UFO entities in the five years since the modern UFO scare had begun with the Arnold sighting. In his *Flying Saucers Have Landed* he writes: 'It was about 12.30 in the noon hour of Thursday, 20th November, 1952, that I first made personal contact with a man from another world. He came to Earth in his space craft, a flying saucer. He called it a Scout Ship.[1]

This encounter with a Venusian UFO pilot seemingly took place at Desert Centre, California. Adamski and six friends saw a bell-like 'scout ship' appear overhead then land. A blond-haired **humanoid** entity emerged and told Adamski by signs and telepathy that his people feared the Bomb, feared to land in populous areas, and believed in God and the transmigration of souls. Brushing against the UFO, Adamski received an arm-numbing shock.

Author Brinsley Le Poer Trench[2] claimed to own a **Project Blue Book** (the USAF UFO enquiry) report of a UFO in the area of Desert Centre that day. In a later book Adamski tells how his new friends took him to UFO bases amid mountains, cities and rivers – on the far side of the **Moon**.

Yet aspects of his lurid adventures are oddly convincing. Describing a space journey he reports 'billions and billions of fireflies . . . flickering everywhere'.[3] This was some years before, in 1963, US astronaut John Glenn returned from his space flight, reporting 'fireflies' as described by Adamski.

A coda to Adamski's tale occurred in England. On 24 April 1965 Mr E. A. Bryant of Scoriton, Devon, out walking, met a UFO which appeared out of thin air and landed near him. Three figures in 'driving gear' emerged. One said his name was 'Yamski', and that it was a pity 'Des' or 'Les' wasn't there, as he would have understood the visitation. Oddly, George Adamski – who collaborated with *Des*mond Leslie in writing *Flying Saucers Have Landed*, had died the day before.

1. *Flying Saucers Have Landed*, George Adamski and Desmond Leslie, T. Werner Laurie, London 1953
2. *The Flying Saucer Story*, Brinsley Le Poer Trench, Spearman, London 1966
3. *Inside the Space Ships*, George Adamski, Abelard-Schuman, New York 1955

AETHERIUS SOCIETY (*See* **KING**)

AFTERLIFE (*See* **NEAR-DEATH EXPERIENCES, REINCARNATION**) What is meant by the concept of 'life after death'? If it means survival of death by our individual egos with memories and personality intact, then probably our entire notion of what constitutes *life* (and thus 'death') is flawed.

Evidence for the existence of orders and states of being other than those presently recognized by science is considered elsewhere. Of interest here is that, despite three centuries of reductionism, millions around the world still believe in some form of afterlife. At the least, this suggests the failure of scientific method to encompass the inner life of human beings.

Since early times the idea has prevailed that *some* aspect of *mind* survives physical death. Perhaps such belief is a psychological necessity: we cannot endure life's brevity or find meaning without it. Virtually all **religions** promise joy in the hereafter . . . or eternal damnation for those who misbehave while alive on earth. Virtually all social morality is ultimately posited on supernatural sanction: Christians are promised heaven or hell; Islamic zealots from Hashishins to Hezbollah are told that dying for Allah leads to Paradise; even Buddhism threatens evil-doers with ever-renewed earthly incarnations (implying not only the undesirability of life on earth but its essentially illusory nature) so long as they fail to see through the veils of Maya to the transcendent truth. Even now militantly atheist cultures find such belief impossible to suppress. In short, belief in life after death is essential to the functioning of societies. Without it, cynicism and self-seeking inevitably corrode the body politic.

No such belief proves the reality of an afterlife. Yet neither does it merely reflect common fear of personal death. For plainly such fear does not reduce the incidence of murder and other crimes where punishable by death. As **Koestler** pointed out,[1] large-scale murder (in war) is usually committed not for greed or selfishness but through devotion to ideals that transcend personal interest. Many unmoved to rob and kill for *personal* gain will do so when caught up in the mass hysteria of (holy) war. Such a psychological switch would be impossible without some deeper belief which holds that some things are worth killing (and dying) for. Such ideals may be a matter of local religious, national or economic advantage – but still a wider dimension of belief must be invoked to justify the shame of murder. Ordinary morality is denied: the extraordinary is invoked. That this can be done suggests implicit belief in purposes transcending the ordinary.

Yet all such 'evidence' proves only the strength of the belief. The question is: What is the purpose of such belief? Why, since time immemorial have the dead been supplied with food and gear for their voyage to the land beyond, or with rites to send their soul safe through the gates? Did the ancient Egyptian obsession with life beyond death possess no utility? How could mere neurotics retain social stability for nearly three millennia? How in China did belief in the Ancestors (real or imagined) control social morality for centuries? In Europe, two millennia of history have been affected by the myth of a man killed then reborn. Without popular belief in afterlife, **Christianity** lacks all sanction. The (cannibalistic) rite of Communion invokes *vicarious* experience of universal rebirth. Life annually plunges into death, then returns to life again.

Belief in afterlife is part and parcel of daily life.

1. *Janus*, Arthur Koestler, Hutchinson, London 1978, pp. 77ff

AGRIPPA, Cornelius (1486–1535) This restless German Renaissance occultist was court secretary to the Holy Roman Emperor at the age of nineteen. Sent as an Imperial spy to Paris, he reached Dôle in France. Here, study of **gematria** and **Qabalah** made him a Doctor of Divinity. Denounced by the Franciscans, his peripatetic life never got any easier. His *De occulta philosophia* ('On Occult Philosophy'), a major survey of Renaissance magic, was written by 1510 but unpublished until 1533.

In it he divides the universe into three worlds – elemental, celestial and intellectual; each affected by that above it. Magicians may draw upper world virtues down by manipulating the lower ones. The elemental world is revealed through medicine and natural philosophy; the celestial world via **astrology** and maths; and the intellectual world by religious ceremonies.[1] Through rejecting the evil uses of knowledge thus gained, he advocated using **demonic magic** to attract intellectual power. 'If you would call any evil spirit to the Circle,' he writes, 'it first behooveth us to consider and know his nature, to which of the planets he agreeth, and what offices are distributed to him from the planet.'[2] As for imagination's power to affect the body, he writes (Chapter 63): 'The fantasy, or imaginative power, has a ruling power over the passions of the soul, when these are bound to sensual apprehensions.' Imagination 'according to the diversity of the passions, change(s) the physical body with a sensible transmutation.'[3]

This assertion that bodily health is subject to imaginative will not only presages modern psychotherapy but Aleister **Crowley**'s definition of **magic** as, 'The science and art of causing change to occur in conformity with the will.' Impure thought guarantees a corresponding bodily impurity: the practice of holy ceremonial **religion** is the route to pure thought and firmness of spirit, without which personal disaster is inevitable.

Denouncing the techniques of the ancient **Magi** as false compared with current Catholic faith, Agrippa was yet bold enough to state that there was much good in them, at least to those able to sift truth from lies. Such *caveats* did him no good. Notoriety always pursued him. The Wandering Jew was said to have visited him: another tale claims that a student, secretly using his book of **spells**, inadvertently summoned a **demon** and was strangled. Finding the corpse, Agrippa apparently ordered the demon to revive the student who, walking in the market-place, collapsed dead of a heart-attack. Examination of the corpse indicated strangulation. Agrippa was again forced to flee.

His enforced travels, the death of two wives and the failure of a third marriage, plus endless conflict with the Church, left him ruined. Unable (like **Paracelsus**) to keep his mouth shut, driven from every town he tried to settle in, his desire for peace proved elusive – unsurprising, given his rash claims to contact the dead and converse with demons. Amazingly, he died not in jail (though often jailed) or at the stake (like **Bruno**), but of bitterness and exhaustion, at Grenoble in 1535. In a late book, *De vanitate scientarium* ('On the Vanity of Sciences and Arts') (1530) he claimed, Faust-like, that knowledge brings only disillusionment.

1. *Giordano Bruno and the Hermetic Tradition*, Frances A. Yates, Routledge Kegan Paul, London 1964, pp. 130ff
2. *The Secret Lore of Magic*, Idries Shah, Citadel Press, New York 1970, p. 226ff, quoting Turner's 18th-century translation
3. *The Occult*, Colin Wilson, Hodder and Stoughton Ltd, London 1971, p. 306

AKASHIC RECORD (*See* **COLLECTIVE UNCONSCIOUS, UNIVERSAL MEMORY**)

ALBERTUS MAGNUS (1206–80) (*See* **ALCHEMY**) Canonised in 1931, this Dominican friar was (*pace* Roger Bacon) thirteenth-century Europe's leading visionary, scholar and magical philosopher. He held that all things in nature and human art arise from celestial influence, that Man is a microcosm of the universe and that God acts through natural phenomena. He advocated using **astrology** to learn when to undertake particular tasks; **drugs** to produce **visions** to find valuable metals, herbs, dreams, magical stones and other **occult** media to bring about desired results. Where such practices failed, he said the defect lay in those misusing natural magic. In *Speculum astronomiae* ('The Mirror of Astronomy') he rejected books then attributed to the legendary **Hermes Trismegistus** as containing diabolical magic. Like Bacon it was said of him that he made a brazen head which spoke. A prolific author on subjects as diverse as physics, psychology, zoology, astronomy, botany and minerals, he was (unsurprisingly, given his era) influenced by Aristotle.

ALBIGENSIANS (*See* **CATHARS**)

ALCHEMY Originating in ancient China and in Alexandria's **Neoplatonic** schools, the term 'alchemy' derives from the ancient name for **Egypt**, *Khem*, meaning 'black earth'. Alchemy is thus 'the art of the black land'.

Alchemists always had two main aims: one, to turn base metal into gold (or seem to do so); two, to find the elixir of life. This led to two kinds of alchemist. Pragmatists laboured for years in smoky laboratories, laying the basis of modern chemistry as they did so; while the theorists, scorned in the sixteenth century by **Paracelsus** for carrying 'golden mountains in their heads before they had put their hands to the fire',[1] speculated about finding the magical transformative ingredient, the 'Philosopher's Stone'. The symbolic smoke-screens erected by the latter, along with the secrecy in which alchemists habitually indulged (in order to stay alive), make it hard today to know what they thought they were up to.

Were they all charlatans? Certainly by the sixteenth century many claimed to practise a divine art established by the legendary **Hermes Trismegistus** – but their Graeco-Roman forebears were initially concerned only to imitate gold. This they did by producing yellow alloys of base metals, by using impure gold, or by colouring metals and alloys. That the technology was advanced is clear from Egyptian recipes for colouring glass and glazing pottery. Even so, the dream of producing real gold from base metal was always seductive, and was considered possible by the first known writer on chemistry, Zosimos, in the third century AD.[2] This dream inspired the desire to discover the *prima materia* said to underlie all physical matter. It seemed justified by the Greek notion of an underlying unity in nature.

During the 'Dark Ages' the Arabs developed practical alchemy. Geber (eighth-century) developed the processes of distillation, sublimation and calcination. He said the alchemist's chief qualities should be patience and perseverance, but also perpetuated a myth that the key to transmutation lay in combining mercury and sulphur. Such combination never led to gold, but the idea grew that what was needed were *specific essences* of sulphur and mercury. Thus developed the mystification later given such a boost by the 'discovery' of works attributed to the legendary **Hermes Trismegistus**.

First mentioned in the West in *De Mineralibus*, a treatise attributed to **Albertus Magnus** (1206–80), who with Ramon **Lull** (1235–1315) and Roger **Bacon** (1214–94) dominated thirteenth-century **occult** thought, the legend of Hermes took off a century later when Ficino translated ancient writings (the *Pimander* and the *Asclepius*) said to be by Hermes. Here, perhaps, is where alchemy went transcendental.

Frances Yates has shown that European alchemy developed from ancient **mystery** teachings taken up by **Gnostics** in the early Christian era. However Ficino and others believed these texts written by Hermes, an Egyptian sage alive three generations after Moses. The era lacked reliable history or scientific knowledge. The mystic appeal of a lost Golden Age was quite as potent as the notion that gold might be created out of lead. So began a mystique lasting till the seventeenth century, when men like Robert Boyle in his *The Sceptical Chymist* (1661) at last poked large holes in the alchemical dream. After which the only defence, in an increasingly hard-headed world, was that alchemy was really not about the transmutation of *physical* matter, but of the ***psyche*** of the alchemist. It was acknowledged that alchemists had developed laboratory equipment and technique, and added to the sum of scientific knowledge – but all, it was said, for the wrong reasons. This is one viewpoint. Another is as follows:

Exoterically alchemy (the Great Work) concerns transmutation of lead to gold. But this requires the alchemist to change his own **consciousness**. By hard self-discipline, **dream** and **vision**, he seeks to create in himself the 'Philosopher's Stone' by which the transmutation is effected. Assuming universal unity in the *prima materia*, the Great Work involves reducing the self (the 'metal') to that primal substance, then rebuilding it into any desired element. Starting in springtime, the process involves pulverising the chosen *prima materia* and heating it in a sealed vessel (i.e. let the sun heat the earth; let **inspiration** heat and fertilise the soul).

Most descriptions of the process are ambiguous, equating the **symbolic** with the physical. In old texts the sun (sulphur) and the moon (mercury) are shown as king and queen lying in a dissolving bath together. In the purifying heat of new growth they merge chemically into hermaphroditic form. The new creation (idea: body) manifests through heat into whiteness – *albedo*: the 'white stone'. Thus over years such mind-body control is gained that the **psychokinetic** transmutation of matter becomes possible.

Unlikely? Natural transmutation occurs all the time, as in the decay of radioactive elements to lead. Bombarding elements with neutrons, high-energy physicists can (at great cost) turn one into another. But what of alchemical claims? Helvetius, the seventeenth-century physician to the Prince of Orange and at first a sceptic, tells (in *Of a Transmutation*) how a stranger showed him three sulphur-coloured lumps of stone, claiming these to be the fabled Philosopher's Stone. Stealing a fragment, Helvetius heated it in a crucible with six drams of old lead. What emerged was said by a goldsmith to be pure gold. The philosopher Spinoza, investigating this odd event, attested to the reality of the transmutation. It is generally agreed that Helvetius was above suspicion. If he was tricked, nobody knew how.

In 1782, one James Price invited a group of distinguished men to his Surrey house. They saw him turn mercury to silver by heating it with a white powder, and into gold with a red powder. The ingots produced were genuine. Pressed to produce more powder, Price said to do so would damage his health (suggesting the psychokinetic aspect). Stressed by the resulting controversy, he committed suicide by drinking cyanide before three members of the Royal Society who had been sent to study his claims.

Why? *Because he was a charlatan?* Or because he was exhausted?

The seventeenth-century Scottish alchemist Alexander Seton travelled Europe with a lemon-yellow powder with which he and others produced gold before witnesses. The Elector of Saxony demanded the secret. Seton refused and was tortured and jailed. A student named Sendigovius helped him to escape and, when Seton died soon afterwards, was given the remaining powder – but not the secret. In his *Dictionary of Occultism* Lewis **Spence** says Seton refused to tell the secret as, 'it was impossible to him as an adept to reveal the terms of the awful mystery'.[4] This again suggests that such transmutation (if genuine) is produced by magical, not chemical means – i.e. through interaction with the *prima materia* of the adept's own will and imagination.

What sort of interaction? In 1850 a book, *A Suggestive Enquiry into the Hermetic Mystery With a Dissertation on the More Celebrated of the Alchemical Philosophers*, was published by Mary Anne South. With her father Thomas she had studied ancient Mystery religion and alchemy and concluded that Mystery initiates often used **hypnotic trance** states. When her father read the book he burned all the copies he could find. When he died soon after she made no effort to reprint it. Later occultist A. E. **Waite** denied that the Mysteries contained any trance element, and took her statement that 'The alchemical process is thus a secret method of self-knowledge which the **soul** follows far through its realm of being' to mean that the alchemical quest is purely psychological and metaphoric.

In which case, why did her father try to suppress the book? What did he fear? In 1936 Israel **Regardie** concluded that the secret they had found – the ancient alchemical secret – was that in trance the alchemist can take on 'demiurgic' powers and directly affect the matter in the crucible. The essential process is psychic, not chemical.[5] More recently, poet Kenneth Rexroth has claimed that the 'forbidden secret' is sexual.[6] Introducing the work of seventeenth-century alchemist Thomas Vaughan, he points out that Hindu **tantrics** use **kundalini yoga** to raise sex energy up the spine to the brain and produce illumination. Uncontrolled, this practice (considered a form of alchemy by the Chinese) may cause madness or serious illness. (Remember the fate of James Price, and his fears for his health?) Rexroth says that Vaughan came close to admitting similar practice in the West. Colin **Wilson** identifies a passage in Vaughan's *Aula Lucis* (House of Light) in which the author writes that the 'Vessel of Nature', in which the operation occurs, is a 'menstruous substance . . . wherein you must place the universal sperm as soon as it appears beyond its body'. Is this merely metaphorical language?

If indeed the heart of alchemical consciousness-raising involves sexual intercourse (the king and queen dissolved in the bath, remember?) or some analogous sexual operation, then it is hardly surprising that Thomas South, and many an alchemist before him, feared to admit this in public.

1. *The Alchemist*, Ronald Pearsall, Weidenfeld and Nicolson, London 1976, p. 85
2. *Ibid*., p. 9
3. *Giordano Bruno and the Hermetic Tradition*, Frances A. Yates, Routledge and Kegan Paul, London 1964
4. *The Occult*, Colin Wilson, Grafton Books, London 1989, pp. 317ff.
5. *Mysteries*, Colin Wilson, Grafton Books, London 1989, pp. 400ff.
6. *Ibid*., pp. 432–5

ALIEN ANIMALS (*See* **ABOMINABLE SNOWMAN, BLACK DOGS, LOCH NESS MONSTER, UFOs**) Every year all over the world people report encounters with beasts either unknown to zoologists or of such ambiguous reality that those involved in such encounters are usually suspected of hoax or **hallucination**. In some cases the beasts encountered are of known species but appear so misplaced where encountered that the sightings are suspect. In all cases there is a characteristic lack of objective evidence: i.e. no bodies are found, and photographic or other such evidence is usually open to question. Another characteristic aspect (one shared with UFO sightings) is a strong sense on the part of observers of the dreamlike nature of their encounter.

In their survey of this phenomenon authors Janet and Colin Bord define five main categories of such creatures. These are: lake monsters; phantom black dogs; giant **birds** and birdmen; 'big hairy monsters' (BHMs); and big cats that leave tracks but can't be caught.[1]

Well-known examples are described elsewhere. Yet the Loch Ness Monster is but one of many; the Abominable Snowman appears to have cousins around the world; 'Mothman' is not the only 'birdman' reported in recent times.

Taking lake monsters first: well over 300 are reported the world around, in Africa, Australia, Russia, Canada and the USA. Irish loughs, especially in Galway (over twenty), seem to be full of them; over twenty Scottish lochs other than Loch Ness are reputed to host them.

One Scottish non-Loch Ness encounter occurred in August 1969 to two men fishing Loch Morar: a humped creature some twenty-five feet long and with a rough dirty skin struck their motor cruiser: Duncan MacDonnell, one of the fishermen, broke an oar trying to fend it off; Bill Simpson fired a rifle at it and saw it sink slowly away. 'I don't want to see it again,' he said later, 'I was terrified.' Some thirty-three sightings of 'Morag' have been reported over the last century: Loch Morar, over 1,000 feet deep, is one of a group of west coast lochs from all of which monster-sightings have been reported.

F. W. Holiday, investigating reports of the Irish water-monster called the *peiste* (pest) in Connemara, was told by librarian Georgina Carberry of a creature she and others saw in Lough Fadda in 1954. She said the whole body had 'movement all over it'; that it was 'wormy' and 'creepy', and that for weeks afterwards she had recurring nightmares. Similarly a woman who photographed the sea-monster *Morgawr* in Falmouth Bay, Cornwall, said she did not 'like the way it moved'. This common response by witnesses of lake- (or sea-) monsters, of automatic repugnance and a sense of intrinsic evil, reminds one of old English **dragon** legends about the 'loathly worm', or of the Welsh legend of the wyvern (two-legged dragon) of Cynwch Lake.

This, seen on land (as Nessie has been seen), would creep with 'hateful, stealthy movements . . . jerking its cumbersome form into uncanny humps . . . and leaving a slimy trail behind it'. Such revulsion, dread – and respect – is testified to by lake-monster observers all over the world, from Okanagan Lake in British Columbia to Lake Labynkyr on Russia's Sordongnokh Plateau.

The mystery of these beasts is compounded by the apparent lack of food available in many lakes where they are said to dwell or are sighted; also by the seeming difficulty of photographing them, far less finding bodily evidence of their physical existence. Some theories as to their origin and nature are taken up in the account of the Loch Ness Monster.

That commonly they seem other than physical, and that sightings of them are oddly reliant (as with some types of **ghost**) on the mental state of the observer, is often observed: the theory that they and other 'alien animals' are **phantoms** is emphasised by the 'black dog' phenomenon, associated in England with churchyards, old green ways, **megalithic** sites and **ley lines**. Often connected with presages of death, they usually appear and disappear at the same places, and at the same times of day and night, as if imprinted there like tape-recordings.

The many sightings round the world of giant birds and, specifically, of 'birdmen' – weird winged creatures with *some* human aspects – compound the sense that such creatures are **paranormal**. In the cases of birdmen like the **'Jersey Devil'**, a 'hideous' flying creature with a long thin tail seen by many in New Jersey during 1909, or (just as horrid) the red-eyed 'Mothman' haunting West Virginia in 1966, it is hard to deny parallels with mediaeval talk of **demons**. The encounter in which a witness saw the Jersey Devil's tail touch an electric railway track, then vanish in an explosion melting twenty feet of track, suggests the same kind of electrical anomaly reported in some UFO and black dog encounters.

Less alarming by comparison are the many sightings round the world of hairy man-apes: yeti in Nepal and Tibet; Bigfoot or Sasquatch in western US mountain regions; Chuchuna in north-east Siberia; the Yowie in Australia (over 3,000 sightings); and other unnamed BHMs in Africa and elsewhere. A Yowie seen in 1912 had a face like 'that of an ape or man, minus forehead and chin, with a great trunk all one size from shoulders to hips, and with arms that nearly reached to its ankles'. Many other descriptions have been given, from all round the world, suggesting (however unlikely it may seem) that BHMs are a natural phenomenon, survivors in various forms in remote regions of our anthropoid ancestors, possessing enough *nous* to avoid *homo sapiens* as much as possible. If so, who can blame them? In the UK there are (not unnaturally) few BHM reports; though the Big Grey Man (*Fear Liath Mhór*) of Ben Macdhui in Scotland's Cairngorm Mountains has cast his eerie spell over not a few mountaineers stumbling through winter mists.

As for big cats, sightings in England began in 1962, when the 'Surrey Puma' first appeared, frightening people and attacking farm animals. Seen by many but never caught, by 1964 there were so many sightings that a zoo break-out seemed the only sane explanation. No such event was reported.

Pawmarks in sand seemed to be those of a puma; frightful howlings were heard; but all efforts to find and catch the beast failed. Inevitably, theories took on a paranormal tinge: time-slips, **thought-forms**, and **Bermuda Triangle**-type interdimensional vortices all being invoked; while a 1973 survey of mystery cats sighted in the Bournemouth region showed that (as with black dogs) all such sightings occurred close to ley lines.

Yet, at least in North Scotland, unknown types of large, wild, feral cat do exist. In one recent case two such cats were shot on a Grampian estate: the corpses were sent south to London's Natural History Museum for identification. They fit no description of the wildcat still prowling the Highlands. Perhaps they were survivors of the Wangye, as in a local hill, 'The Hill of the Wangye'. Either way, it seems foolish to presuppose the 'paranormal' when human ignorance remains more prevalent than we like to admit. These cats had survived unclassified.

1. *Alien Animals*, Janet and Colin Bord, Granada, London 1980

ALLENDE, Carlos (*See* **PHILADELPHIA EXPERIMENT**)

ALTERED STATES (*See* **HALLUCINOGENS, LEARY, LILLY, SHAMANISM**) American publication in 1969 of **parapsychologist** Charles Tart's *Altered States of Consciousness* came amid the so-called 'psychedelic' revolution. Many young people had rejected orthodox Western morality to experiment with hallucinogenic ('mind-expanding') **drugs** and to investigate **occult** or eastern **mystical** practices. Tart's well-timed scientific enquiry into the consequences of such experimentation was accompanied by other texts on the subject by Leary, Lilly, and others. These followed the experiments of US psychologist William **James**, (1842–1910). His enquiry into the effects of nitrous oxide mark him as the first modern experimenter in this field, and connect him with ancient shamanic and **mystical** traditions, involving the quest for altered states via drug-use, physical austerities, dancing, ritual or self-immolation. Early **Christian** saints mortifying their flesh or sitting atop a pillar for forty years (St Simon Stylites) did so in order to induce the altered state of mystical ecstasy, so growing closer to God.

But this age-old quest does not necessarily imply the search for a higher morality, though it may disguise itself as such. Hassan i Sabbah, the 'Old Man of the Mountains', a twelfth-century Persian warlord, terrorised the Crusaders and neighbouring Muslim potentates. From his name come the words 'hashish' and 'assassin'. Sending young men drugged with hashish into his gardens where lovely women seduced them, he would later tell them they had entered Paradise, and could re-enter it only by infiltrating enemy courts as trusted servants, waiting many years if need be, then (if Hassan demanded) assassinating the enemy monarch when the time came.

Recently, popular perception of the hubristic dangers involved in such research or experimentation was highlighted in the 1980 movie, *Altered States*, in which actor William Hurt becomes a self-destroying beast after submitting to the scientific glamour of **sensory deprivation** experiments.

The quest for 'expanded **consciousness**' is glamorous in the imagining, but can prove dangerous if undertaken frivolously. All the old *caveats* about 'Here there be Dragons' apply. Yet every time we drink a shot of whisky or even a pint of beer we enter an 'altered state', however slight it may be in comparison with the effects of drugs like LSD–25.

ALTERNATIVE UNIVERSES (*See* **ANTIMATTER, DIMENSIONS**)

ANCIENT ASTRONAUTS (*See* **ENOCH, SIRIUS, UFOs, VON**

DÄNIKEN) The idea that 'Gods from Outer Space' once intervened in human affairs was not invented by Erich von Däniken, but is common to many human cultures.

In Genesis vi, 2 it is said: 'That the sons of God saw the daughters of men that they were fair; and they took them wives of all which they chose.'

These 'sons of God' are described in the Books of Enoch, suppressed by the early Church for claiming the fallen angels (**Watchers** or *Nephilim*) to be physical beings capable of sexual intercourse with humans. Rediscovered (in an Ethiopian Coptic monastery) in the early nineteenth century, these texts date from the second century BC but derive from older material. Enoch himself (the father of Methuselah: Genesis v, 18–24) was an early abductee: it is said: '. . . he walked with God and he was not, for God took him'.

The text tells how 200 Watchers 'descended on' Mount Hermon (bordering Syria, Lebanon and Israel). They were **Elohim**, 'Shining Ones': men could barely face them. Against their leader Shemyaza's advice, led by Azazel, they 'went native', teaching forbidden arts and taking human wives who bore 'giants'. Subsequently God told the scribe Enoch to 'tell the Watchers of heaven, who have deserted the lofty sky (and) been polluted with women'[1] that their children must die and that they would receive no mercy. Sent to heaven by the Watchers to plead for them, Enoch, driven by 'agitated stars and flashes of lightning', reaches a crystal wall surrounded by 'vibrating flame'. Through this he passes into a 'spacious habitation', also built of crystal. Here One, 'Whose robe was brighter than the sun', orders him to tell the Watchers: 'You ought to pray for me, and not men for you . . . [*for*] you from the beginning were made spiritual, possessing a life which is eternal, and not subject to death for ever. Therefore I made not wives for you, because, being spiritual, your dwelling is in heaven.'[2] The Lord's judgement is duly carried out by his *satans* (prosecutors) on Earth. The Watchers are imprisoned to await the Day of Judgement; their progeny is destroyed, but from the corpses issue evil spirits that plague us still.

Subsequently the early Christian Church fathers suppressed the Enochian account so entirely that *c.* AD 325 St Jerome was able to declare the account apocryphal. Talk of *sexual* relations between men and '**angels**' was out of order to an institution deriving its authority from a supernatural myth.

Other accounts survived, notably by the Chaldean priest Berossus in his now-fragmentary *Babylonian History*. Writing *c.* 300 BC he claims civilisation was founded by alien amphibians. Led by *Oannes* (later Dagon, a fish-tailed Philistine God), and collectively called *Annedoti* ('repulsive ones'), they were physically abominable. Berossus (*via* Alexander Polyhistor) wrote, 'The whole body of the animal was like that of a fish; and had under a fish's head another head, and also feet below, subjoined to the fish's tail. His voice too, and language, was articulate and human . . . When the sun set, it was the custom of this Being to plunge again into the sea, and abide all night in the deep, for he was amphibious.'[3]

In *The Sirius Mystery* (1976), Robert Temple adduced beliefs of the Dogon, a Malian tribe, as evidence that aliens from a planet of the star-system of **Sirius** once came to Earth to civilise their ancestors. Oddly, the Dogon knew that Sirius has a companion star, invisible to the naked eye, small, dense and immensely heavy, which circles Sirius A in a fifty-year orbit. They also say there is a third Sirian star they call the '*emme ya*'. Sirius B was unknown to Western astronomy until 1862 and not photographed until 1970. Yet knowledge of it has apparently informed Dogon **ritual** for centuries, also knowledge of Saturn's rings and Jupiter's four large moons. Their sand-drawings showing the descent to Earth of the 'arc' carrying the Nommo – fish-tailed, like the Oannes – convinced Temple. Drawing on evidence the Dogon gave French anthropologists Griaule and Dieterlen (work begun in 1931, published 1950), he concluded that Dogon mythology records an alien intervention 5,000 years ago. His conclusions convinced many but were debunked by writers like Carl Sagan and Ronald Story, who claimed the Dogon had heard about Sirius B from local French schools before Griaule and Dieterlen began recording their beliefs in 1931 and simply incorporated the information into their 'ancient' rituals.[4]

The matter remains unproven. The very existence of argument suggests a mystery challenging all preconceptions. Writers like von Däniken may be dismissed for distorting evidence or Barry Downing for claiming that Old Testament prophets like Elijah and Ezekiel spent their time cruising in UFOs: their theories do not prove that such contacts never took place. The discovery of Sirius C would aid the Dogon/Temple thesis, but to date there is no sign of it.

Some claim the 'sons of God' continued to influence the world after Enoch's time. Christian O'Brien argues that latterly the Elohim travelled the globe educating human populations; that they were the Tuatha de Danaan, the magic Irish tribe, and that Mesopotamian ziggurats, Egyptian pyramids, and **Stonehenge** and **Avebury** were built as a result of their teaching.[5,6] Similarly the late T. C. **Lethbridge**[7] speculated that the 'sons of God' were stranded on Earth after a 'war in heaven', building **megalithic** circles as navigational beacons energised by 'bio-electronic force' released by human dance and **ritual**. Such accounts remain fascinating, if inconclusive.

1. 1 Enoch xii, 5–6
2. 1 Enoch xv, 2–7
3. *The Sirius Mystery*, Robert K. G. Temple, Futura Books, London 1978, p. 204
4. *Guardians of the Universe?*, Ronald Story, Book Club Associates, London 1980, pp. 113–127
5. *The Megalithic Odyssey*, Christian O'Brien, Turnstone Press, London 1983
6. *The Genius of the Few*, Christian O'Brien, Turnstone Press, London 1985
7. *The Legend of the Sons of God*, T. C. Lethbridge, RKP, London 1972

ANGELS (*See* **DEAMONS, DEVIL**) Belief in angels (Greek: *angelos* = *messenger*), supernal beings who mediate between God and man, is ancient, widespread and **archetypal**, referring to our sense of higher spiritual forces operating in and through us; forces that challenge, protect, guide or harm us, according to how we approach them. That they link higher and lower spheres of **consciousness** is seen in Jacob's **Dream** of the Ladder, on which angels both climbed and descended. In wrestling with the Angel, Jacob engaged in primordial battle with his own inner self, a battle known to **shamanic** tradition the world over.

The names and identities of the great angels are not peculiar to the **Christian** religion alone. The prophet Mohammed received the Koran from God via the archangel Gabriel, who also told Mary she would be Christ's mother. Mohammed told how Gabriel 'descended in his own form, of such beauty, of such sacred glory, of such majesty, that all my dwelling was illuminated. He is of a whiteness brighter than snow, his face is gloriously beautiful, the waves of his hair fall in long tresses, his brow is encircled as with a diadem of light on which is written "There is no god but God".'

This anthropomorphic vision of angels as shining winged human beings is common in every age and in many cultures. The Peruvian hawk-spirit Koakiti appears to the Campu shaman as a winged man; the Four Thunderbirds of the North American Sioux are seen as winged men. 'I looked up at the clouds', the Sioux visionary **Black Elk** told biographer John G. Neihardt, 'and two men were coming there, headfirst like arrows slanting down; and as they came, they sang a sacred song and the thunder was like drumming'.[1]

Angels are often represented as **birds**. To the North American Tlingit, *Raven* both enlightens and confuses mankind, is both benefactor and hoaxer. In ancient Egypt man's soul or higher self was shown as hawk or eagle. The ***devas*** of eastern tradition (hence '*devil*'), embrace a tradition of angels as **elemental** nature spirits, their wisdom neither conscious nor bound by human morality. Another perception of the angel is as a disc. The Old Testament prophet Ezekiel describes certain angels as '. . . a wheel in the middle of a wheel', moving amid a firmament the colour of a 'terrible crystal'.[2] At **Fatima** in Portugal in 1917, after a vision of the Virgin Mary experienced by three young girls, a huge crowd saw the sun (a disc) descend close to earth: close encounters with **UFOs** may represent a modern perception of the same **archetype**. But whatever the culture and its background, the phenomenon of transcendental visitation by winged messengers persists. One explanation may be that it represents a vital projection into consciousness of intelligent but unconscious content. The numinosity of the experience is constant: the form varies according to the contactee's capacity to define the event and translate it comprehensibly. Always the experience is ambiguous. Angels belong to another order of being, but the boundary is permeable. Angels (like Lucifer, who refused to bow to God's new creation, Adam) may fall or be cast down; humans may ascend. So, some humans are said to have climbed Jacob's Ladder (the **Tree of Life**) and become angels. The prophet **Enoch**, charged by God to warn the **Watchers**, whose sin was to take human wives, was taken to heaven to become the archangel Metatron. **Hermes Trismegistus** (alias Mercurius, the winged naked youth of alchemical transformation) inhabits a mythic terrain between angelic and human, actual and metaphoric.

Angels represent idealised projections of positive human imagination, just as **demons** represent the negative pole. So the idea of the 'Guardian Angel' refers to that inner guide, our **intuition**, which helps us steer a course through life. It involves the sense that a higher knowledge exists, albeit unconscious in most of us, and to deny it condemns us to folly and loss.

Angelic meaning and functions were anciently organised in hierarchies reflecting human values. The **Neoplatonist** Dionysus the Areopagite wrote in his *Celestial Hierarchies* that angels exist in nine orders. First, the Seraphim, Kerubim and Wheels (discs) or Thrones; then Orders, Dominions and Powers; and last Principalities, Archangels and mere Angels. But what does all this mean?

The Seraphim are a force inspiring mortals towards divine love. The Kerubim represent wisdom. The Wheels or Thrones form the fiery boundary of this upper triad, corresponding symbolically to the supernal triad in the **Qabalistic** Tree of Life. These symbolise primordial forces in our psychic order. Each sphere on the Tree has its resident 'angel', **Tarot** trump, vibratory colours, **correspondences** with minerals and totem animals, and so on, all building a store of images specific to particular conditions of inner life. The function of magic **ritual** is precisely to tap these pre-established images. The traditional attributes of particular angels operate as guiding symbols as specific as those in a road-map. Thus Uriel (earth and material matters) rules the North; Michael (fire and high places associated with **dragon**-energies) the East; Gabriel (water and the subconscious powers) the South; and Raphael (air and spirit) the West.[2]

Lucifer, sinister yet fascinating, represents the human ego, 'fallen' (separated) from the Light by intellectual pride, yet capable of being 'saved' (raised again) in each of us, once we learn ego is not everything. For even the **Devil** plays a necessary part in evolution. Likewise the Angel of Death (in Jewish folklore standing between heaven and earth with a poison-dripping sword) is not evil, but an expression of universal law.

Thus, though the 'sons of god' may have been actual physical beings, the images of angels may primarily refer to primordial forces as organised psychically as molecular structure is materially.

1. *Black Elk Speaks*, John G. Neihardt, Lincoln, Nebraska 1961
2. *Angels*, Peter Lamborn Wilson, Thames and Hudson, London 1980

ANIMA (*See* **ARCHETYPES, COLLECTIVE UNCONSCIOUS, DREAMS, JUNG**) In the Middle Ages it was said, 'every man carries a woman within himself'.

This female element in the male unconscious C. G. Jung named the 'anima'; and the male element in the female unconscious the 'animus'. The anima thus personifies feminine traits in the male **psyche** – vague feelings and moods, prophetic hunches, feeling for nature, and relation to the unconscious.

The anima may appear in dream, fantasy or art in beneficent or malefic form. In general a man's anima is shaped by his feeling as to his mother's positive or negative influence. In benevolent form it may appear as helper, guardian **angel**, priestess, guiding the male mind through the inner world, initiating him to higher values. So Beatrice guided Dante; so the goddess **Isis** appeared in dream to Apuleius, author of *The Golden Ass*. The anima is a mediator between ego and deeper Self. Just as the Self usually expresses itself (as Jung noted) by a fourfold structure, so four stages mark anima development. Images of Eve (instinct-biological), Faust's Helen (romantic-sexual), the Virgin Mary (*eros* raised to spiritual devotion), culminate in anima as Sapientia or the **Gnostic** Sophia – transcendent wisdom.

Negative anima is met in images of Salome, the Lorelei of Teutonic myth whose songs lured men to death, or as the *femme fatale* as in *Orphée*, Cocteau's film. It is described as *mysterious, tantalising, alluring, wanton*. It appears in unreal longing for love, happiness, or maternal warmth, and may show up in a waspish or poisonous attitude that devalues everything. The anima of a man over-dependent on his mother may manifest in sentimentality, over-sensitivity, or intellectualism. If a man's feelings remain infantile, the anima may manifest in pornographic fantasies. As with the shadow, the anima may be projected by men on to a particular woman, as in cases of 'love at first sight'. 'Fairy-like' women especially attract such projections.

Likewise the animus, the male image in the female unconscious, may be positive or negative. Unlikely to manifest as erotic fantasy, it may show as hard, cold, stubborn conviction, not to be contradicted. This may arise from the influence of the woman's father. Female fantasies of the handsome stranger (Heathcliff in *Wuthering Heights*) or sadistic Bluebeard who kills all his wives, are the animus-equivalent of the anima as wanton, devouring Lilith, leading to a cocoon-like dreamworld and rejection of actual men. Negative animus may make a woman stop her children marrying, or wish harm or death on others – 'When one of us dies, I'll move to the Riviera,' a woman told her husband[1] – or may manifest as deep insecurity, hopelessness and a sense of personal worthlessness. Yet, as in myths of the prince turned into a beast by **witchcraft** but redeeemed by a virgin love – Cocteau's film *La Belle et La Bête*, for example – the animus too has positive and transformative capacities. Enterprise, courage, truthfulness and spiritual depth characterise positive animus. It too is epitomised by the fourfold growth process, from Tarzan-images of physical power, to the romantic initiator of action (Shelley or Hemingway), to the manifestation of 'the Word' (professor, statesman, or clergyman) and fourth: the guru or sage, mediator of spiritual meaning.

1. *Man and His Symbols*, ed. Carl G. Jung, Aldus Books, London 1964, pp. 177–194 (from '*The Process of Individuation*' M. -L. von Franz)

ANIMAL MAGNETISM (*See* ANIMAL POWERS, BIRDS, MAGNETISM)

ANIMAL POWERS (*See* ELECTROMAGNETISM, PRECOGNITION, PSI)

The sensitivity of domestic animals to **paranormal** phenomena is well known. Pets often react to the distant death of their owners; or predictively to the death of a loved one nearby. An old farmer, whose dog was his constant companion, said one day he was not getting up any more and would soon die. Brought to him, the dog nuzzled him, then retreated howling. It howled until 9.30 that night, when it died. The farmer died half an hour later.[1]

Commenting on such cases, Stan **Gooch** suggests death may be presaged by an electromagnetic disturbance of the human **energy-body** or subtle anatomy which unpleasantly affects the animal's energy-body. He notes that clearly the animal knows something is wrong, and that **telepathy** may sometimes be involved. When in the late nineteenth century actor William Terries was stabbed to death in London, at his home in Bedford the family fox-terrier began to dash frantically about, yelping in rage and fear. It transpired later that this occurred exactly when his distant master was attacked and killed. In many other cases the onset of the animal's odd behaviour is equally sudden and abrupt. Likewise there are cases when a pet suddenly exhibits joyful behaviour at the exact moment a distant master begins to return home. The **telepathic** contact appears to be continuous, becoming conscious only when the news is exceptionally good or bad. Most such cases involve dogs.

In cases involving cats, the situation is usually in reverse: the human 'owner' responds to the cat's agony. A man going abroad gave his cat Timmy to a vet-friend. A year later he wrote because of a dream he'd had three nights in a row, of Timmy, head bandaged, trying to get in to him through a shut window. The vet wrote back to say that on those nights Timmy had been dying of meningitis – head bandaged. A British inventor, off to New York on business, left his cat with his housekeeper. One night he dreamed of the cat struggling in the hands of a white-coated man with a goatee beard. On returning home, he learned the cat had refused to eat in his absence. The housekeeper had called a vet to have the animal put down. The vet, a man unknown to the inventor, had a goatee beard.[2]

Another remarkable phenomenon, well-authenticated by organisations as diverse as the RSPCA and the Parapsychology Laboratory in the USA, involves 'psi trailing' – the capacity of animals abandoned or lost to find their way home or to their owners' new home, sometimes over thousands of miles. On 6 August 1923 a collie dog, Bobbie, was lost by his American family in Indiana. Six months later he turned up at the family home in Oregon, 3,000 miles away. An anonymous ship's cat, left behind in Australia, walked up the gangplank of the ship two months later – in London. The tale of *Hector, the Stowaway Dog* is at least as remarkable. Hector was seen boarding four different ships in the Vancouver docks by a ship's officer called Kildall, whose own ship, the *SS Hanley*, now sailed. Next day, Hector was found to be on board. Though cared for, he refused to befriend the crew. However, nearing Japan, he became excited. The *Hanley* dropped anchor in Yokohama, near a Dutch vessel from which a boat put out. Hector jumped into the sea and swam to it. In the boat was his lost owner.[3]

How did he do it? Did he home in on his wandering owner by means of an electromagnetic tracking signal of some sort? Perhaps every organism has its own magnetic fingerprint, like a beacon broadcasting its whereabouts. But in Hector's case and that of the ship's cat **precognition** also seems to be required. Was Hector's owner's ship at anchor in Yokohama when Hector chose the *Hanley*? How did the dog choose the exact ship that *in the near future* would coincide in physical proximity with his owner's ship?

Animal precognition *has* been established. In one experiment, mice were introduced singly to a box. From it they could move to one of several other boxes. Once in the new box they could not return. The choices of the first batch were randomly correlated by computer as 'correct' and 'incorrect'. The mice drawing 'incorrect' were painlessly put to death. Notes were kept of the sex, weight, size, colour and so on of mice avoiding *random* death-selection. Fresh mice were tested on the basis of these characteristics. The new group avoided random death at a level well above chance. Similar tests with rats and goldfish involving threat of *random* shock also indicate that the numbers avoiding shock far exceed chance expectation.[4]

Animals also seem sensitive to **ghosts, ghouls**, and suchlike **astral** or **electromagnetic** manifestations. Experiments at the Psychical Research Foundation in Durham, South Carolina, suggest they can detect the presence of human or other **entities** in

out-of-body conditions: in *Transformation*, Whitley **Streiber** relates how, following invasion of his country house by 'visitors', his cats were terrified, one hiding for twenty-two hours. In trying to explain their response he refers to reports by Desmond Morris as to feline sensitivity to the Earth's magnetic field, and disturbances therein.[5] A fuller understanding of electromagnetism and of the **subtle** or **astral** body might well enlarge our view of these animal mysteries, in ourselves as well as in animals. For animal perceptions, after all, are not subject to the static interference caused by intellect. They pick up subtle phenomena on a wavelength which in human beings seems all too subject to *civilised* interruption and wilful denial.

1. *The Secret Life of Humans*, Stan Gooch, Dent, London 1981, p. 135
2. *Ibid.*, pp. 139–140
3. *Ibid.*, pp. 106–7
4. *Ibid.*, pp 143–4
5. *Transformation*, Whitley Streiber, Arrow, London 1989, pp. 128–130

ANIMA MUNDI (*See* **GAIA**) Literally, 'the Spirit of the World' or 'World-Soul', this **alchemical** idea embraces the notion of Planet Earth itself as repository and ground of the **collective unconscious**. As Above, So Below: as with human skull, so with terrestrial globe; the physical Earth embodies mind and spiritual purpose and is thus a vessel in and through which transformation of **consciousness** occurs. This idea was associated **alchemically** with the *argentum vivum* or Mercurius, the quicksilver messenger, symbol of such transformation. At another level the idea of Planet Earth as a conscious being whose natural processes are not random but purposeful and intelligent has lately been revived (in modified scientific form) by Gaia theorist James **Lovelock**.

ANIMISM This ancient doctrine maintains: (1) that all vital phenomena are produced by the action on matter of an all-pervasive, immaterial **spirit** distinct from matter while giving matter its energetic form; and (2) that purposeful intelligence indwells supposedly inanimate objects and natural phenomena.

Thus to the *animist*, wind, wave, thunderstorm, mountain and forest are literally alive with the particular spirit or spirits indwelling them and giving such phenomena distinct identity. Personifications of such nature spirits include sylphs (air); undines (water); gnomes (earth); salamanders (fire). All who embrace **pagan** beliefs or practice **shamanistic** tradition and knowledge are, by definition, animists. That such belief may be held as arising out of the projection of unconscious content does not invalidate it – in fact, the opposite, given increasing evidence as to the degree to which our perception of the world is organised by unconscious forces, and given the parallel evidence that our denial of such forces makes us sick. Animism at least demands that minimum respect for the natural world without which (since ultimately it is more potent than we are, for it bears us) we are unlikely to survive, far less prosper and fulfil our function.

ANIMUS (*See* **ANIMA**)

ANNUNCIATION (*See* **ANGELS, CHRIST, INCUBI**) At the core of **Christian** belief is the tale of how the angel Gabriel 'was sent from God' (Luke i, 26) to visit a *virgin*, Mary, then resident in a town called Nazareth in Galilee and married to a carpenter, Joseph. Gabriel let her know that she had 'found favour with God', who had chosen her to 'bring forth a son' called Jesus, of whose kingdom 'there shall be no end'.

Mary, understandably scared by this angelic visit (later known as the *Annunciation*), less understandably (she was married) asked, 'How shall this be, seeing I know not a man?' Gabriel said, 'The Holy Ghost shall come upon thee, and the power of the Highest shall overshadow thee.' Whereupon Mary arose, went forth, and duly conceived a man-child. Jesus the **Christ**.

This event may be regarded as literal truth, or as metaphor. Seen as the latter, it is consistent with **myths** of the unconscious as expressed in every age. Impregnation of the human by the divine – as in the Greek myth of how Zeus, in the form of a swan (a solar bird, sacred to Aphrodite), had his way with Leda – was a common metaphor long before Christians adopted it for their own purposes. Mary was 'virgin' not just in flesh but also in spirit; i.e. pure in heart and mind. The Annunciation (and her impregnation by the Holy Ghost) refers not to the celestial cuckoldry of her earthly husband Joseph but to her own perception of and healthy relationship with the holy spirit (animus) underlying and refining her earthly, physical life. Thus the **myth** of the Annunciation refers primarily to a psychological event.

By this view, moral myth and psychic metaphor are misinterpreted as physical fact. Annunciation occurs wherever and whenever individuals open themselves to receive information brought by 'angels' (messengers) from the wider, deeper realms of Universal Self.

Thus 2,000 years ago, Gabriel; thus today, it may be, **UFO entities**.

Yet at the same time the literalist argument cannot be rejected out of hand. Tales of actual human sexual contact with non-human or supernatural beings are universal, ancient and modern. Not only gods and angels but **demons, incubi and succubi, fairies** and UFO entities are said to have enjoyed sexual relationships with humanity. **Abductions** by such beings, or magical workings to invoke them, are often involved in these accounts.

Is there any truth to them? Perhaps all that can be said is that the Holy Ghost is not to be laid by rational or scientific assertion alone.

ANTHROPOSOPHY (*See* **STEINER**) This system of spiritual science, developed and propounded by the Austrian scientist and mystic Rudolf Steiner after his split with the **Theosophical Society** in 1909, is named from the Greek: *anthropos* (man), and *sophia* (wisdom). It explains human evolution as advancing through seven epochs and seven civilisations – not that far from Theosophical notions of the '**root races**'. Essentially **dualistic**, the system employs the image of Lucifer as the eternal enemy of human spiritual progress. **Reincarnation** and life in the spirit worlds between incarnations is another basic aspect of the teaching which, however, *outré* it seems to the pragmatically minded, has established itself in a worldwide system of schooling for the young – 'Steiner schools'.

Today some 400 Steiner schools (*Waldorfschule*) offer a well-established alternative to more conventional educational systems.

1. *Anthroposophy: An Introduction*, Rudolf Steiner, Rudolf Steiner Publications, New York 1983

ANTICHRIST (*See* **APOCALYPSE, DEVIL**) **Christianity** denies **dualism** yet invokes duality. The image of **Christ** as Saviour implies the counter-balance of Antichrist, the Destroyer. There is nothing wrong in this: Destruction and Creation are part of the nature of God, as Eastern **religions** recognise. No Hindu hates Siva for being Siva – it would be like hating a rock for being a rock, or the sea for being the sea. The Destroyer is necessary. But exoteric Christianity denies this, as it denies that God has anything to do with evil. *Antichrist* seeks to destroy *God's Plan*, as if that Plan never included destruction. Esoteric Christians who see it otherwise are not outspoken, not in public, especially in the USA, where Christian fundamentalism is a potent populist force. Lately a US President called an opposing world power the 'Evil Empire': with that power now rendered ineffectual as a spiritual opponent, Antichrist is now located in more familiar biblical territory – the Middle East.

The symbol of Antichrist dates back not only to the Book of Revelation, but also to Sibylline tradition, each telling how in the Last Days there will arise an arch-enemy of God, the Antichrist. The Christian tradition seems to derive from the Old Testament **prophecy** of Daniel's dream, which speaks of a king 'who shall exalt himself, and magnify himself above every god'.[1] That this referred to the megalomaniac Antiochus Epiphanes was soon forgotten: the image of the God-hating tyrant of the Last Days became part of Jewish-Christian apocalyptic lore, merging with the figure of Satan, the ten-horned dragon, 'that old serpent', to fascinate the Middle Ages as an image of demoniacal tyranny, his coming tensely awaited. Tyrannical kings and popes were commonly called Antichrist; Luther was called Antichrist – it was a stock insult for centuries; then, with the dawning of the Age of Reason, fell into disuse, or so it seemed – for now the image is revived.

In books sold in every US supermarket fundamentalists like Hal Lindsey propagate a biblical interpretation of world events holding that the Last Days are nigh and that Armageddon and the Second Coming approach. Lindsey (over 5,000,000 copies of his *The Late Great Planet Earth* sold) identified the EEC (when it consisted of ten member-states) as the ten-horned Beast of Revelation:[2] Antichrist (say seeress Jeane **Dixon** and others) was born in the Middle East in 1962, and will soon engulf the world in **apocalyptic** war. But in 1999 the Image of the Cross will be seen in the eastern skies, Antichrist and his legions will be destroyed at the Battle of Armageddon (Megiddo, near Haifa in Israel). Amid worldwide carnage Jesus will return, physically, to establish the Millennium. Meanwhile the Righteous will have been saved from the carnage by the Rapture, literally rising up 'in the middle of the air' to meet Jesus and go to Heaven. Some fundamentalists say the Rapture occurs only after the final defeat of the Antichrist.

The power of such ideology should not be underestimated. Millions, with the apocalyptic year AD 2000 so close, not only believe this scenario but plan their lives according to it.

1. *In Pursuit of the Millennium*, Norman Cohn, Paladin, London 1970, p. 33
2. *The Late Great Planet Earth*, Hal Lindsey, Zondervan, Great Rapids, Michigan 1970

ANTIMATTER (*See* **BLACK HOLES**) Matter consists of atoms, which consist of combinations of three principal particles – positively charged protons, neutral neutrons and negatively charged electrons. In a stable atom the number of protons in the nucleus equals the number of electrons orbiting it; thus the atom is electrically neutral. But the same balance would arise if protons were negative and electrons positive, giving rise to *antimatter*, consisting of *antiparticles* – the first of which, the positron (positively charged electron) was found in 1932. Such antiparticles spin in the opposite direction to particles. In theory, some galaxies in our universe may be made of antimatter. But as both obey the same laws, an 'antimatter' galaxy would be indistinguishable from a 'matter' galaxy – save if they collided, for matter and antimatter annihilate each other on contact. There is little antimatter in our part of the universe! Such antiparticles as are known are shortlived and rare.

In 1949 Feynman proposed that antiparticles travel (due to reversed spin) not from past to future, but vice versa. Another idea is that antimatter is truly rare in our universe, and that **time** (if linear) points one way only. But *oscillating universe* models (which envisage a 'chain' of universes, each a link in the chain, creating a 'multiverse'), suggest the possibility of a matter/antimatter alternation between one link or universe and the next. Thus our 'matter' universe may be partnered on either side by 'antimatter' or alternate universes in which time (to us) runs backward.

Such theories seem like a modern version of the mediaeval concern with estimating how many angels can dance on the head of a pin.

APOCALYPSE (*See* **ANTICHRIST, NOSTRADAMUS, PROPHECY**) Meaning *revelation* (from Greek *apokalupsis*, 'to uncover'), this term is loosely associated with end-of-the-world cataclysm via the potent imagery of the last book in the New Testament – the Revelation (Apocalypse) of St John, a second-century Greek **mystic**. Ever since, his imagery – the Breaking of the Seals, the seven **angels** blowing their trumpets over the Earth; the horrors of plague, earthquake and mass-destruction, the War in Heaven between St Michael and the **dragon**; the beast whose number is 666; the Fall of Babylon and the New Jerusalem – has fascinated and terrified people.

Apocalyptic fervour is most intense when the date nears a round number, like AD 1000, or AD 2000. In AD 999 fear of End Times so gripped Europe that rich men gave away their wealth! Yet it persists whenever life grows hard. Throughout the Middle Ages and early modern era **millenarian** groups exploited disasters from the Black Death to the Thirty Years War to claim the imminence of the **Second Coming**. People sought salvation by flagellation and self-mutilation.

Today we are wiser – or are we? Pollution, global warming and nuclear weaponry encourage the sense that our activities may be causing, if not the end of the world, at least the end of ourselves. Apocalyptic anxiety is once again easily exploited. Signs of the End are sought and found. Prophecies of doom by Nostradamus, the Monk of Padua, Edgar **Cayce** and others abound.

When doom is in the air, whenever war, plague, famine and social strife rage out of hand, St John's 'apocalyptic' imagery is readily applied by fundamentalist **Christians** who, in every generation, believe that the end of the world is at hand, and that the Rider on the White Horse is about to descend from heaven, to trample the nations, cast Satan into the abyss for a thousand years, and raise up those who have not worshipped the Beast.

'Apocalypse Now' has been a popular cry for 2,000 years, not least because many of us remain personally reluctant to believe that the world will carry on without us after we die.

APPARITIONS (*See* **CRISIS APPARITIONS, GHOSTS, KÜBLER-ROSS**)

APPORTS The projection of objects into visible material space by **psychic** means. Many nineteenth-century **Spiritualists** and **mediums** (including Madame **Blavatsky**) claimed this power. Today, research into **psychokinesis** (PK) suggests Mind *can* move Matter, though not necessarily as easily as in old magical tales.

ARCHETYPES (*See* **ANIMA, COLLECTIVE UNCONSCIOUS, DREAMS, JUNG**) Early in his career C. G. Jung found *potent primordial images* manifesting in his patients' dreams and fantasies. These did not arise from personal memory or experience, but seemingly from a vast, ancient, universal store of imagery located deep in the unconscious. **Freud** considered them useless 'archaic residues', psychic equivalents of the appendix: Jung decided they were vital, living centres of psychic life, arising from a collective, non-egoic mental level at which all beings unconsciously join with each other and with natural forces. Typified by their *numinosity*, these *archetypes*, as Jung named them, are so vivid and organised as to be personified in forms common to every culture, or era. Each such form, Trickster, Earth Mother, Wise Old Man, etc., brings its own character and distinct message from the **collective unconscious** into the conscious individual mind. Gods and devils of world mythology are instinctive/intuitive representations of archetypes; Greek mythology offers perhaps the most accurate, detailed and differentiated model. Jung considered that denial of archetypes and their values and messages causes that (peculiarly modern) sense of life as empty and meaningless: a state which Africans call 'loss of soul' and which they consider the worst disaster that can befall a human being. Derangement and neurosis may thus be seen as measures of individual estrangement from the full unconscious self.[1]

1. *Man and his Symbols*, ed. C. G. Jung, Aldus Books, London 1964, p. 67ff

ARIGÓ, José (d. 1971) (*See* **PSYCHIC SURGERY, SPIRITISM**) José de Freitas, nicknamed 'Arigó', became a national hero in Brazil during the 1950s for his exploits as a **psychic surgeon**. An uneducated ex-miner from Congonhas do Campo, he performed thousands of complex operations with table-knives or scissors in totally unsterile conditions. In **trance** while diagnosing and treating the sick, he said a Dr Adolphus Fritz, a German who died in Estonia in 1918, spoke in his right ear, telling him what to do. Twice jailed for practising illegally (despite testimony from those he'd cured, and despite no evidence that his unorthodox techniques had caused any harm), after his second sentence in 1965 he turned exclusively to diagnosis. In 1968 a team of doctors led by the New York neurologist Andrija **Puharich** saw him treat a thousand patients. Without touching any, and taking on average under a minute per patient, he diagnosed and advised appropriate treatment for each. In cases that could be verified, Puharich says, 'we did not find [one] in which Arigó was at fault.'[1] Puharich also found Arigó phenomenally accurate in making prescriptions, many of them complex. In those few cases where Arigó diagnosed but refused treatment, Puharich and his team confirmed that every one was hopelessly terminal.

Earlier Puharich had seen Arigó practise surgery: 'The people step up – they're all sick. One had a big goitre. Arigó just picked up the paring knife, cut it open, popped the goitre out, slapped it in her hand, wiped the opening with a piece of dirty cotton, and off she went. It hardly bled at all.'[2] Similar operations were not only verified by other observers and authors,[3] but filmed independently, with blood samples identified as belonging to the patients involved. There was no fraud or hallucination. Arigó gave no explanation but credited Jesus and Dr Fritz (whose existence remains unverified). Apparently unaware of what he did while in trance, when once he saw film of himself performing an operation, he fainted. Thus the source of his talent remains as mysterious as his death – he died in a car crash in 1971, having told several people they would not see him again.

1. *The Romeo Error*, Lyall Watson, Coronet Books, London 1976, p. 212
2. 'Arigó: Surgeon Extraordinary', Roy Stemman, *The Unexplained*, Orbis partwork, London 1983, p. 379

ARNOLD, Kenneth (*See* **UFOs**)

ARTHURIAN MYTH (*See* **CELTIC MAGIC, HOLY GRAIL, MERLIN**) Was there ever a 'real' King Arthur? In 1485, soon after the first publication of Malory's *Morte d'Arthur* the printer Caxton remarked, 'Divers men hold opinion that there was no such Arthur.'[1] By then the **myth** was already well developed. In his *History of the Kings of Britain* (1135) Geoffrey of Monmouth, not averse to tall tales, had traced British kingship back to Brutus the Trojan. For his main theme he had drawn on the myth of one *Arth Vawr mab Uthr* (Welsh: 'The terrible Great Bear') who, Lewis **Spence** believed, was the central figure of a late British **pagan** cultus, perhaps representing an older hero-god or sun-god.[2] Mistranslating 'mab Uthr' as 'son of Uther', Geoffrey's romance of Arthur took cultured Europe by storm.

Later writers like Chrétien de Troyes, Wolfram von Eschenbach, and the unknown author of *Sir Gawain and the Green Knight* elaborated the chivalric, magical aspects of this 'Matter of Britain' and of the 'Quest for the Holy Grail'. By the time of Malory (he introduced the Round Table theme), these themes and the tales of **Merlin**, Percival, etc., had become the vehicle of ideas which, though Christianised, were at root thoroughly **pagan**. Thus the sword Excalibur derives from the Irish *Caliburn*; the original Celtic Arthur raids Annwn, Land of the Dead, to steal a magic cauldron (grail) once owned by the Irish Dadga or 'Good God'; while the tale of Arthur hunting the boar Twrch Trwyth predates AD 800, being mentioned by Nennius. Malory was the first to identify the Isle of Avalon as **Glastonbury** (*Ynys Witrin*: 'The Isle of Glass') where, in 1191, monks claimed to have found the coffin of Arthur and Guinevere: a claim that brought the monastery good pilgrim trade! Yet more likely Avalon derives from Celtic tales of the Isles of the Blest (Mag Mell, Tir nan Og, etc.) mythically located in the western (Atlantic) ocean.

The Arthurian mythos thus provided a bridge between pagan Celtic and **Christian** imagination, tapping sources so deep that it has fired European imagination for a millennium. Did a 'real' Arthur live? Does it matter? Perhaps there was a Romano-Celtic war-leader who *c*. AD 516 defeated Anglo-Saxon invaders at Mount Badon; perhaps there was a poet-**shaman**, Myrrdin (Merlin), driven mad after the defeat of his king at Arderwydd and thereafter roaming the Forest of Celydon (in Scotland) – but does it matter? Arthur, Merlin and so on live in our collective imagination as source and epitome of another, magical way of life; potent **archetypes** telling us of something lost or lacking in ourselves and our view of the world. As such the entire myth remains active, not least in the training methods and ritual practice of various esoteric and occult groups in the UK and elsewhere.

To such groups 'The Arthur' (like 'The Christ') is not an historical figure but an elevated state of inner being: the exemplar of a spiritual condition; a Quest-figure appropriate to those brought up in the British group-mind as other such figures are appropriate elsewhere. Such myths are potent: their colour, romance and implications activate vital aspects of human nature and potential that reason alone cannot reach.

1. *Religion and the Decline of Magic*, Keith Thomas, Peregrine, London 1978, p. 508
2. *The Magic Arts in Celtic Britain*, Lewis Spence, Rider, London 1946
   King Arthur and the Grail, Richard Cavendish, Paladin, London 1980
   The Mists of Avalon, Marion Zimmer Bradley, Sphere, London 1984

ASTRAL BODY (*See* **AURA, DOPPELGÄNGER, KA, KIRLIAN, MONROE, OOBEs**) When we **dream**, say occultists, we leave the physical for the *astral* body, to find ourselves **levitating** or travelling instantly to distant places.

Only dreaming? Is it? There is much to support the worldwide ancient belief that the physical body is built round a subtle energetic framework co-existing with it yet not wholly reliant on it. **Kirlian** photographs of the **aura**, out-of-body experiences (**OOBEs**), the manifestation of **ghosts, doppelgängers** and other mechanically inexplicable phenomena all suggest that the physical body is but the gross material layer (the onion's outer skin) of several such 'bodies' we inhabit; each progressively more refined and energetic; each with its own characteristics, rate of vibration, and sphere of influence. Some systems postulate more 'subtle' bodies, others less, but usually three are defined: *physical, astral* and **etheric**. The astral body (given the prejudice the term evokes) may more usefully be called the *energy body*. It constitutes the energetic (**electromagnetic**) blueprint round which the physical body forms; it is occultly seen as the vehicle of **prana** or life-energy; and is said to be so tied to the physical body that it survives the death of that only by some forty days before itself dissipating, leaving the *etheric* body as the vehicle of consciousness.

On the **astral plane** thoughts and desires, unhindered by physical laws, act directly.

What you think is what you are: what you dream is what you do.

One theory suggests ghosts arise from the activity of people physically deceased yet ignorant of this or refusing to recognise it. Via the power of thought and desire such people maintain obsessional contact with living persons or past 'haunts', imposing themselves as ghosts until 'exorcised'. When persuaded of their situation, they move on to the realms that await them.

But the terminology remains vague. *Astral* is applied to conditions that others call *etheric*: neither term means anything to rationalists who deny any sort of non-material existence. Persistent *scientific* disbelief in events arising from Mind's habitation of and movement between its different wavelengths of body mean such phenomena remain 'scientifically' dubious – a Catch–22 situation. The vested interests involved are as profound as those which got Galileo in hot water when he tried to get the Church doctors to acknowledge the existence of Jupiter's moons.

Likewise today the implications of the new physics, as demonstrated by **Planck, Einstein, Heisenberg** and others, while accepted in the creation of nuclear weaponry, have not been applied with sufficient rigour to Mind-Body complexities. The problem is fear of the unknown. Until we get over it, individually and collectively, we are stuck with a materialistic belief-system that not only cannot do (our) Nature justice, but will continue to regard **Gaia** as a lump of exploitable clay.

ASTRAL PLANE (*See* **EARTH SPIRIT, ELECTROMAGNETISM, GAIA**)
As the **astral body** is to the individual, so the *astral plane* is to **Gaia**. It is the energetic blueprint from which the physical Earth derives. As such it has its own laws and occupants. In all ages visionaries, **mystics**, poets and others have been affected by it, consciously or not. Encounters with and visions of **fairies, angels, demons** and **UFO entities** may all involve life-forms existing on this other wavelength. It so entirely coincides with our own *normal* wavelength-world that still we remain perplexed. Events like UFO **close encounters** are so ambiguous and bizarre that contactees often doubt their sanity even before running foul of other people's disbelief.

The 'astral' and physical worlds shift in and out of each other with an ease terrifying to those of us brought up to believe in a fixed and stable physical universe. Parallel **dimensions** with different natural laws run together: we are still like cavemen exalted or terrified by the sky in our emotional urge to believe or disbelieve the evidence without examining it.

How can we face the cosmos as outlined by probability and **quantum** theory? It's fine on paper, but the failure of Newton's laws to guarantee a physical world obeying constant and fixed laws collides with our need for emotional security. Abruptly we face not a simple physical universe, but a *quantum multiverse* in which **ghosts**, demons, and other weird entities and conditions (however defined) return like wolves to the sheep-fold. Seventeenth-century Reason did not, after all, succeed in rejecting them. Is neurosis only the product of cultural background and physical environment? Could it not also arise from **elemental possession – vampiric thought-forms** that we unconsciously create – or from trauma caused by forgotten tragedies in previous lives?

We are all familiar with the astral plane, at least, in our sleep.

Occultly, the *astral plane* is not especially elevated. It lies only one vibratory range up from the range of wavelength from which the matter of the 'gross physical' world is formed. Many other worlds of Mind lie above and beyond it. Yet we have to start our recollection somewhere.

ASTRAL PROJECTION (*See* **MONROE, OUT-OF-BODY EXPERIENCES BRUNTON, GARRETT, GREAT PYRAMID, MULDOON**)

ASTROLOGY (*See* **BROWN, F., CYCLES, GAUQUELIN, JONAS,**

NELSON) 'As above, so below.' This ancient hermetic epigram sums up the essential principle of astrology – that the cosmos is a unity, governed by specific laws and interconnected in all its parts. Astrology is thus the science or study of the relationship between celestial cause and terrestrial effect. Though among the oldest of studies (it was practised in Sumeria *c*. 4000 BC), since Newton's time it has been termed a pseudo-science, as no mechanisms governing such a relationship have readily come to light. Its persistent popularity in corrupt form as a means of predicting the personal fate of those born under each of the twelve Sun signs (as found on the horoscope page of daily newspapers) has deepened scientific prejudice against its basic axioms. Yet now this situation is changing. Research in areas such as biology, meteorology and **electromagnetism** increasingly suggests that the motions and cycles of celestial bodies (especially the Sun, Moon and major planets) have measurable effect on terrestrial organisms and conditions.

There are several forms of astrology. *Natal* astrology links the solar, lunar and planetary positions (seen against the background constellations) at the moment of birth with the personality and fate of individuals. This is the type most commonly invoked (and corrupted). *Astrometeorology* deals with prediction of earthquakes, volcanic eruptions, and climatic conditions in general. The work of John H. Nelson, an RCA radio engineer, has proved illuminating in this area. *Horary* astrology interprets 'specific questions in terms of a chart erected for the moment the question is asked'.[1] *Medical* astrology concerns diagnosis and treatment of disease. *Electional* astrology seeks to find appropriate times to start specific activities. Thus in 1558 the magus John **Dee** was hired by Queen Elizabeth to determine the best date for her coronation. *Cosmobiology*, a new field, correlates cosmic cycles and radiations with animal behaviour and biological rhythms in general. In this latter area US biologist Frank Brown has shown how the metabolism of animals fluctuates according to lunar cycles and other geomagnetic factors; Czech Eugen Jonas in the 1960s pioneered an effective technique of birth control based on estimating the lunar cycles of individual women.

Common to most types of astrology are the ideas of the *zodiac* (Greek: '*circle of animals*') and the *houses*. In apparent motion against background stars, the Sun, Moon, and planets occupy a narrow band of constellations which form the *zodiac*. This circle of sky, the ecliptic, is divided into twelve sectors, each of 30°, each forming one zodiacal sign. These signs, widely known as 'star signs', are: Aries (Ram), Taurus (Bull), Gemini (Twins), Cancer (Crab), Leo (Lion), Virgo (Virgin), Libra (Scales), Sagittarius (Archer), Scorpio (Scorpion), Capricorn (Goat), Aquarius (Waterbearer) and Pisces (Fishes). They are sub-divided into four categories of Earth, Air, Fire and Water. Thus, Aries, Leo and Scorpio are Fire signs; Taurus, Virgo and Capricorn are Earth signs; Gemini, Libra and Aquarius belong to the Air; and Cancer, Sagittarius and Pisces to Water. Between them they form the basis of interpretation in popular daily newspaper horoscopes.

For natal interpretative purposes the sky both above and below the horizon is also divided into twelve further sectors, the *houses*. The first house is that sector immediately under the horizon at the moment of birth: the houses are labelled anticlockwise. An individual birth chart is drawn up in circular form, in two rings. The zodiacal signs (beginning with that constellation touching the eastern horizon at the moment of birth, called the *ascending sign*) occupy the outside circle, and proceed clockwise. The houses occupy the inner circle. The positions of the planets at the time of birth are placed accordingly on this circular diagram. Each thus fits not only a sign but a house. The interaction of planets, signs and houses (each ascribed general psychological characteristics derived from the past experience of astrologers through the ages) creates a complex picture, as individual as a fingerprint, and made more so by further subdivisions that the astrologer interprets. The *formal* image thus presented is only part of the interpretative process. The astrologer's own skill and **intuition** play a major role. A birth-chart is a blueprint, not the fleshed-out being.

Of the subdivisions to aid interpretation: (1) the twelve zodiac signs are subdivided into four elements – earth, air, fire and water, each with its own psychological characteristics; (2) influences *below* the horizon are said to be *unconscious* aspects of the personality; those *above, conscious*; (3) the place (in sign and house) of the Sun at birth is a major reference point; (4) the strengths, weaknesses and potential of the individual whose chart it is are further defined by the *aspects* of the planets in regard to each other on the chart.

Planets close together are in *conjunction*; they are in *square* if 90° apart; in *opposition* if 180° apart. *Trine* (60°) and *sextile* (120°) define intermediate angles of relationship. The former are said to be *difficult* aspects; the latter, *easy*. But 'difficult' or 'easy' aspects do not guarantee 'failure' or 'success' in life – the person with a 'difficult' chart may well be driven, by the need to integrate conflicting influences, to a greater success in life than one in harmony to begin with.

Different house systems and disagreements in interpretation add to the complexity of a system which is necessarily as broad and varied in its interpretative possibilities as is human nature itself. Here we are a long way from the simplistic daily Sun sign horoscopes of the sort denounced as violently by the prophet Jeremiah 2,500 years ago as by sceptics today. Which brings us to the history of astrology.

Natal astrology is old. A Sanskrit text by the Indian sage Parasara, *c.* 3000 BC, employs the 'equal house' system of twelve equal 30° signs. The astrology we know began in Sumeria. The Chaldeans built ziggurats (pyramidal stepped towers) from which to watch the motion of stars and planets. From them we get our mythology of stars and planets as gods. Called *bibbus* (goats) by the Chaldeans, the wandering planets amid the sheep-like steadfast stars seemed like self-ruling gods, each going its own way, seeming to reflect (and control) human behaviour. When Nerval (the Chaldean Mars) dominated the night, war was near. Ishtar (Venus) shone after sunset, when the time of love approached. As for Nabu (Thoth, Hermes, Mercury), he was so fast and hard to see that he was clearly a sharp-witted trickster. Marduk (Jupiter) in his bright, reliable course was as remote as the god-king on the throne. Saturn, that old slow man, so heavy yet potent, was a fearful reminder of cold death.

Yet more than fantasy was (and is) involved. The Chaldeans became the great ancient astrologers because their measurements of celestial motion were the most accurate. (**Stonehenge**, Callanish, Carnac and other European **megalithic** observatories may have been as accurate, but nothing was left in writing). Chaldean myth was taken up by others – Babylonians, Egyptians, ultimately by Greeks and Romans. People were eager to borrow any system that explained the cosmic mystery more fully. The twelve-sign zodiac of 360° appears to have arisen 'independently' from China to Britain about the same time. But there must have been a fight. The number of such signs (as with the number of **chakras** (energy centres) ascribed to the human body) varied according to the culture. They were based on the number of months in the year, giving either twelve or thirteen, depending on the solar/lunar allegiance of the culture. Today we agree on twelve such signs – a solar opinion – even though, **moon**-wise, there are thirteen ($13 \times 28 = 364$ days) months in a year.

US author James Vogh has argued that anciently there was a thirteen-sign lunar zodiac, the 'missing' sign being that of Arachne, the Spider, said to lie between Taurus and Gemini, and epitomised by psychism. He suggests that the thirteen-sign lunar zodiac was purged during a conflict between solar and lunar priesthoods (man-mysteries *vs* woman-mysteries) so profoundly won by one side that evidence, far less memory, of the debate, has been not only lost, but turned into inherited superstition so profound that even today the number '13' is often missed out in new housing developments.[2]

Which returns us to the present. The reconciliation of astrology with science? Nothing is certain, but the signs are more hopeful than for centuries. New scientific discovery slowly leads to a hard-won new respect for old perceptions. (The work of Gauquelin, Jonas, Nelson and Brown is considered elsewhere.) More recently, Dr

Percy Seymour, an astronomer at the University of Southampton, has advanced the theory that Earth's magnetic field responds to the gravitational pull of the planets, arguing (as **Kepler** did 500 years ago) that the *music of the spheres* is an **electromagnetic** reality – a precisely scientific/poetic description of the way in which Gaia's geomagnetic lines of force respond, like a harp, to the influence of the orbiting cosmic bodies. He uses the findings of astronomy to vindicate astrological teachings and implies that many other scientists would do likewise if they did not fear for their careers.

Reporting the work of British astrophysicists Gribbin and Plagemann, who in *The Jupiter Effect* (Fontana, London 1977) developed a theory linking earthquakes to the motion and position of the planets, he quotes Plagemann who, working for NASA, was approached by a colleague. 'You know,' said the man, 'I've been working on predicting solar flares for years, and I've a file of evidence which shows a definite relationship with Jupiter–Saturn alignments. But I daren't put that in my report – it's more than my job is worth.'[3]

1. *The Dictionary of Astrology*, Fred Gettings, Routledge Kegan Paul, London 1985
2. *The Thirteenth Zodiac*, James Vogh, Granada Mayflower, London 1979
3. *Astrology: The Evidence of Science*, Percy Seymour, Arkana, London 1990

ATLANTIS (*See* **CAYCE, VALENTINE**) Ten thousand years ago, it is said, in the course of 'a single day and night' the mighty isle of Atlantis and its proud peoples were swept by earthquake and flood into the depths of the ocean. Whether or not this happened, the **myth** of the drowned island continent exercises a deep fascination. It resonates with the idea of knowledge lost ('drowned') in the subconscious mind. It also epitomises (Tower of Babel) our guilty sense of 'the wages of sin'.

Did Atlantis really exist? Nobody really knows. Some claim its empire embraced parts of the Americas, Africa, Europe and even Asia; that its red-skinned people had deep occult powers; that their abuse of a **crystal**-based technology led to the final disaster, and that **Stonehenge**, the pyramids of **Egypt**, and all **magic** and ancient wisdom derive from the knowledge of the few Atlanteans who escaped the cataclysm.

Many recent expeditions have sought Atlantean remains,typically near the Azores or the Bahamas where in 1968, in the shallow waters of the Grand Bahama Bank, many finely jointed stone slabs were found, making what has been called the 'Bimini Road'. Some call this proof of Atlantis, and point to predictions by Edgar Cayce that rediscovery of Atlantis between 1958 and 1998 would presage global chaos. Others, more sanguine, speculate that Atlantean myth is based on imperfect folk-memory of the cataclysmic eruption of Thera (Santorini) in the Aegean during the fifteenth century BC, an eruption which may have destroyed the island (thus *Atlantean*) civilisation of Minoan Crete, ninety miles to the south.

The tale we have was first recorded (or invented) some 2,400 years ago by Plato in the *Timaeus*. He tells of a journey to Egypt by the statesman Solon *c*. 600 BC. 'You Greeks are all children,' an old priest at Saïs in the Delta told Solon, '. . . you have no belief rooted in old tradition . . . And the reason is this. There have been and will be many different calamities to destroy mankind, the greatest of them by fire and water.' The priest then described 'an island larger than Libya and Asia combined' which once lay 'opposite the strait which you call the Pillars of Heracles'. Here a great empire had arisen. Invading Europe, it had been opposed by ancient Greeks, until 'there were earthquakes and floods . . . and in a single dreadful day and night all your fighting men were swallowed up by the earth, and the island of Atlantis was similarly swallowed up by the sea and vanished.'[1]

Plato describes Atlantis in detail. Ten kings ruled the empire. The capital city occupied ground within three circular canals; metal-clad walls guarded the circles of land; the largest temple on the central island was dedicated to Poseidon and Cleito; the royal palace had hot and cold running water; wild bulls were kept in its grounds.

Etcetera. Some say the detail is such that Plato couldn't have invented it – yet his pupil Aristotle was among the first to imply it was fantasy, invented by Plato to moralise on the nature and consequences of overweening human ambition.

If so, it proved compelling. For centuries thereafter it was generally thought factual. People wanted to believe it. Mediaeval sea-charts showed unknown Atlantic isles. Like the **Celtic** Isles of Youth and Happiness, they were thought to possess ideal climates and ways of life. Portuguese charts in the fifteenth century showed Antilia, a mythic isle. Francis Bacon's *The New Atlantis* (1624) describes an ideal society, or *utopia*. Did he believe it?

Modern popularisation of the legend began with the publication in 1882 by American Congressman Ignatius Donnelly of his *Atlantis: the Antediluvian World*. Siting Atlantis on the Azores, he tried to prove (with a mass of loosely connected ethnographic detail) that old European and pre-Columbian American societies had all been critically influenced by the diffusion of Atlantean culture. His book remains in print.[2] Occultists like **Blavatsky** and **Steiner** subsequently developed the myth of lost continents, with **Mu** in the Pacific playing second fiddle to Atlantis. The revisionist notion that Atlantis was in fact the Minoan civilisation of Crete first appeared in a London *Times* article by K. T. Frost in 1909. This alluring theory is still popular, but it assumes that Plato (or Solon or the priests of Saïs): (1) couldn't tell the difference between 10,000 BC and 1500 BC; and (2) couldn't distinguish betwen the *Mediterranean Sea* and the *Atlantic Ocean*.

It may not really matter if Atlantis ever existed in *physical fact*. The myth – of a proud civilisation destroyed not only by its own flaws but by the inexorable power of Nature, unacknowledged until too late – has its own potency.

1. *Timaeus and Critias*, Plato, trans. Desmond Lee, Penguin, London 1971
2. *Atlantis: The Antediluvian World*, Ignatius Donnelly, Sidgwick and Jackson, London 1970 (1882)

AURA (*See* **ASTRAL BODY, KIRLIAN**) Traditionally shown by artists as an ethereal, coronal light surrounding images of **angels**, saints and other extraordinary, beneficial beings, the aura may now be seen not as unusual at all, but as a natural attribute of the electrical activity of the energy-body associated with all organisms (human beings included) that on Earth do dwell. Though invisible to common sight (as radio waves are invisible), this energetic body, permeating and surrounding all kinds of organic physical body, has always been sensed by **psychics** like **Daskalos**, who interpret its individual condition (bright, muddy, spotted, with *this* or *that* colour predominant) as a guide to the physical, mental and emotional health of the individual involved.

Kirlian photographs show how auric discharge varies according to mood. Such evidence (the aura of a youth attracted to a girl lights up, as does the aura of someone who has just had a drink) offers only the start of a scientific investigation into what has always been known. For example we may call the personality of a person 'magnetic' or 'dull'.

AUTOMATIC WRITING In **trance** states some people produce writing not of their own will but via 'dictation' from what are often claimed to be discarnate spirits. Either that, or the ego of the writer is subordinated to the interruption of organised unconscious content. **Blavatsky, Bailey** and other prolific **occult** writers have all claimed that their published material came not from them but from **discarnate** 'secret masters', 'Tibetans', etc. Thus too the claim of London housewife Rosemary Brown, who since 1964 while in trance states has 'transcribed' many new musical works seemingly by Beethoven, Brahms, Liszt, Chopin and others. Whether her compositions come from 'dead composers' is questionable: her own musical background is rudimentary. However composer Leonard Bernstein and others have been impressed not only by her sincerity but by the power and integrity of such 'posthumous' works.

B

BACH, Charlotte A new twist was given to the notion that human evolution arises from inner conflict (**Gooch**) by Charlotte Bach who in 1948 left Hungary for England and in 1965 began compiling a dictionary of psychology. Baffled by how to define sexual perversions, her studies led her to Plato's remark that men and women were originally halves of one creature: now, god-divided, we all wander about looking for the other half. Assuming sexual attraction to be the desire of each half to become the other, she found sexuality fitted an eightfold pattern starting with two main categories: those resisting unity with the other sex and those affirming it – thus four basic types, two in each sex, each carrying its own psychophysical paired/unpaired duo of male-female. So, a drag queen is a *male negative denialist* – physically male, psychologically the opposite, denying maleness. All such crossovers she concluded arise as 'spillover activities' due to energy overflowing from its original purpose into seemingly pointless roles.

But why all this imbalance? The concept of neoteny (humans are anatomically undeveloped apes, Peter Pans) suggested why. Perversion seems self-defeating, but the dull *equilibrium* of 'normal' sexual behaviour is also oddly incomplete.

On reading **Eliade** on **shamanism** and mystical ecstasy, she realised that *this imbalance is evolutionary;* sexual frustration mothers invention. To deal with this chaotic inner conflict people shunt it aside and block it (deviation), cage it in low equilibrium (normality), or, as in 'asexual' shamans and great artists, harness and resolve it at a higher level, as unified creative force. Blocking it may gain role-equilibrium but further growth is impossible. Caging or quenching it also makes further growth impossible. In many this evolutionary dynamic leads to unbalanced, self-conflicting states. Writer Negley Farson was told by a doctor: 'I could cure your alcoholism, but I'd probably "cure" your talent for writing at the same time.' However neurotic imbalance need not persist. The inner conflict remains, but may be resolved, as the great mystics, artists and **shamans** have always demonstrated.[1]

1. *Mysteries*, Colin Wilson, Grafton Books, London 1989, pp. 514–23

BACH, Johann Sebastian (1685–1750) 'But Papa Bach, how do you manage to think of all these new tunes?' a young admirer asked. 'My dear fellow,' J. S. Bach replied, 'I have the greatest difficulty not to step on them when I get out of bed in the morning.'[1]

An oddity of the Baroque style in which he composed emerged when Bach was asked by an insomniac Russian envoy, Count Kayserling, to compose music to help him sleep. When played by harpsichordist Johann Goldberg (thus the name: *Goldberg Variations*), Kayserling was asleep in minutes. Recent study of the aria starting and ending the piece shows it to induce a meditative state. The slow movements in some other baroque music have a similar effect. Bulgarian scientist Georgi Lozanov and Soviet psychologist I. K. Platonov believe the rhythm of such movements (about sixty beats a minute) induces the effect, not the music itself. And **'plant consciousness'** research suggests that plants grow better to baroque music speeded up.

1. *Jung and the Story of our Time*, Laurens van der Post, Penguin 1978, p. 125

BACKSTER, Cleve (*See* **PLANT CONSCIOUSNESS**) In 1966 this ex-CIA employee, an instructor in the use of polygraphs (lie-detectors), connected one to a house plant to see how it took up water from the soil. A polygraph measures blood pressure, respiration, involuntary muscular movements, and small changes in the electrical conductivity of the skin. Watering the plant, he expected increased conductivity as water rose into the plant tissues, but instead measured a *decrease*, like the response of a human being to a pleasant experience. Wondering how it would react to threat, he decided to burn it. At his thought the polygraph pen jumped: a reaction in a human indicating fear. More experiments suggested it could read his mind and differentiate between real and pretended intentions. He rejected **ESP** as a description and named this plant-**telepathy** 'primary perception'. To test plant reaction to the death of living tissue he rigged an electronic randomiser to drop live brine shrimp into boiling water. The plant responded to immersal of living shrimp, but ignored immersal of dead shrimp. A pet philodendron he handled only with care, deputising someone else to 'hurt' it. Soon the plant got 'agitated' if the assistant entered the room, but seemed to 'relax' when Backster approached.[1,2]

1. *Supernature*, Lyall Watson, Hodder and Stoughton, London 1973, pp. 247–48
2. *The Secret Life of Plants*, Peter Tompkins and Christopher Bird, Harper and Row, New York 1973

BACON, Roger (1214–94) This English Franciscan friar was a prototypical Renaissance man. In combining the study of philosophy, mathematics and physics with **alchemy** he made his lesser contemporaries so nervous that, as with Ramon Lull (1235–1315), supernatural legends sprang up about his name. Educated in Paris before returning to England, his heterodox studies led to the myth that he had succeeded in creating a robot, or 'brazen head', that not only spoke but predicted the future. Seized by the Inquisition, he died in a dungeon.

Six centuries later in 1912, Wilfred M. Voynich, a New York dealer in antique manuscripts, purchased in Europe a quarto vellum-covered manuscript that, in black ink script and coloured diagrams, described the medical and mystical qualities of plants and their preparation. The script was in an unknown language or code. Circumstantial evidence suggests that the author of this 'Voynich Manuscript' was Friar Bacon, and that he had used a self-devised code to conceal his **alchemical** researches. With little success.

The medieval sleuth called 'William de Baskerville' in Umberto Eco's bestselling 1984 novel *The Name of the Rose* seems to be based on the **myth** of Roger Bacon – a man of scientific insight trapped in a mediaeval milieu. If so, the later portrayal of William de Baskerville by actor Sean Connery in the movie of the book presents excellent insight into what it was like to be – as Bacon was – an original thinker in an age of rigid Aristotelian and ecclesiastic dogma. Like **Kammerer, Reich** and **Velikovsky** 650 years later, he suffered the consequences of antagonising Establishment thought.

BAILEY, Alice (1880–1949) (*See* **INNER PLANES, THEOSOPHY**) An English occultist and author (*Esoteric Astrology; Glamour – A World Problem; A Treatise on White Magic; A Treatise on Cosmic Fire*, etc.) whose works she gave out as 'revealed' to her by the Tibetan Master and other Inner Plane entities, Alice Bailey never stopped writing while bringing up a family, running an international correspondence course, and lecturing. She also founded the Arcane School to further her received knowledge, which remains a source for many seeking depth in esoteric cosmology.

BANSHEE (*See* **CELTIC MAGIC**) The Gaelic name means 'supernatural woman'. A Celtic spirit of the dead whose dismal wailing foretold death, the *banshee*, in Argyll called *cointach* or 'keener', usually appeared with sunken nose, scraggy white hair, huge hollow eye-sockets, a tattered white sheet flapping about her, walking by those she met on the road, keening and clapping her hands, repeating the name of the doomed one. Sometime she was the *bean-nighe*, the washerwoman, crouched by a ford washing bloodstained garments; sometimes the *glaistig*, a gruesome and dolorous ghost. Originating in the ancient Irish crow-goddess of battle and slaughter, the *badb* (meaning 'rage', 'fury', 'violence'), the *banshee* suited the Celtic soul. All the best Irish and Scottish families had their own. Lesser folk had only the hoody crow.[1]

1. *Magic Arts in Celtic Britain*, Lewis Spence, Rider, London 1970, p. 81

BAPHOMET (*See* **KNIGHTS TEMPLAR**)

BARDO THODOL (*See* **TIBETAN BOOK OF THE DEAD**)

BATCHELDOR, Kenneth (*See* **PHILIP THE IMAGINARY GHOST, POLTERGEISTS, PSYCHOKINESIS**) Since publishing his 'Report on a Case of Table Levitation and Associated Phenomena' in *The Journal of the Society for Psychical Research* in 1966, this British psychologist has investigated many cases of psychokinesis, **levitation**, and **poltergeist** phenomena. Using infra-red photography, audio/video recordings, and sensitive touch-pads, he has recorded violent movements by heavy tables and brief total levitations.

BEARDEN, Thomas (*See* **JUNG, PSYCHOTRONICS, UFOs**) Drawing on the 'many worlds' interpretation of quantum mechanics this retired US Army Officer and nuclear engineer in the 1970s constructed what he calls a 'psychotronic' model of reality, a theoretical framework accommodating **psychokinetic** phenomena, thought-materialisation (given enough coherence to breach the quantum threshold), and the exertion of **poltergeist** effects by the personal unconscious. He gives as examples of psychotronic phenomena UFOs and the **Loch Ness Monster**.

He wrote, 'The more interest there is, the more photos that are taken, and the more investigation that is done, the easier it is to find evidence of Nessie . . . It appears that Nessie is on the way to being permanently tuned in; a family of plesiosaurs is going to wind up living in Loch Ness, whether or not there are enough fish in the loch to support them.'

UFOs he sees as unconscious mental forms materialising whenever the **collective unconscious** is under stress. Thus UFOs began to appear at the start of the Cold War in 1946–47. Flying saucers (discs) he sees as female mandalas modulated by US national unconsciousness: he noted the eruption of UFO contactee cases in 1973 during the international crisis of the time. He thought the USSR possessed psychotronic weapons, including a machine able to broadcast disease patterns and generate earthquakes, and explained the mysterious wave of **cattle mutilations** occurring in the USA during the late 1970s as violation of the female symbol (cow) arising from collective unconscious expectation of a Soviet attack on NATO.[1]

Though his political views seem overtly to the fore, Bearden's view of UFOs and other forms of paranormal activity as rooted in and manifested by the collective unconscious echoes conclusions reached by C. G. Jung.

1. Quoted in *Lifetide*, Lyall Watson, Coronet, London 1980, pp. 362–65
An approach to understanding psychotronics, T. E. Bearden, privately published, 102 Willis Road, Huntsville, Alabama 1977
Species Metapsychology, UFO waves and cattle mutilations, T. E. Bearden, privately

published, 102 Willis Road, Huntsville, Alabama 1977

BENDER, Hans (*See* **POLTERGEIST, PSYCHOKINESIS, RAUDIVE**)

BENNETT, J. G. (*See* **GURDJIEFF**) Biographer of Gurdjieff, he founded the Institute for the Comparative Study of History, Philosophy and the Sciences to make known Gurdjieffian techniques, but later embraced *Subud*, calling Pakh Subuh (its founder) the forthcoming Avatar, heralding the end of the present age in world history. Later he abandoned Subud for Roman Catholicism and Eastern **mysticism**. He said his work remained Gurdjieffien in that it evolved from one question: What is the sense and significance of life on earth in general and of human life in particular? Some doubt if his later approach via group-work and meditation remained true to Gurdjieff's goal of 'overcoming sleep'.[1]

To explain **precognition** Bennett postulated a fifth **dimension**: 'inner freedom', a state unbound by the other four thus allowing choice between different time-tracks.

1. *Mysteries*, Colin Wilson, Grafton, London 1989, pp. 599–600
   Witness, J. G. Bennett, Turnstone, London 1974
   Gurdjieff: Making a New World, J. G. Bennett, Turnstone, London 1973

BERMUDA TRIANGLE (*See* **ATLANTIS, DIMENSIONS**) A western Atlantic area between Bermuda, Puerto Rico and the Florida coast, also called the 'Devil's Triangle', notorious for the many ships and planes lost in it leaving no wreckage or survivors, the loss sometimes preceded by garbled radio reports of strange fogs, electronic failures, power-loss, the sea looking odd, and so on. Theories of **paranormal** causes peaked, amid much publicity, in the 1970s, despite continued local Coastguard insistence that unexplained losses in the region are due to heavy traffic, sudden violent weather and the Gulf Stream, which can carry a disabled ship rapidly off course, dispersing wreckage too fast for retrieval. Such reassurance was drowned in popular speculation, namely that some unknown force destroyed or misled the lost vessels, or translated them to another dimension, time or space; this achieved either via **electromagnetic** anomaly and space/time warp or, more prosaically, in the bellies of giant invisible **UFO**s. Some claimed that shipping was deranged by submarine Atlantean **crystal** generators still going 10,000 years after submersion: others insisted that official denial of such odd events proved cover-up, either of ignorance or complicity.

Interest in the Bermuda Triangle (so named in 1964 by Vincent Gaddis) began on 5 December 1945. Training Flight 19 of five US Navy Grumman TBM–3 torpedo-bombers from Fort Lauderdale was lost after odd radio messages from the flight leader: 'We seem to be off course. We cannot see land . . . We don't know which way is west. Everything is wrong . . . even the ocean doesn't look as it should.' Fading inter-flight messages suggested that magnetic compasses and gyros in the planes were 'going crazy'. A thirteen-man Martin Mariner went out and was also lost. A huge search party found nothing. 'They vanished as completely as if they had flown to Mars,' said a Naval Board member. The myth thus began grew with each succeeding 'unexplained' loss. In time documentaries, novels, movies and a board game came out. The Bermuda Triangle vied with Uri **Geller** for media prominence . . . then slipped down the charts to the graveyard of mysteries milked for all they're worth.

Many still wonder how with so many losses no wreckage or survivors are *ever* found, but evidence of distortion and inaccuracy in most loss-reports is undeniable. Flight 19 in fact involved an inexperienced crew, rough weather, poor radio conditions, a flight-leader uncorrected when wrongly thinking he'd flown off-course. A storm blew up, night fell, the planes ran out of fuel and ditched in heavy seas which tore them apart. Forty-six years later, in mid-1991, the wreckage of Flight 19 was located on the seabed.

The radio messages cannot be traced beyond a 1962 magazine article. Another famous case relying on distortion is that of the Japanese freighter *Raifaku Maru*. Lost in 1924, its last radio-call (supposedly: 'Danger like dagger now . . .') was actually logged as: 'Now very danger . . .' And though the barque *Freya* was indeed found abandoned at sea in October 1902, it was in the Pacific.

Despite some evidence of magnetic anomalies in the area it may be the Triangle's main anomaly is **psychotronic** human imagination collectively and unconsciously at work . . . or play.

The Bermuda Triangle, Charles Berlitz, Granada, London 1975

BEROSSUS (*See* **ANCIENT ASTRONAUTS**)

BESANT, Annie (1847–1933) (*See* **BLAVATSKY, QUARK, THEOSOPHY**)
Annie Besant's's claim that with **Theosophist** Charles W. **Leadbetter** she psychically observed fundamental particles no longer fazes some particle physicists working on **quark** theory. The structure Besant and Leadbetter related to the **Qabalistic Tree of Life** and called the 'micro-*psi*' hydrogen atom consisted of two intersecting triangular arrays, each of three bodies, each of these consisting of three particles they termed 'ultimate physical atoms' or *anu* (Sanskrit: *atoms*). This model, some scientists believe, accurately prefigures the quark landscape.[1]

Born Annie Wood in London, fanatically Anglo-Catholic at fourteen, married at twenty to Anglican cleric Frank Besant and separated at twenty-three, she threw herself into atheism and free thought. By 1875 Vice-President of the National Secular Society, in 1877 she published *The Gospel of Atheism* while charged with obscenity for advocating birth control in another book. Declared an unfit mother, she lost custody of their daughter Mabel to Frank Besant. She led the match-girls' strike in 1888, enrolled at London University and joined the Fabian Society. Her affair with George Bernard Shaw stimulated another startling, sudden change of direction. She became a Theosophist, maybe finding the loins of Intellect and Received Religion equally dusty.

In 1888, reviewing *The Secret Doctrine*, she visited the author, Madame Blavatsky, who was dying, and knew it. She countered Besant's initial dislike by saying, 'Oh, my dear Mrs Besant, if only you would come among us.' Besant duly entered the Esoteric Section of the Blavatsky Lodge; and when Blavatsky died in 1891, she emerged as leader of the Theosophical movement, save for some US factions. From the 1893 World Parliament of Religions in Chicago she went on to India. Here (where Blavatsky had tried to meld West and East) she was asked but refused to lead a Hindu national movement.

Appointed President of the Theosophical Society (by the Hidden Masters) and confirmed by majority vote of members in 1907, in 1910 in India she and Leadbetter were impressed by the **aura** of the Brahmin-child **Krishnamurti**. Adopting him, declaring him Avatar and World Teacher, they brought him to the West. The Theosophical movement split. Rudolf **Steiner** broke away to found Anthroposophy. Pitching lower, Besant adopted Indian nationalism, in Madras declaring: 'Wake up, India!' Aged sixty-nine, in 1916 she formed the Home Rule for India League. Released from internment she became President of the Indian National Congress, even as Gandhi travelled about the land.

Latterly she was hit by two defections. Disowned as Bishop by the Old Catholic Church, in the early 1920s Leadbetter took many Theosophists into his own Liberal Catholic Church. Then in 1929, when Besant was over ninety, Krishnamurti renounced the god-business entirely.

Besant not only assumed Blavatsky's mantle but also developed her insights on the

'root races', and with W. Scott-Elliott wrote much about **Lemuria**. Her remarkability is not in doubt. Maybe the Rev. Besant gave her no more than a name; maybe her secular activism was more socially useful; but both sides of her nature, devotional and militant, found fruitful expression in Theosophy.

1. 'The Hunting of the Quark', Stephen M. Phillips, *The Unexplained*, Orbis part-work, London 1983, pp. 1834–7

BIOFEEDBACK This is a technique for mechanically monitoring body states and emotional-physiological reactions so that the user gains somatic self-control. Thus by monitoring the rise and fall of one's blood-pressure during varied moods it becomes possible to raise or lower blood-pressure at will. In that it works by objectifying inner states (via monitors) and bringing them to the user's awareness, it is a modern hi-tech version of older **yogic** techniques.

Equipment is not cheap. But the approach has value. Simple measurement of galvanic skin response (GSR) objectifies tension levels that are usually unconscious or automatic, so extending the user's capacity to identify and control states causing such tensions. The technique may be used to slow the heart via electro-cardiac feedback, halt migraine attacks and control pain levels, or attain altered states of mind by monitoring brainwaves.

Autosuggestion is involved. Like a **dowser**'s rod the monitors amplify and objectify, but no more. The machines serve the mind-body system's need to know itself by offering data in a form that the technologically oriented can grasp and apply. Like the psychedelic to the **shaman**, the monitor is a helper, not the end in itself. Thus, as pioneered in its simplest form as 'autogenic training' by Dr Johannes Schultz in the 1920s, biofeedback does not in the first place imply *mechanical* monitoring.

Dr Schultz's 'Relax and give your imagination full rein' approach has led to some cancer specialists encouraging patients to fantasise the rout and destruction of their diseased cells as vividly as they can. No miracle cures are reported, but evidence suggests that heated, vivid imagination can indeed influence bodily states by stimulating the release of *endorphins* – chemical messengers that carry the 'placebo effect'. So science proves the force of that old magical injunction to 'enflame thyself with prayer', if you want to change something important – like yourself.

BIOLOGICAL PLASMA (*See* **AURA, ENERGY BODY, KIRLIAN, MAGNETISM**) A Russian concept restating what has been called **animal magnetism, orgone energy,** *odic force*, etc. It also has corollaries with concepts of the **astral body** – unacceptable in terms of dialectical materialism.

In physics a *plasma* is a gaseous collection of positive and negative ions, sometimes seen as a fourth state of matter, being neither molecular solid, liquid or gas. The stellar atmosphere out to interstellar space is plasmic. The idea that a coherent plasma body might surround and interact with biological organisms arose in 1944 from the work of physicist V. S. Grischenko. It was developed theoretically by Dr Victor Inyushin, biophysicist at Kirov State University. Biological plasma is said to be a coherent, organised system with a minimum of the chaotic particle-dance typical of inorganic plasma. The bioplasmic body is said to be quite stable, but susceptible to electrical and magnetic flux.

The Roots of Consciousness, Jeffrey Mishlove, Random House, New York 1975, pp. 232–3

BIORELATIVITY (*See* **POLE SHIFT**) A concept with metaphysical and **pagan** undertones; this term was coined by US **'psychic archaeologist'** Jeffrey **Goodman** to denote the **psychokinetic** interaction of people and environment via the energy of thought. In other words, thought can move mountains. **Psychics** say that we produce thought-forms constantly whether realising it or not; forms impressing themselves on the energy matrix sustaining the physical world. Loving thought helps create a harmonious biosphere; violent, angry, selfish thought disrupts the fabric and may, in accumulation, cause earthquake and great destruction.

This concept, older than Sodom and Gomorrah, is born in our intimate, primordial relationship with Mother Earth, **Gaia**. It arises from the depths of **intuition** disfavoured in recent centuries by left-brain-dominated Western thought-patterns of a sort leading to what William **Blake** called 'heaps of smoking ruins/in the night of prosperity and wantonness'.[1]

Such a fate may be inevitable so long as we fail to see the planet and its life-forms as a *single living organism*.

Native Americans call this, 'Walking in balance on the Earth Mother'.[2,3]

1. 'The Song of Los', William Blake, *Poems and Prophecies*, Everyman, Dent 1972
2. *Pole Shift*, John White, W. H. Allen, London 1980, pp. 375ff.
3. *We are the Earthquake Generation*, Jeffrey Goodman, Seaview, New York 1978

BIORHYTHMS Turn-of-the-century work by Dr Hermann Swoboda in Vienna and Dr Wilhelm Fleiss in Berlin established that human biology is subject to twenty-three and twenty-eight-day rhythms, the peaks and troughs of which influence our thoughts, moods and activity. The twenty-three-day cycle governs the *physical* state; the other, of twenty-eight days (or nights) the *emotional*. Later in the 1920s engineering teacher Dr Alfred Teltscher added a third, thirty-three-day cycle, based on observation of student *intellectual* performance. These cycles are known as biorhythms.

To understand the cross-linkages of these cycles and their effect on us may improve our self-knowledge. Japanese industrialists pioneered the laying-off of workers on days when biorhythm charting shows combined lows in all three cycles, suggesting actuarial risk of accident and loss.

The principles of biorhythmic theory lie as close to ancient **astrology** as to **Gauquelin** and modern quantification of the absurdly true. They are: (1) before birth, all three internal clocks are at zero; (2) the traumatic change of birth sets them ticking on separate cycles to clock the life that follows. In their unique rhythm borne of the moment they set up individual *patterns*. In each such pattern, each of the cycles rises positive, falls negative. Twenty-three, twenty-eight and thirty-three interact through a whole cycle of 21,252 days, or just over fifty years. Biorhythmic technique may help you plan your month ahead by charting and observing coming combinations or shades of rhythmic high and low. Though not **fortune-telling**, it may at least help in making common-sense decisions, if help is needed.

Controversy arises not over the existence but the interpretation of biorhythms. As with other **New Age** 'bio'-disciplines, the name is new but the substance not. For in new cloth old mantic disciplines live again.

BIRDS (*See* **MAGNETISM**) Birds have always symbolised the transcendent and spiritual. Winging free between heaven and earth they represent: the soul; divine manifestations; spirits of the air; spirits of the dead; and the ability to communicate with gods or enter higher states of consciousness. They have been messengers and guides; their wings adorn angels, the heels of Mercurius, and the Ghost Dance costumes of nineteenth-century Native Americans. In **shamanistic** journeys a bird-robe may be worn to aid the flight of the soul; in **Egypt** the human-headed bird represented the power of the soul (***ka***) to take wing from the body at will.[1]

The symbolism is dual. Storks may bring new-born babies but flocks of starlings or a raven beating against the window may presage death. Plato says a cage of birds represents the mind; and though 'A little bird told me a secret', the claws of the Harpies tore folk to pieces. The ancient Irish war-goddesses were collectively called *badb* (pron. *bive*), meaning 'rage' or 'violence', epitomised by the hooded crow rending battle-carrion. Large birds are often identified with solar, thunder and wind gods – beating wings the storm, tongues the lightning; by settling they confer divine power on the World-Tree, and they are often used to symbolise the State. Ironically the symbol of the USA, the bald-headed eagle, is now threatened with extinction by the dark side of our attitude to birds. The urge to fly vies with the urge to bring down and eat what flies.

But the mystery of birds lies in the birds, not in our symbols. Reptilian, they lack mammalian cortex and mid-brain, but fly on what in humans survives as the **cerebellum** or old brain, the seat of instinctual behaviour. Obeying it, some birds annually migrate thousands of miles to a precise location, steering by sun and moon. They need not even have been that way before. In North America the indigo bunting finishes nesting in August; late in September the adults depart for Brazil, leaving many chicks behind to make their own way, which they do quite well, flying by night, sheltering by day. They fly by night to avoid predators, but also because they respond to the North Star and navigate by it, ignoring all others.[2] The cerebellar programme leads them all the way.

Birds are biologically sensitive to the Earth's weak magnetic field. Robins caged just before migration perch facing their destination even in a blackout, but are disorientated by distortion of the surrounding magnetic field. Between the eyes of the homing pigeon, able to wing 1,000 kilometres straight home even if blinded by frosted glass contact lenses, lies a tissue containing over a million bar-shaped lumps of magnetite (lodestone), a permanently magnetised mineral of iron anciently used as a crude compass – sufficiently sensitised for the bird to detect variations in the magnetic field. That the magnetite works as a compass is unproven; no neural pathways have been traced. But pigeons with bar magnets strapped to their backs get lost, while those carrying an equivalent but non-magnetic brass bar get home as usual.[3]

Tests on humans show we too possess this 'field sense' as, probably, to varying degrees, does all life within Earth's magnetic field. But given its poor sense of smell the bird's 'field sense' has to be as highly developed as its cerebellar programming. The effect of both is seen in flock-behaviour. A warning message flashes through the flock in an instant: all take wing *as one entity*. A flock of starlings darts and dives as one entity. Motion of one is the motion of all. There is a meaning in it that escapes us. They fly naturally, we only imitate; they respond to currents we barely sense, yet we seek those currents, feeling ourselves encaged.

'How can the bird that is born for joy Sit in a cage and sing?[4]

1. *An Illustrated Encyclopaedia of Traditional Symbols*, J. C. Cooper, Thames Hudson, London 1979, p. 21
2. *Beyond Supernature*, Lyall Watson, Hodder and Stoughton, London 1986, p. 113
3. 'The Sense to Survive', Gill Nevill, *The Unexplained*, Orbis partwork, London 1983, pp. 1010–13
4. 'The Schoolboy', William Blake, *Songs of Experience*

BLACK DOGS (*See* **APPARITIONS, LEY LINES, UFOs**) Tales of meetings with huge, shaggy, fiery-eyed phantom black dogs abound in England and Wales. Black Shuck, Gally-trot, Guytrash and Skriker are among the regional names given to this **apparition**. Seen near water, or at boundaries, crossroads and wayside burial places, they may haunt churches, being once thought of as 'church grims', spirits guarding churchyards from the **Devil**. Algarkirk and Northorpe in Lincolnshire both have resident black dogs; the Moddey Dhoo of the Isle of Man haunted a church passageway. They patrol stretches of old lane and green ways associated with **ley lines**, and haunt **megalithic** sites like Doghill Barrow near Stonehenge. Appearing and disappearing always at the same place, they may presage a death. They may seem unaware of human presence or they may gaze direct into the face.

In 1972 a farmer struck with an iron poker at a black dog invading his Dartmoor house one winter night. There was a burst of light, a crash of breaking glass and the phantom vanished. The man then found a complete electrical failure (as in many **UFO close encounters**) in the house, every window broken and the roofs of house and outbuildings badly damaged.

Ivan Bunn, East Anglian researcher, noted that fifteen out of sixty-two reported sightings were near a main river, fifteen on or near the coast and sixteen within a mile of it. This seeming connection with damp places led T. C. **Lethbridge** to speculate that black dogs are manifestations of the site itself. Damp places, he believed, are especially receptive to the 'imprint' of strong thought or emotion. Janet and Colin Bord believe that the phenomenon is in some way connected with ley lines. Certainly detectives investigating the 1945 'witchcraft murder' of Charles Walton close to Oxfordshire's Rollright Stones (long associated with weird events) saw such an apparition.[1]

UFO researcher Paul Devereux connects UFO phenomena with geological faults and the ancient megaliths often found sited on such faults, through which, he believes, **electromagnetic** phenomena erupt, which he terms 'earthlights'.[2] Directly affecting the brain, these assume the *objective* form willed on them (consciously or not) by the observer. Such 'phantoms' may persist for millennia, maintained by continued human belief and unconscious interaction.

Are black dogs such a phenomenon? Their connection with approaching death (half Bunn's witnesses said a close relative had died soon after their encounter) certainly suggests that the black dog image or **archetype** may be summoned and manifested by subconscious premonition of death, at a place charged with that image over millennia of use.

So the connection of black dogs with ancient sites of known magnetic or 'holy' potency, or with tracks connecting such sites, is not accidental. They appear where they do because the geomagnetic conditions are right; and in the 'black dog' form courtesy, maybe, of a psychic technology developed by the megalith-builders to tap and *use* the earth currents. According to this theory, when a charged ball of 'planetary ectoplasm' leaps from the fault through the air and we're caught in its energy-field, unknowingly we convert its raw stuff into UFO, Black Dog, or even mass vision of the Virgin Mary, as at **Fatima**.

Black dogs are not figments of the imagination but part of what Janet and Colin Bord call 'forces operating below the surface', of the landscape and of our lives, forces we had forgotten and now barely begin to remember.

1. *Alien Animals*, Janet and Colin Bord, Granada, London 1980, pp. 80–108
2. *Earthlights*, Paul Devereux, Turnstone Press, London 1982

BLACK ELK (*c.* 1862–1950) (*See* **HOPI, SHAMAN**) This Oglala Sioux shaman, cousin of Crazy Horse and warrior at Custer's Last Stand, travelled to Italy, France and England with Buffalo Bill's Wild West Show. Yet he never spoke English. Unlike other men, as a child he had **visions**, and was instructed in the meaning of his people's spiritual heritage. He became a shaman. Through his visions he gained powers to be used for the good of his people – at the worst of times.

To induce vision he would sit by a **tree**, symbol of the cosmic pillar. Up it in **trance** he'd rise through a tunnel-like aperture, led by a spirit-guide in **bird**-form, to a 'flaming rainbow tepee' to communicate with the 'grandfathers'. The vision, involving painful apparent dismemberment, led to spiritual rebirth and renewed energy. Sometimes he would return to Earth on a 'little cloud'. (The parallels with **UFO abduction** cases are plain enough, except that the shaman induces the experience deliberately.)

In visions he saw the Hoop of the Nations broken. He saw the tribes dispersed. His visions came true. He lived to lament the broken hoop. It seemed his ancient culture was to be swallowed by the American Way. Yet it remained his responsibility to 'bring to life the flowering tree of his people'. This weighed on him. How could he bring his people back to 'the good red road', back to the Great Spirit *Wakan Tanka?* He decided to speak out. The result was *Black Elk Speaks: The Life Story of a Holy Man of the Oglala Sioux*, as told to John G. Neihardt (1932). In 1947, still living a hard life in South Dakota, through Joseph Epes Brown he made known the Seven Rites of the Oglala Sioux, including the sun dance, the purification rite and the 'keeping of the soul'. He told Brown he had anticipated his coming. Shortly before his death in August 1950 he said, 'It is my prayer that through our sacred pipe . . . peace may come on those peoples who can understand . . . Then they will realise that we Indians know the One True God, and that we pray to Him continually.'[1]

1. *The Sacred Pipe*, Black Elk's Account of the Seven Rites of the Oglala Sioux, recorded and edited by Joseph Epes Brown, Penguin, London 1971

BLACK HOLES Conceived in 1783 by English astronomer John Michell and first described mathematically by Laplace, 'black holes' were not taken seriously until 1971, when the first orbiting X-ray telescopic observatory (*Uhuru*) located a bright X-ray source in the constellation Cygnus, flickering on and off a thousand times a second. As information about when to turn on and off could cross the source, named Cygnus X–1, no faster than light-speed, Cyg X–1 could be no more than 300 kilometres in diameter. Something asteroid-sized was hurling X-rays over interstellar distances – but what?

In the same place in the sky is a hot blue supergiant star, shown in visible light to be tugged gravitationally one way then another by a close, invisible companion ten times heavier than the Sun. Such an object the size of an asteroid had to be a black hole, its X-rays perhaps generated by friction in the disc of gas and dust accreted round it from the supergiant.

Black holes are thought to arise principally from the collapse of stars which have exploded through the supernova phase. When gravity reaches 10^{10} gs the collapsed matter and all forms of radiation fall through the 'event horizon' or 'Schwartzschild Radius' and vanish from our universe, creating something like a bottomless pit. Nothing, not even light, can escape the immense gravity. It literally warps space-time and crushes all matter down to a mathematical singularity; time slows as the gravity mounts, and at the event horizon stops entirely. A person seen from outside would take forever to fall in, being seemingly caught at a point where all clocks, biological or mechanical, stop. To the falling person (if somehow conscious amid the maelstrom of radiation and gravity), the passage of time would seem normal. But once beyond the event horizon, deep inside the black hole, there is no escape: collapse into the singularity is inevitable.

It is thought the Big Bang's pressures must have created black holes, and that black holes put in proximity tend to unite. This has led to the idea of 'super black holes' at galactic centres, continually expanding by gobbling lesser black holes formed as stars go supernova. The implication that the cosmos may thus be swallowed into the total timeless night of the ultimate black hole seems to accord with the ancient Hindu tradition of the conflagration that hurls the known universe into the Night of **Brahman**.

But what happens *beyond* a black hole singularity? Cosmic gushers, some say 'White Holes' from which erupt the stuff of new creation. How else to explain highly energetic cosmic sources where matter apparently emerges from tiny central regions? This also accords with Hindu tradition that, from Brahman, the uncreated unmanifest void, new creation emerges.

Speculation about sending a spacecraft into a spinning black hole to be spat out elsewhere in the universe, thus achieving instantaneous travel, to date remains speculation. So does the very existence of black holes.[1,2,3]

1. *Cosmos*, Carl Sagan, Macdonald, London 1981, pp. 241–2
2. *Timewarps*, John Gribbin, Dent, London 1979
3. *White Holes*, John Gribbin, Paladin, London 1977

BLACK MADONNA (*See* **CHARTRES, ISIS, MOON**) Discreetly in many churches across France and Western Europe stand images of the Virgin with black or dark face – black madonnas, symbols of female power and majesty harkening back to **pagan** goddesses. In St Germain des Prés, built AD 542 on the site of a Temple of Isis and the oldest church in Paris (*Par-isis = Grove of Isis*), a black statue of Egyptian Isis was worshipped as the Virgin until destroyed in 1514. One of two black madonnas at Chartres Cathedral, Nôtre-Dame de Sous-Terre (Our Lady Underground) in the crypt sustains the pre-Christian Chartres tradition of a virgin birth. The wooden statue stands near the 'Puits des Saints Forts' well in the oldest part of Chartres, which is traditionally claimed to be the ancient **Druid** capital of France (Gaul). In Toulouse, the Church of La Daurade was a troubadour centre in **Cathar** times (twelfth century) when the Pays d'Oc all but escaped Church control. Initiates paid court to '*La Reine Pédauque*', or *Goose-Foot Queen*: a pagan goddess of many disguises (Lilith to the Queen of Sheba) today half-remembered as Mother Goose. The present Nôtre-Dame La Noire in La Daurade is the latest of several such images in the church, the first being a statue of Athene (?) found in a drained lake in 109 BC. Today, though over 400 Black Virgins are known worldwide, the Church remains reticent about the matriarchal and pagan origins of these potent images.[1]

1. *The Cult of the Black Virgin*, Ean Begg, Arkana, London 1985

BLACK MAGIC (*See* **EVIL, MAGIC, QLIPHOTH**) If magic is the art or science of causing change to occur in conformity with the will, black magic simply means magic undertaken for destructive or selfish purposes; to dominate or harm others; or out of greed or other base motive. A less negative derivation may be from the 'black art', **alchemy**; Khem, ancient name for **Egypt**, means '*land of black earth*', hence 'The Art of the Black Land'. But in general, black magic implies the pursuit of power, wealth, knowledge, etc., for personal gain, by any effective means, without care for others. Thus defined, it is a practice more prosaic than **occult**.

The magical element may not be obvious as such. A man trying to attract a woman (or vice versa) uses male magic, exerting his will and **magnetism** to *influence* her. This instinctive magic she meets with her own. This is natural. *Black* magic lies in any attempt to *force* the will of another. The rites of inverted cross, Black Mass, black cock, etc., are as B-Grade in reality as in the movies. Props and channels to amplify and direct the magical will may be useful, whatever form they take and to whatever end, but they remain secondary: the will initiates.

Occultly, black magicians are those who follow the 'Left-Hand Path' or 'Path of the Shadows', meaning the path of Matter (often called 'shadow' or 'shadows' by esotericists). 'Brothers of the Shadow' are instinctively drawn to this path of selfish materialism. They stand in sharp contrast to the 'Sons of Light', or 'White Magicians' . . . such as William **Blake**, who nonetheless claimed that his poetic energy came from the **Devil** . . .

BLAKE, William (1757–1827) (*See* **DEVIL**)

Trembling I sit day and night, my friends are astonish'd at me,
Yet they forgive my wanderings. I rest not from my great task!
To open the Eternal Worlds, to open the immortal Eyes
Of Man inwards into the Worlds of Thought, into Eternity . . .[1]

Engraver, **visionary**, radical **prophet** and poet of the 'dark satanic mills', Blake was born and lived in London all his life, save for four years at Felpham on the south coast. The gifted, self-willed child of a hosier, he was apprenticed for seven years to the engraver Basire. In 1780 he was one of the mob that stormed Newgate Jail during the Gordon Riots, and in 1782 married Catherine Boucher. Thereafter for forty-five years he earned a precarious living as an engraver. Thick-set, fiery-haired and energetic, in earlier years he thought nothing of a forty-mile Saturday stroll but feared his loudly radical opinions might land him in jail. As for his inner life, he knew even his friends and supporters thought his Prophetic Books incomprehensible. His earlier *Songs of Innocence* (1789) and *Songs of Experience* (1794) ('Tyger, Tyger, burning bright/In the forests of the night . . .') spoke in a simple, popular voice, but the complex mythology of books like *Jerusalem* and *Milton* baffled his contemporaries as *Finnegan's Wake* baffles people today. These books, illustrated, engraved and published by Blake himself, are certainly hard to penetrate, but repay study.

A century before **Einstein**, Blake rejected 'Single vision and Newton's sleep'. Claiming 'All deities reside in the human breast', in his Prophetic Books he dramatised the war in the human soul by characterising Reason, Feeling, **Intuition** and Sense as the four Zoas – Urizen, Luvah, Urthona (*Earth-Owner*?) and Tharmas. In this psychology (presaging **Jung**'s four-fold division of faculties) each Zoa (Greek, pl., '*living creatures*') has a negative counterpart (spectre), sons, daughters, and an 'emanation'.

Of the Zoas, Urizen (Your Reason; also Greek; 'to limit' – horizon), born of Los (Divine Imagination: *Sol* (Sun) backwards?), suppresses the other three by rule of Logic and Reason. Blake thus maintains **Gnostic** values, deploring not **Christ** (forgiveness) but Jehovah (intellectual wrath and ambition). Denouncing 'All Bibles or sacred codes' for demonising our human energies as evil and born of the **Devil**, like **Gurdjieff** a century later he sees humanity as lost 'in Deadly sleep', bound down in Chains of Reason. His poetic answer is to invoke the return of the old free spirit of Britain, Albion. But Albion lies buried in the landscape and deep in our minds by 'Reasonings like vast serpents' that 'infold around my limbs.'

He opposes not Reason but its tyranny over the other human faculties. Urizen, denying love and stifling all energy with iron rules, is miserable, makes everyone else miserable, but won't quit . . . or learn. He will destroy the world unless Albion, the ancient wholesome spirit, awakens . . . in us all.

Politically outspoken and anti-monarchist, Blake was said to have aided the escape from England to revolutionary France of Tom Paine, author of *The Rights of Man.* This seems to be an unsubstantiated hero-myth. In 1804 he was tried for sedition (denouncing the king in public) but was acquitted. His beliefs were probably thought too eccentric and abstruse to bother about. The political outlook of poems that begin:

And did those feet in ancient time;
Walk upon England's mountains green;

or

The shadowy daughter of Urthona stood before red Orc
When fourteen suns had faintly journey'd o'er his dark abode:

was unlikely to raise the masses. He was left in peace to his visions, of which he spoke as bluntly as on other subjects. The relief-etching now known as 'Urizen Creating the

Universe' (bearded creator leans from heaven to measure the Earth's circle with compasses) came from a vision which, his Victorian biographer Gilchrist claims, Blake reported had 'hovered over his head at the top of his staircase', on a blank wall.[2] Gilchrist also reports how one day Blake's patron Thomas Butts called to find the Blakes naked in the sunhouse at the bottom of their garden.

'Come in!' cried Blake, 'It's only Adam and Eve, you know!'

Whether true or not this tale seems to marry with Blake's dictum that: 'Energy is Eternal Delight' save when dammed by Urizen.

1. *Jerusalem*, v. 16–19, *Poems and Prophecies*, William Blake, J. M. Dent, London 1972, p. 165
2. *William Blake: A new kind of man*, Michael Davis, University of California Press, Berkeley, 1977

BLAVATSKY, HELENA PETROVNA (HPB) (1831–91) (*See* **THEOSOPHY**) Co-founder of the Theosophical Society, remembered today as 'HPB', this flamboyant occultist was born Helena Hahn in Russia, her father a colonel, her mother a novelist. **Clairvoyant** as a child, at sixteen she married forty-year-old General Blavatsky; and at eighteen left him, wandering apparently to Mexico, Texas, Canada, India and Tibet. In 1850 in Cairo, American painter A. L. Rawson met a Madame Blavatsky who dressed as an Arab, claimed to be a Russian princess, smoked hashish and studied occultism. Her cousin, Count Witte (later Russian Prime Minister and **Rasputin**'s friend) said that she had ridden bareback in a circus until a fall ruined her womb, had taught piano in Paris and London, assisted **medium** Daniel Dunglass **Home**, and had run an artificial flower factory in Tiflis in Georgia.

Bigamously marrying an opera singer, Metrovich, in July 1871 she was among seventeen survivors of 400 passengers on the passenger ship **Eumonia** when it blew up in the Adriatic. Metrovich was not. In 1873 she reached New York. At the Vermont farm of the Eddy Brothers, famous 'materialising mediums', she met **Spiritualist** lawyer Henry Steel Olcott (1832–1907). Impressed as much by HPB as by her tales and 'spiritual miracles' (she now weighed over 230 pounds, was foul-mouthed, and chain-smoked) Olcott began supporting her despite the farce of another bigamous (but platonic) marriage, to a young Georgian, Michael Bettanelly. Calling sex 'a beastly appetite that should be starved into submission', she soon abandoned the arrangement.

Olcott was soon wholly under her thumb. Notes apparently from secret Mahatmas she'd met in Tibet would drop from the air, detailing her needs. Olcott left his wife and family in September 1875 and after hearing a lecture by a Mr Felt on the secret dimensions of Egyptian pyramids and on invoking spirits by the 'laws of proportion', he suggested forming a society to study these things. They took the term 'theosophy' (from Greek *theos*, 'god'; *sophia*, 'wisdom') and established the Theosophical Society. HPB set out to write Theosophy's bible. Written rapidly, she had her hugely erudite *Isis Unveiled* published in New York in 1877.[1] In it she blended many doctrines into a mix of esoteric cosmology. She held that, since the 'Lords of Flame' impregnated Earth with life eighteen million years ago, five '**root races**' have emerged. The first, from the North Pole, was of invisible fire-mist; the second, from Siberia, invented sex; the third were ape-like **Lemurian telepathic** giants; the fourth the **Atlanteans**, destroyed by **black magic**; we today are the fifth; the sixth will evolve from us to live on Lemuria; and the seventh will quit Earth for Mercury. She asserted that Spiritualist phenomena were known of old; that old **alchemical** and magical texts hid scientific and spiritual truths known to her; and that she was charged by the **discarnate** Mahatmas to regenerate spirituality in the material world. She also asserted the truth of the doctrines of **karma** and **reincarnation**.

Theosophy flourished, but not as well as HPB had hoped. Upset by an attack by the medium D. D. **Home**, in 1880 she decamped to Bombay. Here she and Olcott merged the Society with the Arya Samaj movement despite the scepticism of its leader, Swami Dayananda Sarasvati. Impressing journalist A. P. Sinnett and others by her materialisation of objects out of thin air, she passed letters from such converts on to the discarnate 'Secret Masters'. Voluble replies mysteriously appeared, often written by the discarnate Mahatma Koot Hoomi Lal Singh (whose letters are now preserved in the British Museum).[2]

It didn't last. The Swami denounced Olcott and HPB as frauds; in 1884 her housekeeper Madame Coulomb also denounced her to the Bombay editor of the *Christian College Magazine*. The **Society for Psychical Research** sent Richard Hodgson to investigate her; his report ruined her reputation. Now dying of Bright's Disease, she fled back to Europe. In England poet W. B. **Yeats** recorded how her cuckoo clock hooted at him when he was alone with it, though unweighted and not ticking. In 1888, she published *The Secret Doctrine*, and met Annie **Besant**, who later led the Society.[3]

HPB died 8 May 1891, aged sixty. Some at least of her **psychic** ability was genuine; her disciples were not all fools; 'things happened around her'. Her personal magnetism is obvious; she stimulated a huge growth of interest in the causes as well as the effects of 'occult' phenomena.

1. *Isis Unveiled*, Theosophical Publishing House, USA 1972 (1877)
2. *The Occult*, Colin Wilson, Hodder and Stoughton 1971, pp. 430–41.
3. *The Secret Doctrine*, Theosophical Publishing House, USA 1988 (1888)
4. *Collected Writings Vols*. 1–14, Theosophical Publishing House, USA 1966–85

BLOXHAM, ARNALL (*See* **GLOSSOLALIA, HYPNOSIS, REINCARNATION**) 'The Bloxham Tapes', a 1976 BBC TV documentary, examined claims by Cardiff hypnotherapist Arnall Bloxham to have 'regressed' hypnotised subjects to their former lives. Tape-recorded accounts made during regression were offered as evidence. Graham Huxtable, a swimming instructor, had 'become' an eighteenth-century sailor caught up in battle with a French ship; he screamed in agony as he was 'wounded'. Historian Oliver Warner could not trace 'HMS *Aggie*' (*Agamemnon*?), but believed the tape authentic. In the programme and the book that followed the best evidence of reincarnation reposed in the accounts of former lives given under hypnosis by a young woman, 'Jane Evans'. Of seven such lives she 'remembered' particularly those as Livonia, a Roman wife in fourth-century Britain; Rebecca, a York Jewess murdered in a church crypt during the 1190 massacre; and Alison, servant to a fifteenth-century French merchant prince, Jacques Coeur. Her detailed period knowledge convinced Bloxham, herself, author Jeffrey Iverson and others. It was claimed that as Rebecca she had died in a crypt of St Mary's Castlegate, undiscovered until after her public account of it. A vaulted space was indeed found, but errors in her tale suggested that **cryptomnesia**, not reincarnation, was involved. No historical proof of the existence of any of her former selves emerged.[1]

Jane's 'memories', it seems, came from historical novels she'd read and forgotten. 'Livonia' began with *The Living Wood*, a 1947 novel by Louis de Wohl (hired by the Allies to forge anti-Nazi **Nostradamus** quatrains). She had so deeply identified with and unconsciously edited de Wohl's characters that, under hypnosis, she recalled them as her own far 'memory'.

Does cryptomnesia explain all such 'memories'? Other regression cases – Bridey **Murphy**, the **Guirdham** accounts and Lydia Johnson's **glossolalia** – suggest the phenomenon is not so easily dismissed. Indeed, it remains startling enough to lead some to suppose that hypnotic regression involves access to the **collective unconscious** of the species.

1. *More lives than one*?, Jeffrey Iverson, Souvenir Press, London 1976

'Past lives: an open book?', Melvin Harris, *The Unexplained*, Orbis partwork, London 1983), pp. 2698–2700

BOEHME, Jacob (1575–1624) Amid a state of exaltation on Trinity Sunday, 1600, this great Silesian mystic realised that 'in Yes and No all things consist'.

Aurora, the book he wrote to describe his experience, led the council of his home town of Görlitz to forbid him to write any more. Taking up the life of a travelling merchant he learned **Qabalah** and **Paracelsian** doctrine, becoming as much an **occultist** as 'by far the greatest and most original of Protestant **mystics**'. Convinced of the four-fold nature of existence he held man to have originally been a pure angel, bisexual, balanced between Light and Dark. However a double Fall had occurred, first into material form and sexual division; then into sin and death. His desire to reunite Catholics and Protestants was bitterly attacked. Yet, ignoring all prohibitions, he wrote extensively, producing some thirty books and pamphlets.

BOHM, David Contemporary British physicist and devotee of **Krishnamurti** whose book *Wholeness and the Implicate Order* proposes, in trying to explain **quantum** paradoxes, that the 'apartness' of things is an illusion. His revival of this ancient insight matches the 'hologrammatic universe' theory of Californian brain-specialist Karl **Pribram**, who suggests that the world about us is a hologram and the reality 'behind it' an interference pattern.

BOOK OF CHANGES (*See* **I CHING**)

BOND, Bligh (*See* **GLASTONBURY, PSYCHIC ARCHAEOLOGY**)

BRAHAN SEER (*See* **PROPHECY, SECOND SIGHT**) Scotland most famous **seer**, his prophecies are still anxiously quoted today. Coinneach Odhar Fiosaiche (Sallow Kenneth the Enchanter), alias Kenneth Mackenzie of Brahan in Ross-shire, may or may not have lived in the seventeenth century, may or may not have been executed in a barrel of burning tar by Isabella, Countess at Brahan in Easter Ross, and may or may not have issued the terrible **curse** leading to the doom of the Seaforth Mackenzies over a century later.

In the time of its fulfilment the curse was certainly known, to Sir Walter Scott and Sir Humphrey Davy among others. It told of four sons predeceasing their deaf and dumb father, the lands to be inherited by a 'white-hooded widow from the East' who 'is to kill her sister', all in a time of four great lairds, one buck-toothed, another hare-lipped, a third half-witted, the fourth a stammerer.

In 1816 Francis Humberston Mackenzie (deaf since childhood) followed his sons to the grave: his daughter, married to the lately deceased Admiral Hood, returned from India to take over the Brahan estate – literally white-hooded (in mourning) and from the East. Years later she was driving a pony carriage near Brahan; the pony bolted; her sister was thrown and killed. A memorial still stands by the main Inverness–Ullapool road at Brahan.

It is said Coinneach was born on Lewis, had a magic white stone through which he *saw* the future, that his sharp temper and tongue were feared, that he worked as a labourer at Brahan but fell foul of Kirk and Countess.

The sole evidence that he lived lies not in the seventeenth century when the above events seemingly occurred, but a century earlier, when 'Keanoch Owir' (English spelling of the Gaelic name) was arraigned as an 'enchanter'. It seems likely that this 'Keanoch' took on mythic status round which, by the nineteenth century, hundreds of prophecies by many different seers had accreted.

Certainly, none were formally recorded until Mackenzie's *The Prophecies of the Brahan Seer* came out in 1877. Many spoke of events already achieved – railways, bridges, canals built. Others awaiting fulfilment warn of disasters: 'When there are seven bridges over the Ness, Inverness will be consumed with fire from the black rain and tumble into the sea.' When the construction of a seventh bridge began in 1984 there were anxious letters to the Press. For of the many predictions attributed to the unknown seer, the 'Black Rain' still causes most speculation.

'Sheep shall eat men, men will eat sheep, the black rain will eat all things,' is the short version. A longer version details the takeover of the Highlands by sheep, desolating the country, whereupon 'the people will emigrate to Islands now unknown, but which shall yet be discovered in the boundless oceans after which the deer and other wild animals in the huge wilderness shall be exterminated and browned by horrid black rains'.

The Highland Clearances and dispersal of the clans overseas brought about most of this two centuries ago. As for the black rain, some say it means acid rain, some claim oil and some predict nuclear fallout.[1,2]

1. *The Prophecies of the Brahan Seer*, Alexander Mackenzie, Constable, London 1977 (1877)
2. *Ravens and Black Rain*, Elizabeth Sutherland, Corgi, London 1987

BRAHMA (*See* **YOGAS**) The root of this Sanskrit word, *brih*, means 'expansion', and stands for the spiritual consciousness of our solar system. The 'Egg of Brahma' is the solar system. A Day of Brahma, composed of seven rounds, equals one *kalpa*, a period of 4,320,000 years. A Night of Brahma is of the same length. Seven such Days make one Solar Kalpa; one Year of Brahma equals 360 Divine Days, said to be the duration of a planet's life. The Life of Brahma (alias the created universe) equals one hundred Divine Years – 4,320,000 times 36,000 times 2. The Life is said to be half over, and we are at the bottom of the cosmic cycle, on the lowest plane.[1]

The related word *Brahman* refers to that part of the Unmanifest which initiates manifestation during the Brahmas: the expansion of the One into the Many. Brahman is ultimately unknowable, the Void or absence of being from which being emerges.

1. *Occult Glossary*, G. de Purucker (1933), Theosophical University Press, Pasadena, California 1969, p. 20

BRAIN MYSTERIES (*See* **DREAMS**) 'Man', wrote neurobiologist Paul Maclean in 1962, 'finds himself in the predicament that Nature has endowed him essentially with three brains which, despite great differences in structure, must function together and communicate with one another . . . Speaking allegorically of these three brains within a brain, we might imagine that when the psychiatrist bids the patient to lie on the couch, he is asking him to stretch out alongside a horse and a crocodile.[1]

Of these structures the cerebellum may be said to deal with instinct, the mid-brain with emotion, and the two cortical lobes with reason and intuition.

The cerebellum, or 'little brain', also called the 'Reptile Complex' (R-Complex) by Maclean, is the oldest and least understood. Hidden behind spinal column and reticular system, it regulates heart-beat, breathing, sneezing, yawning and coughing. It functions as an alarm system, alerting the cortex to bodily crises, and as a 'robot'. It takes over when you drive 'absent-mindedly', handing back to the cortical 'thinking cap' if crisis looms. Despite its simple structure it remains a mystery, receiving data not only from cortex but the mid-brain emotional centres. What has a robot to do with emotion?[2]

US psychologist Dr James Prescott, noting the connection between cerebellar damage and social deviance in monkeys reared in isolation, claims that lack of emotional stimulus as an infant causes cerebellar damage which may lie behind many criminal or aggressive human behaviours.[3] The instinctive R-Complex may cause the robotic behaviour of people caught up in 'mob-consciousness'. 'Don't you know,' asked **Jung**, 'that if you get one hundred of the most intelligent people in the world and get them all together, they are a stupid mob? Ten thousand would have the collective intelligence of an alligator.'[4]

The mid-brain includes the pituitary and **pineal** ('third eye') glands and is found above cerebellum and brainstem, under the cortex. From it the hypothalamus emits hormones (chemical messengers) regulating the pituitary, which in turn chemically controls lower glands – thyroids, gonads, and adrenals. The process is two-way. Some hormones boost nerve-impulses and others inhibit them. Some brain-produced hormones affect the body; some body-produced hormones affect the brain, as in the gonadal hormones that affect sexual orientation. Though separately developed, mid-brain and cerebellum are often lumped together as the 'limbic system': a maze of clues to '**paranormal**' processes. A bridge between instinct and the ego-personality as seated in the left lobe of the cortex, this 'inner brain' controls olfactory sensations, oral perceptions, sexual behaviour and 'body-language', generating a profound range of emotional response (grief, joy, fear, rage, ecstasy) without which drama, music, romance, dance or ritual could not exist. As such, it may be seen as the 'guardian of the threshold' between conscious and unconscious worlds. In Egyptian myth, the jackal-god Anubis met the dead at this threshold. The jackal may have been chosen due to its ability to smell water in the desert. Later the Greeks chose the three-headed dog Cerberus (three heads = three brains?) as companion of Charon, who ferried those recently dead (to ego-personality?) into the 'afterworld' of the limbic system, and beyond.

Crowning the brain-castle, the cortex is split into two lobes, left and right. Each mirrors the other but generates entirely different states of consciousness. The left lobe rules the right side of the body physically, also governing egoistic, rational, linguistic manipulation of the external physical world. The right lobe controls the left side of the body and seems to be the seat of egoless processes like dreaming and intuition.

The growth of this 'thinking cap' (it literally caps the older brains, overlapping them on all sides) has been so fast (half-a-million years[5]) that some anatomists talk of a 'brain explosion' or 'tumorous growth'. By means of this 'tumorous growth' we build cities and dispute abstractions, like the relationship between 'brain' and 'mind'. We also inherit the headache of hosting four separate autonomous systems – counting left and right cortical lobes as separate systems. Thus Maclean's remark about horse and crocodile. The reptile in us emerges when a **Hitler** overrides the cortex by means of 'magical' **rituals** like the Nuremberg Rallies which evoke mass instinctive R-Complex reaction. Reason's control is unstable and easily upset, contested as it is by partners whose aims and values are quite different. Indeed, left lobe reason is so new that 'history' may be seen as its record of its war or 'right' to control the other brains.

The notion of 'warring' brains may help explain mediaeval masculine (left-lobe) paranoia as seen in witch-hunts against women (representing right-lobe functions) and as in the tendency to see devils and **demons** (eruptions of unconscious, instinctual content) everywhere. The intellect, its light emerging from dark instinct, fought so successfully to separate itself that now it denies that the 'magical' faculties of the other brains ever existed save in fantasy.

The right and left lobes, though physically connected by a tangled mass of nerve-fibres (the 'commissures' or '*corpus callosum*') are so separate in function and perception that we are all, literally, 'split-brained'. Is this due to bad engineering, as **Koestler** thought? This split (maybe the source of the sign of Gemini, the Twins) exists in most animals. But in humans it increases tensions. Caught between different sets of biological orders, we fight ourselves in a perpetual war. Why? British psychologist Stan **Gooch** suggests an evolutionary purpose. The war between cortex and cerebellum, he claims, drives us on. Perhaps. If so, what is the role of the right lobe? Antechamber to the unconscious and instinctual?

Nineteenth-century scientists like Kekulé (who discovered the structure of the benzene molecule) and Henri Poincaré acknowledged the part played in their discoveries by the dream, or 'flash of intuition' – both right-brain activities. Visionaries like **Goethe, Blake** and **Swedenborg** expressed intuitive unease about the takeover of the world by scientific (left brain) attitudes. Blake's villain Urizen (*Your Reason*) suppresses the other human faculties (of instinct, emotion and intuition), and rules a materialistic wasteland. This tale of lost four-fold unity is found in **Grail** legends and other myths describing the left-lobe takeover. Today, 'Reason' prevails to such an extent that phenomena generated by the other brains are often defined as 'superstition'. 'Magical thinking' is frowned on by the left lobe.

Yet lately the left lobe has begun to realise it shares the house with other tenants. In the 1950s Roger Sperry of the University of Chicago took up the work of 1930s brain surgeons. Severing the commissures to prevent transmission of epileptic attacks ('brainstorms') from one lobe to another had proved successful, oddly without loss of performance. Functions like memory, once thought located in specific areas of the cortex, transferred unaffected from damaged regions, especially in pre-adolescents. Studying a man whose brain was split to prevent epileptic attacks, Sperry found the man could read with his right eye, but not with his left. If he bumped something with his left side, he did not notice. A split brain patient's right brain was shown a picture of a naked man: she blushed. Asked why she blushed, her left lobe said she didn't know.[6] Sperry realised what poets have long known: *We are all dual, even multiple personalities*. The left lobe deals with the outer world, the right with the inner. When we wake up suddenly from a dream, it takes a second or more before we 'remember who we are' and reassume our daily left-lobe ego. Murderers who claim: 'I didn't know what I was doing', like **seers** and **psychic healers** who claim ignorance of their acts while in 'trance', are often honest. Their left brain doesn't remember or know what the **psychic**, dreaming right brain drove them to do. Is this more surprising than the fact that we can function *at all* while so literally at war with ourselves.

The practice by the 'primitive' Malaysian **Senoi** of daily 'dream analysis' created a crime-free society. They exemplified an older wisdom that integrates the functions of the different brains. Urizen had not yet seized them. They still rightly saw their 'dream-giants' as *real* and paid heed. The brain is like a movie-complex with four different shows at once. Left-brain logic says you see one and miss the rest. Yet **mystical, yogic** and **shamanistic** tradition tells us to employ all four at once. The brain's biocomputers are all functional, but the neocortex, literally 'New', rides an uneasy tandem on limbic system and cerebellum.

1. *The Natural History of the Mind*, Gordon Rattray Taylor, Granada, London 1981, p. 29 *et. seq*.
2. *ibid*., p. 9
3. *The Secret Life of Humans*, Stan Gooch, Dent, London 1981, p. 127
4. Quoted in 'The brain's generation gap: some human implications', Paul Maclean (1973), *Zygon – Journal of Religion and Science* 8 (2) 113–27
5. *Janus: A Summing-up*, Arthur Koestler, Pan Books, London 1979, p. 82
6. *Frankenstein's Castle*, Colin Wilson, Ashgrove Press, Bath 1980, p. 21

BROWN, Frank (*See* **BIRDS, CYCLES, MAGNETISM**) Operating from Northwestern University at Evanston, Illinois, since the 1950s, this US biologist has demonstrated the influence of remote environmental or even celestial factors on terrestrial life. Connecticut oysters he removed from their seabed opened their shells in his laboratory, a thousand miles from the sea, *at the time of Connecticut high tide*. They were inexorably linked to the lunar **cycle**. He also demonstrated that the potato tuber 'knows' the **moon's** position in the sky at any time, and that its metabolism is subject to lunar influence.[1] Later he proved that rats, fiddler crabs and oysters also obey lunar rhythms. Though kept in sealed environments with pressure, light, humidity and temperature constant, these life-forms still responded to basic biocosmic imperatives, their metabolism fluctuating in response to lunar cycles and other subtle factors perhaps geomagnetically orchestrated.

He noted, 'fluctuations in intensity of primary cosmic rays entering the earth's atmosphere were dependent upon the strength of geomagnetism. The magnetic field steadily undergoes fluctuations in intensity. When the field is stronger, fewer primary cosmic rays come in from the outer atmosphere; when it weakens, more get in.'[2]

His work has been attacked by behavioural biologists who insist that such influences cannot affect animals in sealed environments.

1. *Supernature*, Lyall Watson, Hodder and Stoughton, London 1973, p. 29
2. *The Biological Clock – Two Views*, Brown, Hastings and Palmer, Academic Press, New York 1970

BROWN, Hugh Auchinloss (1879–1975) (*See* **POLE SHIFT**) American electrical engineer who believed that the weight of the ice-caps will soon tip the Earth over and destroy us all. In *Cataclysms of the Earth* (1967) he wrote, 'The growing South Pole ice cap . . . is the creeping peril, the deadly menace, and the divinely ordained executioner of our civilisation.' Believing that every 7,000 years or so the Earth undergoes a catastrophic pole shift, he claimed the Sudan Basin – a depression that covers nearly 4,000,000 square miles, with Lake Chad in the south – as a former ice cap. Depressing the earth, it had formed watercourses and Lake Chad by run-off. He suggested both Caspian Sea and Hudson Bay as former polar sites. In *Cataclysms of the Earth* he cited Siberian discoveries of fast-frozen mammoths, the myths of Noah and Deucalion, and the excavation of Ur as evidence of past deluge and **pole-shift**. He concluded the planet has a naturally recurring cycle, about 7,000 years long, that begins and ends in cataclysm. His theory of Antarctic disaster rests on the assumptions that: (1) that the south polar ice-cap is growing; and (2) in time it will develop enough off-centre mass to overcome the stability of the planet's spin axis. A pole-shift, he said, would occur in a single day, causing a running earthquake or ground-wave some thirteen miles high, the ice caps ending up near the present equator. The oceans slosh out of their basins as the planet capsizes: only Noah stands a chance.

There may be errors in his calculation of the weight of the ice cap; it remains unclear if the ice cap is growing. The strongest objection to his theory lies in radiometric measurements of rocks overlying and so younger than Antarctic glaciers. They are at least ten million years old.[1]

1. *Pole Shift*, John White, W. H. Allen, London 1980, pp. 66–84

BRUNO, Giordano (1548–1600) Appropriately born at Nola in the foot-hills of Vesuvius, this irascible revolutionary proved too fiery for his own good and eventually burned at the stake. Entering the Dominican Order in 1563, he found **Neoplatonic** and **hermetic** teachings more profound than Church dogma. In 1576 he was accused of heresy on 130 counts and fled Italy. For fifteen years he wandered in Germany, Switzerland, Bohemia, France and England, advancing radical ideas about the cosmos and inner man. He propounded evolutionary theory, holding that spiritual evolution should unfold concomitantly with the development of form, because 'the divine perfection of the individual soul is the aim of all progression'. Before Harvey he taught

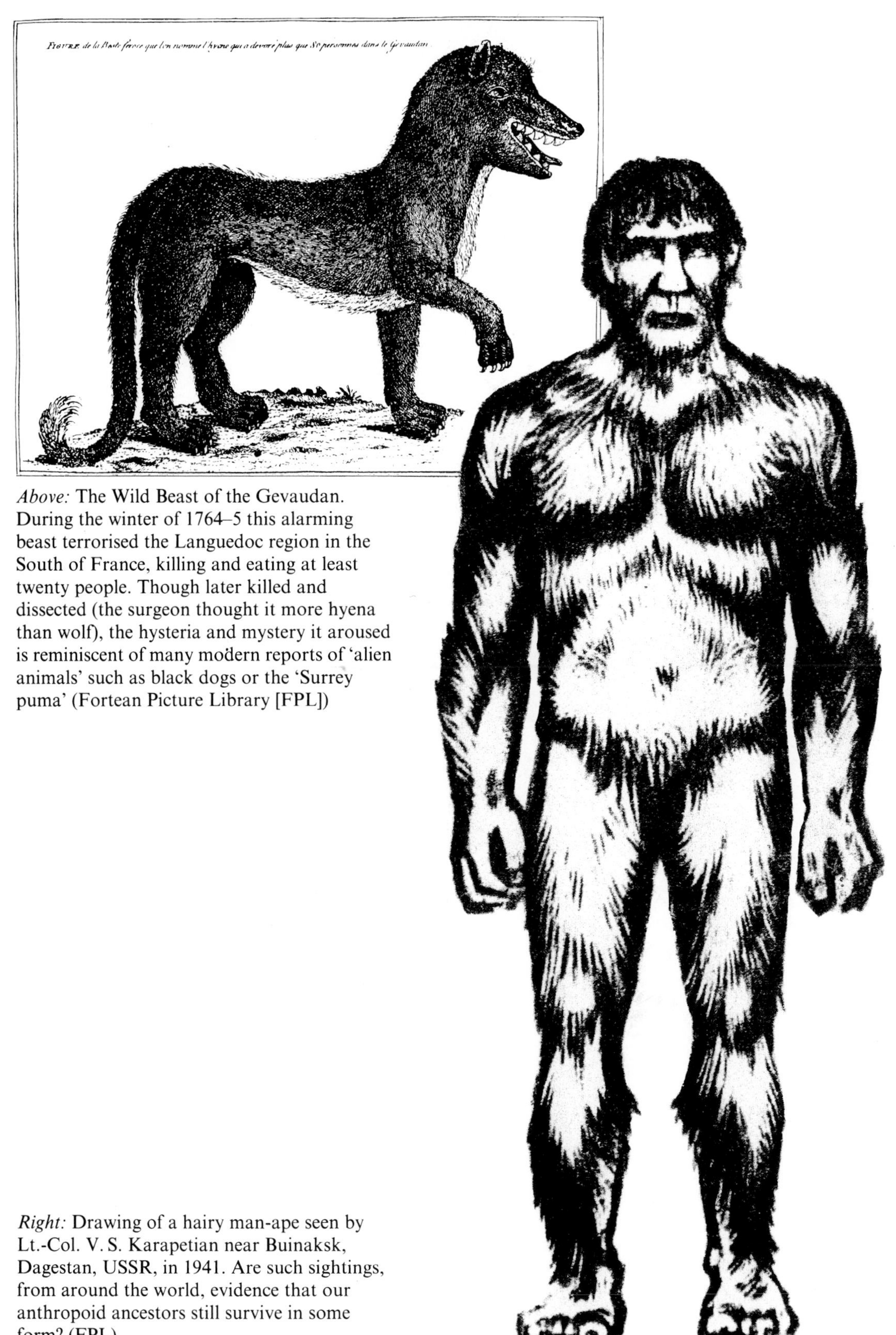

Above: The Wild Beast of the Gevaudan. During the winter of 1764–5 this alarming beast terrorised the Languedoc region in the South of France, killing and eating at least twenty people. Though later killed and dissected (the surgeon thought it more hyena than wolf), the hysteria and mystery it aroused is reminiscent of many modern reports of 'alien animals' such as black dogs or the 'Surrey puma' (Fortean Picture Library [FPL])

Right: Drawing of a hairy man-ape seen by Lt.-Col. V. S. Karapetian near Buinaksk, Dagestan, USSR, in 1941. Are such sightings, from around the world, evidence that our anthropoid ancestors still survive in some form? (FPL)

Angels are forces linking the higher and lower spheres of consciousness, numinous messengers from another order of being which feature in many cultures as winged creatures with human form. Here (*left*) the Archangel Michael liberates the bound souls of the dead, and (*below*) the Archangel Gabriel is shown as an alternative interpretation of the constellation of Pegasus in Julius Schiller's *Coelum Stellatum Christianum* of 1627 (Images)

The only known specimen of the Devil's handwriting, from *The Devil in Britain and America* by John Ashton, 1896 (Fortean)

In this example of psychic graffiti from Borley Rectory, the receiver of the messages entered into a dialogue in an effort to clarify the bizarre writing being recorded (Mary Evans)

Marianne

I CANNOT UNDERSTAND
TELL ME MORE

Marianne.

I STILL CANNOT UNDERSTAND
PLEASE TELL ME MORE.

A detail from the bronze door of the Church of San Zeno in Verona shows a demon being exorcised through San Zeno's mouth (Images)

William Etty's 1840 image of a young girl's dream shows satyrs exposing her body – Jung wrote that a dream is 'a little hidden door in the innermost and most secret recesses of the psyche' (Images)

A modern Druid ritual involving members of the Order of Bards, Ovates and Druids at Spring Equinox (FPL)

These mysterious sigils were used by John Dee, Queen Elizabeth I's magus, to evoke the Enochians, allegedly an order of angels (Images)

The wedding of Tom Thumb and Minnie Warren, in an American photograph of 1865. Folktales of fairies, pixies and elves may have their roots in ancient memories of dwarf races (Mary Evans)

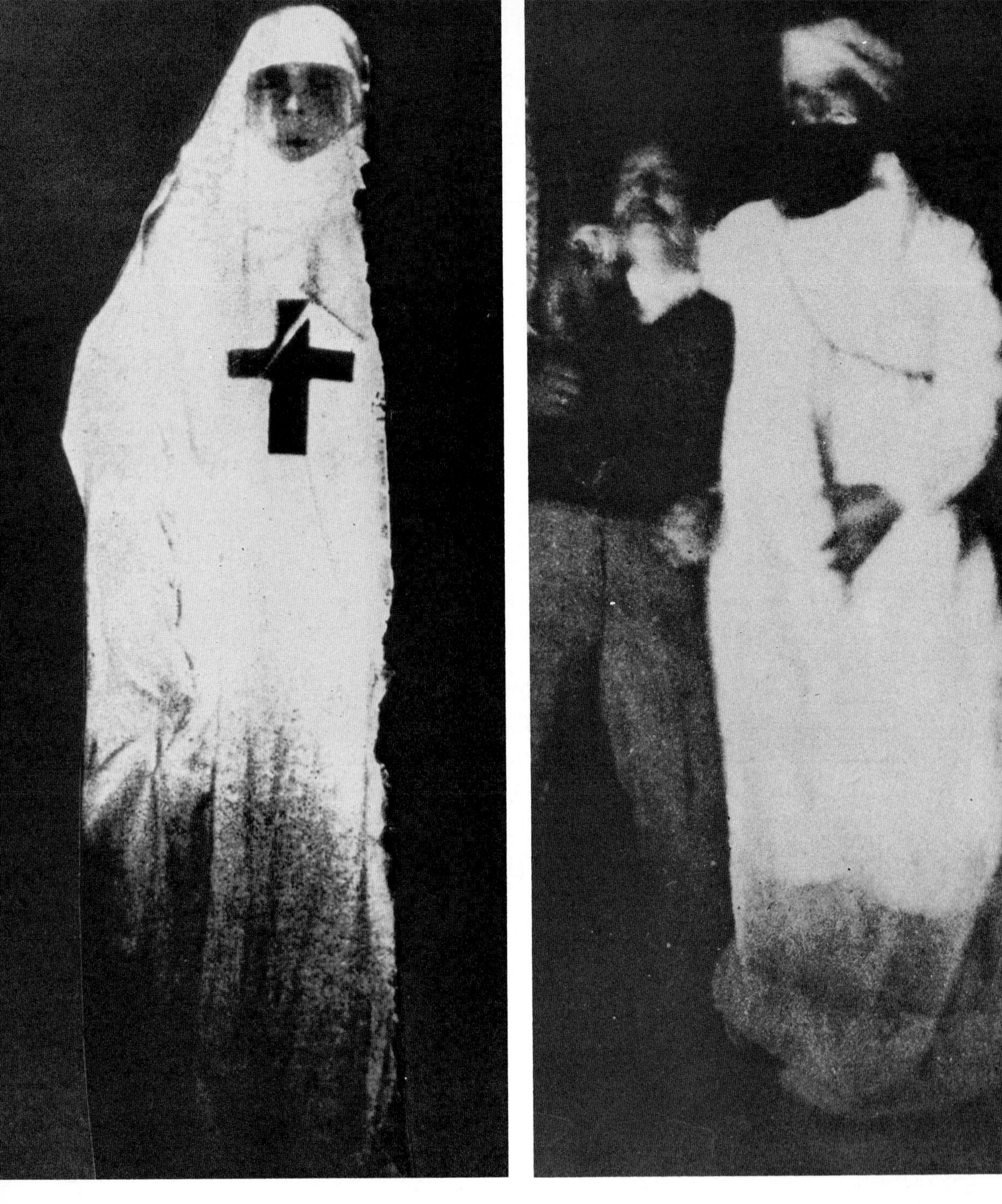

Above left: The ghost of a nun which materialised at a seance in Lisbon, 1918; and, *above right,* ghost in Arabic dress which appeared at a seance held by the medium Eglington in 1878 (Images)

As this picture of medium W. M. Marriott with his 'materialisations' shows, fake photographs of ghosts were only too easy to create in the early years of camera technology. As a result, genuinely intriguing phenomena have perhaps been too easily dismissed (Mary Evans)

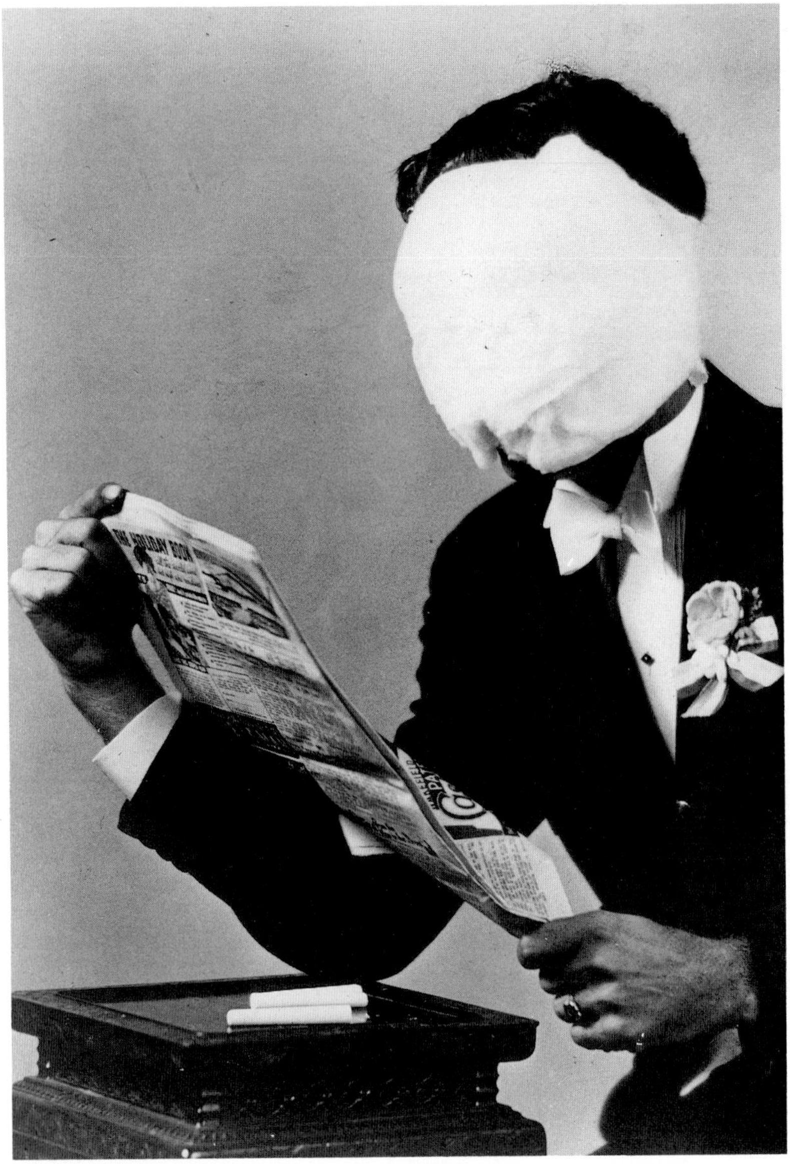

Above: Telepath Kuda Bux reads a newspaper while blindfolded. *Right:* Zener cards are used in experiments to test telepathic skills more scientifically, although tests have been vulnerable to accusations of fraud (Mary Evans)

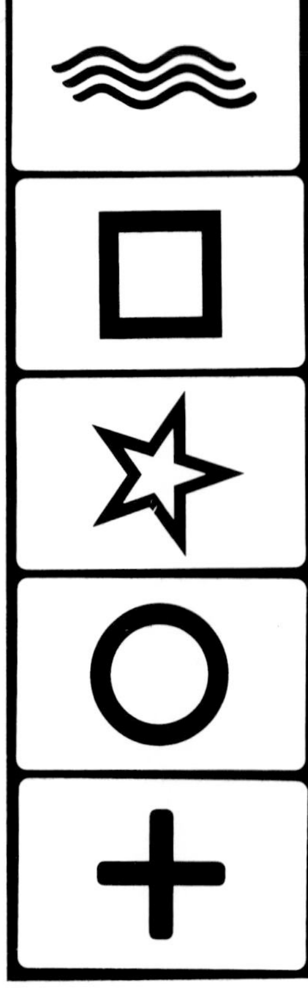

the circulation of the blood as a consequence of his views on cosmic cyclic rebirth. He held the sun to be the centre of the universe, which he thought infinite and containing other solar systems. He said living beings on other planets would see their home world as the universal centre. In a major work, *The Art of Memory*, he said what **Paracelsus** had only dared to hint: the human mind is divine, holding in it the starry heavens. By means of a magical art of memory he aimed to tap the cosmic power emanating from the 'seals', or images of the stars (**archetypes**?). He would open the **psyche**'s 'black diamond doors', burn with 'heroic frenzy' and save the human race.

Rash enough to publicise this mission, he disputed and made himself unpopular wherever he went. In 1591, emboldened by heroic frenzy, he returned to Italy. In Padua he prepared for the inevitable clash with the Church by magical rites meant to gain him charismatic powers. His 'links with **demons**' brought him an invitation to Venice by a nobleman, Mocenigo, who betrayed him to the Inquisition. Tortured into denying his 'heresies', he underwent seven years solitary confinement in Rome's Castel Sant' Angelo. In 1599, required to abjure eight heretical propositions drawn from his work, he was again tortured. Later withdrawing his retractions, he was sentenced as an impenitent heretic and burned alive on the Campo de' Fiori in Rome on 17 February 1600.

'It is with far greater fear that you pronounce, than I receive, this sentence,' he told his judges, who perhaps recalled what he'd written in *The Triumphant Expulsion of the Great Beast*. 'Let us be converted to Justice, because since we have departed from her, we have departed from ourselves; so that we are no longer gods, are no longer ourselves.'

1. *Giordano Bruno and the Hermetic Tradition*, Francis A. Yates, Routledge Kegan Paul, London 1964

BRUNTON, Dr Paul (*See* **ASTRAL PROJECTION, GREAT PYRAMID**) In the 1930s this widely travelled English **occultist** and author arranged to spend a night in the King's Chamber of the **Great Pyramid** – one of the last to get permission. He fasted for three days then, locked into the pyramid, climbed the galleries to the King's Chamber, sat by the granite coffer and put out his light. Awful **elementals** crowded him in the darkness. Then benevolent beings in the regalia of ancient Egyptian high priests came to lead him through secret passages equating to secret passages of the mind.

The experience involved an **astral projection**. He describes how 'a paralysing lethargy' crept over him and he entered a semi-somnolent state: 'I felt myself sinking inwards in consciousness to some central point within my brain . . . There was a final mad whirl within my brain. I had the sensation of being caught up in a tropical whirlwind and seemed to pass upwards through a narrow hole; then there was the momentary dread of being launched into infinite space . . .'

This account of a 'narrow hole' is central to **shamanic** tradition.[1]

1. *A Search in Secret Egypt*, Paul Brunton, Rider, London 1969

BUDDHA The word derives from the Sanskrit root *budh*, 'to perceive', 'to awaken', 'to recover consciousness'. It signifies the spiritually awakened being freed from 'living death'. 'Enlightened Ones' are in Nirvana and have no need of the world but may choose to incarnate to aid humanity. The person laxly called 'The Buddha' is but one of many *buddhas* . . .

Born in Nepal *c.* 563 BC, Prince Siddhartha Gautama lived in closeted luxury. One day he wanted to visit the town. His father tried to hide its ugliness from him, but he saw age, sickness and death – the transitory world. Shocked, he met a begging ascetic who had renounced the world, and declared he must follow the same course. His father, fearing to lose him, locked him up with the pleasures of the palace. He escaped. As the ragged monk Gautama he wandered. Rejecting the doctrines of the **Yogis**, for six years he fasted by a river. Near death, he realised his austerities were pointless. He accepted a bowl of rice from a village girl who pitied him. He bathed in the river. His five disciples abandoned him. He came to the bo-tree (*ficus religiosa*, a type of fig-tree rich in **serotonin**, a nerve hormone produced in the brain by the **pineal gland** or 'Third Eye') and sat under it, swearing never to move until he attained what he sought. All day the **demons** tempted him. As night fell Enlightenment dawned. He saw the way of things, the cause of rebirth. He remembered his former lives, he grasped the cause and effect of **karma**. By dawn, a Buddha, he knew how worlds begin and end. He meditated for a week, stayed by the tree a month. He chose not to enter *nirvana* instantly but to remain in the world to guide others. He retained the physical body for eighty years, dying *c*. 483 BC.

BUDDHISM (*See* **DALAI LAMA, TIBET, TIBETAN BOOK OF THE DEAD**) The system initiated by Gautama the Buddha is metapsychology rather than charismatic religion, and so less clad in imagery or hid in symbolism than **Christianity**. It is essentially a guide-book or DIY course in clearing out illusory ideas about the world. It is about seeing straight.

In Benares *c*. 530 BC Gautama 'set in motion the wheel of the Law'. He preached on the need to avoid extremes – austerity or hedonism – by taking the Middle Way to enlightenment. This Way consists of the Noble Eightfold Path, meaning: Right Views, Right Intent, Right Speech, Right Action, Right Livelihood, Right Effort, Right Mindfulness and Right Concentration.

Four truths underlie the Path: *all life is suffering; the cause of suffering is desire; suffering ceases when desire ceases*; and *the Noble Eightfold Path leads to cessation of desire*.

Three Trainings – morality, concentration and wisdom – focus the mind on the Path. These involve **yoga** (Sanskrit *jog*, 'to yoke'). *Siddhis* may develop. These (powers called '**psychic**' or '**paranormal**' in the West) fall into six categories: **telepathy, clairaudience, clairvoyance**, far memory, and magic powers including **levitation,** *tulpa*-projection, **shape-shifting** and suspended animation. All such powers are said to be distractions, and to be ignored. But did early Buddhism so strictly dismiss *siddhis*? The myth of Gautama's later life includes magical contests with wizards of other beliefs, much like St Patrick's magical battle with the **Druids**.

Today Buddhism is of two branches, Northern and Southern. The Southern retains the 'Buddha's Brain' or 'Eye-Doctrine'; an exoteric philosophy for the outer world. The Northern retains the 'Heart-Doctrine' – the hidden heart-blood and inner doctrine of the teaching.

The difference between the two is the difference between mountain and plain, ice and fire, intellect and sensuality – similar, it may be argued, to the essential difference between Protestant and Catholic Christianity. The Northern doctrine is of the Himalayas and high plains, and is colder, more pure, austere and refined intellectually. The Southern arises from hotter, more populous areas in which mercantile ambition, hot climate, and crowded streets insist on a more worldly approach.

Neither branch is superior. Like **Yin and Yang**, they are two sides of the same coin.

BULWER-LYTTON, Edward (1803–73) This mid-Victorian novelist (*A Strange Story, Zanoni, The Coming Race*) was influenced by French occultist Eliphas **Lévi**, whom he fancifully portrayed as the magician in *The Haunted and the Haunters*. In this short tale, set in London's 50 Berkeley Square (still known as a haunted house), he implied a definite relationship between **hauntings** and haunted. In *The Coming Race* (1871) the hero enters a underground world inhabited by nasty beings who control

'Vril fluid', a magical energy that strikes over distances. 'Vril' was probably derived from what Lévi called the 'astral light'. It also suggests **Kundalini**-fire. This novel inspired various **occult** groups, among them the 'Luminous Lodge' or Vril Society in Nazi Germany, whose members thought Bulwer-Lytton had described an Aryan super-race inhabiting the lost world of Thule. Bulwer-Lytton led his own magical group and contributed towards the occult revival that led to the **Golden Dawn** and influenced the careers of **Mathers, Crowley, Yeats** and others. He is also said to have known the Comte de **Saint Germain**, widely though to have survived death in 1784.

BURIAL MOUNDS (*See* **EARTHWORKS, MEGALITHS**)

BUTLER, W. E. (*See* **FORTUNE , Dion**) Adept and initiate of the Society of the **Inner Light**, Ernest Butler worked all his life to spread interest in **occultism**. In his *The Magician: His Training and Work* (1959) he published the essentials of esoteric training. Later, encouraged by an **Inner Plane** contact, he formed the **Servants of the Light**. For this organisation (led since his death in 1978 by Dolores Ashcroft-Nowicki) he wrote a *Practical Course on the Mystical Qabalah*, a wide-ranging practical study text involving elements of **yoga, meditation**, ritual, and the inner activation of **Grail** and **Tree of Life** metapsychology. Teaching that 'The way of occultism is the Middle Way,' his style was practical and humane, requiring students to assess and correct themselves rather than take orders. 'There seems little point in developing psychic or mental powers if the physical vehicle for these powers is allowed to get into a slipshod or poor condition,' he wrote. Despite persistent ill-health he completed much valuable work.

The Magician: His Training and Work, W. E. Butler, Aquarian, Wellingborough 1959

BUTTERFLY EFFECT (*See* **CHAOS THEORY**)

For want of a nail, the shoe was lost;
For want of a shoe, the horse was lost;
For want of a horse, the rider was lost;
For want of a rider, the battle was lost;
For want of a battle, the kingdom was lost!

The Butterfly Effect[1] as a concept arose through work by MIT meteorologist Edward Lorenz. His research since 1960 on weather forecasting indicates that no model yet created can take account of all the minor details – like the tiny flutterings of a butterfly's wing – that in combination add up to *reality* in terms of a correct forecast. His computer modelling of weather conditions, sound over two or three days, predictively fell apart in a week. While understanding the programme simplifications, he sought a wider cause to explain failure. In so doing, he joined a wider debate. Meteorological rationalists like Von Neumann had assumed computerisation and calculation as the keys to weather prediction. Lorenz showed it was not so easy. For no matter how much data came in, variables remained. This is true too in all other areas involving computer modelling and prediction, including the financial flow and social disposition of nations.

No model existed that could take into account all the variables not yet realised and programmed as such. The variables extend forever. This is one basis of **Chaos Theory**. However deep you go, there's more going on. The butterfly's wing is the slightest thing that ever led to the fall of a king. That which starts a motion cannot be measured by those in motion – while they remain in motion. In Greek, *Kaos* = chasm, or space. In China, the **Taoist** Chuang Tzu dreamed he was a butterfly dreaming it was a man.

1. *Chaos*, James Gleick, Cardinal Books, London 1988, pp. 9–33

C

CABBALA (*See* **QABALAH**)

CAGLIOSTRO, Count Alessandro Di (1743?–1795?) (*See* **FREEMASONRY**)
Either the 'King of Liars' (Carlyle) or 'One of the great **occult** figures of all time' (Lewis **Spence**), Cagliostro was born Giuseppe Balsamo, to a poor family in Palermo, Sicily. 'While not actually handsome,' wrote a hostile witness, the Baroness D'Oberkirch, 'his face was the most remarkable I have ever seen. His eyes . . . were indescribable – all fire and yet all ice.'

His death in an Inquisition prison (probably by strangulation) only added to his legend despite claims by his Inquisition biographer and others that he was just a rogue falsely claiming occult powers.

Early expelled as a monastic novitiate for blasphemy, he travelled in Egypt with a Greek alchemist, Altotas, and entered high society circles. Married at twenty-six to Lorenza Feliciani (aged fourteen), a year later Casanova met the pair in France and thought them persons of rank. In London he worked as a painter and was jailed for debt. An M. Duplessis brought them to Paris but seduced Lorenza. Balsamo applied for royal redress; Lorenza spent a year in jail. A skin lotion containing borax made him money. When Lorenza was released they returned to Italy, Balsamo now calling himself the Marchese Pellegrini. It seems Lorenza had forgiven him. But in Palermo a goldsmith he'd swindled had him thrown in jail.

In 1776, now calling himself Cagliostro, he returned to London, where he discovered Freemasonry. After years of wandering, at last he found himself. Believing Masonry to have originated in ancient **Egypt**, he discovered or invented 'the Egyptian rite'. His new self-belief increased his powers of **second-sight** and **clairvoyance**. In Leipzig he said if the Lodge failed to adopt the Egyptian rite, its master would feel the hand of God before the end of the month. Soon after the master, Scieffort, killed himself. Cagliostro toured European masonic lodges triumphantly.

Even his defenders admit he used fraud to recruit followers, though it seems he took no personal profit. He used young boys or girls (*colombes* = doves) to **scry** for him by gazing into bowls of water: at least twice the *colombe* involved declared it was all fake and he had to brazen his way out.

On 19 September 1780, preceded by liveried servants on black horses, he entered Strasbourg in his black coach. From a room in a poor quarter he distributed alms and cured the sick, snubbing wealthy men who had called him a fake. When **Goethe**'s friend, the philosopher Lavater, approached him, he said: 'If your science is greater than mine, you have no need of my acquaintance; if mine is the greater, I have no need of yours.' So too he rebuffed the Cardinal de Rohan, a powerful man in liaison with Queen Marie Antoinette. Yet both Lavater and the Cardinal became his disciples.

The hostility of local doctors drove him on to Paris where involvement in Rohan's plot to gain the Queen's love led to his downfall. His craven behaviour at trial and a year in the Bastille made him a laughing-stock. He wandered about Europe, still propagating Freemasonry. In 1789, repeating the error of **Bruno** in 1592, he returned to Italy. Arrested, he was thrown, like **Bruno** two centuries earlier, into the Castel Sant' Angelo.

Transferred to the Castel San Leo, he was locked in a cell cut out of solid rock. Lorenza died in 1794 in a nunnery; he died a year later.

His tale is common in European history – that of the **seer** who finds no place in a society that defines '**paranormal**' insight as, at best, oddity, and at worst, subversion of prescribed social norms. Reports on the lives of such individuals are always suspect, given not only their own bombastic nature but the widespread hostility they stimulate.[1]

1. *The Occult*, Colin Wilson, Grafton, London 1979, pp. 377–409

CALLANISH (*See* **MEGALITHIC MYSTERIES**)

CAMPBELL, Joseph (1904–1987) 'Joseph Campbell and the Power of Myth', a six-part TV series posthumously screened (UK BBC2 1990), made clear the cross-cultural authority exercised by this great student of mythology. Born in New York, working from the Sarah Lawrence College for almost forty years, his insights into the global similarities between the 'hero' myths of different cultures were expressed first in his *The Hero with a Thousand Faces* (1949) and developed in his ground-breaking, essential four-volume work, *The Masks of God*.

'Religions, philosophies, arts, the social forms of primitive and historic man, the very dreams that blister sleep,' he wrote, 'boil up from the basic, magic ring of myth . . . the flavour of the ocean is contained in a droplet . . . the whole mystery of life within the egg of a flea.'[1]

1. *The Hero with a Thousand Faces*, Joseph Campbell, Abacus, London, 1975, p. 13
   The Masks of God (4 vols.), Joseph Campbell, Penguin, London 1976

CAPRA, Fritjof (c. 1940–) In the 1970s this Austro-American researcher in the field of high energy physics published *The Tao of Physics*, an influential synthesis of ancient mysticism and modern science. In it he pointed out how deeply the insights of modern particle physicists, artists and philosophers echo and reflect the 'religious' world-view of old esoteric teachings. Rejecting what 200 years ago **Blake** called 'Single vision and Newton's sleep', in a later work, *The Turning Point*, Capra applies a holistic, systems-based approach to many of the problems in contemporary life created by a purely mechanistic world-view. Given his popular influence he is among the more important thinkers involved in attempting to wrench Western thought out of its over-rational and increasingly sterile tram-tracks. His main theme is 'the fundamental change of world-view that is occurring in science and in society, the unfolding of a new vision of reality and the social implications of this cultural transformation'.[1,2]

1. *The Tao of Physics*, Fritjof Capra, Fontana, London 1976
2. *The Turning Point*, Fritjof Capra, Fontana Flamingo, London 1983

CARNAC (*See* **MEGALITHIC MYSTERIES**)

CASTANEDA, Carlos (c. 1940–) (*See* **DASKALOS, DRUGS, SHAMAN**) In 1970 emerged the first in a series of remarkable accounts describing the techniques of a Mexican *brujo* or **shaman** – *The Teachings of Don Juan: A Yaqui Way of Knowledge*. Submitted as a Ph.D. dissertation at the University of California by Peruvian anthropologist Carlos Aranha, who had acquired US citizenship in 1959, it was so bizarrely thought-provoking that publication brought its author (now Carlos Castaneda) instant bestsellerdom, fame and persisting controversy. Does this book and its sequels (*A Separate Reality*, *Journey to Ixtlan*, *Tales of Power*, etc.) constitute trailblazing psychedelic anthropology or a cynical exploitation of the public hunger for marvels?

If Castaneda's magical apprenticeship occurred as described or even at all remains dubious. Yet his thesis was screened when first presented: his examiners were convinced, and though author Richard De Mille (*Castaneda's Journey*, 1976; *The Don Juan Papers*, 1980) has poked holes in his account, still the question put by the two-faced god and his acolytes (**Cagliostro, Crowley**, etc.) remains. *What is true? What is false?*

Castaneda tells how initially he persuaded an old Yaqui Indian *brujo* (man of power), Don Juan, to teach him a magical system relying on three **hallucinogens**, peyote, jimson weed and psilocybin. Each of these were doors to communication with specific entities or forces, called 'allies'. Communion with these forces led to vision beyond surface reality into the 'way of the warrior' and to magical powers like **shape-shifting**. In later books, while Castaneda's adventures grow ever more fantastic, the emphasis on hallucinogens is abandoned. He is told by Don Juan that this approach was needed because of his western cultural preconceptions. Yet it may be noted that by the mid–1970s, when this shift took place, a disillusionment with the psychedelic experience *per se* had taken root. It is tempting to consider Castaneda an attractive fraud.

Yet his accounts are remarkable, and even if read only as fireside romance may move the imaginative mind to genuine growth. Certainly, there is no doubt Castaneda did his magical homework. His description of magical systems and shamanistic techniques, however derived, have an authentic ring. Perhaps in the last analysis it matters not at all whether 'Don Juan' actually lived and taught Castaneda as claimed: what matters is the teaching, that the **magician** must be always alert to the world and the techniques he uses, ensuring that his journeys into the hidden realms are subject to his will, and always understanding the nature of the power he wields.[1,2]

'Will is what makes you invulnerable,' says Don Juan. 'Will is what sends a sorcerer through a wall; through space, to the moon if he wants . . .'

1. *Don Juan, Mescalito and Modern Magic*, Nevill Drury, Arkana, London 1985
2. *The Teachings of Don Juan*, (*et seq.*), Carlos Castaneda, Penguin Books, London

CATHARS (*See* **GNOSTICS, GUIRDHAM, REINCARNATION**) Exterminated by the Church in the thirteenth century, the Cathars of the Pays d'Oc in France not only saw themselves as the only true Christians, but were the last sect to proclaim the tenets of classical **dualism** in public. Believing in **reincarnation**, the equality of good and evil as basic universal principles, and that the Creator of the physical world is the **Devil**, alias the Old Testament Jehovah, they took their **Gnostic** and **Manichaean** faith from the Bogomils of Bulgaria. Their priests, called *Perfecti* or 'perfect ones', were vegetarian, chaste, and espoused non-violence. They thought the crucifixion fictitious and that Jesus had never lived as a man. Their rule of travelling in pairs of the same sex led to the calumny that they were homesexual – 'buggers', from 'bougres', meaning 'Bulgarians'. This arose also from their rejection of marriage and sexual relations as tending to the incarnation of more poor souls in *hell* – for so they saw this earthly life. In fact such abstinence was asked only of the *Perfecti* who had undertaken the *consolamentum*: a rite which most believers undertook only on their deathbed. The faith, though **mystic** in its attitude to **Christ**, was entirely practical in terms of human psychology: requiring nothing of those unable to overcome their nature.

As such, it became so charismatic that it threatened the power of the Church. It seemed as if the entire Pays d'Oc was about to fall to Cathar control. In 1208, following the murder of a papal envoy, Pope Innocent III declared a crusade. The resulting forty-year war waged by the King and barons of north France (interested more in grabbing land than in converting souls) led to the establishment of the Dominican Inquisition and to the razing of over 400 villages by Simon de Montfort.

The destruction began with the sack of Béziers in 1208, the Church's attitude being enshrined in the remark supposedly made by the Abbé de Cîteaux. 'Kill them all,' he told soldiers complaining they couldn't tell between Cathars and Catholics, 'God will know his own.'

The last important Cathar stand took place at the Pyrenean castle of Montségur. At its fall in March 1244 over 200 Cathars were burned alive. It is said a treasure was removed from Montségur before the capitulation. What it was remains the subject of occult speculation. Some claim it was the **Holy Grail**.

Their interest today arises from: (1) a rebirth of interest in Gnostic beliefs; (2) their apparent connection with esoteric movements such as the troubadours and **Knights Templar**; (3) their place in a mythology rendering Montségur as mystical as **Arthurian** Camelot; and (4) the odd events recorded by English psychiatrist Arthur **Guirdham** in the 1960s, suggesting that some of his patients, disturbed by recurrent dreams, were reincarnated Cathars who had lived and died in the years preceding the fall of Montségur.

Apart from these aspects Catharism is remembered for its attempt to maintain in Europe a spiritual path that the Church Militant crushed so utterly that for over seven centuries it was as if dead and gone – forced underground. That it and its tenets survive to require reassessment today only goes to show that spiritual belief is hard to destroy.[1,2,3]

1. *The Medieval Manichee*, Steven Runciman, Cambridge University Press, 1947
2. *The Great Heresy*, Arthur Guirdham, Spearman, London 1977
3. *The Albigensian Crusade*, Jonathan Sumption, Faber and Faber, London 1978

CATTLE MUTILATIONS (*See* **BEARDEN, CORN CIRCLES**) Reported across the western USA, this 1970s phenomenon was as odd as the more recent appearance in England of corn circles. Cattle were found not only dead on the range but mutilated with inexplicably sadistic precision. Wrote investigator Ed Sanders: 'Tongues, eyes, ears, tails, genitals were removed – all perfectly snipped as with a tailor's shears. The rears of the animals were sometimes bored as if the perpetrator were using a razor-sharp geologist's core sampler.'[1] Large numbers died: in a small Colorado area fifty cattle were found mutilated in one year. Nerve gas apparently caused at least one death, degenerative chemicals were involved in others. Coyotes and buzzards would not touch the quickly decaying corpses.

Cause and purpose remain unknown. Some claimed **UFO** sightings in areas where mutilations occurred, Bearden blamed 'tulpoid symbology' emanating **psychotronically** from the US collective dream-pool. Others blamed weird, unknown, but unfortunately human 'blood cults'. Yet human sadism and the copycat tendency fail to explain *all* the deaths. The precision, number and geographic scale of the mutilations would have required a gang of skilled delinquent surgeons to be rushing from one remote area to another in order to perform pointlessly brutal virtuoso operations on illegally slaughtered cattle. This being unlikely, the phenomenon remains unexplained.

1. Quoted in *Mysteries*, Colin Wilson, Grafton, London 1979, p. 559

CAYCE, Edgar (1877–1945) (*See* **ATLANTIS, POLE SHIFT, PROPHECY**) **Trance healer**, **psychic** and prophet of cataclysm, America's 'Sleeping **Seer**' was born on a Kentucky farm. As a child he had 'visions', telling his parents he spoke to dead relatives. At sixteen, injured by a blow on the head, suddenly he told his mother to apply a specific type of poultice. Next day, though cured, he had no memory of ordering the poultice. At twenty-one, he suffered paralysis of his throat muscles. Medicine and hypnotism both failing to cure him, he asked a friend to help him enter the type of self-induced trance that had helped him memorise his schoolbooks. In this state he prescribed his own cure. It worked. Local doctors took advantage of his talent and found he needed only the name and address of the patient to diagnose at a distance. By 1910 he was nationally famous. His diagnoses often contradicted orthodoxy but usually proved correct. Like **Arigó**, his cures are too well attested to remain in doubt. Many of his prescriptions were orthodox, but the source of his knowledge was not, and it led him into areas that *are* controversial.

From giving medical readings he went on to evaluate individual fate by means of 'life readings'. In trance he described not only the **past lives** of his patients (including some on **Atlantis**) but prophesied coming global chaos. An orthodox Christian when awake, he was disturbed by all this, but kept records, leaving at his death in 1945 over 14,000 stenographic records of trance readings for over 8,000 people. These (grist for the **apocalyptic Christian** mill) included prophecies of dire earth changes between 1958 and 1998 including Californian superquakes and submersal of New York and Japan.

He saw Northern Europe changed 'in the twinkling of an eye'. World War II battlefields would be 'ocean, seas and bays'. Cataclysmic **pole shift** in 1998 would lead to a better life for the few survivors. Prior to this chaos Atlantis would start to rise again in 1968 or 1969, near Bimini. Palaeontologist Dr Manson **Valentine** and underwater cinematographer Dimitri Rebikoff subsequently found and supervised exploration of the 'Bimini Road' – long, regular walls of cyclopean blocks (some weighing over eighty tons) in shallow water off the north-west tip of Bimini Island. Whether or not these belong to an outpost of drowned Atlantis remains unproven. As for Cayce, in trance he saw himself reborn in post-apocalypse Nebraska *c.*AD 2100.[1]

1. *Edgar Cayce on Prophecy*, Mary Ellen Carter, Warner Books, New York 1988

CELTIC MAGIC (*See* **BANSHEE, DIVINATION, DRUIDS, SECOND SIGHT**) 'Martin relates, that the natives of South Uist believed that a valley called Glenslyte, situated between two mountains on the east side of the island, was haunted by spirits, whom they called the Great Men, and that if any man or woman entered the valley without first making an entire resignation of themselves to the conduct of the Great Men, they would infallibly grow mad. The same writer mentions a universal custom among the inhabitants of the Western Isles, of pouring a cow's milk on a little hill, where a spirit they called Brownie, was believed to lodge, which spirit always appeared in the shape of a tall man, with very long brown hair.'[1]

The Celts appeared in Europe *c.* 1300 BC but probably originated further east, their poetic metres and marriage customs being similar to those of the Brahmins in India. Celtic place-names (*nemeton* 'grove') are found as far as central Turkey. Sweeping through Europe, they fought naked, took heads, loved to boast and speak in riddles. They honoured warriors, bards (poets) *vates* (diviners), and **Druids** (philosophers). Holding the human soul and universe to be indestructible, they did not fear death, and would stab a victim to read auguries from the death-convulsions.

Settling Europe's western shores, from the mid-sixth century BC Goidelic Celts (Gaels) entered the British Isles. Irish myth records invasions by the sons of Partholon, the Nemedians, the Fir Bolg, the magical Tuatha de Danaan, and the Children of Mil from Spain. Later came the Brythons, their tongue the basis of modern Welsh and Breton. Taking over the remains of the old **megalithic** society which had completed **Stonehenge** a millennium earlier, their **Druids** acknowledged the greater power of those before them.

Believers in **reincarnation**, their reported powers of **shape-shifting, divination, second sight** and **invisibility** perhaps arose out of techniques as used in **yoga**. Popular belief in such powers and in the spirit-world persisted among the Celts due to an imaginative temperament and proximity to nature. While others built cities, the Celts on Europe's wild fringe remained close to the elemental forces. The wailing wind was the **banshee**'s cry; 'accidents' were signs and messages; a shouider-blade of mutton picked clean reflected the future; grain was sowed in the moon's increase; cattle-diseases were cured by forcing new fire and burning juniper; green mounds where the *Sidhe* (**fairies**) lived were best avoided. Such beings were to be treated with respect, or they'd sour the butter and steal your child. Deep in the dark loch lurked the kelpie or waterhorse, luring women and children to death, swelling the flood to drown travellers; the bard's resonant curse was feared even by kings; on the peak where mist and snow lingered all year the Great Ones waited to destroy the unwary and carry them west, though not to blessed Tir nan Og, the magical Land of Youth reserved for heroes . . .

Most cultures retain remnants of belief in a '**magical**' knowledge-system denied by modern rationality and science. But the Celts retain more than most, as is shown by the persistence of the second sight (Gaelic: *an-da-shealladh* = 'the two sights') in Highland areas – and also perhaps by events like the case of the Hexham Heads.

In 1972 an eleven-year-old boy weeding a garden in Hexham, near Newcastle-upon-Tyne in North England, unearthed two heavy, quartz-rich stones carved as human heads. When taken indoors these became the focus of weird events. Objects shattered, the heads turned spontaneously, and where they had been found a strange flower bloomed at Christmas. A 'half human, half sheeplike' entity materialised, touching and terrifying a neighbour. The heads were removed (and the house was exorcised). Celtic scholar Dr Anne Ross took charge of them. She thought them 1800 years old, survivors of some Celtic 'head-cult' ritual. One night she awoke to 'a dreadful atmosphere of icy coldness'. Looking to the door she saw a creature, half-wolf and half-man, covered with black fur and about six feet tall, leaving the room. She had to follow it despite her terror, but it vanished. Soon after her daughter underwent a similar experience. This house too was exorcised. An inorganic chemist, Dr Dan Robins, took over the heads. He believed, like **Lethbridge**, that some minerals can 'tape-record' information (*see* **black dogs**), and he wondered if the quartz-rich heads were the nexus for a '**curse**' anciently imprinted and still electrically operative. This seemed more likely when, putting the heads in his car to take them home, he turned the ignition and found it dead. 'Stop it!' he told the heads, and the car started.

Later a Mr Craigie who had lived in the first house said he had made the heads as toys for his daughter in 1956. Either way, that they had stimulated **poltergeist**-type phenomena was not in doubt.[3]

1. *History of the Highlands*, James Brown, Glasgow 1838, pp. 106ff
2. *Magic Arts in Celtic Britain*, Lewis Spence, Rider, London 1970
3. 'Curse of the Hexham Heads', Paul Screeton, *The Unexplained*, Orbis partwork, London 1983, pp. 2326–9

CEREBELLUM (*See* **BRAIN MYSTERIES**)

CETACEANS (*See* **DOLPHINS, WHALES**)

CHAKRAS (*See* **KUNDALINI YOGA, QABALAH, YOGA**) Originally a Sanskrit term meaning a 'wheel', today in both Eastern yogic and Western magical systems *chakras* are seen as energy centres located at specific points up and down the vertical axis of the human body. Chakras are said to mediate the absorption, transformation and distribution of the universal *prānic* energies through the psychophysical body. Those trained to perceive them describe them as vortices of shifting colours, sounds and densities, spiralling into our *subtle* anatomies. However East and West disagree as to their number, location, description and function.

Hindu systems define seven chakras, each outwardly manifesting in the seven major physiological glands of the body. These are: Crown (*Sahasrara*: **pineal** gland), Brow (*Ajna*; pituitary), Throat (*Vishuddha*: thyroid), Heart (*Anahata*: thymus), Solar Plexus

(*Manipura*: pancreas), Base (*Muladhara*; adrenals and endocrines) and Generative (*Svadhishthana*: sexual glands).

The *Base* or *Muladhara* chakra, also called the 'root' chakra, is said to be the chakra anchoring the body to the physical plane. Physiologically at times of crisis the adrenals pump the body full of chemicals stimulating survival reflexes. Also here at the base of the spine lies the root of kundalini, the dual male-female **serpent** energy that (as in the caduceus) spirals up the spine to the brain, its evocation causing enlightenment or madness. In fact the adrenal nerve-endings climb the spine in that same double-helix pattern found in DNA. The caduceus-serpent exists.

More basic still, the Generative chakra as exteriorised in the sexual glands causes huge confusion if ignorantly invoked. Students working on these disciplines may find their **gurus** or leaders irresistibly attractive once this chakra is ignited – and it is the easiest to ignite. The Church tried, with some success, to channel this tendency into 'Bride of Christ' symbolism, thus (for good or ill) transcending physical sexuality.

Of the others, the *Manipura* chakra governs 'gut feeling'; the *Anahata* the 'heart', seeks needs beyond the self; while the *Vishuddha* marks the shift, and need of harmony, between body and mind. Activation of the *Ajna* chakra is required for conscious self-integration of the foregoing, while what goes on in the Crown or *Sahasrara* chakra remains as mysterious now as in the past. Associated with the pineal gland, anciently seen as the 'seat of the soul', which even Descartes saw as the link between the body and the 'rational mind', this chakra is effectively our gateway to the cosmos. But whether we can go through it, given our left-brain/right-brain split, is another matter.

Western esotericism, employing the **Tree of Life** as image of humanity's **subtle body**, co-ordinates five chakras with its Middle Pillar imagery. In **Qabalistic** terms these relate to the crown (*Kether*: over the head); throat (*Daath*); heart (*Tiphareth*); genitals (*Yesod*) and feet-on-earth (*Malkuth*)[1] (*See* **Qabalah**).

1. *Rhythms of Vision*, Lawrence Blair, Warner Books, New York 1977, pp. 186–95

CHANNELLING (*See* **MEDIUMS**)

CHAOS THEORY (*See* **BUTTERFLY EFFECT**) Classical science, seeking laws of universal *order*, was long at a loss to understand *disorder* – in the atmosphere, the turbulence of the sea, the fluctuation of wildlife populations, the oscillations of heart and brain. In the 1970s scientists in varied disciplines began seeking connections between different kinds of disorder. New insights led to the movement now called Chaos Theory. This holistic science of the global nature of systems reverses the trend to reductionism, seeking common patterns in apparently unrelated phenomena. Its most fervent supporters hold that it constitutes the twentieth century's third great revolution (after **relativity** and **quantum** mechanics) in the physical sciences. The study of **consciousness**, free will, determinism and other imprecise or philosophical areas rejected by 'hard' science is again respectable, as is the ancient realisation that from tiny initial causes (acorns) can grow great effects (oaks). Chaos Theory seeks to cross that apparent gulf between the small and the great.

This quest is nothing new. The mediaeval theory of **correspondences** reflects a similar outlook. In the seventeenth century **Leibnitz** imagined that a drop of water contains an entire universe. A century later William **Blake** (in 'Auguries of Innocence') wrote, 'To see a World in a Grain of Sand/And a Heaven in a Wild Flower . . .'. The mythopoeic consciousness of visionaries and poets has always perceived such connections between the infinitely vast and the infinitely small. Yet in recent times the rule of purely mechanical outlook has led to denial of whatever cannot be measured by material sense alone. That Chaos Theory is essentially a modern reassertion of ancient insight is implied by Polish theorist Benoit Mandelbrot who, in explaining how he arrived at conclusions that fired this new discipline, insists that 'The irrational fertilized the rational'.

Born in Warsaw in 1924, in 1975 this mathematical outsider and jack-of-all-trades, having moved to the USA, coined the term *fractal* to describe a geometry of broken or fragmented shapes. A *fractal curve* implies order amid apparent chaos. By 'looking in the trash cans of science' and using his intuition, he drew data from physiology, botany and other sources to create a new way to see into infinity. His book *The Fractal Geometry of Nature* (1977) soon became the bible of Chaos Theory.[1]

Breaking through barriers of scale into a universe of ever finer detail and self-symmetry repeated in transformations across scale, photographs of the 'Mandelbrot Set' reveal an infinity of patterns within patterns, never-ending **mandalas** . . . a universe organised, beautiful and meaningful at every level. No matter how far microscopic magnification is extended, new detail of astonishing beauty and complexity is revealed. In apparent chaos lies realms of order hitherto unglimpsed save by mystics and poets.

Yet entry to this wonderland requires a willingness to recognise that reason and measurement alone do not a universe make. Imagination and the capacity to credit dream and intuition are as important.[2]

1. *The Fractal Geometry of Nature*, Benoit Mandelbrot, Freeman, New York 1977
2. *Chaos Theory*, James R. Gleick, Cardinal, London 1988

CHARDIN, Teilhard de (1881–1955) In *The Phenomenon of Man* this great Jesuit palaeontologist and theologian argued that the human race is on the verge of a leap of consciousness of cosmic dimensions. Hypothesising the existence of the *noosphere* (sphere of mind) as a sort of collective mental atmosphere surrounding the globe, his attempt to reconcile Roman Catholic theology with the discoveries of modern science is worthy but hard to understand.[1]

1. *The Phenomenon of Man*, Teilhard de Chardin, Fontana, London 1968

CHARM A charm consists in any word, sentence, act or object said or believed to have **occult** power to gain a desired end or ward off evil. In human terms 'charm' is a suspect quality, often associated with promises unfulfilled. In this it is cognate with terms like 'romance' and 'glamour', specifying desire for an unreal world, offering easy victimisation of those eclipsed by such desire. People seeking to dominate others may try charm where crude force seems unlikely to work. Belief in charms belongs to magical thought, being a substratum of the unconscious. Given belief, charms may prove effective.

One of the theoretical sub-atomic particles (entities?) called **quarks** is now named 'charm'. This is *charming*, but is it *scientific*?

CHARTRES (*See* **BLACK MADONNAS, EARTH-SPIRIT, LEY LINES**) Perhaps the greatest Gothic masterpiece, the cathedral at Chartres is also among the most mysterious. It alone among French cathedrals has neither king, cardinal nor bishop interred in it. Anciently *Carnut-Is*, sacred site of the Carnutes and a **Druid** sanctuary, in 1904, a Celtic well, the *Puits des Saints Forts*, was rediscovered deep in the mound now crowned by the cathedral itself. Near it is found the **Black Madonna** of Chartres, Nôtre Dame de Sous-Terre. The myth of a mystic **virgin birth** at Chartres predates Christianity. Meaning what? Some claim the mound was first recognised as a holy place because here a particular telluric current rises. This, the *Wouivre* (**serpent**), is the same earth-energy called in China **lung mei** (the **dragon** current) – part of the geomagnetic nervous system, manifestations of which some researchers associate with paranormal phenomena from **UFOs** to **black dogs** and other apparitions. The presence of a black madonna may symbolise Mother Earth's capacity here to give birth, fertilised only by the cosmic radiation of 'Heaven'. Likewise in the pre-biblical Garden of Eden, as shown on Sumerian seals, Eve (Mother Earth) was fertilised by the Serpent, representing the same cosmic force. Adam, Jehovah and the Fall were later Judaic insertions.[1]) 'Chartres', wrote Canon Bulteau, 'is the classic place of the Incarnation in the West.' As such, like **Glastonbury** and **Carnac** and other ancient sites, Chartres was considered 'holy' long before Christianity arrived, the site itself being a power-place, as is plain to anyone who lets this literally awesome cathedral 'speak' to them. For here more than perhaps at any other 'Christian' site the boundaries between what is **pagan** and what is **Christian** blur and become irrelevant.[2]

1. *Occidental Mythology*, Joseph Campbell, Penguin, London 1976, pp. 12–14
2. *The Mysteries of Chartres Cathedral*, Louis Charpentier, Avon, New York 1975

CHEIROMANCY (*See* **PALMISTRY**)

CHEMICAL WEDDING (*See* **ROSICRUCIANISM**)

CH'I (*See* **ACUPUNCTURE, GEOMANCY, PRANA**) A Chinese term for a universal energy which, solar-generated, manifests in the human body in negative/positive (**yin-yang**) polarity. Manipulation of it underlies **acupuncture** treatment and also the Chinese yogic system of *Ch'i Kung* which, as in **kundalini yoga**, aims to raise Ch'i up through the **chakras** to attain enlightenment or magical powers. The concept of Ch'i is similar to that of the Hindu prāna; it is essentially the same energy that flows through the Earth's 'body' and manifests, in the body of Earth or a human being, at key nodal points, as at **Chartres**.

CHRIST, Jesus (4BC?–AD29?) The Greek word *Christos*, 'the anointed one', refers directly to an act performed in the workings of the ancient **Mysteries** of the Mediterranean world – the unction of an initiate. The Hebrew word *Māshīahh* (Messiah) means exactly the same thing. Esoterically *Christos* or *Christ* refers not to one specific individual but to the divine *individuality* within every human being. Unity of the personal ego with this individuality creats the Higher Ego or 'Living Christ'; in Buddhist terms a Mānushya-Buddha.

Exoterically, *Christ* means *Jesus of Nazareth*, historically a shadowy figure, the myth of whose miraculous birth, life, death and resurrection underlies the **Christian** religion. Lately, it has been suggested that Jesus (or Yeshua) was an *Essene* initiate involved in the militant Zealot movement opposing Roman occupation of Judaea during the reign of Tiberius; a man who sought to fulfil Old Testament prophecies of the coming Messiah in order to free the Jews politically and spiritually. These included Daniel's vision of 'one like a man coming with the clouds of heaven'. The Aramaic term for 'one like a man' – *bar enash* – is often translated 'son of man'. This only means what it says. That Jesus had Zealots among his Apostles is suggested by the Gospels – 'Simon Zelotes' is *Simon the Zealot*; 'Judas Iscariot' may refer to the *sicarius*, a curved dagger used by Zealots for assassinations.

According to this theory and its variants Judas betrayed Jesus so that prophecy might be fulfilled: likewise the crucifixion was essential. But death on the cross was not necessarily part of the plan: it is no new idea that: (1) not Jesus but another died on the Cross (this remains orthodox Islamic belief); or that (2) Jesus was drugged (sop of wine) on the cross, then, apparently dead, was quickly removed, entombed and later revived.[1]

A recent bestseller insists that Jesus survived crucifixion and went to France with his wife, Mary Magdalene, there to raise a family which in time birthed the Merovingian dynasty. That this theory could seem shocking two millennia later indicates the extent of the West's emotional investment in orthodox Christian **myth**.[2] It and similar theories also mark the public resurfacing of a perennial dispute as to the divinity of Jesus. Many early Christians, despite the charismatic evangelisation of St Paul, saw Jesus as a man who was born and died like any other man. Such belief (the 'Arian heresy', after Bishop Arius) was condemned by the Church at Nicaea (AD 325): from then on the supernatural myth of virgin birth and resurrection from the dead alone was orthodox. Freethinkers from **Gnostics** to **Cathars** who dared speculate otherwise usually died at the stake or in other foul manner for their pains. **Mystics** from St John on avoided the historical question by perceiving Jesus as incarnation of the primeval *logos*, or Word. The prosaic historical truth as to *who* Jesus actually was remains unclear.

1. *The Armageddon Script*, Peter Lemesurier, Element Books, Shaftesbury 1981
2. *The Holy Blood and the Holy Grail*, Baigent, Leigh and Lincoln, Corgi, London 1983

CHRISTIANITY (*See* **ANNUNCIATION, APOCALYPSE, CHRIST, DEVIL**) One of the world's most influential religions (**Buddhism, Hinduism** and **Islam** being the others), Christianity today exists in a multitude of forms and sects many of which deny the others as Christian at all. For a religion that has as one of its basic tenets: 'Love thy neighbour as thyself,' and which teaches the community of all humankind, Christianity has, since its birth two millennia ago, proved oddly prone to schism and doctrinal conflict.

Its basic message is of love and redemption. It is said that **Christ**, born to a Virgin, was sent to earth by God the Father to suffer and die so that sinful humanity might be redeemed. Resurrected from death on the third day after Crucifixion, **Christ** appeared to his disciples, charged them to spread his Word, then was translated to heaven. It is said he will return at the end of time (the '**Second Coming**') to judge humanity and to raise true believers to Heaven.

This message is expressed in the Bible in the four synoptic Gospels of Matthew, Mark, Luke and John. Here begin the problems of interpretation. Composed up to a century after Christ's ministry, they underwent extensive textual alteration before attaining their modern form, and are only four among approximately 140 such gospels of the life and sayings of Christ now known to have existed. Many other so-called **Gnostic** gospels, suppressed by the increasingly powerful Roman Church during the early era AD but lately rediscovered, deny the conventional image of Christ.

Further, the influence of St Paul on the development of Christianity was so profound that to some it seems the religion is better described as 'Paulianity'. Taking the Christian message to the Gentiles, or non-Jewish people, he insisted that humankind is born in a state of **Original Sin** redeemed only by Christ's love. Denouncing 'many foolish women', he also encouraged the increasingly *masculine* bias of the emergent Church.

Schismatic belief characterised the religion's early years. **Gnostic**, Coptic, Byzantine, Celtic and **Dualist** churches all vied for pre-eminence or at least the right to worship as they chose. Yet by *c.* AD 800 the Roman Church, claiming direct inheritance of Christ's authority as vested in the Papacy via the 'Apostolic Succession', had emerged as the most powerful, at least in Europe, having subdued or anathematised all other interpretations of Christianity, and having colluded in the destruction of the **Merovingian** dynasty, today claimed by some to be Christ's direct bloodline.

Yet Gnostic (insisting on the primacy of individual conscience) and **Dualist** (insisting in the universal co-equality of Good and Evil) beliefs persisted among Manichaeans, Bogomils, Patarenes and **Cathars**, until the latter were exterminated at Rome's instigation in the mid-thirteenth century. For a time the idea of 'Christendom' was virtually synonymous with the state of European civilisation, being maintained not least (when internal social pressures grew too great) by frequent crusades against Islam. But, in sixteenth-century Germany, Luther's revolt against Rome gave rise to new religious wars and to 'Protestant' interpretations of Christianity. Calvinists and Puritans, and later many other schismatic or evangelical sects (Methodists, **Mormons** and Adventists, etc.) ensured that, today, Christianity is not a unity but as much a patchwork of differing beliefs as ever it was in classical times.

The religion was always steeped in magical beliefs. Virgin birth, **miracles, Resurrection**, Pentecostal speaking in tongues, bodily elevation to heaven and so on were in the first place part and parcel of many other popular religions of the ancient world. Virgin birth and resurrection in particular were the cornerstone of Mithraism, the Orphic **Mysteries**, and **Isis**-worship, with all of which early Christianity had to compete. The call to abandon old gods and embrace a higher morality was not made in a vacuum. The great success of Christianity lay in its capacity to absorb and transform older **pagan** beliefs within its own body of dogma. Thus, for example, cannibalistic blood-rites found a new and less vicious expression in the Christian rite of Communion, the Body and Blood of Christ (the died-and-reborn corn-god) being consumed no longer literally but symbolically.

Even so, the argument (*Transubstantiation*) as to whether Communion is symbolic or actual led to bloody European war only 350 years ago. Cathars, **witches** and other 'heretics' were tortured to death to sustain the myth of the Loving Saviour. Yet it would be superficial to blame the religion for the excesses committed in its name. The power of Christianity, however viewed, is that for almost 2,000 years it has absorbed all human behaviours within its own potent myth.

CHURCHWARD, Colonel James In 1926 this ex-British army officer published a bizarre book, *The Lost Continent of Mu*. In it he claimed that on a continent now lost under the Pacific Ocean a civilisation superior to our own once flourished. Though not the first to have 'discovered' the tale of **Mu** (called **Lemuria** by the **Theosophists**), he argued its case so vigorously that his name has remained linked to it since. His interest began when as a young officer in India in the1880s it seems he found ancient tablets (the 'Naacal Tablets'). These, in the language of a forgotten culture, described Man's appearance some 50 million years ago on the continent of Mu, which had extended from north of Hawaii as far south as Fiji and Easter Island. Some 12,000 years ago Mu was destroyed by earthquake and submersion. **Atlantis**, a colony of Mu, suffered a similar fate a millennium later. Churchward said he had studied these tablets under the tutelage of a '*rishi* priest', who, with two cousins, were the sole survivors of a 70,000-year-old esoteric order founded on Mu itself, the 'Naacal Brotherhood'. Later he alleged that a collection of stone objects found in Mexico carried extracts from the 'Sacred Inspired Writings of Mu'. In this he echoed the account by the French archaeologist Augustus Le Plongeon who in the 1880s 'translated' the Mayan *Troana Codex* to 'prove' the existence of Mu. In his five books on Mu Churchward annexed existing history, **religion** and **occult** belief to back up his case, telling the history of this 'Motherland of Man' in such exotic detail that one can enjoy his fantastic account without believing a word of it.[1]

1. *The Lost Continent of Mu*, James Churchward, Paperback Library, New York 1968

CLAIRAUDIENCE This means 'clear-hearing', and is said to be a spiritual faculty enabling the 'hearer' to tune into sounds physically inaudible, such as the sounds of grass growing or the 'music of the spheres' of the planets in motion. It is assumed that every element, atom or particle has a characteristic tune accessible to the clairaudient initiate.

CLAIRVOYANCE (*See* **ASTRAL PLANE, MEDIUMS, SPIRITUALISM**) This 'clear-seeing' implies a spiritual capacity of inner vision, to see behind or beyond the veils that mask spiritual reality from the material world of the five senses. As such it may involve vision of events at a distance, in space and/or time; a vision in no way physical, nor relying on **telepathy**, in that the clairvoyant **seer** is the only individual involved.

CLOSE ENCOUNTERS (*See* **ABDUCTION, HYNEK, UFOs**) In 'Project Blue Book', a USAF examination of and report on UFO phenomena chaired by J. Allen **Hynek** and published in 1968, three categories of UFO encounter were defined – *Close Encounters of the First, Second and Third Kinds*. Later, the Centre for UFO Studies, directed by Dr Hynek, developed a bibliography of over 60,000 separate reported UFO events. A case-by-case evaluation of the reports in USAF files left only five per cent unexplained as 'UFO'.

The rest were dismissed as 'IFO' – Identified Flying Objects. Yet the remaining, unexplained *Close Encounter* cases numbered in the thousands.

A Close Encounter of the First Kind (CE I) is defined as perception of a UFO in close proximity (within 500 feet) of the witness. The object is visible but does not otherwise influence the environment. It may show oval or disc shape, and is characterised by: hovering; rapid acceleration; steep ascent/descent; silence (no matter how close); and by rotation.

A CE II fits the foregoing but also influences the environment, usually by leaving physical evidence of its presence or by causing **electromagnetic** interference. Many cases involve interference with electric power. In cars the engine may suddenly die. Physical effects may include damaged sites (circular, oval, burned, depressed or dehydrated); damaged trees/plants; soil imprints (often three or four); residues (sometimes rare artefacts); footprints, radioactivity and odours. Physiological effects may include nausea, headache, burns, eye irritation, numbness, shock and feelings of weightlessness. Electrical damage or magnetised metal may result. In some cases displacement or **teleportation** of objects is reported. Electrical equipment typically regains function when the UFO encounter terminates.

A CE III (made famous by the Spielberg movie) involves a CE I or CE II with 'occupants' or entities associated. The UFO either flies close enough to reveal occupants, or lands and disgorges occupants, or alien entities are otherwise associated with the encounter. Such entities (as assessed from over 1,200 reports) belong to one of three groups. The first are three to four feet tall, with large heads on spindly bodies. The second are five to six feet tall and appear normally human. The third group covers all other such manifestations, from giants to robot-like machines. The behaviour of such entities towards human contactees is usually evasive or shy. Virtually all such *Close Encounters of the Third Kind* occur at night.

Cases of physical communication or **abduction** are sometimes defined as CE IV. Other categories of UFO sighting were defined by Dr Hynek as: Nocturnal Light (NL); Daylight Disc (DD), and Radar Visuals (RV).[1]

1. *The UFO Handbook*, Allan Hendry, Sphere Books, London 1980, pp. 7–12

COINCIDENCE (*See* **SYNCHRONICITY**)

COLLECTIVE UNCONSCIOUS (*See* **CONSCIOUSNESS, JUNG, UNIVERSAL MEMORY**) 'The collective unconscious', wrote C. G. Jung, 'is part of the **psyche** which can be negatively distinguished from a personal unconscious by the fact that it does not, like the latter, owe its existence to personal experience and consequently is not a personal acquisition. While the personal unconscious is made up eventually of contents which have at one time been conscious but which have disappeared from consciousness through having been forgotten or repressed, the contents of the collective unconscious have never been in consciousness, but owe their existence exclusively to heredity.'[1]

Adopting this idea from his discovery in **dreams** and **myths** of recurrent patterns suggesting the existence of unconscious **archetypes** (a kind of collective inherited memory), Jung was never able to suggest a mechanism for such inheritance. Lately **Sheldrake** proposed such a mechanism in terms of his hypothesis of **formative causation** or morphic resonance.

Jung regarded the collective unconscious as common to all humanity but also saw it as differentiated between racial types. His disciple Marie-Louise von Franz postulated that below the personal unconscious lies a 'group unconscious' (families, tribes); below that a 'common unconscious' of national units, and, below that, 'the sum of those universal psychic archetypal structures that we share with the whole of mankind'.[2]

More simply, as John Donne put it, 'No man is an island'.

1. Quoted in *The Presence of the Past*, Rupert Sheldrake, Vintage, New York 1989, pp. 250–1
2. *ibid.*, p. 253

COMETS (*See* **DISEASE**)

CONSCIOUSNESS (*See* **BRAIN MYSTERIES, ZEN**) This phenomenon is a mystery to itself. Some physicists think of it as a basic property of matter. Vitalist biologists claim it as a fundamental property of protoplasm. Behavioural psychologists have denied its very existence. Yet without possessing it they could not deny it.

Current theories see it as an emergent evolutionary function, created by the combination of various biological ingredients, each important but none by itself 'conscious'.

So, what is 'consciousness'?

Usually associated with the **brain**, it has been defined as awareness of self and environment. This only begs more questions. If a function of the brain, in what part does it lie? How many levels or types of it exist? What mechanisms decide if we are 'conscious' or 'unconscious'? Even the latter concept breeds confusion. In one sense, it implies lack of consciousness. In another, it implies a substratum of mind operating by its own rules, without 'conscious' intervention but affecting consciousness by seeding it with collective **archetypal** imagery. Again, most but not all theories of consciousness assume it to be so intimately part of a biological organism that it cannot survive bodily death. Such theories conflict with **mystic** notions of consciousness as a spiritual condition interacting with the physical body but not ultimately reliant on it. From this viewpoint biological life in fact 'lives' only due to its infusion by consciousness.

Whatever it is, we possess it, in greater or lesser degree, as a result of laborious evolution over many millennia. Functionally it may be seen as a feedback system, allowing organisms to include models of themselves in their simulation of and interaction with the world. In that it is capable of modelling variations in its own state, from a psychological viewpoint it may be seen as incompletely developed in that in most of us it embraces only part of the **psyche**. This implication is supported by the concern of major religions and **yogic** systems with self-activated consciousness-growth towards 'enlightenment' as epitomised by the **buddhas** or **Christ**.

In the West's materialist tradition we tend to connect it with reason and egoism, implicitly personal: the self-aware, unique 'I'. But so-called 'primitive' cultures see it not as a unitary possession of each individual, but as a state conjoined with the 'consciousness' of the world about. Thus individual consciousness is extended into trees, beasts, the very elements. So too in '**New Age**' thought some see the Earth itself (**Gaia**) as conscious in that its systems seem to demonstrate a capacity for self-regulation.

Historically, association of consciousness with left-brain ego and thus with reason and science is recent. This development, seen in the building of the **Great Pyramid** and the solar worship of Akhenaton, marks separation from and conflict with the older right-brain ***dream***-state In effect now we are all literally at war with ourselves, as Sperry's work on divided brains suggests. Dr Julian Jaynes, in *The Origin of Consciousness in the Breakdown of the Bicameral Mind* (1976) claims this conflict began as late as 1000 BC, and that before then people lacked self-awareness. Thus Greek heroes like Ulysses heard 'voices' sent by the right lobe of the brain to the left, and assumed them to be god-voices. Jaynes mentions how in a stone altar dated *c.* 1230 BC the Assyrian king Tukulti-Nunurti is shown kneeling before a god's empty throne. The god (of intuitive perception?) is gone. A contemporary cuneiform tablet says: 'One who has no god, as he walks along the street, Headache envelops him like a garment.'[1] A century later the Assyrian king Tiglath-Pilesar no longer hyphenates his own name with that of the god; he walks alone, godless, his exploits those of egotistic cruelty.

Jaynes may be incorrect in saying ancient man had no sense of 'I', but it seems a new form of consciousness *had* taken over, causing 'headache' and an acute sense of loss. Centuries later when the Greeks surmised that the sun, not the earth was the centre of the universe, the idea was abandoned (until Copernicus) due to its *emotional* unacceptability. People simply could not bear to abandon the old, earth-centred consciousness so fast. The new 'head'-consciousness demanded cruel shifts in perspective. But the revolution was underway, and in the West the Church became its prime mover. History became the account of a new consciousness struggling for supremacy over older, intuitive forms. Stained glass, the pointed Gothic arch, and the Inquisition were among the means employed to elevate public awareness.

By AD 1600 Descartes (*cogito ergo sum*: I think therefore I am) located consciousness in the 'third eye', or **pineal** gland.[2] Reductionism was well under way. By the early twentieth century the cerebral cortex was the favoured seat of this 'ghost in the machine'. Subsequent research suggests that, if consciousness is located in the brain, it must be in the brain-stem. Back in 1892 Polish physiologist Friedrich Goltz kept dogs alive several years after removing their cerebrums. These dogs continued to walk, eat, sleep and reject unpleasant food. They were conscious. Yet they had lost their memory and showed no fear. Likewise human infants born without the cerebrum show limited consciousness; but consciousness all the same. The point may be that increased complexity of brain-structure increases the potential for consciousness, but that of itself it does not necessarily guarantee growth. We possess the means but not necessarily the will. Here is where **magical, yogic, mystical** and **shamanic** insight becomes essential, as does recent work into 'consciousness-expansion' and 'altered states'. Fasting, dancing, rhythmic drumming, **hallucinogenic** drugs and **sensory deprivation** are among the techniques used since time immemorial to produce such **altered states**.

1. *Starseekers*, Colin Wilson, Book Club Associates, London 1980, p. 74
2. *The Natural History of the Mind*, G. Rattray Taylor, Granada, London 1981

CONSTANT, Alphonse Louis (*See* **LÉVI, Eliphas**)

COOK, Florence (*See* **CROOKES, FRAUD, MEDIUMS**)

CORN CIRCLES (*See* **CATTLE MUTILATIONS, MEGALITHIC MYSTERIES, UFOS**) This phenomenon remains mysterious despite all efforts to record or catch it in action. Perfect circles of corn are found pressed horizontal (stems unbroken) with no evidence of human intervention. The circles may be linked by straight avenues. UFOs have apparently been sighted: the area most affected is rich in megalithic remains. However meteorologist Dr Terence Meaden has suggested that the cause is a rare species of atmospheric vortex.

In 1975 a Hampshire farm-worker at Headbourne Worthy noted a clockwise swirl in a field by the A34. In 1978 he found one big circle surrounded by four smaller ones. Such circles (up to twenty metres in diameter) began appearing all over southern England. By 1990 'corn circles' were big news. Engineers Pat Delgado and Colin Andrews, researching the phenomenon, have found no answers but point out that the circles favour particular sites year after year. These are often associated with unexplained road accidents involving only one car or, as in 1987 at Winterbourne Stoke in Wiltshire, the death of a Harrier jump-jet pilot who had mysteriously ejected, leaving his plane to fly on. Andrews took home soil-samples from one circle: a burglar alarm in the hut where he put the sample persisted in going off at 4.15 a.m. His dog, taken against its will to the centre of another ring, began to vomit. Noises like electrical static have been heard. Delgado and Andrews believe the circles are made by an *intelligent* force, nature and purpose unknown.[1]

But UFO researchers Jenny Randles and Paul Fuller insist that all such talk is deluded and that the 'Meaden Vortex' (a local, temporary whirlwind formed during hot weather, often at the base of hills) is a more likely cause. Farmers in the affected Warminster area have observed whirlwinds causing similar damage. If so, the mystery lies not in the corn but in the human mind and its desire to believe in alien intervention.[2]

1. 'Ever-Increasing', Elizabeth Dunn, *Daily Telegraph Weekend Magazine*, 8 July 1989, reviewing *Circular Evidence*, Delgado and Andrews, Bloomsbury, London 1989
2. *Crop Circles*, Randles and Fuller, Robert Hale, London 1990

•

CORRESPONDENCES People have long tried to understand the world by classifying its features in terms of gods or forces thought to control them. The oldest, most basic part of this system sets out links between planets, metals and colours. So:

Planet	*Metal*	*Colour*
Sun	Gold	Gold/yellow
Moon	Silver	White
Mercury	Quicksilver	Grey/neutral
Venus	Copper	Green
Mars	Iron	Red
Jupiter	Tin	Blue
Saturn	Lead	Black

Some of these linkages arise from obvious analogy – Sun/Gold; Moon/Silver; Mercury/Quicksilver, etc. Copper belongs to Venus because the Greek Venus, Aphrodite, was connected with Cyprus, the classical world's chief source of copper. The colour of Venus, nature's mistress, is green. Mars, the red or bloody planet, was the god of war: iron its metal because iron weaponry defeated bronze. Blue, the sky-colour, belongs to the sky-lord, Jupiter: tin may belong to Jupiter because of the planet's colour. Dark heavy lead belongs to dark heavy Saturn, as does the colour black.

This basic system was extended indefinitely to include birds, beasts, trees, plants, numbers, geometrical shapes, psychological states and so on. *Black* crows belonged to Saturn, their carrion connections an additional ill-omened association: the winter festival (death of the old year) was the Saturnalia. Magicians working to destroy an enemy use iron **wands** and wear scarlet robes embroidered with pentagrams (5-pointed stars, 5 the number of Mars) in red-draped rooms, to arouse the force of Mars. Such associations work to focus the will and imagination required in such operations.[1]

1. *The Magical Arts*, Richard Cavendish, Arkana, London 1984, pp. 25–7

COSMIC JOKER (*See* **FORT, SYNCHRONICITY**) Heard the one about American Civil War General Sedgewick who, raising his head over the parapet at the enemy lines, declared: 'They couldn't hit an elephant at this dist . . .'? Or the shop-lifter who tried his luck in a store in Barnsley, Yorkshire, to discover too late that the store was holding a meeting for store detectives? Or how in 1911 the three men hanged for the murder of Sir Edmundbury Godfrey at Greenberry Hill were named Green, Berry and Hill? Or how in 1968 the Royal Society for the Prevention of Accidents held an exhibition in Harrogate, but the entire display fell down? Or how in 1967 Essex policeman Peter Moscardi, when his station number was changed to 40116, told a friend the number was 40166, and later, while one night checking a factory left inexplicably unlocked and lit, answered a ringing phone, to find it was his friend, ringing him at the factory number, 40166?

These and other absurd events are so common that some researchers have hypothesised an intelligent force, the 'cosmic joker'. Charles Hoy Fort (1874–1932) spent a lifetime chronicling such lunacies, coincidences and unlikely rains (from fish to human flesh), concluding that the human race is the property of a childish, cruel celestial joker who just likes to play with us. Certainly some people (like the Kennedys) seem accident-prone to a degree inexplicable by normal expectation. To be 'bedevilled by bad luck' was once a literalism. Satan himself was thought to cause such tragedies. Today **UFO** researchers like John **Keel** suspect that mischievous, hostile **elementals** are behind such nasty pranks, their techniques for teasing and even destroying human beings being continually updated.

Whatever the truth, such events seem designed just to baffle us – or maybe to shock us out of our assumptions about the world. If the latter is true, the 'Cosmic Joker' may not be so childish. And what if our own **unconscious** is to blame? After all, Sir Peter Scott's Latin name for the **Loch Ness Monster**, *Nessiteras rhombopteryx*, is a perfect anagram of 'monster hoax by Sir Peter S.' Was the punner cosmic . . . or Sir Peter?[1]

1. 'Laughter in Heaven', Lynn Picknett, *The Unexplained*, Orbis partwork, London 1983, p. 697ff

COTTINGLEY FAIRIES (*See* **ELEMENTALS, FAIRIES**) 'Elsie and I are very friendly with the beck Fairies,' eleven-year-old Frances Griffiths wrote on the back of a snapshot sent to a friend in South Africa, where she had lived before her family had moved to Yorkshire, 'It is funny I never used to see them in Africa. It must be too hot for them there.'

The snapshot, taken in July 1917 and developed by her cousin Elsie's father Arthur, showed Frances, chin propped on hand, with four butterfly-winged little dark-haired people dancing on the foliage of a bush in front of her. The initial image was unclear: Arthur Wright made nothing of it. But a month later Elsie photographed Frances sitting under old oaks with a little winged gnome dancing on the grass before her. This time Arthur got cross. He and his wife Polly searched the girls' bedroom looking for cut-outs to explain the pictures, but found nothing. Both girls insisted there really *were* fairies at the bottom of their garden. Arthur told Elsie she couldn't use the camera again until she told the truth.

In 1919, at a meeting of the **Theosophical Society** in Bradford, Polly Wright (who had experience of **astral projection**) heard a lecturer say that fairies are simply a form of **elemental** spirit perceived by **clairvoyants**. She mentioned her daughter's '**fairy** photographs'. Prints made by Arthur reached Arthur Gardner, President of the London branch of the Theosophical society. Suspecting fakery, Gardner sought expert advice, which suggested that the (sharpened) photographs were genuine. Hearing about them, Sir Arthur Conan **Doyle** (creator of Sherlock Holmes), preparing an article on fairies for the *Strand Magazine*, asked to see them. Subsequently Gardner went to Yorkshire to test the girls, providing them with cameras and sealed film-plates. The results, showing more fairy activity, were thought to be genuine by Gardner and Conan Doyle, whose article in the *Strand* caused a controversy. On 5 January 1921 *Truth* magazine declared, 'For the true explanation of these fairy photographs what is wanted is not a knowledge of occult phenomena but a knowledge of children.' Arthur Wright was sad that the great Sir Arthur Conan Doyle had been, 'bamboozled by our Elsie, and her at the bottom of her class'. Conan Doyle, still dubious, yet concerned to advance his own ideas about the **occult** to an unsympathetic public, sent a well-known clairvoyant, Geoffrey Hodson, to Cottingley, where he talked to the girls and saw fairy forms . . . but no new photographs appeared. By now both Elsie and Frances were tired of the whole business, later admitting to deceiving Hodson in terms of telling him what he wanted to believe. It was apparently all over. In 1922 Conan Doyle published his *The Coming of the Fairies*, but there was little reaction. Most people thought the creator of Sherlock Holmes had gone soft. Both girls stopped seeing fairies.

Forty-four years later the case was reopened. In 1966 *Daily Express* journalist Peter Chambers rediscoverd Elsie. She had since lived in India then come back to Yorkshire. She said the fairies were 'figments of my imagination', but denied that the photographs had been faked. In 1971, BBC's Nationwide programme interviewed both Elsie and Frances. Their public statements after half a century remained ambiguous. In 1976 Yorkshire folklorist Joe Cooper persuaded them both to appear on TV. Asked why she had never tried to grab the fairies, Frances said: 'You couldn't. It's like grabbing for a ghost or something.' Asked if she had faked the photos she said: 'Of course not.'

This case remains eminently open to **quantum** and **chaos** theorists.

CRISIS APPARITION (*See* **NEAR-DEATH EXPERIENCES, GHOSTS**)
Perhaps the most common form of ghost, a 'crisis apparition' occurs when a person either dying or under great stress appears to a loved one, relative or friend, typically as a **vision**, perhaps as a disembodied voice. Many cases exist of soldiers appearing to their wives or mothers at the moment of their deaths on distant battlefields. Unusually the apparition is of a stranger. Famous heart surgeon Dr Christian Barnard told an Italian TV audience in 1985 of such an experience eighteen years earlier: 'I was in a private room with a door and a window. My bed was near the window and there was some light coming from outside. Around 10 p.m. a woman entered the room. She walked toward my bed, put her hand on my chest, and began pushing against it. I looked up at her and saw she was very thin and pale, with blue eyes and grey hair. She was pressing strongly on my chest. I took her wrists in my hand. They were very fragile. I pushed her back and realised she was extremely light. Then, as if she were reacting to my pressure, she **levitated** and disappeared through the window.'

He rang for a nurse, but had to wait. On arrival the nurse apologised for the delay, saying, 'a woman was dying in my ward when you buzzed'. Asked about it, the nurse described the woman who had just visited Barnard. He concluded, 'there was no question of my ever having seen the woman before. She had been in the women's ward, while I was in a private room.'[1]

Cases of **apparitions** appearing after death, often to a person tired or ill, have led psychic Ingo **Swann** to comment: 'The appearance of the spirit of a departed loved one is so common it's a wonder it's controversial.'[2]

1. *Intangible Evidence*, Bernard Gittelson, Simon and Schuster, London 1987, p. 282
2. *op. cit.* p. 283

CROISET, Gerard (1909–80) This famed Dutch 'psychic detective' was said to have located by **telepathy** and **psychometry** hundreds of missing persons, dead and alive. However his reputation rests on claims by **parapsychologist** Wilhelm Tenhaeff (d. 1981) of Utrecht University to have accurately documented Croiset's work over many years. Yet Tenhaeff embellished and manipulated data on Croiset; a process abetted by the popular press. When in 1979 Croiset tried to help find the 'Yorkshire Ripper', *Sun* reporter Derek Shuff wrote claiming his 'most famous case was to describe the killer of a young Dutch girl found dead beside her bicycle'. In the case in point (Wierden 1946) the girl was not in fact killed: Wierden's chief of police had long since debunked Dutch press accounts claiming Croiset had solved it.

Croiset was also said to demonstrate **precognition** in 'chair tests' by which he tried to describe a person who at a specific future time would sit in a specified chair. Despite a few clear hits, the evidence as a whole is dubious, Tenhaeff suppressing 'misses', inventing non-existent 'hits' and ignoring procedural errors. None of this proves Croiset a **fraud** lacking in genuine **psychic** capacity. But many of his 'successes' just did not occur, or not as described: other 'predictions' required not **ESP** but simply the interpretation of available information. Such confused research only helps sceptics to deny the existence of psychic abilities in any form.[1]

1. 'Croiset: double Dutch?', Piet Hein Hoebens, *The Unexplained*, Orbis partwork, London 1983, pp. 2630–2633

CROOKES, Sir William (1832–1919) (*See* **SPIRITUALISM**) Another case possibly involving **fraud** concerns the endorsement by Victorian physicist Sir William Crookes of **medium** Florence Cook. Crookes, a highly respected young scientiest, began investigating **Spiritualist** phenomena in 1871 by studying medium Daniel Dunglass **Home**. To the dismay of many, in the *Quarterly Journal of Science* (July 1871) he declared himself convinced by Home's repertoire of **levitation**, fire-handling and other such feats. In 1874 he went further, publishing in *The Spiritualist* an account of the materialisations by pretty teenage medium Florence Cook of one Katie King, apparently once the daughter of a pirate. At the start of a séance in the Cook family home in London, Cook would be tied up behind a curtain. With lights out, 'Katie' would emerge, wearing white robes, face, hands and arms bare, thoroughly physical, and looking rather like Cook. Crookes, insisting that Katie was taller and of fairer complexion than Florrie, persuaded Florrie's parents to let her move into his house for further study. His evidence may be taken three ways. One, as good evidence of life after death (Count Louis Hamon, the **palmist** Cheiro, said Cook was genuine: other witnesses also attested that Katie King and Florence Cook were different individuals). Two, that Cook was a fraud and Crookes her dupe. Three, that the whole business was an attempt by both of them to cover up an illicit affair. In 1922 Francis Anderson, claiming an affair with Cook in 1893, told the **Society for Psychical Research** that she had admitted to a liaison with Crookes and had also said that the séances were a fraudulent cover for it.

The controversy did nothing for Crookes' reputation. 'Katie King' announced that her three-year association with Cook was over: Florence Cook secretly married another man, and Crookes gradually redeemed his scientific reputation.

CROWLEY, Aleister (1875–1947) (*See* **DEMONS, GOLDEN DAWN,**

MAGIC) Edward Alexander Crowley (Aleister' came from Shelley's 'Alastor') was born in Leamington Spa, Warwickshire, to devout Plymouth Brethren. His father, a successful brewer, was an active evangelist. His strident mother kept saying he was as bad as the Great Beast in the Book of Revelations.

Later he had the title 'The Great Beast', printed on his visiting cards, and became notorious as 'The Wickedest Man in the World'.

Mountaineer, poet, magician and traveller, he is remembered primarily for his scandalous life. He loved to shock, baffle and tease, yet has been called one of the century's most important original thinkers.[1] He said he despised women and 'hated the God and Christ of the people I hated'.[2] Yet the ambivalent symbol of Mother dominates his work: the rigour of the God-fearing Brethren characterises his work; while the self-imposed sufferings of his magical exploits suggest a fundamentalist guilt he never shook off.

When he was eight his father died: his mother took him to live with her brother, Tom Bishop, apparently a degenerate bully and liar. In *A Boyhood in Hell*[3] he describes schooldays so harsh as to imply that only will-power brought him through. Inheriting his father's brewing fortune, at Cambridge University he broke with his family, gaining a reputation as a mountaineer and for poetry (*White Stains*) famed more for its shock-value than intrinsic merit. He also began to transform his unwanted identity. Edward Alexander Crowley died, save in worldly law: Alastor, Spirit of Solitude, Wanderer of the Wastes, was born – the prototype of later grandiose identities such as Frater Perdurabo, the Logos of the Aeon of Horus, and the Great Beast 666.

In 1898 he joined the Hermetic Order of the Golden Dawn, rose up its ranks, argued with Macgregor **Mathers** and W. B. **Yeats**, (who called him 'an unspeakable mad person'), then went his own way. In Mexico, Ceylon, China and the Middle East he studied magic (calling it Magick) and **Tantra**, and wrote unrelentingly, his wit and sharp eye for hypocrisy soon apparent. 'It never occurred to the **Buddha** . . . to advise his pupils not to practise in a flat with a wireless next door.'[4]

In 1902 with Oscar Eckenstein he tried to climb the Himalayan Chogo Ri. For sixty-three days they survived on the Baltoro Glacier. Climbing alone to 22,000 feet, he was driven back. The peak remains unscaled. In 1905 he tried Kangchenjunga (the world's third highest peak, unscaled until 1954). Perhaps its evil reputation attracted him. Men died; there was mutiny. Perhaps here he felt confirmed in his mission as the Great Beast 666. For in Cairo the year before his wife Rose Kelly had, in **trance**, led him to a museum in which was a statue of **Horus**, the Egyptian God of Youth. It was numbered 666: the 'Number of the Beast'.

In trance she had dictated messages allegedly from 'a preternatural intelligence', Aiwass, who told him to work the magic of sexual polarities, and who apparently confirmed him as 'the Logos of the new Aeon of Horus'.

This third age, after the Mother-Age of **Isis** and Father-Age of **Osiris**, would be a New Age of Youth, based on union of male and female energies. As Beast (Sun, male principle 666, Logos, Will) he had to seek sacred union with the female principle, alias the Whore of Babylon. Thus he wrote *Liber Legis* (*the Book of the Law*). It contains his famous dictum: 'Do what thou wilt shall be the whole of the Law. Love is the Law, Love under will.' In it he claimed that war, chaos and the discredit of orthodox religions and moral codes lay ahead. 'I am the warlord of the forties,' Aiwass told him, 'The eighties cower before me and are abased.'

Now as 'messenger of the Lord of the Universe', Crowley felt able to 'speak with absolute authority'. Perhaps this hubris led to the disaster on Kangchenjunga. Driven by his mother's **animus**, he could never brook in others any weakness such as he despised in himself. He showed no mercy to those unable to face their own hidden inner nature as he felt he had done.

Foretelling humanity's approaching release from age-old obsessions with Sin and Fear, he founded the A. A. or Argentinum Astrum (Silver Star). In 1909 he flouted

Mathers and the Golden Dawn by publishing their Second Order secrets. Open espousal of sexual magic followed contact with Dr Karl Kellner's German *Ordo Templi Orientis* (Order of the Temple of the East) – OTO – in 1912. He had already unknowingly published their main secret in his *Book of Lies*, speaking of the magic of sexual polarity hidden by the symbols of the rood (phallus) and mystic rose (vagina). Approached by Kellner's successor, Theodor Reuss, Crowley took over the OTO. Only in 1946, the year before his death, did he give up control, to Kenneth Grant.

Acting the role of Logos of the Aeon of Horus, he founded the 'Abbey of Thelema' (Will) at Cefalu in Sicily, a commune whose scandals were avidly milked by the 1920s press. Mussolini, playing righteous moralist, kicked him out. The more lurid allegations later proved false, but many found association with Crowley disastrous. His trail is littered with suicide and insanity. His own grotesque behaviour played a part: less clear is how many of those attracted to him sought self-immolation. Homosexuality and derision of women governed his relationships; yet his excesses were part of his appeal to **mystical** authority. 'When you have proved that God is merely a name for the sex instinct,' he wrote, 'it appears to me not far to the perception that the sex instinct is God.' In this he practised what **Reich** preached: that he survived seventy-two years of self-abuse testifies to his will.

Proudly he proved his 'control' of habits fatal to others. Deep in heroin use he went mountaineering, no drugs involved. On return he took to the drugs again. Once, to test the Ego, he decided to slash his arm with a razor each time he said 'I'. On the day appointed, by noon he had slashed himself almost thirty times. Then he gave up. Even for Crowley this (like Kangchenjunga) was too much.

Aggrandizing himself shamelessly in autobiographical novels that threw public salacity back in its own face (*Diary of a Drug Fiend*, *Moonchild*), he was no victim. Capable of anticipating public reaction to his behaviour, he remained unrepentant, welcoming the trials he brought on himself.

Suing actress Nina Hamnett for claiming he was a **black magician**, he lost, the defence producing more than enough evidence of his bizarre and scandalous life. In April 1934 he was declared bankrupt. The Beast looked threadbare. Yet many stayed loyal. When he died (Hastings, Sussex, on 1 December 1947, aged 72), he expressed no regrets. Still using enough heroin to kill an ox, he was busy to the last. In *The Book of Thoth* (1944) he explains his version of the **Tarot** (produced with artist Frieda Harris).

Gardner, Summers, Regardie and others continued to visit him. In 1946, alarmed by the activities of US **occultists** Jack Parsons and L. Ron **Hubbard**, he wrote to Karle Germer, US head of the Ordo Templi Orientis: 'Apparently Parsons or Hubbard or someone is producing a Moonchild. I get fairly frantic when I contemplate the idiocy of these louts.'[5]

Crowley still makes people uneasy. He worked on what is still seen as the wrong side of the fence, denying social rules still generally observed. He flaunted characteristics hidden and unadmitted in most of us. Twenty years after he died he became one of the exemplars of the 1960s 'youth'-movement. What had seemed mere egotism was held up as honest insight. 'Love is the Law, Love under Will,' 'Aiwass' had proclaimed. Yet though he insisted this was not to be taken as an excuse for hedonism, his own behaviour suggests otherwise. Though brilliant and learned, in many ways Crowley seems to have remained trapped in his childhood all his life.[6,7]

1. *The Eye in the Triangle*, Israel Regardie, Falcon Press, Las Vegas 1989 (from the *Introduction* by Robert Anton Wilson)
2. *ibid.*, p. 46
3. *ibid.*, p. 48, (from *The World's Tragedy*, Aleister Crowley)
4. *ibid.*, p. 259, 286 (from *Eight Lectures on Yoga*)
5. *Bare-Faced Messiah*, Russell Miller, Sphere, London 1987, p. 161

6. *The Great Beast*, John Symonds (1951: many editions since)
7. *Aleister Crowley*, Charles Richard Cammell, New English Library, London 1969 (1951)
Confessions of Aleister Crowley, Aleister Crowley, Arkana, London 1989
Magic without Tears, Aleister Crowley, Falcon Press, Las Vegas 1984
Magick In Theory and Practice, Aleister Crowley, Arkana, London 1990
The Book of Thoth, Aleister Crowley, Weiser, Maine 1984

CRYPTOMNESIA (*See* **BLOXHAM, REINCARNATION**) Some cases of apparent memory of past lives are attributable to this condition, whereby the subject taps previously absorbed information (as from a book) which, forgotten by the conscious mind, is mistakenly attributed to personal experience.

CRYSTALS (*See* **MEGALITHIC MYSTERIES, REICHENBACH**) Associated with the **New Age** movement is a huge upsurge of interest in the supposed **healing** and **occult** powers of crystals and gemstones. As with so much other belief translated from the magical or pre-scientific past, this interest is not new. Throughout known history, crystals have been worn as talismans against evil, or used to focus **clairvoyance**, or to enter states of trance-like **meditation**. The inner light that glints fascinatingly from cut diamonds, emeralds, rubies or sapphires has always given such stones a value remote from any obvious practical application. Their gleaming depths are so entrancing that *romantic wealth* is anciently measured in terms of their possession. In tales like *King Solomon's Mines* (by nineteenth-century English novelist Rider Haggard) it is assumed that hardship and death in the search for such gems are justified by discovery of the treasure, and that such discovery renders the finders rich forever after. They have struggled through to crystalline truth. The gems change **consciousness**.

Implicitly we imbue these inert compressions of mineral activity with **supernatural** authority. Within such stones the future is said to be seen, or glamorous desire may be realised, or transcendent knowledge sought by **prophets** – like the **Brahan Seer** – who rely on their 'hollow stone'..

Today, personalities like Tina Turner or Shirley Maclaine take their 'pet' crystals with them wherever they go. So too in the past many a realm was lost by those who cared more for their store of sparkling gems than for the outer realm of deprived people who, sacking palaces, thought only of ransacking the treasure-house of its glittering treasure of jewels.

Since ancient time specific qualities have been ascribed to different jewels. Occultly, each is seen as a living **entity**, conveying different healing qualities. Sapphires are anciently thought to cure eye-diseases, emeralds to cure dysentery, rubies cure liver problems, and amethysts cure snakebite 'when used in a pendant suspended on a dog-hair cord'.[1] Since time immemorial many cultures have insisted that crystalline stones and rocks offer life-bringing potencies.

What is the underlying truth? What *are* crystals?

Regular geometric forms, spontaneously generated and self-replicating in stable fashion, crystals exemplify Nature's power of self-organisation. Indeed, evolution of life on Earth, suggests Glasgow scientist A. Cairns-Smith, may have involved a process of replication starting not with organic DNA – a fragile molecule – but via the crystallisation of 'inert' matter.

In clay beds, developing crystal patterns not only replicate innovative information about the particular bed and its mineral content (leading to the acquisition and inheritance of new characteristics) but, if changed by environmental pressure, they replicate the change too. This odd process may perhaps be explained by **Sheldrake**'s theory of **formative causation**.

Glycerine, first extracted from natural fats in the eighteenth century as an oily colourless liquid, resisted all attempts to crystallise it into solid form. But early in the twentieth century a sample in a barrel *en route* from Vienna to London spontaneously crystallised. Chemists could now seed their own glycerine samples, which solidified at 18°C. Two scientists inducing crystallisation on one glycerine sample found that all their other samples crystallised spontaneously, even when sealed in air-tight containers. It was almost as if these samples had responded **telepathically**.[2]

Quartz crystals were always thought to hold a special power. As with gems, their glittering interior entrances the mind. Thus occultists from John **Dee** to modern practitioners of 'crystal power' have used crystals to communicate with **angelic** entities, to induce trance-**healing**, or via the 'crystal ball', to **scry** the future. In 1845 Baron Karl von Reichenbach announced that **psychics** perceive an energy emitted by crystals and magnets. His findings, though replicated, were dismissed by sceptical materialists.

Yet the ubiquity of quartz in prehistoric **megaliths** suggests knowledge of the mechano-electric properties of crystals to be ancient. Found in many forms in all types of rock used in standing stones, it is associated with the 'tingling' sensation felt by those **dowsing** megaliths.

This may arise from *piezo-electricity*. Electrical charge applied to quartz changes its shape or curvature. Compression produces an electrical charge across its faces. Pressure applied fast and hard (as by a hammer) can generate several thousand volts. The resulting spark can light a gas jet. Charging a pressurised crystal causes an oscillation that can produce a regular flow of electronic or mechanical pulses.[3]

Many stone circles stand above fault-lines or crossings of underground water. Dowsers note that in open country lightning always strikes directly above the intersection of two or more water-lines. Some circles and stones (as at Crickhowell in Wales) generate measurable field activity. Others produce infrasound and ultrasound when struck by the rising sun. Crystal content in the stones is implicated in this activity.[4]

Edgar **Cayce** held that **Atlantean** science was based on 'crystal power', and that the Lost Continent drowned through the abuse of it. Interestingly, the west wall of the Queen's Chamber in the **Great Pyramid** is infested by salt crystals, for reasons that remain unclear, while Soviet research in the 1960s suggested that the entire Earth is a giant crystal.

1. *The Power of Gems and Crystals*, Soozi Holbeche, Piatkus, London 1989
2. *Lifetide*, Lyall Watson,Coronet, London 1980, pp. 52–59
3. *Needles of Stone Revisited*, Tom Graves, Gothic Image, Glastonbury 1986, p. 78
4. *Earth Magic*, Francis Hitching, Picador, London 1977, pp. 105–107

CSICOP The Committee for the Scientific Investigation of Claims of the Paranormal operates from Buffalo, New York, and maintains that all seeming **paranormal** events are explicable by 'normal' means or by **fraud**. Conjurer James 'The Amazing' **Randi**, who denounced Uri **Geller** during the 1970s, offers $10,000 to anyone who can prove paranormal powers. CSICOP insists that *all* **psychics** claiming to do 'cold readings' (i.e. of clients never met before) operate fraudulently, producing general statements refined by client feedback, thus telling clients what they want to hear. So in the 1850s scientist Michael Faraday opposed **spiritualism** and, in the 1920s, **Houdini** the **mediums**. Opponents insist CSICOP is concerned only to debunk, whatever the truth.

CURSES (*See* **JINXES, KAHUNAS, VOODOO**) A curse involves wishing evil or destruction on an enemy. Part of the **psychic** arsenal traditionally used by priest or **magician**, some say a curse works only if the victim *believes* in it. Just as a cancer-sufferer sure that the disease is fatal is more likely to die than one who fights the illness, so a primitive tribesman, cursed by the witch doctor, is said to die simply due to lost hope. But there are many cases of curses working where the victim either does not know of or believe in the curse. In such cases it appears that the malevolent thought, the curse, has somehow been *imprinted* on the victim. There are also cases where the curse seems not to have been laid by any living human agency at all, or is aimed not at a specific individual but at anyone who inherits a cursed object, or is born to a cursed family.

In January 1960 fifty-three-year-old nightclub proprietor Finis P. Ernest was admitted semi-conscious to an Oklahoma hospital, suffering from asthma. He was soon discharged, seemingly cured. Six months later, having been in and out of private hospitals, he returned, suffering from fits and convulsions. The doctors found nothing organically wrong. Again recovering he went (it later emerged) straight to his mother's home. Within forty-eight hours he was back in hospital utterly depressed and near death. Allowed out to visit his mother, another relapse followed. Realising what was going on, the doctors allowed him out only on condition he avoided his mother. At 6 p.m. on 23 August he phoned his mother. At 6.35 p.m. he was found gasping for breath. By 6.55 p.m. he was dead.

Dr James P. Mathis learned Ernest's father had died with the boy in his teens, leaving him 'man of the house'. Twice married against his mother's will and twice soon divorced, aged thirty-one and with his mother as partner, he opened a successful night-club. Aged thirty-eight he married a woman approved by his mother. For fifteen years all went well. Supported by his wife, he accepted an offer to sell. 'Do this', his furious mother warned, 'and something dire will happen to you.' Within two days asthma struck him, but he went ahead with the sale. 'Something will strike you!' his mother shouted. The visits to hospital began. The attacks and convulsions, and the inability of the doctors to help, convinced him that Mother was right. As for the last phone call, his wife told Dr Mathis that he'd found the nerve to tell his mother he meant to re-invest the money from the night-club sale in a new venture, excluding her. His mother ended their conversation by reminding him of her warning of 'dire results'. He was dead within the hour. Dr Mathis found that he had to label this case a 'sophisticated version of voodoo death'.[1]

Even odder is the curse affecting those taking stones from the Hawaiian volcano Mauna Loa despite local warnings that this angers Pele, the volcano goddess. In summer 1977 Ralph Loffert of Buffalo, New York, with his wife and four children, ignored this warning and returned home with several stones. Mauna Loa erupted. One of the Loffert boys, Todd, developed appendicitis, had knee surgery, and broke his wrist; another, Mark, sprained his ankle and broke an arm; the third son caught an eye infection, and the daughter lost teeth in a fall. In July 1978 they sent the stones back to Hawaii, despite which the disasters continued. When Mark confessed he still had three stones, these were returned and the trouble ended. A Mrs Allison Raymond of Ontario and her family also took stones from Mauna Loa. Her husband died in a car crash, her mother of cancer, her younger son broke a leg – again, the trouble only ended when the stones were returned.

These are not the only cases. Naturalist John Erickson of the Volcanoes National park in Hawaii says he receives daily up to forty packages of stones returned by frightened tourists who have taken them home.[2]

There are many cases of objects – including, in modern times, cars, ships and planes – seemingly cursed which, passed from one hapless owner to another, perpetuate the original bad luck. The curse may not in the first place be intentional, but imprinted by violent accident or death. Such cases may best be defined as **jinxes**, and are considered elsewhere.

1. *Arthur C. Clarke's World of Strange Powers*, Fairley and Welfare, Book Club Associates, London 1985, pp. 19–21
2. *Mysteries*, Colin Wilson, Grafton, London 1979, p. 456

CYCLES (*See* **BIORHYTHMS, BROWN, F., GAUQUELIN, JONAS**) Cyclic rhythms dominate our lives. Most obvious in their effect on us are the diurnal rhythms of night and day, the cycles of the **moon** and of the seasons, year in and out. Less obvious are the planetary cycles, sunspot activity, biorhythms and other periodicities, great and small, which orchestrate phenomena affecting our lives in the most basic (but often unrealised) ways. Stock-market crashes go in cycles; we are born, live and die in cycles; epidemics and even historical process appear to be cyclic.

Since the 1950s the Foundation for the Study of Cycles, affiliated to the University of Pittsburgh, has correlated apparently unconnected data to establish the rhythms that condition all our activities.

A cycle of 9.6 years connects incidence of heart disease, barometric pressure highs, ozone measurements in Paris, overflow of European rivers, tree rings in Java and salmon and lynx abundance in Canada. The 3.86 year cycle ties Norwegian lemming suicides to sudden growth in North American lumber pines. Rise and fall of hemlines, incidence of traffic accidents, and volcanic activity obey the 11.1 year sunspot cycle. The 1348 Black Death and 1665 Great Plague coincided with solar turbulence: flu, cholera, diptheria and typhus epidemics show similar correlation (due to magnetic disturbances?). Russian scientist A. L. Cizevskij, studying correlations between solar activity and human history from the fifth century BC to AD 1962, claims wars and social unrest also obey the 11.1 year cycle.[1]

The effect on us of diurnal, lunar and annual cycles is profound. Our body temperature obeys a regular circadian pattern, rising (with heart beat and urine production) with the sun to peak in early afternoon, falling to its lowest level at 4 a.m. – the hour preferred by secret police for arrest and questioning, also when, the body being most relaxed, most babies are born.

Lunar cycles profoundly affect bodily behaviour. The moon has been called 'the great midwife'. Data on over half a million births in New York hospitals between 1948 and 1957 showed more births occur during the waning moon, with a maximum just after the full moon. Likewise most births on Germany's North Sea coast occur at high tide, as the moon passes overhead. The length of the menstrual cycle, and thus probability of conception, is also moon-influenced.

Blood flow, like the tides, may also be subject to lunar influence: bloodletting was always done with the moon on the wane; while the influence of the moon on the mind is so widely recognised that 200 years ago English law distinguished between 'insanity' (incurably psychotic) and 'lunacy' (moon-struck). Crimes committed at full moon were treated more leniently. Modern research shows that such crimes as kleptomania, arson and dangerous driving all peak at full moon, cloudy nights providing no protection.

The annual cycle also affects birth. Not only are more children in the Northern Hemisphere born in May and June than November and December (and conversely in the Southern Hemisphere) but they tend to be heavier and taller, due to an annual rhythm in the production of hormones involved in pregnancy. In New England, those born in March tend to live some four years longer than those born in any other month.[2]

Such discoveries, allied with the work of Gauquelin, Brown, **Nelson** and others suggest that **astrology** (call it 'cosmo-rhythmology' if you prefer) and the ancient aphorism of 'As Above, So Below', are not merely unscientific superstition. Our lives are affected, at every level, by much more than meets the eye. We live in a shifting, energetic environment in which there is no static balance. The ancient Chinese, postulating the interplay of **Yin** and **Yang**, knew this.

1. *Rhythms of Vision*, Lawrence Blair, Warner Books, New York 1977, pp. 78–80
2. *Supernature*, Lyall Watson, Hodder and Stoughton, London 1973, pp. 44ff

D

DALAI LAMA (*See* **BUDDHISM, DAVID-NEEL, TIBET**) This Mongolian term for the Tibetan spiritual ruler means 'Broad Ocean'. His Tibetan name is Gyalpo Rimpoche or 'Precious King'. In exile since 1959, the present Dalai Lama was born in June 1935 in Chinghai Province, China, and in 1937 recognised as the fourteenth incarnation of Avalokitesvara, the Bodhisattva of Compassion. Brought to Lhasa, he was forced to flee in 1950 when the Chinese invaded Tibet. He returned, but had to flee again.

How was he chosen? On dying Thupten Gyatso the thirteenth Dalai Lama was, as custom demanded, seated in the Potola (his Lhasa palace) facing south. One day his head was seen facing east, towards China. Two years later, Tibet's Regent went to Lake Chö Khor Gye to **scry** the future in its waters. He saw a three-storeyed monastery with golden roofs, and nearby a Chinese peasant house with carved gables. Entering China, search parties found these buildings in the village of Takster. Disguised as a servant, Lama Kewtsang Rinpoche of Sera Monastery entered the house. Crying 'Sera Lama, Sera Lama', a two-year-old boy took from him a rosary belonging to the thirteenth Dalai Lama and hung it round his own neck. This suggested that he was the true **reincarnation** of the Dalai Lama. The boy not only chose other items belonging to Thupten Gyatso but also had large outstanding ears and moles on his trunk. These were identified as vestigial traces of the four-armed Bodhisattva's second pair of arms. Paying the Chinese provincial governor 100,000 Chinese dollars to take the child with them to Lhasa, when the governor demanded a further 300,000 dollars, the monks paid up.[1]

Today the Chinese have destroyed almost all Tibet's 6,000 Buddhist monasteries. The fourteenth Dalai Lama (awarded the Nobel Peace Prize in 1989) forgives them for killing a million Tibetans and reducing the remaining six million to poverty: 'If I get too much anger', he said in 1990, 'that would not harm the Chinese, it would harm me.' He adds, 'If you take compassion as the essence of **religion**, then a religious society is possible.'[2] Seeing life as an endless circle of suffering and desire, he ignores faction. The real horror of Tibet, he says, is not the fate of the Tibetans but that of their murderers. The Chinese hook out the tongues of Tibetans about to be executed, fearing that before dying they may express long life to the Dalai Lama and Tibet. Western governments deny him official audience for fear of offending the Chinese. The fourteenth Dalai Lama, the Incarnation of Compassion, laughs at this. Oddly, it was predicted of old that the fourteenth Dalai Lama would be the last.

1. 'A Glorious Giggler Among Deaf Diplomats', interview by Brian Appleyard with the Dalai Lama, *Sunday Times*, London, 16 September 1990
2. *Seven Years in Tibet*, Heinrich Harrer, Reprint Society, London 1955, pp. 296–300

DASKALOS (1913–) (*See* **ELEMENTALS, HEALERS**) Spyros Sathi, a Greek Cypriot **magus** and healer known as Daskalos (Greek *teacher*) is said to be able to diagnose latent disease visible only in the victim's **aura**, and (in the **etheric** state) to dematerialise then rematerialise diseased organs and bone. Claiming to remember his many **reincarnations**, he says his powers come to him from an entity called Father Yohannan – the biblical St John – and that what the healer requires is *love of humanity*.

The account of him by US-Cypriot academic Kyriacos Markides is reminiscent of **Castaneda**'s tales of Don Juan, but is more accessible in that his system agrees with **Sufi, Christian** and **Qabalist** esotericism. He says **death** means separation of physical body and 'etheric double', the latter taking about forty days to dissolve. In the resulting 'psychonoetic' state feelings, now undiluted by physical limitations, create a subjective heaven or hell. The dead person may not realise he is dead, and may haunt the world until moving on to higher planes. In time the 'Masters of Karma' order him back to Earth via a new incarnation. He emphasises the reality of archangelic hierarchies, the Akashic Record or Universal Memory, and says there is no evil, only ignorance and experience. He explains elementals as human thoughts and desires which, consciously or otherwise, take on life of their own. A person brooding on any strong desire creates 'psychic matter', the basic stuff of the universe, which may act positively or negatively.

Initially sceptical, Markides became convinced by Daskalos. One day he dreamed Daskalos was talking to him then suddenly vanished: he turned and saw Daskalos approaching from behind. Telling Daskalos about it next day, the magus said, 'Oh yes, I was trying to give you a lesson on the nature of space in the fourth dimension.' Another time Daskalos described in detail Markides' home in Maine: back in Maine Markides got a letter from Daskalos' apprentice Iacovos saying Markides' wife Emily (who had a problem with her knee) should see a doctor. Emily's pains vanished three days later.

In 1981, ill with a foot-wound that would not heal, Daskalos said he had deliberately taken on the illness to relieve a son-in-law of a '**karmic** debt'. To demonstrate the power of mind over matter, he went into deep **meditation**, passed his hand over the infected part, then hopped vigorously round the room on the wounded foot. Returning to bed he said: 'Now I must get the Karma back', and that it would take about another week to exhaust.

As **Ouspensky** to **Gurdjieff**, as **Castaneda** to **Don Juan**, so Markides to Daskalos. The more time he spent with Daskalos, the more he too experienced odd events, lucid **dreams** and **synchronicities**. Such events seem so remote from common reality that, read about, they are hard to swallow. But so many of his claims accord with phenomena and teachings witnessed elsewhere that they should not be dismissed out of hand.[1,2]

1. *The Magus of Strovolus*, Kyriacos C. Markides, Routledge Kegan Paul, London 1985
2. *Homage to the Sun*, Kyriacos C. Markides, Arkana, London 1987

DAVID-NEEL, Alexandra (1868–1969) (*See* **DALAI LAMA, TIBET**) Born in Paris, from an early age this extraordinary woman wanted to 'go beyond the garden gate in search of the Unknown'. Following studies at the Sorbonne she journeyed widely through India, Indo-China, Sri Lanka, Burma, China, Korea and Japan. One of her journeys, lasting fourteen years, was spent largely in Tibet, then visited by few Europeans, let alone European women. At the Indian border she met the thirteenth Dalai Lama (then in exile) who until then had refused audience to any but Tibetan women. He told her to learn the Tibetan language, and offered an interpreter, Dawasandup (translator of ***The Tibetan Book of the Dead*** into English) to accompany her into Tibet.

Once in the 'Land of the Snows' she immediately felt 'at home'. She spent years studying Tibetan mystical doctrines, philosophy, occult lore and customs. Her account of these in *Magic and Mystery in Tibet* (1931) remains fascinating. For it and other works (such as *My Journey to Lhasa* describing her exploration on foot of the vast wilderness between China and India) she was awarded a gold medal by the Geographical Society of Paris and was made a Knight of the Legion of Honour. In addition, in Tibet, she was granted the rank of lama.

The marvels recounted in her many books may suggest she was credulous. She underwent the terrifying *chod* initiation – a **visionary** experience that involves being eaten alive by **demons** – and summoned up a **tulpa**. Yet this 'original travelling sceptic', as one commentator calls her, insisted: 'I affirm nothing. I only relate what I heard from people I found otherwise trustworthy, but they may have deluded themselves in all sincerity.'[1]

Commenting on a **clairvoyant** awareness of hostile forces about her she writes: 'Some people would, perhaps, have seen in this the effect of **occult** activities . . . I attributed these phenomena to fever or neurasthenia due to brain fatigue and the annoyance at my plans being upset.'

A political anarchist, she was also an acclaimed operatic soprano.

1. *Magic and Mystery in Tibet*, Alexandra David-Neel, Abacus, London 1977

DEATH (*See* **DASKALOS, NEAR-DEATH EXPERIENCES, REINCARNATION**) The physical death of all biological organisms guarantees evolution. The matter cast off by vitality returns to the elements to be recycled into new forms which in turn live and die. **Consciousness** of whatever sort withdraws into a primal energy-matrix, the nature of which remains unclear. In human terms death occurs (barring mortal accident or suicide) after a period of conscious withdrawal from life. Clinically, death occurs when the heart no longer beats and blood fails to reach the brain. Unconsciousness follows. Yet briefly the brain and its memory-store remain active. It may be during this brief period that the review of the life just lived takes place. The accounts of those revived from clinical death suggest an automatic process whereby the personality leaving the now-dead body gives itself up to a wider sphere of non-egoic consciousness. The '**soul**' flees the failed body but remains active, albeit in a manner inexplicable to science, which holds that the end of physical/biological activity means the end of *all* activity.

Occultism speaks of a process involving several deaths. The matter may be abandoned but the **spirit** persists in forms inaccessible to any material definition, undergoing changes which may or may not lead back to the world. *Death* as such is a transition between one state and another, part of the cyclic motion of things. Nothing stands still or is annihilated – indeed, belief in such annihilation is a form of 'death-in-life'; a denial of the processes orchestrated by Nature; a denial arising from the ego's desire to believe that it alone lives, and that, when it is gone, so is all else.

Such belief is a perversion peculiar to our age, found in few cultures and in few ages. Death as inertia does not exist, as the universe is not inert, but is part of a wider life-process. Physically manifested beings are composites of different principles that come together for a time and then embark elsewhere, their temporary allegiance dissolved. This belief is common to most cultures in most eras: why do we deny it?

DEE, Dr John (1527–1608) This Elizabethan philosopher and **occultist**, his reputation long tarnished by suspicion of **necromancy**, is today ranked with **Paracelsus** and **Bruno** as a tragic Renaissance **magus** caught between magic and science.

A 'magician' in that '**magic**' offered him a field broad enough for his genius, this Welsh-born mathematician was at nineteen a Fellow of Trinity College, Cambridge, before lecturing in Paris in 1550. Back in England he met the occultist Jerome Cardan, and began seeking spirit-contacts to aid his work and finances. When his patron the boy-king Edward died, he cast Queen Mary's horoscope, but also rashly visited the future Queen Elizabeth (then under house arrest) to do likewise. He narrowly escaped the stake.

At Mary's death in 1558 he calculated Elizabeth's coronation date and became an Admiralty spy (code-number 007). As map-maker, naval defence planner and author of navigation guides he moved in an influential circle including Sydney, Raleigh, and the explorers Davis and Gilbert.

Now married and settled at Mortlake, he grew obsessed with **crystal**-gazing and spirit contacts. In 1582 (married again) he hired as **scryer** Barnabas Saul, then an Irish apothecary's apprentice, Edward Kelley, whose ears had been cropped for forgery. A natural trance **medium**, Kelley worked as Dee's scryer for £50 a year, apparently contacting an **angel** called Ave who dictated, backwards, the *Enochian* magical language. Visiting Bohemia in 1585, Kelley persuaded Dee that a spirit-guide, Madimi, wanted them to swap wives. Jane Dee was furious. In 1589 the Dees returned alone to England to find house burgled and library destroyed. Granted wardenship of Christ's College in Manchester, Dee's last years were spent in poverty and under threat due to his reputation as a **sorcerer**. Yet his European travels bore strange fruit. In Bohemia and Germany the philosophy expressed in his *Monas Hieroglyphica* presaged the **Rosicrucian** movement. No charlatan, in effect he founded modern **psychical** research. Even so, his career marks the end of the Renaissance era of **hermetic** magic.[1,2]

1. *John Dee*, Peter French, Owen, London 1972
2. *The Rosicrucian Enlightenment*, Frances A. Yates, Routledge Kegan Paul, London 1972

DELPHIC ORACLE (*See* **ORACLES**)

DEMONS (*See* **ANGELS, DEVIL, INCUBI, ELEMENTALS**) In classical Greece a *daimon* was a morally neutral elemental force. The *daimon* of **Socrates** was his *genius* or inspiration. But under Christianity (following Hebrew tradition) *daimons* became malign entities – *demons*. Once God had been held to create all things, including evil. Now it was held that God, the source of good, could not cause evil. So the hierarchies of Hell were invented: evil was explained by the **myth** of the rebel angels who, led by Lucifer, had been cast from heaven to the earth to work against God and man alike. To the mediaeval mind, bad habits, thoughts and deeds, ill luck and disasters were all caused by invisible demons. Huge numbers were thought to plague the world. On one estimate, of an original total of 399,920,004 angels, 133,306,668 had fallen with Lucifer, all now plaguing humanity. At Vienna in 1583, 12,652 demons were expelled from a sixteen-year-old girl; her grandmother went to the stake for housing those demons as flies in bottles. In 1610 Sister Madeline de la Palud of the Ursuline convent at Aix-en-Provence was found to host a full legion of 6,666 demons, including Beelzebub, Leviathan, Baalberith, Asmodeus and Astaroth.[1]

Knowledge of demonology – the cataloguing and classification of demons – was thought essential to investigate **witchcraft**. A catalogue given in the *Testament of Solomon* (*c*. AD 100–400) tells how an angel gave Solomon a magic ring giving him power over demons by making them tell him their real **names**. Such names come from Jewish, Greek, Egyptian, Syrian and Babylonian sources. The functions of each demon are listed – firing crops, strangling babies, wrecking ships, causing **disease** – which itself was thought to be a demon infesting the body. In later *grimoires*, or magical textbooks, like the *Grimorium Verum*, Lucifer, Beelzebub and Astaroth are named as the chief powers of evil. If summoned, Lucifer appears as a handsome boy, Beelzebub as a gigantic fly and Astaroth as a human being pied black and white.[2]

As angels were classified in nine orders, each of three hierarchies, so (by some demonologists) were demons. Others claimed all demons to be different aspects of Satan/Lucifer. Thus Leviathan (writes Alphonsus de Spina, fifteenth century) is avarice, Asmodeus lust, Behemoth gluttony, Diabolus pride, Astaroth sloth, Baalberith murder and blasphemy. Most originated as other people's gods. Thus Beelzebub, Lord of Flies, was once a Philistine god. Baal (toad-headed, imparting wisdom and invisibility), was a Canaanite fertility-god. Astaroth, a Phoenician goddess, became a male demon, lovely but with foul breath, who reveals the future. Asmodeus (feet of a cock) and Belial (demon of lies) were always seen as evil spirits. The **Gnostics** thought Jehovah, demiurgic creator of this world, the worst demon of all.

Few demonologies agree in all characteristics, but all blame demons for human defects and vices; all believe that **black magicians** could summon such spirits for evil purposes; all believed that demons could (by forging new bodies or by borrowing human corpses) enjoy carnal relations with human beings, appearing as incubi or succubi – 'demon lovers'.

Such beliefs led to witch-hunts in which thousands died. Some now claim there never were witches, far less *demons*, and that the horror arose out of mass neurosis caused by the Church's suppression of human sexuality.[3] Either way, those denying the existence of demons were as much at risk from the Inquisition as those accused of relations with demons. Only in the eighteenth century, with the advent of the 'Age of Reason' did belief in demons begin to fade. Yet some like **Crowley** later did their best to keep up the bad work.

With his pupil Victor Neuburg in Algeria in 1909, Crowley conjured up a 'mighty devil', Choronzon, who, seemingly possessing Crowley as he sat in a triangle drawn in the sand, boasted and raged (in Crowley's voice), 'From me come leprosy and pox and plague and cancer and cholera and the falling sickness.' Neuburg saw not Crowley amid the triangle but a lovely woman. He refused her flattery. Choronzon changed into a naked Crowley, invaded Neuburg's protective circle, and tried to tear out the poor man's throat with his 'fangs'. Finally defeated, Choronzon disappeared. Neuburg never really recovered: Crowley claimed that throughout this episode he had 'dwelt apart' and knew nothing of the attempted murder.[4]

Delusion? Though today we may see demonology as a confused attempt to classify not malign entities but human psychopathology, disbelief in demons has not rid us of the vices and pathologies they supposedly ruled.

The popularity of horror movies like *The Exorcist, Rosemary's Baby* and *Nightmare on Elm Street*; our fascination with 'human monsters' like Saddam Hussein or the Yorkshire Ripper, and the demonic aspect reported of some UFO entities all suggest that such powers remain credible. Our cultural fascination with depravity has simply refocussed itself in new forms. In short, we remain as infested with 'demons' as was mediaeval Europe.

1. *The Powers of Evil*, Richard Cavendish, Routledge Kegan Paul, London 1975, pp. 234ff.
2. *The Magical Arts*, Richard Cavendish, Arkana, London 1984, p. 260
3. *Europe's Inner Demons*, Norman Cohn, Paladin Books, London 1976
4. *op cit.*, ref. 2, pp. 255–6

DERVISHES (*See* **SUFIS**) These Sufi mystics form independent orders and temporary schools, linked by a force called *baraka*, each school practising distinct forms of training designed to produce the perfected human being. The word 'dervish' implies an Islamic holy man, though there have been Christian Sufi schools. The famous 'whirling dervishes' in fact belong to one order alone, the Mevlevi; 'howling dervishes' are associated with the Rufais. These activities are forms of **yoga**, involving rigorous training and inducing **trance** states, the ultimate aim being the creation of the perfected man or woman.

DEVAS This Sanskrit term means 'shining one' or 'celestial being'. From it derives the Latin *Deus* (God), and also, in all probability, the word *Devil*. **Zoroastrians** used the term to refer to malevolent entities. The Gypsies, whose Romany language is of

Indo-European origin, call God *Duvel*. The moral ambiguity in this duality of meaning is highlighted by the old **magical** tag: *Demon est Deus Inversus* ('The Demon is God reversed').

More recently the great folklorist W. Y. **Evans-Wentz** believed that the vision of God and Jesus experienced by Joseph Smith, founder of the **Mormon Church**, was in fact a vision of the devas. And today the term has been rehabilitated by the Findhorn Community in Scotland to refer to helpful nature spirits.

DEVIL, The (*See* **ANGELS, DEMONS, DEVAS, EVIL**) The idea of a personified principle of evil ruling the material world and called Satan, Lucifer, Mephistopheles or the Devil, is deeply rooted in **Christianity. Christ** called Satan 'the prince of this world'; St Paul named him 'the god of this world' – admissions later used by **Gnostics** to support their **Dualist** claim that Evil not only rules the world but created it, God being busy elsewhere. But this belief and even orthodox Catholic belief in Satan as the rebellious fallen angel, inspiring all worldly ill, has always been contradicted by Isaiah xlv, 7: 'I form the light, and create darkness: I make peace, and create evil: I the Lord do all these things.'

The Devil is a mental construct developed by early Church fathers as a scapegoat for human nature and as an image terrible enough to make **pagans** abandon their (devilish) gods and embrace Christ. Insofar as the concept reflects Ahriman, the **Zoroastrian** personification of lies and destruction, and also many older nature-spirits and devas, it is not peculiar to Christianity. However, the Christian Church has made the concept very much its own, distorting older traditions to do so.

The origins of the names *Satan* and *Lucifer* show this clearly. *Satan* in Hebrew means 'adversary', and originally implied an accuser of men (as in the Book of Job). The satan, God's prosecution lawyer, was only gradually magnified, in later Jewish and early Christian writings, into *Satan*, God's Adversary, the source of all evil. *Lucifer* (in Hebrew *Helel ben-Shahar*, 'day-star, son of the dawn', the beautiful morning star who walked in Eden) is Latin for the planet Venus, meaning 'light-bearer'. The passage in Isaiah: 'How art thou fallen from heaven, O Lucifer, son of the morning', predicts doom for the King of Babylon, oppressor of the **Jews**, employing as metaphor the daily eclipse of this brightest planet by the greater light of the rising Sun.[1]

The passage was later used, as was the **Enochian** myth of the fall of the Watchers, to demonise Lucifer as the proud angel fallen to Earth, there in darkness to oppose God (the Sun) in eternal contest for human souls.

Thus grew the myth that Satan and his angels were expelled from heaven for refusing to worship Adam. This was yoked to the tale that the **Serpent** tempted Eve to persuade Adam to eat the Apple and so gain knowledge of good and evil (self-consciousness). It is not said in Genesis that the Serpent (who proves Yahweh a liar) is the Devil: this came later, as did St Paul's dogma that Adam's **original sin** plunged all later generations into the power of the Devil, to be redeemed only by Christ. Very convenient, as was the now-logical association of the **serpent**, or **dragon** (originally a symbol of natural energy fertilising Eve, the Mother Goddess Earth, or **Gaia**) with the by-now thoroughly-blackened 'satanic' or 'luciferian' principle.

The Book of Revelation completes the link: 'And the great dragon was cast out, that old serpent, called the Devil, and Satan, which deceiveth the whole world: he was cast out into the earth, and his angels were cast out with him.' Meanwhile in the unchristianised East the **dragon** retained its beneficent image of life-fertilising energy.

With this construct in place the young Church could now tame the wild, impulsive gods of the old nature religions – meaning the wild, impulsive aspects of human nature. Thus the Great God Pan, horned and cloven-hooved, became the conventional Christian Devil, alias 'Old Nick' – Nik being a title of the pagan English god Woden.[2] Everywhere Christian missionaries went, local nature gods were demonised or absorbed. Failed missions were blamed on the Devil; i.e. that part of human nature resisting repression. So fear of the Devil proved effective in enforcing submission to the God of Love, with fear of the stake a useful back-up. Fire was used to fight fire, fear to end fear, and lies to birth truth – a devilish strategy?

1. *The Magical Arts*, Richard Cavendish, Arkana, London 1984, pp. 286–7
2. *An ABC of Witchcraft*, Doreen Valiente, Hale, London 1973, p. 85

DIANETICS (*See* **HUBBARD, SCIENTOLOGY**)

DICK, Philip K. (1928–82) (*See* **PIKE**) In 1974 science fiction writer Philip K. Dick experienced 'an invasion of my mind by a transcendentally rational mind, as if I had been insane all my life and suddenly I had become sane'.

Prior to this Dick, a brilliant exponent of metaphysical speculation, had produced a huge body of work that typically denied any objectively real world. His obsession with life's seeming pointlessness caused him deep anguish. Then, as he claimed, 'Some transcendent divine power . . . intervened to restore my mind and heal my body.' Subsequently before his early death he wrote several novels (*Valis, The Divine Invasion, Radio Free Albemuth*) exploring the event in autobiographical terms so bizarre as to cause many of his peers (not unused to weird notions) to think he had gone crazy. He said this **entity** spoke Hebrew, Greek and Sanskrit, had memories dating back two millennia, originated the **Christ**-initiative, and that its intervention in human affairs had been suppressed but not destroyed by the Roman Empire. Highlighting the **Gnostic** view of the world as a prison-planet occupied by a hostile power manifesting anciently through the Roman Empire and today in the state power ('The Empire never ended') of the USA and USSR, his account of how he was 'bushwhacked by the Living God' in order to oppose the Empire suggests paranoid megalomania. Yet his examination of his predicament and that of the world in terms of a Gnostic metapsychology abandoned at least since the Renaissance may yet prove profoundly insightful, as psychological metaphor if not necessarily as factual history.

DIMENSIONS (*See* **ABDUCTIONS, FAIRIES, QUARKS, UFOs**) Global folklore old and new tells of people entering or abducted to worlds coincident with yet not of *our* world. King **Arthur** to Avalon, True Thomas into the **fairy** knowe, Barney and Betty Hill into the UFO: all find realms of topsy-turvy physical laws inhabited by **entities** who know more about our world than we know about theirs. Typically there are specific times, such as twilight or after midnight, or at solstices and equinoxes, when the gate or window between the worlds is open. Those returning from the other world suffer amnesia, or are amazed to find their forty-eight hours in the other world has seen a year and a day, or a century and a day, pass in this. What is never in doubt is the *spatial* congruity of the different worlds. One need merely step over a threshold . . . between dimensions. In the case of the *Narnia* books by C. S. Lewis, you only have to walk through the back of a wardrobe.

Are all such accounts purely imaginary? If so, then imagination *per se* constitutes a different dimension to the four – length, breadth, depth and **time** – that we acknowledge. Yet, given not only some basis of truth in the tales of such travels bequeathed by generations, but also given a need to explain the UFO enigma, and the very real paradoxes made apparent by modern relativity and high-energy physics, perhaps it is 'time' to start thinking in terms not of a *uni*verse but a *multi*verse.

Physicists, faced by the mischievous behaviour of elementary particles that deny Newtonian rules by insisting on being in two places at once or by arriving before they started, now speculate about 'superstrings' and about multiple dimensions in a way that would be familiar to ancient Norse *skalds* who told of a nine-dimensional universe of congruent but separate worlds, each with its own intelligent inhabitants and physical laws.

In 1919 Albert **Einstein**, then working on general relativity theory, received a letter from Soviet mathematician Franz Kaluza, proposing a five-dimensional theory of gravity. He wrote back, 'The formal unity of your theory is startling.' In 1926 Swedish mathematician Oscar Klein suggested that the fifth dimension is imperceptible because it is 'curled up' in a circle too small to observe. In 1957 Hugh Everett and John Wheeler of Princeton University proposed a 'Many Worlds Interpretation' of **quantum** mechanics, whereby the universe is viewed as constantly branching through alternate realities. Today physicists involved in superstring research believe that the universe evolved from an unstable ten-dimensional string. In *Beyond Einstein*, Dr Michio Taku and Jennifer Trainer speculate: 'Six dimensions have curled up, leaving our four-dimensional universe intact.'[1]

So what happened to the other six? Is it still unscientific fantasy to believe you can walk through the back of a wardrobe to another world where lions talk? After all, as the Rev. Edwin Abbott indicated a century ago in his romance *Flatland*, Flatland's two-dimensional inhabitants do not take kindly to the radical news from a square who, visited by a Thing from Upper Space, returned from the impossible world of the Third Dimension . . . only to be imprisoned as a menace to society. And how do we explain not only UFOs but the interruption of our 'reality' by rains of stones, fish and other **Fortean** phenomena that don't fit the acceptable pattern?

1. *Dimensions*, Jacques Vallée, Sphere Books, London 1990, pp. 284–6

DISCARNATES (*See* **GHOSTS, SPIRITUALISM**) Another term for the spirits of those dead who maintain contact with the living by **paranormal** means for paranormal purposes.

DISEASE (*See* **CYCLES**) The causation of disease and epidemic has been connected not only to the 11.1–year sunspot **cycle** and the malicious activity of **demons** but, lately, to the invasion of the biosphere by hitherto-alien organisms carried on and developing within the evanescent snowy bodies and million-mile-long tails of those celestial outlaws, comets. Organic molecules may make up to thirty per cent of the mass of a comet: their survival and even growth in such a specialised environment is not impossible. Astronomer Fred Hoyle believes that comets provide a sufficient environment for the growth of life-forms such as photosynthetic bacteria which, at every cometary passage close to the sun, are volatilised and blown by the solar wind into the long, diffuse cometary tail, subsequently to adhere to any solid body, like Planet Earth, which passes through that tail. This notion of biological invasion, though new to science, is not new to folklore. All over the world since the most ancient times the interruption of the sky by comets has been regarded with fear. The Navaho of Arizona, the Bushmen of the Kalahari and the Tukano of the Amazon all carry myths suggestive of cometary insemination of disease.

The speed of travel of mediaeval pandemics is hard to understand, on the basis of a person-to-person infection, given the slowness of land- and sea-travel then available. Hoyle and Chandra Wickramasinghe have suggested that the answer is provided by extraterrestrial biological invasions, in 'the form of new viral and bacterial infections that strike our planet at irregular intervals, drifting down to the surface in the form of clumps of meteoric material.'[1] The theory remains unproven but plausible.

1. *Lifetide*, Lyall Watson, Coronet, London 1980, pp. 39–42

DIVINATION (*See* **DOWSING, PRECOGNITION, PROPHECY**) Means any system for enquiry into hidden matters other than by use of the five senses. Inspiration, magical ritual, **intuition, dream** or **trance** may be employed in conjunction with or boosted by 'mechanical' aids such as (in dowsing for water or other hidden matter) rods, **wands** or **pendulums** or (in seeking information on the future or other obscured matters) systems based on what **Jung** called an 'acausal connecting principle' like the **I Ching** or **tarot**. In the past and in primitive cultures such systems have included divination of **omens** by **crystal**-gazing: by the state of entrails and liver, or by marks on the shoulder-blades (scapulimancy) of slaughtered animals; or by the casting of bones or 'omen-sticks'. It is said the **Druids** divined from the appearance of tree-roots or clouds, by the howling of dogs and the way smoke rose from a fire, and sometimes by stabbing a man and observing his death-convulsions. Another Druid technique involved incantation and the trance-process called 'illumination of rhymes'.[1]

1. *The Magic Arts in Celtic Britain*, Lewis Spence, Rider, London 1970

DIXON, Jeane (*See* **PRECOGNITION, PROPHECY**) In 1956 this American **seeress** made a prophecy in *Parade* magazine: 'As for the 1960 election, Mrs Dixon thinks it will be dominated by labour and won by a Democrat. But he will be assassinated or die in office "though not necessarily in his first term".' John F. Kennedy was elected in 1960 and assassinated in 1963. A sceptic might say that surely Mrs Dixon knew of the 'presidential death cycle' – the odd fact that *every* US President elected at twenty-year intervals since President William H. Harrison in 1840 had died (Harrison, Harding, Roosevelt) or been assassinated (Lincoln, Garfield, McKinley) in office. Kennedy was the seventh . . . and Reagan was nearly the eighth. Shot by a would-be assassin in 1981, in his first term, he survived, thus breaking the 'curse'. (Of the remaining twenty-nine Presidents *not* elected in the twenty-year cycle, so far only *one* has died in office.)[1]

On 5 February 1962, Mrs Dixon, a devout **Christian**, had a vision that told her of the birth in the Middle East of a man she terms **Antichrist**. She said that in the 1990s this man will dominate the entire world, leading to global conflict resolved only in the year 1999. She also predicted that by the end of the century one Pope would be wounded and another killed, and is credited with predicting Watergate, the Apollo 13 near-disaster, and (as did Edgar **Cayce**), the Christian reform of the USSR and its détente with the USA. On the other hand she also predicted that, about 1985, a comet would smash into the Earth, creating huge earth tremors and tidal waves.

With Jeane Dixon, as with other prophets, it is hard to know to what degree her 'successful' prophecies arise from genuine psychic faculty, or if what is involved is an astute, though perhaps unconscious, capacity to extrapolate existing trends and probabilities. It seems likely that both angles are involved, complicated by partisanship one way or the other.

1. *Rolling Thunder*, Joey R. Jochmans, Sun Books, Santa Fé 1980

DOGON (*See* **ANCIENT ASTRONAUTS, SIRIUS**)

DOLPHINS (*See* **ANIMAL POWERS, LILLY, WHALES**) Some seventy million years ago a warm-blooded mammalian ungulate returned to the sea, in time evolving into **whales** and dolphins. The latter in particular have always maintained benevolent contact with humanity, as is acknowledged in global folklore. From age to age tales persist of dolphins, the King of Fishes, rescuing drowning men, guiding or towing them safe to shore. In return, humanity has generally recognised the dolphin as divine or semi-divine. In Celtic myth it was associated with well-worship and the power of the sea; in **Egypt** it was an attribute of the Goddess **Isis**; in Greece it was thought to guide souls to the Isles of the Blessed, and possessed erotic symbolism in association with Aphrodite, the Goddess of Love who rose from the waves. The Greek goddess Thetis rode naked on a dolphin, which also represented the feminine principle and the womb due to the assonance between *delphis* (dolphin) and *delphys* (womb). In addition it was a masculine attribute of the gods Poseidon (sea-power), Dionysus and Apollo Delphinos, the light of the sun. To the Romans it represented the soul's journey over the sea of death: more anciently, the Sumerians used it as an alternative to the fish as image of the being Oannes, said to have emerged from the ocean bringing civilisation to humanity.[1] Further east, in the **Hindu** *Shrimad Bhagavatum*, the dolphin's body is recognised as one especially well-suited for spiritual pleasures: elsewhere in this same text the sphere of the heavens is said to represent the shape of a dolphin.[2]

The dolphin's friendliness, remarked on by Plutarch and Oppian 2,000 years ago, is today apparent in 'dolphinariums' round the world, or as in cases like the wild dolphin Opo, who in 1955–6 befriended many bathers at Oponami in New Zealand (especially children), before stranding herself on the shore and asphyxiating. It seems she died because she liked people too much. Likewise the coastal **Aborigines** of Australia still ask the dolphin to help them catch fish, claiming that when they beat the water with pieces of wood, the dolphins respond by driving fish inshore.

As to their intelligence, Dr John **Lilly** insists that a bottle-nosed dolphin has learned to speak English, albeit with a strong Hungarian accent apparently derived from Dr Kert, the Hungarian-born physicist leading a research team at Marine World in Redwood City, California, in the 1980s.

The size-ratio of a dolphin's neocortex to its limbic system is greater than in most human beings. They may be more 'intelligent' than we are, but their playful, ecstatic intelligence lacks the malignity often manifested by humankind. Certainly, today we take advantage of this friendly creature in ways that would appal our ancestors. Where not wiped out by pollution or by asphyxiation in fish-nets, or caught to entertain us, the dolphin is *intelligently* trained to further human prowess in undersea warfare.

In 1984, ex-naval US naval intelligence officer C. B. 'Scott' Jones, working in Galveston, Texas, with a bottle-nosed Atlantic dolphin, conducted interspecies **telepathic** communication tests. Of six sets of instructions sent by human transmitter to the dolphin, the outcome of four were agreed as hits, the dolphin carrying out instructions as designed and in the time requested. Another outcome was correct, but was achieved *before* the human transmitter opened the sealed instructions. The dolphin knew better than the man what was going on.[3]

Currently the world's dolphin population is at risk of extermination due to human greed and stupidity. It is worth remembering that in ancient Greece the slaying of a dolphin was considered an act of murder.

1. *Illustrated Encyclopaedia of Traditional Symbols*, J. C. Cooper, Thames and Hudson, London 1984
2. *The Phoenix Returns*, Kristina Gale-Kumar, Cardinal Enterprises, Hawaii 1983, pp. 181–4
3. *Intangible Evidence*, Bernard Gittelson, Simon and Schuster, London 1987

DON JUAN (*See* **CASTANEDA, Carlos**)

DOPPELGÄNGERS (*See* **CRISIS APPARITION, *KA*, POWYS, STRINDBERG**) Doppelgängers – 'doubles' or 'phantasms of the living' – are commonly reported but remain mysterious. They may take the form of the crisis apparition, as in cases where the distinct image of a distant loved one, at that moment on the point of death or in mortal peril, suddenly appears before their family or friends. Yet crisis is not invariably involved, and on occasion the double may be projected consciously without the projector knowing how the apparition is created. **Telepathy** seems to be involved, and usually a close emotional link between 'projector' and 'perceiver'.

American writer Theodore Dreiser told how, one evening in his New York apartment, British novelist John Cowper **Powys**, leaving after a convivial evening to catch a train home, said, 'I'll appear before you, right here, later this evening. You'll see me.' Dreiser laughed. 'Are you going to turn yourself into a **ghost**, or have you a key to the door?' Powys said: 'I don't know. I may return as a **spirit** or in some other astral form.' Two hours later Dreiser looked up from his book to see Powys in the doorway, surrounded by a pale white glow. Approaching the ghost he said: 'Well, you've kept your word, John. You're here. Come on in and tell me how you did it.' The spectre vanished. Dreiser then phoned Powys at his country home. 'I told you I'd be there, and you oughtn't to be surprised,' said Powys. Dreiser later said that Powys refused to discuss this event, perhaps because he didn't understand it himself.[1]

Dangerously ill in Paris in 1895 and longing to be home in Sweden, playwright August Strindberg projected the apparition of himself into his distant home. His mother saw it and wrote to ask if he was ill. In this case a form of crisis apparition was involved, caused by the desperate emotional longing of the projector.

In other cases the 'double' appears without its originator's knowledge. French teacher Emilie Sagée lost eighteen jobs in sixteen years because her 'double' kept appearing where she wasn't. Once, picking flowers in a garden in view of girls whose teacher had left the room, her double occupied the teacher's chair. Later she said she had noticed the teacher was away and had felt worried about class discipline. In this case, projection was unconscious, as it may also be in many cases of hauntings by ghosts.

At Christmas 1973 this author tried such a projection from Scotland to London. For twenty minutes I concentrated on visualising the interior of the house into which I had lately moved, and on imagining myself there amid the social activity of the evening. The purpose was trivial: it was to say 'Happy Christmas' to my new flat-mates, none of whom I knew very well. But it was in another London house that suddenly my girlfriend and her mother both clearly heard the clatter of my typewriter from an upstairs room where I'd lived and worked a year earlier. There was no mistaking the staccato rhythm that typifies my typing. They rushed upstairs, but of course the room was empty. Disturbed, aware of the circumstances under which crisis apparitions can occur, they rang immediately to find out if I was well. The phone, by which I had been sitting, rang as I stood up on abandoning the effort. It is curious that the projection apparently worked, but was perceived not visually but in auditory form, and not by those for whom it was intended, but by two people with whom I had close emotional links.

1. *The Occult*, Colin Wilson, Grafton, London 1979, pp. 67–9

DOWSING (*See* **EARTH SPIRIT, GEOMANCY, LEY LINES, MAGNETISM**) Dowsers are widely employed to seek out underground water, minerals, buried artefacts or power cable failures. In general they do so by walking over the chosen site holding a forked stick, L-shaped rods or a **pendulum**. At the key point, the 'divining rod' twists in the hand. If a pendulum is used, it starts to twirl. But pendulum or rod are secondary: they only amplify bodily responses to the subtle forces involved. These, probably magnetic, are in varying degrees registered by all living organisms on Earth.

Research by Dutch geologist Solco Tromp, and by Czechoslovak physicist Dr Zaboj V. Harvalik, shows that the human body functions as a magnetic detector. Tiny variations in the earth's magnetic field cause muscular 'twitches' that promote visible reaction in rod or **pendulum**.

English dowser Guy Underwood held the art to be 'the sensation of **electromagnetic** radiations' emanating from the earth's core. He held that varying frequencies of this 'earth force' result from its interruption by faults and rock fissures, creating energetic patterns to which the dowser reacts. He found that 'water lines' or underground streams as tracked by dowsers often converge at 'knots' under sacred sites marked by churches or **megalithic** henges, where the 'earth force' is strongest. His findings strongly support a connection between 'water lines' and ley lines.[1]

That perception of this 'earth force' as a natural biological function is strongly suggested by plant and animal behaviour. Offshoots from main subterranean water lines ('whorls') are called 'positive' or 'negative' nodes. Gnats and other insects hover above positive nodes, returning if blown away. Ants build their nests, bees swarm, and wild animals prefer to give birth at these locations. Negatives nodes ('black springs') are favoured by plants or trees like the weeping willow, but adversely affect the health of people in houses ignorantly built over them. Mice placed in an enclosure half on and half off such a zone will not sleep in it. Celery, cucumbers, onions, maize and ash trees hardly grow at all in such areas.[2]

Learning that his dowsing rod reacted to electrical current, Harvalik experimented on friends. He found *all* could dowse a current stronger than 20 milliamps, and some a current as low as 2 milliamps; most improved with practice. Sensitivity increased if the dowser drank water before dowsing; a shot of whisky drunk by non-dowsers stimulated their latent faculty just by relaxing the body. Work with German dowser Wilhelm de Boer suggested that the water-detecting organ involved in dowsing is the adrenal gland. He found that aluminium foil wound round the head above the ears blocks the signals, as does a square of foil pasted on the centre of the forehead.

De Boer can detect signals down to a thousandth of a milliamp, and can also dowse different radio stations. Harvalik told him which frequency to look for: de Boer turned until facing the chosen station. Harvalik himself has shown how accurate dowsers can be. He not only indicated the direction and distance (12.6 miles) of a reservoir in Sydney, Australia, but, asked by the water board engineer the depth of water in the reservoir, estimated sixty-eight feet. Checking his booklet, the engineer said the depth was seventy-five feet. On visiting the reservoir they found the water down by seven feet.[3]

Expert dowsers can *choose* what they want to locate; 'tuning in' on the precise signal of water, or gold, or even bodily remains in a long-lost burial site. This may be no more remarkable than our 'normal' capacity to hear a particular conversation in a noisy bar.[4] Yet it raises questions.

T. C. **Lethbridge** tried to answer some of them by practical experiment. In his books this ex-Director of Excavations for the Cambridge Antiquarian Society explained how a pendulum may be tuned to 'some field or force round a given object' by setting it to respond only to that object.

Seeking truffles, he found a 'rate' of seventeen inches; meaning a pendulum held at the end of a seventeen-inch cord reacted to truffles. Testing this 'rate', he found that the larva of the *Bolboceras* beetle (it feeds on truffles) also caused reaction at the seventeen-inch rate. So did beech trees and beech nuts, on which grows the truffle mycelium. Dung beetles and cowpats both responded to the sixteen-inch rate. Testing his pendulum over a *painting* of dung beetles, he found it responded – at the sixteen-inch rate. Testing over a *painting* of *Bolboceras*, it responded – at the seventeen-inch rate.[5]

Map-dowsing is even odder. How, seeking minerals or missing persons, can a dowser gain information by moving a pendulum over a map until, at a particular point, it reacts? What has this to do with electromagnetism or the adrenals? A map is a **symbolic** construct. Yet map-dowsing works. Does the human thought involved in creating the symbol (map) somehow 'charge' the map (or painting) with the 'rate' of the landscape depicted? What is going on? This question is considered separately.

'Is everything,' Lethbridge asked, 'man, beast, bird, fish, tree and rock directly under control by the Earth itself? Does the Earth arrange how they shall be formed and how they shall develop?'

Such ideas remain radical. Yet there is mounting evidence that our bodies respond to energetic processes the existence of which orthodox science still refuses to recognise. But whatever the *how* and *why* of it, one thing *is* generally accepted – dowsing works.

1. *Needles of Stone Revisited*, Tom Graves, Gothic Image, Glastonbury 1986, p. 24
2. *Supernature*, Lyall Watson, Hodder and Stoughton, London 1973, p. 115
3. *The Divining Hand*, Christopher Bird, Dutton, New York 1973, p. 273
4. *Beyond the Occult*, Colin Wilson, Corgi, London 1989, p. 158
5. *A Step in the Dark*, T. C. Lethbridge, Routledge Kegan Paul, London 1967, p. 13ff.

DOYLE, Sir Arthur Conan (1859–1930) (*See* **COTTINGLEY FAIRIES, HOUDINI**) The creator of Sherlock Holmes, the world's most rational fictional sleuth, was fascinated by the supernatural. Born in Edinburgh and brought up Roman Catholic, Conan Doyle trained as a doctor. Practising medicine from 1882, by 1890 the growing popularity of his Sherlock Holmes stories led him into full-time writing and, increasingly, the pursuit of his **psychic** interests. Latterly he embraced **Spiritualism** and **parapsychological** research, being convinced of life after death when at a **séance** in 1919 he heard the voice of his dead son, Kingsley, and with two other observers saw the apparition of his mother and a nephew.

That same year he took up the case of the Cottingley Fairies. His assertion in a *Strand Magazine* article that the 'fairy photographs' taken by Frances and Elsie Griffiths were genuine did his reputation no good, yet he persisted in his stance. In 1920 he met the escapologist Harry Houdini: the two men liked each other. Yet Houdini, wishing to unmask all **mediums** as frauds, thought Doyle hopelessly gullible. Doyle, though not disputing that Houdini was 'a very skilful conjurer', insisted that he was not only 'the greatest medium-baiter' of modern times, but 'the greatest physical medium'.[1] He claimed that the speed and consistency with which Houdini routinely performed complex, death-defying feats indicated psychic powers of which Houdini himself was either unaware or driven to deny. Certainly no stage-magician since has been able to duplicate Houdini's feats.

A member of the **Society for Psychical Research**, Doyle became president of the London **Spiritualist** Alliance, the British College of Psychic Science and the Spiritualist Community. He travelled the world lecturing on the subject, showing slides from his vast collection of **spirit photographs**, and until the day he died lobbied for more liberal laws regarding mediums.

1. *The Edge of the Unknown*, Sir Arthur Conan Doyle, John Murray, London 1930

DRAGON (*See* **DOWSING, EARTH SPIRIT, GEOMANCY, LEY LINES**) Here too **symbol** coincides not only with mysteries of earth-energy but with variant human perceptions. The dragon, or 'winged **serpent**', is a complex metaphor for the relationship between matter, spirit and energy. In the first place the dragon represents life-giving energies; the fertilisation of Earth/Water (serpent) by Air/Fire (**bird**, phoenix).

In Eastern symbolism dragon and serpent are one, representing wisdom, benevolent heavenly power, and the fertilising earth-currents (*lung mei;* now in the West identified with ley lines). A dragon emerging from the Yellow River, the alphabet inscribed on its back, brought literacy to China (as Thoth/Hermes brought literacy to Egypt/Greece). It became the imperial emblem; the Son of Heaven. The two 'contending dragons', are the **yin-yang** forces of **dualism**, as with Egyptian Set and **Osiris**. Neither are **'evil'**: each represent Nature's necessarily polarised potencies that in contention lead to creation. Ever-energetic, the Eastern dragon was never demonised.

But in the **Christian** West, since the Serpent was blamed for the Fall, the dragon has been seen not as winged fertility symbol but as 'loathly worm', or the **Devil**, a sterile guardian of buried treasure (lost **pagan** knowledge?), and as an Enemy fought by (solar) heroes from St George and Beowulf to Bilbo the Hobbit. It persists as national symbol of the Welsh (the Red Dragon), and as symbol of lightning, mountain-tops and high places controlled (as at **Glastonbury**) by St Michael, a solar dragon-slayer. The lance of the dragon-slayer, like the stake driven through the **vampire**'s heart, 'fixes' the serpent current (earth-spirit) in one location, so as artificially to increase the earth's fertility. How we regard the dragon depends on whether we wish to *control* and *alter* Nature or *accept* what She brings us. In trying to control dragon-Nature, we make an enemy of it/her. So long as we fear or demonise the dragon we cannot love or tend the Earth: indeed, we seek to spear our own nature through the heart.

DREAMS In the first dream recorded in the Bible Jacob saw a ladder reaching from earth to heaven, 'the **angels** of God ascending and descending it', and above it God telling him 'I am with thee.' This is the source of all the Bible's visionary material. But what does it mean? What is a dream?

C. G. **Jung** wrote, 'The dream is a fragment of involuntary **psychic** activity, just conscious enough to be reproducible in the waking state,' and went on, 'Of all psychic phenomena the dream presents perhaps the largest number of "irrational" factors. . . . Dreams that form logically, morally, or aesthetically satisfying wholes are exceptional. Usually a dream is a strange and disconcerting product distinguished by . . . lack of logic, questionable morality, uncouth form, and apparent absurdity or nonsense.'[1] He thought '[It] probable that we continually dream, but consciousness makes, while waking, such a noise that we do not hear it'.

All mammals dream. The opossum sleeps twenty hours a day and dreams for ten, its dreams apparently simulating (practising?) flight from danger. Prey-animals dream less; their predators (more secure?) dream more. Cats, especially lions, enjoy long dreams. Dreaming as wish-fulfilment may also occur in most mammals, as with the whimpering, twitching dog chasing dream-rabbits. 'Of what', asks a proverb, 'do geese dream?' The answer: 'Maize'.

Humans like other mammals dream several times each sleep session, in 'active sleep', as distinct from 'quiet sleep'. Active sleep involves short rapid brain waves, irregular heart beat, and rapid eye movement (REM) behind closed lids. REM is usually associated with dreaming, though dreams may occur independently of it. Dreaming begins after an initial period of quiet sleep; the dreams we remember are usually those that precede waking. Children woken from active sleep are soon alert, but are usually confused if aroused from quiet sleep. The foetus seems to spend most of its time dreaming; it appears that this persistent stimulation leads directly to the rapid development of the mammalian brain and central nervous system.[2]

Dream-activity may invade the waking mind, as in day-dreaming; or as hypnogogic imagery between sleep and waking. Here, the distinction between dream and **hallucination** is unclear; both involve the image-making faculty, which may be lost due to injury. Vivid waking dreaming has been reported in a patient after cingulectomy, an operation involving removal of part of the brain, and also following use of the tranquillising drug librium.[3]

Conversely, waking **consciousness** may persist amid sleep and dream. In this state (*lucid dreaming*), dream-content may be consciously influenced. The Russian occultist P. D. **Ouspensky**, dreaming he was in a room with a black kitten, decided: 'If I am dreaming, let me transform this kitten into a dog.' Instantly the kitten became a large black dog; the wall vanished to reveal a mountain landscape. He tried to remember why the landscape was familiar but knew if he tried too hard he would forget he was dreaming and fall into a true dream. Then he felt himself flying backwards and awoke.[4]

Since ancient times much has been made of the **symbolic** aspect of dreams. Flying dreams, dreams of flood, or of transformation into animal form; dreams of the dead and sexual dreams – all have been interpreted, as by **Freud** and Jung, in differing ways. For where both these great modern psychoanalysts saw dream-symbols as a royal road to understanding the unconscious mind, Freud interpreted such symbols solely in terms of sexual conflict, whereas Jung saw them as the text of a primordial language. He wrote: 'The dream is a little hidden door in the innermost and most secret recesses of the psyche, opening into that cosmic night which was psyche long before there was any ego consciousness.'[5] In this he was (as in so much else) in tune with the experience of all 'primitive' societies.

In the 1930s anthropologist Kilton Stewart reported how, among the **Senoi** of Malaysia, daily dream-analysis maintained a healthy society. The Senoi claimed they had known no crime, murder or intercommunal conflict in over 300 years.[6] They said sexual dreams should move through to orgasm; that in falling dreams the dreamer should let himself fall (a rapid way to contact the spirit-world); and that a dreamer endangered in a dream should advance and attack, calling friends for help if needed. The enemy thus killed or overcome would become the dreamer's friend or ally. The Senoi approach mirrors that of other ancient cultures, such as the **Aborigines** with their Dreamtime. 'You know', a Kalahari hunter told Laurens van der Post, 'there is a dream dreaming us.'[7]

Similarly, Jung comments that: 'One does not dream, one is dreamed. We undergo the dream, we are the objects.' Yet despite his work we in the West still have little understanding of our dreams; a failure leading to mental illness and 'loss of meaning'. We see dreaming as a garbage-dump for the day's events, or as a fragmentary, meaningless state of semi-consciousness.

Cases of **precognitive** dreaming suggest otherwise. John Godley, later Lord Kilbracken, while an Oxford undergraduate in 1946, began dreaming of future race-track winners. In his first dream he read racing results in Saturday's evening paper and saw that two horses, *Bindal* and *Juladin*, had both won at 7 to 1. The next day was Saturday. He got the papers and found both horses due to run. He told his friends; bets were placed; the horses won. Later dreams proved equally accurate. One time he wrote down a prediction, had it timed, witnessed, and taken to a Post Office, where it was sealed in an envelope, stamped by the Postmaster, and locked up in a Post Office safe. Both his horses won as predicted.

When at his sister's house in St Louis, American writer Mark Twain dreamed he saw his brother Henry laid out dead in the sitting room, in a metallic coffin set on two chairs, a bouquet of flowers on his breast with a single crimson bloom in the centre. On awaking he told his sister about it. Weeks later the boilers exploded on the *Pennsylvania*, a ship carrying Henry up the Mississippi from New Orleans. Fatally injured, Henry died in Memphis, where ladies of the city provided a metal coffin (the other dead were given simple wooden coffins). When Twain viewed Henry's body in Memphis, he found it as in his dream, save there was no bouquet. Even as he stood there a woman entered and laid on Henry's breast a bouquet of white flowers with one red rose in the centre. The one discrepancy between reality and the dream was that fulfilment came in Memphis, not St Louis.

J. W. **Dunne**'s *An Experiment With Time* details many precognitive dreams, like that of the man in 1879 who left a train at the last stop before the Tay Bridge, which then collapsed with the train on it. He had dreamed of the disaster. More recently on 21 October 1966 at Aberfan in Wales a coal-tip avalanched, killing 144 people including 128 children. Over 200 people claimed foresight of the disaster. Many had dreamed of the event, several such premonitions being written down before it occurred.[8]

Many artists have profited by dream-inspiration. Coleridge composed 'Kubla Khan' in a dream but as he wrote it down was disturbed by the infamous visitor from Porlock and forgot the rest. R. L. Stevenson's *Dr Jekyll and Mr Hyde* began in a dream. Science likewise offers examples of dream-borne insight. Nineteenth-century chemist Friedrich von Kekulé spent years seeking the molecular structure of benzene. In 1865, dozing in his carriage, he dreamed of snakelike chains of atoms, one swallowing its own tail (like the Worm Ourobouros, the mythic **archetype**). He awoke realising the structure of benzene was a closed carbon ring. Physicist Niels Bohr first realised his model of the atom through a dream: inventor Elias Howe developed the sewing machine following a dream in which cannibals, giving him twenty-four hours to invent the machine or else provide them with their supper, danced round him with spears which, he saw, had eye-shaped holes near their tips.

No wonder so many ancient (and some modern) cultures thought of dreams as divine messages, as in Jacob's Dream of the Ladder linking heaven and earth, the angels both ascending and descending it. Laurens van der Post asserts that this dream meant that from then on humankind and the source of its meaning ('God') would forever be in communication, creator and created in partnership – a two-way affair.[9]

Such partnership is impossible for cultures so benighted they deny the meaning and purpose of their dreams, or else try to interpret them through the needle's eye of left-brain logic and reason alone. Ill-health and self-destruction are the inevitable results. We ignore our dreams at our peril. For when we dream, like Jacob's angels we can move freely up and down the ladder of mind, released from the space/time jail in which our waking intellectual consciousness imprisons itself. Deny our dreams and we throw away the key to the door of our cell.

1. *Dreams*, C. G. Jung, Ark Books, London 1985, p. 68
2. *Lifetide*, Lyall Watson, Coronet Books, London 1980, pp. 222–243
3. *The Natural History of the Mind*, Gordon Rattray Taylor, Granada, London 1981, p. 219.
4. Quoted in *Mysteries*, Colin Wilson, Grafton Books, London 1979, p. 370
5. *Civilisation in Transition*, C. G. Jung, Collected Works, Vol. 10, Princeton University Press, Princeton, New Jersey
6. *Pygmies and Dream Giants*, Kilton Stewart
7. *Jung and the Story of our Time*, Laurens van der Post, Penguin, London 1978
8. *A Sense of Something Strange*, Archie E. Roy, Dog and Bone Press, Glasgow 1990, pp. 96–8, 116–7, 127–37
9. *op. cit.*, ref. 7, p. 6

DREAMTIME (*See* **ABORIGINES**)

DRUGS (*See* **CASTANEDA, LEARY, LILLY, SHAMANISM, VOODOO**) Aldous **Huxley**'s *The Doors of Perception* described his experience of *mescalin*, the active alkaloid of the peyotl cactus, when he first took it in 1953. It ushered in the modern interest in 'mind-expanding' drugs.

In fact **hallucinogenic** drugs have been used since time immemorial to enter **out-of-body** or **trance** states, to prophesy or converse with spirits. In Mexico the *peyotil* cactus has been used since Aztec times; a century ago Dr Rafael Bayon, working in Colombia, claimed that peyote-drinking shamans could see distant events. *Psilocybin*, the active agent of the Mexican sacred mushroom *Psilocybe Mexicana; ololiuqui*, the South American morning glory; *teonanacatl*, a mushroom found on cowpats; *caapi*, an Amazonian vine chemically identical to *yageine, harmine* and *banisterine* – all these drugs have long been used in the Americas. Psilocybin, peyote and *yerba del diablo* (Jimson Weed) were used by Don Juan, the Mexican *brujo* (sorcerer) made famous by Carlos Castaneda. *Bufotenin*, a venomous secretion of certain toads is chemically identical to **serotonin**. Nature provides many mind-changing drugs.

One such used world-wide to attain trance-vision was *amanita muscaria* (fly agaric). Drunk as an infusion in Siberia, among the ancient Celts this poisonous white-spotted red mushroom (often featured in fairy tales) was called 'food of the gods' or 'hundred-spotted toad'. Viking warriors chewed it to cause berserk battle-rage: scholar John M. Allegro associated it with his thesis that **Christianity** was originally a mushroom cult.

Many other naturally occurring drugs have been used to stimulate a wide variety of 'paranormal' effects from vision to forgetfulness. Tetradoxin causes 'out of the body' sensations and, in large doses, apparent death. Found in blowfish tissue, this notorious 'fugu' poison of Japan is esteemed as an aphrodisiac. It also forms the core of the Haitian **zombie** poison.

The range of such substances and their effects is enormous. Enough to say that people have always used any means to hand to alter their mental states – even the humble English hop plant contains a hallucinogen – and that casual experimentation may prove dangerous.

DRUIDS (*See* **CELTIC MAGIC**) 'It is especially the object of the Druids to inculcate this', wrote Julius Caesar in *De Bello Gallico*, speaking of the Celtic priesthood, 'that souls do not perish, but after death pass into other bodies, and they consider that by this belief more than anything else men may be led to cast away the fear of death and become courageous. They discuss many points concerning heavenly bodies and their motion, the extent of the universe and the world, the nature of things, the influence and ability of the immortal gods; and they instruct the youth in these things.'

Reaching Western Europe a full millennium after the final decline of the **megalith**-builders, the Celts acknowledged their mysterious predecessors as representing a greater wisdom. Yet Druid teachings were respected. Many Romans sent their children to be educated at the Druid colleges in Ireland. The three orders of Druidism comprised bards (poets), *vates* (augurers), and Druids (philosophers). Training involved a minimum of seven years arduous apprenticeship. A bard had to memorise some 500 tales or poems to qualify; a bardic **curse** was feared by kings even into historical times; the modern Irish respect for 'the word' (of power) may descend from this.

The name 'druid' may derive from the Welsh *derw*, 'oak'; thus, 'men of the oak'. Maybe they revered the oak for its connection with lightning (growing above water, it attracts it) and mistletoe as a plant growing on the oak, on the fire-tree. Never touching the earth, it symbolises Man, who lives between heaven and earth.

The Druids were said to be able to cast dense fogs, raise storms, take animal form and create illusion by 'glamouring' the eyes of men. By the rite of *taghairm*, wrapped up all night in a newly flayed bull-skin, they would emerge at dawn roaring and prophesying. By the *'fith-fath'* spell, standing on one leg, pointing with one finger with one eye shut, they could cast invisibility about themselves. They were said to carry a '**serpent**'s egg'; a **crystal** ball capable of defusing curses; and to carry yew-staffs with magic powers. The archetypal druid was later personified in the form and **myth** of the wizard **Merlin** – born of **demons**, **seer** and commander of **dragon** powers and, though finally defeated by female wiles, never killed but suspended in a crystal cave to return at a future time – at least in the potency of myth, as in Boorman's *Excalibur, That Hideous Strength* by C. S. Lewis, and so on.

Such myth not only marries with their doctrine of **reincarnation** but with the way their beliefs were superseded by **Christianity**. The tale of St Patrick's magical battle with the Irish Druids is as well known as the Druid prophecy of Christ's coming. Perhaps the latter was invented by an Irish monk *c.* AD 700. After all, the monks of the Celtic Church inherited Druid tradition. Even after the Synod of Whitby (AD 664) many Celtic monks maintained not the Roman but the Druid tonsure (shaving not the crown but the forehead in an ear-to-ear line), and did not easily take to celibacy or hierarchic rule. As the descendants of Druids turned Christian hermit, alias *culdee* (Gaelic *cil*, 'cell', *dee, deus*, 'god'), they recorded what by then was already all but lost in the mists of the past. Today many tales of Celtic and Druid magic remain extant. As for those modern white-robed 'Druids' greeting midsummer sunrise at Stonehenge today, they have as much connection with true Druidry as Hollywood (*via* Indiana Jones) has with the **Holy Grail**. Still, the memory persists.

DRYADS (*See* **ELEMENTALS, LETHBRIDGE**)

DUALISM (*See* **CATHARISM, GNOSTICISM**) A philosophy derived from the old belief in the existence of two co-equal universal powers of good and evil, alias light and dark, dualism regards the material world as a creation of the dark, or evil power; and thus the appetites of the flesh as a distraction from spiritual life. It permeates European thought from Pythagoras (sixth century BC) to the **Cathars** (twelfth century AD), en route affecting the philosophy of the **Essenes**, Gnostics, **Neo-Platonists** and **Manichaeans**. Continuously opposed during the last two millennia by the Christian Church, dualism cannot be said to have perished, being in the first place a spontaneous, **archetypal** human reaction to the *natural* dualism inherent in the succession of Day and Night, Life and Death, and other oppositions routinely observed by human intelligence.

DUNNE, J. W. (1875–1949) (*See* **DREAMS, PRECOGNITION**) An aeronautics engineer convinced of his destiny to bring humanity an important message, one night in 1899 he dreamed his watch stopped at half past four. He awoke to find this had happened. This was the first of many precognitive dreams convincing him that in dreams the human mind can foresee the future. Collecting dreams from friends he concluded that many of them symbolically presented distorted fragments of everyday experience, and that such fragments were as easily drawn from the future as the past. In 1927 he published *An Experiment With Time*, describing precognitive dreams. In 1940, in *Nothing Dies*, he presented the notion of a serial universe. In this he argued for precognition on the basis that time flows like a river. This idea is dismissed today but his work with dreams remains influential.

An Experiment With Time, J. W. Dunne, Macmillan, London 1981

DWARVES (*See* **ELEMENTALS, FAIRIES**) Traditional European tales of human interaction with dwarf races cannot be simply dismissed as fantastical folklore. After all, pygmy peoples still inhabit tropical African rain-forests. Despite denial by most historians and archaeologists, European legends of dwarves as a small, dark, muscular race skilled at war and in metal-working may have a factual basis. Biblical, Indian and Celtic texts describing these folk abound. In the eleventh century Adam of Bremen described this race, inhabiting Northern Europe before the Celtic invasions, as having 'large heads, flat faces, flat noses, and large mouths'. They were also described as 'black people'. It seems not impossible that, in the warm climate of the megalithic era, the descendants of folk now found only in Africa ranged further north, before being driven south by chill weather and invasion. The problem today in accepting such a thesis (as in accepting the historical reality of elves, pixies, etc.) lies in the way such beings have been relegated to the realms of **'fairy tale'**, magical romance, and folklore of a sort no longer taken seriously as true historical memory. Yet it should be noted that in many areas folklore and the oral tradition have proved quite remarkably accurate in passing on the unwritten history of our ancestors.

E

EARTH SPIRIT (*See* **DOWSING, GAIA, GEOMANCY, LEY LINES**) 'The earth is not a dead body,' declared the mediaeval alchemist Basilius Valentinus, 'but is inhabited by a spirit that is its life and soul. All created things, minerals included, draw their strength from the earth spirit. This spirit is life, it is nourished by the stars.'[1]

The spirit of 'Mother Earth' was honoured by all ancient peoples. To mine or otherwise violate her body was thought sacrilege. Where mining was needed, e.g., to acquire red ochre (haematite: *blood of the earth*), **ritual** propitiation was conducted; later the mine was filled in; the wound in her body healed. To do otherwise was to court disaster by upsetting the balance of the **spirit** energies pervading matter. Certain 'primitive' peoples have maintained this opinion in the face of Western materialism. 'You ask me to plough the ground. Shall I take a knife and tear my mother's breast?' asked American Indian prophet Smohalla. Today such a view no longer seems so odd.

The remote Kogi people of Colombia, tending a region they call the Heart of the World, having noted the dearth of vegetation on the high peaks of their land (from drought perhaps due to global warming), lately abandoned their long social seclusion to warn the world that the Earth is dying due to industrial pollution and our ignorance of the earth spirit.[2]

How did we forget about it? Settled in cities, folk lost their innate relationship with nature's energies and **cycles**. Rural wisdom was categorised as folklore and fairy tale; reason denied whatever could not be weighed and measured. The process was gradual. Catholic *conquistadors* destroyed entire human societies but at least rededicated the holy places of those conquered, for the health of the land and those living in it. They were guided by the female image of the Virgin Mary. But the Protestants who seized North America scorned Earth Mother notions as **pagan**, fey or silly. They took but did not give: today we inherit an 'energy-crisis'.

Now old notions of *power-places, holy wells* and *spirit-paths* revive. Traditionally such sites are marked by reports of **psychic** activity; rural folk in Ireland and elsewhere termed certain paths **fairy** paths, marking a seasonal flow of telluric energy. Those obstructing or building on such paths risked illness or worse. Now it is known that people living by high-frequency power cables are more prone to suicide; the belief that certain places are good or bad for the health again makes good sense. In England, 'green ways' and 'old straight tracks' are associated with **ghosts, black dog** apparitions, and so on. Such traditions suggest remnants of knowledge of the magnetic currents that follow geodetic lines at known times of the year. Cosmically orchestrated, these currents flow through the Earth, as **ch'i** (or **prāna**, or the *wouivre*, or **dragon** current, etc.) flows through human bodies. The properties of streams, lakes and rivers vary seasonally, as Ovid remarks in the *Metamorphoses*; shrines, oracular sites like Delphi, and other centres always regarded as holy all have a specific season of power when the 'god' or spirit is in residence.

1. *The Earth Spirit*, John Michell, Avon Books, New York 1975, p. 4.
2. 'From the Heart of the World', BBC1 TV, London, 4 December 1990

EARTHWORKS (*See* **EARTH SPIRIT, MEGALITHIC MYSTERIES**)

Evidence of ancient earth spirit worship is found globally in the form of huge earthworks often associated with human burial but sometimes seeming purely **symbolic**. The Ohio **serpent**-mound, weaving over hundreds of yards of ground, is one of many American animal effigy mounds best viewed from the air. Invoking the fertility symbolism of egg and serpent, the Ohio mound may have been meant to procure in reality the fertility it symbolised.

In England the huge mound of Silbury Hill, near Avebury in Wiltshire, is said by some to represent the pregnant Earth-goddess. 130 feet high, covering five acres, its flat top 100 feet across, this largest of European prehistoric man-made mounds is dated *c.* 2750 BC – later than Newgrange in Ireland and Callanish in the Outer Hebrides, but before **Stonehenge**. That it was a burial mound remains unproven; yet it is a centre for alignments of standing stones and straight tracks associated with **ley lines** and the flow of geomagnetic current. In China such mounds were erected on **dragon**-paths *lung mei* (*see* **geomancy**). Silbury's connection with the pregnant Earth-goddess may be no more fantastic than claims that its atmosphere is sometimes 'evil'.[1]

Of the other 40,000 or so earth-mounds surviving in Britain alone, many *do* contain burials. Others were apparently erected on sacred sites as the meeting (*moot*) mounds of a locality. Tales of **fairies** or **giants** attach to many, indicating not only the awe in which generations of people have held their unknown builders, but also their association with **psychic** phenomena. The 'giant' connection may arise from the vast labour obviously involved in their building. Some hills of oddly artificial appearance (like Butthouse Knapp in Herefordshire) or capped by prominent earthworks (the Wrekin in Shropshire) are said to have been created by the Devil; **Glastonbury** Tor is another hill which appears too regular to be natural: some occultists claim that the paths winding up round the hill constitute an initiatory maze.

Many *long barrows* (some over 300 feet) are said to have giants buried in them: tradition claims that some when opened have disclosed skeletons of men over 8 feet tall. Archaeologists are still confused by these barrows; their stone burial chambers occupy only a tiny part, the rest seemingly consisting only of earth.[2] Even more mysterious are Britain's so-called 'hill forts'; some 1500 in England alone. These often consist (as at Croft Ambrey in Herefordshire) of great hilltop enclosures surrounded by steep earth banks and ditches. They are called 'Iron Age', and thought to be defensive sites, though few appear to have been used as such.

Strangest of all are North Scotland's *vitrified* hill-forts, like Tap O' Noth in Aberdeenshire. A steep climb up this bare hill (1,848 feet) brings you to a summit area the size of a football field, banked about by a wall of tumbled boulders, many fused into a glassy slag. The heat required to vitrify them must have been not only intense but sustained. One can just envisage timber-laced walls set alight to burn for months amid some ancient war. But where did the timber come from? The slopes are bare for 750 feet below. Was neolithic Scotland warmer? Did forests grow to the top of such now-barren hills? Even odder, in many such sites (over fifty are known) the vitrification suggests a burning *from above*. Fire from heaven? Having struggled up to such a site one realises the improbability of keeping such a fire going for months, round a 300–yard perimeter, at the temperatures needed to fuse loose stones into the slag still visible today.

Apart from *how, why* was it done? The questions remain. Were there 'giants in those days'? Even the name *Tap o' Noth* is mysterious. Does it echo *Gwyn ap Nudd*, ancient Welsh God of the Dead? For Welsh was certainly spoken in 'Scotland' before the Anglo-Saxon conquests – and, like Silbury, Tap o' Noth can strike the heart with an inexplicable terror, as expressed in local woman Betty Allan's poem about her visit there: 'Ghaists o' Noth'.

> Some ither mither's terror, strang and stairk,
> Cauldrife and seenister, smored me aa aboot;

An eldritch dreid, a fleg [fright] the likes o me
Could niver ken in my douce, ordered life.[3]

1. *The New View over Atlantis*, John Michell, Thames and Hudson, London 1983
2. *Mysterious Britain*, Janet and Colin Bord, Paladin, London 1974, pp. 69ff
3. *Discovering Aberdeenshire*, Robert Smith, John Donald, Edinburgh 1988

EGYPT (*See* **GREAT PYRAMID, KA, ISIS, OSIRIS, PYRAMID PROPHECIES**) Ancient Egypt has exercised its **occult** fascination for over two millennia. Sphinx, pyramids, pharaohs, exotic animal-headed gods and goddesses, the preoccupation with afterlife and mummification of the dead, the Mysteries of Isis and Osiris: even the origin of the land once called Khem ('black earth': thus **al*chemy*** and *chem*istry) still evokes a mystique stimulated by Hollywood epics, pyramidological theory, Tutankhamun's **curse**, and so on.

The romance began in Greece. 'Oh Solon, Solon,' said the old Egyptian priest of Saïs claimed in **Plato's Timaeus** as the source of the **Atlantis** tale, 'you Greeks are all children . . . You are all young in mind, you have no belief rooted in old tradition and no knowledge hoary with age.'

Describing to Solon ancient cataclysms recalled only by the Egyptians, the priest continued, 'The age of our institutions is given in our sacred records as 8,000 years, and the citizens whose laws . . . I will now briefly describe to you therefore lived 9,000 years ago.'

Even in Plato's time many doubted the truth of the bizarre Atlantis tale. But the existence of the enigmatic Great Pyramid the first known account of which is by Herodotus, could not be doubted. There it was . . . and is.

Four hundred years later Alexandrian **Neoplatonist** texts introduced the myth of **Hermes Trismegistus**. In his name Renaissance occultists developed schools of **magic** later rejected by seventeenth-century rationalism, but still nobody could explain away the Great Pyramid. In 1798 Napoleon bled Egypt militarily, but the glamour of Egyptian **myth** conquered Europe culturally once again.

Discovery of the Rosetta Stone led to the decipherment of hieroglyphs; pyramidology and tomb-plunder saw the rebirth of **occult** themes even as Reason seemed to have won all. Magical systems seemingly as dead as the pharaohs were reborn even as many of those dead pharaohs were paraded round Western museums.

In this century alone Edgar **Cayce** has claimed in **trance** that the first Egyptians were Atlantean survivors; that an ancient 'hall of records' will be found between the Sphinx and the Nile, and that the building of the Great Pyramid was begun not *c.* 2650 BC but in 10,490 BC. Jeane **Dixon**, in her 1962 vision of the birth of **Antichrist**, saw the child's parents as Nefertiti and her husband Ikhnaton, the pharaoh who dismissed traditional Egyptian polytheism to worship the Sun as 'one god'. And it was in Cairo in 1906 that **Crowley** claimed he was empowered as the Beast 666.

The best evidence of Egyptian occult wisdom is the Great Pyramid. But what if the Great Pyramid dates from a much earlier period and other Giza pyramids (like Chephren) are later, inferior copies? Was dynastic Egypt a culture in millennia-long decline? Orthodoxy claims the 'Two Lands' (Upper and Lower Egypt) united *c.* 3100 BC; and that the great period followed. Yet was the subsequent culture any greater than that found in India, China or even Babylon? Dynastic Egyptians could clearly build great buildings and maintain an agrarian economy based on the Nile's fertility, yet tales of dynastic Egyptian magic imply not transcendent wisdom but rather a culture living off the bones of the past, increasingly superstitious and reliant on ever vaguer memories of a much earlier, greater era.

Until we re-examine our Western assumptions about *history* and *progress* (linear *vs* cyclic) we may never perceive the wider, more extraordinary timescape of human history which – perhaps – awaits acknowledgement.

The *true* history of 'occult Egypt' may begin long before the known dynastic period. Would this be so surprising? Barely a century ago much of Europe was shocked by evidence that the world had not, after all, been created as recently as 4004 BC.

EINSTEIN, Albert (1879–1955) 'God does not play dice with the universe,' claimed Einstein, implying a purpose to creation beyond the mere mechanics of the Newtonian system which had prevailed since the seventeenth century and which in effect he superseded. In its place he, **Planck, Heisenberg** and others established a new world-view still so '**paranormal**' that it remains imperfectly assimilated.

Born at Ulm in Germany, in 1905 Einstein proposed his Special Theory of Relativity. Examining the physics of bodies moving relative to each other at *uniform* speeds he concluded (following the Michaelson–Morley experiments determining light-speed as 186,325 miles per second) that nothing in the known *physical* universe travels faster than light. Then he sought to explain how bodies move relative to each other in *accelerated* motion and, still in 1905, he introduced his famed equation: $E = mc^2$ (E is *energy*, m is *mass*, and c the *speed of light*). This stated that if one can annihilate a mass, then the energy emitted ($c \times c$) is enormous. Thus the birth of the atom bomb.

Can he be blamed for the misuse by others of his findings? Oppenheimer and others who applied his theories in making the Bomb detested their own compromise. Nobody blamed Einstein, who usually forgot where he had left his toothbrush. The Bomb was a spin-off from his early work, but untypical of its direction. He lived not so much in the clouds as the cosmos.

Special Relativity abandons the conventional idea (by which most of us still live) of Space and Time as fixed and reliable dimensions. Einstein's physics posit events as existing in no *absolute* state, but in a referential flux between varied points of definition equally in flux. Einsteinian time is not absolute, but varies according to an observer's view of the speed of bodies moving relative to himself. Likewise, the measurable *mass* of bodies varies according to their speed as measured relative to such an observer.

One consequence of Einstein's theories was *physically* proven in 1945. Yet *psychological* relativity (as in human interaction) remains without general social application of a sort implying the need to tolerate the views of others. Prejudice of every sort arises from lack of relativistic views. 'Love thy neighbour as thyself,' said Christ.

The first proof of general relativity came in 1918 when astronomer Sir Arthur Eddington used a solar eclipse to prove the light of stars 'behind' the sun during the eclipse were sufficiently bent by the Sun's mass to appear visible. This 'Einstein Shift' did much to validate his theories. He spent the rest of his life trying to develop a 'Unified Field Theory' which would tie up all known forces and effects into a single theorem. The notion of 'The **Tao** of Physics' began with Einstein.

ELECTROMAGNETISM (*See* **UFOs, MAGNETISM**) In discussing the effect on each other over empty space of electricity and magnetism, physicist Michael Faraday in the 1830s advanced the idea of an electromagnetic field, its power determined by the proximity and length of magnetic 'lines of force'. He thought space to be filled with such lines, light and radiant heat being vibrations travelling along them. The Scot James Clerk Maxwell (1831–79) derived equations that proved light to be an electromagnetic wave: in 1888 Heinrich Hertz managed to generate *radio* waves both longer and shorter than light.

Electromagnetism has been invoked as an (unproven) factor in a range of **paranormal** events. These include the often-reported failure of electrical systems in UFO **encounters** – an event first recorded in a *novel*, Bernard Newman's *The Flying Saucer* (1950); and speculation as to the nature of the energy or **astral body, ghosts** and other 'afterdeath' phenomena. The human brain emits extra-low-frequency (ELF) electromagnetic waves at a frequency between 1 and 30 hertz. So does the Earth itself. Is electromagnetism involved as a force not only in our perception but in our *interpretation* of psychic phenomena? UFO researcher Paul Devereux has suggested that UFOs are geomagnetic events with which our brains interact, so producing forms (elfs or **elementals** or UFOs) that accord with our unconscious preconditioning. Such an approach might explain many anomalies.

ELEMENTALS (*See* **FAIRIES, EARTH SPIRIT**) Mediaeval **occultists** hypothesised four categories of invisible beings: **angels**; devils or **demons**; the souls of the dead; and nature's elemental spirits. Once the physical world was seen as the visible manifestation of the earth spirit, its activity springing from the interplay of the four elements: earth, air, fire and water. This interplay and events arising from it, from the wave bursting on the shore to the wind in the woods, was thought to be orchestrated by the appropriate elementals, or nature **spirits** – natural forces personified as intelligent entities, existing in several orders and occupying a realm between man and God. Lacking free will they maintained seasonal processes and the systems of wind, wave, earth and fire that bore them. Thus deep in the earth dwelt the slow, dark *gnomes* (from the Greek *gnoma*, knowledge); temperamental *sylphs* (Greek *sylpha*; butterfly) rode the air; in the sea the *undine* (Latin *unda*, wave) surged; in the fire the *salamander* (perhaps from Greek *salambe*, fireplace) flamed. The latter, visualised as a lizard, or little dragon, was also called the *fire-drake*.

Paracelsus said elementals are 'of an elastic semi-material essence, ethereal enough so as not to be detected by the physical sight, and they may change their forms according to certain laws'.[1] In Celtic belief such entities as **fairies** were 'spirits who could make themselves seen or not seen at will. *And when they took people they took body and soul together*.'

The human relationship with these forces was both intimate and remote. If well-treated, they would help people, but they were capricious, to be respected, as in the Highland Scots tradition of referring to the fairies as the 'Good Folk'. The plough broken by a rock, the ship lost at sea, the house burned down; such events were seen not as 'accidents' but as caused by *human* failure to placate the elementals. Woe betide the housewife who forgot to leave out milk at night for the household brownie!

In **theosophical** usage the term refers to beings starting evolutionary growth, thus in an *elemental* stage. Men too were once elemental beings, entering the created universe on the lowest plane of being to begin their climb up the stairway of life: from elemental to human to god.[2]

An intriguing view of elementals is given by Cypriot magus **Daskalos**. He claims elementals consist of thoughts and/or feelings projected by individuals who, brooding on any strong desire, create *noetic* (**psychic**) matter – the basic stuff of the universe. The 'elemental' is thus in the first place an inner mental image. Such images can take on life of their own and may exist independently (as Alexandra **David-Neel** discovered) of the individual creating them. One type is created subconsciously, with desire uppermost in its formation; the other is constructed and projected deliberately, with thought in control. The latter sort last longer and are more powerful. But the most common sort is that produced subconsciously. Such elementals, often the result of negative emotion like envy or hatred, tend to return to their creator to dwell in the creator's subconscious and form habits and obsessions. This tendency of elementals to return to their source makes the law of **karma** possible. Daskalos claims that our present personalities and circumstances are the sum total of all the elementals we have constructed since our earliest incarnations in the material world.[3]

His view (as with **Tibetan** and modern ideas of **thought-forms**) sheds light on the notions of researchers like **Lethbridge**; that psychic events often result from our own mental *projections* (conscious or not) acting in ways experienced as haunting or similar manifestation. It also suggests why gnomes, elves and other traditional forms of elemental are now seen less commonly than the ubiquitous UFO. The images projected by individuals and maintained by group-belief have changed. But the basic process stays the same. The fairies and their ilk were *literally* diminished in stature and *reality* by the loss of popular belief in them – yet the mind-stuff of which they and other elementals are formed remains active – in us.

In placating the 'Good Folk', it may be our ancestors were in effect placating the unruliness of their own half-glimpsed subconscious activity.

Such a view also offers insight into the nature and effect of **curses**.

1. *Dimensions*, Jacques Vallée, Sphere, London 1990, p. 90
2. *Occult Glossary*, G. de Purucker, Theosophical University Press, Pasadena, California 1933, pp. 43–4
3. *The Magus of Strovolos*, Kyriacos C. Markides, Arkana, London 1985, pp. 34–46

ELIADE, Mircea (1907–86) This Romanian-born author, appointed Professor of the History of Religions at the University of Chicago in 1958, wrote widely on subjects such as **yoga, shamanism** and **mysticism**.

ELOHIM (*See* **ANCIENT ASTRONAUTS, DEVAS, QABALAH**) The Hebrew term 'Elohim' as applied in the Book of Genesis to the Most High is usually translated as 'lord' or 'god'. In fact it is the feminine plural of the word 'el', a term of common significance in many ancient languages. In Sumerian it means 'brightness' or 'shining'; in Old Cornish 'an **angel**'; likewise the Anglo-Saxon 'Aelf' (*elf*) means 'a shining being'. So what is it doing in the Bible? In Hebrew script it first appears in Genesis i, 1, reading (1966 *Jerusalem Bible*): 'In the beginning, God created the heavens and the earth.' Or in Genesis i, 26: 'God said, "Let us make man in our image, in the likeness of ourselves." '

There is something odd here. The plural form of *el*, *elohim*, apparently means 'The Shining Ones'. Thus: 'In the beginning, the Shining Ones created the heavens and the earth'; or, 'The Shining Ones said, "Let us make man in our image, in the likeness of ourselves." '

This anomaly (the term *Elohim* appears some thirty times in the Pentateuch) sheds dubious light not only on the early beliefs or history of pre-Mosaic Hebrews but on the motives of biblical translators through the ages. Was extraterrestrial intervention deliberately misrepresented in order to fit an emergent religious ethos? Did the early Church fathers work to suppress any belief that 'God' and the 'angels' might have been anything other than 'supernatural'? If so, why?[1]

1. *The Genius of the Few*, Christian O'Brien, Turnstone Press, London 1985.

EMERALD TABLET (*See* **HERMES TRISMEGISTUS**)

ENERGY BODY (*See* **ASTRAL BODY, AURA, ETHERIC BODY, *KA***)

ENOCH (*See* **ANCIENT ASTRONAUTS, ANGELS, ELOHIM**) Mentioned in Genesis (v, 18–24) as father of Methuselah and as one *walking with God (Elohim)* the apocryphal books associated with this early Hebrew scribe give full account of the **Watchers** (the 'angels' who mated with the daughters of men), and of his personal visit to Heaven. 'Then he vanished because God [again Elohim; 'Shining Ones'] took him.' (1966 *Jerusalem Bible*.)

The early Church denied knowledge of the Enochian account of angelic fallibility to its growing flock. Rediscovered in an Ethiopean Coptic monastery in the early nineteenth century, today the Book of Enoch provides a contentious source of material for those insisting that human evolution has been both caused and accelerated by the intervention of extraterrestrials disguised as 'God'.

ENTITIES A catch-all term for (intelligent) alien beings interacting with humanity, their source and purpose undisclosed. The word is vague enough to evoke foreboding without demanding specific definition and may thus be used to imply interruption of human affairs by intelligences belonging to no known system of reference.

ESP (*See* **EXTRA-SENSORY PERCEPTION**)

ESSENES (*See* **PROPHECY**) This mystical Jewish brotherhood of the immediate pre-Christian and early Christian era, now associated with the settlement at Qumran and the Dead Sea Scrolls, believed in the imminent appearance of a great Teacher of Righteousness – the Messiah. The idea that **Christ** was an Essene (so similar are Essene teachings to those of the New Testament) has been developed by Peter Lemesurier. He suggests that Christ's entire worldly mission was a deliberate attempt to fulfil Essene prophecy; an attempt which went wrong when he died on the Cross. Lemesurier asserts that the Essenes viewed **prophecy** (messianic or otherwise) not fatalistically (that is, as a set of events that occur willy-nilly, due to acts of God or Chance beyond human influence), but as a blueprint to be fulfilled only by the deliberate action of those aware of the prophecy and working to bring it about.[1]

This attitude (whether true of the Essenes or not) begs some important questions. What of our own response to prophecies by **Nostradamus, Cayce**, etc. as to the global cataclysms predicted for our immediate future? Does prophecy function as inexorable foresight of predetermined events (few fit such a view; most fail miserably); or do *we* ourselves justify them, either by acting upon, or by ignoring, the warning or promise they project.

1. *The Armageddon Script*, Peter Lemesurier, Element Books, Shaftesbury 1981

ETHERIC BODY (*See* **ASTRAL BODY, OOBEs, STEINER**) **Occult** muddle surrounds theories of the **subtle** bodies said to be owned by human beings in addition to the physical body. Phenomena like **out-of-body experiences**, far vision and faith **healing** all suggest that under certain conditions consciousness does inhabit another 'body', one interpenetrating the physical, but with different qualities and powers due to its (possibly) **electromagnetic** nature, such as ability to move instantly through space and **time**. This is sometimes called the *astral body*, sometimes the *etheric*.

Attempts to clarify this conceptual anarchy have been made by, among others, Rudolf Steiner. Teaching that man possesses four bodies; physical, etheric, astral and ego, he said that in sleep we split into two bodies: and that the astral and ego bodies separate from the physical and etheric.

The etheric body he regarded as architect of the physical body: 'All the physical organs are maintained in their form and shape by the currents and movements of the etheric body.' In his view a human being consisting only of physical and etheric body would be literally a vegetable. He said that **consciousness** lies in the astral body: the ego-principle providing a necessary continuity (of the 'I'-sense involved in daily action and memory).

The Hawaiian **Kahunas** also teach a four-body system: the physical body and three 'spirit'-layers – the 'low' self (instinctual unconsciousness); the 'middle' self (conscious ego); and the 'high self' (superconscious ego). The 'middle' self is unaware of the existence of the other two. The 'low' self equates to Steiner's version of the etheric body, interpenetrating the physical body and providing vital force (***prāna, ch'i***) to keep the physical body going while also acting as the seat of the emotions.'

That man has a 'fourfold' nature (however defined) is among the oldest and widest of perceptions. From Buddhist mandalas to **Blake**'s 'four-fold vision' and **Jung**'s four-fold psychotypology, this image keeps emerging as an **archetype** in every culture and age.

1. *Afterlife*, Colin Wilson, Grafton, London 1987, pp. 71–3

EVANS-WENTZ, W. Y. (*See* **TIBETAN BOOK OF THE DEAD**) This American Oxford scholar went far beyond the groves of academe to those of Pan. In 1909 his *The Fairy-Faith in Celtic Countries* broke new ground in its open-minded reporting of subjects elsewhere denied as spurious superstition. A sympathetic interviewer as well as assiduous researcher, his record of Celtic folk-beliefs remains a source-work for all seeking serious insight into such matters. Later he lived in India where his studies into Tibetan **Buddhism** resulted in translation into English of *The Tibetan Book of the Dead; The Tibetan Book of the Great Liberation;* his biography of *Tibet's Great Yogi, Milarepa*; and his study of *Tibetan Yoga and Secret Doctrines*. These texts, along with the interpretations of Chinese occultism by Richard **Wilhelm**, remain of seminal importance to any Western understanding of Eastern mystery. Walter Evans-Wentz spent his latter years in Southern California.

EVIL (*See* **BLACK MAGIC, DEMONS, DEVIL, DUALISM, QLIPHOTH**) Is *Evil* merely a state of ignorance, a lack of well-being, an infliction of adversity by blind circumstance? Or is it an intelligent force working to cause harm, sickness and suffering wherever possible; a force served by the human agents of 'supernatural' beings whose aim is to oppose *Good*, however defined? The latter is the common belief throughout history. The obvious example of an evil **supernatural** being always meddling in human affairs is the **Devil**, or Satan, with his legions of subordinate **demons, spirits**, and other purposefully malign entities existing only to cause human misery and to lead people astray. Less directly personified but commonly regarded as evil or hostile to human welfare are the implacable, inescapable, universal workings of Death and *Fate* (though these too have been personified; Death as the Grim Reaper, Fate as the Norns, or as Nemesis [*moral equilibrium*], or as Night's Three Daughters: Clotho, Lachesis and Atropos).

In the West, the Christian Church has usually been regarded as the main defence against both kinds of evil – but while promising (via good works, repentance, etc.) escape from the Devil and his minions, the Church has never pretended that death and fate are avoidable. Indeed it claims that those doing evil during life will, if failing to submit to **Christ**, be tormented in hell for all eternity hereafter. And though in recent centuries belief in malign supernatural beings was said to have declined due to the rise in agnostic rationalism, the modern revival of interest in the **occult** and in **magic** suggests that such beliefs endure in our basic **psychic** framework.

In researching the subject author Richard Cavendish was struck by the recurrence of specific themes in regard to popular belief about the powers of evil. He notes the connection between evil and the animal world; the dread of being devoured; the links between death, evil and sex; the fear of chaos; the ascription of accidental harm to evil entities through refusal to believe in chance, and so on.[1]

The theology of evil varies between West and East. In **Buddhist** terms there are no 'evil' beings *per se*: evil or misfortune arise merely out of our addiction to illusion, failure to perceive reality, and the necessary workings of **karma**. Thus evil, like *sin*, is only misdirected action, like an arrow fired wide. In the West, the concept of evil (*Devil* minus the D) as a deliberate force is possible only to those who, knowingly or not, are dualists; i.e., they view life as an endless conflict between two equal and opposed universal forces, *Good* and *Evil*. It may also be noted that, without belief in evil, it is very hard to believe in good. Like ***yin*** and ***yang***, up and down, night and day, the one justifies and guarantees the other.

1. *The Powers of Evil*, Richard Cavendish, Routledge Kegan Paul, London 1975

EVIL EYE Fear of the magically dangerous glance was once common. In Egyptian **myth** the creator-god Atum had a detachable eye, both an agent of his creative power (humanity was formed from its tears) and of his fury. Its power was passed on to the god Horus. A spell from one of the Coffin Texts reads: 'I am the all-seeing Eye of Horus, whose appearance strikes terror.' The eye was later associated with Satan, a leader of angels and stars, the 'eyes' of the night sky. So the peacock is connected with Satan due to the 'eyes' on its tail, while in modern **occult** symbolism the **Devil** is linked with the Hebrew letter *ayin*, traditionally representing an eye.[1]

Belief in the 'evil eye' was common among the Celts, being thought to arise from envy or malice on the part of its owner, who might be unaware of owning this power. It was usually attributed to (old) women; those thought to be witches were frequently accused of it, especially if their eyes were of different colours. If a child (typically the prettiest) or beast (the finest) fell suddenly ill, the evil eye was often blamed. Horses afflicted would sweat, tremble and daily grow weaker. Such a glance turned ale or milk instantly sour. **Charms** against it included rowan and juniper, burning cloth, iron and horseshoes. The power, which could be cast at a distance, was usually regarded not as an instrument of deliberate **sorcery** so much as the effect of pure malice. In Irish myth Balor, king of the Fomorians, had one of his eyes always closed because its glance slew whoever it fell upon.[2] In Greek myth the gaze of the serpent-haired Medusa turned men to stone.

1. *The Powers of Evil*, Richard Cavendish, Routledge Kegan Paul, London 1975, pp. 166–167
2. *The Magic Arts in Celtic Britain*, Lewis Spence, Rider, London 1970

EXORCISM (*See* **POLTERGEISTS, POSSESSION**) In 1975 in Barnsley, Yorkshire, Michael Taylor joined a local revivalist group. He grew convinced that a girl in it had psychic influence over him. Approached by Taylor for help, the Rev. Peter Vincent decided that Taylor was possessed by forty devils. After an exorcism ceremony lasting all night Taylor ran home, murdered his wife, and was later found unconscious and naked in the street. On trial he seemed normal; apparently the forty devils had left him. The judge, committing him to a mental home, said that the priest should have sent for a psychiatrist instead of attempting exorcism.[1]

Popular belief in the reality of spirit-possession and in the efficacy of exorcism as a means of 'casting out devils' remains potent. Disturbed but otherwise 'normal' people call on their local vicar to rid them of the inexplicable force wrecking their peace of mind. But often such a course proves harmful as well as inappropriate. Exorcism takes many forms. It may require only a sympathetic ear for the fears of those overwhelmed by their imagination. In poltergeist cases, exorcism is generally useless – the '**spirit**' involved simply laughs. The unconscious mind of the person unwittingly creating the phenomena is unpersuaded by the rite. In other cases, where an interfering external spirit *may* be involved, it will not depart unless mastered by a stronger personality. Why should it?

Full exorcism is not authorised by the Anglican Church without thorough examination, usually involving reports from a GP, local vicar and a social worker. Michael Taylor's case shows why. The forces involved, however defined, are complex and dangerous. Vicars over-eager to attempt a rite of which they have little experience can compound the danger. In Hastings, Sussex, in 1979, a canon so plagued a menopausal, drug-addicted woman with his wish to exorcise her that she ended up in a clinic. A 'priestly cure' may only make things worse – it depends upon the knowledge of the priest.

A mere twenty per cent of exorcisms are now considered to be successful.

1. *Mysteries*, Colin Wilson, Grafton, London 1979, p. 485

EXTRA-SENSORY PERCEPTION (*See* **PRECOGNITION, TELEPATHY**)
The term Extra-Sensory Perception (ESP) was coined by J. B. **Rhine** (1895–1980) as part of his ground-breaking work to define and scientifically research faculties (like telepathy, precognition, **clairvoyance**) whereby information is transmitted by means other than via the 'five senses'. In 1927 Rhine and his wife Louisa began a full-time investigation of ESP at Duke University, North Carolina, work continuing until Rhine's death in 1980. Their method involved use of twenty-five **'Zener'** cards (named after a Duke University researcher) divided into five sets of five cards. Each set bore a different symbol: star, circle, cross, wavy lines or rectangle. Shuffled, these were seen one at a time by the sender (agent). In another room the receiver (subject) pointed out the card he thought the sender was viewing. The laws of chance predicted five correct answers out of twenty-five if only guesswork was involved. If the subject had ESP abilities, the number of correct answers should exceed chance. One subject, called Linzmayer, liked to be distracted while making his guesses. Rhine would drive him into the country, then stop the car to conduct impromptu tests. On one such occasion Linzmayer named all fifteen cards Rhine viewed – suggesting *telepathy*. He also scored above chance when asked to name cards before the sender turned them over – suggesting *precognition*.

Publishing his results in 1934, Rhine was accused of faulty techniques. His statistical methods were validated, but in 1955 medical researcher G. R. Price publicly called Rhine and British parapsychologist G. R. Soal frauds. Later Rhine convinced Price: in 1972 Price published an apology. But in Soal's case, Price's doubts were correct. The card-guessing tests Soal conducted from 1941 to 1943 apparently proved ESP – but twenty years later one of his researchers said she had seen Soal altering the figures. A study by Betty Markwick (1978) concluded that 'the experimental series in card-guessing carried out by Dr Soal must, as the evidence stands, be discredited'.[1]

Duplicitous efforts to prove ESP harm its scientific credibility. Yet research by Targ and Puthoff at Stanford Research Institute in California increasingly substantiates its reality. Their work with psychics like Uri **Geller** and Ingo **Swann** remains controversial, as does the work of Charles Tart with Robert **Monroe**. But maybe the oddest thing about ESP is how we practise it all the time without realising it. 'Oh,' we say, on meeting a friend unexpectedly, 'I was just thinking about you . . .'

1. 'In Search of the Sixth Sense', Roy Stemman, *The Unexplained*, Orbis partwork, London 1983, pp. 12–15

EYSENCK, Hans (*See* **ASTROLOGY, GAUQUELIN**)

F

FAIRIES (*See* **ABDUCTIONS, COTTINGLEY FAIRIES, ELEMENTALS, FAIRY TALES, UFOs**) 'There never seems to have been an uncivilised tribe,' wrote folklorist W. Y. **Evans-Wentz**, 'a race or nation of civilised men, who have not had some form of belief in an unseen world, peopled by unseen beings.'[1]

Today few people believe in fairies. But the enigma remains. There are several possible approaches. One is that fairies are literally 'such stuff as dreams are made on'; being but our imaginative characterisation of natural and elemental forces. Another is that fairy-myths are glamorised folk-memory of early cultures wiped out, driven underground, or absorbed by conquering Iron Age tribes. Again, fairy-lore may constitute our imperfect knowledge of and relationship with tricksy, meddling beings of a realm tied to but separate from our world. Today they manifest not as 'fairies' but as UFO entities. The description changes: the mystery persists.

Taking these approaches individually:

1. Fairies as images or thought-forms projected by human subconscious processes are considered in the entry on Elementals.

2. Tales of fairies and their ilk (dwarves, elves, gnomes, goblins and pixies) suggest distorted folk-memory of older races overwhelmed by invasion. Collating tradition we get a picture like this: the fey folk varied in stature but were said to be physically strong. They had no towns, iron tools or weapons, but lived in mazy earth-houses hidden under grassy mounds. Shy, sly and quick, they were elusive but knew the land intimately and demanded respect. The 'elfshot' of their archers was deadly. The tiny (poison?) arrow had only to prick human flesh. They were said to be able to raise storms and mists. They stole human babies, leaving a 'changeling' behind (sensible, if survival lies in genetic assimilation). They could be malicious – curdling milk, making the mare barren, playing mean tricks – but, if approached with sympathy, friendly. A man taking a fairy bride was warned that to speak of her origin was to lose her. The shortest and most broad-shouldered (dwarves, gnomes) were skilled craftsmen who worked best at night. Wise men placated them, calling them the 'Good Folk', or (in Scotland) *Daoine Sith* ('Men of Peace'). Housewives left food out for them at night, next day to find food gone and kitchen swept – by the 'Brownie', the domesticated fairy, collaborating with the conqueror.[2]

Poison arrows; hidden earth houses; nocturnal excursions; theft of 'human' babies; intermarriage with men; diffidence about their origin – it all suggests an older folk fighting to survive, being in time so absorbed (save for giveaway signs like green eyes and the talent for **second sight**) that their existence became a remote myth, a romantic memory exploited by J. M. Barrie and Walt Disney. Yet on the Orkneys in the 1920s a storm blew away sand to reveal the Bronze Age 'village' at Skara Brae. Its tiny rooms suggest a folk the size of Ituri pygmies. It was hidden, 'made invisible', by its mounded roof. If you seek an archaeologically researched, Carbon–14–dated, genuine *fairy knowe*, Skara Brae seems a good place to start.

3. Yet belief in intelligent, invisible beings (perhaps spirits of the dead) who occupy a realm other than yet coincident with our own is found from Mexico to Russia, Australia to Ireland: a realm obeying other laws of space and time, accessible to humans at specific places and 'in-between' times like twilight. Typically, humans abducted into this other realm (like True Thomas) emerge after hours or days to find years

passed in the human world. It was said that the fairies could englamour human eyes to see old hags as beautiful girls; dross as gold; shabby caves as magnificent palaces. So 'fairy gold' came to mean evanescent wealth; to be 'away with the fairies' now means one who lives in a dreamworld; a 'fey' person is dreamy and strange. But the fact that in mediaeval Europe many folk were accused of (and executed for) association (sexual and otherwise) with '**demons**' suggests the tenacity of belief in and tension associated with the human-fairy relationship. Celtic tradition shows how strongly people believed in the effect of fairy doings on human welfare. As late as 1846–7, during the Irish potato famine, some blamed the disaster on disturbance in the fairy world. One man claimed that before the disaster he 'saw the *Good People* and hundreds like me saw them fighting in the sky over Knock Magh and on towards Galway'[3].

The endurance of such belief despite centuries of discouragement by the Church may arise only from the common sensation that misfortune arises from unknown (**supernatural**) causes, and to a tendency to personify such causes as the work of evil beings. But is that all? In 1691 the Rev. Robert Kirk of Aberfoyle in Scotland wrote *The Secret Commonwealth of Elves, Fauns and Fairies*. In it he defined the nature and organisation of the **entities** so plaguing local society that few denied their reality. He concluded that fairies: (1) have a nature between man and angels; (2) have light, fluid bodies, and can appear or vanish at will; (3) are intelligent and curious; (4) can steal whatever they like; (5) live in caves reached by any opening where air passes; (6) once had their own society and agriculture; (7) are unable to stay in one place and travel constantly (i.e. are nomads); (8) are physically immaterial; (9) are divided into tribes and have children, marriages and burials; (10) have houses normally invisible to human eyes; (11) speak with a whistling sound; (12) have habits and language that to humans seem human; (13) say nothing dies, that all evolves and is forever renewed; (14) have chiefs but no organised **religion**; (15) have books for pleasure and philosophy; and (16) may be commanded to appear at our will.[4]

Kirk thus takes the view of **Paracelsus** and others that such beings can be commanded. Concluding that relations with these beings would become as natural as our relations with any other new discovery, like the printing press, he died the following year (1692), apparently of a heart attack, while out at night on a known fairy knowe. A legend persists that 'the fairies took him'. What else?

Evans-Wentz maintained that 'fairies actually exist as invisible beings or intelligences', and held that our own visible world is immersed like an island in an unknown ocean peopled by species of living beings beyond our comprehension. Today, with innumerable UFO reports to add to fairy tales through the ages, the scientific evidence from **Relativity** to **Chaos Theory** increasingly suggests we inhabit a universe in which material explanations of things are *not entirely reliable*.

So . . . watch the bottom of your garden . . .

1. *The Fairy Faith in Celtic Countries*, J. Y. Evans-Wentz, 1909
2. *Witchcraft Today*, Gerald B. Gardner, Rider, London 1954
3. *Dimensions*, Jacques Vallée, Sphere, London 1990, p. 83
4. *The Secret Commonwealth of Elves, Fauns and Fairies*, Robert Kirk, Observer Press, Stirling, 1933

FAIRY TALES (*See* **FAIRIES, MABINOGION, MYTH**) Fairy tales are more than fanciful romances of magical lands and beings. In every culture they well up from a common ground of human experience. Their origin is lost in time. Implicitly moralistic, inhabiting a **pagan** multiverse, their **archetypal** themes spontaneously reoccur in every age.

So Jack forever climbs a Beanstalk (like the **shaman** climbs the **Tree of Life**) to kill the Ogre in the Cloud-Castle; princes are always defeating evil witches to wake and win Sleeping Beauties; princesses meet talking frogs who seek love, not money. As recorded in Europe since the late seventeenth century by Perrault, the Brothers Grimm, Hans Christian Andersen or Andrew Lang, the cautionary element in fairy tales is explicit. Hansel and Gretel stray in the Wild Woods; Little Red Riding Hood meets the Big Bad Wolf; but Beauty meets the Beast and learns not to judge by appearances.

Today fairy tales not only survive in new forms (fantasy and science fiction), but continue to express underlying popular responses to horrific events. Take the progression expressed by three popular modern fairy tales spanning 1910 to 1980: Barrie's *Peter Pan*, Tolkien's *Lord of the Rings*, and the *Star Wars* movies directed by George Lucas. In the shadow of World War I, Tinkerbell led the Lost Children to the Never-Never Land where Peter Pan never grows up (*a flight from reality*); before World War II Frodo began to fight Sauron and Gollum for the Power of the Ring (*the decision to stand up against tyranny*); in 1982 (near the end of the Cold War), Luke Skywalker in *Return of the Jedi* learns Darth Vader is his father (*evil lies within*).

From ancient Irish myth of the hero Cuchullin's exploits to the latest Schwarzenegger movie of robot violence or unreal domains on Mars, the major fairy-tale themes are universal. Thus *transformation*. The **Shape-shifting** Siberian shaman Morgon-Kara: the Welsh myth of Gwion Bach's shape-shifting flight from the angry goddess Cerridwen; Zeus deluding Leda in swan-form; the trickster-god of Kalahari Bushmen who makes men fight by seeming black to one and white to another . . . all are variants of the same tale, in which basic psychological truths are recast from myth into popular form.

Entertaining and spell-binding, fairy tales advise, warn, encourage and educate. A favourite theme is of the simple man or woman who accepts a challenge to journey into magic domains. *En route* realising his own latent strengths and aided by an ambiguous supernatural helper (the two may be the same), he overcomes all obstacles to defeat a supernatural foe. The ogre, wicked witch, evil magician, **dragon** or other monster is slain, bound to obedience or transformed into nobler guise. A **curse** is lifted, treasure is won: the hero returns to his own world, time and kind: Nature flowers.

The **fairies** themselves, if present, are usually not malign but tricksy and unreliable, their advice untrustworthy unless their obedience be bound by trick, **spell**, **curse**, oath or winning jest that earns their respect.

Such tales inhabit a land of dreams in which a wardrobe leads to Narnia or a toad may talk; in which people may really be deer, seals, or wolves; in which normality is surrounded by magical domains obeying different laws. Relative values are emphasised. The penalties, dangers and possible gains invoked by crossing the boundaries into the fairy realms are emphasised, as is need of a stout heart and shrewd mind. Magical helpers, threats, omens, prohibitions and marvels abound. Some **entities** in this magical multiverse are benevolent: none may be taken for granted. They are, after all, the gods, **demons** and **elementals** of **pagan** belief, thinly disguised.

Of course in many tales the prince or princess is the cradle-tyrant who doesn't want to grow up. Thus Peter Pan imagery, and the moral or nursery aspect of the fairy tale. Who needs a princess who wakes up the household because of a pea under her mattress? Or a prince who won't fight the ogre or kiss the Sleeping Beauty because he's scared?

Fairy tales have often been bowdlerised and diminished due to their frankly pagan content, or due to horrors thought too scary for the infant mind, or because the original meaning is lost. Thus Mother Goose of the nursery rhyme was once La Reine Pédauque (La Reine du Pays d'Oc), or Goose-Foot Queen, inspiring troubadours in twelfth-century Provence. This Queen of many disguises goes back to Queen Sibylla, ancestress of all magicians; to the Queen of Sheba who entranced King Solomon; and ultimately derives from the shadowy ancient Lilith, Adam's first wife.[1]

If Mother Goose has such a distinguished pedigree, how many others?

1. *The Cult of the Black Virgin*, Ean Begg, Arkana, London 1985, pp. 32ff

FAITH HEALING (*See* **HEALING**)

FATIMA (*See* **PROPHECY, UFOs, VISIONS**) On 13 October 1917 70,000 people at Fatima in Portugal witnessed the climax of a sequence of visions begun on 13 May 1917 with the appearance to three sheep-herding children (Lucia dos Santos, aged nine, Francisco Marto, eight, and his sister Jacinta, six) of a lovely young woman who told them she came from heaven. This **apparition** had been preceded during the previous two years by several other visitations, apparently of an '**angel**', whose visits had left the children exhausted (as is typical both in **fairy** and UFO encounters). The encounters occurred at the head of a valley in a hollow pasture called Cova da Iria, the *Cave of St Irene*, an ancient sacred place.

Appearing in a cloud of blinding light she promised to return on the thirteenth of each month for five months. They swore to keep quiet. But Jacinta blurted out the tale, so when the children returned on 13 June, some fifty witnesses heard Lucia address an unseen, unheard entity. At the end of the 'dialogue' all heard an explosion and saw a small cloud rise from a tree – the centre of subsequent manifestations. On 13 July, with the 'Lady from Heaven' now commonly identified as the Virgin Mary, 4,500 people met. Some reported a 'buzzing or humming sound, a decrease in the Sun's glow and heat, a small whitish cloud about the tree of the apparitions, and a loud noise at the Lady's departure'.[1,2] The children reported receiving a fearful vision of hell and three prophecies. One claimed the First World War would soon end. The second warned that a worse war would begin in the reign of Pope Pius XI (d. 1939), presaged by an *unknown light* in the night sky. These, unrevealed until *after* alleged fulfilment, are unconvincing. The third, passed on to the Vatican, remains unrevealed, but is said to refer to awful wars in the late twentieth century, and perhaps to inundation of land by sea.[3]

On 13 August 18,000 people were present, the children having been locked up by an official who wished to end the 'nonsense'. In their absence a clap of thunder was heard, followed by a bright flash, and 'coloured light like a rainbow on the ground'. One witness (under oath during a canonical enquiry) said he saw a luminous globe spinning through the clouds. Six days later the children, released, were again with their sheep. The 'Lady' appeared amid the glowing light. On 13 September 30,000 people met. Two sceptical priests chose higher ground to watch. At noon the sun grew dim; a globe of light advanced down the valley to the tree; shiny white 'petals' fell out of the empty sky but vanished as people reached out to catch them. The children again saw the Lady amid the globe of light: she promised them a miracle. The priests saw the globe and were much shaken.

On 13 October 70,000 people witnessed the best-attested 'miracle' of modern times. At noon a flash of light accompanied a sweet fragrance; the pouring rain ceased; the clouds parted; the sun appeared as a silver disc. Casting off revolving beams of coloured lights, abruptly it plunged down 'in zig-zag fashion to the earth and the horrified spectators'.[4] Even as they thought their last hour had come, the disc reversed its motion and vanished up into the real sun. All below found their clothes dry.

Many lives were changed. Diseases were cured. Folk up to thirty miles away saw the flash. Today Fatima is a major centre of pilgrimage. Yet it is only one site where the visions of children, apparently of the Virgin (in Catholic lands an obvious symbol for *nurturing*) have led to collective **vision**, miraculous cures and prophetic warnings. At Knock in Ireland, La Salette and Lourdes in France (in the nineteenth century) and recently Medugorje in Yugoslavia similar phenomena have been experienced by so many that talk of collective **hallucination** only begs wider questions. As UFOlogist Jacques **Vallée** points out, the Fatima event is consistent with many 'non-religious' reports of UFO visitations. 'Suffer the little children to come unto me.'

1. *The Sun Danced at Fatima*, Joseph Pelletier, quoted in ref. 2.
2. *Dimensions*, Jacques Vallée, Sphere, London 1990, pp. 195–206
3. *Transformation*, Whitley Streiber, Arrow, London 1989, pp. 62–3
4. *op.cit.* ref. 2, p.200

FENG-SHUI (*See* **GEOMANCY**)

FIREWALKING Firewalking and other techniques of bodily ability to withstand heat without harm have been practised the world over since earliest times and fall into three categories: ceremonial fire-walks, in which participants step over beds of hot coals; trials by ordeal, requiring suspects to hold heated iron bars or plunge their hands into boiling water; and as proof of **trance**-powers, those involved permitting fire to play about them.[1]

The first modern tests of firewalking were conducted in 1935 by Harry **Price** of the University of London Council for Psychical Investigation. The Indian fakir Kuda Bux demonstrated before journalists and scientists that he could walk barefoot over a pit of burning coals. Surface temperature of the fire was measured at 806°F, the body of the fire as 2552°F – hot enough to melt steel. Kuda Box took four steps across the pit; his feet were not burned. The event was recorded on film. He claimed he could convey such immunity to others who followed him, but all suffered *minor* burns. Another Indian fakir, Ahmed Hussain, repeated the experiment over the same twelve-foot trench. The temperature of his feet was found to be 10°F *lower* after the firewalk than before. Thus encouraged, several 'amateurs' now found they could cross the pit without burns. Yet when the length of the burning pit was increased to twenty feet, Hussain suffered minor burns.

Price concluded that 'any person with the requisite determination, confidence, and steadiness, can walk unharmed over a fire as hot as 800°C. The experiments proved once and for all that no **occult** or **psychic** power, or a specially induced psychic state, is necessary in a firewalker.'[2]

But Price's opinion that successful firewalking is reliant solely on a brief contact time between foot and fire is as unsatisfactory as the notion of Marcus Terentius Varro (second century BC) that firewalkers use a liniment to protect their feet. More recently Sir James Frazer (author of *The Golden Bough*) asserted that the feet of firewalkers possess 'a sort of leathery or horny substance which is almost callous to heat'.[3]

Such explanations do not satisfy. Self-regulation of bodily reactions is certainly involved. In the nineteenth cenutry Lord Adare described how the medium D. D. **Home**, 'went to the fire, poked up the coals, and putting his hand in, drew out a hot burning ember, about twice the size of an orange; this he carried about the room . . . we all examined it. He then put it back in the fire and showed us his hands; they were not in the least blackened or scorched.'[4] Recent Californian 'coal-strolls' involve preparatory indoctrination: mind over matter. Trance immunity invoked by group support and ceremonial (singing, dancing) is not out of the question.

1. *The Hidden Power*, Brian Inglis, Cape, London 1986, pp. 188–92
2. *Fifty Years of Psychical Research*, Harry Price, pp. 250–62, as given in ref. 3.
3. *The Roots of Consciousness*, Jeffrey Mishlove, Random House, New York 1975, pp. 157–9
4. *op. cit.* ref. 1, p. 189

FLAMMARION, Camille (*See* **SYNCHRONICITY**) In *Death and its Mystery* this early twentieth-century French astronomer and **occult** researcher published many well-attested **paranormal** incidents, most of them however too anecdotal (i.e., M. Fortgibu: *see* **Synchronicity**) to command scientific respect. Investigating the medium Eusepia **Palladino** he reports how, during one séance, she got so angry that the phenomena became violent: 'The sofa came forward when she looked at it, then recoiled before her breath; all the instruments were thrown pell-mell upon the table; the tambourine rose almost to the height of the ceiling; the cushions took part in the sport, overturning everything on the table.'

Providing little in the way or original theory, Flammarion did set down a wealth of internally consistent anecdote regarding the reality and common acceptability of **paranormal** events.[1]

1. *Death and its Mystery*, Camille Flammarion, Unwin, London 1923

FLUDD, Robert (1574–1637) One of the last of the true Renaissance men, Fludd lived in an era when older hermetic or magical beliefs were giving way to the new rational sciences. Passionate in his magical beliefs, he persisted in regarding the *Corpus Hermeticum* and the works ascribed to **Hermes Trismegistus** as of ancient origin even after Casaubon in 1614 dated them post-Christian.

A voluminous writer on a wide range of esoteric subjects, practising **Paracelsian** physician and self-proclaimed **Rosicrucian**, he published the last great work on the 'Art of Memory' – the system whereby preliterate folk accurately held in mind for generations information never put down in writing. His 'Memory Theatre' displays how precise, unvarying information could be remembered and passed down over centuries. The process lies in the art of controlled **visualisation**. A book is a house. The chapters are the rooms of the house. The themes are specific furniture in each room. The paragraphs, arguments and sentences are the details of each item in the room. Visualising the specific items calls to mind the texts associated with them by 'magical' memory. The chair is *this*; the alcove *that*. Every material item carries symbolic, memory importance.[1]

Fludd disputed with **Kepler**, who taunted him, calling his 'pictures' and 'hieroglyphs' of the unknown world an insufficient explanation compared with Kepler's own mathematical formulations. Fludd was often derided. Yet he had a genius for expressing his philosophy graphically: his copiously illustrated works remain worthy of study today.[2]

1. *The Art of Memory*, Frances A. Yates, Peregrine, London 1969, pp. 310ff
2. *Robert Fludd*, Joscelyn Godwin, Thames and Hudson, London 1979

FLYING SAUCERS (*See* UFOs)

FORMATIVE CAUSATION (*See* **CRYSTALS, HUNDREDTH MONKEY**) This hypothesis, advanced in 1981 by British biologist Rupert **Sheldrake**, states that the form, development and behaviour of all living organisms are shaped by *morphogenetic fields* (or 'form fields': from Greek *morphe* = form; *genesis* = coming-into-being). Though unrecognised by orthodox or mechanistic physics, these fields, claims Sheldrake, are as real as magnetic or gravitational fields, and are responsible for transmitting forms and behaviours *through repetition and across space and time*. Thus a developing embryo 'tunes in' to the form of past members of the same species via the process Sheldrake calls *morphic resonance*. So too the fields organising an animal's nervous system and activities derive from the instinctive 'memory bank' or 'pooled memory' of past members of that species. Thus, he claims, when a group of animals has learned a new behaviour-pattern, other animals of the same species all over the world should learn the same behaviour more easily.

That this is the case is strongly suggested by the '**hundredth monkey**' syndrome. In Britain in 1952 some dairies began delivering milk in foil-capped bottles. Some blue tits learned how to peck through the cap to get at the milk. Abruptly this behaviour exploded throughout the European blue tit population – a phenomenon inexplicable by one-to-one imitation alone.

Sheldrake has explained the relationship between genetic material and morphic resonance by analogy. Just as the images on a TV screen arise not from the hardware (wiring, transistors, etc., corresponding to bodily DNA, protein molecules, etc.) in the set itself but via signals transmitted from far away, so too, Sheldrake says, genetic factors cannot by themselves fully account for inheritance of form and instinct – though they may affect such inheritance by altering the 'tuning' or distorting the 'reception'. Another factor – the information signal resonating through the morphogenetic field – is needed. This hypothesis of formative causation, positing as it does new fields and forms of 'action-at-a-distance' unrecognised by physics, remains controversial, not least as it seems to suggest the truth of the old Lamarckian heresy of 'acquired characteristics'.[1,2]

1. *A New Science of Life*, Rupert Sheldrake, Blond and Briggs, London 1981
2. *The Presence of the Past*, Rupert Sheldrake, Times Books, New York 1988

FORT, Charles Hoy (1874–1932) A timid child often punished by his father, Fort grew to hate authority and its attitudes. Leaving home in Albany, New York State, he settled in New York City and in 1897 began researching weird phenomena denied by orthodox science. By 1915 he had amassed many notes and written two books: (*'X'*, devoted to the idea that Earth-life is controlled from Mars; and *'Y'* suggesting that a **hollow-earth** civilisation once existed at the South Pole). Often rejected, both manuscripts were lost (or, according to another tale, burned). He wrote *The Book of the Damned*, which novelist Theodore Dreiser persuaded a publisher to issue in 1919. Few knew what to make of it. Gleaned from Fort's notes, it was written in a choppy, ironic style, raging against science's denial of phenomena ('the damned' of the title) that failed to fit existing **paradigms** of belief. The many cases he presented included reports of things falling from the sky (frogs, fishes and stones, etc.); lights seen on the **moon**; **stigmata**; people appearing and disappearing; **spontaneous combustion**; **UFO**s; **teleportation**; **levitation**; and other alleged miracles. Anticipating by 50 years **von Däniken**'s **ancient astronaut** thesis, he claimed Scotland's vitrified forts had been destroyed in an ancient space war, and that *the human race is property* – an idea elaborated in his later books (*Lo!, New Lands, Wild Talents*). In the latter (1932) he wrote, with typically aggressive cynicism, that:

'I now have a theory that, of themselves, men never did evolve from lower animals: but that, in early and plastic times, a human being from somewhere else appeared on this Earth, and that many kinds of animal took him for a model, and rudely and grotesquely imitated his appearance, so that today, though gorillas of the Congo, and of Chicago, are only caricatures, some of the rest of us are somewhat passable imitations of human beings.'

Offering no consistent argument or theory, his technique was to serve up amazing facts followed by the 'expert' explanation, if any, then to give his own fantastic theories. His primary concern was not to explain these facts but to stimulate lay curiosity and provoke 'anger and distress' among scientists (alias his heavy-handed father). Needless to say they ignored him. When in 1931 Dreiser launched the Fortean Society, Fort refused the presidency. A year later he died. When in 1947 the UFO scare began, Fort was remembered. His work at last became relevant to a wider public. Today he is known as Prophet of the Unexplained. Colin **Wilson** concludes that 'Fort's Principle goes something like this: people with a psychological need to believe in marvels are no more prejudiced and gullible than people with a psychological need *not* to believe in marvels.'[1]

1. *Mysteries*, Colin Wilson, Grafton, London 1979, pp. 199–201
2. *The Complete Books of Charles Hoy Fort*, Dover, New York 1974

FORTUNE, Dion (1891–194?) (*See* **GOLDEN DAWN, QABALAH**) Born Violet Mary Firth to Christian Science parents, aged twenty this English **occultist** clashed with the **yoga**-trained headmistress of a private school where she taught; this led to breakdown and an interest in **Freud**. Intuiting that assertions of her incompetence were literally **vampiric**, she abandoned Freud for **Jungian** mysticism, then turned to occultism. Joining the Order of the Golden Dawn, she found it to consist of 'squabbling greybeards'.

Influenced by **Crowley**, she decided Golden Dawn rituals were invalid and that **Christianity** had lost its way by denying its esoteric, **Gnostic** aspect. By 1918 a lay psychotherapist, in the 1920s she set out on her own, founding the Society of the Inner Light, which survives today.

Promoting worship of **Isis** as the image of dynamic Womanhood, she considered ritual sexual union of Isis with suitable male partners as capable of 'effecting profound transformations in human **consciousness**'.[1]

Believing that human beings form in layers ('vehicles'), that match the emanations of the Qabalistic **Tree of Life**, she concluded that the human task is to learn to operate through ever-higher vehicles of consciousness. Her factual texts (*Psychic Self-Defence*, 1930; and *The Mystical Qabalah*, 1935) and her occult novels (*The Moon Priestess*, etc.) present and explain extraordinary material in a down-to-earth way.

She tells how, brooding on someone who had hurt her, she 'formulated a werewolf accidentally'. Lying in bed imagining Fenrir, the wolf-monster of Norse myth, she felt a large grey wolf manifest. 'I knew nothing of the art of making **elementals** at that time, but had accidentally stumbled upon the right method – the brooding highly charged with emotion, the invocation of the appropriate natural force, and the condition between sleeping and waking in which the **etheric** double readily extrudes.' Elbowing the wolf she told it, 'If you can't behave yourself, you will have to go on the floor.' Pushed away, the beast vanished through the wall. Later another household member said she had seen its eyes in the corner of her room.

Summoning the beast back, Dion Fortune saw a thin cord joining it to her. Imagining that she was drawing the life out of the wolf along this cord, she dissolved it, meanwhile resisting a violent emotional demand to run berserk and destroy 'anything and anybody that came to hand'.[2]

Like **Daskalos** and **David-Neel** she explains such **entities** as the human production of elemental thought-forms that come to exist independently, their creators too often unconscious of the power they have set loose.

Regarding Qabalism as a path appropriate to the 'psycho-physical make-up' of the 'European city-dweller', she wrote: 'The Western occultist does not try to escape from matter into **spirit** . . . he wants to bring the Godhead down into manhood.'[3]

1. *Don Juan, Mescalito and Modern Magic*, Nevill Drury, Arkana, London 1985, p. 130, quoting *The Magical Revival*, Kenneth Grant, London 1972, p. 175
2. *Psychic Self-Defence*, Dion Fortune, Aquarian Press, Wellingborough 1977
3. *The Mystical Qabalah*, Dion Fortune, Benn, London 1966, p. 10

FORTUNE-TELLING (*See* **DIVINATION, *I CHING*, ORACLES, PROPHECY, TAROT**) Human anxiety to know the future has led in all times and places to the practice of a usually spurious trade relying on the desire of seekers for reassurance. *Fortune-telling* by definition implies debasement of whatever divinatory art may be

Above: Reconstruction of a medieval laboratory as used by alchemists and apothecaries; and, *right,* a plate from the *Mutus Liber* of 1677 showing alchemists making the four elements from the Nostoc (Images)

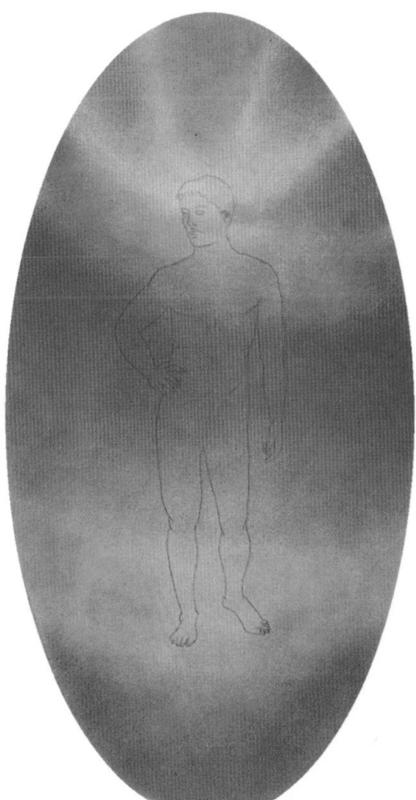

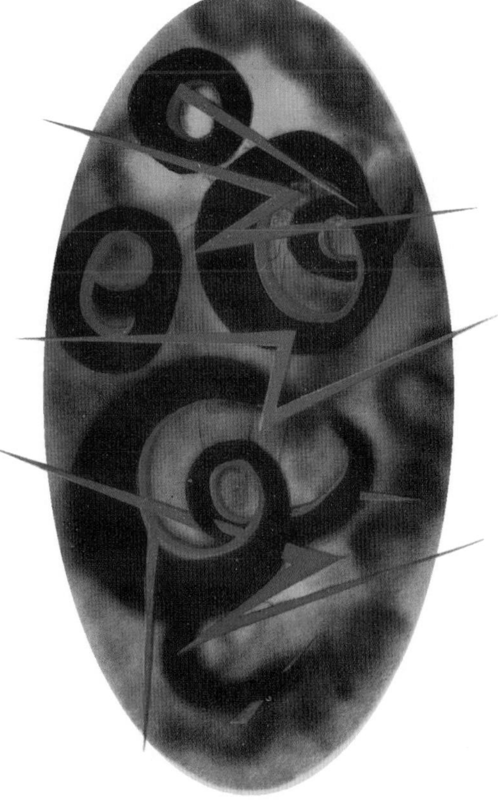

Left: the astral body of an 'average' man; and, *right,* the same astral body registering extreme anger. The astral body is defined as the electromagnetic blueprint of the physical body, an expression of its psychic energy (Mary Evans)

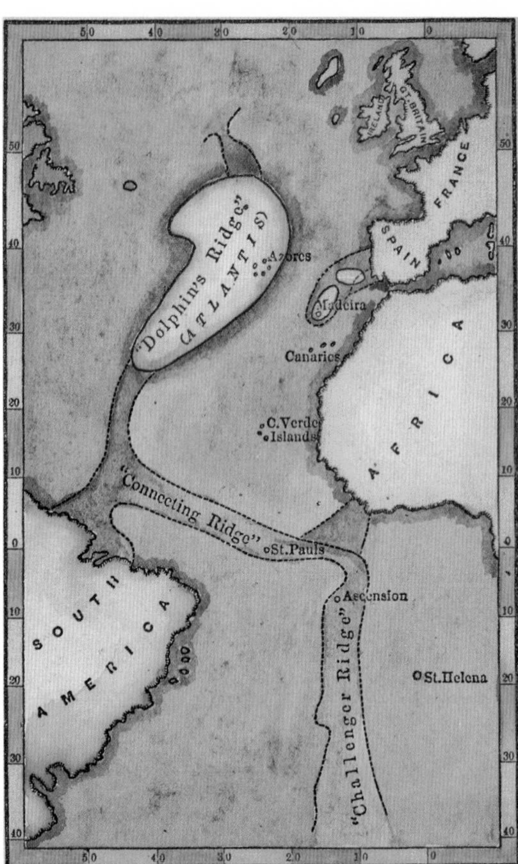

Left: A late-eighteenth-century map of Atlantis, based on Plato's indications as to the whereabouts of the mythical land (Images)

Below right: Gichtel's diagram of 1696 shows human centres of energy (or chakras) as they relate to the planets and the elements. Eastern chakra systems are more complex, but both are said to mediate the absorption and distribution of universal energies through the human mind and body (Mary Evans)

Below left: This qabalistic Golem figure has the word 'Ameth', meaning 'Truth', on its forehead; converting 'Ameth' to 'Meth' – 'Death' – enables the forces of evil to be overcome (Images)

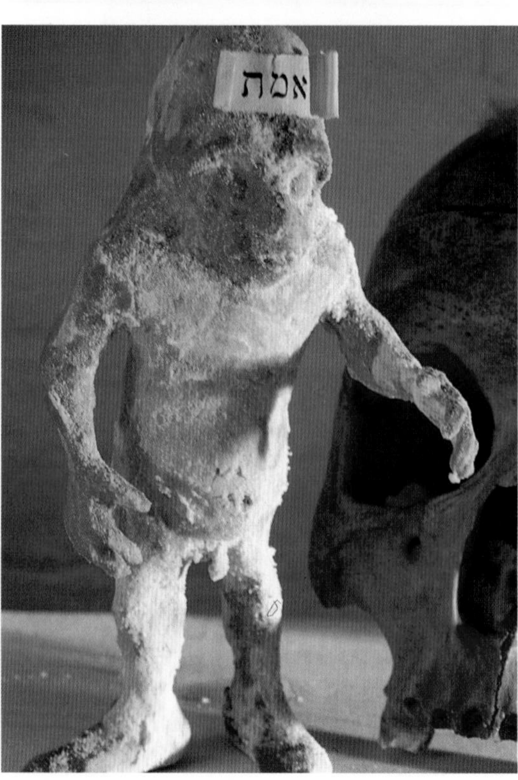

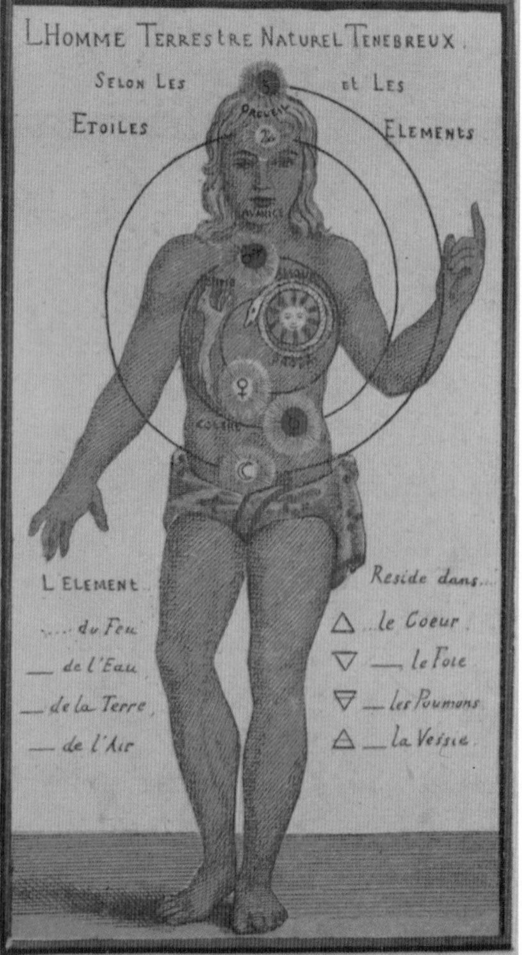

Corn circles at Cheesefoot Head, near Winchester in Hampshire, summer 1990. There is still no fully accepted explanation for this captivating phenomenon which has grown in frequency and complexity over the last ten years. Are the circles made by atmospheric 'vortices', alien intelligence, or ingenious hoaxers? (FPL)

Above: Whatever the mystery behind the corn circles, dowsing in them has repeatedly shown evidence of the presence of highly focussed forces, perhaps electromagnetic (FPL)

Right: Hamish Miller dowsing at Sancreed holy well in Cornwall. The divining rods respond to subtle interactions between fluctuating magnetic forces in the earth and the body's own force field (FPL)

Two great magicians separated by over three centuries: *left,* Dr John Dee (1527–1608) magus to Queen Elizabeth I and the founder of modern psychical research; and, *right,* Aleister Crowley (1875–1947) the self-styled 'Great Beast' and '666' (Images)

Signorelli's graphic fresco in Orvieto Cathedral shows demons torturing human souls. 133,306,668 demons were believed to have fallen along with Lucifer to plague humanity (Images)

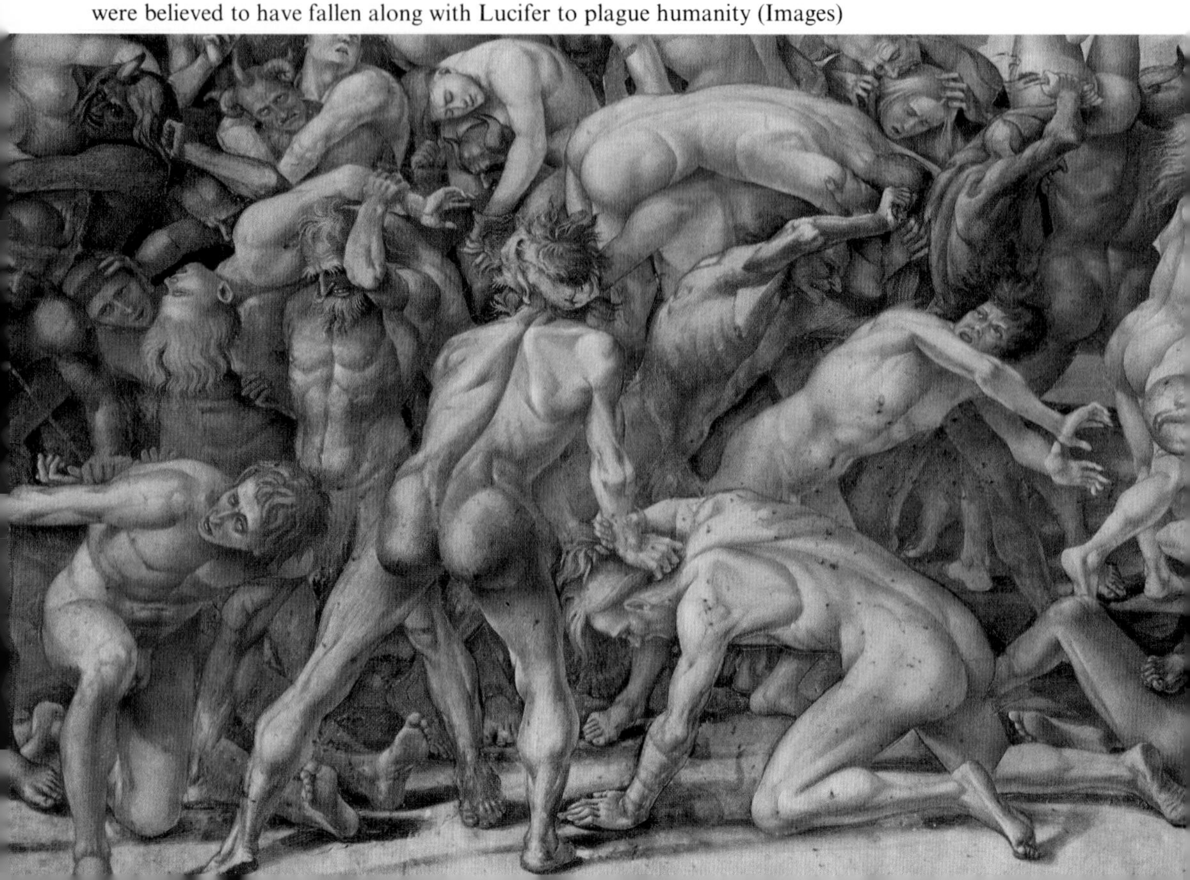

If this photograph is a hoax, no one has as yet adequately explained how it was put together. Taken in 1975 in Adelaide, Australia, no one present was aware of the phantom hands at the time (FPL)

This rare modern 'ghostly' image showed up when the photograph, taken in 1986 at Limassol Bay in Cyprus, was developed (FPL)

Left: In a classic example of the necromancer's art, Edward Kelly (scryer to John Dee, also accused of necromancy) and Paul Waring call up a newly-dead man at Walton-le-Dale, Lancashire, to question him about hidden money (Mary Evans)

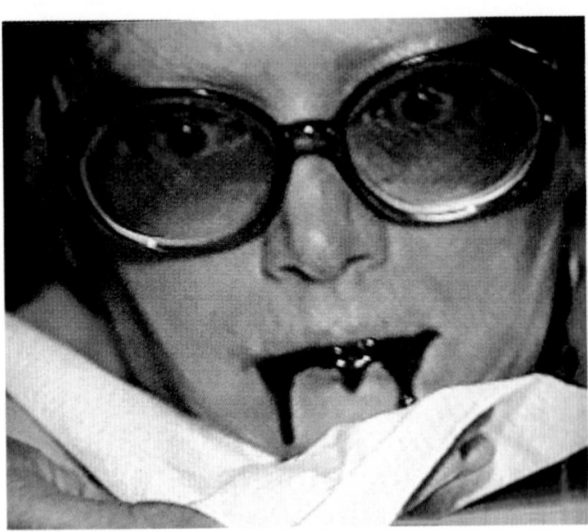

Below left: Blood drips from an Italian medium's mouth as Prince Raimundo de Sangro de Severo, a seventeenth-century alchemist and freemason, appears through him (FPL)

Below: The weeping statue of Our Lady, Rosa Mystica, at Maasmechelen, Belgium (FPL)

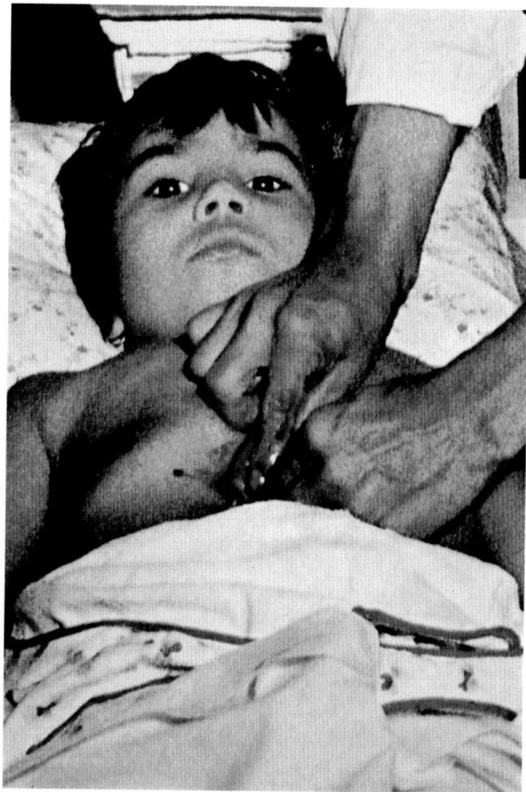

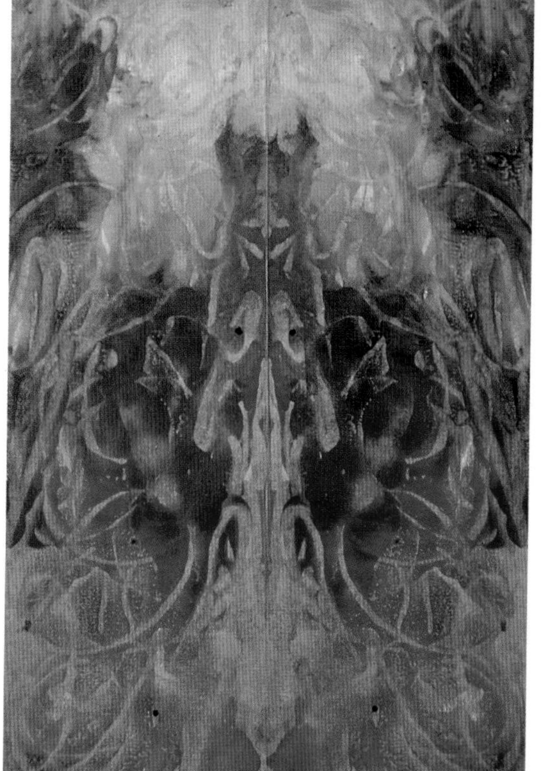

Above left: Upended furniture and scattered belongings were evidence of severe poltergeist activity at this house in Dodleston, Chester, in May 1985, during a period in which computer messages were being received from a sixteenth-century predecessor (FPL)

Left: K. N. Narayana Murthy, a psychic artist, sees his paintings, such as the example shown here, as mirrors into which to project one's own paranormal perceptions (FPL)

Above right: Psychic surgeon Edivaldo Silva operates on a young boy, apparently without the aid of medical facilities. In Brazil, the Philippines and elsewhere such operations have confounded investigators but also seem to provide rapid relief with no serious after-effects (Mary Evans)

Below: A magical pentagram from Eliphas Levi's book *Transcendental Magic* (Images)

Right: Britain's best-known megalithic structure, Stonehenge, a model of sacred geometry and also a precise calendrical and astronomical computer (Images)

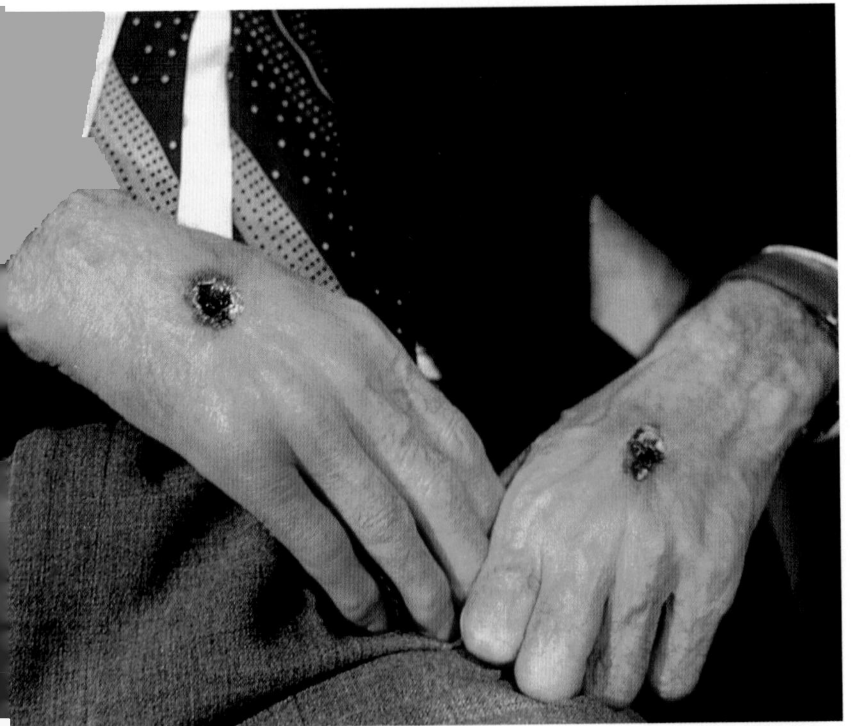

The swastika, an ancient symbol (variant of the cross) implying the fourfold unity of creation. In the early twentieth century it was hijacked and degraded by the Nazis (Mary Evans)

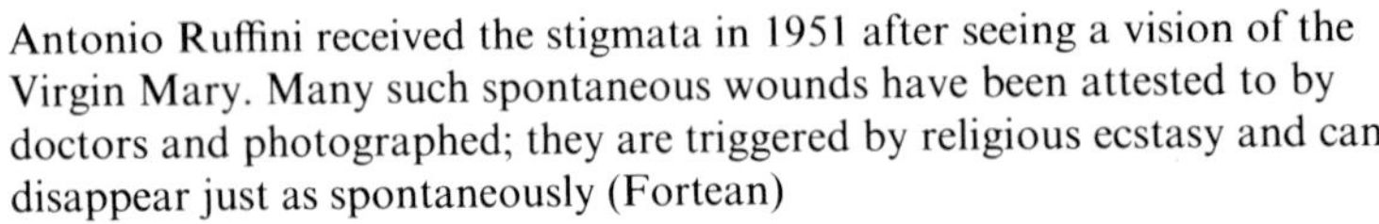

Antonio Ruffini received the stigmata in 1951 after seeing a vision of the Virgin Mary. Many such spontaneous wounds have been attested to by doctors and photographed; they are triggered by religious ecstasy and can disappear just as spontaneously (Fortean)

involved. Personal prediction, whether by ***I Ching***, **Tarot,** tea leaves, **palmistry,** phrenology, **astrology** or other means, usually requires distortion or ambiguous interpretation of events, whether accurately foreseen or not, to give the customer satisfaction – a need too often in conflict with hard or unpleasant truth to guarantee accuracy.

FOX FAMILY (*See* **SPIRITUALISM**)

FRAUD From Simon Magus to Uri **Geller psychics** or magicians whose acts seem too astounding for belief have been readily accused by sceptics of fraud. It is certainly true that, given human credulity, the field of the **paranormal** is rich in possibilites for fraud, as is established in the cases of many famous **mediums** and **psychics. Blavatsky,** Cook, **Croiset, Crookes, Crowley** and others have all been damaged by intimation of fraud or self-delusion. The sceptical assumption is that a psychic once caught out in fraud must therefore lack any genuine powers whatsoever, and that, by extension, *all* psychics are therefore frauds. Yet it is often insisted that few psychics work well under 'cold' test conditions, and that some may resort to fraud to duplicate results of which they are normally genuinely capable.

Four points: (1) the history of science is littered with cases of fraud or 'cooked-up' results (i.e. educational psychologist Sir Cyril Burt (d.1971), who in 1976 was found to have faked research to prove his view that intelligence is hereditary, not environmental); but nobody claims such cases prove *all* scientific research invalid; (2) likewise, proof of dishonesty in one man does not prove *all* men dishonest; (3) predisposition to believe in fraud is as irrational as predisposition to believe in miracles; (4) the principle of *caveat emptor* applies as much in this field as in any other.

FREEMASONRY (*See* **ROSICRUCIANISM**) The obscure origins, bizarre rites, and secrecy cloaking Freemasonry still encourage a belief (especially among conspiracy theorists) that masons not only work to dubious ends but are privy to **occult** powers. At various times masons have been associated with **Knights Templar, Illuminati,** Rosicrucians and other secret societies, real or imagined, that supposedly work towards ends profound, sinister or both. Such beliefs arise from Freemasonry's mystique as an ancient, exclusive male order supposedly dating back to Hiram Abiff, builder of Solomon's Temple, and guarding mysteries hidden from the uninitiated.

Masons were once a guild of itinerant mediaeval builders using secret signs and passwords to establish their mastery of their craft which, as seen in the great Gothic cathedrals, must certainly have seemed occult to the uninitiated. The association of masonry with the **hermetic** mysteries as such seems first to surface *c.* 1638 in a poem by Henry Adamson of Perth:

> For we be brethren of the Rosie Crosse;
> We have the Mason word, and **second sight**,
> Things for to come we can tell aright . . .[1]

Given doubts that the 'brethren of the Rosie Crosse' ever really existed, it may be that these lines were never more than romance. Certainly by the end of the seventeenth century 'Operative Masonry' – the functional practice of the Craft – was changing into 'Speculative Masonry', as evolved in Scotland (Scotch Rite). Such lodges were *possibly* a repository of Templar lore: they certainly did require loyalty to the Stuarts; thus to the Jacobite cause. The formation in 1717 of the English Grand Lodge arose as a Whig/Hanoverian attempt to break this Jacobite monopoly: by 1723 the original four English lodges had grown to fifty-two; in 1733 in Massachusetts the first American lodge was formed . . . and in 1776 masons played a prominent role in establishing the US constitution. Masonic symbols like the Eye in the Triangle remain conspicuous on the dollar bill to the present day.

But what was it all about? Not even masons are sure of the origins of the Craft and its rites. In effect, in its modern form, it constituted a nexus (complete with ancient mystique) for the trading gentry of Europe's emergent middle classes to meet in exclusive clubs, the better to further their business in private association. Such secrecy excited alarm from the start, and still does (Freemasonry was banned in all Communist and remains so in most Catholic countries), as much on grounds that it constitutes an alternative church as through fear of subversion of political life and honest trading by 'insider dealing' between members of the lodges.

Freemasonry insists on the brotherhood of man. It also requires the purification and enlightenment of its members *via* the 'seven steps of Solomon's Temple'. These are: discretion, obedience, morality, love of mankind, courage, generosity and love of death. A third aim is to work towards the regeneration of mankind. Modern Freemasonry is divided into three 'Craft' degrees – Entered Apprentice, Fellow Craft and Master Mason. These are under jurisdiction of the United Grand Lodge of England (its present Grand Master is the Duke of Kent). Several 'optional' or 'higher' degrees are overseen by other Freemasonic bodies, such as the Royal Arch. Britain's 700,000 masons work through the three degrees and may then move on to the higher degrees.

1. *The Temple and the Lodge*, M. Baigent and R. Leigh, Corgi, London 1990, p. 168
2. *The Brotherhood*, Stephen Knight, Granada, London 1983

FREUD, Sigmund (1856–1939) (*See* **JUNG**) The author of *The Interpretation of Dreams* and father of psychoanalytic technique was publicly ambivalent about the **paranormal**, reviling what he called 'the black tide of mud of **occultism**'. In argument with C. G. Jung in 1909 he called it 'sheer bosh'. In fact the subject interested him deeply. His favourite pastime was to tell uncanny tales late at night, in justification quoting Hamlet: 'There are more things in heaven and earth, Horatio,/Than are dreamt of in your philosophy' – but he remained reticent about it, being reluctant to expose psychoanalysis to further attack. This reluctance was shared by many of his more conservative followers. When he published an article favouring **telepathy** his English disciple Ernest Jones criticised him. Freud replied that he had to tell the truth as he saw it.

He derided the 'untrustworthiness, credulity, and unconvincingness' of reports of phenomena like **precognition**. But his own inner ambivalence was notable. Once, as Jung described the preservation of long-dead human bodies in Danish peat-bogs, Freud fainted clean away. It seemed as if with his ground-breaking work into the unconscious he had gone as far as he dared in confronting the 'black tide' as he found it in himself.

Even so, in 1921 he wrote in a letter to **psychic** researcher Hereward Carrington, 'If I were to live all over again, I should devote myself to psychical research rather than to psychoanalysis,' adding, 'it would be a great satisfaction to me if I could convince myself and others on unimpeachable evidence of the existence of telepathic processes'.

FULCANELLI (*See* **ALCHEMY**) The identity of the alchemist 'Fulcanelli' who in 1926 published *Le mystère des cathèdrales* (The mystery of the cathedrals) remains as unknown today as in the early 1920s when rumour swept Parisian **occult** circles that an actual master, who had manufactured the **Philosopher's Stone**, was among them.

These rumours originated with Eugène Canseliet, a young alchemical student, and his older friend, impoverished artist Jean-Julien Champagne. They claimed that Fulcanelli was their master. Sceptics doubted that he existed, but the vast learning and unique qualities shown in the book – an interpretation of the symbolism of

Europe's Gothic architecture as coded revelation of alchemical secrets – made many think again. In the preface Canseliet claimed that Fulcanelli had attained the Stone, been illuminated and had vanished. Speculation about his identity focussed unsatisfactorily on various men, including the writer J. H. Rosny the elder (1856–1940), and on Canseliet and Champagne. But Canseliet seemed too young to possess the erudition shown in the text, while Champagne – who liked to claim he was Fulcanelli – was a noted braggart, drunkard and joker, his character out of keeping with the gravity of the author. Indeed, three years after the 1929 publication of a second Fulcanelli book – *Les demeures philosophales* (The dwellings of the Philosophers) – Champagne, aged fifty-five, died in poverty of gangrene induced by absinthe and pernod addiction.

Canseliet never offered any clues as to Fulcanelli's identity. Flatly denying Champagne's authorship, he asserted that on several occasions in later years he had met the Master who, by his account, had grown visibly *younger* over a thirty-year period, and had an androgynous appearance – which is reportedly a side-effect of taking the Elixir of Life.

There is no evidence that Canseliet gained financially or otherwise from his claimed association with the mysterious Fulcanelli, whose name became widely known in 1963 with the publication by Pauwels and Bergier of their best-selling *The Dawn of Magic* (alias *The Morning of the Magicians*).

If Fulcanelli is still about, he must be over a century old, and may perhaps be sharing an other-dimensional apartment with the Comte de **Saint-Germain** . . . either way, *Le mystère des cathèdrales* remains in print, while the controversy shows that the mystique of alchemically induced longevity or even immortality remains persistent even today.[1]

1. *The Morning of the Magicians*, Pauwels and Bergier, Granada, London 1979

G

GAIA (*See* **EARTH SPIRIT**) *Gaia*, or *Gē* (as *ge*-ology, *ge*-ometry and *ge*-ography), was in Greek **myth** the Earth-goddess who mated with Ouranos, the sky, and brought forth life. In 1969 the name was revived by English Earth-scientist James Lovelock. He proposed that Planet Earth is a self-regulating system (*Gaia*), the seemingly random processes of which in fact combine 'intelligently' to regulate and maintain life.

In support of his theory he noted such 'homeostatic' factors as Earth's steady surface temperature (15°C–35°C) despite increases in solar heating; the steady level of ocean salt (about 3.4 percent) despite continual inflow of salt from rivers (if the level exceeded 6 percent, organic cell walls would disintegrate); the stable oxygen concentration in the atmosphere at 21 percent (less, and insufficient energy would be available for animal and insect survival: more, a global forest fire would erupt); the atmospheric presence of exactly the right amount of ammonia to neutralise sulphuric and nitric acids detrimental to existing life-forms; and the presence in the upper atmosphere of the ozone layer, which shields surface life-forms from excess solar ultra-violet radiation harmful to DNA and other basic biological structures.[1]

These factors suggest that Gaia's climate and chemistry are organised so as to provide optimal conditions for the survival of life as we know it. This concept of Gaia as a single living organism has become a core idea of '**New Age**' thought. To argue that chance alone produces such conditions is like arguing that a house is built by randomly throwing bricks and mortar together, the bricks and mortar themselves being products of chance. It seems that not only poetic but scientific truth rests in the rediscovered image of the dancing goddess Gaia, our organic mother.[2, 3]

1. *The Awakening Earth*, Peter Russell, Ark/Routledge Kegan Paul, London 1984, pp. 10–11
2. *Gaia*, Elisabet Sahtouris, Pocket Books, New York 1989, p. 23
3. *Gaia*, James Lovelock, Oxford University Press, London 1979

GANZFELD STATE (*See* **ESP**) This condition of **sensory deprivation** is employed by **parapsychologists** researching ESP faculties. Resting on a mattress, the subject's eyes are covered with half ping-pong balls on to which soft coloured light is shone; the gentle hiss of 'white noise' is fed into his ears. In this state, without visual or auditory distraction, supposedly the subject – now in the *Ganzfeld State* – may more easily receive *telepathic* signals from a distant agent focussing on some picture chosen at random. In one such experiment conducted at Cambridge University by Dr Carl Sargent, the subject was able to name the picture being 'sent' – *The Ancient of Days*, by William Blake.[1]

1. 'Putting the power to work', Roy Stemman, *The Unexplained*. Orbis partwork, London 1983, pp. 135–6

GARDNER, Gerald Brousseau (1884–1964) (*See* **WITCHCRAFT**) Born near Liverpool, Gerald Gardner (GBG) claimed descent from Grissell Gairdner, burned as a witch in Scotland in 1610. A tea and rubber planter in Malaya, his eye for odd lore led in 1936 to a book: *Keris and other Malay Weapons*. Settling with his wife in

Hampshire in 1936, he learned that the British witch-cult still existed. Neighbours belonged to the Fellowship of Crotona, a neo-**Rosicrucian** cult led by 'Brother Aurelius'. Part-founded by Annie **Besant**'s daughter Mrs Besant-Scott, the Fellowship ran a community theatre which Gardner joined. Here he met Co-Masons: an order begun by Annie Besant to enable women to participate in the **Masonic** tradition. They had followed Mrs Besant-Scott into the Fellowship of Crotona and subsequently contacted a surviving New Forest witch coven. Keeping this secret (not until 1951 was the last UK Witchcraft Act repealed), however they confided in GBG.

Betraying their confidence, in 1949 he published a novel, *High Magic's Aid*, and on repeal of the Act publicised the Craft's survival via books, broadcasts, interviews and his Museum of Magic and Witchcraft on the Isle of Man. In 1954 his *Witchcraft Today* restated Dr Margaret Murray's thesis of witchcraft as a Stone Age fertility religion. His efforts led to many new 'Gardnerian' covens, also to an enduring split in the Craft. Critics did not deny his good intentions, but deplored his publicising practices they felt best kept secret (like ritual nudity, which he thought healthy), and denied the authenticity of rites he developed in collaboration with **Crowley** before the latter died in 1947. Some claim these rites reflect the sado-masochistic sexual interests of both men. GBG said the rituals he had received were fragmentary, requiring new material inevitably reflecting his and Crowley's personalities. As to publicising the Craft, he felt new blood was needed. Supporters point out his lack of malice or exploitation of the **occult** for personal gain, his trusting, childlike nature, and his refusal to pretend he had magical powers, which some say he possessed.[1]

1. *Witchcraft Today*, Gerald B. Gardner, Rider, London 1954

GARRETT, Eileen (1893–1970) (*See* **LeSHAN, MEDIUMS**) Raised in rural Ireland by an aunt who whipped her for 'telling lies' about her **second sight**, she moved to London where, at the age of sixteen, she married a man who told her to give up her 'visioning' or risk going mad. Yet when her second son was born she sensed he would die young. Soon after, both sons died of meningitis.

Divorced, during World War I she married a young army officer who went to the Front. In a vision she 'saw' him blown up. Two days later she heard he was missing. Married again, she had a daughter, who caught pneumonia. Holding the dying child, she sensed a presence and heard a voice say: 'She must have more air. Open the window.' She did. Her daughter recovered.

Falling asleep at a **spiritualist** meeting, on awakening she was told the dead had spoken through her. Consulting a Swiss **clairvoyant**, Huhnli, she again 'fell asleep'. When she awoke Huhnli claimed a spirit, Uvani, had spoken through her as her 'control', saying he wanted to 'do serious work to prove the theory of survival'. Furious, her third husband said she was going mad. She broke down into illness. Recovering, she sensed, 'the **trance** state might be part of a psychological pattern which had its inception in my early childhood. I began to understand how the pain and suffering of these early days had made me withdraw from the world of people . . . the first time I had been successful in escaping the pain of the punishment inflicted on me by my aunt was when I so separated myself that I could see her lips moving as she scolded me, but not a word penetrated my ears.'[1]

Warned by **psychic** James Hewat Mackenzie that 'controls', if spirits of the dead or not, are often stupid and unreliable, she told him she feared 'Uvani' was only a split-off fragment of her own mind. Divorced again, and though loathing the triviality of her sitters, she became a full-time medium. But her disgust persisted: she decided to abandon spiritualism to remarry. On the day the banns were published she developed a mastoid: her husband-to-be fell sick and died a week later, as predicted by the same inner voice which had warned of her son's death. She could not escape.

Now thirty-eight, she went to America. Persisting as a medium to earn a living, she met psychic researchers Hereward Carrington, then working with Sylvan **Muldoon** and J. B. **Rhine. ESP** tests (**astral projection, automatic writing, telepathy**) led her to conclude, 'the **subconscious mind** was a vehicle capable of expanding indefinitely and able to contact all possible realms of understanding which it might choose to reach'.[2]

Later in the USA she worked with Lawrence **LeShan** and Andrija **Puharich**. In 1951 she helped establish the Parapsychology Foundation, an institute devoted to the scientific study of **psi** powers.

Garrett was pragmatic about, even sceptical of her unwanted psychism. Unimpressed by **occultists**, she sought scientific or psychological answers to explain the powers she manifested in **trance**.

Was fear of the aunt who had whipped her so deeply lodged she could never accept her abilities at face value? The evidence of her life denies this negative view. Garrett rose above the misery of her early life and marriages, retaining integrity when a split into **multiple personalities** might have been a more predictable response to the pain she had endured.

1. *My Life*, Eileen J. Garrett, Psychic Book Club, London 1939
2. *Beyond the Occult*, Colin Wilson, Corgi Books, London 1988, p. 413

GASPARETTO, Luiz Antonio During the last twenty years this Brazilian psychologist has performed many **trance**-painting sessions in public, rapidly (in periods ranging from five minutes to half an hour) executing 'new' masterpieces in the style of old masters like Leonardo or Rembrandt, or of modern painters like Modigliani or Picasso. Painting with feet as well as hands, on occasion he 'channels' one artist through one arm, another through the other, and a third through his feet – at the same time! Insisting that the '**disincarnate** masters' paint through him to prove that life survives death, he describes how:

'At the onset I feel a **telepathic** invitation to work. This is followed by my sensing the fluidic presence of other **spirit**-artists. Immediately a force overpowers my arms, moving them automatically . . . It is clear to me that my will is free and that I can stop if I want to.'

An observer of one such session in San Francisco in 1986, resulting in eight pictures in forty minutes, describes how: 'The lights were turned down and Luiz put on a tape . . . an assortment of classical music . . . The combination of the music, the lighting, Luiz' movements, and the heat seemed to have an almost hypnotic effect of the audience . . . Luiz's hands move incredibly fast, and his body moves and gyrates while he works . . . a man steadied the paper or canvas for him . . . he seemed to work in time with the music. Most of the time, but not always, he looked away from a piece while he worked on it. The first drawing, a "Rembrandt" in one colour, was drawn upside down. The two faces in another were drawn simultaneously, using both hands . . . the works were for sale and . . . all proceeds, minus expenses for supplies, go to charity.'[1]

1. *Intangible Evidence*, Bernard Gittelson, Simon and Schuster, London 1987

GAUQUELIN, Michel (1928–) (*See* **ASTROLOGY, BROWN, JONAS, NELSON**) This French psychologist's work suggests that the positions of the planets at our birth do indeed influence our characters and career. That scientists are typically born with Saturn rising or at midheaven, doctors likewise under Saturn or Mars, sportsmen under Mars, soldiers under Mars or Jupiter, and writers under Venus or the Moon, is now seen as likely even by some of Gauquelin's former opponents. In 1975 psychologist Hans **Eysenck** wrote of his work: 'However much it may go against the grain, I think we must admit that there is something here that requires explanation.'[1]

Working since 1950 from Strasbourg's Psychophysiological Laboratory, his interest in planetary rhythms led him to seek terrestrial correlation. His initial nine-year study covered France, Belgium, Italy, Germany and Holland: countries where birth times as well as dates are recorded. From birth registers and professional directories he got 16,336 timed births of 'eminent' professionals, and 24,961 of 'ordinary' professionals. Splitting up this data by profession, he analysed first the births of 576 successful doctors (members of the French Academy) and found a significant proportion born with Mars and Saturn just risen or at midheaven (zenith of the sky). Another sample of 508 successful doctors showed the same result. Odds against chance were reckoned as ten million to one. A Belgian committee of astronomers, statisticians and demographers repeated the experiment with a new group of 539 doctors and confirmed the findings. However mysteriously, Saturn and Mars *are* implicated in the birth of successful doctors.[2]

Later he confirmed the correlation between specific planets and success in other areas. Of 3,674 scientists, 704 were born in sector one (twelfth astrological house) or sector four (ninth house) of Saturn (odds 300,000 to 1 against chance). Of 3,468 military men, the presence of Jupiter and Mars at birth rated odds of 1,000,000 to one. Of 2,088 sports champions, the presence of Mars produced odds of 5,000,000 to one. And so on. Crucially, these results referred *only* to those eminent in their professions. Control groups of 'ordinary' professionals showed no such disposition.

He has also shown that certain professions 'avoid' specific planets in 'high intensity' positions (sectors one and four). Saturn is 'low intensity' in the charts of artists and writers, and Jupiter in those of scientists and physicians. This is not to say there are *no* successful doctors with Jupiter rising or dominant – Gauquelin deals with the significant *tendencies* only.

Elsewhere Edmund van Deusen studied 163,953 birth-dates of folk born in the USA and Canada. In Britain, sociologist Joe Cooper, with Alan Smithers of Bradford University, has processed 35,000 birth-dates. Combined results produced interesting generalisations. Of 28,000 UK and US army officers, a significant proportion were born in late summer or early autumn, with peaks in Leo and Scorpio. A significant number of 2,696 US bankers were born in Virgo. 8,932 UK and US musicians tended to be born in Pisces, Sagittarius, Capricorn or Aquarius. UK politicians prefer Aries; admen, journalists and lawyers typically fall in Gemini. Librarians (oddly enough) embrace Libra. Teachers tend to be born in Leo or Virgo, while of 3,927 UK and US authors, a significant proportion were also born in Virgo.

In 1977 Hans Eysenck, with astrologer Jeff Mayo, set out to research another old claim: that people born in Cancer, Scorpio or Pisces are often unduly emotional or neurotic. Using a standard personality test developed by Eysenck in 1964, they found correlation between extroversion and odd-numbered birth-signs (Aries, Gemini, Leo, Libra, Sagittarius and Aquarius); and between introversion and even-numbered signs (Taurus, Capricorn, Virgo, Scorpio, Capricorn and Pisces). Cancer, Scorpio, Pisces and (surprisingly) Aries were strongly linked with emotional and neurotic leanings.[3]

Such studies progress despite antagonism from many 'scientists' whose love of truth seems oddly limited. To date only a few, like Eysenck, have accepted evidence that goes 'against the grain' of dogmatism.

1. 'Planets, Stars and Personality', H. J. Eysenck, in *New Behaviour*, 29 May 1975, p. 249
2. *The Cosmic Clocks*, Michel Gauquelin, Peter Owen, London 1969
3. 'The Signs of Success', Brian Innes, *The Unexplained*, Orbis partwork, London 1983, p. 634

GELLER, Uri (1946–) (*See* **CLAIRVOYANCE, PSYCHOKINESIS, TELEPATHY**) This Israeli **psychic** became famous in the 1970s and remains controversial despite retiring from the limelight to **dowse** minerals for corporations like Rio Tinto Zinc. His fame derives from his alleged capacity to bend metal and perform other **psychokinetic** feats both on TV and under controlled laboratory conditons. Many insist his powers are genuine: others like US stage magician James **Randi** denounce him as a **fraud**.

In 1971 US psychic researcher Andrija **Puharich** heard of Geller's stage act. On 17 August he saw Geller perform at a Jaffa discotheque. Impressed only by Geller's final trick (breaking a ring without touching it) he asked Geller to undergo tests. Next day in Puharich's apartment, laying a notepad on the table, Geller asked him to think of three numbers. Puharich chose 4, 3 and 2. 'Pick up the notepad.' said Geller. Doing so, Puharich found 4, 3 and 2 already written down. Apparently Geller had influenced him into choosing these numbers. Geller subsequently raised the temperature of a thermometer by staring at it and by concentration moved a compass needle. By such means he convinced Puharich that his power was genuine.[1]

Claiming his growing awareness and control of this power since infancy, Geller let Puharich 'regress' him. **Hypnotised** and speaking in Hebrew, he told how, playing in a Tel Aviv garden aged three, he had seen a shining bowl-shaped light in the sky above, then a bright faceless figure before him. At this point Puharich and his two colleagues heard an 'unearthly and metallic' voice above their heads. Emerging from hypnosis Geller, hearing what had happened, snatched the tape. Puharich says he saw it vanish from his hand. Geller ran from the room. When found he seemed confused, without memory of the event. There was no tape. Later Puharich and his colleagues reconstructed what they had heard as follows: 'It is us who found Uri in the garden when he was three. He is our helper sent to help man. We programmed him in the garden for many years to come, but he was also programmed not to remember. On this day his work begins. Andrija, you are to take care of him.'[2]

The voice went on to warn, in classic space-visitor style, of a coming world war. Subsequent events reported by Puharich included **teleportation** of his briefcase from New York to Tel Aviv, he and Geller being 'tailed' by a red light in the sky unseen by others, and disappearing tape-recorders. These were apparently caused by the Nine: other-dimensional beings behind the **UFO** sightings since 1947 who 'cannot enter your earth, only appear to you through computerising your minds;[3] This account as published by Puharich in 1974 must cause most readers to doubt his sanity, honesty or both. Yet, as his primary concern was to establish Geller's authenticity, why would he invent such a weird tale, far less publish it, especially as publication only gave Geller's detractors ammunition while damaging his own reputation? Subsequently, amid further weird events, he was told by the Nine (of whom even Geller was sceptical: he called them 'clowns playing practical jokes') to abandon further tests. It may be that the Nine, and their phenomena, emerged from Geller's own subconscious.

Geller became famous. On 23 November 1973 he appeared on a UK TV show: the 'David Dimbleby Talk-In'. Before a vast audience he started up broken watches and bent forks apparently by mind-power alone. The switchboard was jammed by calls from parents of children who, watching the show, had begun psychokinetically ruining the family cutlery. Scientists like Professor John Taylor were impressed. Journalists asked if Geller should be allowed to fly for fear he might distress electronic equipment. Asked to undergo more stringent tests, to the surprise of his detractors he agreed. Already in 1972 in New York he had reactivated the flat battery of a calculator belonging to famed rocket scientist Werner von Braun who, rejecting fakery as impossible, had concluded that Geller could produce electrical current.[4]

At the Stanford Research Institute in California Geller's **ESP** successes were notable. Twelve out of fourteen times he 'guessed' correctly under which of ten empty cans a small object was hidden. His duplication of drawings sealed inside double envelopes was as accurate. Asked to say which face of a die lay uppermost after being shaken up inside a closed box he was right every time. Yet now he suffered reverses. His successes on TV and in scientific laboratories enraged those who denied the existence of such faculties. The forces ranged against him included professional stage-'magicians' such as, in the USA, Charles Reynolds and James Randi, who claimed his 'powers' were explicable by sleight of hand, alias fraud. No surprise that those making their living by magical fraud should be first to accuse him – the shock to them to learn that the powers they fake might be real could prove terminal. Either way: bad publicity eclipsed Geller's star in the mid-1970s. No more was heard of fork-bending. He was forgotten – at least by the media.

Yet since he left the media stage he has become a millionaire, hiring himself out to multinational companies as a dowser for copper or gold. Interviewed in 1985 by author and broadcaster Bob Couttie, an intelligent debunker of **paranormal** claims who doubts Geller's psychic capacity, he said of his dowsing activities, 'I retired six years ago. I really don't have to work anymore. I was very successful . . . out of ten times, for example, I would find [something] three times.'

According to a *Financial Times* report, Geller's terms as a mineral dowser are a £1m advance against royalties, non-returnable.[5]

1. *Uri*, Andrija Puharich, Futura Books, London 1974, pp. 66–7
2. *ibid.*, pp. 94–96
3. *ibid.*, p. 184
4. 'Under the Eyes of Scientists', Colin Wilson, *The Unexplained*, Orbis partwork, London 1983, pp. 666–9
5. *Forbidden Knowledge*, Bob Couttie, Lutterworth Press, Cambridge 1988, p. 8

GEMATRIA (*See* **NUMBER, NUMEROLOGY, SACRED GEOMETRY**) This old science involves conversion of the letters of a word into number equivalents, adding up their sum, then substituting another word realising the same total. Seemingly innocuous passages thus reveal hidden meanings to those aware of the codes. The system as we have it originated with the Hebrew twenty-two-letter alphabet and was later taken up by European **Gnostics** and **Qabalists**. The 'magical' aspect lies in the **correspondence** seen between numbers and cosmic law: by association with number the alphabet functioned simultaneously on a pragmatic daily basis and on a cosmic level.

The Bible (both Hebrew and Greek) abounds in examples. Gematria reveals the ladder Jacob saw reaching from earth to heaven to be Sinai. The letters of the Hebrew words *sulam* (ladder) and Sinai both total 130: so the Mosaic law revealed on Sinai is the ladder from heaven to earth. In the Book of Daniel the name of the contemporary Seleucid king Antiochus IV Epiphanes is hidden in the name Nebuchadnezzar: the Hebrew letters of both names add up to 423. By this means the author of Daniel was able to call Antiochus a tyrant and get away with it; only those 'in the know' would understand.

St Irenaeus, a second-century Gnostic who later became Bishop of Lyons, explains the gematric coding of divine names and principles. The number of the cockerel-headed gnostic god *Abraxas* is 365; that of *Jesus* is 888.[1]

The best-known gematric numbers were 666 and 1080. 666, the famous 'Number of the Beast' of Revelation xiii, 18 ('Here is wisdom. Let him that hath understanding count the number of the beast: for it is the number of a man, and his number is six hundred threescore and six'), refers to the positive, active, *yang* charge of solar energy: also to a masculine polarity associated with tyranny or imperial rule. 1080 represents the opposite, complementary principle: negative, receptive, lunar, **yin**, female. Greek phrases giving 1080 include those for the *Holy Spirit*, the *Spirit of the Earth, fountain of wisdom, Tartaros, the abyss*, etc. The sum of 666 and 1080 is 1746, in Greek equivalent to a grain of mustard seed – the number of fusion and fertile union between the two opposite natural principles.[2]

So the combination of individual words and their gematric equivalents can literally speak volumes. Sadly such an esoteric system is wide open to superstitious misinterpretation. 666 especially remains a source of fear – and insult. Over the centuries this 'Number of the Beast' has been applied (by their enemies) to Nero, Luther, Napoleon, the Pope and **Hitler**. Today Christian fundamentalists so mistrust it that when in 1989 ex-US President Reagan retired to Hollywood's 666 Saint Cloud Road, 666 had to be changed to 669 before he (and Nancy) would agree to move in.

Antiquarian John **Michell** suggests St John used gematria to hide his real meaning in Revelation xiii, 18. In the original Greek text St John tells us to 'count the number of the beast'; yet the number (666) is given. '666' is thus only part of the equation. The gematric value for: 'And his number is 666' is 2368. 2368 is the gematric sum of the Greek letters for the name Jesus Christ. So the *coded* meaning is: 'Here is wisdom. Let him that hath understanding count the number of the beast: for it is the number of a man 2368, Jesus Christ.'[3]

Michell claims that St John, a Gnostic, hated the way the 'Christian' church had turned the image of Christ Crucified into an *idol*; an object of compulsory worship for low material purposes. Thus the 'Christ' he named as the Beast 666 was the false Christ of the Church. He was saying Christ and his message had been perverted by power-seekers. He coded what he said for self-protection. His use of code led to enduring misinterpretation. For 666 is indeed the number of Man – the superstitious beast 666 who, lacking deeper union with Woman 1080, still plunders and rapes the Earth.

So **Crowley's** self-advertisement as the 'Great Beast 666' was perhaps more subtle than at first appears. In Britain today, those applying for personal car number plates find 666 excluded. Nobody can drive on UK roads advertising themselves as ME 666. This may be sensible.

1. *The Magical Arts*, Richard Cavendish, Arkana, London 1984, p. 117ff
2. *The New View Over Atlantis*, John Michell, Thames and Hudson, London 1983, pp. 154–6
3. *The Dimensions of Paradise*, John Michell, Thames and Hudson, London 1988

GEOMANCY Called ***feng-shui*** ('wind and water') in China where until lately the art was best developed, *geomancy* involves the harmonious siting of buildings and other artificial features within a landscape so that even in conditions of dense population both land and people remain healthy. Thus in China geomancers – aware of magnetic currents coursing through the body of the Earth just as **acupuncture** meridians track the human body – sited each building, tomb, tree, wood, post or stone so as best to maintain the land's health. These 'dragon currents' they defined in two forms, **yin** and **yang**, negative and positive, the one represented by a white tiger, the other by the blue dragon. The yang (male) current follows high routes like mountain ridges; the yin follows lower hills: points of intersection are beneficial. Tombs especially were ideally sited at a junction of currents, preferably facing south, a hill behind and attractive lower land in front. In general every construction had to meet geomantic standards of beauty and utility.

In the nineteenth century European businessmen entering China were amazed to hear their factories and railways could not be sited as seemingly rational economic demand dictated. Tunnels could not be put through 'dragon hills', etc. The Chinese were also amazed. Were Europeans so ignorant of geomantic necessity as to see only the *material* surface of the landscape? Why did they want to site a port at Hong Kong? – geomantically a disaster area.

Today many people protest the decisions of planning departments, who build new towns and 'developments' that sprawl inharmoniously, encouraging slum mentality and ugliness. In Britain geomantic intelligence lasted from pre-Roman times to the Middle Ages. Sacred sites from **Stonehenge** to Durham Cathedral were geomantically selected to take advantage of earth-energies which today **dowsers** still contact. Dodmen who in pre-Roman times surveyed the 'old straight tracks' today associated with controversial '**ley lines**' practised that art called *feng-shui* in China, and for the same reasons.

Some influences marry; others do not: any gardener or artist knows it. That *feng-shui* created a land of ordered beauty beyond grasp of rational principle alone is acknowledged by the planner Professor Abercrombie, who said it produced: 'one of the most elaborate landscapes which has ever existed, a landscape which had to preserve certain spiritual values and also to fulfil the practical purpose of supporting a dense population'.

1. *The New View Over Atlantis*, John Michell, Thames and Hudson, London 1983, pp. 59–65

GHOSTS (*See* **ELEMENTALS, GHOULS, LETHBRIDGE, POLTERGEIST**) Ghosts are usually defined as unquiet spirits of the dead, typically bound by past anguish to a place or house which they haunt until **exorcised** or 'laid' (to rest). They may be visible to the living as apparitions, or may manifest via **psychokinetic** events: rappings on walls, objects falling from thin air, etc. The latter type, a poltergeist (German: 'rattling ghost'), is usually associated with unconscious psychokinetic activity caused by disturbed adolescents, and so differs from the classic ghost, which is distinctively understood to be the restless, misdirected **spirit** of a dead person.

As such, ghosts are the acceptable face of the supernatural. Everyone knows a ghost-story; ancestral mansions open to the public cannot justify the entrance fee without offering a haunted gallery. The question: 'Do you believe in ghosts?' is trite because so often asked as a means of learning someone else's attitude to the entire range of phenomena discussed herein.

On what does such a belief rely? If not on personal experience or on the evidence of case-histories recorded by the **Society for Psychical Research** (SPR) and other groups, perhaps in the sense that life's energies transcend material reality alone; maybe too in the suggestion that tragic emotion may violently imprint its repetitive echo on the 'haunted' site involved.

Castle Rushen on the Isle of Man is haunted by a Grey Lady, the ghost of a woman hanged for killing her son. Too late it emerged he had died of natural causes. Obsessed by her wrongful execution, still she haunts the place, unable to 'let go'. Such obsession characterises ghosts. Grievance holds them to continue poisoning the site where in life they suffered.

Only when persuaded (exorcised) that their obsession is irrelevant and harmful do they abandon their haunt and go wherever the dead should go.

Modern attempts to explain ghosts in natural terms are typified by T.C. Lethbridge. In the late 1960s this retired English academic proposed an explanation of hauntings by ghosts, ghouls or elementals. Suggesting that we all own an '**electromagnetic**' aura or field, its strength affected by emotional arousal, he said most hauntings arise from interaction between this personal field and the local earth-field – a magnetic medium in which, like tape-recordings, the emotions of those now long dead continue to play, usually unhappily, to be picked up and replayed as 'ghosts' by the living.

Arguing that such ghost-productive local earth-fields always associate with underground water, he connected hauntings with damp places. He thought that in all cases of place-memory haunting at least two people are involved at different times. The 'ghost', created by unconscious energy-leakage from the **psyche**-field of a disturbed person (the 'projector'), is stored (like a tape-recording) in the relatively weak earth-field of the site. Later, via reverse leakage from the earth-field, it is perceived as sound, image or both (a 'ghost'), or as amorphous emotion (a 'ghoul') by the 'retriever'.

This theory fits many ghost-types, including **black dogs**, but does not explain the classic ghost, or **etheric body** of a departed spirit, clinging to its haunt like a limpet to a rock, so bound by past emotional obsession that it may neither depart in peace nor regret the shock it causes the living. Nor does it explain the ghost perceived as **doppelgänger**.

Antony D. Hippesley Coxe prefaces his exhaustive gazetteer of *Haunted Britain* with his 'favourite ghost story'. This involves a navy lieutenant serving overseas. His wife, always with him, dreamed all the time of a certain house. As the children grew up, 'Mama's dream house' became a family joke. When the father retired they returned to England to look for a house in the country. Approaching one place, the mother said, 'But we're coming to my dream house'. Though derided, she told them the route they'd take, which they did. At the house the estate agent met them. Shown over it, the mother kept remarking on changes made to it. 'But surely the stairs used to come down here? Oh! yes, I remember now, they were altered when we were in Hong Kong; that would be about fifteen years ago.' She was right every time. The children asked if the house was haunted. 'Yes,' said the agent, 'there is even supposed to be a ghost.' They bought the house. Later the mother met the agent. He asked if they were happy. 'Perfectly', she said, adding that the children were disappointed not to have seen the ghost. 'I did not think they would,' said the agent, 'you are the ghost. I have seen you here many times.'[2]

1. *Needles of Stone Revisited*, Tom Graves, Gothic Image, Glastonbury 1986, pp. 102ff
2. *Haunted Britain*, Antony D. Hippesley Coxe, Hutchinson, London 1973

GHOULS (*See* **ELEMENTALS, GHOSTS, LETHBRIDGE**) Derived from the Arab word *ghūl*, in Eastern tales a ghoul is an evil spirit that devours human corpses. It may be an **astral** or elemental **entity** that preys on human energy and substance. In *Journeys out of the Body*, American **out-of-the-body** (OOBE) traveller Robert **Monroe** notes: 'Throughout man's history the reports have been consistent. There are **demons**, spirits, goblins, gremlins and assorted sub-human entities always hanging around humanity to make life miserable. Are these **myths? Hallucinations**?'

During one OOBE experience Monroe felt two rubbery beings climbing on to him. In panic he fought them. They turned into his two daughters, but resumed their former shape when they saw him undeceived. Finally a man in a monk's robe came and pulled them off. Another time he endured a long and exhausting battle with an unseen entity which he escaped only, he reports, by dropping back into his physical body.[1]

Henry James senior, father of the American novelist Henry James and psychologist William **James**, describes how in May 1884, after a family dinner, he sat happily staring into the embers, when suddenly: 'fear came upon me, and trembling, which made all my bones to shake'. He sensed 'some damned shape squatting invisible to me within the precincts of the room, and raying out from his fetid personality influences fatal to life'. In seconds 'reduced to a wreck', he wished to run and shout for help, but controlled his fear and sat it out.

His resulting despair and nervous breakdown lasted two years. Doctors said he had 'overworked his brain'. In time he decided he had undergone the spiritual experience **Swedenborg** calls 'devastation', or 'vastation'.

Researching this story, Colin **Wilson** learned James had this experience in England, at Frogmore Cottage near Windsor. Wilson comments that the area, associated with antlered **pagan** deity Herne the Hunter, is famously subject to ghostly events; that Frogmore Cottage lies a hundred feet from a known **ley line**; and that the event occurred near or even on Mayday, the ancient festival of Bel, when such elemental forces are traditionally strongest.[2]

English researcher T.C. Lethbridge used the term *ghoul* to describe any haunting characterised solely by a nasty feeling. On a muggy January day in the early 1960s, he and his wife Mina visited Ladram Bay on the Devon coast. 'As I stepped on to the beach,' he wrote, 'I passed into a kind of blanket, or fog, of depression, and, I think, fear.' Mina felt it too. 'There's something frightful here,' she said. Later her mother said she too had felt similarly depressed (on a warm, muggy day) in a field near the ancient **megalithic** centre of Avebury in Wiltshire.

The next Saturday (again warm and drizzly) Lethbridge and Mina again visited Ladram Bay. Again he felt depressed, at the same place as before – near a brook that ran on to the beach. Mina indicated the spot where she had felt the 'ghoul'. The feeling had been 'so strong as to make me feel almost giddy'. A tingling sensation had accompanied it.

At the clifftop Mina felt someone urging her to jump. Later Lethbridge recalled the recent odd death of their local 'witch'. She had told him she meant to curse the cattle of a farmer she was angry with. Ignoring a warning by Lethbridge that such **black magic** might rebound on her, she had suddenly died. Since then he had felt an unpleasant sensation about her house – but it had a limit, like a field bounded by a wall. He could step out of it.

All this led him (via **dowsing** experiments) to decide that ghouls arise from the imprint of negative emotion on terrestrial force-fields strongest over underground streams or where damp conditions prevail. The 'ghoul' of Ladram Bay arose from someone who had stood on the clifftop contemplating suicide. Whether or not the tragedy actually occurred, the intention alone had left a 'nasty feeling' sensed thereafter by anyone entering the 'field' saturated in gloom and desperation.[3]

As Lethbridge acknowledged, this explanation of one sort of ghoul does not necessarily invalidate the possible reality of elementals or hungry spirits of the dead which **vampirise** the energies of the living.

1. *Journeys out of the Body*, Robert Monroe, Souvenir Press, London 1972
2. *Mysteries*, Colin Wilson, Grafton, London 1979, pp. 447–82
3. *Ghost and Divining Rod*, T. C. Lethbridge, Routledge Kegan Paul, London 1963

GIANTS (*See* **BLAKE, ELOHIM, ENOCH, MEGALITHIC MYSTERIES**) 'There were giants in the earth in those days,' comments Genesis vi, 4. These were beings so wicked that God sent the flood. This episode is expanded in the apocryphal Book of **Enoch**. The giants were born to mortal women as the 'impious offspring' of the **angels** called **Watchers**. For this the Watchers were damned, for God had 'made not wives for you, because, being spiritual, your dwelling is in heaven'. As for the giants, 'who have been born of spirit and of flesh', their fate was to be 'called upon earth evil spirits, and on earth shall be their habitation . . . The spirits of the giants *shall be like* clouds, which shall oppress, corrupt, fall, contend, and bruise the earth . . . no food shall they eat; and they shall be thirsty; they shall be concealed.'[1]

So in Enoch, giants are not of flesh and blood but are **demons, spirits** of contention 'concealed' on immaterial planes, **vampirising** human energy. In the **fairy tale**, Jack climbs the **shamanic** beanstalk, or **Tree of Life**, to face and defeat the Giant in the Castle of the Clouds: the '**astral**' domain inhabited by such greedy, ogreish entities.

Yet the giant is not necessarily **evil**. He may be a slumbering force of nature locked up in Chains of Reason, a repository of racial instinct and vitality, as in **Blake**'s 'giant Albion', or the giant **pagan** fertility-figures cut into the chalk hills of south England (Cerne Abbas Giant, Long Man of Wilmington, the Gogmagog giant at Wandlebury Camp near Cambridge).

Or he may be Másaw in **Hopi** myth, arrogant caretaker of the Third World who, demoted when that world died to Lord of the Dead, gets a second chance as caretaker of the new, Fourth World . . . as already 'he had the people'.[2]

Or Finn McCool with his seven-league boots, striding through Irish myth to Scotland, where as Fingal with one bound he leaps from the **vitrified fort** of Knockfarrel over Stathpeffer Valley to the heights of Ben Wyvis.

Poets seeking inspiration by spending a night alone on the Giant's Seat high up Cader Idris in Wales infallibly go mad by dawn, it is said. This may only mean: they find what they seek. *Giantism* involves passage beyond local physical boundaries into what others call madness.

Attribution of spiritual mystery, good or evil, to overbearing physical size seems inevitable, given that when a child looks up at an adult he sees a giant, unfairly all-powerful, towering above.

What evidence is there of physical giantism in past human peoples?

Skeletons 30,000 years old (Paleolithic era) give an average height for adult males of 177 cm (5′11″), and for adult females of 165 cm (5′6″). But thereafter, as agriculture replaces hunting, average height falls greatly, only recently recovering. In 1960 American males averaged 175 cm. (5′9″).[1] The children of Chinese and Vietnamese immigrants to the meat-rich USA are notably taller than their rice-nourished parents. The stars of basketball teams like the Harlem Globetrotters are giants by any description. So the folklore of giantism needs to be seen in the context of available protein (which may be why, in so many folk-talkes, giants are cannibalistic ogres).[3]

Giantism also refers to amazing cultural achievement. **Stonehenge** was anciently known as 'the Giants' Dance'. The assumption was not only that the **megaliths** themselves are frozen giants (in Gaelic, *fir chreig*, 'false men'), but that only giants could erect stones of such weight.

Likewise the Baalbek platform in Syria, the **Great Pyramid** and so on. They *must* have been built by giants (or spacemen). Who else could shift such huge stones? Surely not mere human beings!

1. Enoch i, 15, (Laurence translation)
2. *The Book of the Hopi*, Frank Waters, Viking/Penguin, London/New York 1963
3. *Cannibals and Kings*, Marvin Harris, Vintage Books, New York 1978, p. 19

GLASTONBURY (*See* **EARTHWORKS, PSYCHIC ARCHAEOLOGY**) 'The holyest erthe in Englande' – Glastonbury, alias the Celtic *Ynys Witrin* (Isle of Glass) or Ynys Avallon (Isle of Apples) – is England's premier magical site. Though to many living there it is just a small Somerset town, Glastonbury is so drenched in **myth** that objectivity comes hard.

It is said King **Arthur** was buried in the Abbey grounds (probably the invention of twelfth-century monks); that the **Holy Grail** lies in the depths of the Chalice Well; and that the invisible 'Watchers from the Other Side' (long-dead monks) led the archaeologist Bligh **Bond** to uncover the Abbey's original foundations. It is said that St Joseph of Arimathea not only brought the Holy Grail here, making Glastonbury Britain's first Christian site but also planted the thorn tree that, despite its desecration during the Commonwealth, still flowers each year at Christmas.

Such tales marry with the mysteries of the Tor and the initiatory ritual maze that, some claim, winds up its steep, maybe artificial slopes to St Michael's Chapel atop it. Even more extraordinary is the enigma of the vast zodiac, 30 miles in circumference, said to have been anciently laid out in the landscape round the Tor, its giant figures 'discovered' in 1929 by sculptress Katherine **Maltwood**.[1] Some say this huge earthwork was known to John **Dee** and that it is the true Round Table. Others deny it exists at all, save in the minds of those wishing to perceive it.

Glastonbury is so rich in emotively **mystic** symbol and allusion that sense is easily lost amid all the **paranormal** speculation. One commentator writes, 'Glastonbury is one of those highly charged sacred focal points for the generation and transmission of cosmic energies. It is a planetary beacon and powerhouse of the spirit that enlightens all who approach its mysteries with a sense of humble participation and genuine love. It is a dangerous place because of the very potency of its spiritual energies, as those who have despoiled its brooding aura have discovered to their cost. It can generate madness and death as easily as it can produce tranquillity and revelation.'[2]

Such belief annually brings thousands of pilgrims into an area which in most respects is ordinary enough. People live, work and die here: bright-eyed seekers of transcendental mystery have not always met with approval. What to one person is a sacred site to another is just a cattle-pasture. Perhaps in such different perceptions lies the true mystery. Glastonbury is a mirror, reflecting and heightening the expectations of those who visit it. Yet its reputation is not a modern invention. Whatever the truth of the tales, they resonate in all who believe in them, and are not to be casually dismissed.

1. *A Guide to Glastonbury's Temple of the Stars*, K.E. Maltwood, Clarke, 1929
2. *Glastonbury: Ancient Avalon, New Jerusalem*, Anthony Roberts (ed.), Rider, London 1978

GLOSSOLALIA (*See* **REINCARNATION, XENOLALIA**) A term defining the phenomenon of 'speaking in tongues', specifically in *unidentified* tongues, as practised amid the enthusiasm of Pentecostalist and other revivalist meetings. Linguistic analysis of tape-recorded cases prove the sounds involved to be language-types, not languages. As such, glossolalia is distinct from ***xenolalia*** (speaking in real languages unknown to the speaker), and *xenoglossy* (likewise, but under **hypnosis**). The latter is usually attributed to unconscious learning of that language in the past: cases have been cited as suggesting **reincarnation** or **spirit possession**. One persuasive instance of the latter possibility is described by respected US reincarnation researcher, Dr Ian Stevenson, in his *Xenoglossy* (1974).

Hypnotically regressed in time by her husband, doctor Harold Johnson, Philadelphia housewife Lydia Johnson (not their real names) flinched, then screamed and grabbed her head. Twice more the attempt was made. Each time she emerged from **trance** with a headache, describing a scene with water, and old people forced into it to drown. She felt herself pushed down, then hit – thus the scream, and the headache. Regressed to a point ten years before by another hypnotist, she began to talk *in a deep masculine voice* in what proved to be Swedish, a language unknown to her. Calling herself Jensen Jacoby (she pronounced it YEN-sen Yah-ko-bee) she described (to Swedish linguists called in for the purpose) living in a seventeenth-century Swedish village. As Jensen, she displayed the personality and knowledge of a simple peasant. She correctly named various items consonant with the locale and era, but had no knowledge of modern tools, like pliers. Then Jensen began to take her over while she was unhypnotised. He was dismissed by the hypnotists and the experiment was terminated for fear that Lydia's personality would otherwise be permanently possessed by the stranger.[1]

1. *Xenoglossy*, Ian Stevenson, reported in *Reincarnation: the Phoenix Fire Mystery*, Joseph Head and S.L. Cranston, Julian Press, New York 1977

GNOSTICISM (*See* **CATHARISM, DUALISM, ESSENES**) From the Greek term *gnosis* (spiritual knowledge) the word *gnostic* refers to one claiming to possess such knowledge and insisting on the direct personal revelation of it as the only road to spiritual truth.

Specifically used as proper nouns, the terms *Gnostics* and Gnosticism embrace early Christian sects each insisting on the primacy of individual gnosis and conscience, and rejecting the authority of the orthodox Church as sole intermediary between God and Man. Dualist believers in co-equal universal powers of good (spirit), and evil (matter), most Gnostics held this world to be ruled by the demiurge, a false creator, whereas orthodox Christians, also holding nature to be corrupt, blamed this on the Fall of Man, not the Creator. Thus Gnosticism typically involved renunciation of the world. One Gnostic sect, the Ophites, worshipped **Christ** in the form of a **serpent**. Others interpreted the Christian *agape* or love-feast in terms of Dionysian orgy.[1] Drawing doctrines from many **pagan** and pre-Christian sources (Pythagoras, the Essenes, **Zoroastrianism**), and despite frequent bloody persecution, gnostic perceptions are so basic to human psychology that, though the sects were exterminated, their ideas persisted.

Gnostic texts, as found at Nag Hammadi in Egypt in 1945, show the vast differences in early interpretations of Christianity. Buried during early persecutions, and diverse in nature, these texts include gospels, poems, **astrological** treatises, philosophic descriptions of life's origin, **mythical** exegesis and instructions in magical practices. Texts like the *Gospel of Thomas* (beginning with: 'Whoever finds the interpretation of these sayings will not experience death'), and the oddly-titled *Thunder, Perfect Mind* reveal a picture at odds with the orthodox New Testament. Typically, Woman is exalted. 'I am the whore and the holy one,' cries the voice of *Thunder, Perfect Mind*, 'I am the wife and the virgin'. In the *Pistis Sophia* it is said the disciple Jesus loved the best was the Magdalene – hated by Peter and the other Apostles. So too the Gnostic image of Wisdom is female: Sophia.[2]

Gnostic veneration of Sophia (old **Isis**) was one cause of persecution by the patriarchal Church. Irenaeus, Tertullian and other early Christian authorities decry the attraction of Gnostic doctrine for 'many foolish women'.[3] Thus the Church saw to one of the many burnings of the library at Alexandria, a repository of Gnostic lore. In AD 414 in the same city the **Neoplatonist** philosopher Hypatia was murdered by monks who later scraped the flesh from her bones on a church altar.

Yet over the next millennium Gnostic ideas kept resurfacing in the beliefs of Manichaeans, Patarenes, Bogomils and Cathars. At last in the thirteenth century the Church apparently triumphed, establishing the Inquisition to wipe out Catharism. During the next four centuries in Europe, hundreds of thousands of women were burned alive at the stake – for being women. By the end of this era, the patriarchal triumph seemed complete.

Yet the theme has survived, via the symbols of troubadours, **Arthurian Myth, Qabalism, Rosicrucianism**; and, recently, via **Jungian** psychology and the recent explosion of **'New Age'**, **Gaia**-orientated beliefs. Impetus has been provided by the seemingly fortuitous rediscovery, at Qumrun and at Nag Hammadi, of Gnostic texts hidden nearly 2,000 yeas ago. Were they buried to await rediscovery in a time when autocratic Father-God imagery and all it implies is once again critically questioned?

Gnosticism is an attitude of mind. Perhaps today it has more going for it than its sterile modern offshoot – agnosticism.

1. *Creative Mythology*, Joseph Campbell, Penguin, London 1976, pp. 145–71
2. *The Nag Hammadi Library*, James M. Robinson (ed.). Harper and Row, New York, 1981
3. *The Gnostic Gospels*, Elaine Pagels, Pelican, London 1982, p. 80

GOETHE, Johann von (1749–1832) The efforts by this great eighteenth-century German visionary (author of *Faust*) to give scientific expression to his poetic insights stimulates renewed interest today. His theory of colour as a matter of perception, as an 'interchange of light and shadow' (distinguishing between hard physical reality and its variable subjective perception), was rejected by Newtonians who wished to reduce all such phenomena into frequencies of vibration, but has been taken up again by US **Chaos** theorist Mitchell Feilgenbaum. His intuitive venture into evolutionary theory led to answers later regarded as correct, but his lack of practical evidence meant his ideas were ignored until, a century later, he was seen as Darwin's inspired forerunner.

Foreshadowing **Jung** with the notion that the influences on his poetry and research were **archetypal** and universal, Goethe combined the vision of a **mystic** with a scientist's systematic approach. Embracing the Platonic notion that all reality is but a manifestation of Idea, he considered it of primary importance that the scientist develop his own **consciousness** as the most delicate and potent instrument available to perceive the universe. To obtain a better understanding of plant-life he would, at night before going to sleep, visualise the entire cycle of a plant's developments in all its stages from seed to seed. As novelist and dramatist, his *Young Werther* was among the first modern popular tragic romances (causing suicides all over Europe): his *Faust* dramatised the continuing conflict of modern industrial Man who seeks knowledge and material power at the expense of his own soul.

Of his psychism it is told how, walking with a friend in Weimar one wet summer evening, suddenly he began talking to an **apparition** he alone saw. 'My God,' he exclaimed, 'If I were not sure that my friend Frederick is at this moment at Frankfurt I should swear that it is he!' Then he burst out laughing. 'But it is he – my friend Frederick. You at Weimar? But why are you dressed so – in your dressing gown, with your nightcap and my slippers here in the public road?' His friend walking beside him, seeing nothing, thought he had gone mad. He went on dreamingly: 'Yes, I understand . . . it is a **vision**. What can it mean though? Has my friend suddenly died? Was it his **spirit**?' On getting home Goethe found Frederick waiting. His hair stood on end. 'Avaunt, you phantom!' he exclaimed. It emerged that Frederick had arrived at Goethe's lodging soaked by the rain, had changed into the poet's dry clothes and, falling asleep in a chair, had dreamed he had gone out to meet him and that Goethe had greeted him, saying, 'You here! At Weimar? What? With your dressing-gown, your nightcap and my slippers here on the public road?'[1]

1. Reported in *Maps of Consciousness*, Jeffrey Mishlove, Random House, New York 1975, pp. 58–9

GOLDEN DAWN, Hermetic Order of The In 1887 Dr Wynn Westcott, a London coroner and **Freemason**, acquired a coded manuscript which, deciphered, yielded five Masonic rituals. Inviting his friend Samuel **Mathers** to expand this material, Westcott found in the manuscript the address of one Fraulein Anna Sprengel, apparently a famed **Rosicrucian** adept. Fraulein Sprengel subsequently told him to found an English branch of her German **occult** society, calling it the Golden Dawn. Or so Westcott claimed. It now seems likely that Fraulein Sprengel was as non-existent as the coded manuscript; that Westcott concocted his authorisation to compete with Madame **Blavatsky**, who in 1875 had established **Theosophy**.

Yet the Order of the Golden Dawn represents the first serious modern effort to synthesise ancient **mystery** teachings into a system of controlled inner exploration. Active a generation after the Darwin furore confirmed the split between science and faith and even as **Freud** and **Einstein** formulated their early insights, the Golden Dawn offered techniques (mostly developed by Mathers) for systematic, *conscious* exploration of mental realms until then denied by all but those aware of former or eastern occult tradition.

The Order offered its adherents a **transcendental** teaching based not on faith but self-effort, the goal being controlled evolution to a god-like state epitomised by the conventional **Christ** and by other reborn deities such as the Egyptian **Osiris**. To attain this state a system of **ritual** and psychoanalytic techniques allied to a doctrine of universal law underpinned by a synthesis of global esoteric teachings was developed. The knowledge thus gained by the dedicated would lead them beyond both **Christianity** *and* science. Devotees would progress through a series of grades, or states of consciousness, designed by Westcott to coincide with the Sephiroth on the **Qabalistic Tree of Life**, which was used (though not quite as in its Judaic origins) as map and as imaginative geography of the inner journey. These grades consisted of two orders. A third, theoretical order was that of the 'Secret Chiefs', said to inhabit the divine world beyond the Abyss, contact with whom was said to be possible only in a state of **astral** consciousness.

The First Order, from *Neophyte* to *Philosophicus*, involved study journey through the lower Sephiroth, epitomising the animal, instinctual, emotional and intellectual states. Later the aspirant gained admission to the higher grades, named by Mathers the *Rosae Rubae et Aurea Crucis*: the Red Rose and the Cross of Gold. This phase of development, symbolically through the higher spheres of Tiphareth, Geburah and Chesed, was characterised by a rigorous self-analysis leading to mystical transformation of personality.

The work involved ritual, **yogic** meditation, and developed powers of **visualisation**. The elaborate structure and precautionary rituals were not merely for the sake of appearances. Mathers knew very well the dangers of uncontrolled launch into latently chaotic states of mind in which negative influences present in the seeker could prevail. By techniques including invocation and personification of **archetypes** potent in the local culture and collective unconscious (e.g., **Merlin** as Wise Old Man in Britain), the seekers would invoke the guides (guardian **angels**) of their own unconscious in threading a path through the fearful, fertile inner world to enlightened further shores. Much Golden Dawn training was, whatever one thinks of the metapsychology, thoroughly practical and trail-blazing in the context of modern attempts to reintegrate the human **psyche**, especially in the west. Rituals like the Banishing Ritual of the Lesser Pentagram, though they may sound exotically unscientific, constituted an effective means of excluding negative psychic content, however personified. Likewise, a deep grounding in symbolic **correspondences** ensured that the seeker could always (given the will to resist panic) locate and redirect himself amid the inner landscape, just as a driver uses a roadmap in unknown territory.

The work of Mathers and the Golden Dawn arose from the same stream that nourished Einstein, Freud, **Planck** and **Jung**. That it remains obscure indicates the continuing false division between 'Science' and the 'Occult'. Yet, like other magical societies, the Order nursed an inbuilt problem it had been formed to solve – human ego. Those of dominant personality, like Mathers and **Crowley**, too easily assumed they had attained or contacted godhood and became overbearing. When by 1896 the Order maintained temples not only in London (1888) but at Weston-super-Mare, Bradford, Edinburgh and Paris, Mathers (assuming pre-eminence as the author of Golden Dawn ritual) tried to run them all. When his authority was questioned he insisted it came from the supernal Secret Chiefs. By now wearing the kilt and styling himself McGregor Mathers, he *did* admit, 'I do not even know their earthly names . . . I have *but very rarely* seen them in the physical body; and on such rare occasions *the rendezvous was made astrally by them*?

Crowley (also a tartan snob, buying a Loch Ness estate and styling himself Laird of Boleskine) soon argued with Mathers, tried to take over the Golden Dawn, then left to found his own more notorious schools. With Mathers in Paris, the London Golden Dawn broke away, renaming itself the Stella Matutina, which in turn bore further groups and approaches – in particular those developed by Dion **Fortune** and Dr Israel **Regardie**.

Such disputes suggest that the Order was just a hive of inflated egos. Yet it not only offered a model of the mind sufficiently rigorous and valid to appeal to men like William Peck, Astronomer Royal of Scotland, and Sir William **Crookes**, discover of thallium, but established a working synthesis of ancient **mystical/shamanic** traditions with modern scientific attitudes.

As Regardie wrote in *The Art and Meaning of Magic* (1964): '**Magic** is a scientific method . . . If it assists us to become more familiar with what we *really* are, it is a Science.'[1]

1. *Don Juan, Mescalito and Modern Magic*, Nevill Drury, Arkana 1986

GOOCH, Stan (*See* **BACH, Charlotte, BRAIN MYSTERIES, NEANDERTHAL**) This British psychologist specialised in child development before turning to researching the **paranormal**. In his first book, *Total Man* (1972), he argued that man's instinctive nature resides in the **cerebellum**, or 'old brain'.[1] In this and subsequent books (*Personality and Evolution, The Neanderthal Question, The Paranormal, The Secret Life of Humans*, etc.), his approach remained pragmatic even where describing his personal experiences as a spirit **medium**. Claiming that most paranormal and **trance** activities originate in the cerebellum, he has suggested that the innate mysticism of the **Jews** is caused by their direct descent from **Neanderthal** Man, in whom the cerebellum was larger than in modern man. Pointing out that **Swedenborg** equated the cerebrum with *intelligence* and the cerebellum with *wisdom*, he supports his theory of the Jews as descended from Neanderthal Man by the discovery on Mount Carmel in Israel of 35,000-year-old skeletons in which Neanderthal and Cro-Magnon characteristics appear to be equally mixed.[2]

Gooch argues that the evolutionary drive in man arises from the stress caused by conflict between cerebellum and cerebrum, and that creativity and 'peak experiences' result from cooperation between the two. The growth of cerebral intelligence was in the first place not an advantage but a burden. It not only caused hostility among the new being's fellows but required an additional effort of self-adjustment in balancing the new faculty with the old instincts. Such effort and the conflict involved guarantee evolution.

In dealing with the matter of survival of death of the physical body, Gooch points out (in *The Paranormal*) that most of the evidence comes from the unconscious mind, and is ambiguous. Detailing his own experiences of trance mediumship and memories of past lives, he admits a human desire to believe in life after death, but as a scientist he finds the case unproven.[3]

Yet in 1984 his *Creatures from Inner Space* seemed to abandon scientific caution entirely in his description of how, lying alone in bed one morning, he became aware of a woman in bed with him. This **succubus**, a composite of former girlfriends and his ex-wife, faded away as his conscious interest developed. But subsequently, 'the presence of the **entity** was maintained, until finally we actually made love'. He concluded that in this and other cases the entities are not real **spirits**, but are created by the human mind. Likewise he considers a **poltergeist** to be, 'an extension of some form of living energy projected by the nervous system' – an opinion denied by other commentators like Colin **Wilson** and Guy Lyon Playfair. Wilson, persuaded by 'overwhelming evidence that most poltergeists are spirits', thinks Gooch may be right in viewing his succubus as a manifestation of his unconscious mind – but warns that not all such experience can be thus explained.[5]

1. *Total Man*, Stan Gooch, Allen Lane, London 1972
2. *The Neanderthal Question*, Stan Gooch, Wildwood House, London 1977
3. *The Paranormal*, Stan Gooch, Wildwood House, London 1978
4. *Creatures from Inner Space*, Stan Gooch, Rider, London 1984
5. *Beyond the Occult*, Colin Wilson, Corgi, London 1989, pp. 353–4

GOODMAN, Jeffrey (*See* **PSYCHIC ARCHAEOLOGY, POLE SHIFT**)

GRAIL (*See* **GLASTONBURY, HOLY GRAIL**)

GRAVES, Robert (1895–1985) (*See* **CURSES, MOON, SYNCHRONICITY**) The circumstances of the publication of English poet Robert Graves' *The White Goddess* are as remarkable as the book itself. Already well-known for his early autobiography *Goodbye To All That* (an account of life in World War I trenches), and for detailed historical novels like *I, Claudius*, his obsession with the White (**Moon**) Goddess and her influence on primitive **myth** and poetry began in 1944. Though living in Majorca since 1929 he was in the Devonshire village of Glampton while writing a novel about Jason and the Argonauts. This was interrupted by a sudden overwhelming obsession to write about a mysterious 'Battle of the Trees', fought in ancient Britian. In three weeks he completed 'The Roebuck in the Thicket' – the original draft of *The White Goddess*. He had no idea what had prompted this obsession.

On his desk at the time was a small brass box with an odd design on the lid. Atop it he kept the brass figure of a hump-backed man playing a flute. Later he learned that the lid-design represented Ngame, an African moon-goddess; and that the hump-backed flute-player was the herald of the Queen-mother of an African state claiming descent from Ngame.

Items connected with the White Goddess kept coming his way fortuitously. Back in Majorca after the War he felt he was being driven to write the book – a complex elucidation of the connection between old Welsh nature poetry (*The Battle of the Trees*) and the worship of the White Goddess.

The book was written. The **synchronistic** oddities continued. The first publisher who rejected it died of heart failure soon afterwards. The second, rejecting it rudely, hanged himself wearing female underwear. The third publisher – poet T.S. Eliot – accepted it . . . and was awarded the Order of Merit that same year.[1]

1. *The White Goddess*, Robert Graves, Faber and Faber, London 1961 (1946)

GREAT PYRAMID (*See* **EGYPT, PYRAMID PROPHECIES**) At least 4,600 years old, the Great Pyramid at Giza near Cairo in Egypt is the biggest, most written about and most enigmatic building in the world. An encyclopaedia in rock the dimensions of which accurately record basic geophysical data, orthodox archaeologists still insist it is but a huge tomb built *c*.2600 BC for the pharaoh Khufu (Cheops).

454 feet high, its 203 courses long ago stripped of their polished white limestone casing (as still crowns the Second Pyramid of Chephren nearby), the Great Pryamid possesses twice the volume and thirty times the mass of the Empire State Building. Aligned to the cardinal compass points to within one twelfth of a degree (the error caused by axial shift since construction), its thirteen-acre base area is level to within a fraction of an inch. Its estimated 2,300,000 stone blocks weigh on average 2.5 tons: some weigh up to 70 tons. The 115,000 casing blocks covered twenty-one acres, being cut and laid to give joints a fiftieth of an inch thick. This is just the start of the mystery.

Sited at the centre of the geometrical quadrant formed by the Nile Delta, the Pyramid lies on the longest land-contact meridian on the Earth's surface, and at the geographical centre of Earth's land mass including the Americas and Antarctica. The four slightly hollow faces climb at an angle of 51°51′14.3″ to a summit platform. The apex is missing. Some claim the Pyramid was deliberately left incomplete as an image of human imperfection.

By projection to the theoretical apex, the angle of slope gives a relationship of the pyramid's height to the perimeter of its *designed* base equal to the radius of a circle to its circumference. Divide the distance round the base by the height, in other words, and the product is π.

Pi is not the only marvel. Of several units of measurement, the *Sacred Cubit* (25.0265 inches, one ten-millionth of the mean polar radius of the Earth as determined during the International Geophysical Year (1957–8)), is found in multiples establishing the

Pyramid as a textbook of geophysical and astronomical data. The side of the designed base square measures 365.242 Sacred Cubits; the exact number of days in the solar year. Other measurements derived from the 'hollowing-in' of the sides as established in the 1920s by Leeds engineer David Davidson accurately represent the sidereal (365.256) and anomalistic (365.259) years. The *Pyramid* or *Primitive Inch* (1.00106 inches: 1/25 of the Sacred Cubit) is also implicated in the repetition of specific values. Measurements of exactly 365.242"P are found in the King's Chamber complex. Also found is the Royal Cubit: 20.63 British inches.

Measurements derived from these units as expressed in the Pyramid give values for the eccentricity of the Earth's orbit (0.004 minimum, 0.019 maximum); its distance from the sun (92,992,270 miles), and the length of the cycle of the precession of the equinoxes (25,826.4 years).

The Greek historian Herodotus (*c*.440 BC) apparently originated the idea that the Pyramid is but a giant tomb. As an initiate of the **Msyteries** he may have disguised whatever else he knew in metaphor. 2,200 years after the presumed date of construction he says 100,000 men worked on the Pyramid. Modern estimates suggest it took 20–30 years to build. The core-stone was local, but the granite lining the King's Chamber, and the limestone casing, came from elsewhere. The most popular constructional theory involves a mud-brick ramp up which gangs hauled, rocked or levered the giant stones into place. An old belief that the stones were moved by the use of **magic** talismans is echoed by modern claims that they were literally 'sung' into place by a lost science of sonics – as, legend suggests, **Stonehenge** was transported to England by **Merlin**. In short, the method of construction remains as much a mystery as the actual *date* of construction. Did Khufu build the Pyramid, or merely rededicate an older structure?

The seer Edgar **Cayce** claimed building began in 10,490 BC (after the fall of **Atlantis**) and took a century. He also claimed that in the pyramid, in terms of passage-angles, types of rock, and internal distances, was recorded the future of nations and the evolution of world religious thought.

The Great Pyramid differs from others in the Giza complex not only in its precision and size but internally. In all nine Giza pyramids a tunnel descends to a final chamber in the bedrock: the Great Pyramid alone has an *Ascending Passage*. This climbs from the *Descending Passage* to the *Grand Gallery*. Here a horizontal passage leads to the *Queen's Chamber*. Here too the rough-hewn *Well-Shaft* plunges down to join the Descending Passage near the *Subterranean Chamber* and the final dead-end passage. The Grand Gallery continues up, via an *Antechamber*, to the *King's Chamber*, where the red granite coffer lies. Both the Queen's Chamber and the King's Chamber have two air-shafts, these slanting up though 180 feet of solid rock. A mummy does not need fresh air. Another nail in the tomb-theory coffin.

The means of entry was long forgotten. Herodotus (440 BC) mentions a door in the north face. In 24 BC Strabo mentions a 'movable stone' which, 'raised up', gives access to a 'sloping passage'. But in AD 820 Caliph Al-Mamoun (son of Haroun al-Raschid), hearing the Pyramid contained ancient maps of Earth and the heavens, told his men to hack into the seventh course of masonry at the centre of the North Face. They found no passage but, hearing a large stone fall, dug towards the sound to find the Granite Plug blocking an Ascending Passage, seemingly unknown to Herodotus or any other authority. The fallen stone, underfacing the Plug, had been set in the roof of the Descending Passage, hiding both Plug and passage above, both fitted when the Pyramid was built. So Al-Mamoun found not only the Descending Passage and the original entrance (off-centre at the nineteenth course) but entry to the corbelled, twenty-eight-foot high, fifty-yard long Grand Gallery, Queen's Chamber, and King's Chamber, with its empty 'coffin'.

Modern research began with Napoleon's conquest of Egypt a thousand years later. He spent a night alone in the King's Chamber. Nineteenth century scholars (Piazzi

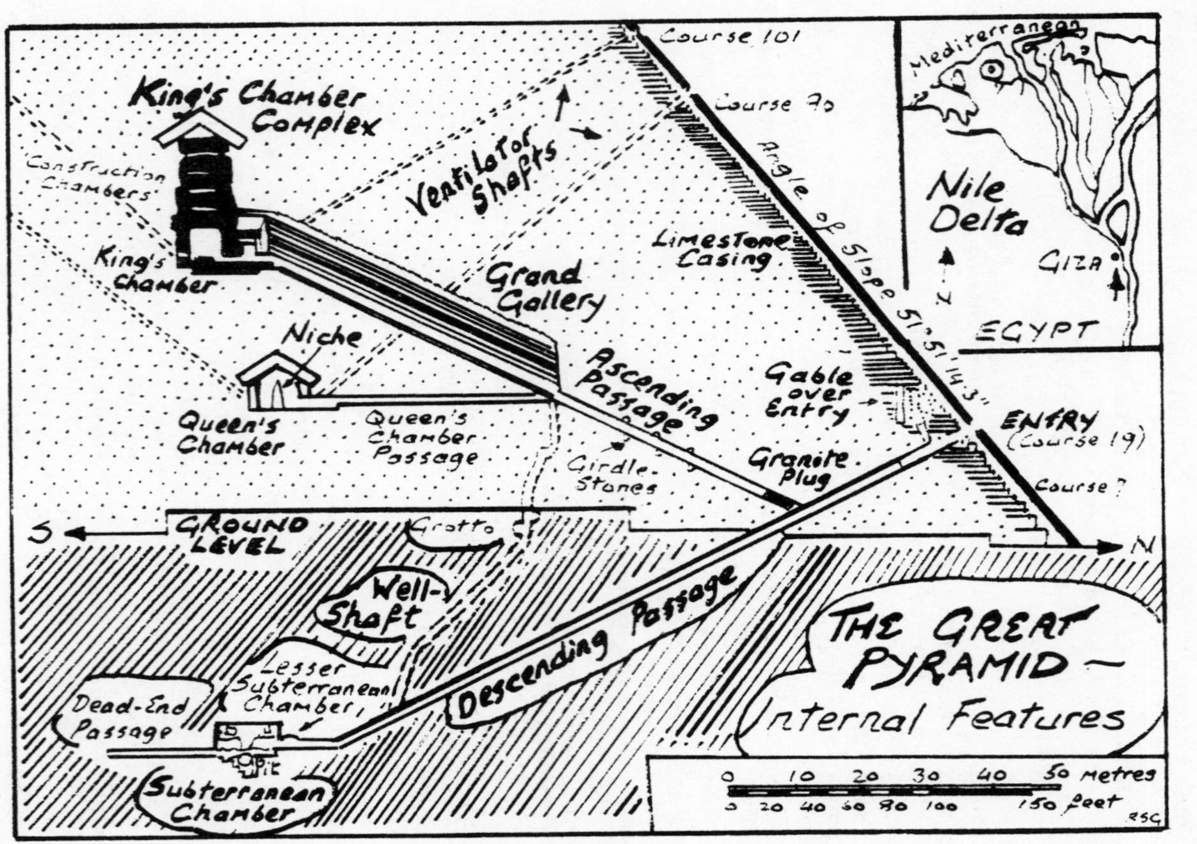
THE GREAT PYRAMID —
Internal Features
King's Chamber Complex
Construction Chambers
King's Chamber
Ventilator Shafts
Grand Gallery
Niche
Queen's Chamber
Queen's Chamber Passage
Ascending Passage
Girdle Stones
Granite Plug
Gable over Entry
Limestone Casing
Course 101
Course 70
Angle of Slope 51° 51' 14.3"
ENTRY (Course 19)
Course 7
Mediterranean
Nile Delta
GIZA
EGYPT
S
N
GROUND LEVEL
Grotto
Well-Shaft
Lesser Subterranean Chamber
Dead-End Passage
Pit
Subterranean Chamber
Descending Passage
0 10 20 30 40 50 metres
0 20 40 60 80 100 150 feet
RSG

Smyth, Flinders Petrie, John Taylor, etc.) surveyed the mystery inside and out. Colonel Howard Vyse (1836) tried to blast his way in. No artefact or inscription was found. But for the 'coffin' (Taylor thought it a standard unit measurement of volume) the Pyramid was empty. Interest turned to deciphering its geometry and dimensions. That these incorporate geophysical and astronomical data was soon recognised.

These data are undeniable. Many wilder claims are made. Some say the Pyramid's internal features constitute a coded **prophecy**; a spiritual blueprint for human progress. These '**Pyramid Prophecies**' seem as bizarre as the discovery (by Walter Siemens) that the Pyramid generates substantial static electricity at its apex; as odd as the theory that geometrical shapes as found in the Pyramid generate their own energy; and as hair-raising as the belief of occultists like **Blavatsky** that priests of the Egyptian **Mysteries** used the structure to initiate candidates into the experience of **astral projection** and the reality of life after death.

The possibility of the latter is suggested by the experience recorded by Paul **Brunton**, while Edgar Cayce, who called the Pyramid the *Hall of the Initiates*, insisted that soon, amid a time of great earth-convulsions, the message of the Pyramid will at last be decoded and an ancient 'hall of records' will be found between the Sphinx and the Nile.

Only a tomb? Perhaps. But of humanity, seeking rebirth. If a tomb, it is **symbolic**, and designed as such, to demonstrate the processes by which – and purposes for which – we incarnate, live and die on Earth. We would be stupid to assume that *we* are more concerned or knowledgeable about the processes of life on Earth than were our ancestors.[1,2,3]

1. *The Great Pyramid Decoded*, Peter Lemesurier, Element, Shaftesbury 1977
2. *Secrets of the Great Pyramid*, Peter Tompkins, Allen Lane, London 1973
3. *Ice: the Ultimate Disaster*, Richard Noone, Genesis, Georgia USA 1982

GREEK MYSTERIES (*See* **CHRISTIANITY, ESSENES, GNOSTICS, QABALAH**) 'Death,' wrote Plato (c. 427–347 BC), 'is one of two things. Either it is annihilation, and the dead have no **consciousness** of anything; or, as we are told, it is really a change; a migration of the **soul** from this place to another.'

Speculation about the **soul**, its origin, nature and destination, is as old as humanity. Yet it is in Classical Greek thought from Homer to Plato and the Atomists that we see the emergence of arguments that ever since have typified the debate (*mystic/materialist; gnostic/agnostic;* ***magic****/science*).

Though the fantastic transformations of Greek **myth** of the same era may be more colourful than the philosophy behind them, it seems appropriate here to chart a course of how particular ideas about the nature of the soul arose and developed.

The poet Homer (eighth century BC) saw man as a composite being embodying three distinct entities – body (soma), ***psyche*** and thumos. The latter was a state associated with the diaphragm or midriff, seen as the seat of will and feeling. A fourth component, the *eidolon* (image), appeared in dreams and, like the Egyptian ***ka***, was thought to survive death. But the early Greeks did not venerate their dead. Hades as punishment for earthly sin (as in the torments of Tantalus and Sisyphus) went hand-in-hand with the notion of the dead as wretched shades condemned to a 'restless purposeless fluttering to and fro . . .'[1] The corn-mysteries of Demeter and Persephone (c.700 BC) did encourage the idea that what is underground (dead) might sprout again into new life, but rationalisation was still remote.

The Mysteries of Dionysus (Bacchus) provided the next step, via the ecstasy produced by wine. Dionysus' drunken followers, roaming Thracian woods and tearing apart whoever they met, believed that, while in a state of *enthousiasmos* (inside the god) and *ekstasis* (outside the body), they tasted the immortal bodiless bliss one day to be enjoyed forever. The distinction thus drawn, between body and soul, hardened into an opposition between the two. Maybe the tendency to awaken next day hung over, bloody and forgetful, invoked a sense of bodily disgust. So this passionate cult, at first seeking fleshly pleasure, came to demand that the soul be purified by denial of bodily impulses. In time this led to the **dualistic** heresies (Manichaeanism, **Catharism**) which later caused the Church so much trouble. Initially, it led to Orphic and Pythagorean asceticism.

The Orphics – Orpheus entranced wild beasts with his music, yet was torn to pieces by his followers – abstained from meat, beans and eggs to purify the body, and practised rites to gain deliverance from the **cycle** of rebirths. Their beliefs strikingly parallel the philosophy given in the **Hindu** Upanishads, while Orphic ideas of personal sin, salvation by asceticism, and initiation by sacrament later influenced **Christianity**. Pythagoras (sixth century BC) followed Orphic thought, holding that the divine human soul is embodied as punishment for sin and condemned to a series of incarnations, animal or human. Abstinence from meat and such plants as beans (in which human souls might reside) aided the quest for deliverance from the circle of necessity. Knowledge might aid salvation; the soul was considered 'a harmony of contrary elements united together in the body'. Empedocles (*c.* 490–430 BC) described himself as a god condemned by sin 'to wander thrice ten thousand seasons [far] from the abodes of the blessed'. He told his followers, 'wretches, utter wretches, keep your hands from beans', and was said by some to have been abducted bodily (like **Enoch** or some modern **UFO**-contactees) into the heavens. Cynics claimed he had jumped into the crater of Etna so that, his death being a mystery, he might continue to pass for a god . . . until unfortunately Etna, in eruption, spewed out one of his sandals!

In Plato's philosophy the idea of the soul attains a high degree of abstraction. By the word *psyche* he usually means the invisible, essential person in contrast to the material body. The soul, he says, 'is one of the first creations, born long before all physical things, and is the chief cause of all their alterations and transformations'.[2] In the *Timaeus* he describes three parts of the soul: reason, emotions and appetite. Plants have appetite; animals, appetite and emotions; but only man (in addition to appetite, located in the belly, and emotions, in the breast) has a rational soul; located in the head, immortal and divine. Yet reason finds it hard to control emotion and appetite. In the *Phaedrus* he compares the rational soul with a charioteer of two horses (as in the **Tarot** trump, *The Chariot*).

The soul, Plato claims, originally inhabited the realm of True Being, source of the 'Forms' (**archetypes**). These are real in contrast with worldly phenomena, which are mere appearances. Losing its home through some unspecified sin, the soul falls into earthly incarnation for at least 10,000 years. Souls choosing in each incarnation the philosophical life may return sooner. The first incarnations are as men; he who lives badly becomes a woman at second birth; persistent sinners become beasts. He said the soul is the true man, and described how at death; 'Our real self – our immortal soul as it is called – departs . . . to the gods below to give an account of itself. To the wicked, this is a terrifying doctrine, but a good man will welcome it.'[3]

The Platonic tradition of soul is **mystical**. On the more 'scientific' side, the Atomists attempted material interpretation, endlessly disputing the nature of the world's basic substance. Thales (sixth century BC) thought it was water; Anaximenes (*c.* 500 BC), air; Heraclitus said it was fire, and that the world endures continual transformation from which the soul, being mixed of the four elements, is not exempt. Only the pure soul, resisting transformation into water, could hope to join the cosmic fire. Parmenides said there is but one Being, eternal, indivisible and homogeneous, and that Heraclitus' doctrine of flux arises from sensory deception; the mind being similar in nature to the body. Empedocles likewise taught that the basic constant is matter, not the migrating soul. Anaxagoras (*c.* 500–432 BC) said that all living things contain Mind (*Nous*), a self-contained unity present in varying degrees in all life's manifestations, and that in death the soul is extinguished, for how can there be *independent* survival of souls if all animated being derives from the single Mind? Democritus (born *c.* 460 BC) said that soul and mind are of the same atomic substance: Aristotle (384–322 BC) defines the soul as the 'form' of the body, inseparable from it and perishing with it; while Epicurus (342–270 BC) considered body and soul to be mutually interdependent – 'Neither can be itself without the other'.[4]

Thus basic positions of argument largely maintained today – the mystic (soul first: body second) versus the material (vice versa) – were well established by the Greeks before the time of Christ. Our attitudes about *normal* or ***paranormal*** remain influenced by this inheritance.

1. *Survival?*, David Lorimer, Routledge Kegan Paul, London 1984, pp. 39–59
2. *Laws*, Plato, Penguin Books 1982, No. 895 (p. 420)
3. *ibid.*, No. 959 (pp. 512–13)
4. *op. cit*, ref. 1, p. 57

GUIRDHAM, Arthur (1905–) (*See* **CATHARS, HEALING, REINCARNATION**) Author of books on healing and psychic factors in mental illness, this West Country doctor became a Senior Consultant in Psychiatry before his retirement. Convinced of the reality of **spirit possession** and its role in inducing serious depression and illness, he asserts that all of his writing is clinically based and insists that much of the **disease** from which people suffer arises from disasters and illness in previous incarnations. In this latter context he is known for a remarkable account of group reincarnation involving eight people (himself included) who, alive in the west of England during the 1960s, had formerly lived and died together as Cathar heretics in the Languedoc region of south-west France during the thirteenth century.

In *The Cathars and Reincarnation* he tells how from 1938 onwards he felt inexplicably drawn to the Languedoc, especially to the castle of Montségur, where in March 1244 over 200 Cathars were seized and burned alive following a long siege by the Church and the French army. The compulsion made no sense to him until 1962 when a 'Mrs Smith', who for twenty years had suffered a recurring nightmare, was referred to him for treatment. It transpired that as a girl Mrs Smith had suffered a rush of **visionary** 'memory' which, though not then realised as such, had been of life in thirteenth-century Languedoc. She knew nothing of Catharism but had written down many of her dreams. She had a dread of the mediaeval period and of the city, Toulouse, which in a dream she called 'Tolosa' – its mediaeval name in Provençal. Checking the detail of her dreams as the Cathar connection began to emerge, Guirdham wrote to French historians. Jean Duvernoy, an authority on the period, was amazed at his knowledge. It included the information (from Mrs Smith) that the robes of Cathar priests (*parfaits*) were dark blue. Common belief was that they were always black: Duvernoy had only just found out (from Inquisition records) that sometimes they were indeed dark blue. 'I could not tell him I had obtained (my knowledge) from a schoolgirl's notes of her dreams . . .'[1]

Subsequently Guirdham found himself the 'magnet' for a group of people all (in the twentieth century) born, or living, or educated, within a dozen miles of Bristol. All of them had apparently been Cathars, persecuted and martyred in thirteenth-century Languedoc. In seven out of eight cases he traced their thirteenth-century identity. Their memories focussed on the period 1242–44, and on the fall of Montségur. He noted how illness and depression in this group manifested at the Spring equinox; when in 1244 Montségur fell and its Cathar defenders were burned alive on a common pyre. He traced his own thirteenth-century identity as one Roger-Isarn d'Arborens, a consumptive who died in an Inquisition jail awaiting trial some time in August 1243.

In later books dealing with this subject Dr Guirdham presents **Gnostic** cosmology as given to him by Cathar 'revenants' – **discarnate** personalities historically described in his earlier texts, including the Cathar bishops Guilhabert de Castres and Bertrand Marty who died at Montségur in 1244.

Justice cannot be done in so short a space as this to the wealth and range of evidence (and philosophy) presented by Guirdham in these books. As in **Castaneda**'s account of Don Juan, and that by Markides of **Daskalos**, one is left with the sensation of inexplicable, candid truth presented by means which reason alone must doubt. But the proof of the pudding is in the eating. Guirdham may yet prove to be a giant among pygmies.[2,3,4]

1. *The Cathars and Reincarnation*, Arthur Guirdham, Turnstone, London 1982, p. 11 (1970).
2. *We Are One Another*, Arthur Guirdham, Turnstone, London 1982 (1974)
3. *The Great Heresy*, Arthur Guirdham, Spearman, Saffron Walden 1977
4. *The Psyche in Medicine*, Arthur Guirdham, Spearman, Saffron Walden 1978

GURDJIEFF, George Ivanovitch (1873–1949) (*See* **BENNETT, OUSPENKY**) 'I saw a man of an oriental type, no longer young, with a black moustache and piercing eyes,' wrote P. D. Ouspensky of his first meeting with G. I. Gurdjieff in Moscow, March 1915. 'He spoke Russian incorrectly with a strong Caucasian accent . . . Not only did my questions not embarrass him but it seemed to me that he put much more into each answer than I had asked for. I liked his manner of speaking, which was careful and precise.'[1]

Ouspensky had travelled widely 'in search of the miraculous'; he had formed his own ideas and philosophy, but it was only on returning to Moscow that he found what he sought – a man who not only talked about but *embodied* real truth. Yet on following Gurdjieff home from the café where they had met to the bare flat where the Master was living, he was not impressed. The clever talk was all very well, but as he entered the flat, it struck him as a bluff. He saw 'three or four young men and two ladies both of whom looked like schoolmistresses'. Yet when one of the young men began to read a tale, 'Glimpses of Truth', he found himself listening . . . and watching Gurdjieff, who sat, silently smoking and drinking coffee. He was hooked.

Ouspensky was neither the first nor the last. Gurdjieff hooked many. Born in Alexandropol in the Transcaucasus, his parents were Greek but his nationality Russian. Fascinated by the **occult**, his early life was spent on the travels described in his book *Meetings with Remarkable Men*. His journeys included visits to monasteries all over Europe and Asia: by the time he met Ouspensky he had formulated his basic philosophy – that most of us live our lives in a state akin to sleep. We do not make things happen: instead, things happen to us. We are the slaves of our own unconsciously determined misfortune: *real* progress is impossible so long as we refuse to break out of our robotic habits to remember ourselves and wake up.

But waking up is hard. The habit of sleep is like a powerful current: trying to swim against it we lose strength and fall asleep again. To wake up *and stay awake* requires huge effort. *Work* is necessary to build up the habit of self-awareness. Speaking of man's three centres (intellectual, emotional and physical) he said each works with its own energy and that they have to be harmonised. Promoting his philosophy via his establishment in Paris (1923) of the Institute for the Harmonious Development of Man, he set his students to exercises and esoteric dance techniques (derived, he said, from the **dervishes, Essenes, Buddhists**, etc.) so rigorous that (it was claimed by French author Louis Pauwels) some of his pupils actually died as a result. One such exercise required members of the group involved to freeze into total immobility at a given signal, and to hold the posture, however difficult, until released by a second signal. A woman novelist who told him she felt more conscious when writing was told: 'You live in dreams and you write about your dreams. How much better for you if you were to scrub one floor consciously than to write a hundred books.'[2] One student, a

Russian emigré called Rachmilevitch, grumbled all the time and irritated everyone. When at last he'd had enough of the pitiless regime and decamped, Gurdjieff had him brought back, saying the way that he upset everyone was useful – it stopped people falling into a routine.

He gave public exhibitions in which his students demonstrated the 'supernormal powers of physical control, co-ordination, relaxation, etc.' he had taught them. 'At his command, they'd race, spread out at breakneck speed from left to right across the stage, and at another low command from him, freeze in full flight as if caught by a race-track camera.'[3] It was clear from these shows that his will dominated them utterly. They would do whatever he told them. This begs the question as to whether they had truly 'woken up' or if they had merely 'borrowed' his own wakefulness.

Writing his philosophy in a vast book (*All and Everything, Beelzebub's Tales to his Grandson*), he deliberately chose a long-winded, complex style forcing his readers to make a huge effort to understand. His cosmology, with its talk of **souls** sucked up to feed the **moon** and its complex **symbolic** structure, has proved too much for most readers, who usually turn to his disciples like Ouspensky or Bennett for clarification.

Gurdjieff was no ascetic. He drank, smoked, pampered his luxurious handlebar moustaches and, near the end of his life, took to driving a powerful sports car. He crashed and ended up in an intensive care unit. Regaining consciousness, he discharged himself. Within a fortnight he was fit and well again. Such tales suggest not the lukewarm saint but a full-blooded **shaman**. Today, his influence persists. The schools he started thrive on the strength of his name.

1. *In Search of the Miraculous*, P. D. Ouspensky, Routledge Kegan Paul, London 1950, pp. 7–8
2. *The Occult*, Colin Wilson, Grafton, London 1979, p. 511
3. *ibid.*, quoting William Seabrook
4. *Meetings with Remarkable Men*, G. I. Gurdjieff, Pan, London 1978
5. *All and Everything*, G. I. Gurdjieff, Penguin, London 1988

GURU (*See* **KRISHNAMURTI, TRANSCENDENTAL MEDITATION**)
From the Sanskrit *gu*, 'darkness', and *ru*, 'light', literally the guru is one who dispels darkness: a teacher who by example assists the disciple towards enlightenment.

H

HADAD After World War II this mass murderer was held at Fort Leavenworth, USA. Psychologist Donald Powell Wilson tells how one day Hadad's body was found hanging from the cell bars. Apparently he had used the belt of a warder he had **hypnotised** earlier. The warder was sure he was still wearing the belt even when it was pointed out that he wasn't. Three days later, in the autopsy room, the surgeons picked up their scalpels, 'Gentlemen,' said the 'corpse' in a fine Oxford accent as it sat up. 'I'd rather not, if you don't mind.'

Explaining he had entered a deep **trance** in which his natural functions had ceased, he offered to prove his powers by stopping all seizures among epileptics in the psychopathic ward for three days. The seizures ceased as promised, then began again. Wilson concluded that, when last in the ward, Hadad had left post-hypnotic commands. In another demonstration he removed his clothes, lay across two desks, and went into a death-like trance. As predicted, the signs of the zodiac appeared across his body in the form of red welts. A punctured vein produced almost no blood. Wilson later heard that Hadad could enter and leave the prison at will. Seen by the prison warden at a concert in a nearby town, he had said, 'I felt it would be such a shame not to go.' Asked why he was in jail, he told Wilson of his mission to wander the world, seeking two 'excessively evil and malign spirits' and 'to relieve them of their corporeal anatomy'. Wilson learned that he had been the 'finger man' of a notorious gang, using his powers to draw victims out of hiding so they could be killed. When caught, the police had riddled his car with machine-gun fire, but he had emerged unharmed. He claimed he had deflected the bullets. Pointing out that he had 'risen from the dead' after three days, he told Wilson he was greater than Christ or Mohammed.

This case is given as fact in Wilson's book *My Six Convicts*.[1]

1. *Beyond the Occult*, Colin Wilson, Corgi, London 1989, pp. 418–20

HALLUCINATION (*See* **DREAMS, DRUGS, LEARY, LILLY, VISION**) Derived from the Latin *hallucinari*, 'to wander in mind', the term refers to the subjective visual or auditory perception of illusory external events as objectively real. Such false perception may arise by confusing a **dream** or personal fantasy with an actual event due to illness, exhaustion, or use of various mind-altering or **hallucinogenic** drugs.

Equally, it may arise in a collective social hysteria, as in mediaeval fantasies about **witchcraft** or (more recently) in the Western fear of 'reds under the bed'. Hallucination is potent globally, not just personally.

As the term implies mental disorder and is thus derogatory, it may be used to denounce or deny any subjective experience considered meaningless or without value, either by the percipient or by others. Such experience may be considered *visionary* by those seeking meaning in it, *hallucinatory* by those who deny such meaning.

HALLUCINOGENS (*See* **DRUGS, LEARY, LILLY, SEROTONIN**) Refers to psychoactive drugs that occur naturally (peyotl, mescal, amanita muscaria, oliliuqui, banisterine, etc.) or to synthetic derivatives (LSD–25, etc.). In whatever form such substances have been used since ancient times in **shamanic** ceremonies to stimulate mystical states of mind; **out-of-the-body** travel; heightened sensory awareness; hallucinatory involvement in subjective or mythical landscapes, etc. By and large they seem to work by inhibiting the brain-function of the nerve-hormone serotonin. Though briefly in the 1950s it was thought LSD produced a psychotic state similar to schizophrenia, this idea has been abandoned. The casual 'recreational' use of such drugs in the West since Dr Timothy Leary told the 1960s generation to 'turn on, tune in, and drop out', and the resulting social furore, has partly prevented proper estimation of their potential value in exploring unusual or **paranormal** states of mind. In fact there is nothing 'unnatural' about hallucinogens and their use; the 'problem' is one of context and preparation; also in their abuse by the unprepared as a 'short-cut' to mystical states. Such abuse can lead to misfortune.

HARMONIC CONVERGENCE (*See* **HOPIS, THOUGHT-FORMS**) In AD 1519 the landing in Mexico of Cortès and his *conquistadores* began the destruction of American pre-Colombian societies, thus inaugurating an epoch defined at the time by the Mayans of Yucatan as the 'Nine Hells' – nine fifty-two year periods, totalling 468 years, during which time it was prophesied that Native American cultures would suffer under the yoke of the white man, who had appeared over the eastern ocean in the guise of the god Kukulcan, also known (to the Toltecs) as Huemac and (to the Aztecs) as Quetzalcoatl.

The 468–year epoch of the 'Nine Hells' ended in 1987, when, the Mayans had prophesied, a new world era would begin. Thus on the 16th and 17th of August of that year celebrations were held by participants in the **New Age** movement at sacred places the world over – **Glastonbury** in England, the Pyramid of the Sun in Mexico. Mount Shasta in California, etc. It was hoped this harmonious uniting of minds would aid world peace and the growth of a new world order by creating a positive energy-field. No doubt it was also hoped that by such means some of the more dire Hopi, Mayan, and other **prophecies** for this era might be offset. We wait and watch.

HAUNTINGS (*See* **GHOSTS, POLTERGEISTS**)

HAUSER, Kaspar (1812?–1833) On Whit Monday 1828 a boy staggered into Nuremberg, unable to speak but holding an envelope addressed to 'the Captain of the Fourth Squadron, Sixth Cavalry Regiment'. Taken to the address he accepted bread and water, but meat and beer revolted him. In the envelope were two letters, each in the same hand. One said the child had been born to a soldier of the regiment on 30 April 1812; the other (supposedly from a labourer who had looked after him since October 1812) said he had been kept locked up and knew nothing of the outside world. Given to the police, he sat motionless and mute for hours in a dark cell. A doctor decided he was not insane or dull-witted, but 'has apparently been forcibly prevented from attaining any personal or social development'. Given paper and pen, he wrote three words, *Reiter* (cavalryman) and *Kaspar Hauser* . . . which was taken as his name. Crowds gathered to watch him eat and sleep as his vocabulary grew. The town council issued a bulletin in which 'Kaspar Hauser' described how he had grown up in a 'hole' where 'he never heard a sound nor saw a vivid light'. Given bread and water and dressed while asleep, he never saw his jailer but, with two wooden horses and some ribbons to play with, was never unhappy. At last one day he stood in Nuremberg, a letter in his hand . . .

Investigation led nowhere. Professor George Friedrich Daumer took him into care and studied him as a good example of a *feral* child. He could see in the dark, hated bright light, and had a sense of smell so sharp he could identify trees by the scent of a leaf and individual people in the dark. Unable to tell between animate or inanimate objects, he was sure a ticking grandfather clock was alive. A photographic memory helped him to learn to read, write and draw. No fool, he now endured speculation that he was the disowned bastard son of the local ducal family. His autobiography (1829) said nothing not already known. On 7 October he was found wounded by an unknown assassin. Lord Stanhope, an English dilettante, toured him round Europe, then gave him to Dr Meyer in Ansbach, twenty-five miles from Nuremberg. On 14 December 1833 he was stabbed by an unknown assailant – tall, with dark whiskers and a black coat. A nonsensical message was found at the place of attack. Kaspar Hauser died on 17 December 1833. Rewards were offered for information on his killer. Nothing was forthcoming. He was buried under a headstone that read: 'Here lies Kaspar Hauser, the riddle of his time. His birth was unknown, his death mysterious.'[1]

1. 'The boy with no past', and, 'Who was Kaspar Hauser?', Graham Fuller and Ian Knight, *The Unexplained*, Orbis Partwork, London 1983

HEALING (*See* **ARIGO, DASKALOS, MESMER**) The power to heal by prayer, laying on of hands, and suchlike techniques has been for so long derided by the medical profession and by organised **religion** that it may seem no more than a superstition of the desperate or naive. So English property consultant Maurice Tester thought – before he suffered a prolapsed disc. After long agony in traction, with his doctors offering no hope of cure other than via an operation with only a forty percent chance of success, he went to healer Ted Fricker in North London. With 'no more pressure than you would apply in stroking a cat', Fricker ran his hand up and down Tester's back. In ten minutes Tester was free of pain. Several visits (including one relapse) brought total cure. His specialist, without being told what had happened, confirmed that (a) the problem was definitely physical and (b) natural remission was out of the question. As baffled as the specialist, Tester asked Ted Fricker for answers. Fricker said he felt his power to heal came from God; and that he heard voices while healing and just followed their directions. He added: 'You're a healer too.'

Forced to examine his preconceptions, Tester later became a well-known healer himself. As he has written: 'One of the dangers of a conventional education is that you learn to think conventionally.'[1]

Healing techniques are certainly odd. Some healers stroke, some **dowse**, some invoke **spirits**. Yet why, with all the evidence to support the reality of healing since earliest times, does Western medical and religious opinion still denigrate it? Maybe because of the old belief that healing involves mind and spirit as well as body. Orthodox medicine treats the body alone. Naturally it tends to oppose practices suggesting that this approach may be flawed or incomplete. Yet why should the Church oppose healing when much of Christ's ministry was devoted to it?

That subtle energies pervade the physical body was known in the ancient world. Indian texts describe how to channel ***prāna*** to cure the sick; Chinese treatment of disease by stimulating and unblocking ***ch'i*** energy persists in **acupuncture**; the Greek physician Hippocrates (fifth century BC) describes how 'the heat which oozes out of the hand, being applied to the sick, is highly salutary'. Yet, though held to be the father of modern medicine, his insights on the healing of the **subtle body** have been ignored.

Of **Christ** it is said that often he healed hundreds of sufferers until too exhausted to continue. Far from claiming this power for himself alone, he said, 'He who believes in me will also do the works that I do.'

The early Church pursued this healing mission, but on gaining material power suppressed it. In the thirteenth century, priests were told not to practise medicine. Roman Catholics are still told that lay healers are in league with the **Devil**. In part this nonsense arose from the Church's desire to stamp out **pagan magic** as practised throughout mediaeval Europe by **charmers** and 'cunning men'. Healing was widely outlawed: the invisible source of a healer's power left him open to charges of **witchcraft**; many whose powers offended Church and medical hegemony died at the stake. Yet belief in healing persisted. 'Charming is in as great request as physic,' wrote William Perkins in 1608, 'and charmers more sought unto than physicians in time of need.'[2] In England it was accepted that scrofula (the 'King's Evil') could be cured by the King's touch; herbalists enjoyed legal protection; and even in puritan times some healers like Valentine Greatrakes (b. 1628) gained fame and influential support. Using his hands in a stroking motion without touching the patient's body, 'The Stroker' (as he was called) was investigated by the Royal Society and found genuine, escaping with no more than ecclesiastical reprimand. Eighty years later Methodism's founder, John Wesley, in his *Primitive Physic* (1747), attacked doctors who 'prescribe drug upon drug without knowing a jot of the matter concerning the root of the disorder'. He asked why physicians did not 'consider how far bodily disorders are caused or influenced by the mind?'[3] In the 1770s Austrian priest Johann Joseph Gassner (b. 1727) treated up to 2,000 people a month in mass healing ceremonies. He claimed divine intervention caused the cures. The Church stopped him practising but Anton Mesmer (b. 1733), experimenting with the effect of magnets on blood flow, heard of him. Insisting that not divine intervention but 'animal **magnetism**' from the planets was the cause of cure, Mesmer's success as a healer in Vienna was ascribed to 'suggestion'. Accused of fraud and witchcraft, he fled to Paris. After his death (1815), doctors continued to sneer at healers: people continued to visit them.

By 1950 **Spiritualist** healer Harry Edwards (1893–1976) got up to 600 letters a day from people asking for 'absent' healing. Insisting that, as he knew little of the processes governing health and **disease**, intervention by spirit beings was involved in his work, of course he offended orthodox doctors. By the mid-1950s he regularly filled London's Royal Albert and Royal Festival Halls. His public healing sessions were dramatic. The halt and lame walked. Many of his cures (of TB, cancer, arthritis, etc.) were permanent. Seeking closer links between 'spiritual healing' and the medical profession, in 1953 he gave evidence to a commission drawn from the Church and the BMA, saying, 'The gift of healing can never belong to the Church of England or to any other denomination. It is God's gift to all humanity.'

The Commission dismissed his case, claiming (like Mesmer's enemies 170 years earlier), that 'cures' arose from 'suggestion'. 'Is the Church Afraid of Faith-Healing?' asked the *Daily Mail*. Today, though the UK ban on cooperation between doctors and healers was lifted in 1977, orthodox medical opinion still insists that cures are due to 'suggestion'. Yet many people given no hope of cure by orthodox means still go for relief to healers. In the UK these include Rose Gladden, George Chapman and Edgar Chase.

A natural **medium**, Rose Gladden feels that she acts 'as a channel for the healing energy. I am convinced that most healing is done through the mind. Your hands guide the healing force and give comfort. But it's the concentration of your mind which is doing the healing.'[4] Also dealing in cases of **possession**, like Dr Arthur **Guirdham** she insists that these are real, though often misinterpreted as mental illness.

Also a medium, Liverpudlian George Chapman heals (as did the Brazilian 'psychic surgeon' Arigo) by surrendering to his 'control', surgeon William Lang, who died in 1937. When working in trance, his personality is Lang's. He is right-handed, but as Lang he works left-handed, performing 'operations' a few inches above the patient's body with invisible surgical instruments. These operations are conducted on the spirit body, through which physical changes are effected. Lang's surviving family and colleagues, when first contacted by Chapman to establish the reality of his contact, were at first stupefied, then reluctantly convinced. 'The man who was in this room was indisputably my grandfather,' said Mrs Susan Fairtlough. 'It was not him physically, but it was his voice, his behaviour. I was so impressed that all I could say was, "Yes, grandpapa, No, grandpapa." ' Confirmed Lang's daughter Lyndon: 'We asked many questions of father about things which only he could know. He knew all the answers.'[5]

Edgar Chase, like Maurice Tester, had no belief in healing until his wife, suffering a twisted spine, was cured by London healer Addie Raeburn, who told him he had the power. A lecturer in cybernetics before becoming a healer, he insists, 'The important thing about true healing is that it deals with wholeness,' and that orthodox medicine's shortcomings arise from a failure to see man as more than a complex biomedical machine, without a spiritual dimension. However he finds that more and more doctors 'accept the view that this therapy can be applied alongside orthodox treatment'.

In some scientific quarters too there is a new willingness to test the claims of healers without prejudice. Even Mesmer's long-derided assumption of a healing force akin to magnetism now appears likely. The Russian healer Djuna Davitashvili qualified as a medical researcher before interesting her colleagues in what she carefully called: 'information-energy interaction with living organisms' via 'contact and non-contact (bio-energy) massage' – i.e., the laying on of hands to transmit the healing force. Reassured by the terminology, her colleagues set up tests proving that her *information-energy interaction with living organisms* could alter pulse rate and blood pressure. Her success was such that ultimately she interacted viably in a bio-energetic mode with the living organism known as President Brezhnev.[6]

Other experiments investigating the healing effect include those at the Mind Science Foundation laboratory in San Antonio, Texas, in which **psychic** Matthew **Manning** (by the laying on of hands) increased the death-rate of cancer cells grown in flasks; likewise he slowed down haemolysis (breakdown of red blood cells) – a process found in malaria and allergic reactions.

Opinions as to the origin of the power vary. Most attribute it to God and believe the healer acts only as a channel: others claim it comes from some outside force, or originates within the healer, the patient, or both. Some say faith is necessary; others deny this. Edgar Chase distinguishes between psychic, or bioenergy healing, and intercessionary healing by which prayers are offered to God for the sick. Rose Gladden sees healing in terms of manipulating **psychic** or auric energies. Methods also vary. Manning uses **visualisation** techniques, such as the flooding of pain with white light. Cypriot healer **Daskalos** claims that he sees inside a wound, then builds a mental image of it healed. This image he mentally 'injects' with 'etheric vitality'. He asks, 'What is that thing that causes the curing? It is something within the body. Call it *etheric*, call it energy, call it magnetism, call it God, call it Holy Spirit, call it whatever you like'.[7]

Parapsychologist Laurence **LeShan** concludes that human beings operate on two distinct but interrelated levels – the *sensory* and the ***clairvoyant***. The first refers to the world of the five senses; the second to that perceived through altered states of **consciousness**. Though the two levels differ they are but aspects of a unitary, greater reality. Paradoxes arise only if we try to interpret the functioning of one level in terms of another. Either way, the reality of healing is beyond doubt. And given the universal human consensus since earliest times about healing power, the **paranormal** question is not about the healers: it is about those who deny their work.

What's WRONG with them?

1. *The Power to Heal*, David Harvey, Aquarian Press, Wellingborough 1983, p. 20
2. *Religion and the Decline of Magic*, Keith Thomas, Peregrine, London 1980, p. 209
3. *op. cit.* ref 1, p. 47
4. *ibid.*, p. 93
5. *Surgeon from Another World*, George Chapman and Roy Stemman, Allen, London 1979
6. *The Hidden Power*, Brian Inglis, Jonathan Cape, London 1986, p. 270
7. *Homage to the Sun*, Kyriacos C. Markides, Arkana, London 1987, p. 12

HEISENBERG, Werner (1901–76) (*See* **EINSTEIN, PLANCK**) In 1927 this German physicist (born in Würzburg) proposed an 'indeterminacy principle' which, along with Einstein's relativity and Planck's **quantum** mechanics, provides one of the ghostly planks of modern physics. He showed that the very fact of assuming that energy moves in discrete quanta means that certain pairs of variables constantly affecting each other, like time and energy, cannot be accurately determined. A degree of indeterminacy must exist in any equation. Mass behaviour (in human crowds as in atoms) can be predicted . . . but not the behaviour of the individual unit. Particles may behave as waves, or waves as particles. Invariably there is a quantity of 'uncertainty'. Faced by this speculation, Einstein rejected quantum theory. As appalled as **Freud** by speculations made credible only as a result of his own revolutionary thought, he said, 'God does not play dice,' revealing a theological preoccupation until then unapparent.

Heisenberg's work has been taken up by **parapsychologists** to justify the reality of 'psychic' activity. In effect, he poked another hole in the solid-state Newtonian wall by which mental/spiritual activity was for 250 years excluded from the scentific **paradigm** of a world operating purely according to material cause-and-effect, 'blind chance', 'random mutation', etc. Since he suggested that particles do not have to behave according to the rules of classical mechanics, they have notably refused to do so. Or maybe it is simply that our perception has changed, and that a change in human perception equals a change in reality. We see what we look for. The prodigal world fits whatever shape we put on it.

HERMES TRISMEGISTUS (*See* **ALCHEMY**) 'That which is above is like that which is below . . . And as all things have been derived from one . . . so all things are born from this thing.'

This, the core statement of hermetic philosophy as derived from a text called *The Emerald Tablet*, was believed by Renaissance scholars to be the work of 'Thrice-Great' Hermes, an ancient Egyptian **magus** dated as living three generations after Moses, and thought greater than Pythagoras and Plato. Works attributed to this mythic figure (Hermes was the Greek name for the Egyptian scribe-god Thoth, inventor of writing and all arts) included (claims Clement of Alexandria, *c.*AD 180) forty-two books: thirty-six containing all Egyptian philosophy and six being on medicine. In the fourth century AD St Augustine attacked one book, *The Asclepius*, as containing diabolical magic.

A millennium later, *c.* 1460, Cosimo de' Medici of Florence received a copy of the *Corpus Hermeticum*, said to be by Hermes. Translated by Ficino as the *Pimander*, this and other texts had profound influence on the growth of European alchemy, **astrology** and **magic** studies, conferring on such work (frowned on by the Church) an aura of antique **mystical** authority. The *Pimander* (first printed 1471) went through sixteen editions by the end of the sixteenth century. In recent times the psychologist C. G. **Jung** found much of value in these texts. Though Frances Yates has established that the works attributed to Hermes in fact date from various **Gnostic** and post-Christian Graeco-Roman sources, their rediscovery and translation was central in stimulating the explosive intellectual climate of the Renaissance.

Giordano Bruno and the Hermetic Tradition, Frances Yates, Routledge Kegan Paul, London 1964

HERMETICA (*See* **ALCHEMY, HERMES TRISMEGISTUS**)

HEYWOOD, Rosalind In her autobiography *The Infinite Hive*, this English **psychic** tells how one evening she and her husband went out to a moor by Okehampton to 'catch the tail-end of the sunset' when 'without warning, the incredible beauty swept me through a barrier. I was no longer looking at Nature. Nature was looking at me. And she did not like what she saw. It was a strange and humbling sensation, as if numberless unoffending creatures were shrinking back offended by our invasion.' So, explaining mentally that she and her husband came as friends, she asked permission to walk quietly on the moor. She felt her apology accepted. Two days later, sitting by a window facing the moor and thinking of its invisible inhabitants, she felt: 'a covey of little invisibles floated in at the window to say "Hullo!" and coax me to play with them. For a moment their visit seemed perfectly normal, but then my analytical mind got going, and at once, for me, they ceased to exist.'

Born into a late Victorian household, Rosalind Heywood's attitude to her **clairvoyance** reminds one of Eileen **Garrett** in its detachment. Persuaded at seventeen that her psychism was only imagination, as a nurse in the Great War she remained sceptical despite witnessing death-bed experiences apparently involving **telepathy** and dying **visions** of distant loved ones. She received mental 'Orders'. In a Macedonian hospital, 'Orders' told her to ask a dying soldier what he would like most in all the world. 'A red rose, sister,' he said. She asked a despatch rider to get one: back came a whole bunch, from the garden of a Greek magnate. The soldier recovered. In this and other cases she acted irrationally but effectively. On leaving her house for a summer holiday, 'Orders' said a water pipe would burst, so she left a key with a builder (who said water pipes do not burst in summer) to repair it when it did. It did. **Precognition**? She remained sceptical. But in the 1930s, with her diplomat husband in Washington DC, at a party she read the palms of a woman called Julia. 'You will never find what you are looking for in this world, will you?' she heard herself ask. 'No,' said Julia. A few weeks later, about to fly to Peru, Julia gave Rosalind a snapshot of herself. 'Orders' told Rosalind to accept it. The plane crashed in the Andes: Julia died. Two days later she was writing to Julia's mother when a woodcut fell off the wall. Its cord was intact, so was the nail which had held it. Puzzled, she heard Julia say: 'Go to my mother now, straightaway, and tell her to stop all this ridiculous mourning at once. I'm very happy and I can't stand it.' Feeling like a fool, she went to Julia's mother's house, to find the blinds down, women in the hall whispering 'and looking like crows'. Julia's mother was in bed, mourning. Rosalind delivered the message. 'I knew it,' cried the mother, her face lighting up. 'I knew she'd hate it and I didn't want it. I shall get up and stop it at once!'

Such experiences persuaded her to abandon her agnosticism. As Colin **Wilson** comments, her 'psychism' went against the grain of her middle-class English upbringing. For years she tried to deny or explain away all the weird events she attracted, yet her experiences of beauty and of 'those presences' continually invading her life were ultimately undeniable. She joined the **Society for Psychical Research**, but was never tempted to develop her **mediumship**. She had too much else to do. Her testimony is convincing because the evidence came unasked. Psychism ran in her family, from her mother to her son. Which begs wider questions.[1,2]

1. *The Infinite Hive*, Rosalind Heywood, Pan, London 1964, discussed in:
2. *Afterlife*, Colin Wilson, Grafton, London 1987, pp. 45–60

HEX (*See* **CURSES**)

HIDDEN MASTERS (*See* **BLAVATSKY, GOLDEN DAWN, MATHERS**)
Magical orders, like political movements, require authority figures. The nineteenth century rise of **Spiritualism** popularised the notion of **discarnate spirit** guides making contact with the living through **mediums**. From this it was an obvious step for some to claim authoritative dispensation from 'Hidden Masters'. Thus Madame Blavatsky,

having written what she called a 'master-key to the mysteries of ancient and modern science and theology' (*Isis Unveiled*, 1887), claimed contact with a secret Brotherhood of Hidden Masters: superhuman Tibetans operating on a discarnate plane who had chosen her as their worldly Messenger. Overseeing human destiny, they dropped messages (often out of thin air) to her whenever she required them.

Macgregor Mathers did likewise. When his authority over the **Golden Dawn** was doubted, he said it came from discarnate Secret Chiefs, contacted only via **astral** consciousness. He thought 'them to be human and living on this earth but possessing terrible superhuman powers'. Rivals like Aleister **Crowley** adopted similar contacts. So not Crowley but an invisible Egyptian entity called *Aiwass* apparently wrote Crowley's *Book of the Law*, dictating it to the Beast 666 via the mediumship of his wife Rose Kelly.

Likewise Alice **Bailey** ascribed her vast output to 'The Tibetan': Dion **Fortune** claimed that her Society of the Inner Light was ultimately run by *Inner Plane Adepti* (including, for good measure, both Blavatsky's Hidden Masters and Mathers' Secret Chiefs); and other subsequent orders also claim access to *Inner Plane* beings to justify their teachings.

The question is: If there is fraud, is it deliberate?

HIGHER SELF (*See* **JUNG, REINCARNATION**) If 'Hidden Masters' truly exist, it may be that they do so as unrecognised manifestations of the *Higher Self* in those whom they 'contact'. The notion of a Higher Self or spiritual essence intermingled with the mundane nature is common in esoteric thought, especially in connection with theories of reincarnation, and may also be linked with ideas of the Oversoul (as the **transcendentalist** Ralph Waldo Emerson called it) or the Guardian Angel. The belief is ancient.

'The knower is never born nor dies,' states the **Hindu** *Katha Upanishad*, 'nor is it from anywhere, nor did it become anything. Unborn, eternal, immemorial, this ancient is not slain when the body is slain. . . . Smaller than smaller, greater than great, this Self is hidden in the heart of man. In all beings it shines not forth; but is perceived by the piercing subtle soul of the subtle-sighted . . . Understanding this great lord the Self, bodiless in bodies, stable among unstable, the wise man cannot grieve . . . He is released from the mouth of Death, having gained the lasting thing which is above the great, which has neither sound nor touch nor form nor change nor taste nor smell, but is eternal, beginningless, endless.'

This perception is expressed by virtually every culture in every age on earth. In the Welsh *Book of Taliesin* (thirteenth century, perhaps from the sixth century), the bard sings of the Imperishable, which lives in him. As the boy Gwion he was swallowed by the terrible hag Cerridwen, only to be reborn as Taliesin. Dying to the ego, he has risen again, in the egoless Self, and as a miraculous child he asks his dumbstruck audience:

> Knowest thou what thou art in the hour of sleep –
> A mere body, a mere soul, or a secret retreat of light?

In 1944 psychologist Carl Jung, while ill and near death, had a remarkable **out-of-the-body** experience. He found himself high above the earth, feeling that 'everything was being sloughed away; everything I aimed at or wished for or thought, the whole phantasmagoria of earthly existence'. Later he dreamed he came to a chapel and saw a **yogi** in meditation. The yogi's face was his own. He awoke realising: 'Aha, so he is the one who is **meditating** me. He has a dream, and I am it.' He concluded that the Self meditates the assumption of earthly form to enter three-dimensional existence, like a diver who puts on a diving suit (the body) to penetrate the material sea.

Or, again, as the *Katha Upanishad* has it:

'Know that the Self is the lord of the chariot, the body verily is the chariot; know that the soul is the charioteer, and emotion the reins . . . the bodily powers are the horses, and . . . the external world is their field.'

A growing number of psychologists suspect that empirical evidence for the existence of the Higher Self is found especially in cases of **multiple personality**, while the theories of Abraham **Maslow** and others concerning the human potential for 'peak experience' increasingly suggest that, when charioteer, chariot and horses all work together, then we are capable of more than ordinary sense alone allows. The Higher Self is the invisible centre of a circle on the perimeter of which we live our daily lives.

HILL, Barney and Betty (*See* **ABDUCTIONS**)

HINDUISM (*See* **BRAHMA, KALI YUGA, KARMA, REINCARNATION, YOGA**, etc.) The oldest and perhaps the most subtle of the world's great **religions**, Hinduism and its traditions, teachings and sacred books offer scope too vast for any easy elucidation. For a start, Hindu cosmology posits a chronology for the created universe of such duration that modern estimates of the time elapsed since the 'Big Bang' are trivial by comparison. Enough here to say that the least division of the chronology involved gives an era of 432,000 years and that Hindu belief holds that currently we inhabit an era called ***Kali Yuga*** (Age of Iron) – an age of degeneration and amnesia which, it is said, will end in universal conflagration, leaving only Brahman, the unmanifest.

Though popularly a faith of many deities, **spirits** and devils, Hinduism teaches that Unity underlies the multitude of manifested appearances. All created beings are subject to the laws of karma and reincarnation – even the 'gods'. The only way to leave the Wheel of cause and effect, death and rebirth, is via the practice of Yoga (Sanskrit *jog* = to 'yoke', as in the English word 'con*jug*al'). **Paranormal** powers ('*siddhis*') may be developed as a side-effect of practising one or another of the many yogic systems. These – as in **Buddhist** yoga – are distractions from the primary aim of **mystical** transcendence. **Fire-walking**, sleeping on beds of nails, snake-charming, the **hypnosis** of audiences involved in the 'Indian Rope-trick', suspended animation and other amazing stunts in the repertoire of an accomplished *fakir* are, for the most part, irrelevant to the primary purpose of yoga, save insofar as the development of such powers aids the yoking of the mind.

HINDU MYSTERIES (*See* **HOPI**) Of late the Hindu Vedas (sacred books) and other old Sanskrit texts have stimulated interest not only for their crystallisation of basic esoteric ideas but for their seeming description of destructive technology all too familiar to us today. UFOlogists and those believing in ancient technology or 'space gods' eagerly annex parts of the *Ramayana* and the *Mahabharata* as proof of their claims. Do they have a case? Sadly, yes. Passages which only a century ago would be dismissed as 'heroic myth' or 'magical tale' now, in the light of modern knowledge, have a disturbingly familiar ring.

The 24,000-verse *Ramayana* (certainly pre-500 BC, possibly pre-3000 BC) involves aerial invasions, dog-fights between 'celestial cars', and the use of '**Brahma's** deathful weapon flaming with celestial fire'. In its theme of the husband's quest for a captured wife whose rape sets the world at war, the *Ramayana* suggests the *Iliad*: did both have a common, earlier source? As for claims that this and other texts are not just fanciful in describing aerial battles and annihilating weapons . . . the more we learn of (and fear) atomic catastrophe, the more these texts seem to describe it. Take this description from the *Droma Parva* (part of the epic *Mahabharata*):

'The valiant Adwatthaman . . . invoked the Agneya weapon . . . The Sun seemed to turn round. The universe scorched with heats seemed to be in a fever. The elephants and other creatures of the land scorched by the energy of that weapon, ran in fright, breathing heavily and desirous of protection against that terrible force. The very water being heated, the creatures residing in [it] . . . seemed to burn. . . . The steeds, O King, and the cars also burnt by the energy of that weapon, looked, O Sire, like the tops of trees burnt in a forest fire. Thousands of cars fell down on all sides.'[1]

This from a translation made in 1888. Further descriptions describe the suffering of the survivors of the blast, the falling-out of their hair and teeth, the poisoning of the waters. Another account in the *Droma Parva* describes the destruction of three 'cities' in the sky by a 'shaft inspired with the **[Kali] Yuga** fire and composed of Vishnu and Soma.' Notes the translator Chandra Roy (again: 1888) in his commentary on another battle, involving a weapon called Brahma's Rod: 'This . . . is infinitely more powerful even than Indra's bolt. The latter can strike only once, but the former can smite whole countries and entire races from generation to generation.'

As, of course, can nuclear fall-out. It is terrible to speculate that as a species we have merely arrived at where we were before, and that the destruction last time was so great that we forgot, or blamed it on 'God'.

'In that dreadful battle those shafts, O King, like the very rays of the Sun, in a moment shrouded all the parts of the compass.'

1. *Gods and Spacemen in the Ancient East*, Raymond Drake, Sphere, London 1973

HITLER, Adolf (1889–1945) (*See* **NOSTRADAMUS**) By 1923 this failed Austrian-born artist and ex-German army corporal was unchallenged leader of the Munich-based NSDAP (National Socialist Workers Party, or Nazi Party). Amid the chaotic inflation of post-war Germany, his rabble-rousing oratory struck a popular chord, inciting violence against **Jews**, Communists and other groups he blamed for German defeat in the Great War. The failed Nazi putsch (military coup) in Munich of 9 November 1923 he later described as 'the greatest stroke of luck in my life'.[1] Jailed in the Landsberg fortress-prison, he wrote his testament, *Mein Kampf*. Few took this rambling, **apocalyptic**, anti-semitic fantasy seriously. Yet on 30 January 1933, Hitler became Chancellor of all Germany. 'We are the last who will be making history in Germany at this time,' he said at the time, even as, backed by Nazi power, he began to put his violent racial fantasies into effect. Within a few years these brought about World War II and its estimated 60 million deaths, including those of 6 million Jews. Despite his ultimate defeat he shaped European politics for the rest of the century.

How did he do it? 'I go the way fate has pointed me like a man walking in his sleep,' he once said. To gain power he awoke the German religious impulse, imposing on it a meaning and function reliant on his primacy as **prophet** of the order he initiated. He did so by use of terror and by *religious* ceremonial on a huge scale. The Nuremberg rallies, held by night, with their banners, flags dipped in blood, and searchlights spearing the sky like cathedral pillars, were implicitly ***ritualistic***: their purpose: to drown individual conscience in a flood of primitive impulse.

'At a mass meeting,' he told Herman Rauschning (a Nazi Party member since 1926 who in 1935 fled via Switzerland to the USA, where he tried to warn the world about Nazism), 'thought is eliminated. And because this is the state of mind I require, because it secures to me the best sounding-board for my speeches I order everyone to attend the meetings, where they become part of the mass whether they like it or not.'[2]

In *Mein Kampf* he wrote, 'One deals with the problem of influencing the freedom of the human will. And that is true especially of meetings where there are men whose wills are opposed to the speaker and who must be brought around to a new way of thinking. In the morning and during the day it seems that the power of the human will rebels with its strongest energy against any attempt to impose upon it the will or opinion of another. On the other hand, in the evening it easily succumbs to the domination of a stronger will . . . The mysterious artificial dimness of the Catholic churches also serves this purpose, the burning candles, the incense . . .'[3]

Said Carl **Jung**: 'Don't you know that if you get one hundred of the most intelligent people in the world and get them all together, they are a stupid mob? Ten thousand would have the collective intelligence of an alligator.'[4] This reptile-intelligence is just what Hitler exploited.

Where did he learn his techniques? '. . . above all from the Jesuits,' he told Rauschning. **Freemasonry**, which he attacked, also taught him methods via its 'hierarchical organisation and the **initiation** through symbolic rites, that is to say without bothering the brains but by working on the imagination and the **symbols** of a cult – all this is the dangerous element and the element I have taken over.'[4]

He did not create but only exploited old German resentments. In 1918, Carl Jung, whose 1913 dream of a 'sea of blood' flooding Europe presaged World War I, had warned against the breakout of 'a blonde beast from an underworld prison.'[5] Later he called Hitler, 'The loudspeaker that makes audible all the inaudible mutterings of the German soul'.[6]

German defeat in World War I had led to social chaos, huge inflation, and loss of national self-respect – yet again. 2,000 years earlier the German race-spirit (Wotan) had been subjugated first by Roman arms then by Roman Christianity. But collective **archetypes** do not die. In 1517 Luther served theological notice on Rome. Two hundred and fifty years later Prussia's Frederick the Great served military notice on Europe. In Bismarck's era composer Richard Wagner and philosopher Friedrich Nietzsche restated German **pagan** beliefs.

Hitler hijacked Wagner, Nietzsche's 'Superman', and any other potent 'German' mythology he could find. Intuitively aware of which mass **psychic** nerves to touch, he gained **the emotive** support of a bruised nation. A self-admitted sleepwalker, he knew (*see* **GURDJIEFF**) *we are all sleepwalkers*. So in his 'madness' he inspired millions to abandon civilised behaviour to embrace the old gods of blood and revenge.

The longer suppressed instincts await release, the more violent their eventual eruption. Repressed, the creative spirit turns into its opposite, glorying in destruction and self-destruction. Such wrath bewilders those whose racial spirit is more happily served. IRA violence bewilders the English; Muslim terrorism bewilders the West; Samson pulled down the temple of the Philistines on their heads and on his own so well. Such violence is **mythic**; proportionate to the sense of (unconscious) grievance. Individually it may manifest only in the **poltergeist** tantrums of a frustrated teenager. Collectively it may lead, if not understood and contained, to global war.

Hitler is not unique. Demonised, he knew how to trigger everyone else's **demons**. That he and his followers were influenced by occult groups – the Order of New Templars, the Thulegesellschaft, or Thule Society, and by Hans **Hörbiger**, was inevitable, given his **magical** preoccupations. Was the ease with which he gained global influence also inevitable? The continuing 'success' of despots like Pol Pot and Saddam Hussein suggests that the mass mind is still all too easily overwhelmed by instinctual impulse . . . and terror.

World War II was ended only by the atomic bomb. As for the man who started it all, his mentality was such that (Jung), he was: '. . . compelled to conduct the war in a manner that would make defeat inevitable'.[7]

1. *Hitler*, Joachim C. Fest, Weidenfeld & Nicholson, London 1974, p. 190
2. *The Messianic Legacy*, Michael Baigent, Richard Leigh and Henry Lincoln, Corgi Books, London 1987, p. 196, quoting Rauschning, *Hitler Speaks*, p. 209
3. *Ibid.*, p. 196, quoting Adolf Hitler, *Mein Kampf*, p. 395
4. Quoted in: 'The brain's generation gap: some human implications,' Paul Maclean,

in *Zygon – Journal of Religion & Science* 8 (2) 113–27, 1973
5. *op.cit.* ref. 2, p. 196, quoting Rauschning, *Hitler Speaks*, p. 237
6. *Jung and the Story of our Time*, Laurens van der Post, Penguin, London 1978
7. *ibid.*, p. 23

HOLLOW EARTH (*See* **BULWER-LYTTON**) One of the many odd or **occult** ideas which characterised the magical worldview of Nazism was that not only is the Earth hollow, but we live in it, adhering to the concave globular surface of a mass of rock extending to infinity, the sun and moon at the centre of its interior.

More common Hollow Earth belief is that the hollow Earth may be entered via holes at the North and South Poles, and that secret societies flourish in it. This idea dates to early times. Egyptian pharaohs were said to be able to reach the underworld via secret tunnels under the pyramids; Greek mythology tells how Orpheus tried to get his dead wife Eurydice back from Hades; the Chaldean hero Gilgamesh visits his ancestor Utnapishtim in the underworld; **Buddhist myth** tells of the paradise of subterranean Agharta.

Modern interest in hollow Earth theory begins in the eighteenth century with mathematician Leonard Euler and Dr Edmund Halley (of Halley's comet), who held that the hollow Earth contains three planets. A century later US Civil War hero John Cleves Symmes almost got government backing for an expedition to prove the Earth hollow; Cyrus Read Teed founded a religion (*Koreshism*) on this basis. The Victorian novelist Bulwer-Lytton used the idea (as did Verne, Poe, and Edgar Rice Burroughs) in a novel, *The Coming Race*, telling of a malign civilisation of superior **psychic** powers inhabiting caves under the Earth. After the First World War a German airman, Bender, took up these theories and that of American Marshall B. Gardner who in 1913 published a book 'proving' that the Sun is inside the Earth, and that the pressure of its rays holds us to the Earth's concave surface. Bender's odd cosmology claimed that the atmosphere extends inwards from the concave surface for forty-five miles and rarefies to a vacuum at the centre, where lies Sun, Moon and a Phantom Universe – a globe of bluish gas pierced by bright points of light the astronomers call stars. Many Nazi leaders believed this – no joke.

Hollow Earth speculation survived the Nazi defeat. In the March 1945 issue of *Amazing Stories* (a US sci-fi magazine) Richard S. Shaver published an article, 'I remember Lemuria'. Maybe influenced by H. P. Lovecraft's 1936 novel *The Shadow Out of Time*, he claimed the caves in the Earth's interior are inhabited by subhumans (*deros*) who abandoned the surface of the Earth 12,000 years ago. Once slaves of a **Lemurian** master race now gone to outer space, the *deros* now persecuted the humans of the outer world and caused the world's troubles. When in 1947 the **UFO** mania began with Arnold's sightings of 'flying saucers' over Mount Rainier, Shaver (he claimed to have visited the world of the *deros*) was in business – obviously the UFOs were not sent by extraterrestials but by an advanced subterranean race gaining access to the surface world via huge holes at the North and South Poles.

Hollow Earth theory gained a new lease of life in June 1970 when Ray Palmer, editor of *Flying Saucers* magazine, reproduced photographs of the North Pole taken by the ESSA–7 satellite and released by the Environmental Science Service Administration of the US Department of Commerce. One of these showed a huge round black hole at the Pole. Palmer asserted this as proof of the existence of the subterranean super race, adducing as further proof the controversy over the polar expeditions of Rear-Admiral Richard E. Byrd (1888–1957). Byrd's reported comment prior to his 1947 flight over the *South* Pole that: 'I'd like to see that land beyond the Pole. That area beyond the Pole is the centre of the Great Unknown.' was exploited by Palmer and others to suggest that Byrd had flown not *over* the Pole but *into* a hole giving access to an 'enchanted continent', a 'land of everlasting mystery', where lay a 'Rainbow City', lush vegetation, lakes, rivers, etc.

Byrd being dead, he could not deny this misuse of his *actual* words; nor were Hollow Earth fans upset by the fact that the image of a 'hole' at the Pole came from a mosaic of satellite TV images taken amid the continuous North Polar night, resulting in a central, circular 'hole of darkness'.

The Earth is not hollow. The only holes involved are in the heads of those believing it is. The womb symbolism involved in such belief is evident. What is disturbing (and relevant to this book) is the ease with which reason is overwhelmed by imaginative desire. Is it *accident* that prominent Nazis sought such a womb-flight from the universe? Such a belief remains irrelevant until those holding it gain military power.[1,2]

1. *The Morning of the Magicians*, Pauwels and Bergier, Mayflower, London 1979, pp. 187ff
2. 'Is the Earth hollow?', W. A. Harbinson, in *The Unexplained*, Orbis partwork London 1983, pp. 530–3

HOLOGRAPHIC THEORY (*See* **BRAIN MYSTERIES, CHAOS, KIRLIAN**) In the early 1980s neuropsychologist Karl **Pribram**, in collaboration with physicist David **Bohm** at London University, developed at his laboratory in Stanford, California, a hologrammatic model of brain-function that may yet provide a working basis for a creative relationship between the insights of **mystics** and the pragmatic discoveries of behaviourists. Insisting that the brain operates according to the same mathematical principles as a hologram (in which the activity of the part describes that of the whole), he argued that his physiological research into brain activity provided a sufficient basis for wider speculation as to the basis of the organisational principle governing processes such as *memory*, *learning* and *knowledge*. This principle he claimed to have found in the hologram.

Speaking of the brain's involvement in perceptual activity, he said in 1979 (in a manner reminiscent of **Goethe**), 'It's not that cells in the visual system are detecting only a certain line. What they respond to is the pattern of shadow and light.' He added, 'The hologram yields a new way of looking at consciousness that is very different from the old behaviorist and phenomological approaches. The behaviorist looks for cause and effect, the phenomenologist, for reasons and intentions. In holography, however, one looks for the transformations involved in moving from one domain to another.' Meaning that neither *behavioural* or *mystic* insights have to be denied or seen as opposed – they simply occupy different domains within the field of legitimate scientific research. Again: 'As a way of looking at consciousness, holographic theory is much closer to mystical and Eastern philosophy. It will take a while for people to become comfortable with an order of reality other than the world of appearances. But it seems to me that some of the mystical experiences people have described for millennia begin to make some scientific sense.'[1]

Well, thank God for that!

1. 'Pribram: the Magellan of Brain Science', Daniel Goleman, *Psychology Today*, USA, February 1979, pp. 76–9

HOLY GRAIL (*See* **ARTHURIAN MYTH**) The cup **Christ** used at the Last Supper which Joseph of Arimathea brought to **Glastonbury**? A **pagan** Celtic vessel that provided endless sustenance (the Cauldron of the Dagda), or a Brew of Inspiration (Cerridwen's Cauldron) or rebirth at dawn for dead warriors thrown into it at dusk (Bran's Cauldron)?

What was the Holy Grail? Mediaeval Grail romance involves imposition of esoteric **Christianity** on **pagan ritual** celebrating life's annual death and rebirth and the belief that the health of King and Land are intimately connected. The anonymous fourteenth-century poem *Sir Gawain and the Green Knight* retells an older **myth** of the giant hero Bran whose decapitated head, put in London's White Tower, ensured fertility. The sexually wounded Fisher King (lanced through the loins) who owns the Grail in various such romances also refers to Bran: his unhealed wound means a sterile land. The Grail itself is invariably ambiguous. Is it cup, dish, stone or cauldron; is it a womb; or a symbolic reflection of all that lies beyond human knowledge?

In the late 1180s, as Jerusalem fell to the Saracens, Chrétien de Troyes wrote *Le Roman de Perceval (Le Conte del Graal)*. Associated with the court of Champagne (as was Hugues de Payens, founder of the **Knights Templar**), he got his theme from Philippe d'Alsace, Count of Flanders. Set in the Arthurian age popularised by Geoffrey of Monmouth's *History of the Kings of Britain* (1135), it tells how Perceval (*Son of the Widow Lady*: a **Gnostic** term later used by **Freemasons**) leaves his widowed mother to win knighthood. He meets the 'Fisher King' who offers him refuge in his castle. That night the Grail (golden, gem-studded, carried by a damsel) appears. Failing to ask who one serves with this Grail, Perceval awakes next day to find the castle empty and the land blighted by his omission. He learns he is of the Grail family and that the Fisher King, who had been 'sustained' by the Grail, was his uncle. There is no mention of Christ in this (unfinished) account.

The first Christian version is the *Roman de l'Estoire dou Saint Graal* (1190–99) by Robert de Boron. De Boron calls the Grail the cup of the Last Supper. In it Christ's blood is caught by Joseph of Arimathea, whose brother-in-law Brons (not Joseph himself, as in the Glastonbury legend) takes it to England. Brons becomes the Fisher King, *Perceval's grandfather*.

In the *Perlesvaus* (its unknown author perhaps Templar), Perceval comes to a castle housing two *masters* and thirty-three other men 'clad in white garments' with red crosses on the breast. One *master* claims to have seen the Grail. Set in Arthurian time, the poem abounds in **magic, alchemical** and Gnostic references – a good reason for anonymity. The crusade against the **Cathars** was about to begin: the Templars were already suspected of magic practices. Here the Grail is a sequence of five visions: a crowned, crucified king; a child; a man crowned with thorns; an unspecified fourth image; and, lastly, a chalice. The Grail here is a mystical *experience*, not an object.

Parzival, by Bavarian knight Wolfram von Eschenbach, is the best-known Grail romance. Composed *c.* 1195–1216, Wolfram says Chrétien's version is wrong and that he heard his own authoritative version from Kyot de Provence (perhaps the troubadour Guiot de Provins). Kyot in turn (Wolfram explains) got it from Spanish Moslem sources, the origin being *Judaic*. As told by Wolfram, 'the Grail is unknown save to those who have been called by name' and is said (a plainly alchemical symbol) to be a '*stone*'. He hints that the Grail is connected with the Crucifixion and with a mission imposed on certain people whom it may call into its service. A specific bloodline is involved. As in the *Perlesvaus*, the Grail is not an object but *knowledge*. Wolfram, writing in a cruel time, holds his cards close, but suggests (like the author of *Perlesvaus*) that Grail-myth means *initiation* into unorthodox *gnosis*. Given the Judaic connection, this implies **Qabalah**; also connection with the courtly movement of *chivalry* (exalting Woman) and the troubadours. These arose in Provence; which is where, say some tales, the Magdalene went from Judaea . . . taking the Grail with her.

Gnostic texts like *Pistis Sophia* claim that 'the disciple Jesus loved most' was the Magdalene, and tell how Peter and other Apostles resented her influence. None of this appears in the synoptic gospels as rewritten by the Church Fathers. Some traditions (as do the Moslems) say that Jesus survived the Crucifixion. According to one recent account, he went with the Magdalene to southern France: the 'Grail' (on a material level) being her womb (cup); its fruit the 'magical' Merovingian dynasty. *Sangraal* (womb; Holy Grail) is thus also *sang raal* (the royal or holy blood of Jesus).[1]

The 'damsel' bearing the Grail is thus the Magdalene: other elements of Grail-myth like the lance or spear likewise refer to what could not be said openly in a time when male hate of Woman (*Nature*) had reached a destructive pitch expressed first in the Inquisition, then by witch-hunts, and today by our consumer rape of **Gaia**. Pagan nature-lore, Gnostic metaphysics, and 'goddess'-worship had to be veiled in myth. The troubadours, Templars and Cathars tried to stem the tide we inherit via the myth of the Holy Grail, creating a body of alternative text which, necessarily dealing in metaphor for the sake of survival, today remains seen as puzzling **fairy tale** despite the evolutionary import of its message. As to the theory that Grail-myth intrinsically involves the great secret that Christ's bloodline survived in the Merovingians and thereafter, this question remains open.[2]

1. *The Holy Blood and the Holy Grail*, Baigent, Leigh and Lincoln, Corgi, London 1983
2. *King Arthur and the Grail*, Richard Cavendish, Paladin, London 1980

HOME, Daniel Dunglass (1833–86) (*See* **FIREWALKING, LEVITATION**) Never caught cheating – the perfect epitaph for a **medium** at work amid sceptics. Brought up in the USA, this Scots genius returned to Britain in 1855. Frequently before witnesses he demonstrated **paranormal** abilities so conclusively that denial is as difficult as acceptance. He played with fire, levitated from one window of a London house and returned via another, elongated his body, and projected tongues of fire from his head. In the latter case the Master of Lindsay, later a Fellow of the Royal Society, observed, 'We all then distinctly heard . . . a bird flying round the room, whistling and chirping. There then came the sound of a great wind rushing through the room.' Home then spoke incomprehensibly before explaining that the performance was a repeat of the first Pentecost, when the Holy Spirit had entered the Apostles as tongues of fire.

Before witnesses of known probity Home also demonstrated:

- movement of heavy objects without physical pressure
- changes of temperature (registered on a thermometer)
- percussive noises – raps, scratchings, detonations
- levitation of furniture without physical contact
- levitation of his own body
- musical instruments played with no body to play them
- materialisations – often of 'hands' taking up those of the observers present, seeming solid before fading (**Crookes**) 'into vapour'
- phantom writing: invisible hands taking up pens to write messages.

In one experiment, Sir William Crookes designed a cage, insulated with copper wire. An accordion was put in it. Home could touch it, but not its bellows. The accordion played, even when Home removed his hand entirely from it. Given the controversy over Crookes in the Florence Cook case, it is easy to assume that such experiments were rigged, or that somehow Home **hypnotised** his observers. But his reputation was good; he was admired by Lytton, Ruskin, Thackeray and Longfellow. Emerson called him a 'prodigious genius'. None attending his séances ever accused him of **fraud**. This alone is notable in an era when all manifestations of supernaturalism were (often correctly) attacked on such grounds. Subsequent enquiries into his reported powers and his character have found nothing to suggest he was less than his reputation says he was: one of the great modern mediums.

HOMING INSTINCT (*See* **ANIMAL POWERS, BIRDS, ELECTROMAGNETISM**) The 'homing instinct' of birds and animals is well known. But what of the same instinct in human beings? Increasingly divorced from our nature, we may not find it easily. Yet it exists, as zoologist Dr Robin Baker proved in the late 1970s. Operating from Manchester University, he led blindfolded people from their homes through twisting lanes to a secret destination at which, supposedly utterly disorientated, they were asked to point the directions of their homes. Despite the blindfold, most did so accurately. In later tests he fitted the heads of some subjects with a bar magnet and others with a brass bar. Those tested were not told which they had. Those with the brass bar (neutral) again accurately indicated their home direction. Those with the genuine magnet attached were confused.[1]

1. *Beyond the Occult*, Colin Wilson, Corgi, London 1989, p. 155

HOPI (*See* **BLACK ELK PROPHECY**) The village of Old Oraibi on a bleak Arizona mesa is the oldest continually inhabited settlement in North America – a millennium old. But the Hopi have inhabited the region much longer. Even their neighbours, the Navaho, who came via the 'Back Door' (the Bering Straits) are said to be newcomers.

Hopi cosmology, legends and **prophecies** are of general concern.

Hopi **myth** tells of three worlds before this present Fourth World. In the beginning was Taiowa, the Unmanifest, who made Sótuknang to create the material universe. He created Spider Woman, Mother Earth, and she birthed the people of the First World (Tokpela, 'Endless Space'). The door in the top of their heads was open to wisdom; they knew no sickness. But language was invented; the animals drew away from them and they from each other. So Sótuknang destroyed Tokpela with fire, but the people survived underground with the ants. Entering the Second World, Tokpa (Dark Midnight), they found it not so lovely, nor was the door in the top of their head so open. They began to trade and barter; evil spread. Sótuknang told the Twins of North and South Poles to leave their posts. The Earth rolled over twice: the sea invaded the land. Again the people survived with the ants, to emerge into the Third World (Kuskurza). Building cities, they became materialistic. There was a great war. Flying machines (*pátuwvotas*) attacked enemy cities. So Sótuknang sent the Flood. Continents sank, but the people survived in hollow reeds that floated on the seas. Seeking land they sent out **birds** which returned, exhausted. But in time Spider Woman brought them to the Fourth World, Túwaqachi (World Complete). They landed in what is now the west of America. The giant voice of Másaw, the guardian of the lands, said they could stay, but only after long pilgrimage. Másaw broke in four pieces a tablet of stone. Each piece sent the white, black, yellow and red races in different directions. It was prophesied that one day they would reunite. So they went their ways . . . and so the Hopi, first to return and find the desert homeland, awaited fulfilment of the prophecy. But when the White Brother (Pahana) returned, he had forgotten. He brought fire, sword, and cruelty. He had forgotten everything. This too was in the prophecy.

'You will hear of a house in the heavens that will fall with a great crash.' The Hopi have long foretold a war begun by 'old countries, which first received the light of knowledge' (Middle Eastern nations). The war will be 'a spiritual conflict with material matters'. Some say 'the house in the heavens' was Skylab. It fell in 1979. A 'Gourd of Ashes', dropped from the sky, will boil the oceans and burn the lands. Then Hopi ceremonial will cease. Yet in the dire time of the Great Purification, marked by the appearance of a 'blue star', Pahana will return, bringing the dawn of the Fifth World to the 'safe' lands of the Southwest.

The Hopi prophecies are carved on Black Mesa in the Four Corners area of their territory. The petroglyphs are reckoned to be at least 2,000 years old. Three signs – swastika, sun and the colour red – were given to signal the approach of the Great Purification. Then the Hopi would release their prophecies and teachings in a final effort to avert disaster.

This has now been done. Notice has been served on all of us, the inhabitants of the Fourth World.[1]

1. *Book of the Hopi*, Frank Waters, Viking Penguin, London/New York 1963

HÖRBIGER, Hans (1860–1931) Supported by **Hitler**, this aggressive engineer-cum-cosmologist (he told Hitler to 'shut up' when interrupted) preached that the universe and all created matter exists due to perpetual conflict between fire and ice, and that originally four moons circled Earth, these having been destroyed by cataclysmic collision with the Earth, the last having fallen 13,000 years ago, destroying **Atlantis** – the original Aryan home, he claimed. He is generally (and probably rightly) regarded as a lunatic – literally, given his belief in falling moons. Who would want to believe in any system that Hitler and Himmler believed? He denied **Kepler**'s laws of motion, yet Hitler held Kepler, Copernicus and Hörbiger(!) to be the three great cosmologists.

Yet it is odd how, in effect, he advanced the same four-world doctrine of epochal cataclysm as North American **Hopis** and the **Hindus** of Asia.[1]

1. *The Morning of the Magicians*, Pauwels and Bergier, Mayflower, London 1979

HOROSCOPE (*See* **ASTROLOGY**) The Greek-derived Latin term *hōroscopus* from *hōra* ('time') and *skopos* ('observer') gives the word *horoscope*, meaning a chart of the disposition of the heavens at a particular moment, usually the moment of birth of an individual. Drawn up, 'erected', or 'cast' for purpose of astrological enquiry into the individual's character and prospects, the horoscope is also known as a 'birth-chart' and as such is considered under **Astrology**.

HOUDINI, Harry (1874–1926) (*See* **FRAUD**) Born Erich Weiss in Wisconsin, USA, this son of a Hungarian rabbi early read the memoirs of magician Robert-Houdin. On beginning his career as an escapologist and stage-magician he took the name *Houdini*. As his fame grew he so regretted this that he wrote *The unmasking of Robert-Houdin*, thus demolishing his old hero's reputation. It later became clear that he had deliberately distorted facts to fit his case that Houdin was a fraud. This attack he later extended to all **mediums**. But why? Because of his mother's death in 1913? Longing to communicate with her, he visited mediums in the hope that she would 'come through'. She never did, or not in a way that satisfied him. After this he spent years unmasking fraudulent mediums, obsessively assuming that they *had* to be fakes. In 1923, returning to the USA from England where Conan **Doyle** had tried to persuade him that not all psychics are frauds, he publicly demonstrated mediumistic 'tricks'. At his suggestion the *Scientific American* offered $2,500 for 'the first physical manifestations of a **psychic** nature produced under scientific control'. Mrs Mina Crandon (as 'Margery' the best-known American medium of the time) took up the challenge. Houdini, the psychic researcher Hereward Carrington, and three others were appointed to investigate. Houdini was caught out rigging the experiment against her. In a new test, Margery, enclosed in a glass cage, levitated objects *outside* the cage. He had to abandon his effort to prove her a fraud, though he claimed he had done so.

In 1926 an alleged **spirit** message was received by Conan Doyle's home circle: 'Houdini is doomed, doomed, doomed!' On 24 October one his allies in the campaign against mediums was sitting in his room when a picture of Houdini fell to the floor. A week later Houdini was dead. But the mystery remains – not only as to his attitude but as to the source of his own abilities. Conan Doyle for one, while accepting that Houdini was 'a very skilful conjurer', was sure he was also 'the greatest physical medium of modern times'. How else, in 1926, did he remain underwater in a sealed container for over an hour and emerge unscathed? He said all he had done was to breathe deeply

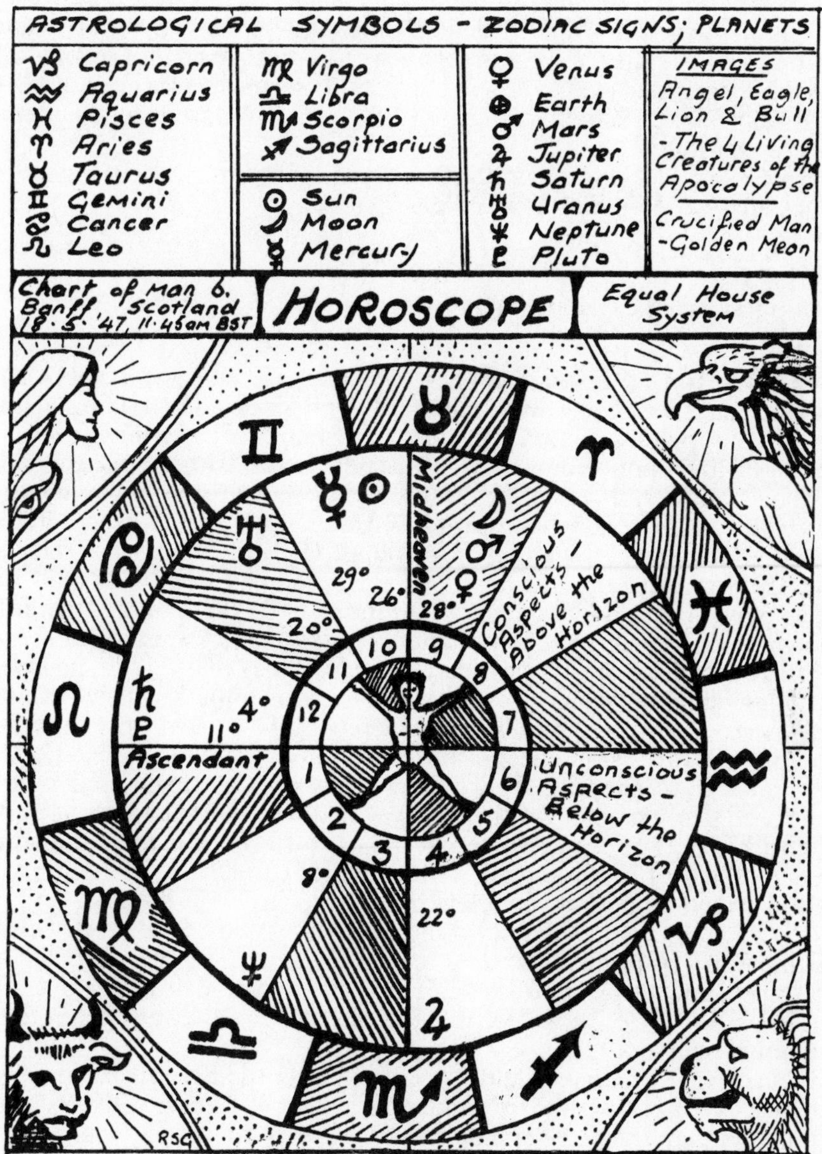
ASTROLOGICAL SYMBOLS - ZODIAC SIGNS; PLANETS
Capricorn
Aquarius
Pisces
Aries
Taurus
Gemini
Cancer
Leo
Virgo
Libra
Scorpio
Sagittarius
Sun
Moon
Mercury
Venus
Earth
Mars
Jupiter
Saturn
Uranus
Neptune
Pluto
IMAGES
Angel, Eagle, Lion & Bull
- The 4 Living Creatures of the Apocalypse
Crucified Man
- Golden Mean
Chart of Man 6. Banff, Scotland 18.5.47, 11.45am BST
HOROSCOPE
Equal House System
Midheaven
Conscious Aspects - Above the Horizon
Unconscious Aspects - Below the Horizon
Ascendant
29°
26°
28°
20°
4°
11°
8°
22°
10
9
11
8
12
7
1
6
2
5
3
4
RSC

before the box was closed, then relax. His fellow conjurers were sure he must somehow have cheated. He seemed unaware that deep breathing is a traditional means of inducing a **trance** state. He did however admit that he had an 'inner voice' which told him what he could or could not do, and that 'so long as he obeyed the voice he was assured of safety' – yet its promptings he regarded solely as 'lucky breaks'. On numerous occasions – including what he claimed was a 'bogus' séance he gave for President Theodore Roosevelt – he seemingly manifested psychic powers (**second sight, levitation**) which he himself denied outright. Again, why? For whatever the source of his powers, they were extraordinary: he remains a household name. No escapologist has ever managed to repeat his feats. It seems he was a genuine fakir who thought all fakirs fake. Either that or he feared that to admit his psychism would destroy his reputation.[1,2]

A modern version of the same ambiguity is seen in the attacks by US stage magician James 'The Amazing' **Randi** on Uri **Geller**.

1. 'Caught in the act', Brian Inglis, *The Unexplained*, Orbis partwork, London 1983, pp. 2521–25
2. 'Was Houdini Psychic?', Brian Inglis, *op. cit.*, pp. 2550–53

HUBBARD, L. Ron (1911–86?) Where does fantasy end and reality begin? The story of science fiction writer L. Ron Hubbard, who invented a **'religion'** with himself as its god, worshipped by millions, makes one wonder. Hubbard's life was one long catalogue of self-invention. For a start he was not, as he claimed, descended from the Norman nobleman 'Count de Loupe', nor was his orphan father a Commander in the US Navy. Himself a US Navy lieutenant in World War II, never in action, he said he had fought the Japanese in the Dutch East Indies. He convinced fellow science-fiction writers like Robert Heinlein and Jack Williamson he had been sunk four times and wounded as often. He said he had grown up in the 'wilds of Montana' (in fact Iowa), been adopted by an Indian tribe, had wandered the East and been taught by a 'personal student' of **Freud**. None of this was true. What *is* true is that, before he invented his successful quasi-religion, Scientology, he wrote tales for John W. Campbell's magazine *Astounding Science Fiction*. Typically, these were rapidly-written 'space operas', full of violent action, or darkly paranoid fantasies (*Fear*, 1940). Another science-fiction editor, Sam Merwin, later recalled, 'I always knew he was exceedingly anxious to hit big money – he used to say he thought the best way to do it would be to start a cult.'[1]

After World War II he was involved in the **occult** experiments of rocket engineer Jack Parsons. Their efforts to create a 'moonchild' earned the contempt of Aleister **Crowley** and ended when Parsons blew himself up in 1952. By 1949 Hubbard was rumoured to be about to unveil a new 'science of the mind'. So in 1950 *Dianetics* was born. In the April issue of *Astounding Science Fiction*, Campbell boosted this new 'science' as a psychotherapy capable of clearing out all mental dross to unveil the latent superman in us all. 'It is', he wrote, 'a coldly precise engineering description of how the human mind operates.'

Arguing that his new therapy could unlock 'engrams' (coded unconscious memories) out of the 'reactive mind', Hubbard claimed in his book *Dianetics, the Modern Science of Mental Health*, that he offered an infallible solution to all ills, physical or psychological. The book was verbose and confusing, but Dianetics became a craze. You could 'audit' (psychoanalyse) your friend and uncover deep memory, then get your friend to do it for you.

Hubbard had charisma. Soon he was making a lot of money. But bankruptcy and FBI investigation followed. Undaunted, he unveiled the Church of Scientology. By calling it a 'church' he gained tax-exemption and freedom from harassment.

Claiming 'scientifically-validated evidence of the existence of the human soul', he now offered an entire cosmology, stating that our true self is an immortal entity – a 'thetan'. Creating the universe for fun, thetans go through thousands of bodies over the aeons, but in doing so get enmeshed in matter and forget their omniscient origin. Scientology aims to restore ('clear') us back to the level of 'operating thetan' or 'OT'.

The auditing process supposed to create 'Clears' involved use of the 'E-meter; a galvanometer which provided technological glamour (and was later implicated in reports that Scientology brainwashed its gullible devotees). Hubbard also wrote voluminous background material. His *The History of Man* reworked evolution. He said many *engrams* went back to a problem suffered by *clams* as to whether to open or close. 'For compressed nonsense and fantasy it must surpass anything theretofore written', commented a 1965 Australian government report into Scientology. Perhaps. But the cult's followers – by 1980 six million worldwide – bought it. Literally. Many still do. Fifty hours of auditing can cost well over $2,000. Some members have paid over $30,000 in seeking to be audited through to 'Clear' status.

The medical profession attacked him. In 1959 (though the CIA and FBI had uncovered little hard evidence of wrongdoing) he moved the cult to East Grinstead in Sussex, England. By 1965 lurid media exposés of its dubious techniques and its claim to be 'the world's largest mental health organisation' led to an Australian ban on Scientology and demands in the UK for an official enquiry. In 1967 Hubbard took to the seas with a private navy. For a decade he was served by nymphets in hot-pants who dressed and undressed him, relaying his orders in his tone of voice. The tale of this 'Sea Org', the cult's subsequent settlement in Florida (under the cover-name of the 'United Churches'), its infiltration of US government agencies, and Hubbard's own disappearance in 1980 is extraordinary . . . and absurd. But the absurdity is unfunny. Those breaking cult rules were humiliated, those trying to leave it were pursued; those on the 'enemies list' were described as fair game for eradication by any means. Journalist Russell Miller, who in 1987 published a critical biography, *Bare-Faced Messiah*, was pursued round the world, spied on and subjected to a campaign to ruin him.

Still in hiding, L. Ron Hubbard died on 24 January 1986. Or so it is said. Truth is hard to come by in the tale of Hubbard and Scientology – save that he used his wit to exploit the gullible and confused. So what is '**paranormal**' about Scientology, or any other such cult? Simply the degree to which individuals like Hubbard can succeed in convincing millions that their own personal fantasies represent a system of *objective* truth worth total devotion. The greater the absurdity, the greater the belief.

1. *Bare-Faced Messiah*, Russell Miller, Sphere, London 1988, p. 172

HUDSON, Thomas Jay For this late nineteenth-century Detroit newspaper editor, '**spirits**' evoked by **mediums** are a creation of the subconscious mind. Admitting his Christian belief that the **soul** survives death, he said that **spiritualistic** phenomena are entirely a mental production. Arguing that man has two minds, which he called the 'objective' and 'subjective', he theorised that the first deals with the external *real* world through the five senses, its highest function being that of reason; and that the subjective operates independently of the senses, primarily via intuition. In 1893 his *The Law of Psychic Phenomena* introduced these ideas and achieved huge popular success. Claiming that the subjective mind has vast power, including that of limitless memory, he argues that our objective (left-brain) mind cramps the subjective (right-brain) mind and inhibits its full flowering. Those people we recognise as geniuses are those naturally free of such inhibition. He tells the tale of the great American orator Henry Clay who, about to speak in the Senate when sick and hardly able to stand, asked a friend to tug his coat-tails to stop him speaking after ten minutes. This friend did so: Clay ignored him. The friend jabbed him gently with a pin. Clay continued. Now the friend stuck the pin hard into Clay's leg. In full flight, Clay did not even notice. At last, after two hours, Clay came to the end of his speech. Exhausted, he fell back into his seat and reproachfully asked his friend why he had not stopped him after ten minutes. Hudson suggested this case as an example of the subjective mind's power over the body. Later, his work forgotten, his theory became acceptable as an explanation of **poltergeist** activity.[1]

1. *Beyond the Occult*, Colin Wilson, Corgi, London 1989, pp. 72ff

HUMAN COMBUSTION (*See* **SPONTANEOUS COMBUSTION**)

HUMANOIDS (*See* **ABDUCTIONS, FAIRIES, MEN IN BLACK, UFOs**) Perception of, meeting with, or abduction by humanoid **entities** whose physical shape, apparent motives, and psychology is *almost* but not quite recognisable as 'human' is a phenomenon reported since earliest times. The wave of reports since the 1950s of UFO **close encounters** of the third or fourth kinds with such 'humanoid' beings does not therefore represent anything new, save in their increase. Such increase may be put down to a growth not only in media capabilities but in media interest: we have simply no way of knowing how common such contactee experiences were in times before modern news media existed, or when such events were perceived primarily in terms of private religious **vision**. It may also be argued in psychological terms that such encounters are primarily an expression of acute anxiety about the insecurity of the world in which we live. *Humanoid* beings per se are often perceived as *alien, threatening* and *disturbing*. They lack the reassuring higher faculty of 'loving-kindness' associated with reports of contact with 'guardian **angels**' or suchlike beings widely perceived as benign. 'Humanoids' tend typically to be *black, headless, scaly, shrouded, masked, winged, unnaturally tall or small* – innately threatening on the biological level; often insectoid. The image is that of 'dehumanisation': an armed soldier in gas mask and chemical warfare suit; a loveless beast threatening death; a **demon**, malign imp, tricksy **fairy**, or carnivorous, cannibalistic **giant**. The term is folklore translated into science-fiction.

HUNDREDTH MONKEY, THE (*See* **FORMATIVE CAUSATION**) Refers to the phenomenon whereby a critical point is reached when new knowledge or capacity, at first painstakingly learned on an individual basis, suddenly explodes throughout the species involved. It derives from an old folk tale in which a monkey, put in a cage and unable to escape, is joined by increasing numbers of monkeys. With the arrival of the hundredth, the cage bursts and all escape. A modern version is told by Lyall **Watson** (among others), of the macaque monkey (*Macaca fuscata*). In 1952 a macaque colony on Koshima island off the Japanese coast was under observation by primatologists. To get the monkeys to come closer raw sweet potatoes were put out for them. Dumped in the sand, these proved unpalatable, but soon a young female monkey (named Imo) learned to wash the potatoes clean of grit. Imo taught her mother and other (mostly young) monkeys the trick. By 1958, all the young monkeys were washing potatoes, but the only adults over five years old to do so were those imitating the young. Also by 1958, Imo had learned that washing the potatoes in salt water added flavour.

Suddenly the trick (until then taught on a one-to-one basis) was common knowledge. As if they'd always known how, overnight *all* the monkeys were washing potatoes. Even more extraordinary, the trick spread simultaneously, as if by **telepathy**, to other macaque colonies isolated on neighbouring islands. Some critical threshold had been reached and broken through.[1]

In Britain (1952) dairies began delivering milk in foil-capped bottles. Some blue tits learned to peck through the cap to the cream. The initial spread of this habit was at a pace explicable by other tits copying it. But suddenly in 1955 all blue tits and most great tits throughout Europe were at it. The knowledge had spread in the same extraordinary manner.

A variant of the phenomenon is seen in human sporting prowess. After many failures, Mount Everest was first climbed in 1953 by a vast military-scale expedition. Of twenty-five further successful expeditions between 1953 and 1980, none involved less than thirty climbers and Sherpa porters; none took less than a month, and all used oxygen to reach the top. But in 1980 Austrian Reinhold Messner climbed Everest solo, without oxygen, in just three days. Since then, similar rapid solo climbs without oxygen have become almost commonplace. The once-impossible becomes commonplace.[2]

The 'four-minute mile' is another example. Once broken by Roger Bannister in 1954, the imagined barrier lost its power to deter not only the body but the (subjective) mind.[3] Within days of his feat, it was duplicated.

So too the tendency for scientific discoveries, long sought after, to be made simultaneously by more than one group or individual; as with the discovery of the planet **Neptune** in 1846 by Leverrier and Adams.

Biologist Rupert **Sheldrake**'s theory of formative causation may help to explain the phenomenon. He postulates an information signal resonating through what he calls *morphogenetic* (or 'form') *fields* as responsible for the instantaneous transmission of 'new' behaviours.

1. *Lifetide*, Lyall Watson, Coronet Books, London 1980, pp. 173–177
2. *Quest for Adventure*, Chris Bonington, Hodder and Stoughton, London 1981
3. *Ibid.*

HURKOS, Peter (*See* **CLAIRVOYANCE, SECOND SIGHT**) In 1943 house-painter Pieter van der Hurk fell from a ladder and fractured his skull. On emerging from coma in hospital in the Hague he found himself second-sighted. Shaking hands with a fellow patient about to be discharged he 'knew' the man was a British agent and in two days would be assassinated by the Gestapo. His correct prediction almost led to his execution by the Dutch underground. Or so he claims in his autobiography, *Psychic*. The State Institute for War Archives in Amsterdam has no record of any British agent being shot at the place and time in question. He claimed that his new faculty meant so many images of other people's lives flooded him that he could no longer concentrate or hold a job. He decided to go on stage. Specialising in **psychometry** and the blindfold description of pictures, in the 1950s he emigrated to the USA to begin a successful career as **psychic** counsellor to Hollywood stars. **Parapsychologists**, save Andrija **Puharich**, remain unconvinced by him. His most celebrated 'successes' do not bear close scrutiny. When in December 1950 the Stone of Scone was taken from Westminster Abbey by Scottish Nationalists, he '**clairvoyantly**' tracked it to Glasgow. Later it turned out to have been hidden in a ruined abbey in Arbroath, eighty miles from Glasgow. Likewise his celebrated 1951 psychic detection of a firebug in Njimegen, Holland, did not occur as claimed. He identified seventeen-year-old Piet Vierboom only after the arsonist's arrest, not *before*.[1]

If his talent is genuine, his exploitation of it and seeming distortion of checkable facts has left him open to scepticism.

1. 'Less sensitive by half?', Piet Hein Hobens, in *The Unexplained*, Orbis partwork, London 1983, pp. 2754–7

HUXLEY, Aldous (1894–1963) This English novelist and essayist, nearly blind for much of his life, is remembered not only for the grim predictions of eugenic tyranny in *Brave New World* (1932), but for his study of the diabolic **possession** of seventeenth-century Ursuline nuns in *The Devils of Loudon* (1952), and particularly for his description and analysis of his experience of the drug mescalin in two essays, *The Doors of*

Perception (1954) and *Heaven and Hell* (1956). Written over a decade after he left Europe for California, these essays relate his **drug**-induced **visions** to the growth of the human religious impulse. Arguing that the brain is a 'reducing valve' that cuts out all information flooding in from the 'mind at large' that is not needed for daily survival, he theorised that **hallucinogens** and practices like fasting and **yoga** annul the 'reducing valve', permitting wider perception of reality. Thus he helped legitimise and popularise psychedelic **drug** use as a route to a 'sacramental vision of reality', but also warning how negative emotions can plunge us into a 'schizophrenic hell'. He also helped pioneer re-evaluation of **shamanic** and **pagan** attitudes to the world as living being. Dying the same day that John F. Kennedy was assassinated, on his death-bed Huxley ingested LSD–25. The title of his essay, *The Doors of Perception*, is from **Blake**: 'If the doors of perception were cleansed, everything will appear to man as it is, infinite.'

HYNEK, J. Allen (*See* **CLOSE ENCOUNTERS, UFOs**) Appointed consultant in the 1950s to the USAF study of UFOs, 'Project Blue Book', Dr Hynek developed the 'Close Encounters' system of definition of UFO sightings, but grew frustrated by the official tendency to explain away or deny UFO occurrences as caused by misidentification of weather balloons, the planet Venus, etc. A typical case (the 'Swamp Gas Scandal') occurred in 1966. Four UFOs were said to have flown over a farm near Ann Arbor, Michigan; one had apparently landed in a swampy area. Researcher Jacques **Vallée** called Dr Hynek who called Project Blue Book. Pressured both by the media and the USAF, Hynek called for thorough investigation but also mentioned that *some* people *might* have seen *swamp gas*. The media attacked him for daring to suggest that an honest farmer might not have seen a *real* UFO. Hynek, who for years had begged the media to report UFO cases more accurately, was taken aback, even as reporters who had earlier sneered at any suggestion that UFOs might be 'real' were beating the bushes in search of alien craft. In Washington a Senate committee decided that NASA should not get involved. Later, following the whitewashing Condon Report (1968) on UFOs, and disenchanted with the variable human reaction at every level to the UFO enigma, Hynek founded the *Center for UFO Studies*. This was, and remains, a *civilian* study group.[1]

1. *Dimensions*, Jacques Vallée, Sphere, London 1990, pp. 228–9

HYPNOGOGIC STATE (*See* **BRAIN MYSTERIES**) Refers to the state of mind experienced between sleep and waking, as when in bed floating to music in a **trance**-like state, or at a concert doing the same. In this floating condition ideas and images drift into the drowsy mind in a manner neither wholly of sleeping **dream** nor waking reason. It is the 'waking dream'. In this state, close to self-**hypnosis**, potent dream-images normally lost on full awakening may be realised and retained for use when awake. This in-between state has been employed by **mystics** like **Swedenborg** who, distressed into a state in which for nights on end he did not sleep properly, for hours lay in semi-trance, watching the images that danced within. These images and the dramas arising from them he remembered and wrote down. 'I once heard loud shouts which sounded as if they were bubbling up through water from lower regions; from the left came the shout: "Oh, how just!", and from the right: "Oh, how learned," and from behind: "Oh, how wise!" ' This led him into a visionary journey to the 'lower earth which is immediately above hell'.

It may be that Swedenborg and other 'mystics' like **Blake** or **Boehme** possess a capacity more refined than in most of us to perceive, remember and *interpret* imagery that flies up from the subconscious depths in which (as in the **Akashic Record**) everything is recorded and known.

HYPNOTISM (*See* **BLOXHAM, MESMER**) The term *hypnotism* (from the Greek *Hypnos*, 'sleep') was coined in the 1840s by the Scot James Braid, but the first report of the phenomenon occurred in 1784. Attempting mesmerism, Marquis Chastenet de Puységur 'magnetised' a subject, 'Victor'. Mesmer's patients usually suffered violent convulsions and spoke in odd voices, but Victor fell into a sleep-like trance. While retaining control of his movements he not only did whatever Puységur *told* him to do but *willed* him to do. This convinced Puységur that Bailly and Lavoisier, in concluding that the 'magnetic fluid' which Mesmer claimed to have discovered did not exist, were wrong. Botanist Laurent de Jussieu was inclined to agree. He saw how when Puységur pointed a finger at entranced subjects, they reacted even if their backs were turned. This suggested to him the possibility of such a force as '**animal magnetism**'. But the control exercised over the subject's will and reported cases of **clairvoyance** and 'community of sensation' (the ability of entranced subjects to 'taste' or 'feel' whatever the hypnotist tastes or feels) smacked of **witchcraft** and the **occult**. So did the claim of mesmerists that persons in whom **trance** had been induced could be operated on without pain. So 'induced somnambulism' joined mesmerism as a taboo subject – and taboo it remained for a century.[1]

In the 1840s Braid demonstrated induction of hypnotic trance without recourse to animal magnetism or any other hidden force, simply by holding a bright object just above the patient's eyeline. He insisted that the trance was a *physiological* reaction. Yet despite his rationalisation he was hard put to explain how some subjects under hypnosis could describe the shape of objects held behind their backs. Hypnotism remained ignored or denounced as fraudulent collusion between 'magnetiser' and subject. But in the 1870s famed German surgeon Rudolf Heidenhain concluded that the trance state was genuine. Asking a magnetiser to hypnotise his younger brother, whose two great loves were beer and his magnificent moustache, he watched while his hypnotised brother not only drank ink, convinced it was beer, but cut off his moustache. On being awakened he was, unsurprisingly, 'greatly enraged'.

Meanwhile in France the neurologist Jean-Martin Charcot showed members of the Academy of Medicine that he could induce the trance state to order in patients suffering from hysterical symptoms. He claimed only hysterics were prone to this state, which was purely neurological. Yet at Nancy in France Professor Bernheim established that almost anyone can be hypnotised, and that non-hysterical symptoms can be treated by hypnotic suggestion. So too the occult aspect was soon revived by one of Charcot's disciples, whose work with 'Madame B', an hysteric, established that she could be hypnotised even if the hypnotist was miles away and merely willed her into trance. Many other experiments later demonstrated clairvoyance and **telepathy** in entranced subjects. These only frightened the scientific community which, while now forced to acknowledge the reality of hypnosis, was rapidly moving to a total materialsm: i.e. behaviourist ideas denying not only **psychic** 'action-at-a-distance' but the very existence of 'mind'.

The increasing association of hypnosis (and self-hypnosis) with a wide range of 'occult' activities (**mediumistic** trance; the trance of **healers** who claim to cure while 'controlled' by **discarnate** beings; use of hypnosis to 'regress' people to past lives, etc.) did nothing to improve its image.

Lately the situation has changed. Hypnotism is, if not respectable (it remains unexplained), at least an acceptable tool. Tennis star Arthur Ashe and cricketer Bob Willis were among the first of many sports stars to use post-hypnotic suggestion in assisting their performance. The 1976 BBC TV documentary studying the claim of Cardiff hypnotherapist Arnall **Bloxham** to have 'regressed' his subjects to accurate memory of previous incarnations aroused a huge public interest, suggesting that superstitious terror of the subject has faded. Evidence that his best-known subject, housewife 'Jane Evans', was remembering not her past lives but historical romances read years before and since forgotten suggests that hypnotism permits access to suppressed **consciousness** (the unconscious) and to faculties normally hidden to the conscious mind. In any case the new interest in hypnotherapy and regression techniques throws up material establishing beyond reasonable doubt that the world of which we are all 'unconsciously' aware is stranger, vaster and more varied than waking consciousness permits us to realise.

Did Bloxham's subjects genuinely recall past lives? Regression work by others suggests cases otherwise hard to explain. One reported by Ian **Stevenson** has been mentioned (*see* **Glossolalia**). Another concerns the successful American publisher Mike O'Mara who, when hypnotically sent back to his 'past life' turns into a nineteenth-century Dublin drunk, Stephen Garrett, arrested for theft and ending up in an institution. Many such cases exist, with a wealth of supportive detail. The hypnotic trance unlocks the imagery of grey areas in the mind otherwise off-limits. Author and **UFO**-contactee Whitley **Streiber** recollected, under hypnosis, absurd events which, whatever their origin, had remained inaccessible to his conscious mind.[2] Likewise Betty and Barney Hill (*see* **Abductions**). The case is clear: whatever the source of buried memories, hypnosis can bring some of them into consciousness.

It is said that hypnotised subjects cannot be made to act against their will. The classic tale is told of how Charcot, putting a lovely young woman into trance before a group of students, was called away on urgent business. He left her to an assistant, who told her to remove her clothes. Her eyes opened, she emerged from trance and slapped his face. This is reassuring!

Yet it is clear that, given the right suggestion, a deeply hypnotised subject can be induced to commit utter mayhem. In a 1950s experiment the subjects were shown what happens to a penny thrown into a bowl of nitric acid. Placed in a trance, they were ordered to throw the acid into the face of an assistant. For obvious reasons, the acid had been replaced by a boiling liquid similar to the acid but innocuous. Direct orders to throw it resulted in the same rejection as met by Charcot's libidinous assistant. But, when told that the assistant was a murderer about to kill her child, one woman, in trance, promptly threw the 'acid'.[3]

Hypnotism is nothing new. An ancient term for it, *mekhenesis*, means 'removal of responsibility'. Individual autonomy is taken over by the hypnotist. In essence, hypnotism involves the overthrow of the conscious mind – biologically a new development. Since ancient time the hypnotist has used suggestion to place the subject(s) in a **dream**-state in which perception is controlled and impossible events become possible – as in the rousing of the German nation by **Hitler**, or as in the Indian Rope-Trick. In any case a receptive, cooperative subject or audience is required.

It is impossible to hypnotise you against your will. Fine. The only problem is – do you know your own will? Are you in control of it? Do you decide things for yourself – or do you let others decide for you?

1. 'A bizarre history of hypnosis', Brian Inglis, *The Unexplained*, Orbis partwork, London 1983, pp. 901–5
2. *Communion*, Whitley Streiber, Arrow, London 1988, p. 122
3. *The Aquarian Guide to the New Age*, Eileen Campbell and J. H. Brennan, Aquarian Press, Wellingborough 1990

HYSLOP, James (1854–1920) (*See* **MULTIPLE PERSONALITY, POSSESSION**) A friend of William **James**, philosopher James Hyslop of Columbia University was sceptical of **psychism** until in 1898, perplexed by Boston **trance medium** Leonore **Piper**, he sought her counsel in disguise. What she told him about his own dead relatives persuaded him that she had genuinely contacted them, or had read his mind. He inclined to the former explanation.

He became involved in the case of Thomas Swain Gifford, a Massachusetts landscape painter who died aged sixty-four in January 1906. Fredric Thompson, an aspiring artist who had briefly met Gifford but did not know he was dead, began painting in Gifford's style, telling his wife 'Mr Gifford' wanted to go sketching. Chancing on a New York exhibition of Gifford's work he heard a voice say, 'You see what I have done. Go on with the work.' Convinced he was insane, in January 1907 he consulted Hyslop who took him to Margaret Gaule, a trance medium. The sitting reassured Thompson that he wasn't mad, but *merely* possessed by Gifford. Thereafter he developed a career painting in a style that experts could not tell apart from Gifford's. Hyslop came to accept it as a case of genuine possession, and turned to the study of **spirit** possession as the root cause of madness and multiple personality.

Working with medium Minnie Soule, he took on the cases of Etta de Camp and Doris Fischer. The former, often ill as a child, experimented with **automatic writing** to a point where pain seized her if she tried to resist the impulse. In 1909 she began writing tales seemingly by Frank R. Stockton (1834–1902), well-known for his whimsical children's stories. What she wrote down seemed to possess the wit of Stockton's work, though she had 'never had any talent that way'. Later Hyslop conversed with 'Stockton' via Minnie Soule: the entity was witty and irreverent, and Hyslop accepted the case as a genuine case of post-mortal influence. Etta de Camp came near to breakdown but later married, living the rest of her life in obscurity.[1]

Hyslop's involvement with the Fischer case and his pact with William James are described elsewhere. His work in dealing with possession was continued by neurologist Dr Titus Bull and psychologist Dr Walter **Prince**.

1. *The Infinite Boundary*, D. Scott Rogo, Aquarian Press, Wellingborough 1988

I

I CHING An ancient Chinese **oracle** available in the West in a number of translations made between 1882 and 1950, the *I Ching* or *Chinese Book of Changes* may be used simply for **fortune-telling**, but has attracted interest as a profound exposition of all matters dealing with human fate. Originating in the old Chinese division of phenomena into negative and positive forces (**yin** and **yang**) its oracular aspect arose from an ancient form of fortune-telling.

Patterns created by heating tortoise shells until they cracked were interpreted as auguries of the future or as answers to specific questions. Eventually these cracks were stylised, or abstracted, into a stack of three lines (*trigrams*), each either broken (*yin*) or unbroken (*yang*).

Oracular study of the trigrams grew alongside the symbolic meanings ascribed to yin (dark, female, moon, unconscious, yielding, receptive,) and yang (light, male, sun, conscious, strong, creative). Chinese philosophy claims that both yin and yang are in continual interplay: neither can exist without the other; the world and its phenomena arise from this interplay.

The meanings ascribed to the eight recognised trigrams were assigned *c.* 1150 BC by Wên, a nobleman jailed by the Emperor. These are: *Ch'ien* (The Creative, Heaven); *K'un* (The Receptive, Earth); *K'en* (Keeping Still, Mountain); *K'an* (The Abysmal, Water); *Chen* (The Arousing, Thunder); *Sun* (The Gentle, Wind); *Tui* (The Joyous, Lake); and *Li* (The Clinging, Fire).

Also combining the trigrams into six-line *hexagrams*, to each of the sixty-four hexagrams thus derived (8 × 8) Wên added a 'Judgement'. Later his son, the Duke of Chou, added commentaries on the individual lines of each hexagram.

So not only each hexagram but each *line* of each hexagram has oracular meaning. Moreover, each line, yin or yang, is held to be either 'at rest' or 'moving'. Lines at rest are ignored: the 'moving' lines, in a state of tension, change into their opposites, thus generating a second hexagram to be interpreted with the first. Thus the oracle can deliver over 4,000 different interpretations to any question without once repeating itself.

The work, now known as the *Book of Changes*, was further elaborated over the centuries, especially by Confucius, who added new commentaries. As such it became a repository of all Chinese morality and insight. 'The essential thing to keep in mind', wrote Hellmut Wilhelm, son of Richard **Wilhelm**, whose German translation is widely considered the most accessible to the Western mind, 'is all the strata that go to make up the book.'

The mystery is how it works not only as a guide to good conduct but as an accurate **oracle**. In his foreword to the Wilhelm edition, **Jung** opined that the Chinese mind 'seems to be exclusively preoccupied with the chance aspect of events. What we call **coincidence** seems to be the chief concern of this peculiar mind, and what we worship as causality passes almost unnoticed . . . The matter of interest seems to be the configuration formed by chance events in the moment of observation.'[1]

How is the oracle consulted? The more complex of two methods involves division of a heap of forty-nine yarrow stalks so as to arrive at a hexagram. Or, simply, three coins are thrown six times. Each throw gives a line, starting at the bottom of the hexagram. Heads count as two, tails as three. Three heads (six) give a 'moving yin' line; two heads and a tail a yang line 'at rest', and so on. With the hexagram complete, reference is made to the Judgement and Commentary on the particular hexagram thrown.

Many have noted how the *I Ching* not only delivers apposite judgements but seems almost conscious, responding directly to queries, or refusing to answer stupid questions. Years ago, writing a novel, several times I tried to ask the *I Ching* what to do next. Each time the answer was Hexagram Four (*Mêng*, or 'Youthful Folly'), with this Judgement:

> It is not I who seek the young fool;
> The young fool seeks me.
> At the first oracle I inform him.
> If he asks two or three times, it is importunity.
> If he importunes, I give him no information.

The *I Ching* offers no easy answers. It offers no false hope and is often obscure. In short, it makes you think for yourself.

1. *I Ching*, German translation: Richard Wilhelm, then into English by Cary F. Baynes: foreword by C. G. Jung, Routledge Kegan Paul, London 1968 (1951)

ILLUMINATI A secret society founded in 1784 by Adam Weishaupt, professing deistic and republican beliefs and organised like **freemasonry**. A term describing those said to possess special powers or enlightenment. Conspiracy theorists claim such groups run the world by **occult** means, as in the *Illuminatus* trilogy; a fantastic 1970s satire by US authors Robert Shea and Robert Anton **Wilson**.

ILLUMINATION Archimedes cried '*Eureka!*'; Saul was struck on the Damascus road. Refers to a sudden event, a split-second eternity, a silent flood of complex feeling, experience, revelation; the mystic experience of heightened **consciousness** St Teresa calls *Union with God*, involving abrupt shift from spacetime to a higher vision, often after fasting, prayer, or other strenuous preparation.

ILLUSION (*See* **CELTIC MAGIC, FAIRIES, HYPNOTISM**) Involves false perception of an unreal external object. Celtic folklore is full of tales of fairies casting illusion – hovel transformed into palace; rags to riches; beans or leaves into gold coin; or crone into lovely girl. Termed 'glamourie' in Lowland Scots and *sian* in Gaelic, such tales, opined Lewis **Spence**, issued from the inherent will-power once believed to reside in magicians and **spirits**. A type of hypnotism may have been involved.[1]

Daskalos tells of an English scientist who complained to him that twice in India he had seen the 'Rope Trick' – the naked fakir playing the flute, the rope uncoiling and rising up like a pole, the boy climbing the rope. But he took photographs which, developed, showed the boy sitting on the ground and the rope beside him still coiled. 'This fakir deceived us but could not deceive the camera,' he concluded.

But Daskalos asked him: 'Why not study this phenomenon carefully, instead of dismissing it as a trick? Why not study the nature of thought, of concrete thought?' He added that the fakir had 'spread his **aura** around and put the audience inside. Then he began to think intensely and he created with his mind all those images you were "seeing".' Daskalos concluded that, as it is possible to make people 'see' things that do not exist, so one can make people *not* see objects or bodies that *do* exist.[2]

1. *The Magic Arts in Celtic Britain*, Lewis Spence, Rider, London 1946, p. 20
2. *The Magus of Strovolos*, Kyriacos C. Markides, Arkana, London 1985, p. 206

IMAGINATION (*See* **MAGIC**)

IMPLICATE ORDER (*See* **BOHM**)

INCUBI AND SUCCUBI (*See* **ABDUCTIONS, DEMONS, FAIRIES**) The image of the 'demon lover' persists. The Latin-derived term *incubus* (male) means 'that which lies upon'. *Succubus* (female) means 'that which lies beneath'. Thus the mediaeval Church described demons or **apparitions** said to enjoy sexual intercourse with mortals.

Tales of amorous contact between humans and **spirits** or fairies are old. In Greek **myth** the god Zeus takes the form of a swan to seduce Leda. Celtic myth is full of amorous fairies. The magician **Merlin** was said to be the son of an incubus. In *The Secret Commonwealth* (1691), Robert Kirk writes: 'In our Scotland there are numerous and beautiful creatures of that aerial order, who frequently assign meetings to lascivious young men as succubi, or as joyous mistresses and prostitutes, who are called Leannain Sith or familiar spirits.'[1]

Likewise Christian dogma claims that **Christ** was borne of a virgin by the Holy Ghost. The Book of **Enoch** was anathematised for telling how the **angels** called **Watchers** mated with human women, who bore **giants**. Yet in the fourth century AD St Augustine wrote, 'It is widespread opinion, confirmed by direct or indirect testimony of trustworthy persons, that the Sylvans and Fauns, commonly called Incubi, have often tormented women, solicited and obtained intercourse with them.'

But, though amoral **pagan** fauns were redefined as malicious demons, the Church remained unsure how to deal with the many cases of demonic intercourse reported during the Middle Ages. Noting the doctrinal ambiguity, mediaeval writer Isodore Lisieux asked: One, is such intercourse physically possible? Two, how does demoniality differ from bestiality? Three, what sin is committed by those engaged in such acts? Four, what should their punishment be?

The theologian Sinistrari said the **Devil**, lacking a body, has intercourse with men and women by borrowing a human corpse, or by forming a new body with other materials. Sinistrari refers not to ordinary erotic dreams: he means *physical* intercourse, as damned in books like the *Compendium Maleficarum*. He said two kinds of people are carnally contacted: sorcerers consciously making a formal pact with demons; or innocent folk who are attacked. He says incubi are not the same as common devils: they ignore **exorcism** and laugh at holy relics. Later, Cardinal Bellarmin claimed that **Antichrist** would be born of a woman having intercourse with an incubus.[2]

By the sixteenth century the Church had decided on its policy. Confessions tortured from women provide much of the lore of sexual contact with the 'Devil'. Giving herself up for execution as a **witch** in Scotland in the 1660s, Isobel Gowdie said the Devil ('a meikle, blak, roch man') was as 'cold within me as spring-well-water'[3]. It is hard to tell if her tale was purely imaginary, or why she admitted it. Either way, she died for it.

Reports of such contacts persist, incubi and succubi commonly now being perceived as **UFO entities**. The experiences of Betty and Barney Hill, Antonio Villas-Boas, and Whitley **Streiber** are typical.

Yet the traditional incubus also persists. In *Creatures from Inner Space* (1984). British psychologist Stan **Gooch** tells how an ex-policeman, Martyn Pryer, inducing **hypnogogic** states while in bed, was 'attacked' by an invisible entity which lay on top of him. Paralysed, he realised it was a woman who wanted to make love to him. Eventually it faded away. Gooch also tells of his own experience of a succubus – a composite of various ex-girlfriends – with whom (or which) he claims he made love. Concluding that such creatures are creations of the human mind, Gooch's testimony suggests the activity of **elementals** or **tulpas**, mind-generated **thought-forms** that take on a life of their own.[4]

Mere sexual fantasy? The question remains open.

1. *Dimensions*, Jacques Vallée, Spehere, London 1990, p. 141
2. *Ibid.*, p. 147
3. *An ABC of Witchcraft Past and Present*, Doreen Valiente, Hale, London 1986, p. 201.
4. *Creatures from Inner Space*, Stan Gooch, Rider, London 1984.

INDETERMINACY, Principle of (*See* **HEISENBERG**)

INITIATION Refers to any rite stimulating the transition of an individual from one stage of development to another. Such rites, especially those connected with puberty, were conducted by most societies, at least until recent, 'civilised' times. Boys might undergo symbolic death by means of ordeal (burial alive for three nights, scarification, circumcision, etc.), from which they awoke as men. American Indian boys would go alone into the woods to fast, seeking a **dream** or **vision** revealing their totem beast and their future path as men, being thus brought into contact with the deeper unconscious layers. Female pubertal initiation was usually less dramatic, being built around a seclusion at the time of first menstruation. Girls were not usually required to formulate their initiatory dream or message consciously.[1] That in Western societies we are no longer helped to grow up in this deliberate way may be a loss, not a gain, resulting in a 'Peter Pan syndrome' – being uninitiated, we never quite grow up or 'find' ourselves.

Initiation rites remain in use among **occult** groups or secret societies (like the **Freemasons**) in order to mark transition from the 'outer world' to the 'inner state'. Ordination of a priest into the Church constitutes such a ritual. Likewise casual initiation continues in many secular areas, as in the 'hazing' ordeals required of children or students new to a gang, school or college. Invariably the purpose, conscious or not, is the same. The child is father to the man: the man cannot thrive until the child dies.

The *gravity* of such **ritual** appears largely lost by comparison with the understanding of it in the ancient world. In the **Greek** and other **Mysteries** seven, even ten, stages of initiation were common. The first three involved teachings alone – a preparatory discipline the Greeks called *katharsis* or cleansing. The fourth degree introduced direct participation in the deeper mysteries by learning to *become* rather than simply being *taught about* the states involved. In higher degrees the power and faculties of the initiant increasingly evolved to a point at which the initiate was considered wholly renewed, or 'reborn'. In India, such men were called *Dvijas*, a Sanskrit word meaning 'twice-born'. In Egypt they were called 'Sons of the Sun'.[2]

Aspects of ancient Mystery initiations survive in various modern occult schools from the **Golden Dawn** on, but the degree to which these accurately reflect ancient teachings is arguable. Perhaps this does not matter: the results are what count, not the slavish adherence to past practice. Rites themselves are important only as an aid to inner transformation.

1. *Woman's Mysteries*, Esther Harding, Rider, London 1971 (1955), p. 70–71
2. *Occult Glossary*, G. de Purucker, Theosophical University Press, Pasadena, California, 1969 (1933), pp. 65–6

INNER LIGHT, Fraternity of (*See* **FORTUNE, DION**)

INNER PLANES (*See* **ASTRAL PLANE**) A term employed in Western occultism and **Qabalism** defining the subtle or higher-energy planes of being, including the **astral, etheric** and other such states. The paths and **sephiroth** of the Qabalistic **Tree of Life** are usually employed as a symbolic map of the conditions involved. While the Outer Planes (physical world) are ruled by material expediency, the Inner Planes represent dynamic spiritual principles at work in many layers from that of unmanifest being to those at which emotional, intellectual and instinctual forces operate. The Inner Planes coexist with and infuse the Outer and have no 'spacetime' location, this being a physical determinant. Initiates of schools of Western Mystery Teachings serve the evolutionary work overseen by a Hierarchy of spiritual **entities** (Inner Plane Adepti, **Hidden Masters**, etc.) on the Inner Planes. Having made the 'Crossing of the Gulf' (a value-transition from expediency to principle), such initiates are said to undergo tests imposed by the Inner Plane Adept who has accepted the individual as a disciple. Such tests befall the initiate as part of the natural circumstances of daily life. Again, the Inner infuses the Outer; there is no separation save by the definitions of the intellect.[1]

1. *Practical Guide to Qabalistic Symbolism*, Gareth Knight, Helios, Cheltenham 1965

INNER SPACE A modern term referring to the vast inner-directed worlds of the mind and its mysteries as opposed to those of 'outer space' – the physical universe as perceived to exist beyond the atmosphere of Planet Earth in terms of solar, interstellar and intergalactic space. Basically implying **psychic** and psychological space as popularised since the 1960s by writers like J. G. Ballard, 'inner space' has been used in Hollywood movies (*Fantastic Voyage, Inner Space*, etc.) to describe a physical realm of microscopic dimensions to be discovered and explored within the human body. As with **Hollow Earth** theory, such movies seem to rely for their appeal on an inversion of the awesome vastness of 'outer space', employing a emotional interiorisation which provides ersatz comfort without true conviction.

INSPIRATION The Latin *spirare* means 'to breathe'. 'Inspiration' is thus a 'breathing-in' of sudden revelation, energy or purpose from an unexpected or unseen source which has no known, rational or logical origin. Thus the process has about it the implicit **aura** of the divine, **supernatural**, or **paranormal**.

Inspiration may arise in a **dream** as in Kekulé's sudden grasp of the structure of the benzene molecule, or in a waking flash, as (again) with Archimedes in his bath shouting '*Eureka*!' – 'I have it!' In each case what is suddenly known with certainty was not known the instant before. The full knowledge is suddenly 'there'. Yet the Law of **Karma** may suggest that such inspiration does not alight on those who have not previously worked hard to gain it. The implication is that long conscious striving to solve a problem so tunes the unconscious mind that, in an unexpected instant, the answer is suddenly delivered. The spirit thus alights on ready-prepared ground.

INTUITION Intuition refers to acquisition of knowledge by instantaneous, apparently unconscious or unreasoned means. It may be, as some psychologists believe, that it involves processes of thought operating too fast for conscious recognition. Yet perhaps this is to try to define in terms of rational intellect a faculty operating by other means altogether. Intuition is holistic. It is *in*ductive, not *de*ductive; abstract, not concrete; lunar, not solar; **yin** not **yang**; proceeding mysteriously, not obviously. It leaps where reason plods. Its insights may prove false or correct in the light of reason, but reason alone, being unimaginative, cannot grasp the initial insight. So intuition is not to be *explained* by reason. The need to guard against such attempts is known in systems like **Zen Buddhism**, in which the tyranny of the rational intellect is undone by the use of teaching devices like **koans**.

Reason is an essential faculty but must not (as **Blake** saw) be allowed to tyrannise other faculties by forcing them to wear its clothes.

Jung defined intuition as one of the four 'compass-points' in his model of the **psyche**, the others being thought, sensation and feeling.

Each of these faculties functions within the whole **psyche** according to its own autonomous rules, and cannot be explained in terms of the others. Any attempt to do so should be avoided. Does a mechanic tell a cook how to create a soufflé, or a cook tell a mechanic how to tune a car?

INVISIBLE COLLEGE (*See* **ROSICRUCIANS**) In 1623 placards announcing the presence of the Brethren of the Rose Cross (rumours of whose existence had lately swept through Germany) are said to have appeared in Paris. 'We, being deputies of the principle College of the Brothers of the Rose Cross', the placards read, 'are making a visible and invisible stay in this city through the Grace of the Most High, towards whom turn the hearts of the Just. We show and teach without books and marks how to speak the languages of all the countries where we wish to be, and to draw men from error and death.'

This was part of what a contemporary writer called a 'hurricane' of rumour that the mysterious Rose Cross Brothers had now reached France. There were said to be thirty-six of these Invisible Ones; it was said that they had sworn before the **Devil** to abjure **Christianity**, in return for which they had been granted powers to transport themselves wherever they wished, to possess purses always full of money, and so on.

In the context of the Thirty Years War and the **witch**-hunts still in progress, such a scare was serious. Yet now it seems likely that the R. C. Brothers never existed, at least not in any organised sense, and that the 'Invisible College' was essentially a serious joke.

Francis Bacon knew the joke: the benevolent brothers of the college in his utopian *New Atlantis* (*c.* 1620) were invisible to the outside word. Descartes had to prove his visibility in order to escape association. Robert **Fludd**, not one for humour, was a self-proclaimed member of what never existed save in the minds of those who believed it did.

The joke took root. The founder-members of England's Royal Society, established some forty years later, were involved in it. They included Boyle the chemist, Hooke the mathematician, the **alchemist** Thomas Vaughan, Elias Ashmole and Isaac Newton. Given the hostility to all matters magical and **hermetic** then prevailing and the recent assault on the reputation of John **Dee**, they had to present a rational 'scientific' front. Yet all of them, Newton included, were immersed in hermetica and **occult** disciplines – thus they did indeed form an 'invisible college'.

Recently the term has been whimsically revived by a group of serious **UFO** researchers appalled by the dogmatic scepticism of the orthodox scientific community. The group includes Dr. J. Allen **Hynek**.

1. *The Rosicrucian Enlightenment*, Francis A. Yates, Routledge and Kegan Paul, London 1972, pp. 103–5

ISIS (*See* **BLACK MADONNA, EGYPT, MYTH, OSIRIS**) In **Egyptian** myth the goddess Isis married Osiris, her elder brother. Osiris was assassinated by their jealous brother Set, who scattered his body in fourteen pieces throughout Egypt. Isis found every piece save for the phallus, reconstituted the body, and performed for the first time in myth-history the rites of embalming, and restored the murdered god to eternal life. Additionally, by union with his corpse, she conceived and bore the falcon-god Horus, who later fought and defeated Set. This most potent magician also tricked the sun-god Ra into revealing his secret **name** and so gained power over him.

Originally representing the rich plains of Egypt fertilised and made fruitful by the Nile (Osiris), this greatest goddess of the ancient world came to absorb the Sumerian Inanna and Babylonian Ishtar. By the Greeks she was identified with Demeter, Hera, Selene and Aphrodite. Normally represented as a woman bearing on her head a throne (later a disc between cow's horns), she was openly worshipped into Christian times. Her temple at Philae was closed only in the reign of Justinian (sixth century AD).[1]

Subsequently her cult persisted in many forms. The name *Paris* derives from *Par-Isis*, 'the Grove of Isis'. The city's oldest church, St Germain-des-Prés, was built (AD 542) over a former temple of Isis. In it, a black statue of Isis was worshipped as the Virgin Mary until 1514. Many such 'black madonnas' derive from Isis-worship, thus perhaps explaining the Church's reticence about them. The immaculate conception by Isis of Horus (a prefiguration of the birth of **Christ**), likewise the way by which her female power overcame Ra, could not please patriarchal Christians.

Like the **Moon**, Isis returns after every seeming extinction. The image of the High Priestess in the A. E. **Waite** version of the **Tarot**, blue-robed and seated between the pillars Boaz and Jachin, the scroll of the Law in her lap, and crowned by the horned disc, is that of Isis.

In **occult** belief this disc, especially when associated with the Winged Isis, refers to **Sirius**, the Dog-Star, said to have been her home, and a source of cosmic power influencing the destiny of this solar system.

From the dream of Isis described by Apuleius in *The Golden Ass* 2,000 years ago, to Isis-rites conducted by **occult** groups today, her image and **inspiration** remain potent. In England in the 1920s Dion **Fortune** founded the Fraternity of the Inner Light in order to re-establish Isis as an image of dynamic womanhood, active rather than passive, and capable of operating as an awakening, transformative power.

Representing the **archetypal** virginity of the feminine side of God, and the receptivity of nature as mirrored by the Moon's reflection of the Sun, Isis cannot be destroyed. More than a **pagan** *Egyptian goddess*, she is one of the great forces of transformation, change and growth; indwelling human **consciousness** at the deepest and highest levels.

As such, Isis is intuitively recognised by each new generation, even if her name and descriptive characteristics are *consciously* forgotten, or if taken over by the more passive, epicene, and one-sided image of the Madonna as proposed by a patriarchal religion that mistrusts Nature.

For, as she told Apuleius, having in his dream 'risen from the middle of the sea' to stand 'poised on the surface of the waves': 'I am Nature, the universal Mother, mistress of all the elements, primordial child of time, sovereign of all things spiritual, queen of the dead, queen also of the immortals, the single manifestation of all gods and goddesses that are. My nod governs the shining heights of Heaven, the wholesome sea-breezes, the lamentable silences of the world below. Though I am worshipped in many aspects, known by countless names, and propitiated with all manner of different rites, yet the whole round earth venerates me.'[2]

1. *Larousse Encyclopedia of Mythology*, Hamlyn, London, 1968
2. *The Golden Ass*, Lucius Apuleius, trans. Robert Graves, Penguin, London 1985 (1950), p. 228

ISIS UNVEILED (*See* **BLAVATSKY**)

ISLAM As with all major world **religions** the origins of Islam are firmly rooted in **supernatural myth** and divine revelation. Before conversion the Arabs held to an **animistic** religion, worshipping stones and trees, and imaginatively peopling the universe with good and evil **demons**, respectively *jinns* and the *Efrit*, who loved taking diverse forms to harm mankind. There were many gods, and a cult of stones. The latter gave rise in particular to worship of the Kaaba at Mecca, which still holds the black stone originally venerated.

Yet though Mohammed the Prophet received the Koran from God via the archangel

Gabriel, whom he described in anthropomorphic terms, and though various forms of **superstitious** belief survived in the new religion, by and large from its earliest days Islam formally denied all **pagan** imagination, anthropomorphic depictions, images of gods, **symbols**, fables and the rest. To ensure the triumph of a pure monotheism and to focus worshippers' minds on Allah alone it confined art solely to that inspired by geometrical form, considering the Law (Shari'a) the sole legitimate expression of truth.

Notably it was the great Arab thinkers like Geber who bequeathed to the still-barbarian West the many elements of **astrology**, astronomy, **alchemy**, mathematics and other studies from which modern science developed.

J

JACK THE RIPPER Some of the theories as to the identity and motives of the mass-killer who terrorised London's East End in autumn 1888 are as bizarre as the murders. The suggestion that the Ripper was the Duke of Clarence, Queen Victoria's grandson, is banal compared to the idea that he was a man possessed by the **spirit** of a mad sixteenth-century monk, or that he was never caught because he was invisible.

The **possession** theory derives from J. F. Brewer's *The Curse upon Mitre Square* (1889). Brewer claimed that the spirit of a monk who in 1530 killed a woman subsequently haunted the area where the murders occurred, seeking out weak-minded men and making them repeat his own crimes.

The invisibility theory suggests the Ripper was a **black magician** who, by performing satanic rites involving human sacrifice, sought the power of invisibility through a 'supreme **ritual**', involving the murder and eating of parts of the bodies of seven women, the killings to be conducted to form 'a Calvary Cross of seven points' – a Christian cross divided in seven squares as superimposed on a map of the East End. This theory Aleister **Crowley** offered in his *Confessions*. It probably originated with him. If so, the Ripper never succeeded: there were only five known killings. In an article written *c.* 1937 (published in 1974), the Beast 666 took this into account by suggesting that not a cross but a reverse pentagram – a five-pointed star with two points upward, a symbol of the triumph of evil – was involved. Also he claimed that the Ripper had achieved invisibility after the second or third murder. This odd notion he may have gleaned from his erstwhile friend and teacher Macgregor **Mathers**, who claimed that the Secret Chiefs (themselves invisible) had taught him how to achieve invisibility. Given Crowley's row with Mathers and his own love of unpleasant pranks, it is odd that he failed to suggest Mathers as the culprit.

Yet he had another target in mind – one 'Dr Donstan'.

The 'Donstan' theory originated with a woman as mysterious as Madame **Blavatsky** (who has also been identified, due to a chance remark made by Crowley, as the Ripper) – one 'Baroness Vittoria Cremers', an adventuress born *c.* 1865 who, in London in the 1880s, had an affair with Mabel Collins, a leading **Theosophist**. Collins was involved with her lodger, an alcoholic occultist calling himself Dr Donstan, an ex-doctor and ex-mercenary soldier cashiered from the British army for cheating at cards. His behaviour was erratic: Collins feared him. His apparent knowledge of the Ripper murders terrified her; one night when he was out she and Cremers broke into a trunk in his room, to find five ties, stiff with dried blood.[1]

Why did the Ripper suddenly stop killing? Crowley knew of tales that Cremers had killed 'Dr Donstan', alias the Ripper, by magical means. But Crowley's own tongue-in-cheek imagination and desire to shock make him a very poor witness. The moral of the tale is: where nothing is known for sure, fantastic belief rushes in to fill the vacuum.

1. 'The Ripper – Black Magician?', Francis King, *The Unexplained*, Orbis partwork, London 1983, pp. 2618–20; also pp. 2638–40

JAHN, Robert (*See* **EXTRA-SENSORY PERCEPTION, PSYCHOKINESIS**) A professor of Engineering at Princeton University, USA, Jahn's interest in parapsychology grew from a **telepathy** experiment in which, with the sender in Paris,

Jahn in the USA repeatedly received a scene 'so unreasonable and implacable' that he was tempted to reject it – of a man in mediaeval armour in a Paris street. The sender's report from Paris made it clear that the allusion was to statuary decorating a building nearby; statuary consisting of a row of warriors, from various periods, one in mediaeval armour.

Since then Jahn has spent over a decade investigating telepathy and psychokinesis. In one test the experimenter concentrates on influencing a machine that randomly generates zeros and ones, the purpose being to generate more ones than zeros. 700,000 such tests to date have led to the generation of a superior incidence of ones at odds against chance of 100,000 to 1.

In a 1990 UK Channel 4 interview Jahn said, 'Certainly the traditional science of the present era does not include human **consciousness** as an active participant in the physical world. It is our view that this is an oversight and needs to be corrected. We believe we're looking at a very common human capability. We need as it were a modern metaphysics that reinserts our human consciousness into the physical system as an active ingredient rather than as a passive observer.'

Of the psychokinetic tests, he says, 'In some way human consciousness can interact with very simple, very rudimentary physical systems to influence rather slightly their performance.' He insists, 'The output of these simple machines does reflect in a characteristic way the intentions and indeed the personalities of their human operators,' and rebukes the sceptics (such as **CSICOP**) for denying evidence for **psi** due to a 'a sense of threat to their own professional investment and to their own personal investment in the contrary **paradigm** that forces them to go to extraordinary extents to find a basis for disqualifying data'.[1]

1. 'Superpowers?', Channel 4 TV, 18 November 1990

JAMES, William (1842–1910) (*See* **HYSLOP**) This American psychologist's *The Varieties of Religious Experience* (1902) is a classic analysis of **occult** and **mystic** phenomena. Brother of novelist Henry James, his experiments with the mind-changing properties of nitrous oxide precede the **hallucinogenic** journeys of **Huxley** and **Leary** by eighty years. A founder member (1884) of the American Society for Psychical Research, his open-minded tests of **mediums** like Leonore **Piper** provided a sensible base for future research into **spiritualistic** phenomena, which he regarded as perfectly natural. While alive he accepted the likelihood of the conscious mind's survival of physical death, and made an agreement with his friend James Hyslop that the one who died first would try to provide proof of survival to the other.

As told by Carl **Jung**, after James died Hyslop grew weary of awaiting the promised proof. But at length Hyslop got a letter from an Irish couple who, both regular **planchette** users, had for months found their experiments dominated by an entity claiming to be 'a certain William James', insisting that they contact a Professor Hyslop in America. The entity had made such a nuisance of itself that finally they had made enquiries about this Hyslop and his whereabouts in order to deliver a message from 'James'.

The message was 'Does he remember the red pyjamas?'

Hyslop made nothing of it. The message seemed trivial . . . until at last he remembered how, as young men, he and James had toured Europe. Reaching Paris ahead of their luggage, they had gone out shopping for necessities like pyjamas. Hyslop had found only some 'really fancy red pyjamas'. James had teased him about his 'dubious taste'. This was an episode Hyslop had entirely forgotten until now, long after James' death.

Jung pointed out to Laurens van der Post, to whom he told this story, that 'red pyjamas' was not such a trivial message. *Pyjamas* suggest night, sleep, and thus death. *Red* is the colour of blood, of life. As for *fancy*, Jung concluded that the discarnate

James had advised Hyslop to look into his 'fancy', or imagination, to see that James lived on.[1]

1. *Jung and the Story of our Time*, Laurens van der Post, Penguin, London 1978, p. 257

JAYNES, Julian (*See* **CONSCIOUSNESS**)

JERSEY DEVIL (*See* **ALIEN ANIMALS**) In January 1909 the state of New Jersey, USA, was visited by an **apparition** which, seen by many, became known as the 'Jersey Devil'. As described by E. W. Minster, the Postmaster of Bristol, Pennsylvania (just over the New Jersey border), the head of this flying creature 'resembled that of a ram, with curled horns, and its long thick neck was thrust forward in flight'.

He continued, 'It had long thin wings and short legs, the front legs shorter than the hind. Again, it uttered its mournful and awful call – a combination of a squawk and a whistle, the beginning very high and piercing and ending very low and hoarse.'

This unknown **entity** was seen and described by many people during the week in which it appeared. It was 'hideous', it 'resembled a kangaroo', or had the face of a German Shepherd dog with large sparkling eyes. Early on the 21st January William Wasso, a track-walker on the electric railway between Clayton and Newfield, saw the beast sniff the rail, and its long tail touch it. An explosion melted twenty feet off the track. The Jersey Devil vanished. Other similar encounters suggest a manifestation wholly visible yet oddly insubstantial – like many **UFOs**.[1]

1. *Alien Animals*, Janet and Colin Bord, Granada, London 1980, pp. 113–15

JESUS (*See* **CHRIST**)

JEWS (*See* **GOOCH, MAGIC, QABALAH**) The root and essence of so much of the Western magical tradition is Jewish. The word 'magic' derives from the Magi, priests of **Zoroaster**, dating back to the fifth century BC. But Jewish lore claims Moses (fourteenth century BC?) as among the first great magicians; Maria the Jewess (also known as Mary, the sister of Moses) is said to have founded **alchemy**, while the *Key of Solomon* (who ruled *c.* 1000 BC) was the best-known magical work in the ancient world, the source of all later *grimoires*, books of conjuration, etc. The Order of **Knights Templar**, the source of so much mystery, was founded in Jerusalem in 1118, its first knights being quartered in a wing of a palace said to be built on the foundations of the Temple of Solomon. Why there, and what did they find? **Freemasonry** dates itself back to Hiram Abiff, legendary builder of that same Temple. And so on. **Gematria, numerology, sacred geometry** – all began (as did **Christianity**) in Israel. The body of esoterica called **Qabalah** is Jewish in origin and was further developed by European Jews in mediaeval times: the *Zohar* (Book of Splendour), a huge commentary on the Pentateuch, was said to be the work of Rabbi Simeon bar Yohai, who died in ecstatic **trance** and left his disciples to write down his wisdom. The *Zohar*, first circulated *c.* AD 1280, constitutes the definitive version of Qabalah – still considered by many to be the foundation of all **occult** science, magic and mystical knowledge, as well as being a 'geography of consciousness'.

Yet what in the Jewish experience so directed them in this exploration of higher or mystical knowledge while all about them were busy worshipping rocks and trees? Did their magical knowledge begin with them or did they get it elsewhere? In **Egypt**, perhaps? Moses is said to have been initiated into the mysteries of **Osiris**; and the Egyptians had, after all, built the **Great Pyramid** – a repository, whatever else it may be, of geophysical and geometric measurements so accurate that its remarkable

Frances Griffiths and the Cottingley Fairies, photographed by her cousin Elsie Wright. Sir Arthur Conan Doyle believed the fairies to be genuine, but Elsie's father regretted that Sir Arthur had been 'bamboozled by our Elsie' (FPL)

At Fatima in Portugal, on 13 October 1917, one of the most extraordinary – and best attested – 'miracles' of modern times was witnessed by 70,000 people: a silver disc appeared in the sky throwing off revolving beams of coloured lights; a sweet fragrance filled the air (FPL)

On 6 June 1936, Indian yogi Subbayah Pullavar levitated for four minutes in front of 150 witnesses. He was in a state of deep trance and, once back on the ground, his limbs could not be unbent (Mary Evans)

Two classic shots of the Loch Ness Monster and a drawing of the infamous Lambton Worm point to possible common origins in Britain's many worm legends. Is the 'worm' an archetype of evil, created in the collective minds of beholders? (Fortean)

A

SYSTEM

OF

MAGICK;

OR, A

HISTORY

OF THE

BLACK ART.

BEING AN

Hiſtorical Account of Mankind's moſt early Dealing with the Devil; and how the Acquaintance on both Sides firſt began.

Our Magick, Now, commands the Troops of Hell,
The Devil himſelf ſubmits to Charm and Spell.
The Conj'rer in his Circles and his Rounds
Juſt whiſtles up his Spirits, as Men do Hounds.
Th' obſequious Devil, obeys the Sorcerer's Skill,
The Mill turns round the Horſe, that firſt turns round the Mill.

LONDON, Printed: And Sold by J. ROBERTS in *Warwick-Lane*. MDCCXXVII.

LE DRAGON ROUGE

(d'après une gravure ancienne).

LE

DRAGON ROUGE

OU

L'ART DE CONJURER LES ESPRITS

DÉMONTRÉ

par des Faits et des Exemples

Par M. ROBVILLE

PARIS.

LE BAILLY, LIBRAIRE-ÉDITEUR

15, Rue de Tournon, 15

Three books of magic spanning two and a half centuries of the occult: *top,* the title page of *A System of Magick,* published in 1727 (Images); *middle,* a popular French magic manual, *Le Dragon Rouge,* from the mid-nineteenth century (Mary Evans); and, *below,* the handwritten endpapers of a modern grimoire with astrological sigils within a lunar node (Images)

Psychokinesis operates in all three images here. The planchette, *above,* aids the transmission of automatic writing, while with the ouija board, *below left,* the communicating spirit swings the pendulum to spell out the answers to questions. *Below right:* Stanislawa Tomczyk levitates a pair of scissors (Mary Evans)

Left: This photo claims to show the burnt remains of an extra-terrestrial following an alleged flying saucer crash at the beginning of the modern UFO cult, in 1947 (Mary Evans)

Below: Vast representations of animals on the Nazca plateau in Peru can only be viewed from the air, leading some to speculate that they may present evidence of ancient spacecraft activity (Images)

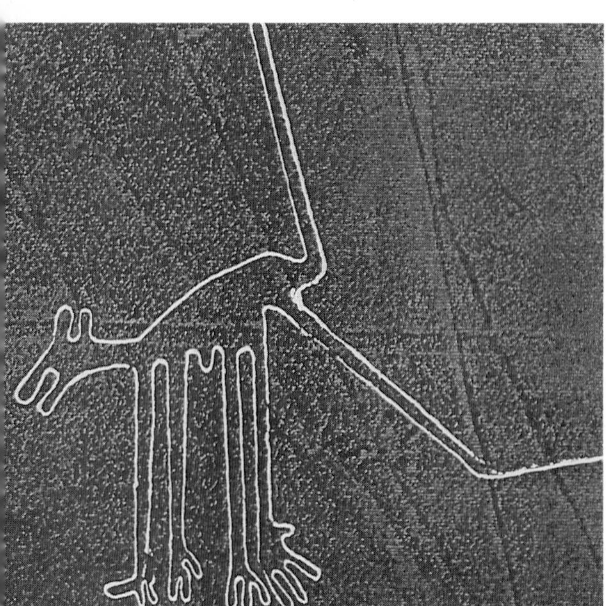

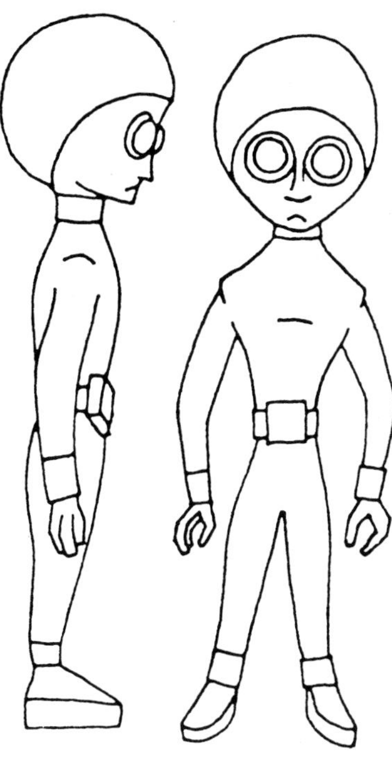

Prof. R. L. Johannis drew this picture of the alien he saw near Villa Santina in Italy in 1947 (FPL)

A further suggestion of ancient spaceships in the form of this Mexican design, known as the 'Palenque Astronaut' (Mary Evans)

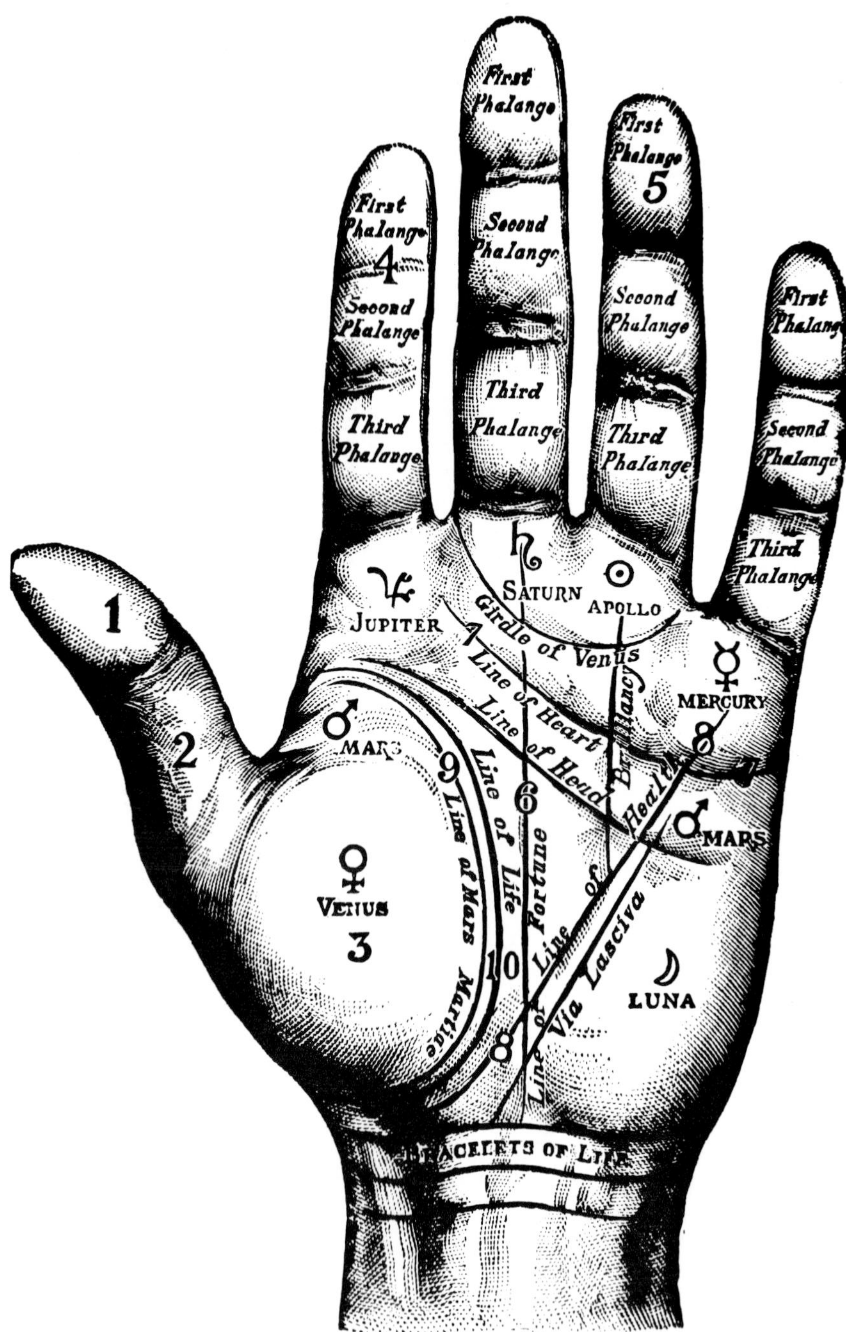

As complex as human nature itself, the interpretative systems of cheiromancy, or palmistry, involve astrology and intuition as well as an understanding of how a lifetime's experience may be etched into the skin. The greatest palmist, Cheiro, not only predicted the abdication of Edward VIII but the exact date of his own death (Mary Evans)

precision is shown only in the light of modern scientific development.

At the very least, the Hebrews guarded, developed and bequeathed to us a body of occult lore superior to any other available in the ancient world. Yet, given evidence of the knowledge not only of the Egyptians, but of the Western European **megalith**-builders of the third and fourth millennia BC, it must be asked: did the Jews originate, or merely transmit, such lore?

The suggestion by Gooch, mentioned elsewhere, that Jewish **mysticism** derives from the greater influence on them of the 'old brain' (**cerebellum**) due to a direct descent from **Neanderthal Man**, is interesting but should be taken with a pinch of salt. Is it not more likely that the experience of the Jews over the last 3,500 years as a wandering, often-persecuted nation, has stimulated their wit and sense of conscious individuality more than is the case with more settled peoples?

Abstract learning is, after all, less essential to landowners than to lost tribes: persecution, whatever else it does, sharpens the mind.

JINXES (*See* **CURSES**) *Jinxes* differ from *curses* in that the bad luck involved rarely arises from deliberately malign intent, real or imagined, but more likely by accident of mischance befalling a person. The agony suffered imprints itself, as in a haunting, on objects associated with the initial disaster, and, like a tape-recording, perpetually 'replays' itself as a run of bad luck.

The jinx also differs from the curse in that usually it snares a specific individual or object. A curse is more general in effect, affecting families or even nations over centuries. Yet at source the two are one. The magical prohibitions (*geasa*) laid on ancient Irish heroes like Cuchullin jinxed them, then fatally cursed and killed them – if they broke the *geas*.

Tales of jinxed or 'unlucky' cars, ships and planes are legion. Take the open red car in which the Archduke Franz Ferdinand was riding when assassinated in Sarajevo in 1914, thus starting the First World War. Its later career involved the death, injury or insanity of all who owned it. The next owner, the Austrian general Potiorek, died insane after defeat in battle; the owner after him died in a crash nine days after buying it; the Governor of Yugoslavia lost his arm in it; the next owner was crushed to death in it; a Swiss racing driver was thrown out of it over a wall and died. Finally the deadly machine ended up in a Vienna museum.

The famous Porsche in which film star James Dean died in 1955 proved deadly even after being dismantled. Slipping while being unloaded from the breakdown truck, it broke a mechanic's legs. The engine was put in another car which crashed in a race, killing the driver; a second car in the same race, containing the Porsche's drive shaft, overturned and injured its driver; two tyres from it, on a third car, exploded simultaneously without apparent cause. The car's shell, used in a Highway Safety display, fell off its mounting and broke a teenager's hip: later, the truck carrying it to another display was in an accident, killing the driver; another truck carrying it slipped its handbrake and crashed into a store, and in New Orleans in 1959 it broke into eleven pieces while on stationary supports.

In June 1859 the *Great Eastern*, the world's largest ship at 19,000 tons, was to be launched, a riveter and his apprentice having vanished during construction. Stuck in the slipway, it took three months to free. When finally launched its designer, Brunel, collapsed on the deck and died a week later. Continual disaster dogged it thereafter. A funnel exploded, killing five men; a man was crushed in the paddle wheel, the captain was drowned. Laying the trans-Atlantic cable, the ship lost it halfway across: storm damage and disaster continued until, only fifteen years old, it was laid up and left to rust. When broken for scrap in 1889, the skeletons of the riveter and apprentice were found trapped in the double hull. During World War II, the German battle-cruiser *Scharnhorst* was dogged by a similar catalogue of disasters ended only when being struck and sunk by a chance British broadside fired at night from a distance of 16,000 yards.

Such events remain unexplained. But they happen.[1]

1. *Mysteries*, Colin Wilson, Grafton, London 1979, pp. 458–60

JOAN OF ARC (1412–31) Born into a poor family at Domrémy in Lorraine, Joan of Arc first heard her 'voices' aged thirteen. They came, she said, from St Michael, St Catherine of Alexandria and St Margaret of Antioch. They stayed with her all her short life: she could summon them at will. At the time, Burgundian and English armies had overrun France: Orléans was under siege. Sometime in 1428 St Michael told her 'she would cause the siege before Orléans to be raised', and to go to Vaucouleurs, where de Baudricourt, the French Captain, would send her to the Dauphin. Reluctantly she obeyed. Within a year she led French armies to the relief of Orléans and to a series of victories that had the English reeling. Yet in May 1430 she was captured: in September the English paid 10,000 francs for 'the purchase of Joan the Maid, who is said to be a sorcerer', then indicted her for trial on seventy counts, mostly of **witchcraft** and **sorcery**, claiming she was in league with the **Devil**.

Of course they wanted her dead; the trial and the charges justifying it were a pretext. Yet many were sure she *was a* witch. What else explained her feats? After Orléans the Duke of Bedford claimed the English retreat was caused by: 'a disciple and lyme of the fiend, called the Pucelle, that used fals enchauntments and sorcerie'. Yet at her trial no reference to witchcraft was made, save in that as a child she had danced under the **'Fairies'** Tree' at Domrémy. Nothing could be proved: she was condemned not for sorcery but for denying the authority of the Church. It is said that after her burning (30 May 1431) the executioner found her heart intact.

Much was odd about her. Her assurance, her success in battle, her 'voices' which she alone heard and which told her what to do, her **second-sight**. On 12 February 1429 she told Robert de Baudricourt at Vaucouleurs that the French army had been defeated at the battle of Herrings, hundreds of miles away. Two days later the news was confirmed. Sent to the Dauphin, she knew his secret prayer – that if he were the true king of France, God would defend him, or at least let him escape the English. On preparing to join the French army, she said her battle-sword would be found hidden behind the altar at St Catherine's Church at Fierbois. So it was, though nobody knew of it beforehand. All this and also her masculine dress stood against her. Thrice she was examined to establish both her sex and virginity; each time both were proved. In fact she made men feel thoroughly uncomfortable. Yet what was the source of her voices? She began hearing them at puberty; they came from saints with whom she was familiar; they spoke in her native tongue. Did they arise from her own subconscious? Was she **'possessed'**, or a 'paranoid schizophrenic' or a 'genius'? Such labels tell us nothing. Whatever their source, and whatever her mental state, her obedience to her voices resulted in one of the most extraordinary (and briefest) careers in documented history.

Joan of Arc, 'La Pucelle de Dieu', was canonised in 1920.[1,2]

1. *Joan of Arc*, Edward Lucie-Smith, Allen Lane, London 1976
2. *Jeanne d'Arc*, W. S. Scott, Harrap, London 1974

JONAS, Eugen (*See* **ASTROLOGY, CYCLES**) More proof, if needed, that our nature obeys hidden natural forces. In the 1960s Eugen Jonas in Czechoslovakia ascertained that women ovulate in tune with the lunar cycle and (more surprisingly) that a mature woman's ability to conceive coincides with the phase of the **Moon** under which she was born.

This discovery was employed initially to establish a contraceptive service. Jonas provided women with (**astrological**) charts based on their own personal lunar rhythms. Thus armed, they could decide when or not to indulge in sexual intercourse, either to conceive or to avoid conception. In contraceptive terms, these charts are said to have proved ninety-eight per cent effective.[1]

Additionally, scanning the birth charts of 250 newborn children, Jonas successfully identified the sex of 217 (eighty-seven per cent) from planetary data alone.[2] Using this method, the Czech government improved prediction to ninety per cent.

1. *Supernature*, Lyall Watson, Hodder and Stoughton, London 1973, pp. 48–9
2. *The Thirteenth Sign*, James Vogh, Mayflower Books, London 1979, p. 105

JOSEPH OF COPERTINO (*See* **LEVITATION**)

JUNG, Carl Gustav (1875–1961) (*See* **ANIMA, ARCHETYPES, COLLECTIVE UNCONSCIOUS, DREAMS, HITLER, MULTIPLE PERSONALITY, SYNCHRONICITY, UFOs**) Strange events marked the death of the great Swiss psychoanalyst and **seer** Carl Gustav Jung. His favourite tree in his garden at Küsnacht near Zurich was hit by lightning: his friend Laurens van der Post, at sea at the time, dreamed Jung waved and said, 'I'll be seeing you' – and next day he learned Jung had died at the time of his dream. Years later he was making a film about Jung at Küsnacht. Lightning struck the garden again even as van der Post was describing Jung's death to camera.[1]

Born 26 July 1875 at Kesswil on Lake Constance, Jung was an odd child. In 1879 his clergyman father moved the family to Klein-Hüningen on the Rhine, where at school he was nicknamed 'Father Abraham'. This reflected his own sense of housing two different personalities: one the awkward, secretive boy; the other a wise old man (later personified as *Philemon*). This inner conflict, exacerbated by his father's demand for faith before reason, found its first resolution in a reading of **Goethe's** *Faust* – 'Two souls, alas, are housed within my breast'. **Psychokinetic** events (which he associated with a fifteen-year-old girl in the house) occurred. A table split, a bread-knife in a sideboard shattered. His interest in psychiatry grew. Krafft-Ebing's dictum that 'psychoses are **diseases** of the personality' fascinated him. So did his **dreams**. In one, aged three, he had followed an underground passage to a chamber where a huge erect phallus stood on a golden throne. Aged twelve, he had a vision of Basle Cathedral shattered by excrement dropped from a gold throne high in the sky. Later he interpreted this to mean that spiritual food as offered by traditional **Christianity** was exhausted. A new religiosity was required.

As a student at Zurich he was angered by the 'lack of ordinary, healthy curiosity' on the part of 'men in command of religious, and scientific and philosophic heights'.[2] He sensed the danger of the European split between *religion* (faith) and *science* that denied individual and subjective meaning, yet saw his intuitions required empirical proof before he could argue them in public. Later he analysed some 67,000 dreams before beginning to theorise about their meaning and function. Even so, and despite the rigour of his observations, for much of his life he was dismissed as a '**mystic**'.

On 12 December 1900 he began work at the Burghölzi Mental Hospital. **Freud** had just published *The Interpretation of Dreams*. Jung studied his colleagues (and himself) as well as his patients. Sensing a pathology in what (then and now) is called 'normal' behaviour, he decided that 'madness always hides a coded meaning and that no remark or fantasy is meaningless. Evolving 'word-association' tests to make hidden material conscious, he saw psychosis as arising from the arrested development of an individual's own story or **myth**. He insisted that '**healer**' and 'patient' enjoy a *sacred* relationship of mutual quest. Using the word 'heal' to mean 'making whole', he commented, 'In the end only the wounded physician heals.'[3]

He supported Freud despite doubts as to Freud's concept of sex as the main subconscious driving force. Freud, after all, had opened a door shut for centuries. Yet where Freud reacted *against* repression, Jung aimed to *transform* it by reconciling opposites which Freud saw as permanent and fixed. They remained outwardly united until one day Freud refused to tell Jung about a dream he'd had, fearing to do so 'would damage my authority'.

Shocked, Jung dreamed of Freud as a peevish Austrian customs official, out-of-date and blocking free **psychic** trade. Later he wrote how, in Vienna in 1909, as Freud argued against **parapsychology**, he suddenly felt as 'if my diaphragm were made of iron and were becoming red-hot – a glowing vault. And at that moment there was such a loud report in the bookcase, which stood right next to us, that we both started up in alarm . . . I said to Freud, "There, that is an example of a so-called catalytic exteriorisation phenomenon." ' Freud called this 'sheer bosh'. Jung intuitively predicted 'in a moment there will be another loud report'. Again the detonation sounded. Freud was aghast. Jung felt 'that I had done something against him'.[4] Soon after this, they parted company.

After publishing *Psychology of the Unconscious*, he entered a time of crisis. Though married with three daughters, he stopped writing, resigned his professorship in 1913, and submitted to a flood of sanity-threatening dreams and **visions**. In one he saw a tide of blood flood Europe from the north, carrying mangled corpses to the rim of the Alps. Dreaming of the land of the dead he met a black **serpent**, a whitebearded man, and a blind girl. The Serpent he identified as his instinctual self; the old man as Elijah (archetype of the 'wise old man') and the blind girl (Salome) as the eternal feminine, his *anima*. Yet why was she blind? The dream seemed to warn against self-denial. Deliberately re-embracing childhood, playing with stones, building a toy-village, he painted and wrote down his dreams in a Black Book then a Red Book. During these years (1913–28) he developed his theories of the collective unconscious, the Shadow, archetypes, the anima, of *individuation* as our common goal, and the four functions of **consciousness** – feeling, thinking sensation and **intuition**. His study of **Gnosticism** and **alchemy** told him that others, from **Plato** to **Paracelsus**, had been this way before, but that ecclesiastical hostility had so denied such enquiry that now it was forgotten or mocked. He saw restoration of this despised knowledge as vital to global mental health.

This work was arduous. His state of mind (even as millions died in the trenches) is highlighted by a bizarre book – *Septem Sermones ad Mortuos* (Seven Sermons to the Dead). Written in the winter of 1916–17, its origin is as weird as its Gnostic language, being heralded by **paranormal** events. Ghostly **entities** were felt in his house by his children as well as himself: the doorbell rang violently one Sunday afternoon, the bell was seen to move without visible cause; a crowd of 'spirits' seemed to fill the hallway, and when he cried, 'For God's sake, what in the world is this?' the answer came 'in a chorus of ghostly voices': 'We have come back from Jerusalem where we found not what we sought.'[5] Thus the opening words of the treatise, its Gnostic **spirit** advertised by the subtitle: 'Seven exhortations to the dead, written by Basilides [a second-century Gnostic writer] in Alexandria, the city where East and West meet.' The text speaks of Abraxas, a Gnostic **symbol** of the union of opposites (also employed by Hermann Hesse in his novel, *Demian*). 'The unlikely likely one, who is powerful in the realm of unreality,' Jung called him. Later he called it 'a youthful indiscretion' (he was over forty at the time). Yet was the 'indiscretion' in the writing or the publication? He may have felt (as did mediaeval alchemists) that wisdom lay in hiding his sources of illumination. Who would take him seriously if it were known that his inspiration arose from quest in '**magical**' areas long condemned?

In 1921 appeared *The Psychology of Type* – an empirical examination of consciousness proposing the idea of extraversion/intraversion; the former state characterising those who seek meaning via outer forms, the latter, those involved in the inner quest. Following ancient formulae, he proposed the division of the Self into four functions: thinking/feeling (Rational), and intuition/sensation (Non-Rational). He said each individual is born with one function in command and another (its opposite) in close support, the third and fourth remaining repressed and unconscious. Health requires the balance of functions by making repressed material conscious.

Thereafter (in *Roots of the Conscious; Archetypes and the Collective Unconscious; Psychology and Religion*; and *Modern Man in Search of a Soul*) he sought to establish the objective validity of the collective unconscious – that vast primordial energy-field underlying the personal unconscious and consciousness itself. He taught that modern Western man, by rejecting the values of natural feeling, has embraced an 'intellectual barbarism'. His African travels 1925–6 confirmed this belief and widened his enquiry. He saw **astrology** as a projected form of human psychology, with the sky as mirror. Gnosticism and alchemy provided continuity between the knowledge of the ancient and modern worlds. In 1928 he read **Wilhelm**'s translation of the Chinese alchemical classic: *The Secret of the Golden Flower*. This and Wilhelm's translation of the ***I Ching***, or *Book of Changes* led to study of eastern **mandala** patterns projecting images of wholeness in nature (and in Man). Yet he warned against substituting oriental wisdom for western science. Some of his conclusions – *Imagination is the star in man* – seem close to those of **occultists** like **Crowley**, and encouraged his detractors. Yet many, particularly women (Aniela Jaffé, M.-L. von Franz, Jolande Jacobi and Toni Wolff), warmed not only to Jung the man (his spontaneous laugh was famous) and his espousal of the feminine principle, but to his intellectual rigour and their intuition that he touched basic truth. Certainly he taught by charismatic example. For in his own journey into the unconscious he had found vast resources of energy, as is demonstrated in his work. But equally his sense of failure in plumbing the **Mysteries** bore out his rediscovery of the 'Shadow' – his term for the mass of unconscious forces rejected by the conscious mind, thus always accumulating and ready to break out. Opposing such 'evils', not as Christ taught ('resist not evil'), provided them with their chance to return. Thus (as he foresaw as early as 1918) Nazism was bound to erupt, reviving long-suppressed Germanic archetypes by blood-rite and Shadow-projection. His solution was to *accept* the hated opposite as an integral part of the hitherto divided self, thus transforming and *redeeming* it by welcoming it as part of the Self. This basic Christian (or **Buddhist**) solution – 'Love your enemy as yourself' – seemingly remains impractical.

Latterly, after a naive flirtation with the Nazis which led to mutual rejection, Jung grew interested in paranormal phenomena as manifested in UFOs, 'synchronicity', and survival after death. In 1944 he had a heart attack. While unconscious, he had a remarkable **vision**. Later he wrote, 'Far below I saw the globe of the earth, bathed in a gloriously blue light. Far below my feet lay Ceylon . . . I knew that I was on the point of departing from the earth . . . The sight of the earth from this height was the most glorious thing I have ever seen . . . I had the feeling that everything was being sloughed away; everything I aimed at or wished for or thought, the whole phantasmagoria of earthly existence fell away or was stripped from me – an extremely painful process. [Yet] something remained.'

In this state, reflecting on the 'long chain of events' of his life, he saw, rising up from the direction of Europe, his doctor, or at least the 'primal form' of that doctor – Doctor H., sent by the earth to deliver a message, 'to tell me there was a protest against my going away'.

'Profoundly disappointed', Jung thought, 'Now I must return to the "box system" again.'[6]

Which he did, for another seventeen years. Those of us still stuck in the box should be glad that he stayed so long. Few of us, when we leave, will have gained such power that lightning strikes to mark our earthly passing.

1. *Jung and the Story of our Time*, Laurens van der Post, Penguin Books, London 1978, pp.263ff.
2. *Ibid.*, p. 104
3. *Ibid.*, p. 128
4. *Memories, Dreams and Reflections*, C. G. Jung, Fontana Books, London, pp.178–9
5. *The Gnostic Jung and the Seven Sermons to the Dead*, Stephan A. Hoeller, Quest Books, Wheaton, Illinois USA, 1982, pp.7ff
6. *op.cit.* ref 4, pp. 320–324

Man and His Symbols, ed. C. G. Jung, Aldus Books, London 1964
Dreams, C. G. Jung, Ark Books, London 1968 (trans. R. F. C. Hull)
Collected Works, C. G. Jung, 20 vols, Princeton University Press, Princeton, New Jersey (various dates: trans. R. F. C. Hull)

K

KA (*See* ***DOPPELGÄNGER, EGYPT***) The ancient Egyptians recognised several **'subtle bodies'**. The *ka* (double) was an image of the *khat* (perishable physical body), and dwelt with the mummified body in the tomb. The *ba* (soul), depicted as a bird, was either the bodily animating principle or a state following death connected with the spiritual soul, *khu*. The imperishable *khu* was part of the spiritual body (*sahu*). The *sahu*, once seen as material in an early literal view of the **resurrection** whereby the *sahu, ba, ka, khaibit* (shadow) and *ikhu* (vital force) came together after 3,000 years, leading to reanimation, came to be seen as purely spiritual, but germinated from the physical body. To ensure this germination the physical body had to be preserved, thus the Egyptian concern with mummification. These complex ideas, as found in the *Egyptian Book of the Dead*, were by and large dismissed by later cultures. Yet the idea of the *ka* seems to equate with the concept of the 'double' or döppelganger.

Wallis Budge defined it as 'an abstract individuality or personality which possessed the form and attributes of the man to whom it belonged, and though its normal dwelling place was in the tomb with the body, it could wander about at will; it was independent of the man and could go and dwell in any statue of him'.[1] In the tomb it needed food and drink, or would wander about seeking sustenance. Flinders Petrie cites the tale of the *ka* of Ahura, buried at Koptos, visiting the tomb of her husband in Memphis. He says the *ka* contains 'the inner mental consciousness and hereditary powers of thought, as apart from the influence of the senses, and continued without the use of the bodily actions'.[2]

In his vast novel *Ancient Evenings* (1983) American author Norman Mailer dramatises the *ka*-state with considerable power and imagination.

1. *The Egyptian Book of the Dead*, E. A. Wallis Budge, Routledge Kegan Paul, London 1969, p. lix
2. *Religious Life in Ancient Egypt*, Sir Flinders Petrie, Constable, London 1924, p.113

KABBALAH (*See* **QABALAH**)

KAHUNAS (*See* **CURSES, MULTIPLE PERSONALITY**) These Hawaiian magician-priests of the Huna religion claim that man has three **souls**. The *low self* (in the solar plexus) corresponds to the unconscious; the *middle self* to ordinary consciousness; and the *high self* to the 'superconscious', in which state **psi powers** may be commanded. After death the low self may become detached from the middle and high selves.

Schoolteacher Max Freedom Long came to Hawaii in 1917 and was soon intrigued by Huna **religion** and especially by the practice of the 'death prayer'. A man thus cursed would first feel a pricking in the feet, which then grew numb; the numbness spread upwards until he died. Checking at the Queen's Hospital in Honolulu, Long found that every year such victims were admitted and that despite medical aid they all died. He also heard of a Christian minister who had used the death curse to kill a Kahuna magician who, by the same means, had been destroying his congregation – a species of 'psychic warfare'.

William Tufts Brigham, a doctor who had studied the Kahunas for years, told Long of a death prayer put on a boy who during a mountain expedition became paralysed. Questioned, he said his local kahuna had warned him that should he work for the hated white man he would die. He had forgotten the threat until now. Brigham determined to save him. Standing over him, he praised and flattered the 'spirits' paralysing the boy's body, telling them the boy was innocent and that the Kahuna sending them was to blame. For an hour he concentrated on this idea. He felt the tension slacken. The boy said he could feel his legs again: the paralysis was soon gone. Enquiring later at the boy's native village Brigham heard the Kahuna was dead. One morning the magician had emerged from his hut to say that the spirits had been sent back on him by the white magician and that, as he had failed to take **ritual** precautions, he must pay the price. Soon afterwards he had died.

Long concluded that the Kahuna system of spirit-psychology offers a satisfactory explanation of multiple personality.[1]

1. *The Secret Science Behind Miracles*, Max Freedom Long, DeVorss, USA 1981; reported in *Beyond the Occult*, Colin Wilson, Corgi, London 1989, p. 308

KALI YUGA (*See* **BRAHMA, HINDU MYSTERIES**) In the Indian epic ***Mahabharata*** and many other texts of the Puranic period (*c.* AD 400) the cosmic cycle of four world ages numbers 12,000 'divine years' of 360 'human years' each, totalling 4,320,000 years. Our present portion of that cycle totals one-tenth of that sum and is considered the last and worst. It is called Kali Yuga, the 'Age of Iron' (following ages of: gold, *Krita Yuga*; silver, *Treta Yuga*; and bronze, *Dvapara Yuga*). In Hindu and Buddhist mythology the Kali Yuga marks the final degeneration of the human race, ending in a time when fire, drought and famine ravage the faithless world. At its conclusion a huge conflagration destroys not only humanity but the known universe, leaving only Brahman, the uncreated unmanifest void from which new creation emerges, establishing a new golden age.

Division by sixty of 25,920 years – the 'Great' or 'Platonic' Year during which the equinox precesses back to its starting-point – gives the sum of 432. The ancient Indian calculation was not arbitrary, though the scale of time involved is huge. The only others to deal so happily in such big calculations have been Mayans, Chaldeans and modern physicists.

KAMMERER, Paul (1880–1926) The tragedy of Paul Kammerer tells us much about the supposed open-mindedness of institutionalised scientific rationalism.

Later stigmatised as a dilettante for his musical training, in 1902 this Austrian biologist joined the Biologische Versuchsansalt, Vienna's Institute for Experimental Biology, known as the 'Sorcerers' Institute'. He soon proved more successful than any biologist since not only in keeping delicate experimental animals alive but in breeding them. This success, the failure of others to reproduce his work, his thesis (*Law of Seriality*) that '**coincidence**' is meaningful and his own high-strung nature all aided his downfall. Most crucial, his controversial experiments with salamanders and midwife toads seemed to prove the hypothesis of the early nineteenth-century biologist Lamarck that acquired characteristics can be inherited. This infuriated neo-Darwinians who (still) insist evolution proceeds by natural selection based on chance mutation. As Samuel Butler wrote a century ago, 'Lamarck has been so systematically laughed at that it amounts to little less than philosophical suicide for anyone to stand up on his behalf.'

In Kammerer's case, the suicide was actual.

He induced modifications in the mating habits, colour or physique of animals by breeding them in environments other than their natural habitat. He claimed adaptive modifications became hereditary sometimes only in one generation. He made the midwife toad, which usually mates on land, breed in water and claimed the toads developed 'nuptial pads': horny swellings enabling the male to grip the female during aqueous intercourse. William Bateson and other neo-Darwinians hinted this work was faked: in 1926 when Kammerer killed himself it was assumed fakery was thus proven, especially when it was learned an assistant had doctored evidence. Yet this unstable man had made previous suicide attempts after failed love-affairs and for financial reasons. His death was conveniently assumed to invalidate his work. Today it remains academic suicide to support Lamarck . . . or Kammerer. Only a few independent thinkers like **Koestler**,[1] who has shown Kammerer's work was discredited not on scientific but emotional grounds, have dared tread on such discredited ground. Neo-Darwinism remains in favour though few seem entirely convinced by the theory of 'chance' mutation.

As for Kammerer, his tragedy is instructive.

1. *The Case of the Midwife Toad*, Arthur Koestler, Picador, London 1973

KARDEC, Allen (*See* **SPIRITISM**)

KARMA This Eastern doctrine asserts that every act (and thought) creates its own consequences. At a material level this is similar to Western belief that causes have effects. But Eastern theologies extend this doctrine to human life and ethics, while Western Christian dogma exempts believers from such law via the Redemption of **Christ**. What this distinction means in terms of social behaviour was suggested by a British Royal Commission in India during the 1880s. Studying murder-rates among different religious groups, it found that murder among Christian and Moslem populations (both without a theory of karma) was three times higher than among **Hindus**, and five times higher than among **Buddhists**. The Commission concluded that belief in karma explained the difference. Christians killed more readily, believing their act might be forgiven. Buddhists killed reluctantly, believing such acts might rebound against them in future lives. Which doctrine is of greater social utility (whatever the basic metaphysical reality of either) may be left to impartial judges.

KEEL, John (*See* **ALIEN ANIMALS, DIMENSIONS, UFOs**) In *Operation Trojan Horse*, this American UFOlogist suggests that UFOs are of earth-origin, crewed not by space beings but **elementals: fairy** beings, natural hoaxers hostile to man who can change their form at will. Once they tricked people by making animals barren or turning milk sour: today, Keel claims, they appear as UFOnauts or '**Men In Black**', and deliberately hoax people to conceal their real origin and purposes. Keel says they are menacing and not to be taken lightly.[1] Similar theories of the UFO-as-hoax have been advanced by Jacques **Vallée** and Whitley **Streiber**. Keel also investigated reports of encounters with winged humanoids in West Virginia during the 1960s 'Mothman Epidemic'. Said to lack arms or head, Mothman apparently had luminous red eyes and was bigger than a man. Keel suggests that such beings enter earth-space through inter-dimensional 'windows' and points out, 'These creatures and strange events tend to recur in the same areas year after year, even century after century.'[2]

1. *Operation Trojan Horse*, John A. Keel, Abacus, London 1973
2. *The Mothman Prophecies*, John A. Keel, Dutton, New York 1975

KELLER, Helen (*c*. 1880–1962) (*See* **NOLAN**) Helen Keller, born in Alabama, was struck deaf and blind when eighteen months old, and soon lost all speech. The last word to go was 'water'. Her parents approached Alexander Graham Bell, the telephone's inventor, himself married to a deaf-mute. He introduced them to Anne Sullivan, once blind herself. Mrs Sullivan taught Helen finger language, spelling on her hand the names of everyday objects. Enraged by her condition, Helen refused to learn until 5 April 1887, when while washing, she wanted to know the name for 'water'. Mrs Sullivan spelled it out, then after breakfast took Helen to the pump-house.

In a letter Anne Sullivan told how then, 'I made Helen hold her mug under the spout while I pumped. As the cold water gushed forth, filling the mug, I spelled "w-a-t-e-r" in Helen's free hand. The word, coming so close upon the sensation of cold water rushing over her hand, seemed to startle her. She dropped the mug and stood as one transfixed. A new light came over her face. She spelled "water" several times. Then she dropped on the ground and asked for its name and pointed to the pump and the trellis, and suddenly turning round she asked for my name. I spelled "Teacher". Just then the nurse brought Helen's little sister into the pump-house, and Helen spelled "baby" and pointed to the nurse. All the way back to the house she was highly excited, and learned the name of every object she touched, so that in a few hours she had added thirty new words to her vocabulary.'

Helen learned to read braille, to write and to lip-read by touching Mrs Sullivan's lips and throat. At Boston's Horace Mann School for the Deaf she learned how to speak, again by touch. Headmistress Sarah Fuller would, if need be, put her fingers down Helen's throat. After ten lessons Helen said, 'I'm not dumb now.' Later she gained a BA, studied philosophy and history, and also learned French, German, Latin and Greek. Constantly with Anne Sullivan, she learned to swim, rode horses, appreciated music by vibration alone, travelled widely, lectured and also, in the course of her astonishing life (she lived to 82), wrote poetry:

> With alert fingers I listen
> To the showers of sound
> That the wind shakes from the forest.

If spoken to, with Anne Sullivan holding her hand, she'd turn her head and smile. Otherwise she showed no response at all. Aged about eight, she was out walking with her mother, who was startled by a boy who threw something.

'What are we afraid of?' Helen hand-spelled.[2]

Her story argues not ***paranormal*** power so much as the suggestion that in us all there are resources rarely tapped, and that these derive from the same ground as other phenomena described herein.

1. *The Story of My Life*, Helen Keller, Doubleday, New York 1954
2. *Superself*, Ian Wilson, Sidgwick and Jackson, London 1989, p. 55–58

KELLEY, Edward (*See* **DEE, John**)

KEPLER, Johannes (1571–1630) The erratic career of the discoverer of the laws of planetary motion well illustrates the ambiguous, magical nature of scientific enterprise during the Renaissance. Kepler's mother was prosecuted as a witch: he practised **astrology** (despite calling it 'the foolish little daughter of astronomy'); and his scientific discoveries arose out of a theological passion to elucidate the divine design of the universe. For years he believed the five regular polyhedra of Euclidean geometry fitted between the spheres carrying the six known planets in *circular* orbits. His heroism was to admit (after years of trying to make Tycho Brahe's calculations fit his preconception) that the astronomical truth is otherwise. In *The New Astronomy* (1609) he broke with tradition in proving that Mars orbited the Sun, and established that it did so in a wholly inelegant *ellipse*. Yet still he sought underlying evidence of divine design, and in 1618 published *Harmony of the World*, relating the velocities of the planets with musical harmony. Thus to his own mind he established the true existence of the 'music of the **spheres**' as discerned by Pythagoras and Plato. That today no value is attached to this vision may say more about modern materialism than Renaissance **mysticism**.

Kepler also wrote an early science fiction novel, *Somnium*, about a dream-journey to the **Moon**. He lived his life in poverty and on the move.

KING, George (1919–) This British **occultist** claims to be guided by the **spirits** of notables such as nineteenth-century **psychic** researcher Sir Oliver **Lodge**. In 1954, alone in his West London flat, he heard a voice say: 'Prepare yourself! You are to become the voice of Interplanetary Parliament.' A week later an Indian swami 'walked straight through' the locked door and gave him facts leading to the foundation of the Aetherius Society. Soon he not only received information **telepathically** from the depths of 'etheric space', but visited Venus and Mars, and engaged in a space battle forty million miles from Earth. He has publicly given **trance** messages from such **entities** as Mars Sector 6, the Master Aetherius and Jesus **Christ**, said to be currently resident on or near Venus.

The society still thrives, concentrating on the 'task' imposed by the Interplanetary Parliament via King's **mediumship**. This task is to store up, in collaboration with the extra-terrestrial entities, 'spiritual energy' in 'spiritual batteries' located in high places, this energy to be released to prevent sickness and suffering all the world round. Society members have undertaken dangerous pilgrimages up high mountains including Kilimanjaro in Tanzania to fulfil their mission as communicated by King.

KIRLIAN, Semyan (*See* **AURA, SUBTLE BODY**) In 1939, repairing an electrotherapy machine in a research laboratory in Krasnodar in the Ukraine, this Russian engineer got his hand too close to a live electrode. The shock he received was accompanied by a spark of light like that in a tube where neon is electrically charged. Another account says the event happened in Krasnodar hospital not to him but to a patient receiving electrotherapy. Either way, he wanted to know what happened if he put light-sensitive material in the path of the spark. With his wife Valentina he set up two metal plates as electrodes and placed photographic film on one. Putting his hand between the plates he turned on the current. The developed film showed a glowing aura round his fingertips. Extending the experiment he found similar effects in a wide range of organic tissue. The stem of a newly cut flower showed sparks streaming from the stem. A dead leaf showed neither spark nor flare. More oddly, the photograph of a newly-torn leaf still showed the part which had been torn away.

Speculation about such phenomena reached the West only when in 1973 two American writers published *Psychic Discoveries behind the Iron Curtain*.[1] It was assumed by many that what Kirlian had captured on film proved the existence of the aura as in mediaeval images of saints, or of the '**astral body**', the spiritual double of our physical selves said by some to survive death. Such excitement was opposed by scientific assertion that the Kirlian effect is explicable by ordinary physics, and already known. Nikola **Tesla** had produced similar effects in the 1890s; in the 1930s George de la Warr discovered weak '**electromagnetic** force fields' round the body; and since the early twentieth century electrical engineers had used a similar technique ('Lichtenburg figures') to pinpoint sudden changes in voltage.

Yet none of this really denied the notion that astral body and aura alike may be essentially electrical or electromagnetic in origin. And yet again 'science' ignored the *emotional* productions of mind as irrelevant.

Recent Kirlian research shows that the 'aura effect' varies according to mood.

Kirlian photos show the aura of young men flaring up if a pretty girl enters the room, and likewise just after they drink a shot of hard spirits. Such 'flares' also emerge at just those bodily points identified as meridians in Chinese **acupuncture**. Kirlian technique is now used by some therapists to diagnose illness before physical symptoms manifest. Success rates are not known.

Dr Victor Inyushin of the University of Alma-Ata, USSR, has concluded that the 'aura' effect of Kirlian photography proves the existence of what he calls '**biological plasma**', his description of which parallels the 'body of **energy**' or 'astral body' described for so long by **clairvoyants**. At the Neuropsychiatric Institute of UCLA, California, Kirlian energy flares have been photographed emitting from the fingertips of **healers** – which may help explain why so many healers are exhausted after such sessions.

1. *Psychic Discoveries behind the Iron Curtain*, Shiela Ostrander and Lynn Shroeder, Sphere Books, London 1973

KNIGHTS TEMPLAR (*See* **DUALISM, FREEMASONRY**) Founded in Jerusalem *c.* AD 1118, this powerful order of crusading monks so concealed their true beliefs that, since their mysterious downfall in 1307, their actual goals have remained obscure. Today Templar influence, real or imagined, persists in Freemasonry and other semi-occult orders.

On the face of it, they fell because they had grown too powerful. With their own fleet and ports, banking for European kings, they over-reached themselves. On Friday 13 October 1307, King Philippe le Bel of France rounded up as many as could be found. Yet those caught were accused not of civil crimes but a range of heresies. Under Inquisition torture they were accused of denying **Christ**, defiling the Cross, perverting the Mass, adoring an idol (Baphomet: a head); also of **ritual** murder, immorality, obscene kissing, and of wearing a heretical cord (as with **Cathars** and **witches**).[1]

The last Grand Master, Jacques de Molay, died at the stake in Paris in 1314. It is said he called King Philippe and Pope Clement V to join him before God's throne within the year. Both died within the year.

Yet most Templars escaped. Where? Who warned them? Why? The mystery of their fate is as profound as that of their origin in the Holy Land.

Guillaume of Tyre (the first 'historical authority' to mention them) says *c.* 1180 that the *Order of the Poor Knights of Christ and the Temple of Solomon* was founded in Jerusalem in 1118 by a French knight of Champagne, Hugues de Payens, and eight companions. Arriving unannounced at the palace of Baudouin I, King of Jerusalem, they demanded recognition as an order to: 'keep the roads and highways safe . . . with especial regard for the protection of pilgrims'. The king granted them a wing of the royal palace – quarters traditionally built on the foundations of the Temple of Solomon. Thus the name: Knights *Templar*. So these poor knights, also blessed by the Patriarch of Jerusalem, got all they wanted. So claims Guillaume.[2]

Supposedly so poor they had to share horses when riding out to protect pilgrims (thus the well-known Templar seal), they were sworn to poverty, chastity and obedience. Contemporary historian Fulk de Chartres does not mention them. Yet in 1128 St Bernard, Abbot of Clairvaux and head of the new Cistercian order, issued a tract 'In Praise of the New Knighthood'. In 1130 Hugues de Payens returned to Europe from Palestine with an entourage of 300 knights. In 1139 Pope Innocent II (once one of St Bernard's monks) absolved the Templars from allegiance to any power but the Pope. Why?

Meanwhile Abbot Suger of St Denis (Paris) rebuilt his church in a new style. Later called 'Gothic', it invoked pointed arch and flying buttress, drawing eye and spirit up. This style was not derived from the preceding Romanesque, with its heavy round arches and barrel-vaults.

The pointed arch first appears in Europe in the Italian Bendictine monastery of Monte Cassino, built 1066–71, two decades before the first Crusade.[3] The geometry was Islamic, as was the astronomy and **alchemy** of the time. Were the Crusades, publicly a war against **Islam**, also a quest for cultural growth? Some claim Hugues de Payens was secretly authorised (by St Bernard?), to found the Order not to protect pilgrims but to glean esoteric knowledge, including the principles of the 'new' Gothic style.[4]

If the Templars were founded to *collaborate* with the infidel, no surprise that a mystery persists. Certainly eastern **dualism** entered Templar philosophy early on: impossible if they or their sponsors were unsympathetic to it.

Their freethinking and the rapid growth of their wealth and power seems to have been *encouraged*. So long as the Crusades lasted they were secure, playing their double game – publicly Christian, privately **pagan**?

Their doctrines were at least unorthodox. In the Second Crusade their zeal was suicidal. They could not surrender, but had to fight to the death. They behaved like dualists, despising earthly life. Another clue to their true outlook is suggested by the fact that the growth of Templar power coincides with the rise in Provence of the dualist Cathars, and of the troubadour romance of chivalry, idealising Woman, and pre-Christian, **pagan** philosophies thinly disguised as Christian by **Arthurian** and **Grail** myth.

It was recently suggested that the Templars were the military wing of a much older **mystical** alliance, the *Prieuré de Sion*, created to protect and promote the interests of those descended from the **Merovingian** dynasty, claimed as the offspring of Christ and Mary Magdalene.[5]

Yet French Templars on trial in 1308 said 'Christ is a false prophet', and that they did not believe in the Cross, 'for it is too young'. Their beliefs seem to be pre-Christian. Baphomet, the bearded head they adored, suggests Celtic head-worship. Like the Cathars, who said Christ never incarnated, but was literally a 'holy **ghost**', they denied the Crucifixion.

In AD 1208 Pope Innocent III preached a crusade against Catharism. Amid bloody war the Inquisition was founded to wipe out the heretics, a task effectively completed by 1244. The Templars survived, but the turning tide ran out completely when in 1291 Acre fell and the Holy Land was lost. For 200 years the Crusades had diverted Europe from domestic wars and let the Templars do as they pleased. Now, with their *raison d'être* destroyed, they were fatally compromised. They could not assimilate into post-Crusade Europe. Learned in Islamic doctrine, **number** and science; Jewish **Qabalah**, Celtic and **Druid** mysteries, their engagement in dualism implied anarchism, above king or pope. Worse, kings resented going to them for loans as much as ordinary folk hated their arrogance. Now at last they were weak. So in 1307 Philippe attacked them, just as 228 years later Henry VIII of England attacked the monasteries, as much for hard cash as political control.

Yet many Templars, warned in advance, escaped. One account suggests many fled to Scotland, and that Scotch Rite Freemasonry derives from their influence. Viscount Dundee, killed at the Battle of Killiecrankie in 1689, was found to be wearing a Templar cross under his armour.[6]

But for over a century their mysticism mattered less than their role as a multinational company, with their own ports, fleet and banks. Inventing the cheque, they were exempt from tithes but imposed their own. Answerable only to the Pope, they lived in increasingly lonely splendour, loathed by all. Yet they were survived not only by the glamour of the chivalric ideal they represented, but by a mystery that still reverberates.

1. *Witchcraft Today*, Gerald B. Gardner, Arrow, London, 1975 (1954), p. 79
2. *The Holy Blood and the Holy Grail*, Baigent, Leigh and Lincoln, Corgi, London 1983

3. *The Mysteries of Chartres Cathedral*, Louis Charpentier (1966), (English trans. 1972), Avon Books, New York 1975
4. *Sacred Geometry*, Nigel Pennick, Turnstone Press, London 1983
5. *op.cit.* ref. 3
6. *The Temple and the Lodge*, Baigent and Leigh, Corgi, London 1990

KOAN (*See* **ZEN**) The *koan* is a device developed by Zen **Buddhist** masters to baffle and corner the rationality of novices seeking enlightenment. It usually takes the form of question without logical answer, such as: '*What is the sound of one hand clapping*?' The search for a rational answer (there is none) builds up mental tension, typically over years, until the aspirant reaches a point where all concepts and words, arising from intellectuality alone, become meaningless and dissolve. Here the answer erupts spontaneously from those deeper, more universal layers of mind formerly subdued or drowned by the tyranny of reason and language. Perceiver and perceived become one.

KOESTLER, Arthur (1905–83) Born in Budapest and educated at the University of Vienna, this original thinker embraced communism as a young man, took up journalism and became foreign correspondent for various British and German publications. During the Spanish Civil War he was caught by the Fascists and condemned to death. In his book *Arrow in the Blue* he describes how to pass the time in jail he scratched mathematical formulae on the wall. While working out Euclid's classic proof that there is no 'largest prime number', he was swept into a sudden mystical exaltation. Entranced by the realisation that Euclid had established an infinite truth using finite means, he slowly remembered that soon he might be shot. This worry seemed irrelevant. 'So what?' he asked himself, 'Is that all? Have you nothing more serious to worry about?'

This experience changed his life. Released due to British protests, he settled in the UK. Later in his essay *The Yogi and the Commissar* he argued that there are two psychological types: the 'Commissar' who believes that the world is changed by influencing others, and the '**Yogi**', who insists that to change the world one must first change oneself. Also from his jail experience came the novel *Darkness at Noon*, published in thirty-two languages and after Orwell's *1984* the most influential political novel of the era.

Abandoning politics, he turned to popularising science and aesthetics in books such as *The Act of Creation* and *The Ghost in the Machine*. These displayed a wide-ranging intelligence but also increasing pessimism about humanity's future. In *The Case of the Midwife Toad* he examined the tragedy of Austrian biologist Paul **Kammerer**, hounded into suicide for apparently proving the 'heretical' Lamarckian theory that acquired characteristics are heritable. In *Janus* (1978), he summarised his views that: (1) humanity is technically schizoid due to design flaws in our nervous system; (2) that our main problem as a species is not excessive *aggression*, but excessive capacity for *devotion* and self-transcending identification with the local group-mind; and (3) that our deadliest weapon is language; every language being a cohesive force *within* the group but divisive *between* groups. Pointing out evidence that most people will obey authority without question even if it conflicts with their morality and causes them distress, he thought it essential that we learn to *reconcile* emotion and reason, 'which have been at loggerheads throughout most of man's schizoid history'.[2]

Latterly struck by Parkinson's Disease, he became involved in psychic research. In the *Roots of Coincidence* he surveyed and extended the work by Kammerer and **Jung** on **synchronicity**. At his death by suicide in 1983 it was learned that he had endowed a Koestler Foundation to encourage further investigation in **parapsychology**. A doctoral programme was subsequently established at the University of Edinburgh, Scotland.

1. Quoted in *The Occult*, Colin Wilson, Grafton, London 1979, pp.560–62
2. *Janus*, Arthur Koestler, Hutchinson, London 1978, pp. 98ff.
   The Act of Creation, Arthur Koestler, Hutchinson, London 1964
   The Roots of Coincidence, Arthur Koestler, Pan, London 1972
   The Sleepwalkers, Arthur Koestler, Penguin, London 1988

KRISHNA, Gopi (1903–?) (*See* **KUNDALINI YOGA**) In his autobiography this Indian **yogi** tells how at Christmas 1937 he was seated cross-legged in a house in Kashmir, meditating on his crown **chakra**, when he felt a strange but pleasant sensation below the base of the spine. When he focused on it it ceased. Concentrating once more on the crown's lotus-image, the sensation began again. He maintained concentration until: 'Suddenly, with a roar like . . . a waterfall, I felt a stream of liquid light entering my brain through the spinal cord . . . I experienced a rocking sensation . . . I felt myself slipping out of my body, entirely enveloped in a halo of light . . . the body, normally the immediate object of its perception, appeared to have receded into the distance . . . I was now all consciousness, without any outline, immersed in a sea of light . . . in a state of exaltation and happiness impossible to describe.'

Returning to normality he felt exhausted and depressed, unable to work, eat, sit still or control his thoughts. 'My consciousness . . . rose and fell like a wave, raising me one moment out of the clutches of fear to dash me again the next into the depths of despair.' Weakened by pain and confusion over the following weeks he fell into a delirium near death, at which point a **dream** suggested he eat milk and a little well-boiled meat every hour. His wife fed him until his strength returned: nonetheless it took him a further twelve years to attain ***samādhi***, or true realisation and self-control.

What had happened? Nowhere in India could he find a **guru** who knew. It seems he had accidentally released an uncontrollable energy-current called *kundalini* which, though sometimes active in the physical body, does not have its source there. This '**serpent**-power' so deranged his nervous system that it almost killed him. He was either luckier or more steadfast than many others who have unwittingly or ignorantly invoked this force'.

1. *Kundalini: the Evolutionary Energy in Man*, Gopi Krishna (1967), quoted in *Mysteries*, Colin Wilson, Grafton, London 1979, pp. 575–8

KRISHNAMURTI, Jiddu (1894–1985) The earliest and among the most impressive of many Indian **gurus** to make their mark in the west during the twentieth century, Jiddu Krishnamurti was discovered in Adyar, India, by the **Theosophist** C.W. **Leadbetter** and Annie **Besant** in 1910. Adopted (or abducted) by them, he was taken to England as a child and groomed as the incarnation of Lord Maitreya, the new World Teacher. He soon attracted thousands of followers who joined the organisation – the Order of the Star of the East – formed on his behalf. He had little to do with it. Remaining sane despite the adulation, he is notable not least for the fact that in 1929 he rejected guruhood, disclaimed spiritual authority, and told his followers to find someone else to worship. Thereafter he went his own way, advising people to reject formal beliefs and **religions**, which in his view only provide substitutes for self-responsibility, and find out the truth for themselves. Thus he proved his Theosophical mentors correct in their initial intuition that they had discovered a remarkable man.

KÜBLER-ROSS, Elizabeth (*See* **NEAR-DEATH EXPERIENCES, SURVIVAL**) At the end of World War II this doctor visited the extermination camp at Maidanek and established a refugee camp on the Vistula River in Poland. She emigrated to the USA where in the early 1960s, revolted by the US tendency to deny death, she invited a twenty-year-old girl dying of leukaemia to her classes at the

University of Chicago. This led to nationwide notoriety and an article in (oddly enough) *Life* magazine. Subsequently she has worked to change the attitudes of what she terms a 'death-denying society'.

In the first place she was sceptical about 'life after death'. Yet her experience through years of attempting to succour the dying and those left behind led her to decide that both **reincarnation** and survival of death are factual. Her conclusions, in books like *Of Death and Dying*, are that:(1) we all know the time of our own death: (2) everyone who dies is met by dead relatives or other loved ones; and (3) that all human beings have **spirit** guides who watch over them and manifest at times of **psychic** stress.

From her considerable personal experience of the dying she also accepts that time in the 'next world' is unlike this world's time, and that the 'judgement' of the dead is a process conducted by the dying individual and not by any other external or **supernatural entity**.

Kübler-Ross has been accused (mostly by men) of emotionalism, but the subsequent researches of **Moody, Sabom**, Stevenson, *et al.*, suggest that in fact her work is ground-breaking and should be respected.

She herself tells how, after the last engagement in a long lecture tour, she was so exhausted she decided she'd have to stop such work. But as she stood in front of an elevator a patient she'd helped to die appeared beside her, greeted her, and stated: 'You can't give up this work for the dying! It's *much* too important.' The **apparition** followed her down the elevator and along a corridor to her room, where it insisted, 'Promise me you won't give up your work!'

Still amazed but looking for proof like any good scientist would, she demanded, 'Give me your autograph.'

After signing the piece of paper she gave it, the apparition went out of the door. Kübler-Ross followed, but the corridor was empty. She stood there with the signed piece of paper in her hand . . . and later risked her professional reputation by speaking about this event.[1] Why?

'Man has not basically changed,' she writes. 'Death is still a fearful, frightening happening, and the fear of death is a universal fear even if we think we have mastered it on many levels.'

1. *Intangible Evidence*, Bernard Gittelson, Simon and Schuster, London 1987, pp.282–3.

KUNDALINI YOGA (*See* **CHAKRAS, KRISHNA, Gopi, YOGA**) This potent **yogic** system involves raising energy up through the body from the base of the spine to the intellectual centres of the cortex in order to hasten the dawning of enlightenment. The Sanskrit term implies a *winding spiral* or *coiling* motion or energy. In effect the yoga involves bypassing evolutionary time by consciously invoking *Kundalini-Sakti*, said to be one of the fundamental ***prānic*** forces of Nature. Underlying physical existence, it continuously expresses itself in many familiar phenomena even though we remain unaware of it. Human beings have developed various neurological defences against energetic input too potent for easy assimilation. The notion of the '**dragon**' or *serpent*-power coiled at the base of our spines, one step up from the sexual centre, is not a metaphor but organic reality.

Such energy, raised to the brain, can lead to enlightenment or madness, depending on the capacity of the individual to carry such current without overloading and burning out. Unskilled attempts to interfere with the normal working of this force in the human body are ill-advised. As in the case of Gopi Krishna, even practised yogis may find difficulty handling the energies thus released. When unconsciously invoked, the consequences are said to be catastrophic.

L

LAW OF CORRESPONDENCES (*See* **CORRESPONDENCES**)

LEADBETTER, C.W. (1847–1934) (*See* **BESANT, KRISHNAMURTI**) This dubious character (an Anglican curate before his **occult** interests led him into **Theosophy** in 1884) 'adopted' **Krishnamurti** in India in 1910 with Annie **Besant**. Later he abandoned Theosophy to found the Liberal Catholic church, taking many Theosophists with him. He became the second Bishop of this organisation, which survives. Claiming the power to see **auras** and communicate with Nature spirits, he wrote on occult matters, but was widely considered a disreputable pederast.

LEARY, Timothy (1920–) Originator of the 1960s injunction to: 'Turn on, tune in, and drop out', this Harvard professor popularised use of LSD–25 and other **hallucinogenic** drugs as a route to mystical realisation. In *The Psychedelic Experience* (1964: co-authored with Richard Alpert, who later emerged as **guru** Baba Ram Dass), he commented, 'Westerners do not accept the existence of conscious processes for which they have no operational terms. The attitude which is prevalent is: if you can't label it, and if it is beyond current notions of space-**time** and personality, then it is not open for investigation.'[1]

Forced to abandon his academic career, he continued advocating use of psychedelics. Arrested and jailed for possession of marijuana, he escaped and fled to Algeria. On return to the USA, publicly repentant, he developed an 'eight-circuit' model of **consciousness**. This has been popularised and further developed by **Robert Anton Wilson**. It defines the human brain as a form of bio-computer taking on 'programmes'. These consist of *imprints, conditioning* and *learning*. The first four circuits (*oral, anal, semantic* and '*Moral*') are traditional, common to all adult human beings; the second set of higher circuits is said to be much newer, less common and, indeed, literally futuristic, in that they *pre*capitulate future evolution.

The higher circuits are typically 'imprinted' via ecstatic or mystical experiences, or by advanced **yogic** discipline, ultimately tuning 'the brain into the non-local **quantum** communication system suggested by physicists such as **Bohm**, Walker, Scarfatti, Bell, etc.'[2]

Whether the Leary/Wilson model represents a genuine breakthrough in perception or merely new icing on an old cake remains to be seen. What is clear is that Leary, like many another, paid the price for preaching a gospel at odds with currently acceptable **paradigms** of reality.

1. *The Psychedelic Experience*, T. Leary and R. Alpert, University Books, New York 1964
2. *Prometheus Rising*, Robert Anton Wilson, Falcon Press, Las Vegas 1983, p. 20
3. *The Politics of Ecstasy*, Timothy Leary, Paladin, London 1970

LEIBNITZ, Gottfreid Wilhelm von (1646–1716) This 'greatest intellectual genius since Aristotle' (Macneile Dixon) claimed that matter is but another name for energy, and that space and **time** are inseparable. He said, 'The world is not a machine.

Everything in it is force, life, thought, desire. The world, in brief . . . is a living society'.

Believing that all living individuals always have existed and always will exist, he regarded death as a longer, profounder version of sleep, in which the continuity of the individual life is not wholly broken. He held the universe to be composed of monads; living and active beings who reflect the universe each from its own angle, each in its own degree.

From his *Monadology*: 'There is nothing waste, nothing sterile, nothing dead in the universe; no chaos, no confusions, save in appearance.'

LEMURIA (*See* **BLAVATSKY, CHURCHWARD, POLE SHIFT, STELLE GROUP, THEOSOPHY**)

LEONARDO DA VINCI (1452–1519) Leonardo, whose genius led him in so many **prophetic** directions, was clearly a believer in **reincarnation**. In his *Notebooks* he wrote: 'Behold now the hope and desire to go back to our own country, and to return to our former state, how like it is to the moth with the light! . . . this longing is the quintessence and **spirit** of the elements, which, finding itself imprisoned within the life of the human body, desires continually to return to its source.' And again: 'Read me, O Reader, if you find delight in me, because very seldom shall I come back into this world.'

LeSHAN, Lawrence (*See* **ESP, GARRETT, HEALING**) In 1964 this American experimental psychologist began to study ESP – out of conscience, not conviction. He felt he should explore every avenue in coming to terms with the way the mind influences the body. His scientific training had convinced him that ESP could not exist.

Instead, he found 'To my intense surprise . . . it became obvious that the material *was* valid. The standards of research were extremely high . . . The only alternative explanation . . . was that the greatest conspiracy in history had been going on for more than eighty years.'

He began work with the **medium** Eileen **Garrett**. He took three plastic boxes: in the first he placed a lock of hair from his twelve-year-old daughter's head; in the second, a tuft of hair from the tail of his neighbour's dog; and into the third a rosebud from his garden. Telling Garrett what was in each, he went behind a screen with the boxes. She put her hand through a narrow hole. Choosing a box at random, he put it where she could touch it. The first box she touched she correctly identified as containing his daughter's hair. She said, 'I think I'll call her Hilary – she'll like that.' LeShan was amazed. His daughter Wendy had once had a crush on a girl called Hilary, and had begged to be called that name. Next, touching the box with the dog-hair, Mrs Garrett correctly identified it, adding that the dog had a hurt paw, and had a Sealyham companion. The neighbours, only just moved in, later verified that the dog, a Welsh terrier, had been hurt, had a septic paw, and that its bone structure suggested the Sealyham breed to dog-fanciers. She also told him that the rose in the third box had suffered from acid soil. LeShan already knew this.[1]

Subsequently LeShan designed and tested his own concepts of **psychic healing**. These are recorded in his book *The Medium, the Mystic and the Physicist*. He divides healing into two categories: 'Type 1', and 'Type 2'.

Type 1 involves the **tranced** healer attempting to unite with the patient in a therapeutic bond designed to infuse the patient with a sense of being at one with the universe, enhancing his/her sense of individual uniqueness.

Type 2 requires a 'healing flow', whereby perceptible energy emanates from the healer's hands to the patient's afflicted area.

LeShan regards Type 2 as a 'cop-out'. Now a healer himself, he thinks that Type 2 (Subject to Object, rather than recognition of Type 1 Unity) involves a convenient *pretence* that 'a flow of energy is coming out of the hands and treating the problem'. He thinks it more likely that problems are solved by recognising an often uncomfortable but natural unity. Healer and patient both obey the same natural laws.[3]

1. *Beyond the Occult*, Colin Wilson, Corgi, London 1989, pp. 36–7
2. *Intangible Evidence*, Bernard Gittelson, Simon and Schuster, London 1987, p. 247
3. *The Science of the Paranormal*, Lawrence LeShan, Aquarian Press, Wellingborough 1987

LETHBRIDGE, T.C. (1901–71) (*See* **DOWSING, GHOSTS, GHOULS**) Honorary Keeper of Anglo-Saxon Antiquities in Cambridge University's Museum of Archaelogy and Ethnology for many years, in 1957 Tom Lethbridge wrote *Gogmagog*, in which he claimed that **Druidism** and **Brahmanism** share a common origin, and that Britain's ancient **religion** was worship of the earth mother (**witchcraft**). Enraged reaction perhaps hastened his 'retirement' to Devon. Here, pursuing an interest in dowsing, a 'witch' told him that a **pendulum** dowses better than a rod and conveys more complex information.

Experimenting, he found specific substances reacting to 'rates' defined by the length of cord between the dowser's hand and the pendulum itself. Silver reacted at the twenty-two-inch 'rate', grass at eighteen, truffles at seventeen, cowpats and dung-beetles at sixteen. A *painting* of a dung-beetle reacted at sixteen inches.

Even odder, he found that objects handled by folk long dead reacted at rates reliant on the emotions and sex of those who had handled them.

Flint implements dated 3500 BC gave male (twenty-four inch) or female (twenty-nine inch) rates for their makers or users. Supposed slingshots from Wandlebury hillfort gave the fourteen-inch rate for silica, also the twenty-four-inch male rate and the twenty-seven-inch rate (the thought put into their use). Pebbles from a nearby beach reacted only at fourteen inches – but when hurled violently at a nearby wall *all* of them reacted at twenty-four or twenty-nine inches depending on whether he or his wife Mina had thrown them. Abstract phenomena also reacted. Light, sun, fire and red at ten inches; life, earth, white and electricity at twenty inches; **Moon**, water, green and sound at thirty inches; death, sleep, cold and black at forty inches. These suggested a purposeful universe. Rates to forty inches implied the first upward circle of a evolutionary spiral. Items in this range had a corresponding, but weaker, rate *beyond* forty inches. Nothing ended at the forty-inch 'death-rate', but continued in a second whorl.

'Brain and mind are not the same thing,' he wrote. 'Mind can work in many **dimensions**. Brain can only function in three.'[1]

The work of other dowsers with his 'rates' suggest that these lengths vary from dowser to dowser, yet that his basic intuition may be sound.

He saw ghosts as **electromagnetic** recordings imprinted in the 'fields' of specific sites. Damp places, carrying 'naiad-fields', take on such imprint. 'You see television ghosts walking about every day and think nothing of it,' he commented. 'Why then is it so strange if you see a picture of someone who isn't there at the time?' Television, he added, 'is only a man-made copy of something which happens naturally on another level of human consciousness.'[2] So too he explained **ghouls** as 'the result of a terrible mental strain projected into another dimension', and lodged in the 'naiad-field' of a stream or the 'dryad-field' of a tree.

Pendulum-dating Cornwall's Merry Maidens **megalithic** circle, with one hand on a megalith and the other holding the pendulum, his hand 'received a strong tingling sensation like a mild electric shock and the pendulum itself shot out until it was circling nearly horizontally to the ground. The stone itself which must have weighed over a ton, felt as if it were rocking and almost dancing about.'[3] Concluding that 'bio-electronic force' energises such megaliths, he wondered: were they erected by the 'Sons of God': extraterrestrials who (Genesis vi, 2), stranded on Earth following a 'war in heaven', guided landing spacecraft via such beacons?

Even as he wrote *The Legend of the Sons of God*, **Von Däniken**'s *Chariots of the Gods* (1969) became a bestseller. Unaware of Von Däniken and of **'ley** hunters' like John **Michell**, he died soon after.

He also proposed that **Stonehenge**'s bluestones came not from Prescelly in Wales but from Tipperary in Eire, being floated round Land's End slung between boats, the water displacing their weight – a logical explanation of the old tale of how **Merlin** brought the 'Giant's Dance' from Ireland.[4]

In his last book he commented, '. . . variants of ideas like mine are held by many people all over the world; but relatively few are prepared to write things which can lead others to regard them as crazy. It is perfectly fair. Many regard Darwinian Evolutionists as too simple to be allowed loose on humanity; but few dare put this on paper.'[5]

1. *A Step in the Dark*, T. C. Lethbridge, Routledge Kegan Paul, London 1967, p. 71
2. *Ibid.*, p. 73
3. *The Legend of the Sons of God*, T. C. Lethbridge, Routledge Kegan Paul, London 1972
4. *Ibid.*, p. 3
5. *The Power of the Pendulum*, T.C. Lethbridge, Arkana, London 1984, p. 2

LÉVI, Eliphas (1810–75) (*See* **MAGIC, QABALAH, TAROT**) A Paris shoemaker's son expelled from the church for heresy, Alphonse-Louis Constant became a radical journalist. Abandoned by his wife after their two children died, in 1850 he met Polish **occultist** J. M. Hoene-Wronski (1776–1853), who claimed to know ultimate truth. Eliphas Lévi (as Constant now renamed himself) accepted Wronski's belief that practice of **ritual** magic can lead to semi-divinity. In 1856 he published his *Dogma and Ritual of High Magic*. Returning to Roman Catholicism, he initiated a magical revival influencing **Bulwer-Lytton**, the **Golden Dawn** and others. He wrote widely on Qabalah and Tarot while accepting dubious texts and claims, asserting that in all ancient teachings 'are found indications of a doctrine which is everywhere the same and everywhere carefully concealed'. Though influential, he never scrupled to claim invented sources as factual.

In 1854 he tried to evoke the spirit of Apollonius of Tyana, a **magus** of the first century AD. By his own account, after three weeks of meditation and dieting, he set about the ritual, clad in white, burning appropriate incense by which the long-dead magician might build himself a body.

'Three times, with closed eyes, I invoked Apollonius. When I again looked there was a man in front of me, wrapped from head to foot in a shroud . . . I experienced an abnormally cold sensation, and when I endeavoured to question the phantom I could not utter a syllable . . . a fainting sensation came so quickly over me, that I sat down, whereupon I fell into a profound lethargy accompanied by **dreams** of which I had only a confused recollection when I recovered consciousness . . .'

Lévi later spoke of the episode as 'drunkenness of the imagination'; warning against such practices as 'destructive and dangerous'. He said they led to 'exhaustion, and frequently a shock sufficient to occasion illness'. Even so, he influenced later occultists. Aleister **Crowley**, born the year he died, claimed to be his **reincarnation**.

Even A. E. **Waite**, not famed as a rigorous thinker, in translating Lévi's books, warned the reader that Lévi was prone to overuse of his imagination.

1. *The Occult*, Colin Wilson, Grafton, London 1979, pp. 423–8

LEVITATION Most of us while asleep have experienced 'flying **dreams**', or the sense of a tremendous lightness. Our feet barely touch the earth as we bound along.

But this happens only in dreams. Or does it?

In 1603 Giuseppe Desa was born in Italy, a sickly, vacuous boy given to 'ecstasies' and ascetic practices. Aged seventeen he was accepted as a Capuchin but soon dismissed, being unable to concentrate. Taken in by a Franciscan order near Copertino he became a monk. One day, in ecstasy at prayer after mass, he floated off the ground and landed on the altar. Taken to see the Pope, again in rapture he levitated. Persecuted by a hostile superior, he lost his gift for two years but regained it when enthusiastically received in Assisi. Tales of his power spread widely and though for twenty-five years he was banned from all public services, he levitated not only before the Pope and his fellow monks but before Europe's titled heads and the philosopher **Leibnitz**. Calling these spells 'my giddiness', he is also said to have been able to lift heavy weights and to make others float. Fortunately for him, the church decided that his levitations were the work of God. As he was dying after a lifetime spent at prayer, the doctor treating him noted that Brother Joseph was floating six inches above the chair. He died saying he could hear the sounds and smell the scents of paradise: 104 years later he was canonised as St Joseph of Copertino.

The great mystic St Teresa of Avila (d.1582) also suffered involuntary levitations. When she felt an 'attack' coming on she would beg the sisters in her convent to hold her down. Feeling 'as if a great force beneath my feet lifted' her up, she said the levitations had at first filled her with 'great fear', and that 'After the rapture was over, I have to say my body seemed frequently to be buoyant, as if all weight had departed from it, so much so that now and then I scarce knew my feet touched the ground.'

Such ecstatic denial of gravity is not limited to those in holy orders. The nineteenth-century **medium** Daniel Dunglass **Home** was, among his other talents, the most famous levitator of all. Like St Joseph, he was a sickly child. His first recorded levitation was unsought. Present as medium at a séance in Connecticut in August 1852, suddenly (reported F. L. Burr, editor of the *Hartford times*) he was 'taken up into the air . . . He palpitated from head to foot with the contending emotions of joy and fear . . . Again and again he was taken from the floor, and the third time he was carried to the ceiling of the apartment, with which his hands and feet came into gentle contact.'

Home often repeated this feat in a public career lasting thirty years. On one famous occasion, witnessed by Lord Adare, Captain Charles Wynne, and the Master of Lindsay (later the Earl of Crawford), he floated out of one window of a London house and back through another. Attempts have been made to discredit the witnesses by quoting discrepancies in their accounts of the event – but even if this case is set aside, there are statements by hundreds of other people who on many occasions saw Home levitate, usually in broad daylight. Neither **fraud** nor any species of **hypnotism** or mass suggestion exercised by Home was ever proved. Home himself said he was lifted up by '**spirits**'. 'I feel, no hands supporting me,' he wrote. 'I am generally lifted up perpendicularly; my arms frequently become rigid, and are drawn above my head, as if I were grasping the unseen power which slowly raises me from the floor.' Though later able to levitate at will, on occasions it apparently occurred without his being aware of it.

But what of photographic evidence? Cypriot Magus **Daskalos** suggests that the 'Indian Rope Trick' involves not levitation but the capacity to generate **illusion** – convincing, but still illusion. What the human senses witness the camera does not.

Yet on 6 June 1936 the *Illustrated London News* published photographs showing levitation by an Indian **yogi**, Subbayah Pullavar. Entering a small tent before 150 witnesses, he was photographed lying in the tent holding a cloth-wrapped stick. The witnesses withdrew. Some minutes later the tent was removed. Subbayah was suspended horizontally a yard above the ground, in deep trance, his right hand resting lightly on the cloth-wrapped stick. After four minutes in this state, photographs being taken from all angles, the tent was re-erected. Through its thin walls photographer P. Y. Plunkett saw the yogi's body appear to sway then slowly descend, still horizontal, taking about five minutes to move the three feet from the top of the stick to the ground. Back on the ground, 'his assistants carried him over to where we were sitting and asked if we would try to bend his limbs. Even with assistance we were unable to do so.'[1]

The ancient world offers tantalising hints of a lost science involving not only the power of levitation (lifting one's body) but of **teleportation** (levitating objects). From **Egypt** to the Andes, from Baalbek to **Stonehenge** tales persist that cyclopean building projects were undertaken by means of a '**magic**' science, perhaps involving sound and the manipulation of magnetic currents, whereby huge stones were moved great distances then set precisely in place. Some of the blocks forming Syria's Baalbek platform are seventy feet long: moving these, as with the blocks found in mountain-top cities, would strain or defeat modern resources. Take with such evidence the tale of the **Druid** Mog Ruith and his flying machine of stone, or of how **Merlin** removed the Giant's Dance from Ireland to **Stonehenge**, and the many tales of levitating rocks (like Oxfordshire's Rollright Stones) found in Britain, and there is at least the suggestion of some definite system of knowledge, now long lost, by which levitation was once routinely accomplished.[2]

Or is it lost? **David-Neel** reported how in Tibet she saw a lama using a novel – or ancient – form of locomotion: 'The man did not run. He seemed to lift himself from the ground proceeding by leaps. It looked as if he had been endowed with the elasticity of a ball and rebounded each time his feet touched the ground. His steps had the regularity of a **pendulum**.'[3]

So, if trance or ecstasy are involved in levitation, perhaps 'flying dreams' are not unreal, but half-buried memory of power latent in us all.

1. 'The art of levitation', Lynn Picknett, *The Unexplained*, Orbis partwork, London 1983, pp. 346–7
2. *The New View over Atlantis*, John Michell, Thames and Hudson, London 1983
3. *Magic and Mystery in Tibet*, Alexandra David-Neel, Abacus, London 1977

LEY LINES (*See* **EARTHWORKS, GEOMANCY, MEGALITHIC MYSTERIES, UFOs**) Controversy over ley lines began one June day in 1921 when Hereford brewer and magistrate Alfred Watkins, riding out near Blackwardine, paused on a hilltop. Meditating on the landscape below, 'in a flash' he saw through the modern patterns of cultivation to an ancient web of lines linking antique sites and sacred places. As John **Michell** describes it: 'Mounds, old stones, crosses and old crossroads, churches placed on pre-Christian sites, legendary trees, moats and holy wells stood in exact alignments that ran over beacon hills to cairns and mountain peaks. In one moment of transcendental perception Watkins entered a magic world of prehistoric Britain, a world whose very existence had been forgotten.'[1]

Marking out sites on a one-inch-scale Ordnance Survey map, Watkins found his perception confirmed. Over short stretches of land up to nine or more such sites would lie in exact alignment. Some lines extended for miles across neighbouring maps, often ending on a peak, or converging with other leys (as he called them) at old sacred sites. Avoiding mystical interpretation (while admitting their association with sacred wells, groves, etc.), he thought them remnants of salt traders' routes laid down in the Neolithic era – thus the title of his *The Old Straight Track* (1925). This and his *Ley Hunter's Manual* (1927) made ley-hunting a popular craze.

Archaeologists hit back. Insisting civilisation began in Mesopotamia, that ancient Britons were ignorant savages, and that all straight tracks had been built by the Romans, they denied all evidence to the contrary. O. G. S. Crawford called Watkins' work 'valueless'. Orthodox wrath increased as it became clear that leys were more than traders' tracks. Evidence that many leys combine to form exact geometric figures laid down over vast areas was bad enough; worse was the discovery that some major British leys carry on into Europe! Not even after Professor Alexander Thom's exact surveys of stone circles during the 1960s proved beyond doubt the sophistication of their ancient builders would the Establishment back down. Professor Stuart Piggott even claimed on TV that 'only professional archaeologists can put forward ideas about prehistory'.[2]

Professional archaeologists remain unimpressed not only by the British evidence, but by the growing evidence that such systems have existed worldwide since early times, from **Aboriginal** 'Songlines' to China's '**dragon**-paths', the mysterious lines at **Nazca** in Peru, or the **Serpent**-Mound in Ohio, USA.

Responding to the criticism that chance alone would provide a number of points in alignment over any stretch of land, ley hunters tightened their criteria. To be acceptable, a ley must join at least five sites known to be ancient. This left Britain spider-webbed by leys. Even so, Crawford's claim that the hypothesis is supported by 'no great evidence' remained tenable so long as data-collection remained haphazard. Prior to the 1980s, the only systematic survey was by John Michell. His study of Cornish sites (see *The Old Stones of Land's End* 1974), unearthed twenty-two leys aligned with 'rifle-barrel accuracy' between fifty-three 'valid' (proven prehistoric) sites. By computer-analysis, Chris Hutton-Squire and Pat Gadsby confirmed all but two of his alignments and added another twenty-nine. One stone, at Sennen near Land's End, had no less than seven alignments running through it.[3]

That such alignments do exist can now be doubted only by those with a vested interest in doubt. As to the more '**paranormal**' claims that leys constitute a neolithic energy-grid, there is *some* evidence for this.

In 1969 John Michell, summarising existing ley research in his *The View over Atlantis*, noted similarities between European leys and Chinese *lung mei*, or 'dragon paths', said to carry a geomagnetic energy that fertilises the earth, much as **ch'i** energy vitalises the human body. The implication was that leys conduct a force which ancient man knew how to tap, divert, augment and utilise, and that (eastern) dragon-**myths** refer to the seasonal motion of this energy. Meanwhile Aimé Michel linked leys and ancient sites to UFOs; **dowser** Guy Underwood connected underground water and associated energy effects with neolithic barrows and henges. The emerging picture of an ancient global energy-grid caused academic derision.

In the 1970s the situation began to change. Imperial College physicist Eduardo Balinovksi, working with dowser Bill Lewis, used a gaussmeter to measure the magnetic field at a megalith near Crickhowell, Wales. Lewis had claimed that the stone emitted a force detectable by dowsing. To his surprise Balinovski found Lewis was right: a measurable magnetic anomaly centred on the stone.[4] 'The people who put (the stone) there', he said, 'knew about its power, even if they didn't know about **electromagnetism**.'

In late 1977 *The Ley Hunter* magazine called a meeting of scientists, dowsers, electronic technicians and others to set up a project to study the forces associated with the ley systems and some megalithic sites. The work of the subsequent 'Dragon Project' is described elsewhere (*see* **megalithic mystries**). To date the question as to the nature and function of leys remains open. Certainly they seem to have been connected with utilisation and channelling of the seasonal flow of geomagnetic energy that 'snakes' through the earth: thus the dragon and serpent symbolism. Only one thing is sure: those who created and maintained the ley system were *not savages*.

1. *The New View over Atlantis*, John Michell, Thames and Hudson, London 1983, p. 23
2. *Needles of Stone Revisited*, Tom Graves, Gothic Image, Glastonbury 1986, p. 50

3. *Ibid.*, p. 51
4. *Earth Magic*, Francis Hitching, Picador, London 1977, pp. 105–6

LIGHTNING CALCULATORS (*See* **BRAIN MYSTERIES**) That many '**paranormal**' phenomena originate in right brain activity seems likely. The left brain analyses, the right intuits patterns which the left denies as spurious. But how else to explain 'lightning calculators', who instantly or rapidly solve complex mathematical questions, often when very young, without education or mathematical training?

Take Zerah Colburn. Born in 1804 to a farmer in Vermont, USA, aged five (unable to read, write or recognise any number written on paper) he performed incredible feats of calculation. Aged six, he was put on show in Boston. Aged seven, he was asked: 'What number multiplied by itself will produce 998,001?' In four seconds he answered '999'. In England, aged eight, at one performance: 'He was asked the square root of 106,929, and before the number could be written down he immediately answered 327. He was then requested to name the cube root of 268,336, 125 and with equal facility and promptness he replied 645.'[1]

Later, asked if 4,294,967,297 is a prime number (one indivisible by any other whole number) instantly he replied that it could be divided by 641.[2]

Asked how he did it, he said he had no idea. He was as much in the dark as anyone. The answers just came into his mind. At the time he did not know how to multiply or divide – at least formally, on paper. Admirers sponsored his mathematical education. His talent declined. Thinking about what he was doing interfered with it.

Karl Friedrich Gauss, whose nineteenth-century work on electrical theory remains influential (he died young in a duel) was three when he told his father, who was struggling with wage calculations, 'Father, the reckoning is wrong.' Truman Stafford (a professor of astonomy at twenty) when aged ten took a minute to calculate in his head the multiplication of a sum with an answer of thirty-six figures. Yet once he received formal mathematical education he too lost much of this ability. Likewise Richard Whately, a nineteenth-century Archbishop of Dublin: a calculating genius when aged five to eight, he lost the talent once corralled into the left-brain educational straitjacket.

Does the hormonal confusion of puberty depress this talent?

Many other examples are available – Willem Klein, who on 27 August 1976 in 163 seconds mentally calculated the seventy-third root of a number of 499 digits (6,729,235, as confirmed by a computer); or George Bidder, born in 1806 the son of an English stonemason and, like Zerah Colburn, exhibited as a 'lightning calculator', who said, 'If I perform a sum mentally it always proceeds in visible form in my mind; indeed I can conceive of no other way possible for doing mental arithmetic.'[3]

Knowledge so derived by right-brain **intuition** (if this is its source), remains largely inexplicable to reason. Yet we fail to value or protect those who manifest it. Easier to call it freak, than see it as evidence of another path of knowledge perhaps latent *in us all*.

1. *Superself*, Ian Wilson, Sidgwick and Jackson, London 1989, p. 43, after E. W. Scripture, *American Journal of Psychology*, 4 (1891) pp. 1–59
2. *Frankenstein's Castle*, Colin Wilson, Ashgrove Press, Bath 1980, p. 72
3 *op. cit.* ref. 1, pp. 43–6

LILLY, John C. (*See* **DOLPHINS**, **LEARY**, **NEAR-DEATH EXPERIENCES**) In 1972 Dr John Lilly, an American neurophysiologist already known for his work with dolphins, published *The Centre of the Cyclone*, an account of his experiences with LSD and **inner space** exploration. Though in some ways he pursued Leary's path, and though attacked for similar reasons, Lilly has since remained academically functional, though controversial.

Accidentally injecting himself with detergent foam after a bad LSD trip, Lilly tells how he went into coma and 'left his body', in which state he 'met other beings, **entities**, or **consciousnesses**', including two beings like guardian **angels** whom he had met before when anaesthetised. They said they were always with him but that he could perceive them only when close to bodily death. In this heightened state (as was **Jung** in his near-death experience) he was aware of past and future as part of the present.

Like Leary and **Wilson** (**Colin**), and much like **Gurdjieff**, he thinks of man as 'a human bio-computer'. In our natural state we live our lives as robots, responding to external stimuli and obeying our 'basic programming' without question.

Where Leary proposed an eight-circuit model of consciousness, Lilly proposed nine levels. Everyday consciousness is one level: above it are four *positive* levels; below it four *negative* levels. He claims to have experienced all nine. Of the positive levels, the first arises through an interest in something (work); the second is a 'blissful' state, a sense of 'belonging', as when falling in love; the third, of deeper significance, is the level of *paranormal* powers and **out-of-the-body experiences**; the fourth is the level of ***samādhi***, **illumination**, union with the divine.

Lilly's negative levels mirror the positive. The first involves common feelings of pain, guilt, fear; the second invokes feelings of isolation, of being trapped in a meaningless world; the third is a purgatory in which the mind is wholly focussed on misery; while the fourth is a negative *samādhi*, 'the deepest hell one can conceive'.

Borrowing Gurdjieff's idea that the universe consists of seven distinct levels of vibration, and that according to one's vibratory rate one is more or less 'free', Lilly also adapted Gurdjieff's numbering of these levels. He labels Gurdjieff's 'earth level', alias 'ordinary consciousness' or 'the bio-computer', forty-eight, the first positive level as twenty-four, and so on to *samādhi*, three, the Trinity. Likewise the minus or negative levels start at ninety-six and so proceed to ever 'heavier' states in which the mind is bound down by an ever greater number of oppressive 'laws' contingent on the level and the mental inability to escape it. According to this system, the lower you fall, the less control you have over your own destiny, and the more likely it is that personality will splinter into a multiple state. Conversely, upward motion through states twenty-four, twelve, and six to three confers an increasingly unified identity ultimately indistinguishable (because realised) from the ground of Mind.

Insisting that LSD is useful only as a way to learn about these states, when LSD was prohibited Lilly turned to **hypnosis**, **meditation** and suchlike techniques to continue his research.[1]

1. *The Centre of the Cyclone*, John C. Lilly, Paladin Books, London 1973

LOCH NESS MONSTER (*See* **ALIEN ANIMALS**) Prehistoric plesiosaurs, giant eels, slugs, **hallucination**, hoax? Whatever the truth, the Loch Ness Monster still eludes positives identification even when pursued by submarines, sonar and powerful flashlights.

Occupying the north part of Scotland's Great Glen, a fault running from Loch Linnhe to the Moray Firth, Britain's largest freshwater loch is deep, dark and cold. Fifty-two feet above sea level, it is twenty-two and a half miles long, one and a half miles broad at most and, in places, up to 820 feet deep. A reading of 975 feet at one point was recorded in 1969. Its dark peaty waters and steep banks restrict the growth of rooted plants; potential food sources consist mainly of fish, plankton and detritus on the loch floor. It is connected to the sea by the River Ness to the north: to the south by the Caledonian Canal.

In April 1933 two local hoteliers saw 'an enormous animal rolling and plunging' in the loch by Abriachan.[1] Their story appeared in the *Inverness Courier* on 2 May. By October, with over twenty sightings reported (including one of the 'Monster' crossing a lochside road), the story was international news. Most sightings reported an unknown animal with long neck, tiny head, and huge black body, as indicated by the famous photographs taken in April 1934 by London surgeon R. K. Wilson, who claimed only to have photographed an object moving in the water. Zoologists were baffled.

The earliest reported sighting dates from Adamnan's seventh-century *Life of St Columba*. He tells how, in AD 565, Columba dismissed a monster that rose from the loch with 'a great roar and open mouth'. A thousand years later, telling of the death of Scotland's last dragon after a 'sair tussle', a chronicler added, 'No one has yet managed to slay the monster of Loch Ness, lately seen'. Further sightings in 1771 (the 'water-kelpie'), 1889 and on other occasions went unpublicised. Only after 1933 were many local folk willing to admit, 'There's many a queer thing in that loch'.[2]

The modern search has provided no body, floating or beached. Doubters ask why, and also ask what such a colony of animals (nobody claims there is but one, near-immortal 'monster'), would feed on. Loch Ness is sparse both in plankton and aquatic vegetation: a herbivorous beast would have a hard time surviving. But salmon and sea-trout are plentiful: many sightings are made off the mouths of rivers in spate: reports of salmon exhibiting bursts of high speed suggest a fish-predator in pursuit. Otherwise virtually all the evidence comes from eye-witnesses. Though many are of known probity (and sobriety), the evidence to date remains imperfect. Hoaxes have not improved the case. Yet the presence in the loch of an unknown, adapted marine fish-predator would not be so remarkable if not for the lack of physical evidence. If it exists, is the monster reptile, mammal or fish?

A popular 'scientific' theory is that a family of prehistoric reptiles (plesiosaurs?) may once have been cut off from the sea and stranded in the loch. Impossible? The discovery of 1938 in the Indian Ocean off Madagascar of a living coelecanth, until then thought dead seventy million years ago, proved the possibility of such survivals. Such a family might have strayed into Loch Ness long before the last Ice Age and adapted to the cold water – the lower depths remain all year round at a constant 42°F (5.5°C).

Environmentally a mammal seems more likely. But long-necked seals, which might account for some sightings, breed on land, while the need to breathe would surely result in more surface activity and thus sightings.

The beast *has* been seen on land – reports suggest something larger than a seal. Local opinion indicates a species of giant eel or slug; while some sonar evidence, of contacts rising from then returning to the bottom, is consistent with the behaviour of eel or the European catfish. Likewise the beast's apparent tendency to surface in calm hot weather is consistent with the behaviour of bottom-dwelling fish such as the catfish.

That there is *something* in Loch Ness has convinced naturalists like Gerald Durrell (he calls the evidence 'incontrovertible'), Peter Scott (with Rines he coined the came *Nessiteras rhombopteryx*: see below) and David Attenborough, who supports the notion of a giant eel.

Yet as a whole the academic establishment denies the beast. Without bodily evidence, this is understandable. But the way in which every new sighting or photographic proof is ascribed to hoax, drunkenness, insanity or hallucination suggests a preconceived desire to disbelieve.

In 1972 Robert H. Rines of the Academy of Applied Science, Boston (MIT), teamed up with the Loch Ness Investigation Bureau. Setting up underwater sonar linked to a camera with a flashlight designed to take pictures once every fifty-five seconds so long as any large moving object remained in photographic range led, on 8 August 1972, to colour photographs apparently showing a diamond-shaped paddle or flipper, four to six feet long, of a rhomboid shape (thus the suggested name: *Nessiteras rhombopteryx*, although this has also been revealed as a perfect anagram of 'monster hoax by Sir Peter S.! see **Cosmic Joker**). Sonar records also recorded the presence of a large moving body. Such evidence then and later was dismissed by zoologists of London's Natural

History Museum as being of 'small gas bubbles' produced by 'the larvae of phantom midges'.[3]

Phantom midges? This is inventing **ghosts** to deny their existence! Yet again, the basic problem: that anomalous phenomena are denied due to vested interest in a particular belief system. Whoever sees anything denied by scientific or social preconception is denounced as a drunk or a **fraud**. Yet who has seen an electron or a quark? Which brings us to F. W. Holiday.

In August 1962 this English naturalist saw the monster. It looked like a black overturned boat. In *The Great Orm of Loch Ness* he claimed Nessie to be a type of giant slug.[4] Noting Britain's many 'worm' legends, and the revulsion with which such creatures were regarded, he examined other tales of loch-monsters in Connemara in Eire, concluding that Nessie is similar to the Irish 'peiste' (Latin: *pestis*: English, *pest*). He also concluded that such creatures represent **archetypes** of **evil**, existing and created at least in part in and by the mind of the beholder.[5]

This seems hard on the many witnesses who report (usually to their own disadvantage) seeing what they did not expect to see. Yet it may help to explain the hostility of the scientific fraternity which, as Gerald Durrell said, when faced with evidence that 'something large and unknown exists in the loch . . . nervously takes refuge behind a barricade of ripples, leaping salmon, shadows, dead stags, logs of wood and what must surely be the most agile and acrobatic strings of otters ever seen . . .'[6]

Loch Ness is not alone in hosting monsters. Similar ambiguous creatures are reported in many lakes not only in Scotland (Loch Morar), but the world around, from Connemara to Canada (Okanagan Lake, British Columbia) and the USA (Flathead Lake, Montana), from Russia (Lake Labynkr, Lake Vorota) to Australia, where in Lake Modewarre lurks the monster locally called Bunyip.

Wherever such beasts are reported, the human reaction is one of dread, and unwillingness to speak of them.

1. *The Loch Ness Story*, Nicholas Witchell, Corgi Books, London 1989, p. 29
2. *Ibid.*, p. 70
3. *Alien Animals*, Janet and Colin Bord, Granada, London 1980, p. 30
4. *The Great Orm of Loch Ness*, F. W. Holiday, Faber and Faber, London 1968
5. *The Dragon and the Disc*, F. W. Holiday, Sidgwick and Jackson, London 1973
6. *op cit.* ref. 1, Foreword by Gerald Durrell

LODGE, Sir Oliver (1851–1940) (*See* **SPIRITUALISM**) Twice President of the **Society for Psychical Research** (SPR), physicist Sir Oliver Lodge was for years a sceptical investigator. He was persuaded at last of the reality of life after death by a case involving his youngest son Raymond. Early in September 1915, with his son an infantry officer in the trenches, Lodge received a letter from Boston **medium** Leonore **Piper**. Her message came purportedly from F. W. H. **Myers** (a co-founder of the SRP who had died fourteen years earlier). It referred obscurely to a poem by the Roman poet Horace about a tree being struck by lightning.

A week later Lodge learned that Raymond had died in action. During the following weeks several mediums relayed messages seemingly from Raymond. Lodge remained unconvinced even when his wife, anonymously at a séance by the medium Mrs Osborne Leonard, received a message from 'Raymond' to say he had met various of his father's friends. Asked to name one, 'Raymond' said 'Myers'. On 27 September 1915, again incognito, Lady Lodge consulted the medium A. Vout Peters, whose guide, 'Moonstone', declared, 'Not only is the partition so thin that you can hear the operators on the other side, but a big hole has been made.'

Lodge was astonished by the similarity of this message to a passage he had written in his *Survival of Man*. At the same séance 'Raymond' referred to a group photo that included himself and mentioned a walking-stick. The Lodges knew of no such photo, but on 28 November the mother of an officer in Raymond's regiment wrote saying her son had sent copies of a group photo that included Raymond. Did they have a copy? If not, she would send one.

Before the photograph arrived Lodge visited Mrs Leonard to ask about it. Through her guide, 'Raymond' said it had been taken outdoors, that he had been sitting down, and that someone had wanted to lean on him.

From this information given via two mediums Lodge wrote a description of how he thought the photo should look. He posted this description to J. Arthur Hill, his secretary for **psychical** matters. On 7 December the photo arrived. It showed twenty-one officers in front of a hut – nine standing at the back, seven seated in the middle, five squatting cross-legged on the ground in front. Raymond, second from the right in the front row, had a walking stick lying across his feet: the officer behind was resting a hand on his shoulder. Lodge was finally convinced. Both mediums had spoken of the photo before Lodge knew it existed, thus ruling out **telepathy**.[1]

Other members of his family sought proof via Mrs Leonard. They too were convinced by the detail 'Raymond' gave. When Lodge published his account (*Raymond, of Life and Death*), many dismissed it as the delusion of a grieving father. Yet it went through six editions in a month, and twelve editions in all before in 1922 being updated by *Raymond Revisited*.

Long before **Lethbridge**, Lodge suggested that **ghosts** may be a kind of 'photograph', an imprint of strong emotions in matter. 'On a **psychometric** hypothesis,' he wrote in *Man and the Universe* (1908) 'the original tragedy has been literally *photographed* on its material surroundings, nay, even on the ether itself, by reason of the intensity of emotion felt by those who had enacted it; and thenceforth in certain persons an **hallucinatory** effect is experienced corresponding to such an impression.

1. *Afterlife*, Colin Wilson, Grafton, London 1987, pp. 141–2

LOURDES (*See* **FATIMA, HEALING**) On 11 February 1858 Bernadette Soubirous, a peasant girl from the obscure village of Lourdes in southern France, had a vision of a young girl, later identified by the local priest as the Virgin Mary. During the ninth of eighteen such visions, before a huge crowd, the apparition told her to dig in the muddy earth. She uncovered a spring which still flows, yielding 27,000 gallons (123,000) litres) a day. Today, over four million pilgrims visit Lourdes every year, many seeking cure in the healing waters of the spring, convinced that the Virgin herself caused it to flow. Investigating claims of miraculous cures, the Medical Bureau at Lourdes has substantiated sixty-five since 1858, many more being claimed. Of those accepted as 'miraculous', a recent case is that of Delizia Ciroli, a seventeen-year-old Sicilian girl. Given in 1982 only three months to live (she had cancer), within a few days of her return from Lourdes she was walking again, all trace of disease gone.

Once again: divine intervention? Or the hidden powers of the mind?

LOVELOCK, James (*See* **GAIA**)

LULL, Ramon (1235–1315) (*See* **ALCHEMY**) Claiming to have found an Art based on fundamental natural patterns which by analogy could be applied to all arts and sciences. Lull hoped to reach an understanding of the nature of God. A system built, as he believed, on elemental patterns combined with divine patterns formed by 'Dignities', the Lullian Art was dynamic and methodical, its concepts continually changing according to their varying combinations between the 'patterns'.

At one time Seneschal of Majorca, legend says that this Muslim-born **alchemist** became a Christian having found and drunk the elixir of life. Seeking out his beloved and begging her to drink the elixir too, he found her in agony with cancer and wishing only to die. Grieving, he wandered the world seeking death but condemned to live until at last God relented and he was released by being stoned to death. So runs the tale.

More prosaically, his chief aim was, by basing his art on principles recognised by **Islam**, Judaism and **Christianity**, to convert all to Christ. This aspect of his work was forgotten, but his Art remained influential as an early attempt to develop methodical thought, using diagrams and letter notations. Both Bacon and Descartes knew of it. Yates claims that the European search for scientific method began with him. Carefully avoiding use of images of the stars in his 'elemental astrology', he insisted that his Art was based on 'natural reasons'. Yet its claim to be a universal key inevitably led it to be seen as a prefiguration of the **hermetic** and **Qabalistic** philosophies of the Renaissance, while the legends about Lull show that, despite his disclaimers, he came to be regarded as a **magus**.'

1. *Lull and Bruno: Collected essays Vol. 1*, Frances A. Yates, Routledge Kegan Paul, London 1982, pp. 4–7

LUNG MEI (*See* **GEOMANCY, LEY LINES**)

LYCANTHROPY (*See* **WEREWOLF**)

M

MABINOGION (*See* **CELTIC MAGIC, MYTH**) First collected and published under this title by Lady Charlotte Guest in the nineteenth century, the eleven tales of the *Mabinogion* were preserved in two Welsh collections, the *White Book of Rhydderch* (written down *c.* 1300–25) and the *Red Book of Hergest* (*c.* 1375–1425). Derived from the bardic oral tradition, parts of the tales go back to the dawn of the Celtic world.

Consisting of *The Four Branches of the Mabinogi* (literally: *the four parts of the tale*), *The Four Independent Native Tales* and *The Three Romances*, the core of the work lies in the Four Branches, telling of the supernatural life and death of the hero Pryderi, and the magical history of the Children of Llŷr and the Children of Don.

Rich in **Celtic magic** and original **Arthurian** myth, the tales tell of the King of the Underworld changing places with an earthly king to beget a wonder-child on a mortal woman; of **spells**, **visions**, **shape-shifting** and the magical desolation of the land; of Blodeuwedd the woman conjured out of flowers and her betrayal of Lleu Llaw Gyffes; of the intrigues of Rhiannon and Arianrhod. Templates for subsequent British folklore and fairytale, these fantastic tales offer a profound insight into the beautiful, magical, grotesque, poetic imagination of the pre-Christian Celts.

Though perhaps containing some historical elements, the Mabinogion is best regarded as folk-myth of a high order, rich in **symbol** and psychology.[1]

1. *The Mabinogion*, trans. Gwyn Jones and Thomas Jones, Dent. London 1949

MACLEAN, Paul (*See* **BRAIN MYSTERIES**)

MAGI (*See* **ZOROASTRIANISM**) The *magi* were the philosopher-priests of the Persian Zoroaster (*c.* fifth century BC). Later the term (particularly in its singular form: *magus*) came to be applied to 'wise men' in general, especially to those involved in **hermetic**, **occult** or magical practices. The terms 'magic', 'magician', and 'imagination' also derive from this root.

MAGIC Magic is the art of influencing the external world (and the magician's own mind) by will and imagination combined. In this context 'imagination' is the mental faculty of forming images of objects or **entities** not immediately present to the senses; 'will' refers to the force of intention directed and focussed by the conscious mind. Thus magic involves creating clear mental images, sustaining them by concentration, and projecting them (by various means designed to maintain and increase the focus) into reality.

The essence of this ancient system is a belief that the external world reflects the inner spiritual realms, and that external effects proceed from forces originating in the **spirit** realm within which Man (Sanskrit *manas*, 'mind') is said to exist. Identification and invocation of such forces (visualised as guardian **angels**, **demons**, etc.) may thus through imaginative demand produce desired effects. Distracted by the trials of the material outer realm, our inner perception is usually occluded or scattered: successful magical working demands preparatory rites and purifications to steady the mind, focus imagination and direct the will.

The practice of magic is ancient and may represent the first deliberate attempt by humankind *mentally* to grasp and control the external world. Thus cave-paintings of deer, bison and other animals as found at Lascaux are probably magical in intent: by painting the image of the beast the artist-hunter sought to 'capture' its **soul** (and identify with it) on the spirit plane, intending thus to invoke successful hunting. The essential process has not changed. To harm someone, a **'black' magician** may make a wax image of that person, ideally incorporating their hair or fingernail-parings. By sympathetic correspondence, destruction of the image is said to result in harm to the victim. The malign intent is channelled through the image. But if the force is deflected by the victim or by a protector, it rebounds on the magician with equal power (*see* **Kahunas**). The force, unleashed, has to go somewhere.

Use of blood-sacrifice or sexual rite in some types of magical working may imply not depravity but recognition that normally inaccessible unconscious powers may thus be most effectively and potently invoked. Moral considerations (as in the application of atomic theory in science) may lead to the exclusion of some types of working as too dangerous or ethically improper; but such concerns of themselves do not affect the potency of the methods. Poet Robert **Graves** once said that men (no doubt women too) unconsciously employ a form of magic as an aid to seduction: they focus their will and imagination on overcoming the will of the desired one to gain sexual union.[1] That **Gurdjieff** was consciously able to direct his will in this way was reported by an American woman novelist seated next to his table in a restaurant. He began to inhale and exhale in an odd way: when she caught his eye, she said, 'I suddenly felt as if I had been struck right through my sexual centre. It was beastly!'[2]

Stan **Gooch** has suggested that magic and **psychic** powers are associated with the 'old brain' or **cerebellum**, and were well-developed in **Neanderthal man**. Certainly such power seems to be a 'lunar' or right-brain faculty, or at least to be channelled through the right-brain. If so, no surprise that 'magic' is denied by left-brain 'solar' reason, which proceeds by deduction and manipulation, not by induction and imagination. *Science* and *magic* both aim to control the natural world but proceed by means as different as day and night. Perhaps in time each will see the other as complementary.

Crowley defined 'magick' as: 'the science and art of causing change to occur in conformity with the Will'. Dion **Fortune** modified this to: 'Magic is the art of producing changes of **consciousness** in accordance with the Will.' The latter is the commonly accepted definition today.

1. *The Occult*, Colin Wilson, Grafton, London 1979, p. 197
2. *Ibid.*, p. 524

MAGNETISM (*See* **CYCLES, DOWSING, ELECTROMAGNETISM, HYPNOTISM**) Magnetism remains mysterious. Like other early civilisations, the Chinese knew of the natural magnetic properties of lodestone, or **magnetite** (a form of iron oxide), and thought it magical. Around 200 BC their fortune-tellers used magnetised 'spoons' (shaped after the Big Dipper) on their divining boards. Later the piece (no longer resembling a spoon) was mounted on a pin or floated on water – thus the first magnetic compass. By the sixth century AD they magnetised iron needles by stroking them with lodestone: in the eleventh they discovered how to magnetise iron by raising it to red heat then cooling it while it was held in a north-south direction.[1]

The first European use of the term 'magnetic pole' is in a treatise by the military engineer Peter Peregrinus, dated 1269. Nothing more appeared for three centuries. In 1600 William Gilbert (born 1540) published *De Magnete*, explaining how every magnet has an 'invisible orb of virtue' around it. He assumed that the Earth itself is a giant magnet.[2]

Nearly 200 years later Anton **Mesmer** (1734–1815) formulated his theory of 'animal magnetism'. Positing a **psychic** ether that pervades space, he said the heavenly bodies cause tides in this 'fluid', which as magnetism flows through the world and all organic bodies. The free movement of these bodily tides results in health; their blockage causes sickness. Trying the effect of magnetism on his patients, he concluded that their bodies were magnets, and that he could cure them by moving the stagnant 'fluid' round their bodies by using magnets (and his hands). Believing this as much as they did, cures *did* occur. His fame grew. He devised an apparatus: a vat of dilute sulphuric acid from which protruded magnetised iron bars to which his patients clung. It worked, but the process was violent. It involved convulsion and hysteria, and (claimed moralising sceptics) overmuch bodily contact – explained as necessary to spread the 'animal magnetism'.

In 1784 a committee of Parisian doctors concluded that though Mesmer possessed strong powers of suggestion, there was no evidence of a magnetic fluid. Mesmer was denounced as a **fraud**: his self-confidence (and thus no doubt his capacity to heal) declined long before he died.

Are his cures explicable solely by suggestion or hysteria? Mesmer did not understand the force he tapped, yet sensed that much illness arises from a blockage of natural forces, and that cure involves setting those forces in motion again. For a century thereafter, 'magnetisers' (**hypnotists**) were ignored by science: the magnetic aspect seemed to have been a red herring.

But was it? The *essence* of magnetism remains a mystery, but ever more is known about its *effects*, particularly in conjunction with electrical current. Gilbert was right: the Earth *is* a magnet, due to the movement of liquid materials in the core. But though huge, it is weak: the geomagnetic field varies between 0.3 and 1.5 gauss; a child's magnet has a strength of 1000 gauss. Yet **electromagnetic** storms and geomagnetic fluctuations affect climate, vegetative growth, animal and human health and behaviour. **Dowsers** associate crossings and 'whorls' of underground water with electromagnetic anomalies: **megaliths** and mediaeval cathedrals alike were erected over such nodes; animals seek out or avoid such places as healthy or harmful; while some UFOlogists connect **UFO** manifestations with magnetic fluxes affecting the brain's electrical and perceptual activity.

Czech physicist Zaboj V. Harvalik has demonstrated (*see* **Dowsing**) that some people can sense magnetic field changes as minute as 1/1,000,000,000 of a gauss. In 1975 biologist Richard Blakemore found that tiny organisms he was examining in a drop of water oriented themselves by reference to magnetic fields; each drop possessing a minute string of magnetite beads (as found in the heads of homing pigeons). A growing plant photographed by time-lapse photography is seen to move in an upwards spiralling motion taking its head through a full circle every twenty-four hours – a response to the daily magnetic cycle. Mental breakdown is more frequent at times of high sunspot activity. It begins to look as if all organisms in the world are sensitive to local and general magnetic fields, not just in broad outline, but down to minute variations.[3]

So perhaps the megalith-builders did tap a force which, waxing and waning, promoted fertility of land and people. Electromagnetic anomalies are associated with many megaliths: for generations childless people went to standing stones, dolmens, or hill-figures like the Cerne Abbas Giant in search of sexual fertility. Is this the origin of the **Grail**-myth that the sexually wounded Fisher King means a sterile land? Tests of **healers** still suggest that positive *attitude* (in both healer and patient) is the primary healing factor, but maybe Mesmer was not so far off. Dr Robert Becker in the USA has found that applying weak electric current to a site of illness speeds up healing and stimulates the beneficial effects of **acupuncture**. Application of electric potential can cause partial regrowth of amputated limbs in *mammals*: application of magnetic fields higher or lower than usually experienced has been shown to: retard aging, cure or reduce some forms of cancer, produce higher activity rates, stunt offspring into the third generation, delay reaction time to stimuli – in short, to influence (for good or ill) almost all biological functions.[4]

Mesmer's 'animal magnetism', and magnetism itself, may be but a manifestation of a vital universal force everywhere known but differently identified as **ch'i**, **prāna**, **odic** force, and **orgone** or **etheric** energy.

The case (as with so much else) remains wide open.

1. *Cambridge Illustrated History of the World's Science*, Colin A. Ronan, Book Club Associates, London 1983, pp. 172–3
2. *Ibid.*, p. 315
3. *The Secret Life of Humans*, Stan Gooch, Dent, London 1981, pp. 98–101
4. *Ibid.*, pp. 102ff

MAGNETITE (*See* **BIRDS, MAGNETISM**)

MAHABHARATA (*See* **HINDU MYSTERIES, KALI YUGA**) Fifteen times longer than the Bible, this ancient (*c.* 1000 BC) Indian epic poem (its name means: 'The Great History of the Bharatas', or mankind) is an enclopaedia of **myth**, folklore and spiritual tradition. The *Bhagavad Gita*, recounting Arjuna's dialogue with Krishna on the eve of battle between the Pandavas and Kauravas, is but a part of it. That it may tell of advanced ancient technology is described elsewhere. Note that 'Mab' (in *Mabinogion*) and 'Mahab' (in *Mahabharata*) both mean 'history' or 'tale'. Do Celtic and Brahminical tradition and language possess a common origin?

MALACHY OF ARMAGH (1094–1148) (*See* **PROPHECY**) In 1139 an Irish Cistercian monk, Malachy of Armagh, travelled to Rome and there left a list of 113 Latin titles, one for every Pope who would reign from his day henceforward. The titles supposedly forecast the names of the popes, their birthplaces, offices held, crests and major events during their pontificates. Thus for Pope John XXIII (1958–63), he offered the designation *Pastor et Nauta* ('Shepherd and Sailor'). John, before becoming Pope, had been Patriarch of the port of Venice. The term *nauta* was earlier used in motto forty-seven, for Pope Gregory XII (1406–15), who was born in Venice.

John's successor, Pope Paul VI, was designated *Flos Florum*, or 'Flower of Flowers'. In mediaeval Church symbology the 'flower of flowers' was the lily. Paul's papal crest sported three lilies.

For John Paul I, who died after only thirty-four days in office, the motto was *De Medietate Lunae*, 'From the Half (or Crescent) Moon.' His secular name was Albino Luciani – in Latin, 'pale white light'. Also the full moon fell exactly halfway through his brief reign (of one month, or moon), meaning that he both succeeded to the papacy and died at the time of the half moon.

His successor, Pope Paul II, was born 18 May 1920; the day of a total eclipse of the sun. His motto is *De Labore Solis* – 'From the Labouring Sun' (or 'Eclipsing' or 'Rising' Sun). Given that he is the first Pope from eastern Europe, the latter interpretation is possible.

Following *De Labore Solis*, only two titles are left on Malachy's list. For the next Pope the motto is *Gloria Olivae*, the 'Glorious Olive'. This may refer to the Benedictine Order, also known as the Olivetan. Or it may mean an olive branch in his insignia, or that his papacy will coincide with a time of peace. If so, it will be brief. The last Pope is identified as *Petrus Romanus*, 'Peter of Rome', like the first. Malachy devotes to him an entire paragraph. The Latin translated reads, 'In extreme persecution of the Roman Church shall sit Peter the Roman, who will feed his flock amid many tribulations; which things being done, the City of the Seven Hills will be removed, and the Great Judge will judge the people.'[1]

This apparently portends a time of dire transformation, perhaps global. Is Malachy reliable? Some commentators think so. Yet it should be pointed out that: (1) cardinals responsible for choosing each successive Pope will know of the prophecies; (2) each new Pope can choose to fulfil the prophecies; (3) Within each given lifetime it is not impossible to find events that fit each given motto.[2]

1. *Rolling Thunder*, Joey R. Jochmans, Sun Books, New Mexico 1980, pp. 26–9.
2. *Nostradamus*, David Pitt Francis, Aquarian Press, Wellingborough 1985, pp. 16–17

MALTWOOD, KATHERINE (*See* **GLASTONBURY**)

MANDALA (*See* **MEDITATION**) An eastern meditation aid of intricate **symbolic** design, usually circular within an inscribed square, possessing a centre, symmetry, cardinal points, and harmonious balance of all elements, often with a fourfold subdivision in which individual motifs are mirrored. The centre (abode of the deity), is contained in the square (palace of inner being), itself surrounded by a set of circles, each representing different levels of **consciousness**.

Jung rediscovered and employed the mandala as a device aiding **psychic** integration. In *The Secret of the Golden Flower* he and orientalist Richard **Wilhelm** present it as therapeutic tool and meditative technique generating focussed concentration and as conducive to attainment of mystic exaltation.

Mandala-forms occur naturally both in microcosmos (subatomic pattern, snowflake) and macrocosmos (spiral nebulae, Planet Earth). Pre-invasion **Tibet** mastered this art of reflecting cosmic creative principle. Mandalas are usually represented pictorially, but may be sketched mentally, or (as in Navaho sandpainting) drawn on the ground. The temples, churches, and stone circles of the world emphasise the basic *integrative* principle.[1]

1. *Mandala*, José and Miriam Argüelles, Shambala (Routledge Kegan Paul), London 1972

MANDELBROT, BENOIT (1924–) (*See* **CHAOS THEORY**)

MANNING, Matthew (1955–) (*See* **HEALING, POLTERGEISTS**) Born three weeks after his mother suffered a severe electric shock, this English psychic was a centre of **poltergeist** activity from the age of eleven. At boarding school he was almost expelled due to the chaos caused by flying objects and moving furniture. At sixteen this phase ended: he began producing **automatic writing** (in languages unknown to him, like Greek and Arabic) and drawing in the styles of Dürer, Goya and Picasso. Watching Uri **Geller** spoon-bending on TV early in 1974, he tried it and immediately succeeded.

In 1976 **Colin Wilson** studied both Geller and Manning. He noted that both lacked full control of their powers, and that electronic equipment in their vicinity manifested inexplicable faults. Dr George Owen, studying Manning's EEG chart as the **psychic** tried to bend a spoon **psychokinetically**, noted considerable theta activity in Manning's brainwaves. Theta rhythms are associated with violence and frustration. More interesting, his EEG chart showed the theta rhythms in phase with his alpha (relaxation) and beta (concentration) rhythms. Somehow he maintained a balance between violence, concentration and relaxation.[1]

Working with US scientists, in one test he killed cancer cells in a glass flask by concentration and laying on of hands. A photograph taken of him when he claimed to be producing healing energy shows a diffuse white radiance shining from his hands. Concentrating on someone across the room, a ball of this radiance, moving over the room, appeared on film. He also quietened or aroused hamsters in another room by thinking about them.[2]

Later he became a full-time healer. In 1980 a woman who had suffered chronic pain in her foot before and after operations to remove growths on her left foot sought his help. He told her she needed no faith, he had his own confidence. In two sessions, of fifteen and five minutes, he 'held first my foot, then the outside of my left thigh between his hands. His hands felt hot. . . . An hour later, it was clear that the big pain was not in the foot. The little pains still were, and the pain in the thigh remained.' After the second treatment: 'It was clear an hour or so later that the pain had gone.' Discomfort did not return, save when she felt tired.[3]

Notably, the polgergeist activity ceased once Manning began to learn to channel his power consciously. The ghost had been laid or earthed.

1. *Mysteries*, Colin Wilson, Grafton, London 1979, pp. 443–5
2. *The Secret Life of Humans*, Stan Gooch, Dent, London 1981, pp. 80–81
3. *The Power to Heal*, David Harvey, Aquarian, London 1983, pp. 137–9

MANTRA (*See* **MEDITATION**) The verbal (silent or spoken) equivalent of a **mandala**, a mantra is a word or phrase which, repeated over and over again, induces meditative calm. Usually associated with oriental esoteric practice, the best-known mantra is probably that associated with **Buddhism**, *Aum mani padme hum*, generally translated as 'Hail to the Jewel in the Lotus' (or: 'Amen the Thunderbolt in the Dark Void'). However the literal meaning is less important than the mind-stilling rhythm induced, and the fact that the syllables run easily from the end of the phrase back to the beginning again. The Catholic practice of telling beads on a rosary while saying *Ave Maria*s serves a similar function. So, on a less elevated or self-controlled level, do advertising jingles or popular songs that 'stick in the mind'.

MAP-DOWSING (*See* **DOWSING, PSYCHIC ARCHAEOLOGY**) That some dowsers can find what they seek simply by focussing on, or using a pendulum over, a map of the area, is mentioned elsewhere. But the faculty is so remarkable that it requires further comment. In his *Pendulum: the Psi Connection*, Francis Hitching describes an experiment undertaken in Britain with dowser Bill Lewis (who worked with physicist Eduardo Balinovski in establishing magnetic anomaly at the Crickhowell **megalith** (*See* **Ley lines**).

Aiming to locate ancient Native American megaliths in the USA by map-dowsing, Hitching obtained maps showing no ancient sites. Lewis was not shown the relevant map until the particular session began. Opening the map, Hitching would ask Lewis to locate the largest standing stone in the area, or to find a burial chamber accessible on foot. Using a pendulum, Lewis then 'felt' his way into the locale, verbally developing a detailed image of the site allegedly involved, describing it as if he were looking at it. At the end of several sessions, Hitching had a list of twenty-two sites and sixty-three specific predictions. As a control, John Stiles of the **Society for Psychical Research**, had on each occasion looked at the same map and made similar predictions (guesses) as 'check sites'.

Hitching went to the USA to check the predictions. Stiles scored one per cent correct predictions – statistically, chance level. Lewis scored thirty-five per cent on correct placing of site, and fifty-five per cent on accurate description of site.

An even more remarkable experiment in **psychic archaeology**, conducted by Jeffrey **Goodman** and Aron **Abrahamsen**, is described elsewhere.

Map-dowsing works – but how? Dowser-contact with the geomagnetic field cannot be involved here. A map is a ***symbol***. Can a *symbol* carry energy? Can focus on it (as on **mandala** or **crystal** ball) generate **clairvoyant** access to **Bohm**'s 'implicate order';

to the 'underlying reality' of the **Akashic Record**? **Jung** held that the **collective unconscious** contains knowledge of everything that ever happens. **Precognition** presents the same problem.

Not just the answers, but the correct *questions* remain unknown.

1. *Pendulum: the Psi Connection*, Francis Hitching, Fontana, London 1977

MASLOW, Abraham (1908–70) The son of a Russian Jewish immigrant to New York, this intuitive, inter-disciplinary psychologist studied Native American culture then taught psychology at Brooklyn College and Brandeis. Disinterested in the study of neurosis and weakness, he focussed on the processes resulting in healthy, fulfilled people whom he termed 'self-actualised'. He taught that the basic human need is for food and security; that satisfaction of this need leads to the urge for a mate; followed by the need for self-esteem and social acceptance. Satisfaction on all these levels results in the growth of 'meta-needs' – intellectual activity, art, philosophy, religion. People become mentally ill if some major blockage hinders this evolution – at *any* level. Thus obstructed, the will runs down, like a battery going flat. But if the way forward is open and there is a strong sense of purpose, the will becomes so highly charged that even minor satisfactions cause a spontaneous discharge or flash of pure delight. This he called the 'peak experience'. Regarding the essence of psychological health as the *activity of the will*, he considered peak experiences to be distinct from mystical experience but thought of their frequent occurrence as the natural heritage of *all* healthy people. That they are not more common is not due to our innate incapacity but to negative expectation. He noted that, as his students began to talk among themselves of peak experiences, they began having more of them.[1,2]

In other words, possession of a positive, well-defined self-image tends to produce that activity of the will whereby life is inherently meaningful, extraordinary and vital. But a vague or negative self-image leads to the robot of habit taking over: a sense of purposeless mediocrity results.

Maslow felt that **Freud** and his followers have 'sold human nature short' by their focus on the negative aspects of the human **psyche**, and that there are 'higher ceilings of human nature' than Freudians acknowledge. Yet he doubted that peak experiences may be induced at will: he thought of the state as a spontaneous 'bubbling over' of irrepressible vitality. **Colin Wilson** for one suspects he was wrong in this, and that we *do* induce peak experiences, yet by a process so subtle we fail to realise how we do it.[3]

Maslow's notion that human beings are *evolutionary* creatures, whose need for fruitful and creative activity is basic, has influenced fields as diverse as health care, business management, marketing and theology. Any society run on the negative assumption that people are stupid and selfish must fail: assume the opposite, he claimed, and the sky's the limit.

1. *Order of Assassins*, Colin Wilson, Panther Granada, London 1975, p. 46ff
2. *Beyond the Occult*, Colin Wilson, Corgi, London 1989, p. 294
3. *Ibid.*, p. 499

MASONRY (*See* **FREEMASONRY**)

MATHERS, Samuel Liddell (1854–1918) (*See* **ABRAMELIN, GOLDEN DAWN, CROWLEY**) 'At the British Museum Reading Room I often saw a man of thirty-six or thirty-seven, in a brown velveteen coat, with a gaunt resolute face, and an athletic body, who seemed, before I heard his name, or knew the nature of his studies, a figure of romance. Presently I was introduced . . . he was called Liddell Mathers, but would soon, under the touch of "The Celtic Movement", become MacGregor

Mathers, and then plain Macgregor. He was the author of *The Kabbalah Unveiled*, and his studies were only two – magic and the theory of war.'

So wrote poet W. B. **Yeats** who, introduced by Mathers to the fledgling Order of the Golden Dawn, soon became a member. Years later he fell out with Mathers, regarding him as 'unhinged', as perhaps he was. Given to extravagant claims of his contact with invisible 'Secret Chiefs' who had commissioned him to lead the Order, his assumption of the kilt and of fake Scots ancestry seems odd in one claiming knowledge of inner truth. Yet (as Yeats acknowledged) he was a remarkable individual. Walking in a field of sheep with actress Florence Farr, he said, 'Look at the sheep. I am going to imagine myself a ram' – with the result that the sheep ran after him.

His scholarship and psychological insight, as revealed in translations he made of *The Book of the Sacred Magic of Abramelin The Mage*, *The Key of Solomon* and *Armadel*, and in the **rituals** he wrote for the Golden Dawn, are as undeniable as his high flown, contentious, elusive, romantic nature. In many ways he typifies the 'magicians' of the era. He was as quarrelsome as Crowley, as over-imaginative as **Lévi**, as domineering as **Blavatsky** – and in one way or another he managed to fall out with all whom he failed to bully, impress, or badger.

Marrying Moina Bergson (daughter of the philosopher), he spent his later years in Paris, far from the Golden Dawn battlefield he left behind him in England, though seemingly supported by members who remained loyal.

He died in 1918, of influenza, or due to astral attack by his enemies – take your pick. Larger than life, he is due a biography.

MEDITATION (*See* **MANDALA, MANTRA, YOGA**) Like prayer, a process of cleansing the mind of daily preoccupation and self-interest by trained focus on the deeper, higher world of the **spirit**. Meditation may be considered in two forms, active and passive. The *active* form is more typical of West than East: it may employ preliminary breathing exercises to still the mind, then invoke controlled **visualisation** processes as a prelude to magical working. Energy is built up – 'Enflame thyself with prayer!' runs an ancient rubric. The purpose is to still the mind prior to some wordly undertaking. The passive form has no worldly goal. In Western **mysticism** as in the East it involves clearing the mind of any thought or intention whatever in order to focus on the Eternal. The process may be assisted by visual focus on a **mandala**, sub-aural chanting of a **mantra**, or by any other means that releases the mind from material preoccupation.

Physiologically the purpose is to synchronise the electrical activity of both the left- and the right-brain. This helps release hormones called endorphins, which function as natural opiates, stilling the mind.

In the ancient Indian *Upanishads* the following advice is given:

'Retire to a solitary place . . . protected from the wind and rain. The place . . . must be pleasing to the eye and quieting to the mind. Seated there, practice meditation and other spiritual exercises . . . Sit upright, holding the chest, throat and head erect. Turn the senses and mind inward to the lotus of the heart. Meditate on **Brahman** (God) with the help of the syllable OM . . . With earnest effort hold the senses in check. Controlling the breath, regulate the vital activities . . . you may see in vision forms resembling snow, crystal, wind, smoke, fire, lightning, fireflies, the sun, the moon. These are signs that you are on your way to the revelation of Brahman.

'As you become absorbed . . . you will realise that the Self is separate from the body and for this reason will not be affected by disease, old age, or death. . . . Know God, and all fetters will be loosed. . . . Meditate, and you will realise that mind, matter and Maya (*imaginative delusion*) are but three aspects of Brahman, the one reality.'[1]

1. *Upanishads*, Prabhavananda and Manchester, pp. 192–3

MEDIUMS (*See* **FRAUD, ROBERTS, SPIRITUALISM**) A Spiritualist term for human intermediaries passing messages between the living and the **spirits** of the dead. The practice is ancient. The Delphic **Oracle**, **shamans** and mediaeval **necromancers** all practised mediumship, commanding respect, fear or (in this *rational* era) disbelief.

For though belief in an **afterlife** has been universally held, mediums today are widely seen as charlatans despite contrary evidence as presented (during the first half-century of the Spiritualist upsurge) by eminent Victorians like **Conan Doyle**, **Crookes**, **Hyslop**, **James**, **Lodge** and **Myers**.

At first sceptical of events like **apports**, table-rapping, **levitation**, **psychokinesis**, production of ectoplasm, physical materialisations, spirit **possession**, direct voice-communications and messages from the dead, these men grew convinced of the reality of survival, even though fraud was common. Mediums holding séances in dim-lit rooms used many tricks. For example: sheeted masks to ape materialised spirits; cheesecloth hidden in the mouth to produce 'ectoplasm' (a term coined by French Nobel laureate Charles Richet to describe the transitory matter produced by mediums in physical materialisations); or hidden strings or wires tied to tables or chairs which, tugged, produced fake psychokinetic effects.

Such tricks persuaded sceptics that these phenomena are *always* due to fraud (for fame or gain). The case was not improved by the use of 'spirit guides' purporting to be deceased Red Indian chiefs or **discarnate** Tibetans. Nor did the cheating of genuine mediums like **Palladino** help. She hated the exhaustion involved in genuine work; her eroticism and open cheating seemed to prove her a fake. Sexual prejudice (many mediums being women) of a sort once leading to witch-trials also denied clear evaluation. Science was honestly masculine: mediumship and the whole business of talking to the dead seemed shady, lunar and disreputable.

Some mediums suffered fraudulent attempts to prove them frauds. Mina Crandon (alias 'Margery') took up **Houdini**'s challenge to produce genuine physical manifestations. She apparently succeeded, but Houdini was caught rigging the test against her. Others like **Garrett**, **Home** and **Piper** were not only never caught out, but produced so many phenomena and information unavailable by normal means that investigators like James, Hyslop, Lodge, and more recently **LeShan** and others, all concluded that genuine mediums have access to knowledge inexplicable other than by **telepathy**, or by the survival of death of those with whom contact is sought.

This conclusion demands consideration, not blinkered rejection.

Whatever material orthodoxy insists, many people still believe that mediums provide contact with those 'on the other side', so much so that today mediums still command massive media attention despite the efforts of James **Randi** and others to prove them frauds.

Born a blacksmith's daughter, Londoner Doris Stokes saw herself as an ordinary person. As did Eileen Garrett, she dismissed **occult** glamour: her attitude to her strange talent was down-to-earth. Known as a ***clairaudient*** (one who hears) rather than a ***clairvoyant*** (one who sees), in the 1970s and 80s on stage and TV she relayed messages 'from the dead' to questioners in her audiences. Though these messages often seemed trivial, their recipients rarely doubted her communication, due to her accurate delivery of names and details known to themselves alone. To her, the spirit world was as real as the physical: she offered consolation to the bereaved, or urgent advice.[1]

Today too, the process called *Channelling* combines mediumship with **New Age** thought to put clients in touch with their personal 'guide', said to be a spirit between incarnations with whom the client has had close **karmic** contact in a former life. In a recent survey, author Joe Fisher concludes (following disenchanting personal experience) that any fakery involved in such work is caused not by the mediums but by the spirits. He concludes that they are not benevolent, but are unhappy souls denying their deaths, clinging to earth-life by tormenting the living, and not to be trusted.[2]

This reminds not only of ancient and mediaeval suspicion of **demonic** activity, but of the theory of **Keel** and others that *some* **UFO** entities are mischievous **astral elementals**. Yet many cases suggest that life after death is as varied and prodigal as is material life here on Earth. There is no simple answer to a complex set of questions.

1. *Voices in My Ear*, Doris Stokes, Futura, London 1980
2. *Hungry Ghosts*, Joe Fisher, Grafton, London 1990

MEGALITHIC MYSTERIES (*See* **CRYSTALS, EARTHWORKS, MAGNETISM, LEY LINES, UFOs**) What *are* the stone circles? Lunar observatories? Calendrical calculators? Navigational beacons erected by extraterrestrials? An ancient, world-wide system for storing and amplifying geomagnetism to fertilise the earth? Or stone needles tapping earth-energy as **acupuncture** needles tap **ch'i** energy in the human body? How about early-warning beacons of earth-shifts built by post-**Atlanteans** obsessed with the danger of earthquake convulsion?

Megalithic theory is so varied and speculative it is hard to know where to start. *Megaliths* ('big stones') are found the world over, either singly (menhirs, standing stones), in circles (**Stonehenge**), rows (Carnac), or as dolmens (usually two uprights and a crosspiece or lintel). In whatever form they are often found to be aligned on other such sites locally or even internationally distant. Typically they stand over crossings of underground water, near geological faults, or tectonic intrusions where the geomagnetic field exhibits measurable anomalies. Usually they consist of stones with a high crystal content generating piezoelectric effects. Such stones were often transported considerable distances to be erected at the chosen site.

Brittany and the British Isles are especially rich in these legacies of a culture which, over two millennia from the building (*c.* 3500 BC) of the New Grange tumulus in Ireland to the final phase of construction at Stonehenge (*c.* 1600 BC), erected mounds, barrows and megaliths for a purpose remaining largely unclear. Nothing is known of the builders save via their enigmatic works which, whatever else they were, demonstrate knowledge of Pythagorean geometry 2,000 years before Pythagoras. Indeed, a legend claims Pythagoras received knowledge from Abaros, priest of a 'winged temple' in Hyperborea, the northern land. Some say the winged temple was Stonehenge, others that it was Callanish in the Outer Hebrides. Yet Abaros must have lived a full millennium after climatic deterioration led to the downfall of megalithic culture *c.* 1500 BC and to a 1000-year hiatus or 'dark age' in Britain and in northern Europe even as Graeco-Roman Mediterranean civilisation developed.

When the Celts arrived in Britain they found only memories of those who had built the circles. The Irish *Book of Invasions* records memory of the magical race, the Tuatha de Danaan. Legends of **giants** and **dragons** cloaked megalithic sites: not even the **Druids** knew their full meaning. The stones were said to be alive; (in Gaelic: *fir chreig*, 'false men') who 'walked' or 'danced' by night, or (as with Oxfordshire's Rollright Stones) sometimes went down to nearby rivers to 'drink'. Odd lights and will-o'-the-wisps – **spirits** of the dead? – were sometimes seen hovering above them.

Early Church missionaries found it hard to deter folk from worshipping at these 'sacred' sites. In AD 601 Pope Gregory ordered Abbot Mellitus: 'that the temples of the idols in Britain should not on any account be destroyed. Augustine must smash the idols, but the temples themselves must be sprinkled with holy water.' Yet difficulties persisted. Saints trying to found a new church away from such sites would find that the **'Devil'** had by night removed the stones from the new site back to the old **pagan** mound or hilltop. What the Church called devilish was loved and respected by the successors of the megalith-builders. Many churches, especially in Wales, ended up being built within megalithic circles (Llanerfyl, Ysbyty Confin), or on pagan mounds

Mary Evans Picture Library

(Cascob, Darowen), or on alignments of standing stones and other ley-features (Darowen, Old Radnor).

Yet gradually the old landscape was absorbed within the new, the old **myths** within **Christianity** and as such both were largely forgotten. Lights continued to flicker above the stones which, seen as the Devil's work, were broken up for new building. Much of the great circle at Avebury was thus destroyed in the seventeenth century by farmers like 'Stone-killer Robinson'. Few enquired about the past until antiquarians like Aubrey and Stukeley initiated a new romantic interest in megaliths, which they thought **Druid** in origin. So **Blake** refers to 'Britain's ancient rocky Druid shore' and to the 'giant Albion' which, like Stukeley and John **Dee**, he saw hidden in the landscape. A 3000-year-old mystery was slowly worming its way back to the light.[1]

This romantic assumption of Druid origin persisted until, in the nineteenth century, a more scientific attitude displaced it. In the 1890s Norman Lockyer proposed the basic purpose of circles like Stonehenge and Callanish to be astronomical, individual stones marking the motions of sun and moon. In the early 1960s a Boston astronomer, Gerald Hawkins, fed Stonehenge data into a computer and showed the complex to be a sophisticated solar/lunar calendar: the later work of Professor Alexander Thom in surveying many British circles and single megaliths proved the geometric and astronomical precision of the megalithic system on a broader scale. Surveying Callanish on Lewis, for example, he found that the main temple and subsidiary circles in the land about form an exact elliptical relationship, and that the main avenue at Callanish could have been used for sighting on the moon to the south and on the star Capella to the north in 1800 BC – as earlier suggested by Somerville and Lockyer. Thom also found evidence of a common unit of measurement in megalithic construction, the 'megalithic yard', of 2.72 feet, employed not only in Britain and Europe but in North America.[2]

So far so good. Orthodox archaelogists disliked but could hardly deny (though they could ignore) the mounting evidence that the megalith builders had practised a coherent science involving knowledge of geometry, astronomy and unknown building techniques. That was bad enough.

Worse was the rising tide of fringe speculation and research suggesting that megalith-builders had not only knowingly tapped energies unrecognised or barely understood by modern science but had done so in a manner making nonsense of the orthodox belief in a linear development of human culture and in diffusion of culture from the Middle East.

The claims from the 1920s onwards by **occultists**, **dowsers** and ley line theorists that megalithic sites were central nodes in a system of 'sacred' science devoted to the amplification and distribution of 'earth-energies' unknown to science seemed absurd. The 'evidence' of folklore and Chinese **geomancy** was simply not considered. In 1936 the occultist Dion **Fortune** described 'sacred sites' as 'power centres' radiating 'lines of force'. This was as unacceptable as Katherine **Maltwood**'s claim, published in 1929, to have discerned a giant **zodiac** anciently carved into the landscape round **Glastonbury**. It was not just that such claims flouted current scientific understanding; they also flouted historical orthodoxy. The speculations of John **Michell** and Aimé Michel in the 1960s, linking megalithic sites and the ley system with UFO sightings, only widened the gap, as did the claim by Michell and dowsers like Guy Underwood that single standing stones were erected to mark places of exceptional magnetic force, often associated with healing. Once again folklore bore out the claim: science denied it.

By the 1970s a new generation of researchers, *au fait* both with occult theory and scientific method, began an attempt to heal the split by testing occult claims scientifically. Following the successful collaboration of dowser Bill Lewis and physicist Eduardo Balinovski in detecting (both by dowsing and by gaussmeter) magnetic anomalies at a monolith by Crickhowell in Wales, in 1977 those involved with *The Ley Hunter* magazine set up the Dragon Project – named after the **feng-shui** symbol for earth energies – to investigate unusual effects at megalithic sites.

Two programmes were set up: one measuring physical quantities such as electric potential; the other using **psychics**, with dowsing a link between these two very different techniques. In 1978 the project began work at the Rollright Stones in Oxfordshire. Early on anomalous radio signals were detected: in 1980 Bill Lewis repeatedly proved able, while placing his hands on one of the 'energy nodes' on the circle's tallest stone, to affect readings given by a voltmeter attached to points on the megalith.

Photographs of the Kingstone at Rollright in 1979 showed a hazy glow round the upper part of the monolith, with a 'streamer' effect rising at an angle from it. This effect manifested at three separate dawns. Photographs taken earlier or later (on the same reels of film) showed no such effect. Tested by a Kodak physicist, they showed no processing faults: no ordinary explanation was found; and attempts to reproduce the effects failed.

Biologist Harry Oldfield, having found that the human body energised by **Kirlian** electrophotography functions as an ultrasonic and radio 'beacon', in 1981 wired a Rollright stone to a Kirlian device, thus inducing electric current into the stone, which was also connected to a decibel meter (to check for ultrasound) and an oscilloscope. The oscilloscope showed an increase in the stone's electrical field when the sun rose. This effect has been repeated, but occurs only at dawn, and at no other time of day.

Research by Paul Devereux (1977) had shown that thirty-seven and a half per cent of leys studied nationwide manifested UFO activity somewhere along their lengths. With geologist Paul McCartney he later found all stone circles in England and Wales to lie within a mile of a surface fault or associated tectonic intrusion. In Brittany Pierre Mereaux showed the Carnac complex to lie on an intrusion surrounded by fault lines, its rows delineating magnetic field changes. Later research by Devereux suggested that aerial phenomena (such as bell lightning) may be caused by piezoelectrical effects produced by pressure on rock crystals (in standing stones) adjacent to fault lines.[3]

Thus a pattern began to emerge, connecting stone circles and individual stones with geological faulting, the 'shear force' of sun and moon crossing the horizon and anomalous aerial lights. Devereux has speculated that UFOs are terrestrial emanations connected with faults and the megalithic system. Such emanations, being **electromagnetic**, may influence the brain directly. This may begin to explain how UFO, **fairy**, **black dog** and similar phenomena often appear in a form appropriate to the cultural preconceptions of the witness. It may also be that the megalith-builders knew of such processes and used them to stimulate **visionary** or altered states of mind.

That megalithic energies were associated with fertility and healing is clear from folk-myth and made explicit by words put in the mouth of **Merlin** in Geoffrey of Monmouth's *History of the Kings of Britain*. Speaking of the Giant's Dance (Stonehenge), Merlin says, 'the stones possess mystical power and are useful for many healing purposes. The giants [who] brought them from Africa and placed them in Ireland . . . designed to take baths among them whenever they were stricken with illness. For they washed the stones and placed their sick in the water, which invariably cured them.'

One night in 1973 while at the Callanish circle on Lewis I touched one of the stones and received a shock. It was like being stung by a bee. I jerked my hand away. The event made no sense. Later I read **Lethbridge**'s account of receiving a similar shock while dowsing Cornwall's Merry Maidens circle. Odder still (given the tale that the bluestones of Stonehenge came not from Prescelly in Wales, nor even from Killaraus in Ireland from whence Merlin is said to have removed them, but from Africa), the Callanish stones, apparently, are *not local* to the remote Hebridean isle of Lewis.

Legend claims that a priest-king and his acolytes, wearing robes made of the skins and feathers of birds, came in ships with the stones and gangs of black men to erect them. A local man told me a legend that they had come from China! –

home of the healing (geomagnetic) 'dragon current'.

What to make of all this? Research of the kind outlined above suggests that many megaliths *do* possess energetic properties and *are* associated with phenomena of the sort long claimed by folklore. It also appears that indeed they were often brought over vast distance to sites the specific geological and energetic characteristics of which were well known. The picture begins to emerge of an organisation, possibly intercontinental in extent, devoted to the world-wide establishment of a healing and fertilising technology.

Speculation? Certainly. Impossible? Only those who designed and built the system know for sure – and they have been dead for 4,000 years.

1. *The New View over Atlantis*, John Michell, Thames and Hudson, London 1983
2. *Megalithic Sites in Britain*, Alexander Thom, OUP Oxford University Press, UK 1967.
3. *Earthlights*, Paul Devereux, Turnstone, London 1982
4. *The Legend of the Sons of God*, T. C. Lethbridge, Routledge Kegan Paul, London 1972

MEN IN BLACK (*See* **KEEL, John**) Some people claiming **UFO** sightings or contact subsequently report surreal visits by sinister beings usually termed 'Men in Black' (MIBs). Typically such visits occur so soon after the encounter that the subject (usually alone at home) has had no time to contact the media or authorities. Generally three in number, the visitors arrive in a large black car, often an out-of-date model, with licence plates which, later checked, turn out to be false. Usually men, they wear dark suits, hats, ties, shoes and socks but white shirts; are dark-complexioned, perhaps oriental and frail. Conforming to a stereotyped CIA image, they claim to be government agents or produce identity cards which also prove false. Their movements are stiff, their manner formal and cold, their stilted speech reminiscent of B-movie dialogue. Their interviews usually consist of an interrogation followed by a warning not to speak about the UFO encounter, or to abandon the enquiry.

This composite description is not invariable. MIBs may masquerade as journalists, insurance salesmen or (in America) USAF personnel; sometimes no threat is offered; or there is no personal visit, only a phone call; or there is no black car, only an abrupt appearance and disappearance.

One evening in September 1976 Dr Herbert Hopkins, consultant in a UFO **teleportation** case in Maine, USA, was alone at home. A man claiming to be a UFO researcher phoned to ask if he could visit to discuss the case. The doctor agreed. Switching on the back porch light, he saw the man already climbing the porch steps. There was no car; the phone call had only just ended. The man was black-suited, bald, had dead white skin, no eyebrows or eyelashes and wore lipstick. He told Dr Hopkins that two coins lay in the doctor's pocket. This was so. He asked Hopkins to put one coin on his hand. Hopkins saw the coin go out of focus then vanish. 'Neither you nor anyone else on this plane will ever see that coin again,' the visitor said. Having asked Hopkins to erase tapes of **hypnotic** sessions on the case, the MIB rose unsteadily. 'My energy is running low – must go now – goodbye.' He left the house towards a bright blue-white light shining in the driveway. Hopkins assumed this to belong to the visitor's car, though he neither saw nor heard it leave. In shock, he erased the tapes and abandoned the UFO case. He never heard from his visitor again. When his family returned, they found him sitting in the fully lit house at a table, a gun to hand. Marks in the centre of the drive, not those of car-tyres, vanished by the next day. The report by this respected doctor remains inexplicable.

No MIBs have ever been caught or interrogated. Is the whole thing a paranoid **myth**? All the reports are by individuals alone at the time. UFO theorist John Keel suggests that MIB behaviour is reminiscent of the '**fairy** hoaxes and games of an earlier epoch'. Author David Tansley suggests that MIBs are a form of **demonic psychic entity**. French researcher Jean Robin points out that many UFO manifestations seem to parody human expectations or achievements. Certainly, MIBs seem to parody Hollywood B-movies with their stilted dialogue and bizarre appearance. Two points emerge: (1) in all reports the MIB has access to information known only to the 'victim'; and (2) such visits are not limited to the modern UFO phenomenon but have been reported for centuries, and have usually been seen as diabolical.

Whether they be but **thought-forms** projected unknowing from the mind of the isolated percipient remains unclear. Surveying the phenomenon, author Hilary Evans suggests that MIB victims who have ignored or refused to obey the threat have not suffered in consequence. If MIBs exist, they operate out of their own realm and their power in this realm is limited.[1,2]

1. 'Who are the Men in Black?', *et. seq.*, Hilary Evans, *The Unexplained*, Orbis partwork, London 1983, pp. 510–13, 526–9, 578–580.
2. *Operation Trojan Horse*, John A. Keel, Abacus, London 1973

MERLIN (*See* **ARTHURIAN MYTH, MEGALITHIC MYSTERIES, PROPHECY**) Did this **archetypal** British **magus** and prophet ever exist? There may have been a sixth-century bard, Myrrdin, who fled into madness and exile in the Forest of Celydon (north of the Solway Firth) following the defeat of his king Gwenddolau in AD 573 at the Battle of Arderydd.[1] *This* historic Merlin, born of earthly mother and father, was no doubt a **seer**, influential in his time. But the Merlin of Arthurian myth is an archetype, not a person: the British Prophet *par excellence*, personifying many earlier magical themes as introduced by Geoffrey of Monmouth in his *History of the Kings of Britain* (1135) – the progenitor of all subsequent Arthurian romance, **Grail**-myth, and later attempts to marry Christian theology with **pagan** memory.

Merlin first appears as part of Geoffrey's elaboration of the **myth** of the semi-historical King Vortigern, remembered as a villain who, in the fifth century AD, collaborated with invading Anglo-Saxons. Usurping the British throne but driven back to Wales by the Saxons, he consulted magicians who told him to build a tower. He did but it kept collapsing. His magicians told him to seek a youth who had never had a father, kill him and sprinkle the stones with his blood to cement the unstable foundations. Merlin, a boy apparently born of union between a virgin and an **incubus**, was brought to Vortigern but told him his magicians were liars, and that under the tower was a pond, into which the foundations were sinking. Digging was done, and the pond was found. 'Command the pond to be drained,' said Merlin, 'and at the bottom you will see two hollow stones, and in them two **dragons** asleep.'

This was done. The red and white dragons, released, fought. And so Vortigern listened to Merlin, the true prophet, who then began to prophesy even as the contending dragon-powers (fertility denied) found release.

The tale of and prophecies of Merlin, as given by Geoffrey, form the basis for all subsequent Merlin-myth as developed by Grail romancers from Chrétien de Troyes (*c.*AD 1180) to Malory in the late fifteenth century.

The myth itself is a compound of earlier tradition: 'Merlin' is a state of mind, a way of knowledge and transformation. In Arthurian tale he often retreats from action, from the daylight waking mind, in time to return from the (unconscious) wilderness with a new insight that creates the Round Table, or sets in motion the Quest for the Grail. His absence is thus more important than his presence. Hidden deep in forest or 'hollow hills', and ultimately tricked into crystalline suspended animation by Nimüe, he is a metaphor of the magical processes underlying and informing mundane human life and death, love and hate, peace and war. His appearances are like the flash of **intuition** – mysterious, illogical, yet potent. His **daemon**-father is **Spirit**, his mother is **Gaia**. A magical gateway to the deeper levels of **psyche**, like Mercury/Hermes he moves between the conscious and unconscious worlds with equal facility, fertilising one with the other. He is neither dead nor alive, but expresses the power that creates both life and death, each relying on the other. He is not dead because he never lived in any form that dies. As such he (and any other equally potent archetype in other cultures) is reborn whenever called upon. Merlin lives in the mind.[2]

1. *The Quest for Merlin*, Nikolai Tolstoy, Sceptre, London 1988
2. *The Prophetic Vision of Merlin*, R. J. Stewart, Arkana, London 1986

MEROVINGIANS (*See* **KNIGHTS TEMPLAR, RENNES-LE-CHÂTEAU**)
The thesis that in 1982 made the book *The Holy Blood and the Holy Grail* a best-seller is as follows: Jesus Christ, the royal descendant of King David and thus literally King of the **Jews**, married Mary Magdalene, sired a family *before* his ministry began, escaped the Crucifixion, and *possibly* went with his family to France, where later his mummified body was *possibly* concealed in the region of Rennes-le-Château in the Corbières. Either way, his bloodline survived among the Sicambrian Franks, surfacing in the form of Mérovée (died AD 438), whose son (of the same name) became Frankish king in AD 448, thus founding the Merovingian dynasty of 'long-haired' kings whose *magical* blood was acknowledged as 'sang raal' or 'sang réal' – *holy* or *royal* blood.

This acknowledgement was common at the time. An aura of holiness seems to have surrounded the Merovingians. Ruling like eastern potentates, their polygamy uncontested by the Church and their wealth enormous, they were not required to *govern but simply to be*. As such, they were a threat to the new temporal order the Church wished to create. It is alleged that the Church knew full well that Christ had married the Magdalene but that to favour its own power had already rewritten gospels (Mark) or suppressed **Gnostic** texts (Thomas, etc.) which hinted that Jesus was the bridegroom at the marriage-feast of Cana, and that 'the disciple whom he loved the most' (his wife) was the Magdalene. Certainly Clement of Alexandria (second century AD) knew of Mark's secret gospel, while insisting on its denial. So it seems possible the Church knew that Christ's bloodline had survived in the Merovingians.

In AD 496 Mérovée's grandson, Clovis I (456–511) converted to Roman Christianity, agreeing to support the Church so long as it supported him as the 'New Constantine' who would preside over a 'Holy Roman Empire'. An indissoluble bond was thus created between Church and State: the Church acknowledging the sanctity of the Merovingian bloodline in return for its militant support of the Church's ambitions. During the following century this agreement was less and less to the liking of those who saw the Roman Church as a new political order. In AD 679 the Merovingian king Dagobert II (who threatened to become powerful) was assassinated with the collusion of Rome. The Merovingians, weakened, continued as Frankish kings until 751. In that year Childeric III was deposed by the Mayor of his Palace, Pepin the Short. Supported by the Pope, Pepin declared himself king. Childeric died in 754. The Merovingian (i.e. Christ's) blood-line was thought to have died out. At Christmas, AD 800, Charlemagne was tricked by the Pope into reluctant coronation as the first Carolingian king. The power-game of the Church had succeeded. From that time onward, the 'blood royal' was whatever the Church sanctified. Christ's blood had become irrelevant. So it is argued.

Yet the Merovingian blood-line survived. This was the great secret of the Middle Ages, giving rise to the coded tales of **Grail**-myth and **Arthurian** romance. The Holy Grail (*San Graal*) was the *sang raal*, or holy blood. The chalice dispensing it was the Magdalene's womb. This secret was kept alive by a mystical alliance, the Prieuré de Sion, of which the Knights Templar were a military arm, and which, the authors claim, survives today in order to protect and further the interests of the true blood royal of Christ.

If true (and much evidence is marshalled to support the claim) then the Roman Church connived at the extermination of Christ's descendants in order to guarantee its own interpretation of Christianity; i.e. to guarantee its own developing temporal power and authority, as based upon the doctrines of **Original Sin** and salvation through the Church alone. The importance of the claim lies in the fact that, if true, it means that European culture and thought for the last two millenia has been dominated by an interpretation of Christianity which not only has had little to do with Christ and his teachings, but which relies on the rejection and murder of both.[1]

1. *The Holy Blood and the Holy Grail*, Michael Baigent, Richard Leigh and Henry Lincoln, Corgi, London 1983

MESMER, Anton (*See* **HYPNOTISM, MAGNETISM**)

METEMPSYCHOSIS (*See* **REINCARNATION**) A term meaning the transmigration of the soul of a human being or animal at death into a new body of the same or a different species.

MICHELL, John (*See* **GEMATRIA, LEY LINES, MEGALITHIC MYSTERIES, STONEHENGE**) An English antiquarian and researcher whose 1969 publication of *The View Over Atlantis* led to a cult-revival of interest in megalithic mysteries, ley line research, **geomancy**, etc. His subsequent studies in gematria, **sacred geometry** and the inner meaning of **number** and measure, and his field research into megalithic technologies, have led to a range of books which are distinguished as much by their speculative power as by their careful presentation of fact, academic command of historical source-material, and imaginative unveiling of the practical meanings of **symbolic** texts.

Arguing that the shared features and common units of measure of stone monuments and ancient earthworks as found across the globe indicate the existence of a once-sophisticated and latterly forgotten worldwide system of applied knowledge, Michell has done as much as anyone to nail once and for all the false belief that our neolithic ancestors were idiots.[1]

1. *The New View over Atlantis*, John Michell, Thames and Hudson, London 1983

MIDDLE WAY (*See* **QABALAH**)

MILLENARIANISM The superstition that the 'end of the world' or '**Second Coming**' coincides chronologically with a thousand (or two thousand) year count since **Christ**'s alleged date of birth. At the end of AD 999 Europe's population went insane with dire expectation. Rich men gave away their wealth, the churches were flooded, there was weeping and wailing and gnashing of teeth. Come the dawn on 1 January, AD 1000, the rich men set about getting back their wealth, and everyone else resigned themselves to continued existence as usual.

Now a millennium later we are (in lands operating Christian chronology) subjected once again to the same fear of death by round number. Prophecies from **Nostradamus** on suggest AD 1999 or AD 2000 as cataclysmic years, dealing in terms of Second Coming, **Pole Shift**, nuclear war or other forms of the Ultimate Disaster. Few such round-number prophets of doom care to indicate that the round number of AD 2000 is appropriate only to Christians. **Jews**, Moslems, **Hindus**, the Chinese, Native

Americans and Scotch Rite **Freemasons** deal in entirely different chronologies with no such emotive impact.

MIND (*See* **CONSCIOUSNESS**)

MIRACLES (*See* **FATIMA, HEALING, LOURDES, MIRACULOUS ICONS**) A miracle is a marvellous event generally perceived both as beneficial and **supernatural** in origin. The divine power may be channelled through the **mediumship**, conscious or not, of saint, **shaman, magus** or innocent child. Typically, as at Fatima, Lourdes, or Medugorje, children perceive an entity later described as the Blessed Virgin Mary. **Apparitions** perceived by large crowds may ensue, accompanied by miraculous **healings** of the sick who *believe* in the miracle. Less frequently, those given up as dead, or dead already, are restored to life, as reportedly was Lazarus by **Christ**, or Christ himself after the Crucifixion. Miracles may also be associated with relics or icons connected with the saints or holy men of **Christianity** or other **religions**. In cases like the **Shroud of Turin**, the icon may be proved fraudulent, yet some may still claim it as miraculous. The power of *belief* appears to play an important role in the efficacy of miracles.

In essence, the miracle is a divine event, contravening or briefly suspending otherwise immutable natural law. By definition, no miracle is ever perceived as **evil** save by those denying its reality or lamenting its social or political effects. In the latter case, disbelievers are likely to condemn those perceiving the miracle as victims of 'mass **hallucination**'.

MIRACULOUS ICONS (*See* **STIGMATA**) How can plaster statues of **Christ** bleed, or images of the Madonna cry? For it seems, such phenomena do occur. In 1968 a 300–year-old wooden crucifix in a church at Porto das Caixas in Brazil began to bleed. Tested, the blood was found to be real. Nine years earlier the same thing occurred to a crucifix in the church of St Ignatius in Rome. In January 1981 a statue of the Virgin at Caltanisetta, Sicily, began to bleed from the right cheek. The same statue was said to have wept in 1974. These flows persisted under close scrutiny.

In April 1975 a plaster statue Christ belonging to Mrs Anne Poore of Boothwyn, Pennsylvania, began to bleed from the hands and continued to do so, especially on Fridays and holy days. Placed in St Luke's Episcopalian Church at Eddystone, Pennsylvania, this image 'bled as long as four hours', claimed pastor Chester Olszewski. 'I have seen the palms dry, then, minutes later have observed droplets of blood welling out of the wounds.'

Philadelphia doctor Joseph Rovito X-rayed the statue but found no trace of a reservoir or any other trick mechanism. As for the 'blood', it proved genuine, but with a low red cell count suggesting great age. 'It's so old we can't even determine the blood type,' Dr Rovito concluded.

In New Mexico in May 1979 a plastic-coated postcard-sized portrait of Jesus began weeping tears of blood. Bought years earlier as a memento by Mrs Kathy Malott for her grandmother, Mrs Willie Mae Seymore, the picture bled, 'just as if I had cut my finger,' said Mrs Seymore. Many people subsequently examined the portrait. The blood seemed to flow directly from the surface of the plastic. Tested at the Eastern New Mexico Medical Centre Hospital, the liquid proved to be 'honest-to-gosh, bona-fide blood'. The 'not too religious' Malott family changed its outlook, especially when Zach Malott dreamed Christ told him the blood was a sign of his **Second Coming**.

Interestingly, such liquids (blood and tears) appear not at random but at the sites associated with them. In images of Christ the blood runs from the hands and feet (nails), forehead (crown of thorns), and side (spear-thrust): the Virgin weeps from her eyes. What is going on? Certainly in some cases suggestible people anticipating such a '**miracle**' may perceive illusory tears or blood as real – but this was not so in the cases outlined above. Even if these manifestations are unconsciously created by the holy ardour of devoted worshippers, the mystery remains actual . . . and profound.[1]

1. *Phenomena*, John Michell and John Rickard, Thames and Hudson, London 1977

MONROE, Robert Allen (*See* **OUT-OF-BODY-EXPERIENCES**) A student of journalism and drama at Ohio State University, in 1937 Monroe went into broadcasting as a writer/director of radio documentaries. After World War II he founded his own successful company. Until 1958 his only unorthodoxy was to experiment with data-learning techniques during sleep. One Sunday, after one such experiment (with his family at church) he was seized by a 'severe, iron-hard cramp'. Three weeks later, again alone on a Sunday, while asleep he was struck 'by a warm light' from 'the sky to the north'. It shook him violently, leaving him immobile and scared. It kept occurring. His doctor said there was nothing wrong with him. Months later, with the vibrations still occurring, one night in bed before sleep he found his fingertips *passing through* the bedside rug and the floor beneath it. He felt a triangular chip of wood, a bent nail and sawdust. Next day he nearly cut a hole in the floor to find if the '**hallucination**' was true. Later, again in bed near sleep, the vibrations returned. He found himself floating up against the ceiling. Looking down at the bed, he saw his wife, asleep, and a second body. Shocked, he realised the second body was *his*.

Fearing death or madness, he fell back to his body and later consulted a psychologist friend who, mentioning **Hindu** notions of **astral** travel, told him to try it again. Despite his fear he 'began to experiment with this strange aberration, keeping notes of each event'. He told his wife, but not his young children. First he explored his familiar world to confirm that events he witnessed out-of-the-body were objectively real, not just **dream** or **hallucination**. Once, visiting a woman friend in her kitchen, she seemed to acknowledge him. To ensure she'd remember, he pinched her. She cried out. Later, 'in the flesh', he questioned her, but she remembered nothing. He asked about the pinch. Amazed, she showed him the bruise.

His range of 'astral' travel broadened. He developed techniques for leaving the body, such as 'rolling out', and identified three different realms or worlds that he habitually visited, which he called 'locales'.

Locale I is the familiar physical world – not, he asserts, an ideal plane for such travel. Familiar views are seen from unknown angles, and despite an automatic '**homing instinct**' (think of someone and you see them: think of somewhere and you're there), astral travel in Locale I is as hard as for a diver going deep without face-mask or oxygen. It can be done, but any stray image becoming even briefly dominant derails the prior intention. Establishing proof is also difficult. Trying to 'visit' **parapsychologist** Andrija **Puharich**, Monroe concluded that he had done so (his recollection of the room he'd visited proved accurate) but Puharich, as with the woman Monroe had pinched, later had no memory at all of the conversation (on the **astral plane**), even though Monroe clearly remembered it.

Locale II, as he describes it, resembles the conventional Purgatory for those newly dead. He calls it the *natural* environment of the 'Second Body'. It interpenetrates the physical world but is not of it. In it, 'reality is composed of deepest desires and most frantic fears': thought is literally action; it is that timeless world of bodiless mind described in the ***Tibetan Book of the Dead***, the realm we visit in **dream**, the natural environment of the **astral body** where personality moves after the physical body dies. Yet often the personality is unaware of its physical death, or is bewildered and anxious. Monroe describes the lower reaches of Locale II as peopled by 'insane or near-insane, emotionally-driven beings', including those still (physically) alive 'but asleep or drugged and out in their Second Bodies, and quite probably those who are dead but still emotionally driven'.

Once in Locale II he found himself in a 'park-like surrounding' where hundreds of people sat about looking disorientated, as if waiting for friends or relatives to take them on to their 'proper place'. He describes a Locale II meeting with a bewildered bedridden boy who asked, 'What do I do now?' and 'Where do I go?' Monroe tried to comfort him, but then had to return to the physical world. Next day he read in the local paper of a boy who'd died of a lingering illness just as he'd begun the experiment.

He comments that Locale II, though frequently full of the antagonisms characterising Locale I existence, is also inhabited by beings who appear ready and willing to assist those seeking to 'move on'. Guardian **angels**? Our own higher selves? **Near-death** researches suggest that this experience of the helper is common; that the ancient conception of **karmic** retribution as arising in the mind of the individual alone is precisely true.

His Locale III is like an alternate Earth in which our personalities are mirrored in a less developed culture. He describes how, ducking through a 'hole' in a wall, black infinity beyond and hands pulling him through it into his apparent alter-ego, he so confused his 'alter ego' that he grew embarrassed, desisted and fell back to the known world.

In 1971 Monroe established a Mind Research Institute at his home near the Blue Ridge in Virginia USA to train others in the art (or science) of leaving the body. Notable for his analytical lucidity and willingness to submit himself to scientific study, his experiences are considered genuine by parapsychologist Charles Tart, author of the classic *Altered States of Consciousness* (1969).[1]

1. *Journeys Out Of The Body*, Robert Monroe, Souvenir Press, London 1972

MOODY, Dr. Raymond A. (*See* **NEAR-DEATH EXPERIENCES**) In the mid-1960s Raymond Moody, a philosophy student at the University of Virginia, began collecting accounts of near-death experiences. His initial interest was aroused by the account of Virginian psychiatrist Dr George Ritchie who, as a soldier in 1943, had 'died' of a respiratory infection. Losing consciousness Ritchie had found himself outside his body and unable to return to it. A ward boy had walked through him; a man whose shoulder he tapped ignored him. Then the room became 'brighter than a thousand arc lights': a figure he identified as Jesus appeared. On reviving he insisted the experience had been real, no **dream**. Subsequently Moody took a medical degree and over the next decade collected about a hundred and fifty such cases. He did not at the time know of Elizabeth **Kübler-Ross** or others working in this field. Struck by the basic similarities in these cases he wrote *Life after Life* which, published in 1977, became a bestseller.[1]

1. *Life after Life*, Raymond A. Moody, Bantam Books, New York 1977

MOON (*see* **ISIS, WITCHCRAFT**) There are not twelve months (or moons) in a year, but thirteen ($13 \times 28 = 364$). The tale of how and why a twelve-month year was created by adding two or three days to each month (save February) illumines a shadowy 3,000-year process whereby matriarchal *lunar* structures and spiritual values were superseded by *solar* patriarchal rule. Today we take for granted the solar, 'rational' basis of our social system, and rarely consider the war that led to it. Yet the evidence exists. The indivisible lunar 'thirteen' is thought unlucky and awkward. The solar 'twelve' is rational, divisible, and easily manipulated. Yet, just as the Sun rules the day and the Moon the night, behind every twelve lies a thirteen. Jesus and his twelve disciples, a judge and twelve jurors: in each case the *whole group* numbers 13. Likewise the astrological zodiac today numbers twelve signs. Yet once there was a thirteenth sign. Arachne the Spider, (*see* **Astrology**) the house of lunar **intuition** and **psychism**, was discarded by the Church fathers, just as they denied many other lunar, feminine elements in the human **psyche**.[1]

A millennium later, women were being burned *en masse* in mediaeval witchcraft trials. The war of solar man against lunar woman seemed thoroughly won. History became the tale of humanity told from a solar masculine viewpoint. Today, men acknowledging the lunar principle in human nature (poets, seers, etc.) are socially suspect: women insisting on their innate lunar wisdom remain likewise suspect even if not (recently at least) burned as witches.

This subjugation occurred throughout the world. Even as Christian fathers suppressed the Moon, so did the Brahmins of India. Women were not only excluded from religious office but were no longer allowed even to read the sacred writings. Perhaps, in a wider evolutionary scale, this was a necessary interlude, allowing solar reason to grow out of the moon-womb.

Yet now the ordination of women into the formerly male bastion of the Church suggests that the purely masculine approach has had its day. The intuitive lunar viewpoint denied for two millennia is making a comeback. The moon, like **Isis**, the great goddess of the ancient world, has survived every solar attack. It is no accident that US Lunar expeditions sent in the 1960s to 'conquer' the Moon were named after Apollo, the Sun-god. Yet the 'conquered' ultimately 'conquers'. The Moon-landings, whatever else they achieved, encouraged remembrance of an outlook denied since some men lost respect for the earth. The beautiful photographic views of the Earth from the Moon helped revive the concept of **Gaia**, the Earth-Mother. For the first time in centuries men felt foreboding and shame about their misuse of the planet. The Moon-landings stimulated this perception.

The power of the Moon is obvious. It controls the tides of the oceans and our bodies: the phases of conception and growth. Words like *menstruation*, *menopause* and *meniscus* drive from *moon*. Human 'prehistory' was ruled by the Moon and its ever-shifting effect on the mind. It stimulated **consciousness**-growth, just like plant-growth.

From the palaeolithic era to the Bronze Age, humanity worshipped the Moon Goddess in her ever-changing forms: Isis, Inanna, Ishtar, Astarte; Demeter, Selene, Aphrodite, Diana; Ch'ang O, Maja Jotma, Tsuki-Yomi; Brigit, Hecate and the Badb. But with the coming of Osiris, Orpheus, Dionysus, Mithras and **Christ** the focus of worship (and thus of the mental sphere of attention) shifted to her son, her husband, and to the priests of new male **religions**. Drowned in the glare of solar reason, apparently cowed and quelled, she became the Virgin Mary, meek and mild, mother and wife, without life of her own, burned at the stake if she got 'above herself' and dared to challenge the power of the Sun (son). Even so she survived as Magdalene, Black Madonna: as houri, strumpet and whore. Her son rejected her but needed her: she was in his blood, in his unconscious. In trying to crush her, he brought misery on himself and the world. Yet she survived in his language, culture and intuitions. Wherever he turned, she underlay him. In love, he *mooned about*, unable to deal with daily affairs. Married, he went on a *honeymoon* (from Teutonic custom: for a *month* after a wedding the community celebrated by drinking honey mead). If *mentally* disturbed, he turned *lunatic*, especially when, at full moon, the electrical potential of his body was deranged and he no longer knew his own mind. Fishermen had to watch the tides, farmer or gardener had to plant in the *waxing moon* to gain the best growth. And so on. All his attempts to curse her only deepened her hold on him. Solar reason and logic could not replace lunar **intuition** and imagination: Sun and Moon must marry to create the whole human being.

Yet what is the Moon? A 'dead' satellite circling the Earth, some 4.6 billion years old, containing (4 billion years old) the oldest rock ever found, on the Apollo 15 mission, christened the 'Genesis rock'.

Did Eve dream the Moon before Adam walked the Earth?[2]

1. *The Thirteenth Zodiac*, James Vogh, Mayflower, London 1979
2. *Moon, Moon*, Anne Kent Rush, Random House/Moon Books, New York 1976

MORMONISM Today 30,000 Mormon missionaries annually gather in some 200,000 converts while the church itself, operating from a twenty-eight-storey headquarters in Salt Lake City, makes an estimated $1.3 billion annually. A far cry from its **miraculous** origins. For on the night of 21 September 1823 the founder of Mormonism, Joseph Smith, was visited by an **angel**, Moroni, who told him of a book (in the form of gold plates buried in a secret place) which contained the history of the ancient peoples of North America. Thrice that night Moroni appeared to him: in the morning, exhausted, Smith fell unconscious, at which his father, told what had happened, ordered him to obey the angel.

Smith found the plates in a stone box but could not remove them. After four years the angel let him take and translate their 'reformed Egyptian' hieroglyphs with the help of special spectacles or stones called 'Urim and Thummim' found in the box. Completed in 1830, the translation (*The Book of Mormon*) told of two Israelite peoples who had migrated to the Americas – the Jaredites, come from the Tower of Babel to Central America; and the Nephites who, fleeing Babylonian captivity in Jerusalem to South America, had split into warring factions, Nephites and Lamanites. In AD 428 in a battle near modern New York the Lamanites, destroying the Nephites, were cursed with dark skins and became the American Indian race. Before dying, the Nephite leader, Mormon, set down this history on the golden plates as found by Joseph Smith 1400 years later.

From this source grew the polygamous cult which, driven successively from New York, Ohio, and Missouri came to Illinois, where in 1844 Joseph Smith (by then with twenty-seven wives) and his brother Hyrum were lynched by an outraged mob. Brigham Young then persuaded the remaining Mormons to follow him to Utah. In July 1847 they reached the Salt Lake Valley. By the time he died in 1877 Young had collected 140,000 followers. Today an estimated 30,000 fundamentalist Mormons believe they cannot enter heaven unless they follow the covenant of polygamy set forth by Joseph Smith in 1843.[1]

1. *Larson's Book of Cults*, Bob Larson, Tyndale House, Wheaton, Illinois 1989, pp. 156–65

MORPHIC RESONANCE (*See* **FORMATIVE CAUSATION**)

MOSES, Rev. William Stainton (1839–92) (*See* **MYERS, SPIRITUALISM**) Always in poor health, a friend of William **James** and initially hostile to **Spiritualism**, the Rev. Stainton Moses called Lord Adare's book on Daniel Dunglass **Home**, 'the dreariest twaddle he ever came across'. Yet in 1872 at a séance he was impressed by an accurate description of a friend who had recently died. Later he realised he was a **medium** himself. His twenty-four volumes of **automatic writing** were edited by Myers as a book, *Spirit Teachings*. He believed the phenomena he manifested (**automatic writing, table-rapping, psychokinesis** and **levitation**) were produced by his unconscious mind. As a clergyman, he distrusted information that came via automatic writing, and took pains to hide the identity of the 'forty-nine communicators' operating through him. It seems they included Aristotle, Plato and a number of Old Testament prophets. Once he argued bitterly with them, calling them 'silly and frivolous, if not mischievous', to which they replied that all human history is a 'progressive revelation of one and the same God'. Insisting on the need to beware of mischievous 'earthbound' spirits who are either unaware that they are dead or who have no wish to move on, he observed that execution is no way to deal with criminals, since all it does is release a vengeful spirit that will continue to try to harm the living.[1]

1. *Afterlife*, Colin Wilson, Grafton, London 1987, pp. 165–7

MU (*See* **BLAVATSKY, CHURCHWARD, POLE SHIFT, STELLE GROUP**)

MULDOON, Sylvan (d. 1971) (*See* **OUT-OF-BODY EXPERIENCES**) Like **Moses** (see above) subject to poor health, Muldoon first left his body aged twelve. Visiting the Mississippi Valley Spritualists' Association in Clinton, Iowa, with his mother, he awoke in the middle of the night feeling paralysed, and realised he was floating in the air above his bed, connected to his body only by a 'shining cord' attached to the base of his brain. After many more such experiences he wrote to **psychic** researcher Hereward Carrington, with whom he collaborated on a book, *The Projection of the Astral Body* (1929). This account of his experiences was followed in 1951 by *The Phenomena of Astral Projection;* a case-book of reports from available literature and from his correspondents, and one of the first in-depth studies of the subject. Sceptical about reports of visits to other higher planes of reality, his own experiences were confined to the earth. Later in life, now famous and financially secure, he completely lost the ability to project his **astral body**. Yet again, the connection between ill heath and psychic capacity is prominent.

MULTIPLE PERSONALITY (*See* **BLOXHAM, JUNG, POSSESSION, PRINCE**) Once the bizarre phenomenon of multiple personality was explained by the invasion and **possession** of the victim by **demons** or **spirits** of the dead. Today it is generally assumed that more prosaic medical or psychiatric explanations suffice. Is this always so?

The term 'personality' derives from the Latin *persona*, meaning 'mask' – specifically the mask worn by classical actors playing god-roles. It was once thought the essence of the god shining from the actor's face would harm or destroy spectators. Thus *personality* is a mask concealing being's true essence. In most of us it becomes fixed at an early age as the mask or face we show the world (and ourselves) thereafter. In healthy people, (early supported by a loving family), the personality *seems* to be singular.

Multiple personality emerges typically where the victim is abused as a child. Psychological unity is lost before it can be developed: the self splits into warring facets, some more potent than others, as with Jekyll and Hyde. Hyde knows about Jekyll: Jekyll does not know about Hyde.

While a student at Zurich, C. G. Jung investigated a female cousin through whom various 'spirits' claimed to speak. Her behaviour changed for each. Jung noted how, with the girl in **trance**, 'spirits' spoke through her, or she would enter ecstatic sleep, later to tell how, as a saintly personality ('Ivenes') she had left her body to move through the spirit world. Unlike the real 'S. W.' (so Jung hid the girl's identity), Ivenes was intelligent and self-possessed. S. W. was shy, unattractive and not very intelligent.

'Ivenes' claimed S. W. as but one of her many incarnations. She had been a Christian martyr, a French countess, and Frederika Hauffe, the 'seeress of Prevorst'. Yet Ivenes claimed this latter identity only after S. W. read a book about the seeress. (This reminds one of 'Jane', the housewife regressed to 'past lives' by hypnotherapist Arnall Bloxham: her 'memories' seemingly derived from historical novels read years earlier and since forgotten.)

Later S. W. developed tuberculosis and died aged twenty-six. Jung suspected her 'spirits' were pubescent fantasies, perhaps compensating for unconscious knowledge that she would die young. Yet as 'Ivenes' she had propounded **Gnostic** philosophy which S. W. could scarcely have grasped.[1]

Notably in many such cases the secondary personality is mature, fun-loving or mischievous; whereas the primary personality is dull and quiet.

Studies over the last century by Jung, **Freud**, William **James**, Morton Prince, Walter F. Prince, James **Hyslop** and others suggest that, though common features emerge, the same explanation does not necessarily cover all cases. Sometimes five or six personalities emerge, all different.

Two famous cases are those of Christine Beauchamp and Doris Fischer.

In 1898 Christine, a depressed student, approached Dr Morton Prince of Tufts Medical School in Boston for help. Hypnotised, she became 'Sally', lively, mischievous, but childlike. Sally would trick Christine by walking far into the countryside then handing over to the bewildered and listless Christine. Then emerged a third personality, a mature girl Prince called 'B–4'. Sally and B–4 hated each other, whereas Christine always passively accepted Sally's tricks. B–4 thought Dr Prince was a man called William Jones. She told him not to climb through the window or he'd break his neck. This was the key. Christine's father had been alcoholic: William Jones a man who had treated her kindly. Aged thirteen, Christine's mother died; at sixteen she fled from home to become a hospital nurse. She still saw William Jones. One night Jones, drunk, came to see her. He climbed a ladder to a window. She saw him leering through the glass. Shocked, she talked to him. He tried to kiss her. B–4 and Sally, who told Dr Prince the story, both recalled the evening. Christine did not and later, said Sally, had become 'queer and moony'. As for B–4, she remembered nothing since.

Prince decided that Christine and B–4 were the 'true selves' and that Sally had to go. Sally fought the **hypnotic** commands of **exorcism**, crying: 'I won't – I won't be dead. I have as much right to live as she has.'

Reintegrated with B–4, Christine again took up nursing. Yet for years afterwards Sally put in occasional appearances, playing practical jokes.

The Fischer case is more complex – and suggestive. Born in Pittsburgh in 1889, one night in 1892 her drunken father tore her from her mother's arms and threw her to the floor. Her personality split in two. Doris was the primary personality, a 'good little girl'. But 'Margaret' emerged, her mischief always getting Doris into trouble. 'Margaret' knew Doris; but not vice versa: Doris was eclipsed when Margaret took over. Doris learned easily: Margaret stopped maturing at ten. In 1906 her mother died: a third personality emerged, 'Sick Doris', who believed herself fatally ill.

'Sick Doris' replaced Doris entirely. 'Margaret' educated 'Sick Doris' about Doris before, but growing jealous of 'Sick Doris', she began making her hit and scratch herself, especially during sleep.

Fleeing her drunken father in 1906, Doris found nearby refuge with the Rev. Walter Franklin Prince, a psychologist. Seeing her scratch herself while asleep, in 1910 Prince tried to exorcise the controlling spirit, telling it he was 'withdrawing' its power. Her face changed. She woke up. Her pulse dropped to fifty-four beats a minute. A new voice burst from her. 'You must get her out of this.' He began shaking her. 'Shake her harder!' it ordered. 'Walk her! Walk her!' He did. Finally 'her' voice said, 'She is coming to herself now. She will be all right soon.'

Doris revived. For the rest of the night she fought him. 'Have you ever prayed against the voices,' he asked. She glared. 'What made you want Doris to pray?' a new voice screamed. He prayed. Doris fell into a deep sleep. Later he told the invader he would rather let her die than give up her **psyche** to it. The invader made Doris start choking herself.

A fivefold hierarchy of personalities emerged – Doris, Margaret, Sick Doris, Sleeping Real Doris (reeling off memories like a tape recorder), and Ariel, apparently the unifying personality telling Prince to 'Walk her!'

'Ariel' knew about the others: none of them knew about her. Insisting she was a spirit sent to look after Doris, she was the most mature of the personalities. Prince had to admit her claim. Doris Fischer, her mind split aged three by her father's violence, was a psychic battleground.[2]

In such cases multiple personality follows traumatic shock. Though, as with **mediums**, the 'spirit' hypothesis is not invariably indicated, rarely does a purely mechanical theory suffice. Current psychology details the wreckage on the floor of the room in the house of the psyche, and explains how the window was broken, but says nothing of the nature of the spirit-wind that bursts through the window.

1. *Mysteries*, Colin Wilson, Grafton, London 1979, pp. 205–7
2. *The Infinite Boundary*, D. Scott Rogo, Aquarian, Wellingborough 1988, pp. 117–55

MURPHY, Bridey (*See* **BLOXHAM, REINCARNATION**) In this famous 1950s case Colorado businessman Morey Bernstein persuaded housewife Virginia Tighe to undergo **hypnotic** regression. Sent back beyond her birth she began speaking with an Irish brogue and identified herself as Bridey Murphy, born in County Cork in 1798. Subsequently wife of a Belfast barrister, she had died after a fall in 1864. In six tape-recorded sessions Mrs Tighe (alias Bridey) provided much detail about Victorian Ireland. She named Belfast shops subsequently found to have existed, used now-redundant terms then in use, described popular songs, farming methods, books, coins and furniture of the time, and much more.

Bernstein wrote a book, *The Search for Bridey Murphy*. Serialised in the *Chicago Daily News*, it became a best-seller in 1956. Yet attempts to track down Bridey Murphy were hampered by the fact that records of Irish births and deaths began only two years after her supposed death. At the same time a rival newspaper, the *Chicago American*, uncovering Virginia Tighe's identity, reported that she had grown up in Chicago with an aunt 'as Irish as the lakes of Killarney' who told tales of Ireland, and had lived opposite an Irishwoman named Bridey Corkell whose unmarried name had been Murphy, and with whose son (John) Virginia had been infatuated.

The Bridey Murphy case collapsed. Virginia was assumed to be a fraud or unconscious romancer. But a *Denver Post* journalist, investigating the exposé, found most of it untrue. Virginia's aunt, Mrs Mary Burns, had grown up in New York and never met Virginia until the girl was eighteen; both she and Virginia denied there had been any Irish tales. Mrs Corkell (whom Virginia denied ever meeting) refused to be interviewed: as for her son John, he turned out to be the Sunday editor of the rival *Chicago American*.

None of this 'proved' Virginia's far memory of being Bridey Murphy to be true. But it *did* show how easy it is to destroy such a case, given the common western disbelief in such matters. Furthermore, the Bridey Murphy case interested other hypnotists like **Bloxham** in regression techniques.

Today, the Bridey Murphy case remains open.[1]

1. *The Search for Bridey Murphy*, Morey Bernstein, Hutchinson, London 1956

MUSIC OF THE SPHERES (*See* **SPHERES**)

MYERS, Frederick W. H. (1842–1901) Founder member of the **Society of Psychical Research** (SPR), Myers researched the **paranormal** as thoroughly as anyone since. His (posthumously published) *Human Personality and its Survival of Bodily Death* remains, says Colin **Wilson**, 'notably the most comprehensive work ever written on the subject of the paranormal'. Aldous **Huxley** called it, 'an immense store of information about the strange and often wonderful goings-on in the upper storeys of man's soul-house'. Considering every aspect of the paranormal and seeking a common pattern, Myers concluded that our powers are far greater than we realise. His work indicated the existence of many layers of **consciousness** both above and below our everyday waking state. He saw nothing mystical in the existence of such powers and layers (save in that we make so little use of them), but regarded them as proven by irrefutable scientific evidence, claiming that the 'substratum' or basement layers are those that survive death and exercise paranormal powers. Researching **multiple personality, near-death experiences**, etc., he investigated many cases of 'survival' before – like others who began as sceptics, including his friends William **James** and Stainton **Moses** – accepting the evidence as watertight, especially through the work of Boston medium Leonore **Piper**.

Appropriately, Myers seemingly survived his death on 17 January 1901. Earlier he had given Oliver **Lodge** a sealed envelope to open only when a spirit purporting to be Myers should claim to repeat the message in it. After he died a friend, Margaret Verrall, tried **automatic writing** to reach him. Messages in Latin signed 'Myers' came through. One said the sealed message contained 'the words in the *Symposium* about love bridging the chasm'. In the envelope Lodge found no quote from Plato, but: 'If I can revisit any earthly scene, I should choose the valley in the grounds of Hallsteads, Cumberland.' Then it was recalled that Myers had referred to the *Symposium*, in a privately printed book dedicated to Annie Marshall, with whom he had been in love. She had lived at Hallsteads and had drowned herself in Ullswater. Other evidence of Myers' survival, received by Mrs Piper was convincing in accumulation but just as frustratingly vague.

Asked why he was not more direct, in one script 'Myers' stated that the difficulties in sending a message were like 'standing behind a sheet of frosted glass which blurs sight and deadens sound – dictating feebly to a reluctant and somewhat obtuse secretary'. 'Myers' continued to manifest through different **mediums** for many years, not least in connection with the death of Lodge's son Raymond in 1915 (as recorded elsewhere).[1]

1. *Afterlife*, Colin Wilson, Grafton, London 1987, pp. 147–83

MYSTERIES (*See* **GREEK MYSTERIES, INITIATION, MOON**) The Mystery cults of the ancient and classical worlds mark early fruition in the long transitional growth of human **consciousness**. In Babylon, **Egypt**, Greece and Rome, the cults of Ishtar, **Isis**, Dionysus and Mithras presage a mental emergence from **animistic** nature worship to more formal intellectual teachings as given (in the East) by the **Buddha** and by **yogic** systems, or (in the West) by **Islam** or **Christianity**. These in turn led to the modern abstract teachings and the attitudes of rational science.

An early Mystery teaching is that of Inanna, Queen of Heaven and Earth in Sumerian mythology. Like Isis and Persephone later, this goddess, or principle of natural activity, must always descend from the *Great Above* to the *Great Below* (the Underworld, Hades, Hell), giving up all her wealth and beauty, stripping herself naked before the Lord of the Dead, imploring the release of Life, her lover, from the annual clutch of wintry death. Dating back to 2000 BC, this myth-cycle explains human existence and suffering by epitome. Even the gods are bound by immutable natural laws. Preparing to descend to the underworld, Inanna cries to Ninshubur her servant:

> . . . If I do not return,
> Set up a lament for me by the ruins,
> Beat the drum for me in the assembly places.
> Circle the houses of the gods.
> Tear at your eyes, at your mouth, at your thighs.
> Dress yourself in a single garment like a beggar . . . [1]

If the Great Goddess herself must die, what of the rest of us? The telling of such a

Mystery to those who heard it anciently justified the daily joys and sorrows; explained the meanings of the seasons; of how spring succeeds winter to flower in summer before giving way to autumn and winter again.

So the Mysteries offered hope. For, of course, She returns. Though defiled, humiliated, and made to bow down low, She returns – every year.

Thus began a process of perceiving natural rhythms in terms of human inner life. Mystery initiates began the abstract interpretation of natural **symbols:** a process which over three millennia led via **alchemy** to Science.

Rising moon, setting sun, pains of birth, death and life: all married in the Mysteries. Modern analysts far from the dreaming, poetic mentality that engendered Mystery rites and **symbols** cannot enter the mythic labyrinth of pre-rational consciousness. The explorations of **Jung** and others begin to rediscover the world as omnipresent *mystery* that those before us knew.

Yet children naturally know the Mysteries, biologically recapitulating the same fears, joys, terrors and ecstasies that once led to the rites of Inanna, Isis, Osiris, Ishtar, Bacchus and Dionysus.

The latter two refer to the Mysteries of alcohol and *enthousiasmos* (a state inside the god) and *ekstasis* (outside the body). These were Greek *masculine* mysteries, devoted to an approach which lately **Leary** and others tried to rediscover via use of **hallucinogenic drugs**.

Little is known of specific Mystery **rituals**. Yet it may be that, long before Christianity tried to tame Western man's more violent excesses by converting cannibalism from *actual* to *symbolic* (Communion: bread and wine, body and blood), some Western Mystery initiates already doubted the value of literal self-sacrifice and Descent to the Underworld. It seems that the old Greek Mysteries of Eleusis (based on Persephone's abduction to the Underworld by Hades) had, even before the birth of **Christ**, abandoned the physically sacrificial aspect of the rite called 'The Opening of the Eyes'.

The rite, involving fire, and death and rebirth of spiritual sight had become symbolic. One documented incident concerns an invitation in 20 BC to an Indian holy man to join the rite. When the fire-rite came, he anointed his body with oils and leaped into the flames. His last words were that in his land they put their whole soul into religion and were not satisfied with symbols alone. His hosts were shocked by such literal zeal.[2]

1. *Inanna*, Diane Wolkstein and Samuel Kramer, Rider, London 1984, p. 53
2. *Moon, Moon*, Anne Kent Rush, Random House/Moon Books, New York 1976, p. 211

MYSTICISM (*See* **BOEHME**) A system of contemplative religious practice directed towards union of the mystic with the greater whole, the Godhead, nirvana. Not reliant on any specific belief system or **religion**, the experience may occur spontaneously but is often sought or triggered through long practice of **yoga**, prayer, or **meditation**. The process, in any era or society, involves the purification of self, the cleansing and humbling of the senses, the journey through the crooked lanes of the **psyche** and symbolic inner landscapes, and the focus and concentration of the energies of transcendent matters. In effect it involves the dissolution and transmutation of the infantile images of the mystic's personal past and the discarding of all psychological baggage.

MYTH (*See* **FAIRY TALE**) 'Myth', wrote Joseph **Campbell** in his classic *The Hero with a Thousand Faces*, 'is the secret opening through which the inexhaustible energies of the cosmos pour into human cultural manifestation. **Religions**, philosophies, arts, the social forms of primitive and historic man, prime discoveries in science and technology, the very dreams that blister sleep, boil up from the basic, magic ring of myth.'[1]

More prosaically, introducing the *Larousse Encyclopedia of Myth*, Robert Graves asserts that myth has two main functions. One is to answer the awkward questions that children ask, like 'Who made the world?' and 'Where do souls go after death?' The other 'is to justify an existing social system and account for traditional rites and customs'.[2]

Myths are thus metaphoric tales that account for events, perceptions and questions which cannot otherwise be explained or answered in factual or historical terms. In his mediaeval bestseller *The History of the Kings of Britain* (1135), Geoffrey of Monmouth claimed that Britons were descended from Brutus the Trojan; likewise the Romans claimed descent from the twins Romulus and Remus, suckled by a she-wolf; and the Sumerians claimed that the fish-god Oannes arose from the depths of the ocean to teach mankind the arts of civilisation. In this sense, mythology is the study of basically incredible heroic or religious foundation legends.

Yet psychologically, as Joseph Campbell spent a lifetime pointing out, myth is the metaphoric history of the journey undertaken by every living human being. The hero-journey at the heart of the mythic quest is always the same. It involves going out from the safe and known world into regions of darkness, strangeness, beauty and terror; confronting the monsters of the subconscious (slaying the **dragon**); entering the underworld (dying to be reborn) and there dealing with Hades (rescuing Eurydice, gaining the gift, stealing the treasure: so integrating formerly separate aspects of the **psyche**); then returning with enhanced powers (treasure or new knowledge) which benefit the common daily world. The process is threefold: separation, initiation, return.[1]

This process is seen in the mythic **Mysteries** of the ancient world whereby Inanna, **Isis** or Persephone leave the daily world to go down into the Land of the Dead (winter) before returning with the springtime; in the **Grail** myths whereby the Knights of the Round Table ride out into a blasted wilderness in Quest of the Cup that will restore life to Land and King; and in the early twentieth-century Dublin streets of James Joyce's *Ulysses*, explored by gentle unlikely hero Leopold Bloom. Likewise the adventures, trials and fate of the Greek hero Hercules mirror those of the Irish Cuchullin or the nineteenth-century American frontier hero Davy Crockett. Each perform their heroic feats, but fall in the end: Hercules to the poisoned cloak; Cuchullin to the *geasa* or magical prohibitions that inevitably, due to their contradictory demands, he breaks; Davy Crockett at the Alamo. And again, the myth of the died-and-reborn god; Bacchus torn to pieces in the midnight grove; **Christ** crucified on the Cross; the Norse Odin hanging self-impaled by his own spear from Yggdrasil, the World Tree; **Black Elk** seated under the **shamanic** tree up which in **trance** he rises, dismembered, to meet the spirit 'grandfathers' and bring their wisdom back to earth.

Typical in all such mythic tales is the sense of awe, terror and pity underlying and informing the fate of Everyman: all mythic heroes being but Everyman writ large, born to grow up, go out, triumph, suffer and die. Yet at the same time the possibility of rebirth is invariably there, even in the darkest night.

The mythical drama informs daily life at its very core and gives it its meaning. A society without myth is dead inside. On the other hand, over-reliance on myth, or over-stimulation of the **collective unconscious** by any specific mythic theme, can prove dangerous. **Hitler** demonstrated this. He aroused the German people through abuse of Teutonic myth; a force which, as **Jung** had foreseen, was ready to explode into the light of day following centuries of suppression and repression. The catastrophe was not in the persistence of the mythic **archetype** but in its centuries-long *exclusion* and thus its unbalanced outbreak.

1. *The Hero with a Thousand Faces*, Joseph Campbell, Abacus, London 1975 (1949), p. 13
2. *Larousse Encyclopedia of Mythology*, Hamlyn, London 1965

N

NAMES Magical thinking holds that a thing's name contains its essence. To know its name is to control it. Once it was thought a man might be harmed by an enemy writing his name on a piece of lead, wax or pottery, adding a **curse** and burying it. This led to the concept of the 'real' or 'secret' name. In ancient or primitive societies a man had two names – one for daily use: the other his real name, whispered into his ear by his mother at birth, and so secret that not even he always knew it. Misuse of it could, after all, kill him. Likewise the names of **supernatural** beings were secret: mediaeval magicians sought the secret names of **demons** to gain power over them. In the *Testament of Solomon* it is said an **angel** gave Solomon a magic ring enabling him to make demons reveal their secret names. Egyptian **myth** tells how **Isis** tricked the sun-god Ra into revealing his secret name. Collecting his spittle, she mixed it with earth to make a serpent that bit him. In his agony he let Isis know his name. Thus she stole his power.[1]

In Judaism the hidden name of God is hugely important. It is literally God, alias the universe: to know it is to control all things. In the Bible God has many names – El ('god' in Assyrian, Phoenician and Hebrew); Elohim (feminine plural: *shining ones*); Sabaoth ('Lord of Hosts'); Shaddai ('the Almighty'); Adonai ('the Lord') – all 'ordinary' names. *Jehovah* (Yahweh) comes from the four letters forming the Hebrew Tetragrammaton, YHVH (*yod he vau he:* ('he is' or 'he exists'). The **Jews** held this name in awe, speaking it, if at all, inaudibly so that it could not be put to **evil** use. By the time of **Christ** the High Priest spoke it only on the Day of Atonement, in the Holy of Holies. For centuries now nobody has known how YHVH is really pronounced – which perhaps means only that nobody has yet understood the universe![2] For the 'name' YHVH is as much a formula as is $E=MC.^2$

Today the naming of names still retains some **magic**. Parents name their children with care, hoping the child will take on a personality reflecting the given name, or to pass on a name important in their blood-line, or to express their religious and cultural beliefs. They might even consult a **numerologist** to find a name bringing good luck. Those entering religious orders take new names in their adoption of new identity. The importance advertisers place on finding the right name for a new product shows how much we still (magically) assume that the name IS what it describes. Politicians use words (names) like 'democracy', 'free world', 'equality' and 'human rights' to **spell**-bind us; generals talk of 'surgical strikes', the army formula of 'name, rank and serial-number' is a control-technique similar to that exercised over demons by the **magus**.

1. *The Magical Arts*, Richard Cavendish, Arkana 1984, pp. 43–5
2. *Ibid.*, p. 124–5

NATURE SPIRITS (*See* **ANIMISM, ELEMENTALS, FAIRIES**)

NAZCA (*See* **LEY LINES**) The vast desert drawings at Nazca in Peru are one of the world's great mysteries. This high bare plateau is covered by representations of birds, animals, of a spider, a monkey and a killer **whale**; by triangles, spirals, and over 13,000 dead-straight lines, some over twenty-five miles long, running without deviation over difficult, hilly terrain. The mystery lies in the fact that from ground level only shallow depressions scraped in the surface to show yellow earth below are visible: the Pan American Highway was built through the desert without the drawings being noticed at all.

Probably designed between 400 BC and AD 600, rediscovered in 1927, they can be seen only from the air. This led Erich **Von Däniken** to claim the Nazca lines to be 'runways' for ancient spacecraft – most unlikely.

So what were they for and who built them? One evening in the 1940s Professor Paul Kosok of Long Island University saw the sun set precisely along one of the lines, apparently confirming his theory that they marked astronomical alignments. In 1946 German astronomer Maria Reiche joined him in cleaning the lines. When he died in 1959 she continued her study of this '**mystery in the desert**' (the title of her book on the enigma). She asserts that the Nazcans were agriculturalists who needed to know when to sow and harvest. Some lines (as with European **megalithic** alignments) indicate the rising- and setting-points of particular stars and planets. Others reveal no such function. Speculation that (as with European leys and Chinese ***lung mei***) they mark subterranean streams of geomagnetic energy remains unproven.

In 1976 Maria Reiche visited Britain to seek clues as to the methods and systems of measurements used by ancient builders. She concluded that the Nazca builders used the 'megalithic yard' (2.72 ft, 83 cm.) as employed in Britain and France – though some 1,500 years earlier. She concluded too that the Nazca builders transferred the design of small-scale models on to the desert floor section by section, each section marked by wooden posts, and claimed to have found the original sections. She also noted that Nazca, though the most impressive, is not the only such site in South America.

As for the vast **symbolic** patterns and animal representations, these lack obvious practical function. Yet they and the gold and pottery objects found in the upright graves throughout the region prove the artistry (and perhaps the religio-magical preoccupations) of the builders. Yet there are mysteries here too. One design is of a monkey, but there are no monkeys in Peru today and probably never were. It suggests (as does the possible use of the megalithic yard) the transmission of cultural knowledge in ancient times on a much wider scale than currently orthodox belief allows.

Yet if the lines, invisible at ground-level, were made as astronomical pointers, how were they used? American businessman Jim Woodman theorised that the Nazcans used hot air balloons to view their work from above. In 1975 (like Thor Heyerdahl using only local, anciently available materials) he built and flew a balloon (of woven cloth; its pores clogged by being 'smoked') and gondola (made of reeds). It was designed from drawings on Nazcan pots. His theory remains hotly disputed despite the success of his experiment. The Nazcans may have flown hot air balloons, but it seems a complex way to determine when to sow and reap. Definite conclusions remain impossible. The purpose of the lines remains as mysterious as that of the figures. Yet again the discrepancies between current theory about the past (whether orthodox or unorthodox), and the *evidence* of the past as revealed by its incomprehensible remains, only increase.[1]

1. 'Sketchbook for the gods', Tony Morrison, *The Unexplained*, Orbis partwork, London 1983, pp. 310–13, also 344–5, 370–73

NEANDERTHAL MAN (*See* **ABORIGINES, BRAIN MYSTERIES**)
Neanderthal Man 'invented' religion. Lately in Swaziland was found buried the skeleton of a child laid to rest some 80,000 years ago.[1] The body was dusted with ash and ochre. Another early burial, in a cave in the south of France and dating back 46,000 years, is of an arthritic Neanderthal male, his body packed about with red ochre – haematite, the 'blood of the earth'. Those who buried him had symbolically

returned him to that bloody state in which he entered the world from the womb. The caking of the dead with red ochre is implicitly an intentional religious act.

Neanderthal Man may have operated primarily by powers we call magical or **paranormal**. It may be that they passed such powers, weakened, into *homo sapiens* by interbreeding before they died out – if in fact they did. The Aborigines of Australia (there for at least 32,000, maybe 150,000 years), claim that the spirits of the Dreamtime (or the **collective unconscious**) were once men much like us who did not vanish but blended in with humanity. Known for faculties like the capacity to navigate trackless desert as well as migrating **birds**, the Aborigines may represent Neanderthal survival. If so, their familiarity with the Dreamtime suggests our forebears operated primarily by (right-brain) dream-perception rather than (left-brain) logic and intellect. Their interaction with the natural world may thus have been both more sympathetic and less ego-bound and 'separated' than our own: and processes that we call 'magical' were their ordinary means of perception.

Evidence? Neanderthal man had a larger **cerebellum** (the wrinkled 'old brain' sited at the back of the head behind the spinal column and under the cerebrum) than does 'modern' man. In his *The Neanderthal Question* British psychologist Stan **Gooch**, boldly theorising that today especially the **Jews** (but in fact all of us) carry Neanderthal genes, specifically associates magical or paranormal activity with the cerebellum. **Swedenborg** asserted that his visionary powers resided there, and Kaspar **Hauser**, the strange visionary boy found wandering in early nineteenth-century Germany, was found after death to have an abnormally large cerebellum. The production of **automatic writing** and other **trance**-activities (*see* **hypnotism, mediums**) has been associated with this mysterious organ. Modern Asiatics possess larger cerebella than most Europeans, and many of the most evolved paranormal systems (***I Ching***, etc.) come from the east. Likewise women, commonly thought to be more intuitive than men, are found to have larger cerebella than men.[2,3]

Perhaps all modern history is about the growth of the left lobe of the cerebral cortex, and its battle for control over the older brain-systems. Our prejudices about 'modern' versus 'primitive' are essentially those of the left lobe – rational, logical, manipulating the world and increasingly alienated from it. We might do well to recapitulate our *Neanderthal* past. This doesn't mean rejecting reason: it means uniting it with the faculties that embrace a wider world-view than reason alone allows.

1. *Lifetide*, Lyall Watson, Coronet Books, London 1980, p. 63
2. *The Neanderthal Question*, Stan Gooch, Wildwood House, London 1977
3. *The Secret Life of Humans*, Stan Gooch, Dent, London 1981, pp. 126–31

NEAR-DEATH EXPERIENCES (**NDE**) (*See* **OUT-OF-THE-BODY EXPERIENCES**) In 1944, unconscious after a heart attack, **Jung** had a vision in which he concluded he was near death. His nurse later said he had been 'surrounded by a bright glow'. Later he wrote: 'It seems to me that I was high up in space. Far below I saw the globe of the earth, bathed in a gloriously blue light . . . I knew that I was on the point of departing from the earth . . . The sight of the earth from this height was the most glorious thing I have ever seen . . . Everything was being sloughed away; everything I aimed at or wished for or thought, the whole phantasmagoria of earthly existence, fell away or was stripped from me – an extremely painful process.'

In this state, reflecting on the 'long chain of events' of his life, he saw rising up below him from the direction of Europe the 'primal form' of his 'Doctor H.', sent to protest his departure. 'Profoundly disappointed,' Jung told himself, 'Now I must return to the "box system" again.'[1]

This disappointment is known to many undergoing near-death experiences, often on the operating table. Many, on recovery, report experiences during their 'unconsciousness' that fit religious images of the **afterlife** rather than any known scientific

paradigm. Such events are increasingly recorded and quantified by doctors and other researchers who until lately denied or ignored them as **hallucination** induced by shock or anaesthesia. But the many accurate accounts by 'unconscious' patients of what goes on round them during their supposed oblivion alerted doctors like Raymond A. **Moody** and Michael B. **Sabom** to examine these 'hallucinations' more closely.

As a whole such accounts seem not only to fit reports of **astral** travel (and the death-process as described in the ***Tibetan Book of the Dead***), but display a remarkable similarity of experience. Typically the sufferer, fully aware of self, alert and not in a **dream**, first experiences a huge physical distress and a loud ringing or buzzing sound, accompanied by the sense of moving through a long dark tunnel. On emerging from this he finds himself outside his body but still in its physical vicinity. In turmoil he views it, typically from above, and the attempts to revive it. Growing used to this condition, he realises he still has a body, but not like the one he has left. In this state he meets 'dead' friends or relatives who comfort and reassure him; also a warm, loving being of light (usually described in terms of his religious preconceptions) who asks non-verbal questions that help him evaluate his life. Simultaneously there appears an instantaneous, panoramic playback of his life's major events. Then, apparently leaving the scene of his 'death', he nears a barrier that seemingly represents the limit between this life and the next. Beyond this he cannot pass. He is told or made to return to his earthly life and body. He resists, being so involved with the freedom of this new state and with the feelings of love, peace and joy that it induces that he has no desire to return to the 'box system' of physical manifestation. Yet back he goes, whatever his regret, then to wake up and find huge difficulty in telling what he experienced.[2]

A vivid account of this state and the barrier met was given by Victor Solow, a fifty-six-year-old New York film-maker and sceptic, who was clinically dead for twenty-three minutes. Drastic efforts to revive him failed. His doctors, sure he was dead, made one last effort. Later Solow described his experience 'over there', doing so without recourse to conventional religious imagery:

'For me, the moment of transition between life and death – what else can I call it – was easy. There was no time for fear, pain or thought . . . I was moving at great speed towards a net of great luminosity. The strands and knots where the luminous lines intersected were vibrating with a tremendous cold energy. The grid appeared as a barrier that would prevent further travel. I did not want to move through the grid. For a brief moment my speed appeared to slow down. Then I was in the grid. The instant I made contact with it, the vibrant luminosity increased to a blinding intensity which drained, absorbed and transformed me at the same time. There was no pain. The sensation was neither pleasant nor unpleasant but completely consuming. The nature of everything had changed. Words only vaguely approximate the experience from this instant on.

'The grid was like a transformer, an energy converter transporting me through form and into formlessness, beyond **time** and space. Now I was not in a place, nor even in a **dimension**, but rather in a condition of being. This new "I" was not the I which I knew, but rather a distilled essence of it, yet something vaguely familiar, something I had always known buried under a superstructure of personal fears, hopes, wants and needs. This "I" had no connection to ego. It was final, unchangeable, indivisible, indestructible pure **spirit**. While completely unique and individual as a fingerprint, "I" was, at the same time, part of some infinite, harmonious and ordered whole. I had been there before . . .'

On 'return' he found life hard to endure. He observed his body 'with suspicion and amazement'. It did things of its own volition; he was only a visitor. After six days he rejoined the world. Yet 'a recurrent nostalgia remains for that other reality, that condition of indescribable stillness and quiet . . . The memory softens the old drives for possession, approval and success. . . . I am glad I am here and now. But I know this marvellous place of sun and wind, flowers, children and lovers, this murderous place of evil, ugliness and pain, is only one of many realities through which I must travel to distant and unknown destinations.'[3]

1. *Memories, Dreams and Reflections*, C. G. Jung, Fontana, London 1971, pp. 320–24
2. *Life after Life*, Raymond M. Moody, Bantam, New York 1977
3. *Reincarnation: The Phoenix Fire Mystery*, S. L. Cranston and Joseph Head, Julian Press/Crown Publishers, New York 1977, pp. 450–51

NECROMANCY (*See* **DEE, DIVINATION, LEVI, PROPHECY**) Necromancy ('divination by the dead'), involves invocation of the **spirits** of the dead, traditionally to discover the future, find buried treasure, or commune with **demons**. There is said to be high risk of **possession**.

Tradition states that for nine days before the rite the necromancer inculcates death's **aura**. He dons grave-clothes stolen from corpses while reciting the funeral service over himself. Avoiding sight of woman he eats dog-flesh, black bread baked without salt or leaven, and drinks unfermented grape-juice. The dog belongs to Hecate, Goddess of Death: the lack of salt implies putrefaction; no leaven or fermentation means matter without spirit and parodies Christian communion. The necessary rapport thus induced, he approaches the grave of the chosen corpse at sunset or immediately after midnight. A circle is drawn about the grave; a mixture of henbane, aloe wood, hemlock, saffron, opium and mandrake is burned. With coffin opened, he touches the corpse thrice with his **wand** and tells it to rise. The body, disinterred, is arranged head to the east and arms and legs in the position of **Christ** crucified: thrice the spirit is told to enter its old body and answer all questions put to it or else suffer 'torment and wandering thrice seven years'. Slowly the body rises upright and in a faint, hollow voice answers the questions. The magician then rewards the spirit by destroying the body (via fire or quicklime) so that it can never again be so abused.[1]

The efficacy of such operations is unclear. Necromancers do not seek publicity. Yet this 'art' is an undercurrent in every magical tradition and charged against those known to 'dabble in spirits'. Roman author Lucan tells in the *Pharsalia* how Sextus Pompey, son of Pompey the Great, sought to learn the future by consulting the dead through the witch Erichtho, who 'kept on good terms with the infernal powers by squatting in tombs'. She insisted that the operation be conducted with the aid of a recent carcass with sound lungs, as older corpses 'only squeak incoherently'.[2]

Elizabethan **magus** John **Dee** was popularly thought to be a necromancer: certainly his **scryer** Edward Kelly was pilloried in Lancashire for digging up and using new-buried corpses. Whether he had done so or not is unclear. Oxford dons of the time, influenced by **Neoplatonists** and **Paracelsians**, thought it possible that the dead might be made to walk. Others lamented such belief as 'still in the mouth and faith of credulous **superstition** at this day'.[3] Today, necromantic practice persists in Haitian **Voodoo**. The attempt by Eliphas Lévi to raise the ghost of Apollonius of Tyana has been described elsewhere. **Crowley** in his novel *Moonchild* describes, in gory and excremental detail, such an ugly operation.

1. *The Magical Arts*, Richard Cavendish, Arkana, London 1984, pp. 267–8
2. *Ibid.*, p. 269
3. *Religion and the Decline of Magic*, Keith Thomas, Peregrine, London 1978, p. 706

NELSON, John (*See* **ASTROLOGY**) In 1946 radio engineer John H. Nelson was commissioned by his employers RCA (Radio Corporation of America) to discover the cause of short-wave radio disturbances, so as better to forecast bad conditions. Sunspot activity was suspected as a cause, but not how or why. Before Nelson began work, sixty per cent predictive accuracy was the best available. By his retirement in 1971, accurate prediction of 93.2 per cent had been achieved.

First he studied possible relationships between planetary positions and stormy ionospheric conditions known to hinder reception. Not only did he find a connection, but it was much as described by ancient **astrologers**. Applying the angular relationships between all the planets, with the Sun as centre, he found that relationships (aspects) between planets traditionally described as 'malign' associate with bad shortwave reception; while those regarded as 'benign' are associated with good reception. 'Bad' conditions accompany oppositions, conjunctions or squares (180°, 0°, or 90°) between prominent planets (Venus, Mars, Jupiter, Saturn: all encouraging sunspot-production); 'good' involve trines or sextiles (60°, 120°). He also found that Mercury is usually the trigger planet for abnormal conditions.

Thus by reapplying an old and derided system he improved prediction of disturbed conditions by over thirty per cent. RCA at least was grateful. Yet, as with the work of **Gauquelin, Brown (Frank), Jonas** and others, the scientific fraternity has remained reluctant to accept the implications.[1]

1. *The New Astrologer*, Martin Seymour-Smith, Sidgwick and Jackson, London 1981, pp. 29–30

NEOPLATONISM (*See* **GREEK MYSTERIES**) Founded in Alexandria *c.* AD 193 by Ammonius Saccas, this school of mystical philosophy has had an enduring influence despite being banned in AD 529 by the emperor Justinian. Also known as the Philalethians, the *Lovers of Truth*, the Neoplatonists did not limit themselves to **Plato** but sought to reconcile all **religions** and philosophies. This task they held to be the real purpose of **Christ**. They embraced **reincarnation** and the idea that all manifestation emanates from a single transcendent source. Origen and Plotinus were early disciples: Iamblichus, Porphyry, Proclus, Eratosthenes, Hypatia, Macrobius and the emperor Julian were later initiates. At first there was no conflict with **Christianity**, Judaic rabbis or older **Mystery** schools. Early in the fifth century the school gained its height of popularity under Hypatia, an Athenian lecturer whose youth, eloquence and beauty proved so potent that in AD 414 *Saint* Cyril, Bishop of Alexandria, had her killed. Monks led by Peter the Reader slew her on a church altar, dragged her body through the streets and scraped the flesh from her bones. This Christian terrorism destroyed Alexandrian Neoplatonism. But, as Plotinus had written, 'Murder, death in all its guises, the reduction and sacking of cities, all must be to us just such a spectacle as the changing scenes of a play; all is but the varied incident of a plot, costume on and off, acted grief and lament. For on earth, in all the succession of life, it is not the **Soul** within but the Shadow outside of the authentic man, that grieves and complains and acts out the plot on this world stage which men have dotted with stages of their own constructing.'[1]

Macrobius (fourth to fifth century) added, 'But all, indeed, in descending, drink of oblivion; though some more and others less. On this account, though truth is not apparent to all men on the earth, yet all exercise their opinions about it; because a defect of memory is the origin of opinion. But those discover most who have drunk least of oblivion, because they easily remember what they had known before in the heavens.'[2]

1. Selection from *The Enneads*, Plotinus, trans. Stephen MacKenna
2. *Commentary on the Dream of Scipio*, Macrobius, footnote in *Select Works of Porphyry*, trans. Thomas Taylor (1821)

NEPTUNE The discovery of the planet Neptune in 1846 by John Adams in England and Urbain Leverrier in France, each working independently, arose from observed irregularities in the orbit of Uranus, discovered by Herschel in 1781. Both calculated where the new planet should lie, and when a telescope was turned to the spot, there it was. This success was seen to endorse Newton's laws and prove that skilful observation and mathematics solves all problems. In part this was so. But the means used by both men to calculate where the new planet should lie were flawed. Both employed Bode's Law, involving the now-disproved idea that the planets orbit at distances from the sun to a scale of proportions rising by a constant increment: 4:7:10:16:28:52:100:196:388, etc. Assuming the asteroid belt to be the remains of a planet once orbiting between Mars and Jupiter at position 28, then all the seven inner planets fit the scale exactly. Thus it seemed reasonable to assume that an eighth planet must lie at position 388. In fact Neptune lies much further out. But when on 23 September 1846 Johann Galle lined up the Berlin reflector, there was Neptune, exactly as predicted, at position 388.

Peculiar, to say the least. Two men working independently with flawed assumptions simultaneously got the right answer. Even odder, neither had considered all the discrepancies of the Uranian orbit: discrepancies caused not only by Neptune but by the ninth planet, Pluto, undiscovered until 1930. Somehow Neptune (now **astrologically** associated with **mysticism** and **magic**) managed to be in the right place at the right time.

NEW AGE (*See* **HARMONIC CONVERGENCE, POLE SHIFT, PROPHECY**) The idea that a New Age is about to dawn or is already dawning has become widespread, especially among those concerned with a range of activities including alternative **healing**, environmental concerns, respect for **Gaia** and feminine wisdom, and the study or practice of various esoteric, **occult** or spiritual traditions. The notion is also embraced in more **apocalyptic** fashion by sects, **Christian** or otherwise, that live in expectation of the **Second Coming** or suchlike world-shattering events. **Seers** from **Nostradamus** to Edgar **Cayce**, Paul **Solomon** and others predict an imminent cataclysm, in Native American traditions referred to as 'the Great Purification', to be followed by a New Age on Earth.

Yet such predictions are not peculiar to the late twentieth century, but persist throughout known history. The idea of imminent spiritual renewal of the mundane world, doing away with war and poverty, is **archetypal**. In Europe alone it is found among early Christians; in the mediaeval era in the predictions of Joachim of Fiore and among groups like the Brethren of the Free Spirit; in the **Rosicrucian** manifestos of the Renaissance; in the eighteenth century amid Enlightenment optimism; among **Transcendentalists** and **Golden Dawn** occultists of the nineteenth century; and so on up to the Beat and 'hippie' movements of the 1950s and 1960s.

Today the idea is particularly associated with 'the dawning of the Age of Aquarius', as announced in the musical *Hair* in the late 1960s. This refers to the **astrological** perception that the Earth is about to move (via what is called the 'precession of the equinoxes') from one zodiac sign to another. This event occurs roughly every 2,100 years. The Age of Pisces, beginning about the time of Christ, is now giving way to that of Aquarius, which, supposedly, will see increasing global harmony and spiritual growth among peoples.

NOLAN, Christopher (1965–) (*See* **KELLER**) In 1987 Irish athetoid spastic Christopher Nolan won the Whitbread Book of the Year prize for his autobiography, *Under the Eye of the Clock*. Born in County Westmeath, Eire, on 6 September 1965, he was nearly asphyxiated at birth. He could not walk, talk, swallow or hold up his head. As with Helen **Keller** his family did not deny him. In 1975 a new anti-spastic drug, Lioresal, relaxed his neck muscles enough to let him move his head in a bowing motion. With a unicorn device (a metal pointer fastened round his forehead), and with his mother Bernadette holding up his chin, he learned to type. On 20 August 1977 he tapped out his first poem: 'I Learn to Bow'.

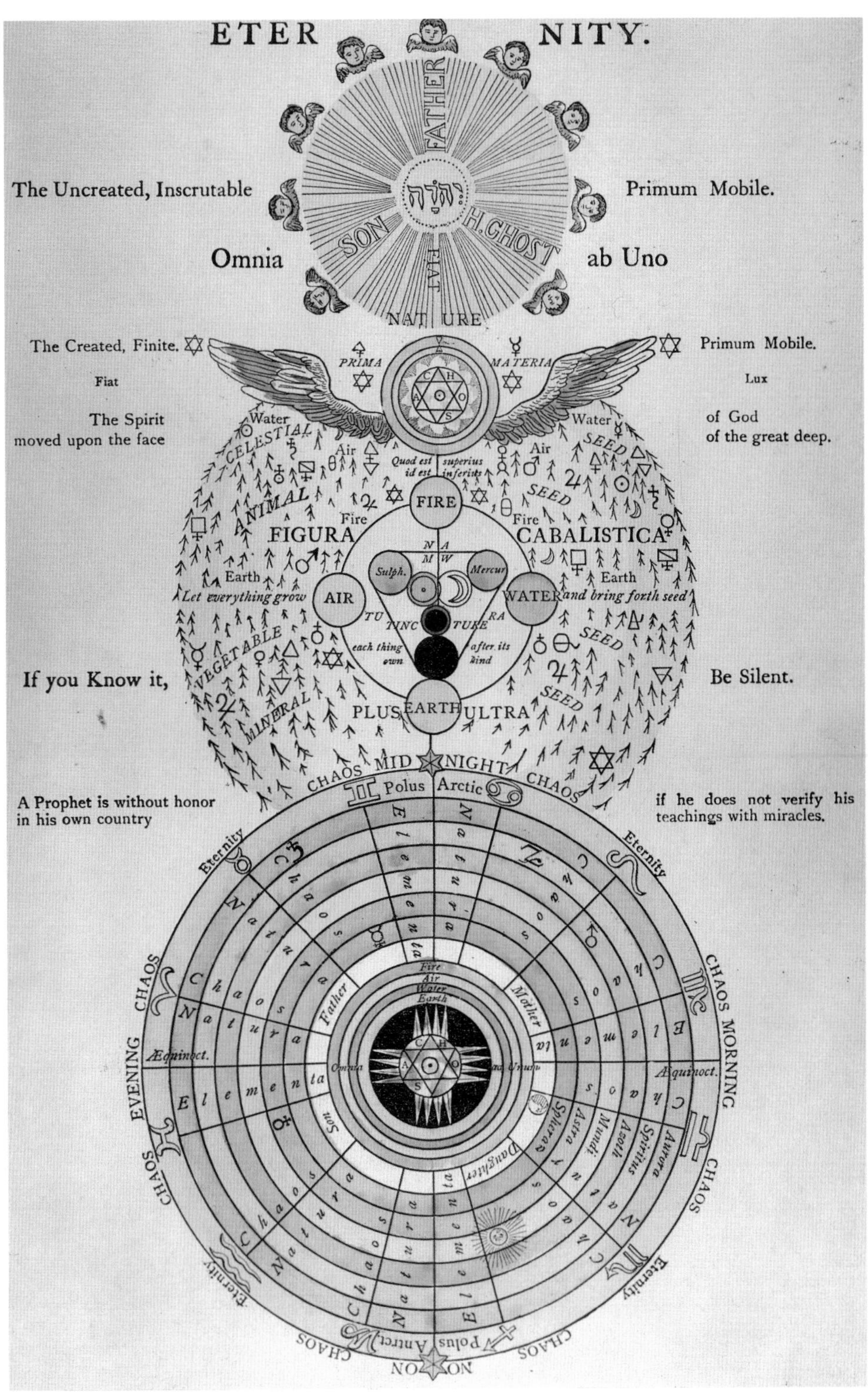

This configuration of the Rosicrucian world order dates from the nineteenth-century resurgence of interest in the seventeenth-century cult of the 'Rosy Cross', a rich mix of alchemy, political science and apocalyptic predictions; it now seems likely to have been a sophisticated literary hoax (Images)

This 1939 illustration by Frank R. Paul in *Fantastic Adventures* may seem comic, but our ideas about the appearance of extra-terrestrials have not altered a great deal since then (Mary Evans)

A UFO photographed above Albuquerque, New Mexico in June 1963. Sightings of alleged UFOs have been linked to ley-lines and ancient megalithic sites (Mary Evans)

Left: Heinrich Nusslein's mediumistic artwork shows the king of an unknown transgalactic civilisation (FPL)

Above: A fork twisted during an experiment in psychic metal-bending (FPL)

Cornish witches invoking the 'Owlman' near Falmouth, 1 November 1980 (FPL)

Magical symbols as used by nineteenth-century magician Eliphas Levi (Images)

Witches dance around a midnight bonfire by Lough Leane, Co. Kerry in 1981 to summon the magical powers of a water spirit (FPL)

Above left: an eighteenth-century witch's 'poppet' used to cast spells (Images); and, *above right*, amulets and remedies for sale in a modern witch-doctors' market in La Paz, Bolivia (FPL)

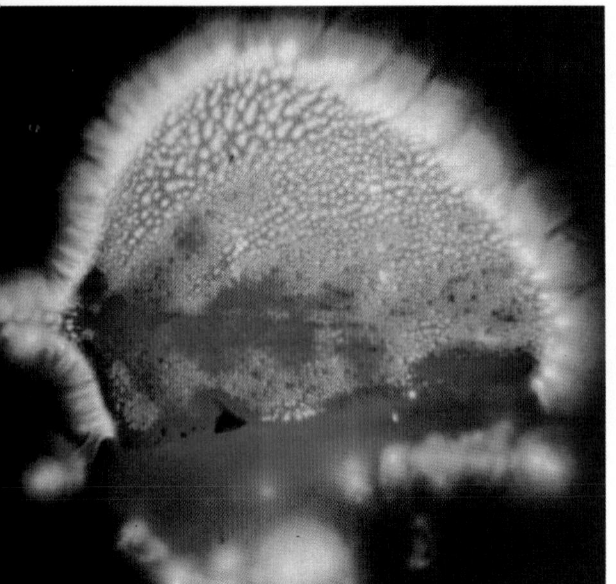

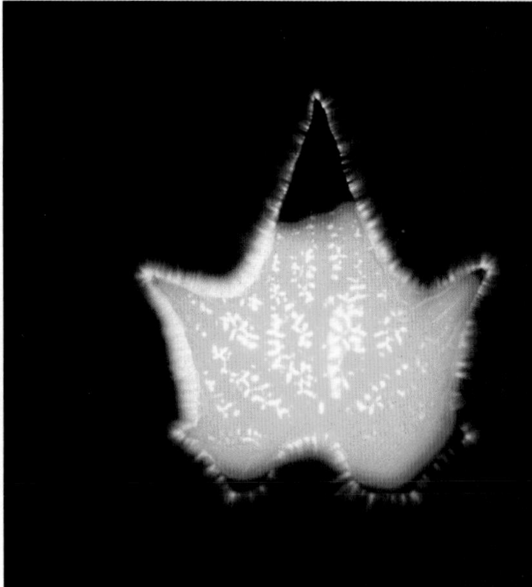

Russian engineer Semyan Kirlian discovered that living tissue emits electromagnetic 'force fields' which show up on photo-sensitive paper. *Above, left and right,* cut leaves still show the outline of the missing segments, prompting suggestions that Kirlian photography reveals the 'astral body' (Mary Evans)

A document, said to have been signed (in reverse Latin) as a pact between the seventeenth-century priest Urbain Grandier and the demons, headed by Lucifer (Images)

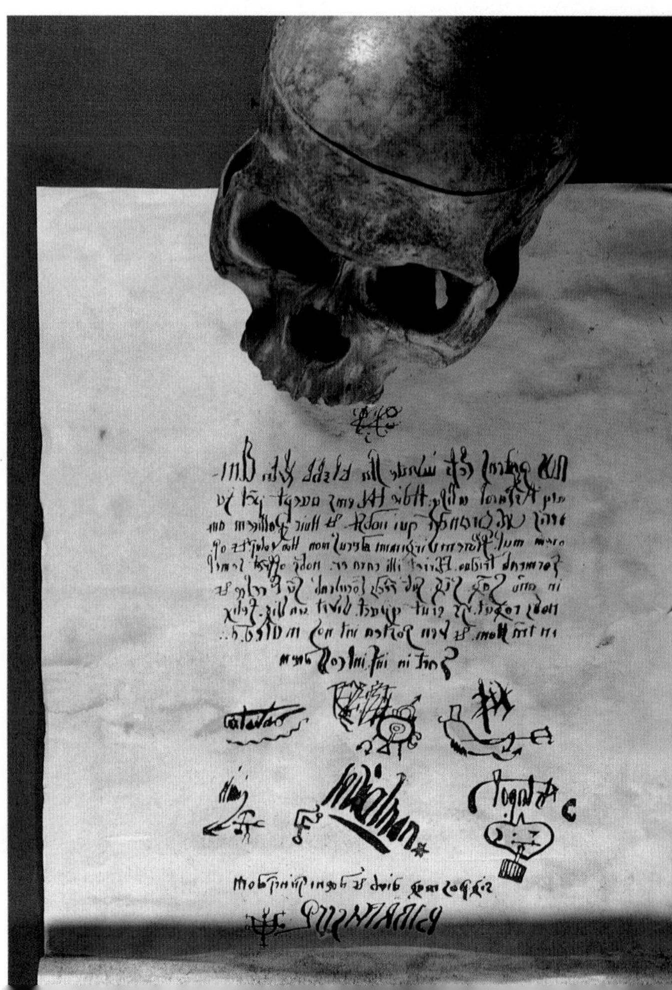

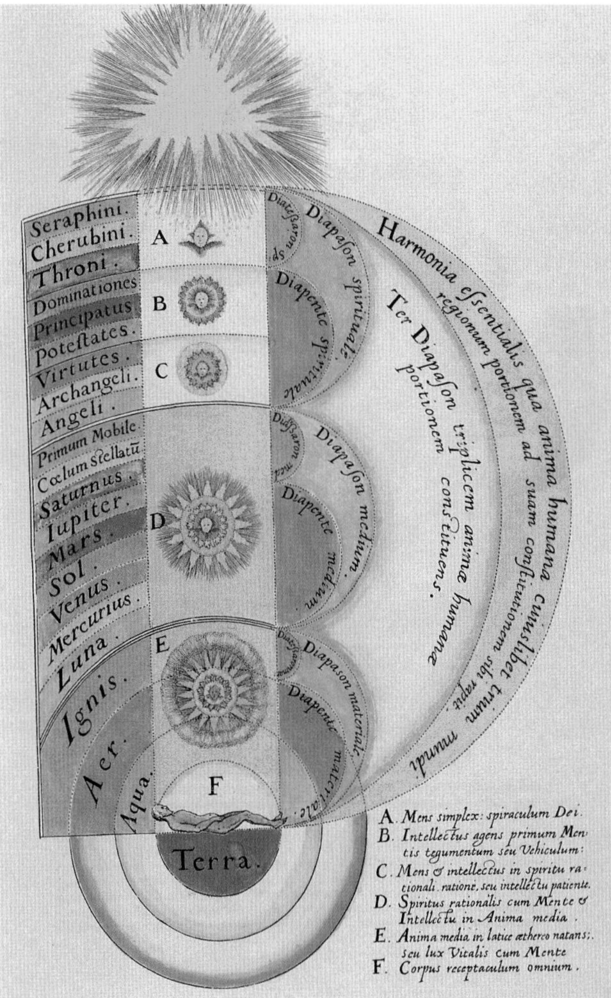

Some symbols of different belief systems compared: *above,* universal harmony is implicit in the medieval concept of the Song of the Spheres, the ever-shifting yet ever-constant celestial interplay; *above right,* the Tibetan Wheel of Life symbolises the six 'palaces' or divisions of life; *right,* a Yin and Yang symbol on a decorative Chinese gate expresses all the eternally interacting pairs of opposites which cannot exist one without the other – male and female, light and dark, passive and active ... (Images)

Lallemant de Betz's zodiac chart (Mary Evans)

Polarised, I was paralysed,
Plausibility palated,
People realised totally,
Woefully, once I totally
Opened their eyes.[1]

Auther Ian Wilson asks if Christopher Nolan's literary gift is *because* of his condition. Does his talent arise from enforced focus on the world of the mind, fed by awareness of his distinction from 'ordinary' people?'

Nolan has said his pain is not just a physical agony but also arises from rejection by the 'healthy'. With others like him through history he suffers the jibe of idiots that *he* is the idiot. In his autobiography he writes, 'Century upon century saw crass crippled man dashed, branded, and treated as dross in a world offended by their appearance, and cracked asunder in their belittlement by having to resemble venial human specimens offering nothing and pondering less in their life of mindless normality.'[2]

As with Helen Keller, Nolan's fight for expression suggests the depth of the reservoir of will we may tap if we must.

1. *Superself*, Ian Wilson, Sidgwick and Jackson, London 1989
2. *Under the Eye of the Clock*, Christopher Nolan, Weidenfeld and Nicolson, London 1987, p. 3

NOOSPHERE A term coined by Jesuit theologian **Teilhard de Chardin** to describe growth of 'world-mind' or 'planetary consciousness'. From Greek *nous*, 'mind', it implies the coming-of-age of **Gaia**'s (human) intellect.

NOSTRADAMUS (1503–66) (*See* **PROPHECY**) Born at Saint-Rémy in Provence to Jewish-Gentile grain merchants, Michel de Notredame, or Nostradamus, graduated from Montpellier University in 1525 as a doctor in a time of plague. Scorning the plague doctor's 'magical robe' and refusing to bleed victims, his reliance on sanitary precautions – pure water, fresh air – aided his growing renown as a healer. Yet when in 1538 his wife and children died (of plague) the Toulouse Inquisition accused him of heresy. He fled and for six years wandered, pursuing **occult** studies until invited to fight the plague in Aix – alone. When the plague abated the grateful city voted him a pension. In 1547 he married a rich widow, Anne Ponsart Gemelle of Salon, where he settled to father a family and start work on the *Prophecies*. First published in 1555 and called the *Centuries* (C) after their intended final organisation into twelve books each of 100 quatrains (Q) (four-line verses), these brought him instant (and enduring) fame throughout Europe.

In 1556 Catherine de Medici, Queen of France, summoned him to explain CI,Q35, a quatrain seemingly predicting the death of her husband, Henri II. He so impressed her that, when in 1559 the king died, his eye pierced by a lance as foreseen, Catherine's protection (she was not so kind to others) spared him the Inquisition's attentions. When in 1566 he died of dropsy he was, as he had predicted, 'trouvé tout mort prés entre le lit et le banc' – found stone dead on the bench he used to climb into bed.[1]

In their final 1568 version the *Prophecies* of Nostradamus comprise 965 quatrains and a few other verses written in an obscure mixture of French, Latin, Greek and Provençal. Their time-sequence deliberately jumbled, they purport to foretell global history up to AD 3797. The death of Charles I, the French Revolution, the rise of Napoleon, Franco, **Hitler** and Mussolini, and the destruction of Hiroshima are among events commonly identified. For the end of the twentieth century they predict the rise of **Antichrist**, a terrible twenty-seven-year war, then a **New Age**. Being mostly published in his lifetime, later interpretation or invention can be checked against the original text.

Yet his explanations of his prophetic technique are as enigmatic as the prophecies themselves. In the first quatrain of the *Centuries* he tells how:

Estant assis de nuict secret estude,
Seul, reposé sur la selle d'aerian?
Flambe exiguë sortant de sollitude,
Fait prospérer qui n'est à croire vain.

('At night, studying alone in a secluded place, and rested on a bronze chair, a small flame comes out of the solitude and brings to pass [predictions] which should not be thought vain.')[2]

The second quatrain, even more ambiguous, suggests a **divinatory** technique used by the fourth-century **Neoplatonist** Iamblichus: seeking **vision** in a bowl of water on a brass tripod. He insists that 'Divine splendour, divinity itself, sits by him', and in his Letter to his son César (preface to the *Centuries*), he says his art 'is governed by the power of Almighty God, inspiring us not by Bacchic frenzy nor by enchantments but by astronomical assurances'.[3] Refusing to name the books he used, he says he burned them on completing the work. Yet, while many prophecies (of aerial warfare, etc.), may be rational deduction rather than occult prescience, it seems he used **ritual magic** – dangerous in an intolerant time. Thus his deliberate ambiguities. Yet the prophecies themselves cover ground wider than any attempted by any other post-Biblical seer; and some at least seem to refer to specific events centuries ahead of his time:

De la cité marine et tributaire,
La teste raze prendra la Satrapie:
Chassez sordide qui puis sera contraire,
Par quatorze ans tiendra la tyranie, CVII, Q13

('From the port under foreign domination the shaven-headed man will take power. He will drive out the squalid revolutionaries, the wind of history having changed, and will rule tyrannically for fourteen years.')[4]

This is thought to refer to Napoleon. Retaking the port of Toulon from the English in 1793, he overthrew the Directory and enjoyed absolute power from the end of 1799 until April 1814. Yet the quatrain is as ambiguous as all the rest. The use of anagram, syncope, aphesis and other word-games offers vast scope for false interpretation. Thus 'Lonole' has been interpreted as Oliver Cromwell or London; 'Hister' as Hitler or the Danube (Ister). The problem of deliberate participation also arises. Dictators have been eager to fulfil quatrains assumed to favour them. Hitler's decision to invade Poland in 1939 was influenced by the 'Hister' verses (CII,Q24, etc.), and by Loog's version of CIII,Q57 (*Die Weissagungen des Nostradamus*, 1921). Both the Nazis and the Allies used 'Nostradamus' for propaganda purposes. Swiss astrologer Karl Ernst Krafft forged pro-Nazi quatrains; the Allies hired novelist Louis de Wohl to produce quatrains that predicted an Allied victory. In 1944 Pierre Laval, the collaborationist French leader, banned the sale of the *Centuries:* they spoke of an old man 'mocked by everyone' (himself?) and 'a general who returned in triumph' (De Gaulle?).[5]

Can our participatory belief in well-known prophecies bring about their 'fulfilment'? If so, we should worry. Take CX,Q72:

L'an mil neuf cens nonante neuf sept mois,
Du ciel viendra un grand Roy d'effrayeur.

Ressusciter le grand Roy d'Angoulmois.
Avant après Mars regner par bonheur.

('In July 1999 a great, terrifying leader will come through the skies to revive [the memory of?] the great conqueror of Angoulême'. Before and after war will rule luckily.')[6]

This notorious quatrain is typically ambiguous. How can war rule luckily? Who is the 'great conqueror? Interpreters disagree as usual. De Fontbrune (his version above: Cheetham differs both in interpretation and 'original' text), explains that Angoulême was once conquered by the Huns, a Mongol race. Thus the text is said to refer to the return of Attila the Hun, or his memory; meaning the coming of one like him – the Antichrist?

But note the apocalyptic similarity of such quatrains to imagery found in *Revelation*. Nostradamus both copied St John's style and used orthodox Biblical chronology, which held that the world, created in 4004 BC, must last 6,000 years until the final battle with Antichrist and overthrow of Babylon, leading to a New Age of peace (the Rule of the Saints) and the Last Judgement. 6,000 years brings us, by this reckoning, to the end of the twentieth century. His date of July 1999 was thus an orthodox choice for Apocalypse and personally astute, given that he was a Jewish doctor suspected of magic and heresy in an intolerant age. His portrayal of our near future is thus (whatever else) a conscious elaboration of **millenarian** Christian tradition, with St John's **Apocalypse** a dominant influence. That it also provides a moral model or warning applicable to any age including his own is another aspect, while (as Pitt Francis points out), since he *copied* rather than *interpreted* the biblical tradition, he had nothing to lose should it later prove false. In any case, by 1999 he would be long dead, unavailable for further questioning.[7] So whether Nostradamus believed the Apocalypse literally due in 1999 must remain an open question. Sufficient to recall his own warning concerning facile interpretation.

Let those who read these verses judge them naturally:
Let the vulgar and stupid rabble not approach them:
And let all Astrologers, fools and barbarians keep away'
May whoever does otherwise be justly accursed.[8]

1. *The Further Prophecies of Nostradamus*, Erika Cheetham, Corgi, London 1985, pp. 78–9.
2. *Nostradamus 1: Countdown to Apocalypse*, Jean-Charles de Fontbrune, Pan, London 1984 (trans: Alexis Lykiard), p. 428.
3. *Ibid.*, p. xxii.
4. *Ibid.*, p. xxix.
5. *Nostradamus: Prophecies of Present Times*, David Pitt-Francis, Aquarian Press, Wellingborough 1985, p. 251.
6. *op. cit.* ref. 2, p. 428.
7. *op. cit.* ref. 5, p. 125ff.
8. *op. cit.* ref. 2, p. 3.

NUMBER (*See* **GEMATRIA, GREAT PYRAMID, SACRED GEOMETRY**), **Names** and numbers grew together. In Babylonian, **Hindu** and Pythagorean tradition Number is the basic principle from which the objective world is born. The underlying harmonies of cosmos, music, art, poetry and human psychology may be expressed in number, numbers being not just quantitative expressions but **symbolic** entities. 'Everything is disposed according to numbers,' claimed Pythagoras. The ancient Chinese considered *odd* numbers as *yang* – male, celestial and auspicious; *even* numbers as *yin* – female, terrestrial, inauspicious. Today in the West the odd number thirteen is thought so unlucky (*see* **Moon**) that it is often left out in the numbering of houses on a street or apartments in a block. Likewise today the manipulation of number ('Number-crunching') is so much at the root of society, whether in terms of finance, physics or **numerological** prediction, that we cannot escape it. Without calculation of Number we have no functional society.

Today Number may be applied 'rationally' but our basic approach to it is 'magical' or symbolic. Every number has a meaning. The mystery of the Great Pyramid is apparent chiefly in that its dimensions express numerical relationships transcending time and historical prejudice to prove beyond reasonable doubt the *number-skills* (and thus philosophical wisdom) of its builders. Numerological doctrine as developed by the Hebrews holds that we each have a *personal number*, much as we have a personal **horoscope**, which indicates our individual character-type and likely fate. Numerology thus implies **predestination**, and for this and other reasons is now usually considered spurious. Yet its debasement into a **fortune-telling** art should not blind us to the ingenuity of those who first established it.

For centuries specific values have been ascribed to particular numbers. What are these values? How are they applied (or misapplied) in numerology?

Zero, alias O, is non-being, the Void, from which *being* springs. No numerological table of character-analysis includes Zero. In **Tarot** the card called 'The Fool' is today numbered Zero. Zero is the empty circle, total abstraction, the Cosmic Egg, latent power unknown to itself.

One is almost as odd. What does it emerge from? One is nothing without Two and Three; they mean nothing without the phenomena derived from them. For One is a point, single-minded primordial unity, the Centre, indivisible Ego, isolation. '**Tao** begets One.' One-people are said to be leaders, creators, arrogant and bold, without close friends, potential tyrants.

Two is duality: above and below, opposite poles, length stretched from One. Sun and Moon, Light and Dark, Yang and Yin, Male and Female. Two is the line, the Tower, the Phallus. Two-people are said to be soft, even-tempered, conciliatory . . . or cruel and malicious if they follow their dark side.

Three is multiplicity, the first potential expression of body, **soul** and **spirit**. Three absorbs One and Two into a mystery: the Trinity, the 'Three-in-One'; the 'Holy Ghost'. In **Qabalah**, Three bears the female design of Binah, the Great Mother, in whose womb-void all material creation commences. Three is Father, Mother, Son: Thrice-Great **Hermes**, Triple Goddess, three wishes, the triangle. Three-people are supposedly brilliant, bold and ambitious.

Four (crossing the **Qabalistic** Abyss) is the blueprint of the practical, four-square, physical world. The 'four-gated city' is an ancient image for the balanced soul, guarded in all directions: static, total, whole, well-ordered, square. There are four cardinal points, seasons, elements, limbs of the body. Four-people are solid, down-to-earth, practical administrators, yet prone to melancholy or sudden rage. Four is Jupiter.

Five is adventurous Mars, the number of Man. The spreadeagled human form as portrayed by da Vinci. Two arms, two legs (four) plus *head*. A five-pointed star. The Pentagram, the human microcosm, the centre of a squared circle. It is individuality, aspiration. Five-people like change, risk and speculation. It is said they are domestically unreliable.

Six is even, is resolution, is the number of **Christ** and of reason, is Qabalistically the midpoint of the **Tree of Life** between High and Low. 666 is the Number of the Beast, alias Man (head, arms, legs and phallus). It is the number of the Sun, of intellect. The symbolic world was created in six days. Six-people are harmonious, loyal, idealistic and affectionate.

Seven is Venus-union of Three (the heavens) and Four (the earth). There are seven heavens, seven hells, seven Ages of Man, seven wonders of the world, seven days in a week. The Pleiades are the Seven Sisters: anciently it was thought there were seven planets. Seven governs **mysticism** and **magic** (the seventh son of a seventh son). Seven-folk are said to be idealistic, world-denying, impecunious, dreamy, aloof, sarcastic, pessimistic.

Eight is double-four, the octagon, a new beginning, but may also mean money and worldly power. Eight-people are said to be hard, material, selfish, unscrupulous, yet with an underlying mercurial eccentricity.

Nine is high intellectual and spiritual achievement, thrice three. Nine is the number the Hebrews (it is said) thought too holy for inclusion in their numerological system. Nine-folk, full of big ideas, may often be found as teachers, scientists or artists. Strong-willed, they are often regarded by others as wild, impractical or impossibly egocentric. The names of US Presidents Lincoln and Kennedy both add up to nine.

Numbers above nine are usually reduced to single digits, but exceptions are made for eleven and twenty-two. Eleven-folk – Winston S. Churchill, **Einstein**, Pablo Picasso – are regarded as visionaries bringing revelation, sometimes at the cost of martyrdom. As for Twenty-two-folk (who might just be ordinary Fours) – these are said to be great *masters*, for good or ill. But use a pinch of salt if you find you're an Eleven or a Twenty-two. Numerological systems today look *silly* – which is not to say Number is silly. Why throw out the baby with the bathwater? Human **superstition** about Number does not invalidate the essential power of Number itself. The ancient art of Gemetria, employing number-substitution for letters as practised in numerology, underlies all code systems and led to the establishment of complex hidden meanings both in the Old and New Testaments of the Bible.

1. *An Illustrated Encyclopaedia of Traditional Symbols*, J. C. Cooper, Thames and Hudson, London 1978, pp. 113–20

NUMEROLOGICAL SYSTEMS Numerological prediction relies on two main sources – birth-date and name. From birth-date your personal number is determined by reduction. If born on 18.5.1947, adding the individual digits gives a total of 35, 3 + 5 = 8. Your number is thus 8. (If born under other calendrical systems – Jewish, Chinese, Islamic, etc. – calculate accordingly!)

Calculating your number from your name requires conversion of the letters of your name into numerical equivalents as set forth by whichever system you choose. Some numerologists follow the 'modern' system, which uses the number 9 and gives the following correspondences:

1	2	3	4	5	6	7	8	9
A	B	C	D	E	F	G	H	I
J	K	L	M	N	O	P	Q	R
S	T	U	V	W	X	Y	Z	

The other system, called the 'Hebrew' system, excludes the number 9 (simply because the Hebrew letters standing for 9 lack equivalents in Western alphabets) and places the letters of the alphabet in a different order:

1	2	3	4	5	6	7	8
A	B	C	D	E	U	O	F
I	K	G	M	H	V	Z	P
Q	R	L	T	N	W		
J		S			X		
Y							

Converting each letter of your name into its number equivalent, add all the digits to find the sum of the name. Take the two digits of the resulting sum. Add them together to find your number. Thus, by the 'modern system', FRED = 6 + 9 + 5 + 4 = 24. 2 + 4 = 6. FRED's number is thus 6. Of course, the Hebrew system will give a different result.[1] The process is arbitrary, to say the least. In short, it is a parlour game, and not to be taken too seriously.

Yet symbolic fact underlies **fortune-telling superstition**. The meanings attributed to individual numbers are not arbitrary. Numerology arises from our natural preoccupation with ***number***, from the amount in our wage-packet, to the number of fingers on our hands, to our suspicion of the number thirteen. Why is thirteen bad luck? Not only because it is an awkward, indivisible number, but because there are in fact thirteen, not twelve, months in a year (13 × 28 = 364), and the thirteen-month year belongs to a former **pagan, moon**-worshipping social system eliminated by the Church and the rational (four-square, twelve-month) *solar* mind.

1. *The Magical Arts*, Richard Cavendish, Arkana, London 1984, pp. 47–53

O

OANNES (*See* **ANCIENT ASTRONAUTS**)

OCCULT From the Latin *occulere*, 'to hide' or 'to conceal', thence by extension inferring secret, esoteric, or mysterious knowledge beyond the range of the everyday: whatever is **supernatural**, mystical, magical or **paranormal**. Also a term used in astronomy to refer to a large body passing in front of a smaller, thus '*occulting*' or *occluding* the smaller.

ODIC FORCE (*See* **REICHENBACH**)

OLCOTT, Henry (1832–1907) (*See* **BLAVATSKY**)

OMEN (*See* **BIRDS, DIVINATION, PROPHECY**) Any event or object said to portend good or **evil**, its meaning interpreted by **divination**. Omens occur spontaneously or are sought. Ancient Celtic **Druids** and Roman augurers sought omens in the flight of birds, marking out a given space and seeking answer to their questions by observing the flight pattern, species and other behaviour of birds impinging on that space. In Ireland, each sound, position and movement of domesticated wrens or ravens had significance. If the bird called from the door, strangers or soldiers were on the way; if it called with 'a small voice', sickness was expected.

'I heard the cuckoo while fasting', remarked a Scot, 'and I knew the year would not go well with me.' In 1814 a minister at Dornoch in Scotland fell ill: a cormorant settled on the church steeple; his rapid death was seen to fulfil the fatal omen. Thirty-five years later the same event reoccurred and the incumbent also died. Likewise in Scotland a raven settling on the roof was an omen of approaching death within the house. A dove that flew round a person's head was also *ominous*. In Devon a swarm of bees alighting in a dead tree was taken as an omen of death, but a strange swarm alighting in the garden was an omen of wealth to come. The Druids derived omens from the chirping of wrens, called *dryw* in Welsh – the 'Druid bird'. Before joining battle with the Romans, Queen Boadicea let loose a hare, which ran off in what the Iceni considered the auspicious direction, so that they 'shouted with pleasure, seeing victory within their grasp', as Dio Cassius reports.

Omens were also drawn from the direction taken by the smoke and flames of sacred fires, from the appearance of clouds, by the howling of dogs, by the shape of tree-roots, by the death-throes of a stabbed man; from **dreams**; the state of the entrails, liver or shoulder-blades of slaughtered animals, and by many other means.[1] In Kenya a *murogi* or **shaman** of the Kikuyu would toss his sandals and derive omens from the way they fell on the ground. So too the throwing of dice, coins or yarrow sticks (as in the ***I Ching*** system of divination) have been universally employed to generate omens.

Underlying such systems is the belief that all events interconnect; the meaning in apparently chance events may be divined by **intuition. Jungian** speculation that the **collective unconscious** knows all things implies that this approach may not be so absurd as rationality alone supposes.

1. *The Magic Arts in Celtic Britain*, Lewis Spence, Rider, London 1970

ORACLE (*See* **MEDIUMS**) From Latin *orare*, 'to speak'; thus a place or person, or both, at and from which **prophetic** advice is given. The great classical Oracle was at Delphi in Greece, a vast establishment focussed on the priestess or Pythoness who, seated in a cave on a tripod straddling a cleft in the earth from which arose **trance**-inducing fumes, answered queries put to her by supplicants, though famously in a way so ambiguous that misinterpretation led many to ruin. Originally in the power of **Gaia**, the Earth-goddess, the Delphic Oracle passed into the hands of the Sun-god Apollo as part of the process whereby male logic and commerce took over female lunar trance-wisdom. Yet the Oracles at Delphi and elsewhere appear to have functioned similarly to **Spiritualist mediums** today, via trance-contact with sources no better understood by Apollonian reason now than then. Apollo took over the Oracle as manager, not as **seer**. The oracles became a profiteering industry, and in so doing gradually lost their power, their contact with the 'gods'.

ORDO TEMPLI ORIENTIS (*See* **CROWLEY**)

ORGONE ENERGY (*See* **REICH**)

ORIGINAL SIN Original Sin refers to the Christian dogma that man is innately depraved because (Genesis iii) Adam ate of the Tree of the Knowledge of Good and Evil (the forbidden fruit), even though God had said: 'Ye shall not eat of it, neither shall ye touch it, lest ye die.' Yet the **Serpent** told Eve: 'Ye shall not surely die.' Eve ate the fruit, then persuaded Adam to do the same. Neither died. In effect, the Serpent proved God a liar.

Advanced particularly by St Paul and embraced by the early Christian Church, this patriarchal idea that Adam lost Paradise because he listened to the advice of Woman is pernicious. To claim that all generations since are born damned, redeemed only by belief in **Christ** (alias submission to the patriarchal Church), compounded the psychological catastrophe. 'Allas, allas, that ever love was sinne!' cries Chaucer's Wife of Bath in the fourteenth century. The Church, for its own ends, thus conferred a permanent guilt on Western Mankind. Yet Yeshua, or Jesus, never condemned anyone for their human nature. Today we in the West remain so mentally colonised by the idea of 'Original Sin' that though we may reject it intellectually, it still affects our outlook. Not least it justified misogyny and denial of 'caring' virtues, and heightened a sense of separation from the Earth-Mother (Eve, *alias* **Gaia**), leading to industrial exploitation and the continuing pollution of Earth.

ORPHEUS (*See* **GREEK MYSTERIES**)

OSIRIS (*See* **ANCIENT ASTRONAUTS, ISIS, SIRIUS**) The Egyptian progenitor of all died-and-reborn God-**myths** from Dionysus to **Christ**, Osiris has been euhemerised by some as a culture-hero, or even an extraterrestrial, perhaps of Sirian origin. The first son of the gods Geb and Nut, it is said he was handsome, *dark*-skinned, and taller than others. On becoming king of Egypt he took his sister Isis as queen, abolished cannibalism, taught agriculture, law and **religion**, and built the first towns and temples. Later he journeyed the world, his gentleness and music (as with Orpheus) disarming people everywhere. Having spread civilisation he returned to Egypt to find Isis ruling wisely, but his jealous brother Set had him assassinated. Set then cut up his body into fourteen pieces which he scattered through Egypt. Recovering them, Isis magically restored Osiris to life and conceived their son, Horus, who later fought Set in wars which some claim were 'space battles'. Resurrected, Osiris chose to reign in the underworld to welcome the souls of the just. As god of the dead he was worshipped in Egypt along with Isis and Horus, thus forming a trinity.

The myth may be based in the life of a pre-dynastic king. As for the extraterrestrial hypothesis, Temple points out that, as Isis was identified with Sirius, Osiris, her 'dark companion', might have symbolised Sirius B, the dark star apparently known to the ancients and to the Dogon of Mali before being discovered by Western astronomers in the mid-nineteenth century.[1]

1. *The Sirius Mystery*, Robert K. G. Temple, Futura, London 1977, pp. 97–102

OUIJA BOARD A device, often used casually as a party game, for communicating with the dead. An ouija board is simply created by placing cut-out letters of the alphabet randomly in a circle on a smooth tabletop. The words 'Yes' and 'No' are included, opposite each other. A tumbler or glass is set upside-down in the centre of the circle thus formed. Seated roundabout, those involved lay a finger of one hand lightly on the glass. Questioning usually starts with, 'Is there anyone here?' The communicating **spirit**, if any, spells out its answers to queries by moving the glass from letter to letter. Sceptics may accuse others of deliberately moving the glass (which no doubt occurs). Yet often those who thought it a party game become disturbed or frightened, either by accurate answers, or by unexpected and apparently **psychokinetic** manifestations (sudden cold draughts in closed rooms, articles falling off tables, etc.) that suggest the presence of a genuinely inexplicable force.

Dr Jerry Goldfisher, chief medical officer at a New Jersey hospital, told how, 'One night when I was in medical school, six other students and I were fooling around with an ouija board for the first time (this was in November 1941), and we asked when the invasion would take place that would stop **Hitler**'s Reich. The board said, "June 6". When the Normandy invasion actually took place on that date in 1944, we called each other, remembering the ouija prediction. I truly can't explain this incident.'[1]

Frivolous use of this and similar devices is not recommended.

1. *Intangible Evidence*, Bernard Gittelson, Simon and Schuster, London 1987

OUSPENSKY, P. D. (1878–1948) (*See* **DREAMS, GURDJIEFF**) Peter Demianovich Ouspensky attempted to synthesise mathematics, religion, science and the **occult** into a unified system of thought. Though known best for *In Search of the Miraculous* (his account of eight years spent studying under Gurdjieff) his books *Tertium Organum* and *A New Model of the Universe* display an original, passionate mind. Impressed by a book on physics aged fourteen, his dislike of the dryness of science led him to study occultism and to wander the east in search of 'esoteric knowledge'.

'I had been living in a desiccated and sterilised world,' he wrote of his early occult research, 'with an infinite number of taboos imposed on my thought. And suddenly these strange books broke down all the walls round me, and made me think and dream about things which for a long time I had feared to think and dream. Suddenly I began to find a strange meaning in old **fairy tales**; woods, rivers, mountains, became living beings; mysterious life filled the night; with new interest and new expectations, I began to dream again of distant travels.'[1]

His account of Gurdjieff remains valuable. Being of independent mind himself, he realised that Gurdjieff was fallible. This refusal to worship blindly adds authenticity to his reports of strange events such as the way in which, in summer 1916, Gurdjieff spoke to him by **telepathy**. 'I heard his voice inside me, as if it were in the chest, near the heart.' Accepting Gurdjieff's claim that the human race is mostly asleep, he also noted that in the presence of Gurdjieff it was impossible to get away with lies or to conceal facts. Once he brought a friend to Gurdjieff, 'A', a clever man who talked all night long. Embarrassed, about to shut 'A' up, Ouspensky eyed Gurdjieff, who 'looked at me so fiercely that I stopped short'.

After 'A' left, Gurdjieff commented, 'He is called a clever man. But he would not have noticed even if I had taken his trousers off him. Only let him talk. He wants nothing else. And everyone is like that. And this one was much better than many others. He told no lies. And he really knew what he talked about, in his own way of course. But . . . perhaps this was the one time in his life when there was an opportunity of hearing the truth. And he talked himself all the time.'[2]

1. *A New Model of the Universe*, P. D. Ouspensky, Routledge Kegan Paul, London, 1969, p. 4
2. *In Search of the Miraculous*, P. D. Ouspensky, Routledge Kegan Paul, London, 1969, p. 273

OUT-OF-THE-BODY-EXPERIENCES (*See* **JUNG, MONROE, MULDOON, NEAR-DEATH-EXPERIENCES**) Can we exist consciously outside the physical body? 'Out-of-the-body-experiences' (OOBEs) are not only remarkably common, but are increasingly subjected to **parapsychological** tests making it hard to dismiss them as **hallucination** or fantasy. Too often 'astral travellers' are seen by others while abroad in their **'subtle' body**, or later offer information impossible to acquire otherwise. Often those near death or clinically dead undergo OOBEs and, after revival, accurately report the desperate attempts made to revive them (*see* **Near-Death Experiences**). Where occurring spontaneously to those otherwise in good health, typically the body is viewed from above, usually during sleep. Typically the subject feels split into two or more aspects. The vacated physical body is one: the others may be described as the mental, **astral**, subtle or **etheric** bodies (definitions of these terms and their implications remain imprecise.) In some cases, but not all, the subject reports a 'silver cord' or 'thread' connecting the subtle body to the physical body: they sense that return to physicality is possible only if this cord remains intact. Also commonly reported is a sense of contact with a 'guardian **angel**' or protective **entity** which, rarely seen directly, insists (often against the individual's will) on return to the physical.

The most common experience is that of seeing oneself from a distance (autoscopy). Travelling OOBEs are rarer, usually arising from a consciously developed facility, as with Monroe and Muldoon. But in most cases, spontaneous or deliberate, the subject is convinced by the experience that personal identity survives death. The experience is not vague or dreamlike, but distinct and vivid: more 'real' than daily waking life, reminiscent of **Gurdjieff**'s claim that waking **consciousness** is a form of sleep.

Literature on the subject falls into three categories: (1) books by authors like Monroe and Muldoon, describing detailed, repeated personal experience; (2) collections of anecdotal material; and (3) laboratory reports claiming to place the phenomenon on a scientific basis. The latter include the work by Charles Tart with Robert Monroe, and reports on **psychics** such as Ingo **Swann**.

Studying anecdotal material, parapsychologist Hornell Hart found 228 published cases of reported '**ESP** projection', ninety-nine containing evidence of correct perception of actions or objects located too far away for identification to have taken place in the physical body. Of 800 cases collected by Robert Crookall, many demonstrated, as with Hart: (1) perception of distant places and persons; (2) perception of an **apparition**; (3) perception from 'outside' of the subject's physical body; (4) the sensation of inhabiting a 'subtle' or 'apparition' body; and (5) that this body defied gravity. Crookall also noted that subjects were often unaware of the moment when separation from the physical body occurred; that **discarnate** entities were often sensed, and that the silver cord, commonly reported, often exercises a 'pull', drawing the dissociated conscious self back into the body.[1]

Monroe's experiences remain perhaps the most notable, but many other accounts exist. In his 1934 novel *Resurrection* William Gerhardie tells how he awoke from a feverish dream, reached out to turn on the lamp, but found himself floating up by the ceiling, attached to his body only by a 'cable of light' from his forehead to the back of his 'neck'. He found he could pass through doors and walls at will, and began memorising details to be checked later. But suddenly, 'pushed up like a half-filled balloon', he found himself out on the street, and knew he could go wherever he wanted. Afraid of losing contact with his physical body, he willed himself back to his bedroom and, 'with a jerk that shook me', found himself re-embodied.[2]

Again, inspired by Muldoon's accounts, every night for a month **psychic** researcher Professor Arthur Ellison tried imaginatively to rotate himself 'about an axis from head to feet' and thus loosen the grip of the physical body. At last he entered a cataleptic state, unable to move a muscle. 'I used my will – or was it my imagination? – to make myself float upwards, and the experience was quite fascinating . . . Slowly I floated upwards, like an airship released from its moorings. I reached the ceiling and floated through it into the darkness of the roof-space. Then I passed through the roof tiles, and the sky, clouds and Moon became visible. I increased my 'willing' (or 'imagining'), and my velocity of ascent up into the sky increased. I have the memory of the wind whistling through my hair clearly to this day.' Later, trying to move beyond what Muldoon called 'cord activity range', he reports: 'As I cleared the window and started the descent to the lawn . . . I felt two hands take my head, one hand over each ear, move me (still cataleptic) back into the bedroom and down into the body. I heard no sound and saw nothing.'[3]

This suggests the same experience reported by those returned from near-death journeys: though wishing to move beyond a point of no return, they *are not allowed to*. They are sent back, though whether unconsciously by themselves or by an 'external' entity (or both) remains unclear.

The notion of protective entities is also reported by British psychic John Heron, who writes of travelling to what he calls '***ka***-domains' at 'very high speed, in something like a rushing energy wind. . . . I only feel the presence, but have no perception, of those who are conducting me on the journey.' Commenting on this report, Colin **Wilson** speculates that OOBEs are simply a version of Jung's 'active imagination', and that the entities sensed are **archetypes** of the **collective unconscious**, generated solely by the mind's 'hidden powers'. Yet, however neat this theory may seem, Wilson notes that he and most other **paranormal** researchers tend to believe in the reality of 'survival', on grounds of **intuition** if not of clear proof.[4]

1. *Survival?*, David Lorimer, Routledge Kegan Paul, London 1984, pp. 229–39
2. *Alien Intelligence*, Stuart Holroyd, Abacus, London 1980, pp. 85–6
3. *Beyond the Occult*, Colin Wilson, Corgi, London 1989, pp. 261–2
4. *op. cit.* ref. 2, pp. 461–3

P

PAGANISM (*See* **BLAKE, ORIGINAL SIN, POWYS**) Derived from Latin *paganus*, 'countryman', *paganism* implies 'heathen' (*of the heath or moor*) Nature-worship, whereby the elements, trees, earth, rivers, sea and sky are perceived as alive, each with their own indwelling **spirits**. Demonised by the **Christian** definition of life as unending conflict between good and **evil**, and by the insistence that nature (including human nature) is corrupt ('Original Sin') and must be corrected, pagan beliefs came to be defined as 'evil'. This negative definition in time provided 'moral' justification for persecution of witches and all beliefs derived from the older fertility religions. Yet mounting unease as to the moral supremacy of a milieu that spawned scientific materialism and 'dark satanic mills' led in the eighteenth century to a poetic revival of the essentially pagan or *pantheistic* notion that God indwells every aspect of the natural universe, and that 'everything that lives is holy'.

Thus wrote William Blake (1757–1827): his Romantic successors like Wordsworth, Coleridge, Keats and Shelley adopted a lyrical paganism, while Walt Whitman (1819–92) likewise celebrated the emergence of the USA. The essence of this pantheistic approach is found in *The Prelude* (Book 1), in which Wordsworth describes how, for days after a midnight boating trip:

> o'er my thoughts
> There hung a darkness, call it solitude
> Or blank desertion. No familiar shapes
> Remained, no pleasant images of trees,
> Of sea or sky, no colours of green fields;
> But huge and mighty forms, that do not live
> Like living men, moved slowly through the mind
> By day, and were a trouble to my dreams.

Twentieth century writers like Robert **Graves** and John Cowper Powys sustained this literary paganism, while today, increasing doubt as to the validity of Christian dogma and science that leads to planet-polluting industries has led to a wider revival of 'pagan' belief, especially among **Gaia**-oriented feminists and **New Age** environmentalists who feel that enough is enough, and that 'paganism' has been slandered unnecessarily.

PALLADINO, Eusapia (1854–1918) (*see* **MEDIUMS**) This controversial Italian medium's mother died giving birth to her; when she was twelve her father was murdered. In 1872 at a London séance the Italian **psychic** researcher Damiani's English wife was told by a spirit called John King of a powerful psychic in Naples, the reincarnation of his daughter. At the given address in Naples Damiani found Eusapia Palladino and helped her develop her dramatic powers. Customarily bound to a chair (to stop her cheating) she manifested **psychokinetic** phenomena so violent that tables rose in the air and seemed to attack observers; suggesting **poltergeist** phenemona as associated with disturbed adolescents. This, given her tragic background, is unsurprising. Though known to cheat if she could, phenomena manifested whatever controls were employed by the researchers investigating her. Parisian physiologist Charles

Richet conducted over a hundred séances with her and concluded her powers were genuine. **Flammarion** reported how, when she got angry, the phenomena became destructive. Sofas, tables and lesser objects rushed about the room; a man was thrown from his chair which 'came up on the table with a great clatter'; limb-like extrusions appeared from her body; human forms and parts of bodies materialised in full view. **Society for Psychical Research** investigators including Hereward Carrington conducted eleven séances with her in Naples in 1908: one of them, Everard Feilding, wrote after the sixth session, 'I have seen this extraordinary woman . . . held hand and foot . . . by my colleagues, immobile, except for the occasional straining of a limb while some **entity** . . . has over and over again pressed my hand in a position clearly beyond her reach.'

Though 'exposed' as a fraud in the USA in 1910, she convinced many that she was perhaps the greatest physical medium of the era.

PALMISTRY Also called *cheiromancy*, this system of **divination** is based on analysis of the lines, pads, texture, shape and colour of the human hand. Originating in India and China over 2,000 years ago, the art was also practised by the ancient Greeks, being used by **Plato** and referred to by Aristotle, and (it seems) by the Hebrews. In Job xxxvii, 7 it is said, 'He seals up the hand of every man, that all men may know his work.'

Taken up in mediaeval Europe as a magical art with **astrological** linkages, by the early eighteenth century palmistry was included in the curriculum at Leipzig University: a century later the young Napoleon had his palm read by Marie-Anne le Normand, who before witnesses predicted he would marry Josephine and become 'the most illustrious of all Frenchmen'.

In the early twentieth century Count Louis Hamon, alias Cheiro, told England's King Edward VII, 'You will not die, sir, until you are in your sixty-ninth year . . . but a namesake will give up his crown for love.' Edward VII died, aged 69, in 1910: in 1936 Edward VIII gave up the throne to marry Mrs Simpson. Cheiro also told Lord Kitchener he would die by drowning: Kitchener learned how to swim, but duly drowned in 1916, when his ship was sunk by a German mine en route to Russia. Cheiro also predicted his own death. Aged seventy, he asked his publisher to get the galley proofs of his most recent book to him quickly because he thought he would die on 8 October 1936. He did.[1]

Given that the uniqueness of the human fingerprint is recognised in law, some claim that palmistry is not so much a divinatory art as a type of scientific character analysis. Certainly, signs of specific physical characteristics are revealed in the hand. Reporting a study that found 'about thirty different congenital disorders . . . connected with particular patterns in the palm, some of which are apparent even before the disease appears', Lyall **Watson** has pointed out that a vast number of nerve sensors are located in the palm of the hand, and surmises that, as the ridges on the skin are formed by the twentieth week of foetal development – at the same time as the brain, nervous system and sense organs develop – then it is 'not at all unreasonable to assume that many internal events will show up externally through the skin'. He adds that there is a close connection between many skin diseases and mental states.[2]

Yet the extraordinary work of palmists like Cheiro and the American Nellie Meier suggest that, though logical method is involved, the skilled palmist (as with the skilled **astrologer** or **Tarot**-reader) also exercises divinatory **intuition** hard to explain rationally. Though 'islands' in the life-line may indicate illness, and a break in it, death; it is altogether harder to explain how Cheiro could predict the *exact date* of his own death. Indeed, the language of palmistry is innately astrological.

Each finger is 'ruled' by a particular planet (index, Jupiter; middle, Saturn; third, the sun; little finger, Mercury); the fleshy pads at the base of the fingers are known in turn, as the Mounts of Mercury, the Sun, Saturn and Jupiter; the thumb-pad is the Mount of Venus: the Mount of the Moon is the heel of the hand; the Mounts of Mars, positive and negative, lie either side of the hand. Different-shaped hands are: 'Earth' (square, few lines); 'Air' (long fingers, fine lines); 'Fire' (short, many lines); 'Water' (narrow, delicate and fine-lined). As for the lines (Heart, Head, Fate, Life, Intuition, Health, Marriage, Mars, etc.), their implications are self-explanatory. The interpretative systems of palmistry, as developed in many lands over two millennia, are as compiex as human nature and activity itself: there are many texts on the subject.[3]

1. *Intangible Evidence*, Bernard Gittleson, Simon and Schuster, London 1977
2. *Supernature*, Lyall Watson, Hodder and Stoughton, London 1973, pp. 189ff
3. *Palmistry*, Francis King, Orbis, London 1979

PARACELSUS (1493–1541) (*See* **AGRIPPA, ALCHEMY, ELEMENTALS**) *Philippus Aureolus Theophrastus Bombastus von Hohenheim* called himself Paracelsus – 'Greater than Celsus' (an ancient Roman physician). Arrogant, aggressive, usually angry, 'Always drunk and always lucid', his motto was 'He who can be his own, should not be another's'. A genius who overreacted to imagined slights and made enemies everywhere, his name, behaviour and contempt for established values gave rise to the word 'bombastic'.

Born near Zurich, he studied at Basel and Würzburg, then worked in the Tyrolese silver mines before travelling Europe. An army doctor in Naples and Holland, he practised medicine in Strasbourg, then in Basel became city physician. Like Agrippa, he was a romantic, seeking the Elixir of Life. He despised theoretical alchemists ('they carried golden mountains in their heads before they had put their hands to the fire'), but praised those more practically minded, 'They are sooty and black like smiths and colliers, and do not pride themselves upon a sleek countenance.' Their duty, he said, was to make not gold but healing drugs. Dropping the '*al*' from alchemy, he coined a new term – '*chemistry*'. He also took the Arab word for black eye-paint, *al-kohl*, and applied it to the spirits of wine – '*alcohol*', and made advances in using alcohol bases to extract the oils of healing herbs.[1]

Yet, like Agrippa, **Bruno** and **Dee**, he was a man caught between **magic** and science. Advising the *cleaning* of wounds, he also relied (despite his attacks on tradition) on arsenic and mercury in cures that killed as often as not. Viewing illness as arising from spiritual imbalance, he emphasised that man is the microcosm of nature and that health arises from maintaining harmony between man and nature. 'Man is not body,' he wrote. 'The heart, the **spirit**, is man. And this spirit is an entire star, out of which he is built. If therefore a man is perfect in his heart, nothing in the whole light of Nature is hidden from him.' Also teaching that each of the four elements has dual nature: one gross and corporeal, the other subtle and vaporous, he said that two quite different worlds intertwine: that of men, animals, plants and minerals, and that of the elementals. He wrote, 'The elementals are not spirits, because they have flesh, blood and bones; they live and propagate offspring; they eat and talk, act and sleep, etc., and consequently they cannot properly be called "spirits". They are beings occupying a place between men and spirits . . . (though) resembling spirits in the rapidity of their locomotion.'

'**Magic** is a teacher of medicine preferable to all the written books,' he wrote, defining magic as a 'power that comes direct from God'; adding, 'Magic is a Great Hidden Wisdom – Reason is a Great Open Folly' – an attitude anticipating **Jung's**, born near Zurich some 400 years later.

Indeed, Jung claimed a sense of inner kinship with this outrageous man. For Paracelsus was outrageous. He began at Basel by burning the books of Galen and other old masters, claiming they were all less gifted than the hairs of his beard. 'You are nothing but teachers and masters combing lice and scratching,' he told his colleagues,

'You are not worthy that a dog should lift his hind leg against you.'[2] Given such an attitude, it is no surprise that, despite his many cures (including the gout of Erasmus) he was driven from Basel. In April 1541 the Prince Palatine gave him refuge at Salzburg. Five months later, aged forty-eight, he died mysteriously. Some say he was poisoned by thugs paid by the medical establishment, others that he was pushed from the top of a cliff. Perhaps like Agrippa he simply died of exhaustion. Later his tomb was found empty. Rumours of **resurrection** may be dismissed. In a time when grave-robbery for medical purposes was common, such a famous body would have been a priority for dissection.

1. *The Alchemists*, Ronald Pearsall, Weidenfeld and Nicolson, London, p. 85
2. *The Occult*, Colin Wilson, Grafton Books, London 1989, p. 312

PARADIGM Derived from the Greek *paradeigma*, 'pattern', this term was introduced in 1970 by Thomas Kuhn in his book, *The Structure of Scientific Revolutions*, to denote any conceptual framework by which a scientific community derives a common model of reality. Subsequently the definition has been widened by **Capra** to suggest: 'the totality of thoughts, perceptions, and values that form a particular vision of reality'. Today (as with the idea of *zeitgeist*, or 'spirit of the times') the definition of *paradigm* has been broadened to suggest any collective idea which, spreading like **magic** (or by **morphic resonance**), creates a vision by which society reorganises itself. Yet again, we have a term that re-expresses an idea fallen into disrepute via the redundancy of an older term expressing the same perception. Thus in the Middle Ages, the notion of 'Christendom' was a 'paradigm', moving folk to positive activity in accord with the idea as expressed in the Word.

PARALLEL WORLDS (*See* **DIMENSIONS, FAIRIES**) The notion of other-dimensional worlds sometimes intersecting our own realm is found in folklore and **occultism** since early times. '**Fairy**land' and the '**astral plane**' represent two of the **archetypes** involved. The one is that of the human being (True Thomas, etc.) translated to a parallel world where he finds adventure and love; the other involves visitation by **entities** from the other world into this. These themes (and sub-themes such as **abduction**) are dealt with elsewhere. The term 'parallel worlds' belongs principally to modern fantasy and science fiction, in which the **mythic** themes are treated in a manner essentially derived from the traditional forms, appealing as much to wish-fulfilment as to fear. The idea has occasionally been used in more innovative forms, as in *Report on Probability A* by Brian Aldiss (1968), in which observers in parallel words study each other, and in other novels by Niven, Laumer, Zelazny, *et al.*, in which the complex physics and psychology of multiple or infinite series of parallel worlds are explored.

PARANORMAL A term describing events or phenomena considered (particularly in terms of the existing western scientific **paradigm**) as beyond the range of 'normal' experience. As such it covers all '**psychic**', '**supernatural**', or '**occult**' phenomena, and is essentially a cultural definition: what is 'paranormal' to one society may be 'normal' to another. Belief in **reincarnation** is 'paranormal' in the West, 'normal' in India. The term says more about the perceptual system of the culture employing it than about the phenomena so described. A blinkered horse has no peripheral vision: likewise any science of reality limited purely to material definition or evidence is predisposed to deny or dismiss peripheral phenomena outside the chosen angle of vision.

PARAPSYCHOLOGY Again, a cultural definition, created by need of an acceptably 'scientific' label for the study of phenomena generally considered outside scientific boundaries. Parapsychology is thus the study of the measurable effect, if any, of **psychic** powers, with a *caveat*: that, to be acceptable in scientific terms, these must first be described in terminology that implicitly denies their existence.

This Catch–22 bedevils all such research into **ESP** and related powers. However the modern revolution in high-energy physics, as begun by **Planck, Einstein** and **Heisenberg**, has created a sufficient area of uncertainty for parapsychology to find a niche. **Telepathy, psychokinesis** and other ESP powers can no longer be ruled out of consideration on grounds of existing scientific dogma. Since J. B. **Rhine** of Duke University began experiments into ESP in 1927 it has become increasingly difficult to insist that all phenomena may be explained in terms of 'physical' cause and effect alone.

Today these researches, though uneasily accepted and often derided, continue in institutes around the world. In the UK, a professorial Chair in Parapsychology was established in the 1980s at Edinburgh University following a bequest by the late Arthur **Koestler**. In the USA, **Jahn, Leshan**, Tart and others produce findings hard to deny even by those who defend the old, purely materialist **paradigm**. In the USSR research has been going on for years in areas as diverse as **acupuncture**, bio-electricity, **Kirlian** photography, psychic **healing**, subliminal perception, paraphysics and psychokinetic events, as detailed in Ostrander and Schroeder's *Psychic Discoveries behind the Iron Curtain* (1970).

The evolution of parapsychology is as slow as was that of material science in the time of Galileo. Today many still refuse to look through the parapsychological telescope. These things take time, as measured in human generations and the death of the old guard, to become acceptable.

PAST LIVES (*See* **REINCARNATION**)

PEAK EXPERIENCES (*See* **MASLOW**)

PENDULUM (*See* **DOWSING, LETHBRIDGE, MAP-DOWSING**)

PHANTOM BATTLES After the 1642 English Civil War battle at Edgehill, Northamptonshire, folk in the area were so disturbed by phantom sounds of battle that a pamphlet was published: *A great Wonder in Heaven, shewing the late Apparitions and Prodigious Noyse of War and Battels, seene on Edge-Hill, neere Keinton, in Northamptonshire*. It told how, for a month of weekend nights, folk visiting the battlefield were plagued by images of slaughter. The visions faded, but the sound of battle was heard at Edgehill into the twentieth century.[1]

One night in August 1951 two English sisters-in-law on holiday at Puys, near Dieppe in France, were disturbed by the sound of battle raging. They heard shelling and shouting 'about 4 a.m.': the noise ceased fifty minutes later. Then they heard bombers overhead and men shouting. Silence fell, broken only by the faint cries of wounded and dying men. Next day they learned nobody else had heard a thing, but that nine years earlier, on 19 August 1942, the Allies had landed 6,086 men in a bloody costly attack. Records showed that shelling had begun at 3.47am and stopped at 4.50am, followed by the bombing between 5.07am and 5.40am. The battle had ended at 6.00am – the time the 'phantom battle' had ended too.

In other reports people step over some invisible boundary-line to find themselves amid phantom battle. If they step back, the disturbance ceases. **Lethbridge, Lodge** and others have suggested that the violent emotion of such events prints itself so strongly on the site's geomagnetic field that thereafter sensitives pick up a 'recording' of the event. It may also be that **precognition** of disasters involves a similar 'ripple' effect.

1. *Beyond the Occult*, Colin Wilson, Corgi, London 1989, p. 154

PHANTOM HITCH-HIKERS This phenomenon is reported all over the world. Motorists give lifts to hitch-hikers who, typically, deliver a prophetic message then unexpectedly vanish *en route*. As with the **Men in Black**, there is rarely a witness to substantiate such encounters. Most appear to fit the ancient pattern of lonely travellers generating imaginary travelling companions. But is this phenomenon purely the result of **hallucination**?

Of his historic thirty-four-hour solo Atlantic flight in 1927, Charles Lindbergh later wrote how he fought to stay awake. In mid-Atlantic, he fell asleep, and a new 'extraordinary mind' thereafter flew the plane. In this state, with his skull become 'one great eye, seeing everywhere at once', he sensed the fuselage behind him crowded with ghostly human presences, appearing and disappearing at will, passing through the walls of the plane, advising him with messages from beyond his walls of bone, bringing up 'old associations, bygone friendships, voices from ancestrally distant times'.[1]

Lindbergh's experience is **archetypal**: a lonely traveller subjected to mental invasion by hitch-hikers from the unconscious, as may affect anyone gone too far from the collective world-view and its psychological support system. Solo Everest climbers and Arctic explorers also report ancestral voices or spirits accompanying them during their extreme effort. Isolated, exhausted and under stress they make contact (like Saul on the Damascus road) with deeper mental forces normally hidden from the conscious mind.

Are such **entities** solely produced by the unconscious mind, or is there (again) sometimes a geomagnetic involvement? Just as with **black dogs** and some **ghosts**, phantom hitch-hikers haunt specific stretches of road. Black dogs may presage death; the hitch-hiker usually delivers a message. This given, he vanishes. **Angels** (messengers) traditionally act in a similar way: typically today the hitch-hiker is Jesus promising the **Second Coming** or a **UFO** entity threatening global disaster if we don't wake up.[2]

It looks as if we want to tell ourselves something – about ourselves.

1. *Reincarnation: The Phoenix Fire Mystery*, S. L. Cranston and Joseph Head, Julian Press/Crown Publishers, New York 1977, pp. 390–91
2. *The Evidence for Phantom Hitch-Hikers*, Michael Goss, Aquarian, Wellingborough 1984

PHILADELPHIA EXPERIMENT (*See* **TELEPORTATION**) A persistent tale concerns Project Rainbow; an experiment in 'electronic camouflage' allegedly undertaken in October 1943 by the US Office of Naval Research at the Philadelphia Naval Yard, and conducted on the destroyer USS *Eldridge*. The purpose was to render ship and crew invisible within an **electromagnetic** 'force field' by applying **Einstein**'s Unified Field Theory.

Allegedly the *Eldridge* vanished from the sight of onshore observers, materialised in the harbour at Norfolk, Virginia, then rematerialised some minutes later at Philadelphia. Not just invisibility but teleportation had been achieved. However many of the crew, exposed to the energy field, reportedly went mad, fell ill and died, burst into flames, walked through walls, or vanished completely. Further research was abandoned.

The evidence for this odd tale? In 1956 UFOlogist Morris K. Jessup received two semi-literate letters from a man signing himself Carl M. Allen or Carlos Miguel Allende, who claimed that, as a seaman on the SS *Andrew Furuseth* out of Norfolk, he had witnessed the experiment and knew the fate of the *Eldrige*'s crew. Allende remains a mystery: Jessup's involvement led to depression and (in 1959) suicide. Allende's main evidence (beyond his own assertions) refers to a newspaper article he read in 1943. Berlitz and Moore claim to own a photocopy of this article. Received anonymously, it is undated and the newspaper unidentified. Under the headline 'Strange Circumstances Surround Tavern Brawl', it describes how Philadelphia city police, answering a call for help from the Navy Shore Patrol to break up a bar fight, arrived to find the bar empty. Two frightened waitresses said the Shore Patrol had already cleared the bar, but not before two of the sailors involved 'just sort of vanished into thin air . . . right there', as one of the waitresses claimed, 'and I ain't been drinking either!'

This story has persisted for half a century, spawning an entertaining sci-fi movie in which two of the sailors involved are cast through time into the 1980s. Albert **Einstein**, said to have been party to this test of his theories, is no longer available for questioning.

1. *The Philadelphia Experiment*, C. Berlitz and W. Moore, Granada, London 1980

PHILIP THE IMAGINARY GHOST (*See* **GHOSTS, PSYCHOKINESIS**) In 1972 members of the Toronto Society for Psychical Research decided to create a 'ghost'. First they invented the story of Philip, a seventeenth-century English aristocrat who, unhappily married, fell in love with gypsy Margo. His wife denounced Margo as a witch; Margo was burned at the stake; Philip leapt to his death from the roof of 'Diddington Manor' in Warwickshire.

Reading books on the period, they visited 'Diddington' Manor and other English sites in the story, sketched 'Philip', and for a year met weekly in communal **meditation**, trying but failing to generate Philip as a 'shared **hallucination**'. In 1973 they read in the *Journal of the* ***Society for Psychical Research*** of similar work by British researchers Hunt, **Bacheldor**, and Brookes-Smith, who since 1964 had produced seeming **paranormal** effects (table-tilting, rapping, etc.) not by meditation but amid jollity, joke-telling, songs, while telling the table to obey them. They said the desired phenomena should be believed in, expected, and that no surprise or rejection should greet any result.

The Toronto group (eight men and women) began holding jovial sittings in full light at a table which they called 'Philip'. The table, their hands resting on it, soon began to vibrate. Someone asked: 'I wonder if by chance Philip is doing this?' A rap resounded from the table top. With one rap established as 'yes', two for 'no', the phenomena now came rapidly. 'Hello, Philip', each person would say, to receive an audible, tangible rap under one hand. At least four group-members were needed for results, but no one person was essential. Sometimes the table lifted off the (carpeted) floor with nobody touching it. Once it chased someone across the room, wedging itself in the doorway. The victim escaped; the others collapsed laughing. Raps were heard from walls or pipes overhead. Coloured lights behind the glass panel of a lighting unit on which Philip's portrait stood flickered when Philip was asked to make them do so. His behaviour relied on who was present. He objected to smoking only when a member allergic to cigarettes was present. When a drinking song was sung, the table bumped up and down, keeping time. Up to three outsiders could be introduced, but then table motions would be reduced.

In 1974 the group made a film (*Philip, the Imaginary Ghost*). Despite the presence of bright lights, cameras and crew, phenomena were generated. Next, Philip appeared on live TV. With table (and group) in the audience, and a discussion panel, on a platform, the table moved about, then climbed three steps to the platform. This was filmed live and broadcast on Toronto City Television. Apparently Philip performed better with a large audience ready to join in the psychokinetic hilarity. Later, other Toronto groups (like the 'Lillith' group) reproduced similar phenomena.[1]

Research established that table-raps produced 'paranormally' died away quicker (lasting on average 0.16 seconds) than those produced 'normally' (0.30 seconds), even if the raps were as loud. It was also apparent that childlike hilarity was more productive than (adult) meditation (supporting the connection between **poltergeist** activity and pubertal emotion).

The Philip experiments beg many questions. How far is 'reality' created by our collective thought-processes? How far do unconscious group **thought-forms** influence the natural laws of the world? Are such phenomena created or mediated primarily by the right-brain world of **intuition** and **dream**?

To date, funds for such research remain tiny.

1. *The Roots of Consciousness*, Jeffrey Mishlove, Random House, New York 1975, pp. 170–71

PHILOSOPHER'S STONE (*See* **ALCHEMY**)

PIKE, Bishop James (d. 1969) (*See* **DICK, MEDIUMS**) In his bestseller *The Other Side* this American bishop described how, after in February 1966 his son Jim committed suicide in a New York hotel room, **poltergeist** phenomena began occurring in his apartment. Books and letters rearranged themselves; part of the hair on his secretary's forehead (Jim had disliked her hair-style) burned off as she slept; she awoke to find her fingernails damaged as if pins had been driven under them. Another night she entered the bishop's bedroom for a book. He sat up asleep and lectured her on the importance of selfishness. It dawned on them that Jim might be trying to communicate. He consulted London medium Ena Twigg. Through her came so many personal references known to him alone that, Pike concluded, either she was reading his mind or Jim really was present. In the séance Jim's first words were: 'I failed the test, I can't face you, can't face life. I'm confused. Very sudden passing . . . God, I didn't know what I was doing. But when I got here I found I wasn't such a failure as I thought.' Later he added: 'I wanted out. I've found there is no way out. I wish I'd stayed to work out my problems in more familiar surroundings.'

Subsequently Pike's secretary, Mrs Bergrud, killed herself. In August 1969, with his new wife Diane, Pike went to Israel. In the wilderness they got lost and exhausted. Diane went for help, but could not find the place she had left him. On 4 September, three days before his body was found, he 'communicated' with Ena Twigg in London, telling her what had happened and where he was. Diane Pike later confirmed that Mrs Twigg's information was accurate. A decade later, before his own premature death, Philip K. Dick fictionalised the strange case of Bishop James Pike in his final novel, *The Transmigration of Timothy Archer*, in which a character remarks: 'Death and fate are not the same thing. . . . He died to avoid fate, because the fate he saw coming for him was worse than dying there on the Dead Sea desert.'[1]

1. *The Transmigration of Timothy Archer*, Philip K. Dick, Pocket Books, New York 1983, p. 225

PINEAL GLAND (*See* **BRAIN MYSTERIES**) Located in the mid-brain (limbic system), this tiny organ (weighing under a tenth of a gram), is identified by **Hindu** tradition as the 'third eye': the centre of the sixth **chakra** and of man's **psychic** and **spiritual** activity.

Metaphor? Maybe not. Anciently in the age of reptiles the pineal was a separate eye on top of the head. In the *Tuatura* lizard of New Zealand it remains visible, under a transparent membrane atop the skull, complete with pigmented retina and lens.[1] In other reptiles (including by extension **birds**) it remains directly responsive to light, lying under a thin shell of skull. In men and other mammals, it was long ago buried deep in the brain, under the cortex. Yet still it uses information from the eyes, exerting odd chemical effects. The testes of a blinded hamster grow smaller, save if the pineal is first removed. Female rats kept in light remain permanently in oestrus, unless pineal extract is injected.[2] Strong light raises our spirit, the lack of it depresses us. A reaction controlled by the pineal? The work of Sir Alexander Cannon shows that **mediums** have larger pineal glands than most people. Autopsies suggest that alcohol abuse causes the pineal to atrophy; in those abstaining from alcohol and other detrimental chemicals the gland is found to be filled with a sand-like substance; in those dedicating their lives to spiritual pursuits it is found to contain a clear fluid.[3]

In the seventeenth century Descartes located **consciousness** in the pineal. A century later, in his *Adventures of an Atom*, Smollett's atom says it can communicate with men only once inside their pineal. Only in 1958 was the pineal established as a gland when Aaron B. Lerner of Yale isolated its hormone, melatonin (meaning: 'darkness constricting), a substance which, if injected into various creatures, turns them a lighter colour. Melatonin is made by the pineal from **serotonin** – an amazing substance in its own right, and one clearly connected to the 'higher' human mental functions. (The bo-tree, *ficus religiosa*, under which the **Buddha** sat, is rich in serotonin.)

All of which begs a question: how did the ancient Hindus know about it?

1. *Frankenstein's Castle*, Colin Wilson, Ashgrove Press, Bath 1980, p. 57
2. *The Natural History of the Mind*, Gordon Rattray Taylor, Granada, London 1981, p. 64
3. *The Phoenix Returns*, Kristina Gale-Kumar, Cardinal Enterprises, Hawaii 1983, pp. 44–5

PIPER, Leonore (*See* **MEDIUMS**) This Boston-born medium not only convinced William **James** and others of the reality of the **afterlife** but is among the few mediums to whom no taint of charlatanry has ever clung – a considerable feat, given the huge efforts made by sceptics then and since to prove all mediumistic activity fake.

A young housewife from a fashionable Boston suburb, she discovered her mediumistic talent on consulting a blind **clairvoyant healer**, falling into **trance** amid one of his sessions. Soon she was conducting private sittings. In 1885 the mother-in-law of William James was so impressed by Mrs Piper that she told the eminent psychologist of her discovery. James and his wife soon visited Mrs Piper and concluded (as with **Crookes, Pike** and others in like circumstances) that either she had read his mind or was genuinely transmitting information from deceased relatives.

'My later knowledge of her sittings and personal acquaintance with her,' he wrote subsequently, 'has led me to absolutely reject the former explanation, and to believe that she has supernormal powers.'

For eighteen months James supervised her mediumship, making the arrangements for clients to sit with her. Concluding that, despite all his checks, she was indeed a mouthpiece for the dead, he contacted the **Society for Psychical Research** in England. In 1889 she was brought to Europe for even more stringent tests. These proved so effective that **Myers, Crookes**, Hodgson and **Lodge** were convinced that she was at least a gifted thought-reader. Later, in 1898–9, **Hyslop** became involved with her, at first attending her séances in disguise, removing his mask only when she was already in trance. Nonetheless she brought through four of his dead relatives, including his father, each of whom communicated in ways entirely typical of their former living personalities. He too was struck by the possibility that she was reading his mind, but concluded, in his 1901 report on Leonore Piper, '[that] the evidence forces us in our rational minds to tolerate the **spiritistic** theory as rationally possible and respectable'. Considering other 'explanations' for her insight, such as **multiple personality** or **telepathy**, he added: 'I prefer to believe that I have been talking to my dead relatives in person; it is simpler.'[1]

Thus applying Occam's Razor, Hyslop and other intelligent men concluded that Leonore Piper was a genuine medium whose communications provided more than sufficient evidence to overcome their initial material scepticism.

1. *The Infinite Boundary*, D. Scott Rogo, Aquarian, Wellingborough 1988, pp. 32–5

PIRI RE'IS (*See* **POLE SHIFT**) In the Moslem year 919 (AD 1513) the Turkish Admiral Piri ibn-Haji Memmed, also known as Piri Re'is, signed his name to a parchment map, a large piece of which in 1929 was found in the old Imperial Palace in Constantinople (Istanbul). It drew attention because, from the date, it seemed to be one of the earliest maps of America. Examination revealed it as unusual for the sixteenth century: it showed South America and Africa in correct relative longitude, despite the fact that navigators of the time had no way to find longitude. In his *Maps of the Ancient Sea Kings*, American author Charles Hapgood reports how, 'In one of the legends inscribed on the map by Piri Re'is, he stated that he had based the western part of it on a map that had been drawn by Columbus.' And, 'Piri Re'is made other interesting statements about his source maps. He used about twenty, he said, and he stated that some of them had been drawn in the time of Alexander the Great, and some of them had been based on mathematics.'[1]

In 1953 Captain Arlington H. Mallery (having indicated in his book *Lost America* (1951) that old maps of Greenland show landforms under the present ice-cap) saw the Piri Re'is map and was struck by community of its features with those on the seismic map of Antarctica. Before going public he asked two astronomers and a cartographer to check his belief that the Piri Re'is map accurately showed coastal detail of Antarctica's Queen Maud Land – not surveyed prior to the twentieth century. In August 1956 on a radio discussion he stated his conclusion that ancient cartographers, 'had a record . . . of every mountain range in northern Canada and Alaska . . . which the (US) Army Map Service did not have at the time when . . . I checked. They have since found them.' Of the Piri Re'is map of Antarctica he added, 'it indicates that the glacier had just begun to appear at the middle of Queen Maud Land, but the bay on the map that Columbus had was still entirely uncovered . . . The ice has added about a mile . . . since that map was made.'[2]

Subsequent seismic data produced by Paul-Emile Victor show Greenland to consist of at least three separate islands buried under the ice – just as indicated by the ancient maps as employed by Piri Re'is.

Yet again: human civilisation is older than orthodox belief admits.

1. *Maps of the Ancient Sea Kings*, Charles Hapgood, Chilton, USA 1966
2. *Pole Shift*, John White, W. H. Allen, London 1980, pp. 38–44

PLANCHETTE This device consists of a small board mounted on wheels or castors, with a pencil attached. Used to facilitate **automatic writing**, the name is simply French for 'little board'. It was invented in France in the nineteenth century.

PLANCK, Max (1858–1947) (*See* **QUANTUM THEORY**)

PLANT CONSCIOUSNESS (*See* **BACKSTER, WATSON**) In 1966 ex-CIA employee Cleve Backster hooked household plants up to a polygraph (lie-detector) and demonstrated their seeming awareness not only of threatening stimuli, but of the *mere intention* of threat. When he decided to burn the leaf of a *Draecaena* plant, the plant reacted instantly, the polygraph needle leaping up. Apparently the plant had 'read his mind'. When he entered the room with matches, the plant again reacted. From this and other experiments he concluded that plants display a form of **telepathy** that he was careful to term, neutrally, 'primary ponception'.

Gardeners and farmers long have known that certain plants germinate only if planted at specific times of the year or under specific phases of the **moon**. The waxing moon is the best time to plant annuals bearing above-ground crops; the waning moon is the time to plant biennials, perennials, bulb and root-crop plants, and pruning and harvesting should be done in the waning moon. Such processes may suggest no more than vegetative response to cosmic rhythms and energies. Yet the response can be extraordinarily powerful. The growing roots of trees can split rocks and dislodge houses. In 1984 a report appeared in the *New Scientist* of a tumescence under the tarmac of an English street. Finally the tarmac burst open to reveal an edible pink-gilled mushroom of a sort which could be crushed between finger and thumb. The mechanism governing such processes remains unknown.[1]

Belief in 'plant consciousness' is ancient. **Neoplatonist** philosopher Plotinus considered that plants 'aspire to contemplation'. In the nineteenth century Gustav Fechner suggested that plants have **'souls'**, a sort of **psychic** identity (a theory to which Findhorn gardeners would subscribe).

A century ago Indian physicist and botanist Jagadis Chandra Bose showed that plants react to 'blows' or 'irritation' much as animals do. Though he called the effect 'electrical', his work was so unorthodox that, once his talk of a 'pervading unity' became known, he was ignored as a **mystic**.

Botanist Joseph Sinel met a similar fate when (in his book *The Sixth Sense*, 1927) he claimed publicly that plants are **clairvoyant**.

Testing to find how a climbing plant finds suitable holds, he observed how a wall-plant grows towards the nearest nail in the wall. 'If there are two nails near each other, it will select the more suitable one, an old rusty and crooked one having the preference.' He also noted how the sticky hairs of sun-dew, an insectivorous bog-plant, usually held upright to seize insects, turn upside-down if insects are unavailable. He wrote, 'If a dead fly is now stuck upon the point of a needle and fixed an inch or two away from the plant, a decided movement of the leaves will commence.' The sun-dew not only has a sense of direction but knows what is or is not edible: Sinel's tests showed that its leaves ignored inedible material.[2]

Such anomalies are usually seen only in terms of 'electric signalling' or 'electrophysiology'. 'Clairvoyance' or 'plant consciousness' is ruled out of court. When Backster's work emerged in the 1960s, his paper appeared in a journal devoted to psychical research. Back-up tests by another team gave negative results. Yet soon the Russians A. P. Dubrov and V. N. Pushkin demonstrated similar effects. Using electro-encephalographs they found that plants react to emotional shifts in human subjects. Further tests were run in answer to objections that graph responses might be caused by chemicals on the subject's skin, or by body heat. **Hypnotised** subjects were asked to identify with one plant only. The recordings revealed that each plant reacted 'only when the emotion of the subject had been directed to it, while there was no response from the other plant'. No physical mechanism was involved: the plants responded directly to human emotion.

The bestselling *The Secret Life of Plants* (1973) was ridiculed for some of its more bizarre claims. Do plants really dislike rock music, but grow well to Vivaldi or Bach? One may ask: why not? Musical rhythms whether rock or baroque derive from natural rhythms to which plants, belonging to the planetary bioenergetic field, respond as do other forms of life. Why 'consciousness' should be narrowly limited in scope to human beings (and denied even to human beings by some behavioural reductionists) is a matter for continuing amazement.[3]

1. *The Hidden Power*, Brian Inglis, Cape, London 1986, pp. 14–20
2. *The Secret Life of Plants*, P. Tompkins and C. Bird, Harper & Row, New York 1973

PLATO (*See* **GREEK MYSTERIES**)

PLOTINUS (*See* **NEOPLATONISM**)

POLE SHIFT (*See* **BROWN, Hugh Auchinloss, CAYCE, PIRI RE'IS, PROPHECY, VELIKOVSKY**) This concept implies sudden displacement of the planet's axis of rotation or a slippage of Earth's crust over the molten interior, causing abrupt positional change of the poles. This could lead to tidal waves, electric storms, hurricanes, earthquakes, lava flows, poison clouds of volcanic ash and gas, plus the rapid melt of displaced ice-caps and global flood.

Despite orthodox uniformitarian belief that all geophysical changes occur gradually, some researchers claim pole shift has happened many times and may happen again. Legends, **prophecies** and **psychics** warn that a pole shift is due, giving 'signs' by which the 'end times' may be known.

Geophysical suggestions of such an event in the past include: (1) the inexplicable Chandler Wobble (irregular rotation of the planetary axis); (2) reversed polarity of the geomagnetic field 170 times in the last eighty million years – its strength is now failing so fast it may vanish by AD 2030 then (presumably) reappear, again reversed, with unknown effect; and (3) the ice ages. At least four have occurred during the past billion years.

Theories explaining ice age causation fall into two camps; 'sudden' or 'gradual'. Sudden pole shift as trigger of an ice-age may explain evidence of former ice-sheets in tropical Africa, India, Guyana and Brazil; also the discovery of coral in Alaska, coal in Spitzbergen and Antarctica; and quick-frozen woolly mammoths in Siberia. In 1900 a landslide seventy miles north of the Arctic Circle exposed the Berezovka mammoth. It was found preserved in the permafrost with unchewed grass and buttercups in its mouth and nine kinds of field grasses (no evergreens) in its stomach. It had been suddenly suffocated, then buried by mud soon after its death some 44,000 years ago. Many 'mammoth boneyards' have been found on islands north of the Siberian coast; some beasts so well-preserved by quick freezing that their meat remains edible. The remains of hardwood trees, including plum, with leaves and fruit preserved, have been found with them.

Carbon–14 dating ranges these deaths from 44,000 to 1,900 BC. Deer and bison in Texas and elsewhere died simultaneously. So cataclysms involving abrupt temperature falls and volcanic activity *have* taken place. Were they caused by pole shift? If so, what mechanisms might cause such an event?

US engineer Hugh Auchinloss Brown (1879–1975) proposed that growing ice-cap weight has tipped Earth over in the past and will soon do so again.

Russian-born Immanuel Velikovsky proposed near-collision between Earth and Venus (fifteenth century BC), then between Earth and Mars (seventh century BC), causing displacement of the axis and crustal slippage.

Charles Hapgood, in *Earth's Shifting Crust* (1958) and *The Path of the Poles* (1970) claimed that the planet's crust has been repeatedly displaced, each shift taking millennia and involving an average distance of about 2,000 miles. Drawing evidence from ancient maps including that of Piri Re'is, he claims that continental drift is a secondary effect of crustal shift.

Other theorists include Peter Warlow (a sudden upending of the Earth following near-miss with some cosmic body), Chan Thomas (pole shift 6,500 years ago produced the Flood), and Adam Barber (who predicts imminent pole shift through an increase in intensity of gyroscopic forces).

Orthodox belief in gradual change is unproven. Does it arise from a wish to believe we inhabit a stable planet? Catastrophism's implications are too uncomfortable, while its association with religious, **prophetic**, and **occult** beliefs discourages those whose outlook is solely materialistic.

One such belief is that human behaviour influences the planet's fate. In Genesis, the

Flood is sent by God to punish human sin. Recent prophets like Edgar Cayce, Gopi **Krishna** and Paul **Solomon** say the quality of human **consciousness** is crucial in assuring or preventing catastrophe.

In Reading 906–7 Cayce says, 'For mind is the builder and that which we think upon may become crimes or miracles.' Gopi Krishna claims, '. . . they [earth changes] are inevitable . . . these unnatural and unhealthy actions of human beings can have no other end except that nature takes recourse to drastic measures.' Paul Solomon sees earth changes as *birth pains*. He says that geological catastrophe helps create a higher humanity.

Native American prophecies speak of the coming Great Purification – a cataclysmic time due, says Chippewa medicine man Sun Bear, to human greed, arrogance and defilement of the Earth Mother. The process, climaxing in pole shift, is 'sealed in the **spirit** world'. 'Sealed' means absolutely certain. The event *must* occur. The only question concerns the degree of severity. **Hopi** legends say that three worlds have perished before this Fourth World, and that the Fourth World's now-imminent end is revealed in ancient prophecies. One such speaks of a time when 'two brothers would build a ladder to the moon'; another of a time when man would: 'put his house in the sky'. The Hopi, believing that Skylab was this 'house in the sky', have stored food in expectation of surviving the final cataclysm.

Students of pole shift point to numerous Biblical references: Psalms xlvi, 2–3, Isaiah xiii, 13, xxiv, 1, and xxiv, 18–20; also to Luke xxi, 25–26; Peter iii, 10, but most particularly to Revelation vi, 12–14, and xvi, 18–20:

'And there were voices, and thunders and lightnings, such as was not since men were upon the earth, so mighty an earthquake, and so great. And the great city was divided into three parts, and the cities of the nations fell. . . . And every island fled away, and the mountains were not found . . .'

Such predictions are an unsound basis of assumption, being often either metaphoric or already seemingly fulfilled by past events. The same problem arises with the prophecies of Mother **Shipton, Nostradamus**, St **Malachy** and others. Even if the text is authentic, most prophecies are notoriously vague. The Nostradamus quatrain about the year 1999 may refer only to his participation in an already-ancient Christian eschatological chronology.

Yet some groups await 'end times' caused by pole shift. Members of the **Stelle Group**, of Illinois, USA, claim descent from **Lemuria**, which they say was destroyed and submerged 26,000 years ago. They expect cataclysmic pole shift, triggered by the 'grand conjunction' of planets on 5 May AD 2000; the gravitational pull of the aligned planets being sufficient to disturb the Earth into pole shift. A similar cataclysm was forecast for similar reasons ('The Jupiter Effect') in 1982. We are still here.

But this is no cause for complacency: global warming aided by the burning of rain-forests shows how human idiocy afflicts the environment: occult warnings are increasingly borne out by the *scientific* evidence.

1. *Pole Shift*, John White, W. H. Allen, London 1980

POLTERGEISTS (*See* **MANNING, PHILIP THE IMAGINARY GHOST**)
This German term ('noisy' or 'rattling' **ghosts**) describes phenomena which typically include domestic bangs, raps, **levitating** furniture and floating domestic objects, showers of pebbles or water cascading from nowhere, and fires lighting up then dousing themselves. Usually more mischievous than dangerous, poltergeists ('the knockabout comedians of the **psychic** world') can be so irritating as to drive people from their homes.

Yet most are now considered not 'ghosts' at all, but manifestations of unconscious mental disturbance usually associated with pubertal teenagers. The haunting ceases when the emotional problems triggering it are solved.

The English psychic Matthew Manning was almost expelled from school due to poltergeist chaos: aged sixteen he began producing **automatic writing**; poltergeist activity declined and later vanished completely when he learned to channel his power consciously, becoming a full-time **healer**.

In October 1965 Anne-Marie Schaberl left a Munich school and began work in the Rosenheim office of lawyer Sigmund Adam. In late 1967 his electrical systems went haywire. Strip-lighting failed inexplicably, there were sudden surges in current, his telephone bill was absurdly high. A device put in to register all numbers dialled showed up to six calls a minute to the speaking clock – an impossibility; it took seventeen seconds at least to get through to it. The relays were being directly affected, but how? When a reporter investigated, a bulb fell from its socket and almost hit him. His story of 'the Rosenheim spook' alerted Professor Hans **Bender** of Freiberg's Institute of **Paranormal** Research. At Adam's office Bender's assistant saw overhead lights begin swinging if Anne-Marie walked under them. Investigation proved the current surges happened only if she was in the office. Tested at the Institute she proved tense, mistrustful and aggressive. Her rural family background was difficult; she hated town living. Though engaged to marry, her relationship was unhappy. Asked about a year she had spent in plaster (with a tubercular hip) she became disturbed. Tested for **ESP**, she showed **telepathic** abilities. She returned to Adam's office: the glitches began again. Fired, she got another job: again electrical equipment went haywire.

Meanwhile her fiancé had dropped her. The patron of an electronically controlled ten-pin bowling alley, he was disturbed at how, whenever Anne-Marie walked in, the board registered random scores and the pin-setting equipment went mad. She took a job in a mill; a man died in an accident. People began to avoid her. Leaving the job, she married, moved outside town, and had three children. The poltergeist activity ceased.[1]

Poltergeist infestation in 1848 at Hydesville, New York State, launched the **Spiritualist** movement. Contact by two children, Kate and Margaret Fox, with (apparently) the spirit of a pedlar who had been murdered and buried under their house led to a spate of rappings and to a 'yes' and 'no' code whereby the dead pedlar's tale was interpreted and made known. Whether or not the 'pedlar' existed is unclear: either way, the Fox sisters were able at will to produce rappings from all about a room, generating such a craze that in London in 1853 Sir David Brewster wrote, 'I have no doubt that there are *thousands* of tables turning every night in London, so general is the excitement on the subject.'[2]

The **psychokinetic** (PK) phenomena produced by Spiritualist **mediums** then and later suggest not so much 'survival' (a different question) as the unknown powers of the human mind. This is further shown by the activities of the 1970s Toronto group who deliberately generated poltergeist or PK phenomena by calling upon **'Philip the imaginary ghost'**.

But do *all* poltergeists arise solely from the unconscious mind? What other factors may be involved? Consider the 'Black Monk of Pontefract'.

In August 1966 a poltergeist struck the Pritchard family of Pontefract in Yorkshire. Joe and Jean Pritchard had two children, Philip (fifteen), and Diane (twelve). Pools of water formed in the kitchen, a white powder 'snowed' in the living-room, lights came on and off, pots levitated, cupboards and wardrobes tottered, there were raps and bangs and the house turned chilly. The first episode soon ended. Two years later the haunting began again. Pots were shattered, a paint brush flew past Jean Pritchard's face, a strip of wallpaper stood up and swayed like a snake; a carpet sweeper flew into the air and swung about as if used as a club by an invisible giant. Yet nobody was hurt during the nine months the affair lasted. The Pritchards got used to the presence of 'Mr Nobody', or 'Fred'. The trouble usually started at bedtime. At an early stage Philip suggested **exorcism**: a local vicar, Mr Davy, visited and was convinced (by floating candlesticks and other phenomena) of 'something evil' in the house. He advised the family to move, but Jean refused. After he left, Diane was going up to bed when the air grew cold. A heavy oak stand floated into the air and pinned her to the stairs. Nobody could move it off her. Yet as soon as she realised she was not being crushed, she relaxed and felt a change in the force that held her down. The stand was easily removed. She was not even bruised.

The 'haunted house' became news. During the following weeks many people experienced Fred's inventive tricks. Family friend René Holden, hearing that Philip and Diane both had a stomach ailment which got worse when the poltergeist appeared, suggested Fred drew energy from their solar plexus and also from a stream under the house. Attempts to communicate with Fred failed, but he demonstrated new tricks; floating eggs from closed boxes and exploding them in mid-air to produce a delicious scent. Further attempts at exorcism were met by increased activity. Several witnesses noted how at night the Pritchard's house glowed dimly while, throughout the nine months of the haunting, the electricity bill for the house was half what it should have been. Latterly Fred appeared to the Pritchards and others as a tall hooded figure. Events reached a climax one night when Diane screamed: Jean and Philip found her being dragged upstairs, her cardigan stretched out in front of her. They pulled at her: Fred let go and all three tumbled down the stairs in a heap, to find Diane's throat covered with red fingermarks. Some days later Philip filled the house with garlic. Oddly, this worked. Fred, perhaps insulted by his unpopularity, vanished and never returned.

A decade later local historian Tom Cunniff, wondering if the Pontefract poltergeist had connection with the priory which had existed nearby between 1090 and 1539, learned a Cluniac monk had been hanged for rape in the reign of Henry VIII. The gallows had been on the hill where the Pritchard's house now stood; the house itself was on the site of an old bridge – 'Priest's Bridge'. He suggested that the Pritchards had been haunted by the monk.

Investigating the case, Colin **Wilson** found no evidence of execution or rape. He concluded that René Holden had rightly identified the underground stream as involved in creating a 'naiad field' (damp place holding a localised **electromagnetic** field) of the sort T. C. **Lethbridge** hypothesised as ideal for 'psychic' imprint of emotional stress. Pointing out that poltergeists seem to manifest only in unhappy households, Wilson noted that Fred's first 1966 appearance coincided with Phillip's puberty and disagreements with his father.

Wilson consulted psychic researcher Guy Playfair, who suggested that a poltergeist is like a 'football of energy', exuded from disturbed teenagers and taken up by footloose, mischievous **spirits** or **elementals**, who 'kick' it about and create havoc. Getting bored, they abandon the game: the football – a form of electrical energy – turns into a pool of water, for example.

Noting the area to be full of tales of **hauntings**, Wilson concluded that the mystery's solution lies in the geomagnetic properties of the site. Such sites, once identified by **megalith** builders as 'holy' places where earth-energies and human mental powers interact, were taken over by the Church and are now associated with '**black dogs**', **UFOs** – or poltergeists.

The force involved was initially triggered by Philip's tensions: the 'entity' invoked took its cues (as to how to manifest and behave) from the preconceptions of the Pritchards and their friends: its power was sustained by the unconscious participation and **medium**istic capacities of Philip and later Diane. When they rejected it, it became inactive again. As with many ghosts, 'Fred' was indeed 'real' – a latent force given expression by the unconscious interaction of human beings with favourable local conditions.[3]

1. *Mysteries*, Colin Wilson, Granada 1979, pp. 466–8
2. *The Hidden Power*, Brian Inglis, Cape, London 1986, p. 76

3. *Poltergeist!*, Colin Wilson, New English Library, London 1982, pp. 137–71

POSSESSION The old belief that the human **psyche** is a house which may be invaded and taken over by psychic burglars if poorly guarded has only in recent times and in the West been rejected as **superstition**. In the Middle Ages much illness both psychiatric and physical was attributed to the possession of the personality by invading entities, usually **discarnate** or **demonic**. In Brazil today many psychiatrists attribute various psychotic disorders to possession, while in the USA and Britain, despite a prevailing materialist orthodoxy, numbers of experienced doctors and psychical researchers are on record as suggesting that **spirit**-possession is the reasonable explanation for a variety of complaints otherwise dismissed (as if explained) by terms such as schizophrenia, or split mind. For what is a *split* mind? How is it split, and into what, and by what? Likewise the analysis in some cases of '**multiple personality**' only begs a wider set of unanswered questions.

The classic post-mediaeval European case of 'demonic possession' was detailed by Aldous **Huxley** in his *The Devils of Loudun*, describing how in the seventeenth century a convent of French Ursuline nuns began to blaspheme and behave as if 'possessed by demons'. The local priest Urbain Grandier (also known as a Don Juan) was called in to **exorcise** them: their accusations that he had caused their possession led to his torture and death at the stake. Huxley surmised that the nuns were seized by a sexual frenzy and that the invading 'demons' did not exist save in that the nuns believed in them.

This also seems true in many modern cases, even when complicated by **poltergeist** phenomena, as in Nova Scotia's 1878 'Amherst Mystery'. Esther Cox, living with her sister and brother-in-law, **levitated** and was stabbed by a teleporting knife before fires, breaking out in the house, landed her in jail for arson despite no proof that she had *consciously* played any part in laying them. Her *unconscious* frustration alone was enough.

But in the Loudun case (here lies the rub) the 'spirits' transferred themselves to the investigators. Not only the unhappy Grandier but others on the case – Dr Mannoury, Father Lactance, Father Tranquille and the Jesuit Father Jean-Joseph Surin – all succumbed. Mannoury, who had pricked Grandier for 'Devil's Marks', saw Grandier's **ghost** and died insane. Father Lactance, a sadist who ensured Grandier's horrible death, died frothing at the mouth a month later, screaming blasphemies. Capuchin Inquisitor Father Tranquille went mad four years after Grandier died, writhing on the ground, barking and hissing; as he died the *devils* left him and entered a friar who knelt in prayer nearby: the friar began writhing and blaspheming. As for Surin, he too fell prey, observing with horror how, if he tried to make the sign of the cross, the 'other **soul**' would push his hand aside or make him bite it savagely. An intelligent man, he wrote, 'the alien spirit is united to mine, without depriving me of **consciousness** or of inner freedom, and yet constituting a second "me", as though I had two **souls**'. For twenty-five years he suffered periodic attacks of insanity (or possession), and only in the last five years of his life was he free.

All such testimony is easily dismissed on the grounds that it belongs to a past and unscientific age. Or is it? Many modern cases suggest that 'possession', if unattributable to poltergeist manifestation originating in the unconscious mind or right brain, is indeed caused by the invasion of the personality by external **entities**, however defined. **Reincarnation** is in some cases implicated; such cases, described elsewhere, are typically found in regions like India where the **reincarnation** hypothesis is not only accepted as fact but in some cases admissible in law. More to the point is a 1970s case in Chicago, where a doctor's Filipino wife began speaking in the voice of a Filipino nurse, Teresita Basa, who had been murdered in her apartment by an unknown assailant. The 'possessed' woman named the killer as Allan Showery, a colleague of the murdered woman at Edgewater Hospital. Arrested and confronted by this 'evidence', Showery confessed and came to trial, the evidence of the doctor's wife being allowed in court.

Though sexual hysteria may have played a large part in the demonology of mediaeval European 'possession', it seems clear that, once we take into account the modern prejudice against such belief, there is no good reason to reject evidence in its favour as advanced (*see elsewhere*) by **Hyslop, James, Prince** and others. More recently Arthur **Guirdham**, for many years an NHS psychiatric specialist in the UK, stated, 'people who insist that possession cannot exist have never seen a case or, if they have, have been so blinkered by prejudice that they have temporarily lost the capacity to assess symptoms'. He details a number of cases in which the possession (as in the take-over of Doris Fischer by 'Ariel': *see* **multiple personality**) proved beneficial. He mentions other cases like that in which a patient, who had savagely attacked her friends, told him, 'Something which is not me gets inside me and makes me do these things.'[1]

In considering the evidence for possession by 'discarnate spirits', it is not necessary to assume that all such spirits are malign.

1. *The Psyche in Medicine*, Arthur Guirdham, Spearman, Saffron Walden 1978, p. 55ff.

POWYS, John Cowper (1872–1963) (*See* **DOPPELGÄNGERS, PAGANISM**) Maternally descended from the poets Donne and Cowper, this English-born author possessed **shamanic** qualities typifying the pagan nature **mysticism** of the Celts, as suggested by his Welsh surname. Spending much of his life in the USA, it was there he wrote his great novels, including *Wolf Solent*, *Weymouth Sands* and *A Glastonbury Romance*. The latter is immense in length, scale and metaphysical depth, all its characters being overshadowed by the age-old mysteries of **Glastonbury** and **Grail** romance.[1]

Of Powys, biographer Wilson Knight wrote, 'Those who have incurred his anger have so invariably suffered misfortune that he has, as it were, been *forced* into a life of almost neurotic benevolence . . . (his) early ambition to become a magician was no idle dream.' In his *Autobiography* Powys confirms this: 'The evidence . . . of my being able . . . quite unconsciously . . . to exercise some kind of "**evil eye**" on people who have injured me – has so piled up all my life that it has become a habit with me to pray to my gods anxiously and hurriedly for each new enemy.'

American novelist Theodore Dreiser told how one night Powys, leaving after a social call, promised to *return later* 'as a **spirit** or in some other astral form', and did so (*see* **Doppelgängers**). Yet his prediction 'that when I die it is the complete and absolute end of me', was perhaps less successful. A month after he died on 17 June 1963, a **medium**, Miss Frances Horsfield was standing by Wilson Knight in Exeter Cathedral when she sensed a man present and proceeded to describe Powys (whom she had not known): 'He has rather gaunt features, with high cheekbones and unruly hair. He *is* a personality. He is nearly controlling me, but I do not want that. He was himself an **occultist** . . . He wrote, didn't he?' Knight confirmed this. She went on, 'He is so close to you . . . His power is so strong that you may well see him yourself some time.' She added that he had a 'wide, gleaming mouth' and a 'beaklike nose'. When Knight said Powys had latterly become a sceptic about 'survival', she said, 'Anyway, he knows all about it now.'[2]

1. *A Glastonbury Romance*, John Cowper Powys, Pan Picador, London 1980
2. *The Saturnian Quest*, Wilson Knight, 1964

PRĀNA A Sanskrit term from **pra-**, 'before'; and **an**, 'to breathe', 'to blow' or 'to live'; prāna is said to be a psycho-electrical field generated by the sun and manifesting in the individual as vitality. Absorbed into the body via the **chakras**, it has affinity with Western concepts of the **aura** or life-field, and with Chinese **ch'i** energy. At death the prāna of the individual body is said to return to the planet's prānic reservoirs.

PRECOGNITION (*See* **DREAMS, DUNNE, PROPHECY, SECOND SIGHT**) Precognition (from Latin *praecognitio*) means prior or previous knowledge. In the **paranormal** sense it means knowledge or **vision** of an event before it occurs.

This baffling phenomenon is well-attested. Second sight in Gaelic culture is (or was) taken for granted. Lord Kilbracken dreamed horse-race winners; Mark Twain dreamed of his brother's death. Premonitions of the Aberfan and *Titanic* disasters were widespread.

The subject was popularised by J. W. Dunne's *An Experiment With Time* (1927). Among the many other accounts of precognition given in this famous book he tells how, as a soldier in South Africa in 1902, he dreamed he was on an island threatened by a volcano. In the dream he 'was seized by a frantic desire to save the four thousand (I knew the number) unsuspecting inhabitants . . . I was at a neighbouring island, trying to get the incredulous French authorities to despatch vessels . . . I was sent from one official to another; and finally woke myself by my own dream exertions . . . All through the dream the number of the people in danger obsessed my mind.' Days later in the *Daily Telegraph* he read of Mount Pelée's eruption in Martinique. 40,000 people were said to be dead. Obsessed with '4,000', he read '40,000' as '4,000' and only years later realised the true reading had been 40,000. Subsequent reports gave a different figure entirely. 'My wonderful "**clairvoyant**" vision had been wrong in its most insistent particular!' he noted, concluding that he must have got the number 4,000 from a mis-reading of the newspaper in his dream.

On 21 October 1966 a coal tip slid down a Welsh mountain and buried the mining village of Aberfan, killing 144 people, 128 of them schoolchildren. Following a visit to Aberfan next day, Dr J. C. Barker appealed in London's *Evening Standard* for those who felt they had foreseen the disaster to write to him. Seventy-six people did so. Seeking witnesses to confirm that these people had spoken of their premonition before the event, he was able to confirm twenty-four cases. These premonitions involved dreams, clairvoyant visions or '**spirit** messages'. They had affected people from all over Britain from five weeks before the disaster to within two hours of it. In several cases the dreams were so vivid that the dreamer awoke screaming. Some reported hearing children screaming. Seven people developed acute stress symptoms from four days to a few hours before the tragedy: some claimed previous premonitions of other disasters.

Following J. Gaither Pratt's conjecture that 'individuals who have convincingly precognised one or more future events are at least as common as left-handed people', Barker called such people 'human seismographs'. He suggested founding a Disaster Early Warning System, quoting Louisa Rhine's 1961 comment: 'If the precognitive ability is developed and directed . . . and if imperfect **ESP** impressions, especially those suggesting disaster ahead could be clarified, intelligent preventative action could follow to the untold advantage of mankind.' In 1967 Barker helped set up the British Premonitions Bureau, which in its first year filed some 500 premonitions.

At the Second International Conference of the **Society for Psychical Research** in Cambridge, March 1978, Professor Hans Bender (of the Anne-Marie Schaberl **poltergeist** case) presented a paper describing a prophecy written down in 1914 by a Bavarian soldier, Andreas Rill. It was made by a Frenchman who had told his captors to 'throw away their guns', as the war would end in German defeat, followed by revolution, inflation and the rise of a man 'from the lower ranks' in 1932, leading to another war in 1939 which in 1945 Germany would lose. A Third World War involving China would break out before AD 2000. Bender said that there were no doubts about the authenticity of Rill's letter.

The sinking of the *Titanic* in April 1912 was presaged by many cases of seeming precognition, among them the 1898 publication of *Futility*, a novel by Morgan Robertson. In this a great liner, the *Titan*, thought unsinkable due to its watertight compartments, hits an iceberg during an April voyage at a speed of twenty-five knots (*Titanic*: twenty-three knots); has only twenty-four lifeboats (*Titanic*: twenty) for its 3,000 passengers and crew (*Titanic*: 2207, but it was only two thirds full); and sinks with huge loss of life. Professor Ian **Stevenson**, commenting that Robertson's tale may be explained as intelligent deduction, collected many other premonitions of the disaster, including the warning given by the **palmist** Cheiro to the editor W. T. Stead that: 'Very critical and dangerous for you should be April 1912, especially about the middle of the month. So don't travel by water then if you can help it.' (Cheiro had also predicted death by drowning for Lord Kitchener, which duly occurred in 1916.) Despite this and other warnings Stead went . . . and died.[1]

Stevenson suggested that such disasters produce **psychic** shocks by their very unexpectedness. But no theory yet 'explains' precognition, or allays our unease at the **predestinatory** implications. Is free will an **illusion**?

Dunne's theory of 'serial **time**' is today generally rejected. **Bennett**, fascinated by **Einstein**'s hypothesis that the ether is a material substance able to go all ways at once at light-speed, postulated a fifth **dimension** at right angles to the space-time we know, offering the freedom of more than one time-track and thus more than one possible future. Parapsychologist Charles Tart has postulated a second time-dimension operating as a channel for **psi** information. In this dimension **consciousness** functions on a wider band, stretching further into both past and future than is usually the case. However Tart's theory fails to explain long-range precognition.[2]

Attempts to explain the phenomenon by existing scientific **paradigms** may be as doomed to failure as attempts by inhabitants of Flatland to explain the Third Dimension in terms of length and breadth alone. That precognitive vision is often dream-borne or said to be brought by 'spirits' from other sets of dimensions interpenetrating our spacetime may be relevant. The idea that thought-activity extends beyond the physical body, partaking of a planetary 'field of mind' in which the *shadow* of the future already exists as part of an 'implicate order', **collective unconscious** or **Akashic Record** may prove helpful, and the study of ancient **symbolically** formalised systems (such as Gaelic second sight) may also provide relevant clues.

1. *A Sense of Something Strange*, Archie Roy, Dog and Bone, Glasgow 1990
2. *Mysteries*, Colin Wilson, Granada, London 1979, pp. 604–8

PREDESTINATION A harsh Calvinistic offshoot of traditional Judaeo-Christian chronology. The latter held the future to be fixed and its fate already sealed by the dictates of the Almighty so that the world, created in 4004 BC, must endure 6,000 years until the final battle with **Antichrist** and the subsequent Rule of the Saints: predestinarians go further than this in claiming that every event and individual fate is immutably decreed in advance, and that only the 'Elect' will be saved, the rest of humanity behind damned. The number of the Elect has been given since Roman times as 144,000. Of course true believers in the system invariably number themselves among the Elect.

PREDICTION (*See* **DIVINATION, I CHING, OMENS, PROPHECY, TAROT**)

PRE-EXISTENCE (*See* **REINCARNATION, THEOSOPHY**) This belief does not in fact imply **reincarnation** but says only that the soul, human or otherwise, existed before its birth on Earth. As such it is found not only in Theosophy but in the teachings of early Church fathers such as Origen, who claimed that the human **soul** pre-exists in the spiritual world before embarking on a series of reincarnations on Earth. This claim was formally anathematised and condemned by the Church *c*. AD 541.

PREMONITIONS (*See* **PRECOGNITION**)

PRIBRAM, Karl (*See* **HOLOGRAPHIC THEORY**)

PRICE, Harry (1891–1948) (*See* **FRAUD, GHOSTS**) A travelling salesman, Price became a prominent member of the **Society for Psychical Research** (SPR). Witty and imaginative, he was also competitive, ambitious for fame and easily slighted. Such attributes upset many of his colleagues, several of whom denounced him after his death as a fraud.

In the 1920s he and Austrian **medium** Rudi Schneider worked with one Baron von Schrenk-Nötzing (known to sceptics as *Baron Shrink-at-Nothing*). The claims that he was a fraud began here. His reaction to accusation of faked photographs fuelled later hostilities arising from his investigation of Borley Rectory (*The Most Haunted House in England*), near Sudbury in Essex. Built in 1863, Price began investigating it in 1929. A decade later it burned down. Phenomena reported included: a phantom coach; a headless monk; a ghostly nun; the **spirit** of a former vicar; eerie lights; odd bells; and water turning into ink. 'The best authenticated case of haunting in the annals of psychical research', Price called it. Others disagreed. His claims were denounced in *The Borley Report* (1956), written after he died by three former SPR colleagues. They alleged that he had faked evidence by burying bones, producing aural effects in the dark by crumpling cellophane, and so on. The widely publicised affair persisted to a point where it had less to do with Borley Rectory than with Price himself.

Yet again in such cases the phenomena examined are so tricksy that the sanity or integrity of the investigators is easily doubted. Price was hated not only for desiring fame, but for his social background, his over-eager imagination, and the shadow of his previous investigations. It remains hard to tell if SPR hostility arose from fair assessment or pure dislike of him.

A later SPR report, *An examination of the 'Borley Report'*, by Robert Hastings (1969) considered weaknesses in the argument against Price but was never separately issued or widely publicised.[1,2,3]

1. *Search for Truth*, Harry Price, Collins, London 1942
2. *Search for Harry Price*, Trevor H. Hall, Duckworth, London 1978
3. *The Occult*, Colin Wilson, Grafton, London 1979, pp. 646–51

PRINCE, Dr Walter Franklin (*See* **MULTIPLE PERSONALITY, POSSESSION**) Historian, clergyman and psychologist, Prince's insight into the multiple personality of Doris Fischer began his lifelong research into the **psyche** and its mysteries. Invited in 1917 by James **Hyslop** to join the American Society for Psychical Research (ASPR), he became the ASPR's chief research officer when Hyslop died in 1920. By then suspecting that many psychological traumas arise from **spirit-possession**, he also believed that such cases could be cured by the power of the psyche itself, aided by suggestion.

In 1922 a Mrs Latimer approached him claiming she was possessed. Guilt at a cousin's death had plunged her into failed relationships and other misfortunes she blamed on a **discarnate entity** whose voice persecuted her. He concluded she was paranoid but agreed to try **exorcism**, hoping that in her case this potent form of suggestion might work. He told her that, by existing psychiatric criteria, her problem lay in her own psyche, but that he would try a makeshift exorcism. He gave her a fifteen-minute sermon, stating and analysing what he saw as her problems, then told her to ignore the invading 'entity' if its voice tormented her further. A hiatus in the treatment led him to write to her in January 1923. She said the voices had gone, but she felt exhausted. By 1924 she seemed cured despite continued production of **automatic writing**, apparently from the invading entity.

Was she cured by exorcism? Had she been 'possessed' by 'spirits', or merely by her own sense of guilt? Prince felt her case would not respond to suggestion or psychology. His *religious* exorcism seemingly succeeded.[1]

1. *The Infinite Boundary*, D. Scott Rogo, Aquarian, Wellingborough 1988, pp. 187–96.

PROJECT BLUE BOOK (*See* **HYNEK, UFOS**)

PROPHECY (*See* **DIVINATION, OMENS, PRECOGNITION, SECOND SIGHT**) Though divination, **fortune-telling**, precognition and other techniques for gaining insight into the future may in general all be considered *prophetic* sytems, *prophecy* in its pure form is distinguished by the moral, social and theological framework within which it occurs. Precognitive events or **dreams** are rarely sought consciously; a diviner or any other **psychic** may have material or selfish reasons for seeking knowledge of the future; and such arts, whether practised deliberately or unconsciously, usually deal with relatively transitory, personal, or local events.

The true prophet, on the other hand, has only one reason to function as he does: to perceive and reveal spiritual truth (the 'Word of God') to his people. Operating as a special instrument with a divine mission, he has to be fearless. Whatever the consequences he must deliver the inspirational messages flowing through him. The form of his utterance is usually moulded in cultural tradition, employing **symbols** relating to **astrology** (cosmic, not mundane), or to the **mythic** expectations of a particular land or people. He is a lantern, a guiding light whose basic aim is to persuade the culture involved to transform itself, or else suffer the consequences prophesied.

Thus prophecy deals not in **predestined** fact or inevitability. The main purpose is (often by dire warning) to set a people into a new course of behaviour and action, thus defusing the predicted misfortune in advance.

Where misfortune is inevitable due to actions which cannot be undone, prophecy seeks to provoke activity by which the destruction is minimised. Thus the true prophet may be widely perceived as false precisely because, due to his warning, people act to avoid the prophesied disaster.

The converse may also be true: a prophecy may be disseminated precisely to realise calculated social changes via the activity of those aware of it and deliberately fulfilling it. Peter Lemesurier has argued that **Christ**'s ministry was an **Essene** initiative to fulfil ancient biblical prophecies of a future Messiah, and that Christ's every act was undertaken to fulfil, to *the very letter*, Old Testament prophecies by Isaiah, Daniel, Amos and others. He rode into Jerusalem on an ass to *fulfil the prophecy* in Psalms 118, 25–26, having been anointed according to prescription in Leviticus. His Last Supper, betrayal, trial and Crucifixion were necessary acts in a preordained symbolic drama. His every act was **ritualistic**, part of a pattern to be physically fulfilled to ensure a coming, prophesied Golden Age.[1]

Such 'participatory fulfilment' (in itself an answer to simplistic **predestination**) is seen in the effect of prophecies by **Nostradamus**, St **Malachy**, the **Brahan Seer**, etc. Napoleon and **Hitler** both thought certain quatrains in Nostradamus prophesied their triumphs. Thus encouraged, they pursued their historic courses. So history was influenced. Whether or not they assumed correctly is unimportant. Their belief was enough.

Any widely disseminated prophecy is essentially a revolutionary act. It breeds political change by its very existence, by the belief placed in it, and by its legitimisation of radical action. Thus in England at the end of the fifteenth century the upstart Tudor dynasty legitimised itself by allegiance with the **Arthurian** mythos, arguing its right to rule as based on ancient prophecy of 'The Return of the King'. The effect of such claims was considerable. During the English Civil War unprecedented acts like the execution of King Charles I in 1649 were justified by 'ancient' prophetic authority, no other authority being available. 'Prophecies [were] many times the principal cause of the event foretold,' wrote Hobbes.[2]

But the prophetic tradition most influencing Western history is that of 'end times' as found in Judaeo-Christian lore, especially in the Revelation of St John. Belief in an imminent **Second Coming** as forecast in the New Testament peaked in AD 999's end-of-the-world hysteria, peaked again during the aftermath of the Black Death in 1348 and is peaking again today.

Jehovah's Witnesses, other Christian sects, **UFO** cultists, **pole shift** theorists, and **New Agers** seize on 'prophecies of doom' as evidence that global warming, pollution, war and over-population constitute *prima facie* moral justification for belief in our imminent collective demise.

Seers like **Dixon** and **Cayce** mix talk of **Antichrist** with predictions of global cataclysm. Sometimes precise dates are given. When these dates pass without disaster, believers usually excuse the 'prophet' involved due to their personal need to sustain a belief-system. The dates of approaching catastrophe as given by Nostradamus (1999), Mother **Shipton** and others are emotively potent, even when (as with Nostradamus) his dating was clearly motivated by pre-existing expectation, or (as with Mother Shipton) there is evidence that all 'modern' prophecies attributed to this shadowy mediaeval seeress were nineteenth-century inventions subsequently rendered more dramatic by modern writers for hoax and profit.[3]

The spurious interpretation of biblical text as prophecy of imminent global doom peaked in 1970 with US publication of Hal Lindsey's *The Late Great Planet Earth* which, 'proving' the EEC to be the ten-horned Beast of Revelation, forecast Armageddon via world war starting in Israel, with Russia ('Gog') and China aiding the Antichrist. This thesis enjoyed forty-five prints in five years and today is said to have sold some twenty million copies, mostly in the USA. Our need to acknowledge the transitory nature of human existence is strong: however the misuse of prophetic texts that originated in the Middle East 2,000 years ago and which referred to then-current events in that region suggests the degree to which we remain a species still confused by lack of distinction between reality and desire.[4,5]

1. *The Armageddon Script*, Peter Lemesurier, Element Books, Shaftesbury 1981
2. *Religion and the Decline of Magic*, Keith Thomas, Peregrine Books, London 1978, p. 501–5
3. *Patterns of Prophecy*, Alan Vaughan, Dell, New York 1976, p. 20
4. *The Late Great Planet Earth*, Hal Lindsey, Zondervan, USA 1970
5. *The Elements of Prophecy*, R. J. Stewart, Element Books, Shaftesbury, 1990

PSI POWERS 'Psi' is a neologism, probably derived from 'psionic', itself apparently a neologism derived from '**psychic**', and perhaps first used in science-fiction writer Murray Leinster's 1955 story, 'The Psionic Mousetrap', then later popularised by the editor of *Astounding Science Fiction*, John W. Campbell.

Psi or psionic powers are **ESP** powers – **telepathy, precognition** and **clairvoyance** in particular; also **telekinesis, teleportation, levitation** and the *pyrotic* capacity to start fires by mind power alone. Their thematic use in science-fiction stories derived in part from the popular discussion of cases of such powers in Charles **Fort**'s *Wild Talents* (1932).

PSYCHE Originally a Greek term referring to ***soul, spirit,*** *mind*; epitomised as a female spirit, or represented with butterfly wings, delicate, evanescent, not easily weighed or measured, the hidden mover, the secret source.

PSYCHIC A noun describing one possessing **paranormal** or **ESP** abilities as described above; an adjective indicating the practical essence of such abilities.

PSYCHIC ARCHAEOLOGY (*See* **LETHBRIDGE, MAP-DOWSING, GLASTONBURY**) This is a term that refers to **paranormal** means of archaeological research or discovery; i.e. by **clairvoyance, dowsing, dreams**, map-dowsing, **psychometry** or **spirit** communications. By such means and without other evidence the researcher is led to dig in the right place.

In 1907 the Church of England bought ruined Glastonbury Abbey for £30,000. This venerated site (*'the holyest erthe in England'*), founded in the fifth century and destroyed by Henry VIII during the 1530s, was by then so plundered that little was left. Architect and mediaevalist Frederick Bligh **Bond** was appointed as Director of Excavations and briefed to find the Abbey's original features.

His success was amazing. Wherever he dug a trench it intersected some buried wall. He found lost parts of the old Abbey and the foundations of St Edgar's Chapel, east of the main building. But in 1918 his delighted employers were shocked when Bond published *The Gate of Remembrance*, explaining his success as due to spirit communications via the **automatic writing** of a friend, John Allen Bartlett. Unseen correspondents calling themselves 'The Company of Glastonbury' or 'Watchers from the Other Side' had drawn (via Bartlett) the unknown original plan of the Abbey and shown him where to dig. Signing themselves 'Gulielmus Monachus' (William the Monk), Ambrosius the Cellarer, Peter Lightfoot the Clockmaker, Johannes Bryant and Abbot Bere (the last abbot but one), they had explained their aim (in Latin and Old English) as the rebirth of Glastonbury as a great spiritual centre.[1]

Outraged by this **necromancy** (maybe too by dislike of Bond's influence in the revival of the Abbey as a mystical centre) Church and archaeological establishment ensured that he was sacked, his excavations grassed over, the Edgar Chapel and his other discoveries removed from official Abbey plans. He was banned from the grounds. Even today, despite modern endorsement of his ground-plan, his books are unavailable at the Abbey bookstall.

Bond did not automatically assume his 'Watchers' to be dead monks; he thought they might be projections from that same part of the unconscious through which dowsing functions. But the unconscious cut no more ice with orthodoxy than dead monks. Embittered, he lectured in the USA, meanwhile receiving new communications from the Company. These concerned tunnels and buried treasure under the Abbey, also material about King **Arthur** and the **Grail**. An American party gained permission to dig in the Abbey grounds, but permission was revoked when their association with Bond was discovered. These later communications remain unexplored.[2]

Since Bond died in 1945 Glastonbury has regained much of its magnetism as a centre for artists, healers and seekers. Meanwhile, the lesson of his dismissal is not lost on today's psychic archaeologists.

In 1971 Jeffrey Goodman, a graduate student in geology and archaeology at the University of Flagstaff in Arizona, dreamed of a prehistoric human settlement site older than any known in the USA. His enquiries led him to contact Oregon clairvoyant

Aron **Abrahamsen**, who told him where to dig in the local San Francisco Mountains. Abrahamsen had never seen the area but clairvoyantly identified human artefacts over 100,000 years old to be found at each level of the dig down to fifty feet, and predicted soil and rock types at exact levels down to twenty-three feet, where evidence of ancient human habitation would be found. He added that the first humans reached Arizona 500,000 years ago, not from Asia but from **Atlantis** and **Lemuria**.

Before starting the dig, Goodman sent Abrahamsen's predictions round archaeologists, anthropologists and geologists throughout the USA. The common response was that the predictions were nonsense. *Then* Goodman dug. Of Abrahamsen's fifty-eight specific predictions, fifty-two proved accurate. If his claims are correct, human habitation of North America goes back at least to 100,000 BC – some 70,000 years earlier than the earliest currently accepted orthodox date.

Did this prove Abrahamsen right about Atlantis and Lemuria? No. Only that he was right about what lay under a site he had never visited.

1. *Poltergeist*, Colin Wilson, New English Library, London 1981, pp. 208–14
2. *Psychic Archaeology*, Jeffrey Goodman, Berkley, New York 1977.

PSYCHIC ART (*See* **GASPARETTO**)

PSYCHICAL RESEARCH (*See* **SOCIETY FOR PSYCHICAL RESEARCH**)

PSYCHIC HEALING (*See* **HEALING, PSYCHIC SURGERY**)

PSYCHIC PHOTOGRAPHY (*See* **SPIRIT PHOTOGRAPHY**)

PSYCHIC SURGERY (*See* **ARIGÓ, HEALING, PUHARICH, SPIRITISM**) The work of 'psychic surgeons' in the Philippines, Brazil and elsewhere has been reported since the 1950s. Healers without medical education or facilities, often with only a 'rusty knife' and often in **trance**, perform complex surgery on patients with a high level of success and few failures. The work of Brazilian José de Freitas, known as Arigó (d. 1971) sustained credibility under outside investigation. Yet the greatest attention has been attracted by Filipino healers like Tony Agpaoa. Using bare hands, seemingly they operate by pulling open the body and removing diseased tissue and organs. Concentrated on the island of Luzon, most belong to the Union Espiritista Christiana de Filipinas, a network of rural **Spiritist** churches – a movement also popular in Brazil.

Their discovery by Western investigators soon led to denunciation. The operations described (and often filmed) *had* to be fraudulent. By the mid–1970s psychic surgery was thoroughly debunked as being sleight-of-hand or suggestion. But **fraud** proven in many cases failed to explain away Arigó's record, nor the eye-witness reports of researchers like Lyall **Watson**.

On three visits to the Philippines occupying eight months, Watson saw over a thousand operations by twenty-two different healers. One involved a middle-aged woman with stomach pains. He saw the healer apparently push his hands deep into her body. A tennis-ball-sized lump of flesh grew between the healer's first and second fingers. Lifting it clear with forceps, an assistant snipped a thread of tissue to free it from her body, and dropped it into Watson's hand. Removing his hands, the healer wiped blood from her body, leaving no visible wound. 'I rub my hand over her skin,' wrote Watson. 'It is hot, but there is nothing on it, not a mark of any kind.' The patient got up and walked away. Typically, 'the whole process lasted about five minutes and is very matter-of-fact. There is little or no showmanship, no music or drums or incense, nothing to divert the attention from what is going on.'[1]

In 1973 Chicago journalist Tom Valentine saw similar operations and dismissed the possibility of sleight-of-hand, hypnosis or hoax. That same year and again in 1975 George Meek led teams of experts to the Philippines. They saw many healers in action and, while deciding some to be fake, agreed that 'the factual existence and daily practice of several types of psycho-energetic phenomena by several native healers was clearly established. The practice of materializing and dematerializing human blood tissue and organs as well as non-human objects was found.' All members testified that there had been no fraud, anaesthetics or sterile precautions, and no cases of infection or post-operative shock.[2]

In his book *Psi Healing*, German investigator Alfred Stelter speculates that the process involves temporary suspension of physical reality leading to a subtle interplay of spiritual and physical energies manipulated by the surgeon. Cypriot healer **Daskalos** claims psychic healing involves mastering the '**etheric** double'. Of a case in which he reset a woman's vertebrae, he told author Kyriacos Markides, 'It would be impossible to place the vertebrae in their right place unless one knows consciously how to employ etheric vitality and also have a knowledge of the structure of the spine.' He added, 'In this case, through the imprinting property of ether, we could create two etheric hands and place them inside the body of the patient. By mastering the sense property of ether, we could then feel on the edges of our etheric fingers the spinal problem and move the vertebrae into their proper place. Four hands are now at work, the material hands outside the body, and the etheric hands inside.'[3]

Bizarre? So is the phenomenon.

1. *The Romeo Error*, Lyall Watson, Coronet, London 1976, pp. 214–9
2. *Ibid.*, p. 218
3. *The Magus of Strovolos*, Kyriacos C. Markides, Routledge Kegan Paul, London 1985, p. 185

PSYCHOKINESIS (*See* **ESP, GELLER, MANNING**) The Oxford dictionary defines this faculty (also called 'telekinesis' and abbreviated as 'PK') as 'the movement of physical objects by mental influence without physical contact'. Meaning: the power of mind over matter, as manifested most famously by Uri Geller and his spoon-bending.

In the seventeenth century Sir Francis Bacon suggested 'shuffling cards, or casting dice' as a way to test 'the binding of thoughts'. In 1854, amid the **Spiritualist** craze, Count Agénor de Gasparin concluded from table-turning experiments that the human will can affect matter at a distance, and that '**spirits**' were not involved. In 1870, **medium** D. D. **Home** convinced Sir William **Crookes** that he could **levitate** people and objects, alter the weight of inert bodies, and produce other genuine PK effects. Crookes also suggested that PK (which he called 'psychic force') implied the existence of other **dimensions**, the observer being 'in infinitesimal and inexplicable contact with a plane of existence not his own.' Later researches by eminent men with the mediums Eusapia **Palladino** and Stanislawa Tomczyk only added to the evidence. A **Society for Psychic Research** team studying Palladino recorded 470 events they considered inexplicable: Tomczyk produced spontaneous effects in her normal state: under hypnosis she made spoons and matchboxes rise into the air by placing her hands near them. It seemed no more proof was needed as to the *reality* of PK: all that was required was to *explain* and *harness* the force.

Yet when in 1934 Dr J. B. **Rhine** published the first results of his **ESP** experiments he was instantly accused of faulty techniques, despite (for his PK tests) devising dice-throwing machines making it impossible for subjects to influence the fall of the dice physically. Throughout his life he went on recording statistically significant results, concluding that PK is an 'oft-repeated demonstrated experimental fact'. But no explanation emerged.

In the 1960s UK psychologist Kenneth **Batcheldor** with several friends succeeded in producing (and recording) table-rappings and **levitations** with no more spiritual aid than patient, positive thinking: later the Toronto **Philip** group recorded similar phenomena publicly on TV. Yet in all such work the PK effects produced tended to get out of control and manifest in unexpected ways, suggesting either subconscious activity or perhaps the genuine presence of **discarnate entities**, as claimed by Spiritualists.[1]

Then came Uri Geller. Tested at the Stanford Research Institute, his powers disturbed US intelligence agencies not for what he accomplished but for the 'almost limitless list of equipment failures' that accompanied his visits, including the wiping of computer programmes. With the Russians also known to be interested in possible military PK applications, the agencies funded further research, a fact hidden until a 1980 article in the *Military Review* revealed that both CIA and Pentagon took the possibility of psychic warfare seriously. In 1982 the position in the USSR was described when the English translation of *Parapsychology and Contemporary Science*, by Dubrov and Pushkin, appeared. Devoting space to the remarkable Leningrad medium, Nina Kulagina, who can produce PK effects to order roughly eighty per cent of the time, the authors made it clear that resistance to the reality of ESP and PK is as common in the East as in the West, excoriating colleagues who refuse to examine the evidence for 'acting like people who have evidence of a crime and hide it', and concluding that ESP and PK are so important: 'that neither science nor mankind have the right to ignore them'.[2]

1. 'Phenomenal Successes', Guy Lyon Playfair, *The Unexplained*, Orbis partwork, London 1983, pp. 1170–73
2. *The Hidden Power*, Brian Inglis, Cape, London 1986, pp. 121–4

PSYCHOMETRY (*See* **LETHBRIDGE, PSYCHIC ARCHAEOLOGY**) A term invented by Professor Joseph Rhodes Buchanan, a nineteenth-century Dean of the Covington Medical Institute, USA. Intrigued by Bishop Leonidas Polk's claim to be able to detect brass in the dark because its touch produced an unpleasant taste in the mouth, Buchanan's experiments showed that some of his students could detect different chemicals wrapped in thick brown paper; also that some of them, holding letters, could describe the writer. His geologist friend William Denton tested his own students with rock samples and found some able to describe, with amazing accuracy, the origin of the samples. Buchanan concluded (as did Lethbridge a century later) that all materials give off 'emanations' affected by human emotion, and that the world's history lies about us, recorded on objects, waiting to be picked up and decoded by the sensitive. Both he and Denton were sure they had found a new science, without **supernatural** aspect: he considered psychometry no more remarkable than the power to hear or see. Yet he failed to hide his **Spiritualist** allegiance: his findings were derided on the usual grounds that the ideas of a man unconvinced by materialist orthodoxy are innately suspect. Yet today psychometry proves to be a useful faculty for **dowsers**, psychic archaeologists and others seeking buried knowledge.[1]

As with dowsing, the technique is simple. Take an object the history of which is known, but not to you. Hold it, or press it to your forehead. Let mental images come as they will. Describe what you see to the person who knows the object's history. The talent improves with practice. (An accurate description may indicate not psychometry but **telepathy**.)

1. *Mysteries*, Colin Wilson, Grafton, London 1979, pp. 385–6

PSYCHOTRONICS (*See* **BEARDEN, UFOs**) Employing **parapsychological** theory as to the bio-energetic power inherent in certain shapes, Czech inventor Robert Pavlita claims to have developed a 'psychotronic generator' which draws on this energy, accumulates it and uses it for purposes as diverse as the removal of pollutants from water to the stimulation of **telepathic** capacity. The theory thus conjoins with the notion of ancient **megaliths** as geomagnetic accumulators creating mind-alerting fields in and about which occur **'ghosts'** or UFO phenomena, these arising from subjective perception of objective events. The term has also been employed by American nuclear engineer Thomas Bearden to describe a model of reality whereby interest in a phenomenon stimulates the emergence into physical reality of that phenomenon. Thus unconscious mental forms combine 'psychotronically' with the energy-properties of particular sites to produce anomalous manifestations which, though failing to obey 'normal' laws of nature, may show up if photographed – or maybe not.

PUHARICH, Andrija (1918–) (*See* **ARIGÓ, GELLER, PSYCHIC SURGERY**) This Chicago-born researcher worked with Aldous **Huxley** and with Eileen **Garrett**, brought the Dutch psychic Peter **Hurkos** to the USA, studied the sacred mushroom cult in Mexico and the Hawaiian **Kahuna** cult, and between 1963 and 1968 investigated the Brazilian **psychic surgeon**, José Pedro de Freitas, known as **Arigó**. He was so impressed he let Arigó remove a benign tumour from his elbow. Arigó, a pocket-knife in hand, asked him not to watch, so he faced the cameraman filming the event. Within seconds Arigó put both tumour and pocket knife in his hand. Puharich was amazed. Though entirely conscious, he had felt no pain. Yet there was a bleeding incision and a tumour. Knowing that the knife was dirty and that Arigó's hands were unwashed, he feared infection, but the wound healed clean in three days.

When Arigó died mysteriously in 1971, 'the tragedy of the death', wrote Puharich, 'awakened my consciousness to become a seeker' (as if he had not been one already). Thus that same year, on hearing of Uri Geller, he flew to Israel and saw Geller perform in a Jaffa discotheque. The association developed into a set of experiences so bizarre that Puharich, in recording them as fact in his 1974 biography *Uri*, must have known that his reputation would suffer. Extraterrestrial or other-dimensional entities ('The Nine'), his briefcase **teleporting** from New York to Tel Aviv, disappearing tape-recorders and time-lapses: the tale would not disgrace a Spielberg movie. Even Geller called The Nine: 'clowns playing practical jokes'. Subsequently The Nine told Puharich to abandon further tests with Geller.

Given Geller's subsequent career, and the evidence that at the time he had little control over faculties elsewhere and in others (*see* **Manning**) manifesting as **poltergeist** events, it may be that Puharich reported to the best of his ability events that really did occur, though not necessarily caused by the **entities** he described. The mystery persists. Puharich's own flamboyant career makes it no easier to understand.[1]

1. *Uri*, Andrija Puharich, Futura, London 1974

PYRAMIDS (*See* **EGYPT, GREAT PYRAMID, PYRAMID PROPHECIES**)

PYRAMID PROPHECIES (*See* **GREAT PYRAMID, PROPHECY**) Some researchers claim that the internal features and passages of the Great Pyramid constitute a coded prophecy; a spiritual blueprint for human progress. Peter Lemesurier (after Edgar **Cayce** and David Davidson) offers the following interpretation.

Entry to the Descending Passage symbolises humanity's Fall to physical matter (Pyramid = Earth). The *Descending Passage* itself (aligned on Alpha Draconis, the Pole Star in 2600 BC) represents rational materialism and its plunge to destruction in the *Subterranean Chamber*. Yet thirty metres down this passage is found, in the roof, entry to the *Ascending Passage*: the way to enlightenment. But this was literally blocked by the Granite Plug. Entry was gained only by Al Mamoun's men physically forcing their way round it in AD 820. Four feet high, the Ascending Passage climbs to the Grand Gallery, which is twenty-eight feet high. This sudden sevenfold increase in height represents an explosion of enlightenment.

The symbolic events outlined by specific features are dates by distance from the entry. Counting one Pyramid Inch per year, with the entry given as 2623 BC, the Ascending Passage starts in 1453 BC (associated by some with the Exodus), and the entry to the Grand Gallery in AD 33 (Crucifixion). At AD 73 (Masada?) the Well-Shaft plunges; a horizontal passage leads to the Queen's Chamber; the Grand Gallery continues up. The downward plunge refers to the physical death; the horizontal path to Pauline **Christianity** and the path of **dualistic** idealism: the continuing climb to the King's Chamber implies the possibility of psychic reintegration and ascent to unknown dimensions.

Today, the chronology suggests, we face material destruction but also the possibility of transformation. The Subterranean Chamber with its rough, broken floor was reached in 1914 – as was the Great Step atop the Grand Gallery. AD 2004–7 sees global civilisation plunge into the 'bottomless pit' of the Subterranean Chamber – yet at the same time we are at the door of the King's Chamber. Potent new ideas and influences manifest from 1985 onwards and lead through crisis to a new, spiritual world order. In this scheme, the lower end of the Well Shaft enables those who wish to, though otherwise trapped in the material catastrophe of the Pit, to ascend to higher possibilities as symbolised by the King's Chamber.[1]

1. *The Great Pyramid Decoded*, Peter Lemesurier, Element, Shaftesbury 1977

PYTHAGORAS (*See* **GREEK MYSTERIES**)

Q

QABALAH (*See* **INNER PLANES, JEWS, QLIPHOTH, QUARK, TAROT**) The Hebrew root QBL signifies 'to receive'; thus the body of teaching known as Qabalah means 'the received'. According to Rabbinical tradition it was first taught to Adam in Eden by the Archangel Gabriel and passed on 'from mouth to ear' thereafter. Jewish in origin, this profound and complex body of knowledge assumed Persian, Egyptian, Grecian, **Gnostic** and **Neoplatonist** elements during its development. It was transmitted orally without being written down until, *c*. AD 1280, Spanish Qabalist Moses ben Shemtob de Leon issued the *Zepher ha Zohar* (Book of Splendour). This vast commentary on the Pentateuch was said to be the work of the legendary Rabbi Simeon bar Yohai, who had died in ecstatic trance some 1200 years earlier.

Departing substantially from orthodox Judaism, the *Zohar* provided a basis for the growth of Qabalah into a system so flexible and sophisticated that today it lies at the heart of the Western Mystery Tradition.

Qabalistic teaching centres on the symbol or glyph known as **The Tree of Life**. This has been called 'a ground plan of the universe and the **soul** of man'. Used as such, it offers techniques for training the mind, a means of correlating different disciplines, philosophies, pantheons and mythologies, a tool for the evocation of spiritual powers and, via its **symbolism**, a map of the **psyche** vital to controlled exploration and work on the inner planes.

According to Qabalist philosophy, positive existence or manifestation emanates from a negative, unmanifest state incomprehensible to the rational mind. From this latter state of limitless undifferentiated being (*Ain Soph*) spring the ten *Sephiroth* (spheres or states of being). With their twenty-two interconnecting *Paths*, these encompass the entirety of manifestation in all its forms, from *Kether* to *Malkuth*, the highest to the lowest, a process seen in terms of the Divine Energy plunging down through one *Sephirah* to the next in a zigzag path: the 'Lightning Flash'. So each Sephirah connects with all the others yet in itself represents a unique condition of manifest being with specific **correspondences – astrological**, psychological and so on. The glyph is rendered yet more complex by the overlaying on the primal Tree of not one but four spiritual worlds – the *Assiatic* (material world); the *Yetziratic* (world of formation); the *Briatic* (creative world); and the *Atziluthic* (the highest world, the abode of uncreated deity).

The Tree is divided into three *Pillars*: Passive (left); Active (right), and Middle. In Qabalistic terms, pursuit of the 'Middle Way' means seeking progress by uniting the extremes without surrendering to them. Thus the intellectual life as expressed in the Sephirah *Hod* (Mercury) is as poorly balanced if pursued as an end in itself as is the sensual life of *Netzach* (Venus); both are best served by marriage of the faculties involved at the '**Christ**'-level of *Tiphareth* at the very centre of the Middle Pillar.

The Sephiroth or spheres are defined in declining sequence, as follows:

1. *Kether*, the Crown, pure brilliance, the fount of creation, the one universal point where life's energies spring into being from the Unmanifest – the Godhead and highest **chakra**, moving into activity in the next sphere;

2. *Chokmah*, Wisdom, the powerhouse of force, phallus, straight line, standing stone or tower: the initiator of action, standing under Kether at the head of the Right *Pillar of Mercy*, from whence the energy flashes to;

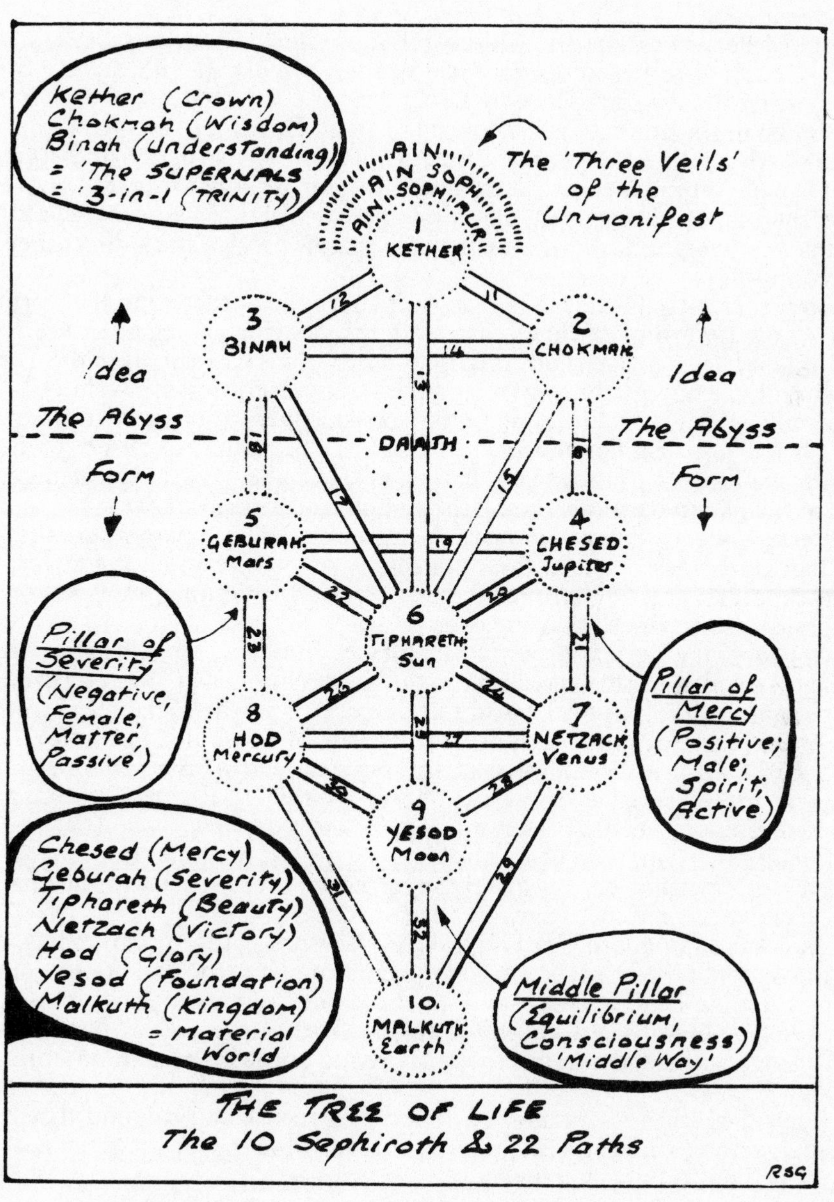

THE TREE OF LIFE
The 10 Sephiroth & 22 Paths

3. *Binah*, Understanding, Great Mother, primal ocean at the head of the *Pillar of Severity* which, fertilised by and taking in the pure spiritual energy of Kether and Chokmah, first manifests the idea of form.

These three Sephiroth stand above the *Abyss* separating Idea and Form: they constitute the Trinity, Triad, Three-In-One, the primal matrix from which all material existence proceeds. Yet it should not be thought that any of the lower Sephirah are any less 'spiritual'. The Tree is One.

Straddling the Abyss on the Middle Pillar is the hidden, numberless, mystical Sephirah, *Daath*, of relatively modern conception, associated with the star **Sirius** and with the positive idea of confidence in the future.

From Binah the lightning-flash shoots on through Daath to;

4. *Chesed*, Mercy, the four-square principle of form, construction and organisation, also worldly rule, mundanely associated with Jupiter. It is also called the Receptive or Cohesive Intelligence because at this level the Supernal forces cohere into (subtle) forms, thus establishing a sort of blueprint for matter before, work done, they cross to Chesed's opposite;

5. *Geburah*, Severity, Mars, the on-rush of energy, destructive in that forms established in Chesed are broken down, assessed and distributed for a further refraction into multiplicity. The image is of a mighty warrior in his Chariot, as in the Tarot card. From Geburah the energy thus refracted pours tranversely downward into;

6. *Tiphareth*, Beauty, the level of Christ-consciousness and the central Sephirah of the Tree, balancing what lies above with what lies below; the aspirations of the human world with the descent of the spirit. Thus it is called the Mediating Intelligence: it is the state of the Self in harmony, being the station transversely above;

7. *Netzach*, a beautiful naked woman, Venus: a dynamic sphere where the coherent love of Tiphareth rays out into the multiplicity of Nature in all her robes; kind or cruel but prodigal, creating natural forces perceived by human imagination as gods and goddesses, from which, crossing over;

8. *Hod*, Glory, the hermaphroditic Mercury of Intellect; the sphere in which men form images of formless truths relating to the Supernal regions. Such images arise not from experience of the physical world but descend from the higher Sephiroth. From Hod the creative energy plunges transversely to the Middle Pillar again, to;

9. *Yesod*, the **etheric** Foundation of the physical Earth, the machinery of forces coordinating the emergence of physical form, source of psychic, unconscious and reproductive energies, leading down to;

10. *Malkuth*, the Kingdom of Earth. Here we are, at the polar opposite to Kether, at the nadir of creation, yet intimately involved at every level with all that goes to make us what we are and seeks to draw us up again.

Yet this is no damnation. For Qabalah, unlike some other philosophies, does not despise the material life of Malkuth. On the contrary, it is the cornerstone of Qabalah that spirit must descend all the way into the depths of matter, that human destiny must be fully realised in Malkuth, before any further progress is possible. In this, Qabalah agrees with **Christianity**,[1] though arriving at the realisation not through faith but through gnosis.

This is an unsubtle presentation of a model of reality so profound that it is quite capable of assuming within its existing formulations the modern implications of high-energy physics and superstring theory.

1. *A Practical Guide to Qabalistic Symbolism*, Gareth Knight, Helios, Cheltenham 1966

QLIPHOTH (*See* **DEMONS, EVIL, QABALAH**) A distorted reflection of the **Tree of Life** is also said to exist. Powers employed in magical workings may be summoned not only for good but for **evil** or selfish purposes: in Qabalistic terminology the latter activity, and the demons thus summoned, belong to the inverse Tree, associated with the word *Qliphoth*, meaning 'harlots' or 'shells'. This state requires no romancing: the results of focus upon it, conscious or unconscious, may be found, as Gareth Knight puts it, 'in the nearest hospital, lunatic asylum, prison, brothel, or slum'. In all cases where the negative aspect of a Sephirah is invoked or appears, the consequence appears to be confusion, disorder and misery arising through a denial of unity. Focus on this area, as on any other form of '**black**' or selfish **magic**, is ill-advised.[1]

1. *A Practical Guide to Qabalistic Symbolism*, Gareth Knight, Helios, Cheltenham 1966, Vol. 1 p. 232

QUANTUM THEORY In 1900 Max Planck, Professor of Physics at Berlin University, suggested that radiation appears not in a continuous stream but in discrete packets or 'quanta' of energy, the number of quanta, and thus the total amount of energy, being greater the shorter the wavelength of the radiation. Thus an ultraviolet quantum contains more energy than a red quantum, untraviolet light being of higher frequency (short wavelength) than red light. The product of the frequency and size of the corresponding quantum (Planck's constant = *h*) appears to be a universal constant. Confirmed as observed fact in 1905 by **Einstein**, the theory established that **electromagnetic** radiation and light should be considered as both wave and particle.

Subsequently developed by Shrödinger, Dirac and **Heisenberg** (who from it derived his indeterminacy principle), quantum theory has since provided a theoretical base for a new model of the universe that includes **ESP** and **paranormal** events. Drawing on the insights gleaned from **relativity** and quantum theory, Lawrence **LeShan** has proposed that two kinds of reality exist, *sensory* and ***clairvoyant***: a theory reminiscent of the belief of **Paracelsus** that each of the four elements has a dual nature; one gross, the other subtle.

In short, the work of Einstein, Heisenberg, Planck and others has so undermined classical Newtonian physics that 'certainty', as such, no longer exists as a constant in natural law. 'I cannot believe that God plays dice with the cosmos,' Einstein is often quoted as having said, thus expressing his dislike of the uncertainties introduced by quantum theory, to which Stephen Hawking more recently retorted, 'On the contrary, it appears that not only does God play dice, but also that he sometimes throws the dice where they cannot be seen.' This does not mean that the derived laws of nature are not generally true or should be discarded; only that there is always – like a slightly open door – an element of uncertainty present.

QUARK (*See* **DIMENSIONS, QABALAH**) Lately theorised as the basic building blocks of the protons and neutrons inside atomic nuclei, 'quarks' (from the Lewis Carroll poem *The Hunting of the Snark*) not only behave without regard to the former basic axioms of physics, but may even prove less fundamental than supposed. 'Subquarks' are now posited as necessary to 'superstring' theory, which claims that the basic particles of matter are a kind of vibration occurring along closed curves in a ten-dimensional space-time continuum. First advanced in 1984 by two physicists: John Schwarz at the California Insitute of Technology and Michael Green at Queen Mary College, London, this theory eliminates a long-standing problem afflicting **quantum** field theory: the idea that particles occupy single points in space. But to do so it invokes the notion that space time consists of ten dimensions, not four, the six 'higher dimensions' occupying infinitesimal distances in order to have escaped detection.

Similarities between this proposed ten-dimensional system and the ten **Sephiroth** of the **Tree of Life** have been noted by some **Qabalists**.[1]

1. 'The Tree of Life: Basis of Superstring Theory', Stephen M. Phillips, *Circles* (magazine of the Theosphical Society in Scotland), Spring 1990

R

RADIESTHESIA (*See* **DOWSING**) In this form of dowsing the operator holds a pendulum over the map, human body, or substance under enquiry. Asking questions of it, he interprets the pendulum's gyrations as answers. Typically such questions require a 'Yes-No' response, given by the pendulum's clockwise or anticlockwise motion.

RADIONICS (*See* **HEALING**) This mechanical version of ***radiesthesia*** was developed in the late nineteenth century by San Francisco neurologist Dr Albert Abrams. Theorising that, as the human body emits radiation, it should be possible to detect changes in the body's energy field caused by illness or physical damage, he became famous for his 'black box' or 'reflexoscope'. Widely manufactured and sold after 1900, it had made him rich by his death in 1924. The 'black box' (a later version, the 'oscilloclast', was used to broadcast healing radiations to distant patients) was said not only to diagnose disease but to deliver appropriate remedies. Consisting of calibrated controls outside, and a maze of random wiring inside, the box was used thus: tapping a rubber pad (like an artificial diaphragm) with his finger the technician adjusted the knobs until receiving response in the form of a 'plonking' sound. This was supposed to suggest both the nature of the illness and the remedy.

In the 1940s, English engineer George Warr (later self-styled de la Warr) studying homeopathic ideas of the effects of the 'minimum dose', decided the theory was rubbish but that homeopathy itself often works.

He hypothesised a vital force permeating all life-forms, stimulated by the homeopathic system of prescribing drugs so dilute their presence cannot be detected by chemical analysis. Believing **electromagnetism** to be the cause, he attached aerials made from his wife's hair-pins to various plants and connected them via an amplifier to a cathode ray tube. He detected no signals at all from the plants. Rather than conclude that there *were* no signals, he decided the 'life radiation' was not electromagnetic, but was more likely connected with the 'electronic reaction' as defined by Abrams.

Later de la Warr revised the Abrams 'black box' by abandoning all the internal wiring. Circuitry led from a rubber pad to containers holding a sample of blood, hair and tissue. Stroking the rubber pad with a finger, the operator turned the first control knob until the finger briefly adhered or 'stuck' to the pad. The number on the knob was noted and the process repeated with the other knobs. The resulting combined number was thought important. This and de la Warr's 'radionic camera' sold so well that by 1960, like Abrams before him, he was rich. An ex-disciple, Miss Catherine Philips, sued him for **fraud**. She lost her case, the judge concluding that de la Warr obviously believed in his boxes. Yet the judge's open doubt as to whether the boxes really worked led to bad publicity and a huge decline in the popularity of radionics by the time de la Warr died in 1969.

Isolated reports of 'miracle cures' continue. It may be that in some cases a 'placebo effect' operates, the patient being cured by belief in the system. Or it may be that some practitioners are genuine healers without knowing it, and attribute their own unrealised powers to the black box.

RANDI, James (*See* **FRAUD, GELLER, HOUDINI**) This American stage conjurer's career as 'The Amazing Randi' was arrested by the rise to fame of Uri Geller. He got his own back by becoming the best-known Geller-debunker and imitator. A founder member of **CSICOP**, he stays in the news by accusing Geller and others of the fraud to which he himself admits. 'I'm a charlatan, a liar, a thief and a fake altogether,' he admitted on TV in 1982. 'There's no question of it, but I'm an actor playing a part, and I do it for purposes of entertainment.'

Parapsychologists Harold Puthoff and Russell Targ found twenty-four factual errors in the twenty-eight-page account Randi gave of the Stanford Research Institute (SRI) tests of Geller's powers in his *The Magic of Uri Geller*. They found that 'in every instance Randi, in his efforts to fault the SRI experiments, was driven to hypothesise the existence of a loophole condition that did not, in fact, exist'. Yet Christopher Evans ('unarguably definitive'), Carl Sagan ('Splendid!') and others publicly approved Randi's 'findings'.

Randi has sustained his success as an 'investigator' despite refusing to face evidence which he cannot explain, and sometimes simply by rewriting history (as when reportedly proving 'thoughtographer' Ted **Serios** a cheat). Taking a leaf out of Houdini's book he has offered $10,000 to anyone who can demonstrate **psi** under controlled conditions. To date the sum remains unpaid. His well-publicised attacks on serious psi research continues. As was noted in the *New York Times* following Randi's Project Alpha, in which he planted two youths faking psi powers on the McDonnell Laboratory for Psychical Research, hoaxing the investigators into publishing spurious data, 'If Mr Randi were a psychologist, the hoax might have landed him in hot water.' As it is, the wish of many to discredit psi by any means guarantees this self-admitted hoaxer an always receptive audience.[1]

1. *The Hidden Power*, Brian Inglis, Cape, London 1986, pp. 252–8

RASPUTIN, Grigori (1870–1916) Associated with charlatanry, excess and with the downfall of the Romanov czars during the Bolshevik Revolution, this Russian **magus** was no fake. Son of a Siberian peasant, he drank and womanised, yet was a genuine **mystic** and **healer**. Married at twenty, when his baby son died he went on pilgrimage to Mount Athos in Greece, called by a **vision** of the Virgin. On return he gained a reputation as a holy man. Accused by a local priest of holding orgiastic prayer meetings, the bishop investigated and found no impropriety.

During subsequent wanderings he developed the power to cure by prayer, kneeling by the beds of the sick. Reaching St Petersburg in 1905, his fame reached the ears of the Tsarina. In 1907 her haemophiliac son Alexei was apparently cured by his prayers. In 1912 Alexei was again near death after a fall. In disgrace and far away, Rasputin was telegraphed. He telegraphed back, 'The illness is not as dangerous as it seems. Don't let the doctors worry him.' It is said Alexei's state improved as soon as the telegram arrived. Again, in 1915, Alexei was injured. With a nose-bleed that would not stop, he declined into fever. Rasputin delayed his visit for twenty-four hours, but as soon as he entered the room, the bleeding stopped.

Certainly he was in no doubt of his own powers, nor is it surprising that he made enemies. There is always hostility to those manifesting such powers; Rasputin was never tactful or discreet, while his involvement at the Romanov court during such a feverish, revolutionary epoch stimulated hatred, especially as his patroness, the Tsarina, known as 'the foreigner' (she was German), was herself hated – her enemies became Rasputin's.

In Siberia in June 1914 Rasputin was stabbed. From evidence given by Rasputin's daughter Maria, **Colin Wilson** concludes that the attack occurred *at exactly the same time on the same day* that, thousands of miles away in Sarajevo, the Archduke Franz Ferdinand was assassinated by Gavril Princip. The archduke's death led to the First

World War: Rasputin was near death for weeks. He recovered to learn that the Tsar had rejected his earlier advice against going to war over the Balkans: Russia had entered the war.

By late 1916 the Russian army was in flight and Russia itself in chaos. Rasputin himself was murdered on the night of 29 December 1916. Before he died he wrote a letter. In it he said he felt he would be dead by 1 January 1917; that if the peasantry killed him Russia would remain a prosperous monarchy; but if the aristocracy (the boyars) killed him, their hands would remain soiled by his blood, no nobles would remain in Russia, and the Tsar and his family would die in two years. Historian Sir Bernard Pares later saw a facsimile of the letter and was inclined to accept its authenticity.

Rasputin's death is legendary. Apparently poisoned by cyanide (in fact no poison was found in his body) then shot, he burst through a locked door. Shot again, beaten with an iron bar, he was dropped into the river through a hole in the ice. When the body was recovered he was found to have died of drowning. His murderer? The aristocrat, Prince Yussupov.[1]

1. *The Occult*, Colin Wilson, Grafton, London 1979, pp. 492–502

RAUDIVE, Konstantin (d. 1974) (*See* **SPIRIT PHOTOGRAPHS**) In 1965 this former professor of psychology at Uppsala and Riga began research based on an odd discovery made in 1959 by Swedish artist and film producer Friedrich Jürgenson. Recording birdsong in the countryside, on playing back the tape Jürgenson heard not only birdsong but faint human voices speaking in Norwegian and Swedish. Repeating the experiment he heard voices addressing him personally and claiming to be dead relatives and friends. His book *Voices from the Universe* (1964) interested Professor Hans **Bender** of the Freiberg **parapsychological** unit in Germany. Bender established that, under differing conditions, a new tape, run through a tape-recorder in a silent environment, if played back contained recognisably human voices yielding visible oscillograph impulses on videotape. Later he decided that the voices were not those of the dead but are caused by 'telepsychokinesis' (TPK) emanating from those present at the recording sessions.

Raudive, once a student of **Jung**, began making his own recordings. Between 1965 and 1974, working with Swiss physicist Dr Alex Schneider and electronic engineer Theodor Rudolph, he made over 100,000 tapes under stringent laboratory conditions. Exhaustively analysed, his work was published in German; the 1971 English language edition came out as *Breakthrough*. But first the English publisher, Colin Smythe, conducted his own tests under the supervision of Pye Records Ltd, who provided equipment and engineers. With Raudive present, the tapes rolled for eighteen minutes.

On playback, over 200 voices appeared, twenty-seven proving totally intelligible to all present. Sir Robert Mayer, chairman of Colin Smythe Ltd, heard the voice of his late friend, the pianist Artur Schnabel. A second test led to similar results. The engineers were baffled. The voices spoke in an odd rhythm, in short sentences, using the native tongues of those addressed.

Raudive, a devout Catholic, evolved a communication technique, asking questions and inviting reply. The answers were short and uninformative: 'The dead live', 'I am alive, Konstantin'. Often they seemed surprised, as if stirred from a daze, and amazed to find themselves conscious.

The Vatican has shown sympathetic interest in this 'voice phenomenon'. But when in the late 1960s two NASA engineers visited Raudive they refused to reveal what they knew. Raudive reasoned that, if on his own relatively simple equipment he could pick up the voices, what might be coming through the sophisticated recorders on Apollo spacecraft?[1]

1. 'The Ghosts in the Machine, Frank Smyth, *The Unexplained*, Orbis partwork, London 1983, pp. 398–400; also 418–20.

REGARDIE, Israel (1907–) (*See* **ALCHEMY, CROWLEY**) An emigrant from London to the USA aged thirteen, in 1926 this student of art and occultism wrote Crowley an admiring letter and in 1928 became the Beast's secretary in Paris. Their stormy three-year relationship, described in his biography of Crowley, *The Eye in the Triangle*, gave him a good education in the fundamentals of modern **magic**.[1] Returning to London, he wrote *The Tree of Life*, still a well-respected introduction to the **Qabalah**.[2]

In 1934 he joined the order of the **Golden Dawn**, then called the Stella Matutina. Soon deciding it was redundant, he published its rites and magic practices. The order collapsed amid recrimination and scandal.

Later he fulfilled his promise as one of the most discerning of writers on modern **occultism**. In *The Philosopher's Stone* he recognised that, though the chemical aspect of alchemy takes place in the laboratory, the essence of the operation is **psychic** or magical. Even so he tended to a **Jungian** interpretation of the forces involved. But in the 1968 edition, describing a seminar at the Paracelsus Research Institute in Salt Lake City, he writes (in vague terms) that what he witnessed there showed him that alchemy is 'not psycho-spiritual' or symbolic, but practical.

In a later preface to *The Alchemist's Handbook*, by 'Frater Albertus', he says plainly that he will not betray the secret of the Great Work (the transmutation of metals), but implies that he had witnessed the operation.[3]

Of magic in general, he wrote, 'Magic is a scientific method. It is a valid technique. Its approach to the universe and the secret of life's meaning is a legitimate one. If it assists us to become more familiar with what we *really* are, it is a Science – and a most important one. And to the scientist, whether he be psychologist or physicist it will open up an entirely new universe of tremendous extent.'[4]

1. *The Eye in the Triangle*, Israel Regardie, Falcon Press, Las Vegas 1989
2. *The Tree of Life*, Israel Regardie, Rider, London 1937
3. *The Philosopher's Stone*, Israel Regardie, Llewellyn, USA, 1970
4. *The Art and Meaning of Magic*, Israel Regardie, Helios, Cheltenham 1964.

REGRESSION (*See* **BLOXHAM, GLOSSOLALIA, GUIRDHAM, HYPNOTISM**)

REICH, Wilhelm (1897–1957) Reich was born to a rich Galician farmer. In 1911 his mother killed herself, apparently after he told his father of her affair with his tutor. Three years later his father died of TB. In 1916 he joined the Austrian army, saw action in World War I, and in 1918 reached Vienna, unable to go home due to new frontiers imposed by the Treaty of Versailles. Joining the Vienna Psychoanalytical Society, by 1920 he was practising psychoanalysis despite lack of formal training. Concluding that civilisation is based on sexual repression, which creates an armour against love and happiness, in 1927 he published *The Function of the Orgasm*. Following **Freud**'s refusal to analyse him, he joined the Austrian Communist Society, visited Russia, and in 1930 moved to Berlin. Publishing *The Mass Psychology of Fascism* in 1933, he was thrown out of the German Communist Party the same year, then in 1934 the International Psychoanalytical Association expelled him. Both groups found his combination of Marxism and sexual theory too hot to handle.

Rejected by both the organisations he had joined, this tormented man developed messianic convictions. Convinced that he had moved 'beyond the intellectual framework of present-day character-structure and, with that, the civilization of the last 5,000 years', in 1938 he moved to the USA, where lucrative therapeutic practice funded his Orgone Institute in Maine.

He divided civilised humankind into two types, mechanists and **mystics**, both of which, he claimed, had rejected bodily life. Thus both science and **religion** failed to acknowledge the importance of orgasm in uniting body and **spirit**. Claiming that only **Christ** and **Bruno** had anticipated his ideas, his own 'martyrdom' was, in a way, preordained by his temperament. Claiming to have found the basic nature of energy and love, he also claimed that he isolated life energy in the form of *bions* (vesicles of bio-energy: *see* **ch'i** and **prāna**). Found in two forms, bions themselves had mass and vitality, but *orgones* were mobile, mass-free and pulsating. A negative, destructive, repressive form of orgone energy (DOR) also existed. He said clouds of DOR literally leach life-force, creating the Keatsian landscape in which 'no birds sing'. Mixing metaphysics with science, he 'invented' a 'cloudbuster' to break up evil DOR and manufactured 'orgone boxes'. The size and shape of telephone boxes, these orgone accumulators were made of alternate layers of organic and inorganic material. Sick people placed in them were supposedly cured and others recharged with vitality.

In 1954, ignoring an injunction put on the distribution of his orgone boxes by the US Food and Drug Administration (on grounds that the claims made for them were fraudulent), Reich was charged with contempt of court and jailed for two years. Diagnosed as paranoid, he was transferred to Lewisburg penitentiary where, aged sixty, he died of heart disease.

Some see him as **prophet** and liberator, martyred by a cynical scientific establishment; others reject him as a charlatan. Either way, his work on psychoanalysis (still widely dismissed due to his controversial insistence on the primacy of orgasm) was considerable. Today his theories have fired **New Age** therapies like Rolfing and bioenergetics.

Yet his orgone research was so flawed by lack of distinction between subjective and objective perception that it is easily dismissed as fantasy. Whether such an energy exists is another matter. Latterly anti-communist, he also rejected his earlier insistence on total sexual freedom, writing, 'If anyone had the guts and power to decree that freedom and self-regulation be established overnight, the greatest disaster in the history of mankind would inevitably swamp our lives like a flood.'[1]

In many ways his life, in its autocratic rejection of authority, in its unresolved conflict between mysticism and science, in its wanderings and unhappy end, seems a recapitulation of the tragedies of Bruno, **Agrippa** or **Paracelsus**.

1. *Reich*, Charles Rycroft, Fontana, Glasgow 1971

REICHENBACH, Baron Karl von (*See* **CRYSTALS, MAGNETISM**) In 1845, a century before **Reich** 'discovered' orgone energy, this respected German scientist announced that crystals, magnets and the human body emit a radiation perceptible to sensitives. He called this radiation 'od' – a name changed by his English disciples to 'odic force'. One case described in the book detailing his discovery was of a sick girl, Angelica Sturman.

Taking a piece of mountain crystal to her home, he put it in a dark room. Brought into the room, she was quickly able to tell him where it was, though Reichenbach and a doctor present could see nothing. She said it glowed blue, with a tulip-like blue light spraying from one point of it and emitting sparks. When Reichenbach turned the crystal upside down, she said she saw a smoky yellow light emanating from the other end.

He experimented to ensure this was not just imagination. With magnets, the blue light came from the north pole, yellow from the south. The blue light felt cool and pleasant to sensitives, the yellow warm and unpleasant. He also found that many people emit a similar radiation or **aura**, which was duller in a sick person than in one in good health.

Other experimenters obtained similar results. But in England, James Braid (who coined the term **hypnotism**) insisted that the same effects could be obtained by hypnotic suggestion. And since **Spiritualists** were quick to seize on odic force as 'evidence' for their own claims, those scientists at first enthusiastic about Reichenbach's claims soon rejected them.

Today there is sufficient evidence gleaned from many fields (**Kirlian** electrophotography, etc.) to suggest that he was not a crank but a pioneer. Unlike Reich, he did not wreck his claims by basing them on easily derided or inept scientific technique.

1. *The Odic Force*, Karl von Reichenbach, University Books, New York 1968.

REINCARNATION (*See* **BLOXHAM, GLOSSOLALIA, GUIRDHAM, MURPHY**) **Hindus** and **Buddhists** believe that human beings are reborn into the world over and over again. They view this prospect with great anxiety, for 'life is suffering', and who wants to suffer? Thus a central function of their religious outlook is to teach (in texts for the dying like the ***Tibetan Book of the Dead***) how to *avoid* rebirth, which is seen as a starkly unpleasant reality. The Western belief that we can escape incarnation after just one cycle of the Wheel of Life is seen as wishful thinking, denying **karmic** law and making life nonsensical. So in the East reincarnation is not thought of as ***paranormal***, but unpleasantly *normal* – a fact of life.

In the West the idea of reincarnation seems fantastic to many due to the influence of Judaeo-Christian tradition and its offshoot, scientific materialism. But the religious ideas espoused by Westerners are even more fantastic. The Christian dogma of the 'resurrection of the flesh' denies the fact that, on death, the body is dispersed by cremation or incorporated 'into the living bodies of worms, sharks or vultures'.[1] Secularists see both doctrines as equally absurd and lacking in proof. Yet while there is no evidence for bodily **resurrection**, there is plenty for reincarnation.

Before considering such proof, some objections need to be faced.

If reincarnation is a fact, why can't we remember our previous lives? Leaving for now cases in which such memory seems to have been proved, it may be asked in reply: how many of us recall infancy? Our sense of present identity is unimpaired by amnesia about our early years, or even by the difficulty in old age in identifying with who or what we were ten, twenty, or thirty years ago. Given our lack of long-range recall of *this* life, how much less likely are we to remember who or what we were before entering it?

If so, surely rebirth is thus in no real sense different to the death of one person followed by the birth of another? But amnesia about an event does not disprove its reality, while the karmic hypothesis suggests that in any case not our memory but our actions are the issue. We may *forget* the choices we made which brought us to our present state: this doesn't mean we never made such choices. Either way the case remains unproven.

The objection (made by Tertullian 1800 years ago as by sceptics now) to reincarnation as inconsistent with population increases is likewise flawed. It assumes the proportion of **discarnate** to incarnate beings as roughly one-to-one. What if this is not so? In the *Phaedo*, Plato suggests that 'many revolutions of ages' ensue between lives. In the *Republic*, he mentions a 1000–year cycle between rebirths. Virgil does likewise in the *Aeneid*. The Bhagavad-Gita speaks of an 'immensity of years'.

Are there balancing forces that regulate such periods, ensuring that, during crucial epochs (such as the present), many more beings are born to take part in the evolutionary process? That such forces exist is suggested by oddities, inexplicable to biologists, such as how after destructive wars more male than female children tend to be born.

Objections based on the materialist hypothesis (*reincarnation cannot occur because there is no life without the body*) assert not proven *fact* but only personal adherence to a *belief*-system that, on balance, seems unlikely to encompass the whole truth of a universe that remains largely mysterious.

As for evidence favouring reincarnation: first there is the age-old **intuition**, found all over the Earth, of the immortality of the **soul**. This profound belief survives all atheistic attack. Of many theories, rebirth or *palingenesis* is by far the oldest and most widely held. It is 'the only system to which philosophy can hearken', as David Hume (the eighteenth century Scots pragmatist) put it. Images of rebirth are found everywhere: in the seasonal cycles, in symbols like the phoenix; in the human conception of died-and-reborn gods from **Osiris** to Tammuz to **Christ**.

So, such intuition no more proves reincarnation than materialistic logic disproves it. Yet the sheer volume of philosophical opinion in favour of rebirth is impressive. Not only Hindus and Buddhists but the Platonists, **Neoplatonists, Gnostics** and many early Church fathers were all convinced reincarnationists; also **Essenes, Sufis** and **Qabalists.** 'Those who doubt [immortality] are dead and they do not know when they will be born again', states the Koran (Sura Nahel). The Bantu speak of the Abakulu-Bantu: the Perfect Men for whom rebirth has ceased. Australian **Aborigines**, Balinese, Eskimos, Iroquois, Dakotas, **Hopis** of North America and others in Central and South America, the early Teutons and the Irish Gaels all hold or held such belief. The list is endless. Nor is belief limited to old or 'Third World' cultures. Many great Western thinkers of near-modern and modern times have likewise committed themselves. **Leonardo, Paracelsus, Bruno**, Donne, Spinoza, **Leibnitz**, Voltaire, Benjamin Franklin, Fielding, Hume, **Goethe, Blake**, Schiller, Hegel, Wordsworth, Coleridge, Shelley, Humphrey Davy, Schopenhauer, Carlyle, Balzac, Emerson, Thoreau, Whitman, Dostoevsky and Tolstoy, W. B. **Yeats**, Russell, **Bennett**, Thomas Huxley, Julian Huxley, Aldous **Huxley**, J. B. **Rhine**, J. B. Priestley, William **James, Freud, Jung**, Hesse: all these (and many others) endorsed their belief in reincarnation or spoke of it as a reasonable theory commanding serious attention.

Today such attention comes from researchers like Ian **Stevenson**, whose *Twenty Cases Suggestive of Reincarnation* (1966) and *Xenoglossy* (1974) arose from his 'growing feeling of dissatisfaction that available knowledge of heredity and environmental influences, considered either alone or together, often didn't account for personality as we see it'. Employing 'the methods of the historian, lawyer and psychiatrist', and gathering evidence from as many witnesses as possible, several of his cases, (*See* **Glossolalia**) are hard to explain save as evidence of reincarnation.

In 1929 Shanti Devi, a three-year-old girl in Delhi, India, shocked her parents by talking of her husband and children. She described a town called Muttra where, she said, she had died in 1925 in childbirth. The 'fantasy' persisted for several years. A test was set up: a man called at the door. She knew him at once as Kedarnath, her former husband. Taken to Muttra, she made her way through it blindfold. With blindfold removed, she found her former home. In it she recognised and named Kedarnath's father, mother and brother. Kedarnath's children by his dead wife Ludgi were produced. She recognised three of them. The fourth, whom she did not know, was the child born as Ludgi died. Claiming Ludgi had buried some rings before she died, Shanti led the Indian government investigators to a spot where they dug. They found the rings. Ludgi's mother identified them as Ludgi's.

In **Tibet** the **Dalai Lama** has always been found by such processes of recognition. Today in the West, the evidence mounts. Cases seemingly of group reincarnation (Guirdham and the **Cathars**) or recall of past lives via **hypnotic** regression (Bloxham, Bridey Murphy) are detailed elsewhere.

1. C. J. Ducasse, quoted in *Reincarnation: the Phoenix Fire Mystery*, eds Joseph Head and S. L. Cranston, Julian Press, New York 1977

RELATIVITY (*See* **EINSTEIN**)

RELIGION Philosophy and science – techniques for researching the Unknown – are both children of religion. Expressing **intuitive**, mystical, and sensual aspects of human nature, religion involves yearning for and striving towards union with God, the Divine All, the First Cause, **Samādhi**.

The term derives from the Latin *religare*, means to 'reconnect' or 'bind back' (with or to the unknown, forgotten primal source). The Roman poet Cicero offers another derivation, from a root to 'select' or 'choose'. Thus religion implies living by a code of conduct (interpreted through exemplars like Rama or **Christ**) as selected, tried and proved by conscience.

The world's religions may show different outer form, but true religion is necessarily the same everywhere, however shaped outwardly by the society expressing it – 'For every thing that lives is Holy'.[1] As for 'organised religion', spiritual impulse may fall prey to worldly demands. The original meaning gets lost in a web of daily business. Part of the West's hidden history involves the war between **Gnostics** assuming the ancient religious primacy of direct personal experience and conscience; and Priests demanding submission to God via His self-elected go-betweens – themselves.

The essential question was put by Joseph **Campbell** in his posthumous TV series (in Britain 1990, Channel 4), *The Power of Myth*.

Do you see the world as an 'it', or a 'Thou'?

1. 'Chorus', *The Marriage of Heaven and Hell*, William Blake

RENNES-LE-CHÂTEAU (*See* **HOLY GRAIL, MEROVINGIANS**) Perched high above the River Aude in southeast France, this hamlet became famous in 1982 with the publication of *The Holy Blood and the Holy Grail*. The authors implied that **Christ** and Mary Magdalene founded the Merovingian dynasty, and that not only Merovingian treasure but Christ lie buried amid this old, dramatically mystic **Cathar** landscape south of Carcassonne.

Rennes-le-Château was a backwater. In 1885 Bérenger Saunière, aged thirty-three, a robustly intelligent local man run foul of his superiors, was made *curé*. He seemed not to mind. Living on a pittance, he hunted and fished. In 1891 he began restoring the old church. Consecrated to the Magdalene in 1059, it stood on sixth-century Visigothic foundations. In a hollow altar-pillar he found four parchments in sealed wooden tubes. Two comprised genealogies from 1244 and 1644. The other two, seemingly by Saunière's 1780s predecessor, the Abbé Bigou, appeared to be pious texts. Discerning codes in these, Saunière deciphered several startling messages including: *À DAGOBERT II ROI ET À SION EST CE TRÉSOR ET IL EST LA MORT* ('To King Dagobert II and to Sion belongs this treasure and he is there dead.')

Showing them to his Bishop at Carcassonne, Saunière was sent on to the Church authorities in Paris. His three-week stay catapulted him into high society. Whatever he'd found, it leapfrogged all ordinary routes to wealth and power. Back at Rennes he went on restoring the church, made mysterious long country treks, began corresponding with new acquaintances throughout Europe, opened negotiations with bankers, and (between 1896 and his death in 1917) spent a fortune. He paid for water and a new road up to the village, built the Tour Magdala and an opulent villa which he never occupied. He entertained Archduke Johann von Habsburg, the French Secretary of State for Culture and the diva Emma Calvé to lavish banquets amid his zoological garden and his collection of porcelain, fabric and antique marbles.

In the restored church he put a statue of the **demon** Asmodeus (guardian of buried treasure), and plaques depicting the Stations of the Cross in subtly heretical fashion.

Called to account, he appealed direct to the Pope who, maybe knowing something Saunière's superiors didn't, supported him. Like an Eastern potentate he lived in pomp until 17 January 1917.

His fatal stroke that day seems to have been presaged, the coffin being ordered five days earlier by his housekeeper Marie Denarnaud.

Saunière died on 22 January. The priest called in to hear his Last Confession emerged visibly shaken, and 'never smiled again'.[1]

Saunière died unshriven. Unknown mourners plucked tassels from his garment during his burial ceremony. Though seemingly penniless when he died, his housekeeper Marie lived in comfort until in 1946 the French government issued a new currency. Unwilling to explain her wealth, seen burning old bank-notes, she ended her days in poverty, her mouth shut on Saunière's secret.

What had he found? Merovingian gold or something more extraordinary? Did he blackmail the Church? Nobody knows or says. For the region itself is profoundly mysterious, saturated not only in Cathar blood and echoes of the troubadours, but with a **Glastonbury**-like resonance. An earth-temple, sophisticated in its **sacred geometry** and covering over forty-square kilometres, is said to exist, its every nodal point marked by church, chateau, mountain, rock outrop or other prominent natural feature, with Rennes-le-Château on its western perimeter. This sacred landscape and its buried meanings spoke to painters like Poussin, who expressed what they knew in cautious **symbols**.

Saunière found something ready and waiting. The essence of the secret may lie not in the Magdalene or even in Christ, but in something older and less easily accessible.[1,2,3]

1. *The Holy Blood and The Holy Grail*, Michael Baigent, Richard Leigh and Henry Lincoln, Corgi, London 1983, pp. 24ff.
2. *The Holy Grail Revealed*, P. and L. Fanthorpe, Newcastle, California 1982
3. *Genisis*, David Wood, Baton Press, Tunbridge Wells 1985

RESURRECTION (*See* **REINCARNATION**) Christian dogma has it that on the third day after his death on the Cross, **Christ** arose bodily and left his tomb. No mortal saw this event: it was only discovered when Mary Magdalene, Mary mother of James, and Salome went to the tomb early on Easter Sunday. They found the stone rolled back and, inside, a young man in a white robe (an **angel**) who told them that Jesus had been raised. The women were disbelieved, but later Jesus resurrected appeared to many, though Doubting Thomas at first refused to believe it.

Today many fundamentalists, believing these events literally true, anticipate their own resurrection. They expect that, following Armageddon (or, say others, after the Tribulation resulting from the seven-year reign of **Antichrist**), they and other true believers will be plucked bodily from the despairing world and be taken up in Rapture to meet their Maker at his **Second Coming**, as in the old blues song:

> Meet me, Jesus, meet me
> Meet me in the middle of the air

The association of Resurrection with Easter (Oestre, a pagan fertility goddess) suggests the doctrine arose in the tradition of died-and-reborn corn gods as represented by **Osiris**, Tammuz *et al*. Resurrection was in the first place not a theological dogma but simple recognition of the seasonal facts of life. Every winter, life dies: each spring it is reborn. This recognition was found in ritualised forms the world over. The Aztec rite of electing a youth king for a year then tearing his heart out amid due pomp and ceremony reflected it. 'The King must die, long live the King.'

Early Christians inhabited a world requiring its god-**myths** to reflect and demonstrate this seasonal resurrection. What use was a **religion** whose myths ignored what everyone knew intuitively?

Was Christ physically resurrected? It is the metaphor that is vital, not the argument over whether the event did or could occur historically.

Indeed, the continuing argument helps to sustain its resonant power.

RHINE, J. B. (*See* **ESP, PSYCHOKINESIS**)

RIGHT-HAND PATH (*See* **BRAIN MYSTERIES, MOON, QABALAH**) Why should *right* (dexterous, dominant, masculine, individualistic) be seen as 'right' and good, and *left* (sinister, witchy, unconscious, communal) be seen as evil and wrong? This is a long story, perhaps rooted in a current phase of our neurological evolution.

Until lately, left-handed children were often forced to become right-handed. Prejudice against the left runs deep.

In superficial **occultism** the Right-Hand Path is equated with all that is benign in mystical search, and the Left-Hand Path with **black magic**. Yet the reality is not so black and white. On the Qabalistic **Tree of Life** the Sephiroth or spheres of consciousness on the Pillars of Mercy (right) and Severity (left) are intimately interconnected by paths running through the mediating spheres on the Middle Pillar. So too the left and right lobes of the brain command different spheres of **consciousness** mediated through the corpus callosum, perhaps through the **pineal**. There is continual dynamic, ebb and flow, electrochemical marriage between Left and Right-Hand Paths.

The terms derive from Oriental **Tantric** practice. Devotees of the Left-Hand path use sexual technique in pursuit of **samādhi**; those of the Right-Hand Path do not. No moral judgement is implied.

RINES, Robert H. (*See* **LOCH NESS MONSTER**)

RITUAL A symbolic, repetitive act or set of acts, consciously or unconsciously undertaken to invoke a desired state of mind or circumstance, to ensure good luck or avert ill. Typical semi-conscious mundane rituals include knocking on wood, pinching salt over the shoulder, or not walking under ladders. Personal ritual may be a source of strength, or may degenerate into habit, fetishism or obsession. On a public level ritual reaffirms the vitality of society or social group: Trooping the Colour or rock festivals are as ritualised as a church service. In religious and magical ceremonial, ritual is characterised by set liturgy, by symbolic clothing and equipment, and by prayer or invocation, aloud or silent. Controlled visualisation may be employed. The purpose is to 'enflame thyself with prayer', to enter the sphere of **consciousness** from which the desired effects will flow, to bring together whatever was apart, to initiate whoever was outside, or to bind and integrate the individual or group-**soul** at a higher level.

RIVAIL, Hippolyte (*See* **SPIRITISM**)

ROBERTS, Jane (d. 1984) (*See* **MEDIUMS**) Between 1963 and her death in 1984, this American medium pioneered North America's current preoccupation with channelled **discarnate** authorities via the famed **spirit entity** or guide called *Seth*. From the early 1970s emerged a stream of 'Seth' books, said to have been dictated by this entity which referred to itself as an 'energy essence personality no longer focussed in physical reality'. This body of work, known as *The Seth Material*, sold in the millions. Preparing the way for wide public acceptance of the 'spirit-guide' phenomenon, Seth's chief message was that through our beliefs and desires we create our own realities.

Yet, by Roberts' own account of how Seth first contacted her, she had no choice in the matter. One September day in 1963 at home at Elmira, New York, she was suddenly ('as if someone had slipped me an LSD cube on the sly') overwhelmed by 'a fantastic avalanche of radical new ideas . . . as if my skull were some sort of receiving station, turned up to unbearable volume'.

In his survey of the channelling phenomenon, author Joe Fisher suggests that such entities are genuinely discarnate spirits of the dead; not the **fraud** or delusion of the medium. Yet at the same time, he concludes, they are not to be trusted. Literally 'lost souls', they are hungry for the vicarious sensual thrills provided by those living beings who accept them as what they claim to be: spiritual guides offering high-minded advice. Yet their true purpose may be **vampiric**, as ancient testimony warns.[1]

1. *Hungry Ghosts*, Joe Fisher, Grafton, London 1990, p. 123, p. 322

ROERICH, Nicholas (*See* **SHAMBHALA**)

ROLLING THUNDER (*See* **BLACK ELK, HOPI, PROPHECIES, SHAMAN**) Accompanying a team of scientists, anthropologist Doug Boyd witnessed this American Indian shaman or medicine man cause a violent storm. Every time Rolling Thunder poked a stink-bug with a stick 'there was a loud sharp crack; a bolt of lightning . . . I might have been watching someone scratching a screwdriver on a battery pole or touching two live wires together.' This led after a few minutes to a 'wild downpour'.

Anthropologist John Welsh accompanied Rolling Thunder to Leavenworth prison to free an Indian jailed for refusing to fight in Vietnam. Prison officers told them they could not see the man: he had been transferred to another prison. Overnight in a motel Rolling Thunder became furious. He told Welsh he had just been inside the prison; the officers had lied for *their* ends, so he would use fear for *his*. In the morning he made Welsh join him in chanting and smoking a pipe by the riverside. From the fire a column of black smoke rose straight in the air. Thunder crashed; clouds gathered. As the two men approached the jail a black funnel-shaped cloud followed them. Rolling Thunder roared; the officers told him to leave. He told them to watch the cloud which, sweeping down at them, caught them in a whirlwind that ripped the prison gate from its hinges. The authorities were persuaded to release the prisoner.

Boyd concluded that Rolling Thunder's powers arise from a relationship with Nature based on recognition that the Earth is a living being.[1]

1. *Rolling Thunder*, Doug Boyd, New York, Random House 1974

ROOT RACES (*See* **BLAVATSKY, THEOSOPHY**)

ROSICRUCIANS (*See* **DEE, INVISIBLE COLLEGE**) In the seventeenth and eighteenth centuries the myth of the Rosicrucians grew so potent that, as with the **Freemasons** and **Illuminati**, it was feared this secret society of magical adepts controlled the world. Today this fear survives as conspiracy theory, though the fascinating shadow is now cast less by the name of the Rose Cross than by fear of the CIA or **UFOs**.

The word 'Rosicrucian' derives from the name 'Christian Rosencreutz' or 'Rose Cross'. The 'Rosicrucian manifestos' which gave rise to the furore are two short pamphlets, first published in 1614 and 1615 at Cassel in Germany, the *Fama Fraternitatis* and the *Confessio Fraternitatis R.C.*

The *Fama* (written in German) claims that 'Father CRC' founded an ancient Fraternity, now revived, which others are invited to join. It is devoted to developing a new light and truth. But the truth is impeded by old authority, tied to Aristotle and Galen. The text tells how Christian Rosencreutz (dates given as 1378–1484), having travelled in the east and laboured towards reformation of knowledge, returned to his native Germany, where he began the Fraternity of the Rosy Cross. The business of this order is attendance on the sick, but also to gain and spread knowledge. Brother Rosencreutz is said to be buried in a mystical vault, the rediscovery of which will signal a general reformation. The *Fama* thus claims to represent advancement of learning, via rediscovery of old **alchemical** and geometrical truths, and via the development of new mechanical ('scientific') knowledge.

The social excitement caused by the *Fama* grew with publication of the *Confessio*. Written in Latin, apparently aimed at a more educated or more international audience, it announces thirty-seven aims. These include an end to hunger, poverty, disease, old age, sectarian and political strife. The **apocalyptic** note is expressed with even greater fervour. The end is at hand, new stars have appeared.

The furore thus aroused throughout Europe (the *Fama* was reprinted three times in 1615) grew in 1616 with the publication of a lively romance: *The Chemical Wedding of Christian Rosencreutz*. Published at Strasbourg, it is the alchemical tale of a husband and wife dwelling in a magical castle.

The narrative, divided into Seven Days, describes the mystic marriage of the **soul** as undergone by Christian Rosencreutz, via **visions**, theatrical performances, **initiation** ceremonies and the social life in the castle. Each Day sees allegorical development. Thus, on the Fourth Day, six people are beheaded and put in coffins: on the Fifth Day they are resuscitated; on the Fifth Day too the narrator discovers a vault lit by huge carbuncles; on the Sixth Day alchemists create life in the form of an alchemical bird; on the Seventh and Last Day the party leave the Castle, gathering on the shore before twelve ships, each flying flags showing the signs of the **zodiac**.

In a time preoccupied by theology, the influence of these pamphlets was huge. Suddenly, Rosicrucians (like Communists in the USA 330 years later) were suspected of being under every bed; the atmosphere grew dangerous, particularly following the outbreak in Prague in 1618 of the Thirty Years War. In 1623 in Paris placards announced the presence of the Brotherhood R.C. and their **Invisible College**. Many believed literally in the existence of Christian Rosencreutz; more sophisticated minds perceived the pamphlets as a serious joke. Today it seems likely the Rosicrucians never existed in the sense of an organisation with affiliated membership.

The author of the pamphlets, then a mystery, is now generally thought to be the Württemburg theologian Johann Valentin Andraeae. Born in 1586, his early work as a writer includes a piece called *Chemical Wedding* (published *c.* 1602), which he described as a *ludibrium*, or jest, of little worth. That later he obscured his authorship of the R.C. manifestos suggests good sense in an era when mere suspicion of heresy or **witchcraft** could lead to the stake.

For few such literary jests have had such potent effect on history. The immediate furore soon died, but the transmission of the ideas involved persisted on several levels. Popularly, the notion of secret societies running the world has never looked back. The jest of the Invisible College influenced the founding of the Royal Society; the R.C. tradition re-emerged in the eighteenth and again in the nineteenth centuries, playing a prominent role in the creation of the eclectic Order of the **Golden Dawn**. So the alchemical tradition of John Dee and other **hermeticists** persisted in the collective European mind, subtly subverting and casting doubt upon purely mechanical or rational thought processes ever since.[1]

1. *The Rosicrucian Enlightenment*, Frances A. Yates, Routledge Kegan Paul, London 1972

S

SABBAT (*See* **MOON, TABOO, WITCHCRAFT**) The sabbat of witches, also the Sabbath-day, derives from the Babylonian *sabattu*, or *Sa-bat*, meaning 'Heart-rest'. Originally the day of rest the moon took when full, neither increasing or decreasing, the sabattu or evil day was the direct forerunner of the 'modern' Sabbath. On this day when, it was said, Ishtar the Moon-Goddess was menstruating, it was unlucky or taboo to work, eat cooked food, or go on a journey – prohibitions placed on menstruating women. Originally observed monthly, this taboo day was later observed at each of the moon's quarters, i.e. weekly, on the seventh day. Later the Hebrews took over this seventh day as that upon which God rested after the creation, thus displacing the feminine, lunar element, which was further still displaced by Christian annexation of the Mithraic Sun-day as the day of rest. In terms of the origin of the day as one of menstrual taboo, Monday, or *Moon*-day, is more appropriately the Sabbath-day; while the witches' sabbat was in fact truer to the feminine spirit involved.[1]

1. *Woman's Mysteries*, Esther Harding, Rider, London 1971, pp. 62–3

SABOM, Michael B. (*See* **MOODY, NEAR-DEATH EXPERIENCES**) This US cardiologist spent five years interviewing 116 patients who had undergone near-death experiences. His resulting *Recollections of Death* followed Raymond M. Moody's *Life after Life* as one of the best popular clinical accounts of the phenomenon yet published.[1]

1. *Recollections of Death*, Michael B. Sabom, Corgi, London 1982

SACRED GEOMETRY (*See* **GREAT PYRAMID, MEGALITHIC MYSTERIES, NAZCA, RENNES-LE-CHÂTEAU** In 1386 the masons of Milan's new cathedral couldn't agree whether to use the traditional *ad quadratum* (square-based) system of sacred geometry, or the newer *ad triangulum*. They got so confused they had to call in outside experts. The first, to get *some* logic back into the conflicting geometry, recommended rounding off the **numbers**. The next, Ulrich von Ensingen from Ulm, was so infuriated by this compromise of true measure that he walked out. The third, Jean Mignot of France, was also enraged when, to justify their aberrant geometry, the local masons argued that pointed arches exert no thrust. '*Ars sine scientia nihil est*,' he spat ('Art without science is nothing.') To which they retorted, '*Scientia sine arte nihil est*.'[1]

Sacred geometry is a set of building principles posited on the harmonic relationship between man, nature and cosmos. Most modern architects dismiss it or have never heard of it. Yet perception of this harmony pervades all sacred and much secular architecture of former times. 'Man is the measure of all things,' wrote Protagoras (fifth century BC). Vitruvius, **Leonardo** and Corbusier later agreed. So today do some scientists. In *Nature* (12 April 1979), B. J. Carr and M. J. Rees discuss microphysical constants found to govern proportional relationshp between galaxy, star, planet, man, and microcosmos. A planet's size is the geometric mean between that of atom and that of universe; a man's mass lies between that of planet and proton.

Coincidence? – or sacred geometry?

To 'primitive' man it was obvious. The Earth-Mother lives. All her manifestations, energies and the relations between them and the cosmos are holy commands to be lived and expressed. One way to express and draw these energies into human recognition is by building temples the proportions of which reveal and resonate with the true measure of Nature.

Geometry means 'measuring of the earth'. Of itself a 'sacred' art, to call a branch of it 'sacred geometry' is tautology born of racial amnesia. If there is 'sacred geometry', then there is 'profane geometry'. What can *that* be but false measure, serving blind human ego first? **Blake** saw this amnesia as 'single vision and Newton's sleep'.

No coincidence that the principles and meaning of 'sacred geometry' were rejected by the heated iron ego of the Industrial Revolution.

Was it to cure our resulting amnesia that the Great Pyramid, was built as an encyclopaedia of measure writ in enduring stone? And what better way to write the measure of history of Earth than by shaping her very rock?

Who can say how many parchments expressing the same geometries perished in the periodic burnings of the Alexandrian Library? But rock is almost as hard to burn and destroy as ideas. In its proportions the Great Pyramid exemplifies a range and depth of true measure (i.e., *science*) that remains continually astonishing. What we discover, we find is only rediscovery. The measure of our 'new' knowledge is found everywhere in the emblems of the past. Khufu's pyramid (was it?) may be the most complete expression of geometry, but the knowledge was known and applied everywhere, in one way of another. Chinese **geomancy**, the **Aboriginal** 'Songlines', Nazca lines and sacred peaks: **serpent earthworks**, megaliths, circles, henges and dolmens; vast terrestrial **zodiacs** and 'landscape **giants**' woven into the land – today those researching such mysteries find alignments, circles, ellipses and triangles swooping through every landmark, natural or 'man-made'.

The sacred geometry of the human landscape was initially the outcome of instinctual pattern, as in animal sensation. The rationale we inhabit now was not part of it. Geometric forms and proportions were not *invented*; they were *perceived* in nature, then reflected upon. 'How' and 'why' came later. Yet our emotional identity with the 'sacred' (i.e. 'real') remained strong despite Greek abstraction and Roman pragmatism. Soaring Gothic cathedrals expressed new spirit while built to the same basic principles, holy because *scientifically accurate*. But by the time of Milan Cathedral Europeans were finding it hard to sustain the old intuitive pantheistic perception. The Black Death of 1348 accelerated the cynicism that became scientific method.

Though during the following centuries Europeans largely discarded their intuitive perception of geometrical proportion as derived from the landscape, elsewhere in the world the tradition still persists, though under constant attack.

In Australia some Aborigines still follow the Songlines, invisible continent-webbing paths formed by many generations singing the ancestral songs of creation, songs to be renewed whenever someone travels. Without such continual renewal the paths and then the land die, and the people too. The harmonies of the songs are geometric: they 'measure the earth'.

'Sacred geometry' creates buildings that sing, accurately transmitting natural harmonies ('truth') that stimulate the growth of a healthy society 'in tune' with nature, cosmos and itself. So what is the secret?

Basic geometric forms (circle, square, hexagon, triangle, Platonic solids and *Vesica Piscis*) all occur in nature or are intuitively obvious. Sun and moon are circular, the square is the image of stability, hexagons are found in honeycomb, triangles focus **elemental** dynamism, and the *Vesica Piscis* (produced by drawing two circles of equal size through each other's centres) formed the genitals of the Mother Goddess, birthing all things.

As such, the *vesica* was essential in founding all holy structures from stone circles to Gothic cathedrals. At sunrise on a preordained day, the site geomantically chosen, the oriented *vesica* was measured on the ground. From it, as from the Goddess, all other structural forms were generated.

Proportional relationships were typically ruled by the dynamic symmetry of the Golden Mean, or Golden Section. This ratio derives from a series of root rectangles produced by compass from a double square and its diagonals. A series of terms in which each number equals the sum of the two preceding is produced. This series (today known as the Fibonacci Series) generates a progression: 1,2,3,5,8,13,21,34,55,89,144 and so on, governing forms from the pads on a cat's feet to the spirals in microscopic shells.

Considered by **Plato** the key to be the physics of the cosmos, in the twentieth century the Golden Mean and true geometry were reapplied by **Steiner** in the Goetheaneum, by Corbusier in his 'modular' system, and by Gaudi in his *Sagrada Familia* in Barcelona. Elsewhere over the world the denial of the art is often horribly obvious.

1. *Sacred Geometry*, Nigel Pennick, Turnstone, London 1980, pp. 104–6
2. *Ibid.*, quoting 'The Anthropic Principle and the Structure of the Physical World', B. J. Carr and M. J. Rees, *Nature*, 12 April 1979
3. *City of Revelation*, John Michell, Garnstone, London 1972

SAINT-GERMAIN, Comte de (*See* **ALCHEMY, CAGLIOSTRO**) Is this mysterious eighteenth-century adventurer still alive today? He appeared in Viennese society *c.* 1740. Perhaps he was the son of a tax-collector born *c.* 1710; perhaps he had learned his skill as a jeweller at the court of the Shah of Persia. Black-garbed and handsome, seemingly in his thirties, he wore diamonds on his fingers and carried loose diamonds in his pockets in lieu of cash. Or so it is said. Claiming alchemical knowledge, he said he had distilled the Elixir of Life. Reputed never to eat in company, he sipped water while others gorged themselves. The perfect ladies' man, **magnetically** attractive, he also had **healing** powers.

In Paris he attended a soirée given by Countess von Georgy, wife of the French Ambassador to Venice in the 1670s. Hearing the name Saint-Germain, she said she recalled it from Venice. Had his father been there? No, said the Count, *he* had; he remembered her as a lovely young girl. Impossible, she said, the man she had known had been forty-five at least. 'Madame,' he said, 'I am very old'. To convince her he recounted details of their last meeting. 'You are a most extraordinary man,' exclaimed the Countess, 'a devil!' 'No such **names**!' he cried, and, seized by a trembling cramp, fled the room.

The legend spread rapidly. He fed it. He hinted that he had known the Holy Family, had been at the marriage feast at Cana, and had 'always known that Christ would meet a bad end'. At the Council of Nicaea (AD 325) he had personally proposed the canonisation of Anne, mother of the Virgin. Yet at the same time he claimed no spiritual mission, only the good of mankind.

In 1743 he moved to London. Perhaps he was already working as a spy for Louis XV. In 1745 during the Jacobite rebellion he was arrested for owning pro-Stuart letters. Claiming they were planted, he was released. The English politician Horace Walpole wrote that he 'will not tell who he is or whence, but professes that he does not go by his right name. He sings and plays on the violin wonderfully, is mad and not very sensible.'

Hereafter working openly as a diplomat for Louis XV, at the Hague he met Casanova, who considered him a charlatan but 'extraordinary'. Falling into royal disfavour he fled back to England then back to Holland. Taking the name Count Surmont he raised money to establish dye factories, vanished with a fortune, then turned up in Belgium as the Marquis de Montferrat. In 1768 he appeared in Russia and (taking the name General Welldone) became a high-ranking adviser. In Nuremberg (1774), masquerading as Translyvanian Prince Rákóczy, he failed to persuade the Margrave of Brandenburg to fund a new laboratory. In 1776 he turned up at the court of Frederick the Great, with similar lack of success. Moving on to Hesse, he died in 1784 while setting up a new paint factory.

Another eighteenth-century charlatan? Over three decades, under many guises and professions (healer, alchemist, jeweller, diplomat, dyer, musician, painter, linguist), he stimulated contrasting opinions in all who met him. Count Warnstadt called him, 'the completest charlatan, fool, rattle-pate, windbag and swindler'. Voltaire wrote, 'C'est un homme qui ne meurt jamais qui sait tout': Frederick the Great replied, 'C'est un comte pour rire.' In 1777 Count Alvensleben wrote, 'Inordinate vanity is the mainspring driving his whole mechanism.' His last patron, Prince Charles of Hesse-Cassel, called him 'perhaps one of the greatest sages who ever lived'.

Parish registers record his death, but the legend that he still lived began immediately. Many saw him in Wilhelmsbad in 1785. It seems he warned Marie Antoinette about the coming French Revolution. In 1789 he visited his friend, diarist Madame d'Adhémar, who noted that he looked like a man of forty-six. He told her he would see her five times more. She claimed this happened, 'always to my unspeakable surprise', the last occasion being before the Duc de Berry's murder in 1820. Sixty years later Madame **Blavatsky** annexed St Germain as one of **Theosophy**'s 'Hidden Masters'. More recently in 1972 a Parisian, Richard Chanfray, appeared on TV claiming to be Saint-Germain. In the USA his myth has been annexed by the syncretic Church Universal and Triumphant. Its leader, Elizabeth Clare Prophet, claims St Germain as 'Hierarch of the Aquarian Age' who (apparently now **discarnate**) channels dire messages of nuclear war, cataclysm and **karmic** evolution through her.

SAMĀDHI (*See* **BUDDHISM**) A Sanskrit term meaning 'to direct towards', signifying a profound depth of meditation and focus on the ultimate unity of things: *Samādhi* is the eighth and final stage of **yoga**. The highest form of self-possession, it involves the abstraction of consciousness from mental as well as worldly concerns, total control of every faculty and complete conscious union with the divine source.

SANGSĀRA Likewise Sanskrit-**Buddhist**, *Sangsāra* means the illusory realm of worldly phenomena and existence, the realm of attraction and repulsion inhabited by incarnate beings, who seek their emancipation from it via enlightenment. Though it is said that in time by normal process of human evolution Man will realise the unreality of the *Sangsāra*, it is the aim of all **yoga** to accelerate the escape from this Ocean of Misery, this Quagmire into which unenlightened lost souls **reincarnate** again and again, to become attached to *Sangsāric* phenomena, of which it is said, 'Indeed, all these are like dreams, like **hallucinations**, like echoes, like the cities of the Odour-eaters, like mirage, like mirrored forms, like phantasmagoria, like the moon seen in water – not real, even for a moment. In truth, they are unreal; they are false.'[1]

1. *The Tibetan Book of the Dead*, ed. W. Y. Evans-Wentz, Oxford University Press, 1960, p. 181

SAUNIÈRE, Bérenger (*See* **RENNES-LE-CHÂTEAU**)

SCIENTOLOGY (*See* **HUBBARD, L. Ron**)

SCREEN MEMORIES (*See* **ABDUCTIONS, STREIBER, UFOs**) When an event too strange or horrible for easy recognition occurs, false or 'screen' memories may be substituted by the unconscious or by **hypnosis** to account superficially for what is otherwise inexplicable. This process has been invoked by researchers into

UFO **Close Encounter** cases to explain the many instances in which contactees suffer amnesia or 'memories' which later prove to be a despairing rationalisation of 'impossible' events.

SCRYING (*See* **PROPHECY, DIVINATION**) This term covers any form of divination that involves staring at a shiny or polished surface to induce **visionary** or **trance** experience.

SÉANCES (*See* **MEDIUMS, SPIRITUALISM**)

SECOND COMING (*See* **CHRIST, RELIGION**) The persistent Christian belief that suffering in this world is about to be terminated by divine invasion and the Last Judgement. In early Christian times it was widely thought that Christ would return within the lifetimes of those who had known him. In AD 999 believers throughout Europe assumed that on midnight of the New Year the Millennium would end and with it the world. The hysteria was such that rich men gave away their wealth. When the new millennium dawned without change, they were quick to get it back.

With the third Christian millennium now at hand, the threat and promise of Second coming is employed by charismatics to influence others. Desire for release from daily life is so common that '**prophets**' offering an escape via belief in imminent cataclysm always get a hearing, however defective their theology, science, or character. But so many cases of false prophets 'crying wolf' make us cynical: how can we recognise the true fatal edge if it is disguised by a multitude of false ego-based calls?

SECOND SIGHT (*See* **BRAHAN SEER, PRECOGNITION, PROPHECY**) 'The Second Sight is a singular faculty of seeing an otherwise invisible object,' wrote Martin Martin in his *A Description of the Western Isles of Scotland* (1703), 'without any previous means used by the person that sees it for that end; the **vision** makes such a lively impression upon the **Seers**, that they neither see nor think of anything else, except the vision, as long as it continues; and then they appear pensive or jovial, according to the object which was represented to them.'

Several aspects of Second Sight are so firmly associated with the Highland Gaels that it may be seen as a precognitive system specific to them. Typically it consists of spontaneous unsought **vision**, premonition of impending disaster, physical changes affecting the seer, and perception of certain **symbols** denoting specific events. These symbols are so systematic as to suggest that Second Sight (*an da shealladh*, 'the two sights') is the remnant of a formerly *organised* and consciously directed precognitive art.

In historical times and though unconsciously practised most of the time, it was so much a part of everyday existence in the Highlands that it was taken for granted. Seers were thought not to be blessed but *afflicted* with a malady which made life problematic for them and everyone else.

Martin, factor to the Laird of Macleod in the Outer Isles at the turn of the eighteenth century, describes this malady and its effects as it existed before the *Gaeltacht* (the old Highland culture) was destroyed. His account invites further quotation.

He continued, 'At the sight of a vision, the eye-lids of the person are erected, and the eyes continue staring until the object vanish [sic]. This is obvious to others who are by, when the persons happen to see a vision . . . There is one in Sky [sic], [who] when he sees a vision, the inner part of his eyelids turn so far upwards, that after the object disappears, he must draw them down with his fingers . . . This faculty of the Second Sight does not descend lineally in a family, as some imagine . . . neither is it acquired by any previous compact. And . . . I could never learn . . . that this faculty was communicable any way whatsoever.

'The Seer knows neither the object, time, nor place of a vision; and the same object is often seen by different persons, living at a considerable distance from one another. The true way of judging as to the time and circumstance of an object, is by observation . . . If an object appear in the day or night, it will come to pass sooner or later accordingly.

'If an object is seen early in the morning . . . it will be accomplished in a few hours afterwards. If at noon, it will commonly be acomplished that very day. If in the evening, perhaps that night . . .

'When a shroud is perceived about one, it is a sure prognostic of death: the time is judged according to the height of it about the person; for . . . as it is frequently seen to ascend higher towards the head, death is concluded to be at hand within a few days, if not hours . . . If a woman is seen standing at a man's left hand, it is a presage that she will be his wife . . . I have been seen . . . by Seers . . . at some hundred miles distance; some that saw me in this manner, had never seen me personally . . . my coming there being purely accidental.

'To see a spark of fire fall upon one's arm or breast, is a forerunner of a dead child to be seen in the arms of those persons . . . To see a seat empty at the time of one's sitting in it, is a presage of that person's death quickly after.

'All those who have the Second Sight do not always see these visions at once, though they be together at the time. But if one who has this faculty, designedly touch hs fellow-seer at the instant of a vision's appearing, then the second sees it as well as the first.'[1]

And so on. There is nothing 'romantic' about it: Martin simply records fact. Other eighteenth-century texts are likewise down-to-earth. *A Treatise on the Second Sight, Dreams and Apparitions* by 'Theophilus Insulanis' (1763) catalogues hundreds of cases, all in a matter-of-fact way. The pseudonym remains unpenetrated: maybe the author knew how strong the tide was running against all matters Gaelic. He may have been the Rev. John Macpherson, a minister of Skye. He is unsurprised that 'deists and freethinkers, who deny all revelation', refuse to credit Second Sight, and 'raise what dust they can to cloud and discredit it'; yet he finds it 'lamentable' that the Church, being based on 'Sacred **Oracles**', should also deny the truth of revelation.[2]

The best-known Highland seer was Coinneach Odhar, the **Brahan Seer**. The many prophecies attached to the name of this **archetypal** figure may however have originated not with him but with a multitude of seers today forgotten. Yet the 'prophecies of the Brahan Seer' are still quoted in the Highlands. And the faculty persists.

In Easter Ross above the Dornoch Firth lives Swein Macdonald. A stonemason (b. 1931) badly injured by a load of bricks dropped on his head in 1970, he claims his second sight comes from his grandfather John, who also saw visions. When he was young, unwanted precognitive vision often struck him. He never relished friends asking him to predict their futures. He began consciously developing the Sight only after his accident. He wrongly predicted that Margaret Thatcher would never become PM, 'because I built myself up strongly that she would not succeed, because I knew that if she were to become prime minister, trouble would lie ahead'.

Asked if he regards the Sight as affliction or gift, he said, 'As a chosen gift to be used wisely, not frivolously, and never for personal gain. By continual use, it has developed in the same way as a muscle. The more you work at it, the more you get out of it.'

'So what is second sight?' author Elizabeth Sutherland asked him.

'Just a vision, an inner vision, a waking **dream** . . . You can't judge it by modern experimentation.'

'Where does it come from, do you think?'

'It goes back to the dawn of time. In prehistoric days most people had it. Minds were not so cluttered in those days.'[3]

1. *A Description of the Western Isles of Scotland*, Martin Martin, 1703
2. *A Treatise on the Second Sight, Dreams and Apparitions*, Theophilus Insulanis, Edinburgh 1763
3. *Ravens and Black Rain*, Elizabeth Sutherland, Corgi, London 1987, pp. 231–46

SECRET DOCTRINE (*See* **BLAVATSKY, THEOSOPHY**)

SEERS (*See* **DIVINATION, PRECOGNITION, PROPHECY, SECOND SIGHT**)

SENOI (*See* **BRAIN MYSTERIES**)

SENSORY DEPRIVATION (*See* **ALTERED STATES, LILLY, SHAMANISM**) A technique for inducing altered states of **consciousness**. The seeker or test subject enters a controlled environment in which all external events are excluded. The five senses are cut off. By this deprivation the mind is focussed on its own activity without distraction. Placing himself in a sensory deprivation chamber while using LSD, US scientist John C. **Lilly** found himself in a black, silent space which he called 'the absolute zero point', or 'the centre of the cyclone'. From this point he moved on to reportedly **paranormal** experiences, including contact with his 'guardians'.

Traditionally, **yoga** aims at similar goals but without using mechanical or psychedelic stimuli; the austerities or sexual rites of some paths may produce similar results. Mostly the work is done by control of the will.

Sensory deprivation techniques have been used to torture or 'break' political prisoners in many lands including Northern Ireland. In the 1970s UK authorities subjected IRA internees to 'white noise' for hours on end while making them stand sleepless, blindfold and spreadeagled against a wall. It seems odd that the state sought by mystics to gain truth should be used by states to break the will of their worldly opponents.

SEPHIROTH (*See* **QABALAH**)

SERIOS, Ted (*See* **SPIRIT PHOTOGRAPHY**)

SEROTONIN (*See* **BRAIN MYSTERIES**) This nerve hormone, a bodily neurotransmitter, belongs to a series of indole alkaloids including psychedelics like LSD–25, psilocybin, and *bufotenine* (the **hallucinogenic** toadskin secretion traditionally used in witches' brews: today literally licked off toads by some US enthusiasts).

Though found more in the body than brain, serotonin's brain-function is crucial. Its varying effects combined with other hormones and enzymes make for uncertainty, but serotonin may tie into the growth of intellectual (and mystical?) capacity. More serotonin is found in primates than in any other creature. Schizoid patients have less brain-serotonin than 'normal' people; 'psychotics' more. 'Bananas and plums abound in serotonin,' biologist John Bleibtrau noted. 'So do figs, and among species of figs none is richer in serotonin than the *ficus religiosa*, known in India as the Bo-Tree, under which the **Buddha** reportedly sat when he became enlightened.'[1]

No surprise then that this hormone is produced (or at least used) by the **pineal gland**, anciently seen as the 'third eye', the opening of which is said to lead to spiritual enlightenment. Today, generally speaking, serotonin is seen as a nerve inhibitor: perhaps Aldous **Huxley**'s 'reducing valve'.[2]

Psychedelics seem to 'block' serotonin and cut out left-brain activity, thus freeing the poetic, timeless **dreamer** in the **psyche**.

Most brain serotonin is in the reticular activating system, helping to regulate the sleep-wake cycle. Too much leads to deep sleep or psychosis. Too little, and we forget to wash dishes, go to work, or care about social relationships. Properly balanced, it helps us orient to the daily world.

1. *The Parable of the Beast*, John Bleibtrau, Macmillan, New York 1968, p. 74
2. *The Doors of Perception*, Aldous Huxley, Chatto and Windus, London 1954

SERPENTS (*See* **DRAGONS, GEOMANCY, LEY LINES**) The serpent has had a bad press ever since Genesis. Coiled round the Tree of the Knowledge of Good and Evil, he perpetually tempts the Eternal Eve to tempt the Old Adam to take a bite, always with disastrous consequences.

This is patriarchal propaganda. The Hebraic Garden of Eden is adapted from the Sumerian Garden of Immortality, with crucial alterations. In the latter, Mother Earth (Eve) is *married* to the Serpent (cosmic fertilising phallic principle, the Lightning Flash of **Qabalah**, snaking from high to low and back). There is no jealous God: all men and women are free to enter the Garden and seek immortality via enlightenment.

In the West the demonised Serpent became 'that old dragon'; in the East the serpent/dragon as fertility-bringer remains revered. Yet even the Biblical scribes had a hard time resolving contradictions over origins. It was the serpent-rod that Yahweh gave to Moses that struck fear in the Egyptians and later drew (**dowsed**?) water from the desert: later Yahweh sent serpents to bite and kill the Israelites, then told Moses to 'Make a fiery serpent, and set it on a pole; and every one who is bitten, when he sees it, shall live.' So Moses made a bronze serpent, and set it on a pole – the image as in *caduceus*, Mercury, Asclepius, Hippocrates and **healing**.[1]

Yahweh/Jehovah defeats in battle the mighty serpent Leviathan – or does he? The Tribe of Levi (Leviathan) recorded Yahweh's doings: when Hebraic images did in time appear of the God who-must-not-be-pictured, they were of a god with serpent legs.

Yahweh *is* the Serpent, but one side only. The other side got cut off, demonised and turned into the Eternal Enemy – generation, procreation, all that is Earthy, natural, instinctive, writhing on the face of the Earth far from the clear heavens of pure Intellect – at least, in some traditions.[2]

1. *Numbers* xxi, 5–9
2. *Occidental Mythology*, Joseph Campbell, Penguin, London 1976, pp. 9–15, p. 30

SERVANTS OF THE LIGHT (*See* **FORTUNE, GOLDEN DAWN, QABALAH**) In the early 1960s some members of the Society of the Inner Light (itself an offshoot of the geriatric **Golden Dawn** of the 1930s) became unhappy with the Society's direction. Including W. E. **Butler** and Gareth Knight, they left it and created a correspondence course, *The Helios Course in Practical Qabalah*, to spread esoteric training in the Western Esoteric Tradition, employing the **Arthurian/Grail** mythos as a basis of the inner journey.

Out of this grew the Servants of the Light (SOL). In establishing it, Butler claimed guidance by an **Inner Plane** Adept. Gareth Knight later left to found his own, more Christianised order. When Butler died, Dolores Ashcroft-Nowicki took over SOL as Director of Studies, basing it in her native Jersey. Controversially publicising **ritual** techniques of inner or **magical** journeys like pathworking (a technique of imaginative quest through **psychic** doorways, formerly maintained as an esoteric secret), she is a

Michel de Notredame – Nostradamus – whose obscure predictions have invited the most wide-ranging and enduring interpretations, including the Apocalypse in July 1999 (FPL)

Rudolf Steiner (1861–1925), founder of Anthroposophy, educationalist and advocate of spiritual self-responsibility (FPL)

Every Friday for thirty-two years Teresa Neumann lost up to a pint of blood from wounds which appeared in her hands, side, feet and forehead and then disappeared by Sunday (Mary Evans)

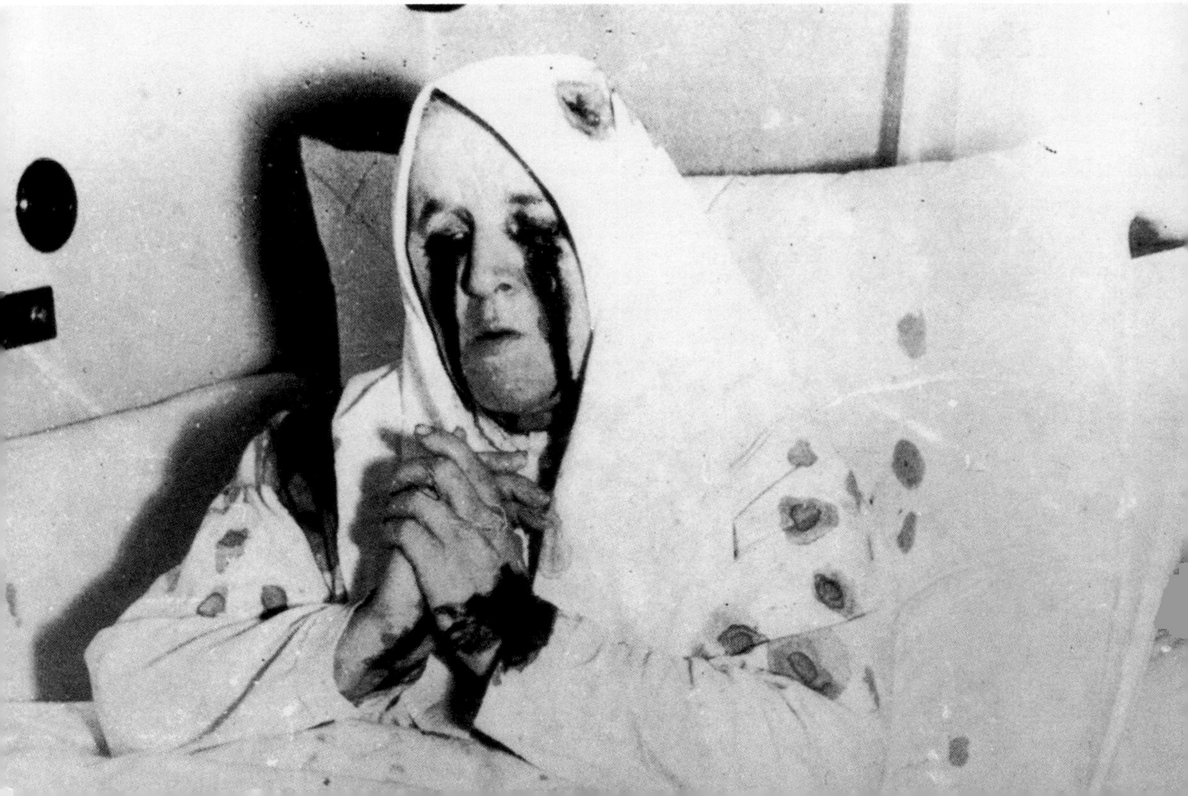

Overwhelming psychological events which in a modern, material society may be interpreted as mental illness can, amongst more 'primitive' peoples, be seen as an initiation into shamanism. Men and women with the ability to contact the spirit-world act as healers and prophets; a shaman is an expert in psychic technology. *Right:* A Siberian shaman's costume (FPL), and, *below,* a Yakut shaman performs a healing rite (Mary Evans)

The remains of Dr John Irving Bentley, believed to be the victim of spontaneous human combustion in 1966. A manifestation of internalised cosmic force triggered by intense emotion? (FPL)

Founded in Jerusalem in 1118 AD, the powerful order of crusading monks, the Knights Templars, were crushed by King Philippe le Bel of France in 1307 and many were brutally executed (*right*). Yet their influence still persists today, in Freemasonry and other semi-occult orders. *Below left:* A thirteenth-century Templar document with its characteristic secret symbols for signatures; and, *below right*, the Templar seal showing two knights sharing a horse – the sign of their great poverty and unworldliness (Images)

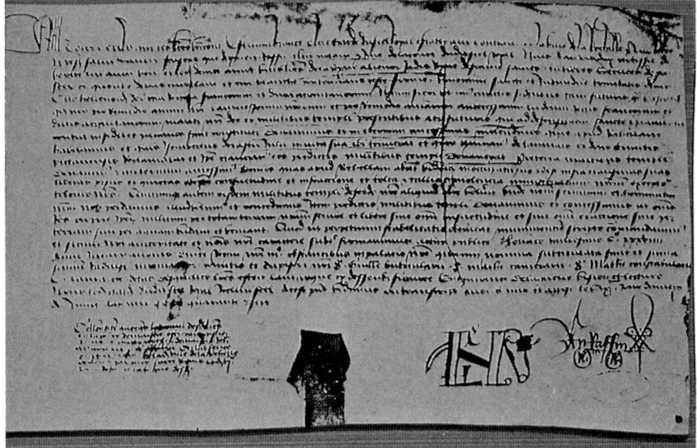

Two great figures of Theosophy: *right,* co-founder of the Theosophical Society, Madame H. P. Blavatsky, whose life-long search for the spiritual truths embedded in esoteric doctrines inspired Annie Besant (*below*) to embrace Theosophy (Images)

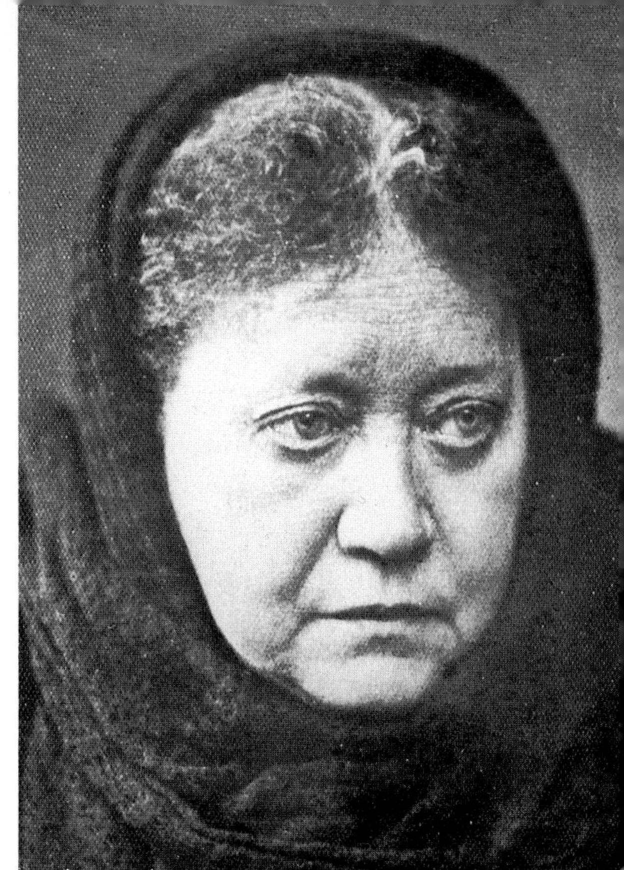

Witches and the Devil flying on broomsticks (FPL)

Bela Lugosi in the classic film interpretation of Count Dracula (Mary Evans)

A zombie, Felicia Mentor, who died and was buried on Haiti in 1907, is shown here in a photograph taken in 1937 (Mary Evans)

A seventeenth-century scene showing werewolves and the means used to eliminate them (FPL)

Although there is nothing paranormal about the ancient Chinese healing art of acupuncture, it contrasts with the purely physical emphasis of Western medecine and serves to highlight the typical Western confusion between what is 'magic' and what 'science'. This eighteenth-century woodcut shows the position of one of the treatment points (Images)

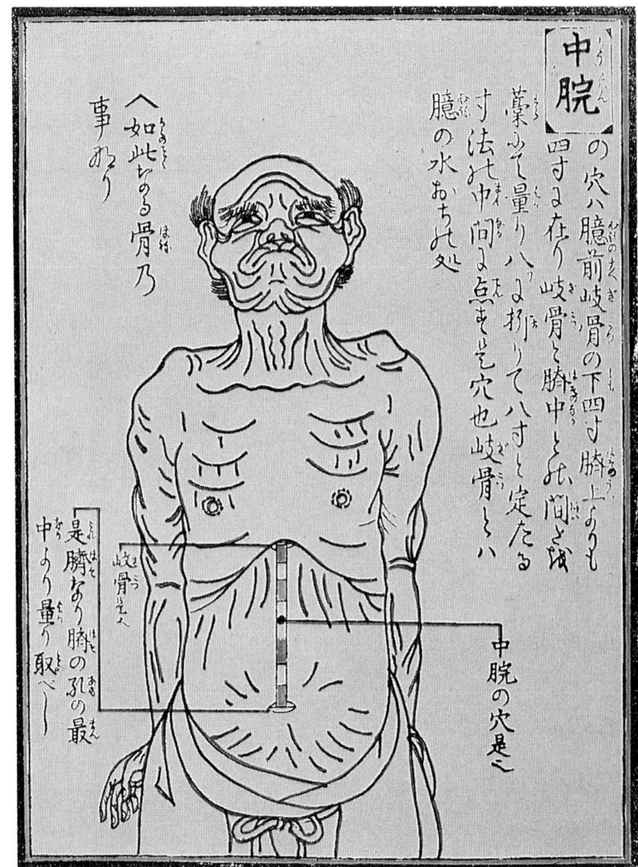

An Indian yogi demonstrates his complete mastery of his physical body by burying his head in sand; his breathing stopped and his pulse slowed to two beats per minute (FPL)

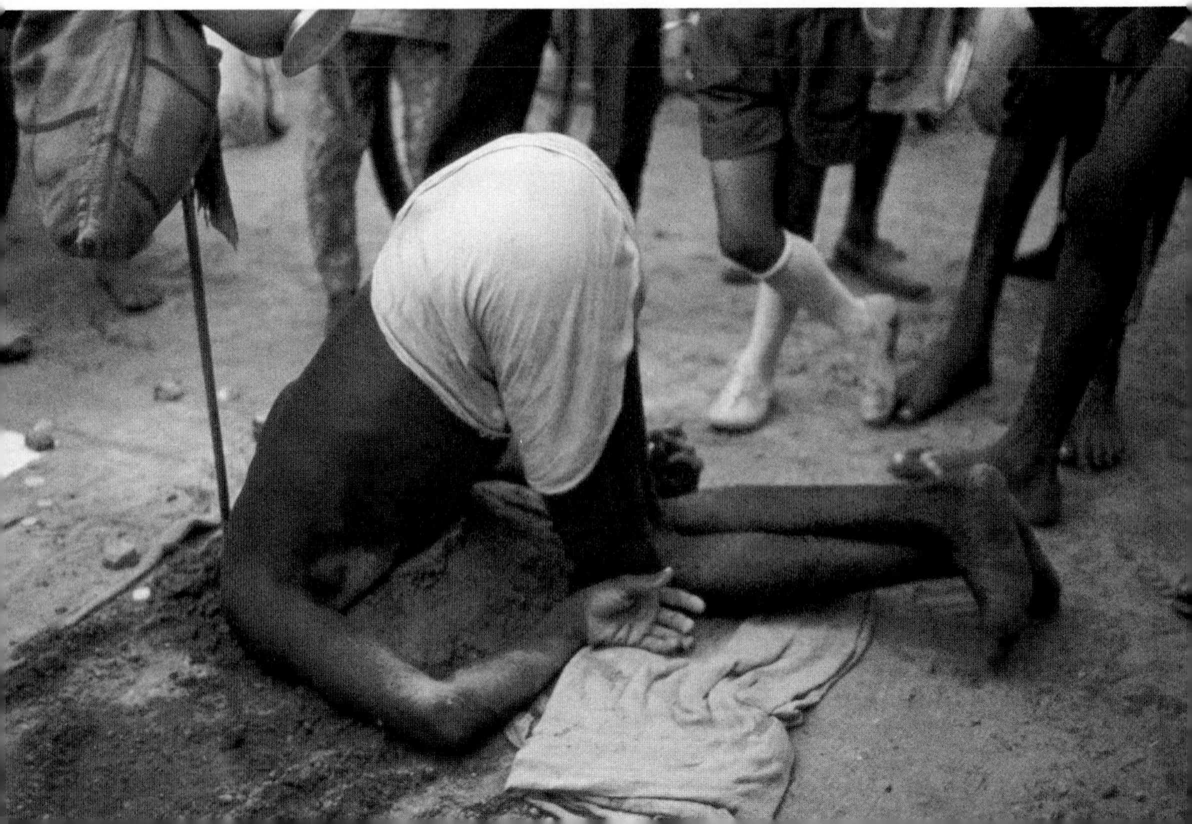

prolific author on the subject: her *The Ritual Magic Handbook* is seen as one of the best currently available introductions.[1]

1. *The Ritual Magic Handbook*, D. Ashcroft-Nowicki, Aquarian Press, Wellingborough 1986

SHADOW (*See* **JUNG**)

SHAMANISM (*See* **BLACK ELK, CASTANEDA, INITIATION, ROLLING THUNDER**) Originally a Siberian term, the word *shaman* is today widely used to refer to those who in primary or 'primitive' societies function as medicine men, witchdoctors, priest **healers, trance**-experts and **prophets**. They may be defined as men and women with the ability, both innate and developed, to contact the **spirit**-world and its inhabitants.

Despite the efforts of first the Church and then rational materialism to denigrate all such **pagan** or **magical** survivals, shamanism still exists in many parts of the world. Not just an outlook on life, it is a form of **psychic** technology authenticated by the common experience of humanity.

The shaman is typically a male who in late childhood or at puberty experiences some overwhelming psychological event that snatches him from society and turns him inward. The event may involve a schizoid crisis amid which **dreams** and other psychic events show him his way thereafter. In a modern material society the crisis, interpreted only as mental illness, is likely to land the 'sick' person in a mental ward, subjected to electrical shock, drug treatment, or even lobotomy as a means of 'cure'. Yet in more 'primitive' cultures the process, once recognised, is encouraged by others who have been through it themselves. The troubled child (*see* **Black Elk**) is watched over by the existing shaman, who seeks to persuade the child that the **visionary** event is not madness, but a 'learning experience', or *initiation*. The child who comes through this event may do so by a number of **vision**-inducing means – use of **hallucinogenic drugs, yoga** techniques, **sensory deprivation**, or yet more hazardous techniques like flagellation, **ritual** sex, self-torture, or burial alive for several days.

In an Australian initiation, the master-shaman assumes the form of a skeleton and places the (magically reduced) candidate inside a small bag. Pulling himself up the Rainbow **Serpent**, he hurls the candidate into the sky, so 'killing him'. Then into the candidate's body he inserts quartz **crystals** – after which they both return to Earth via the Rainbow Serpent.[1]

This typifies a global shamanic initiation procedure whereby the would-be shaman follows a totem-animal, snake, or **bird** into the wilderness; to the underworld, or a celestial domain. Here, amid trance, he meets the **entities** from the worlds beyond, to gain what in oriental literature is called the 'diamond' or 'thunderbolt' body, immune to ordinary ills.

Another universal theme (as in 'Jack and the Beanstalk', or in the **symbolism** of the Indian rope trick,) involves climbing a celestial rope to kill the **giant** at the top, thus taking his power and returning to earth with it. The more violent the encounter, the more power the shaman gains – if he survives. Fear of dismemberment often precedes the encounter with or the **possession** by the initiating spirit. Yet, en route, as in **fairy tales**, he may acquire helping spirits who remain with him thereafter.

Thus returning, now consciously inhabiting the magical spirit-world in which every act, object and intention has resonant meaning beyond its apparent outer face, he gains a place in his society that is both feared and respected. He has seen his sacred animal, met the spirit-beings. He is forever apart from the others who have not died and been reborn, yet remains among them as counsellor, healer and **prophet**.

Among some Apache peoples on the US-Mexican border the shamanic test was simple: you threw yourself over a cliff. Those who died, died: those who lived, survived with spirit-knowledge. In the Sun-Dance of the North American Plains Indians, young braves were suspended by hooks dug deep into their flesh from the roof of the medicine lodge. Through pain it was thought (as by early and mediaeval Christian ascetics) that the doors to shamanic knowledge are opened. Likewise in Norse **myth**, the god Odin (again like **Christ**) gained his shamanic knowledge by self-sacrifice. For nine days and nights he hung, impaled by his own spear, from Yggdrasil, the World-**Tree of Life**. Through this ordeal he gained powers to raise the dead, prophesy the future, fly through the sky and **shape-change** at will.[2]

Having survived death-in-life the shaman is freed to explore the realms of wisdom, power, gods, devils and primal impulse, bringing benefit to the living human world via prophecy, teaching or healing.

The shaman is of course always at risk of crucifixion. But having been crucified by ordeal already, such a fate is unlikely to distract him.

1. *The Shaman's Doorway*, Stephen Larsen, Harper and Row, New York 1977, p. 69
2. *Runes*, Michael Howard, Aquarian Press, Wellingborough 1990, p. 8

SHAMBHALA This ancient Sanskrit place-name refers to a mystic lost land surrounded by snow-capped mountains. Home to superhuman beings, a font of secret wisdom, the hot springs of its hidden high valleys nourish lush vegetation and rare herbs. Yet Shambhala has proved hard to find, even locate. It is variously said to lie in Mongolia's Gobi Desert, China's Kun Lun Mountains, Tibet or further afield. Like Eldorado, Cibola, **Atlantis**, etc. the idea of Shambhala generates a potent allure. Some, insisting it is physically manifest, have set out to find it. A 1923 Russian expedition never returned from beyond the Kokushi Mountains. Rumours that tunnels connect it with Lhasa's Potola Palace persist, and it has been claimed, 'A multitude of aeroplanes might fly over the place without "seeing" it, for its frontiers are very carefully guarded and protected against invasion.'[1]

En route from Mongolia to India in 1928 Nicholas Roerich (designer of Stravinsky's *Rite of Spring* ballet) was told by a lama that Shambhala is not of this earth but another **dimension**. Only those spiritually prepared may find it, for it is lost and found in the mind. Yet maybe it embraces the manifest world. Roerich also met a mysterious lama on the Darjeeling-Ghum road: later the monks of Ghum said this lama was from Shambhala.

Elsewhere Roerich's entire party saw a **UFO**. Moving fast above their camp, it abruptly changed direction.[2] Was it part of the interdimensional Shambhala mental frontier defence and security system?

1. *Occult Glossary*, G. de Purucker, Theosophical University Press, California 1933
2. *Altai-Himalaya*, Nicholas Roerich, Jarrolds, London 1930

SHAPE-SHIFTING (*See* **CELTIC MAGIC, ILLUSION, SHAMANISM, WEREWOLF**) Belief in shape-shifting is probably as old as humanity. On the walls of caves like Lascaux the painted shaman of 20,000 years ago dances as deer or buffalo. Hunters everywhere identify with ('become') their beast in order to slay it: in Celtic **myth**, as elsewhere, human beings regularly transform into deer, wolf, seal or vice versa. Always the relationship is governed by strict pacts and laws. The greatest Celtic Shape-Shifter is Manannan, God of the Sea (so Isle of *Man*). Mantled in fog with rocks all about, he reflects uncanny deadly transitory appearance. What seemed clear passage turns into disaster and drowning. A modern equivalent might be the shifting shapes on global stockmarket screens!

In Welsh myth the goddess Cerridwen by Lake Bala leaves young Gwion Bach to stir her Cauldron of Inspiration and keep the fire going under it while she's away. The brew in it is to revive her drowned husband. 'Never taste it,' she warns. He keeps the fire going and stirs well, until suddenly from the bubbling brew leap three drops, one burning his thumb, which automatically he licks. Instantly, inspired, he sees all things . . . including Cerridwen's fury. In flight from her, he transforms himself into hare, fish and grain of wheat. Pursuing him, she shifts to greyhound, otter and finally hen, in which form she pecks up the grain of Gwion . . . only nine months later to bear him as an infant who, abandoned Moses-like in a coracle and brought ashore, so confounds the king's wise men that he is called Taliesin, Radiant Brow.

Thus runs one tale of how poetry is born, what it is and how many seasonal shapes it has to shift to become what it is.

Likewise **Merlin** helps Uther Pendragon shift shape to deceive Ygraine that he is her husband Gorlois: this deception leads to the birth of King **Arthur**.

Transformations from human to animal, and vice versa, are commonly told and ritualised the world over. Again, it's mentally real. The legends of lycanthropy not only persist in films like *Wolfen* or *The Company of Wolves*, but in everyday talk. Call someone 'wolf', 'sheep', 'fascist hyena', 'male chauvinist pig', 'bitch', 'running dog', 'mouse' or 'loan shark' and we all know what's meant. Nobody likes being 'badgered', 'dogged' or 'ratted on'. Yet few would reject 'lionisation', even if by the 'jackals of the media'.

Shape-shifting runs deep, especially when the **Moon** is full. Science too shifts shapes, as in genetic engineering. We already have the *shoat* (or is it a *geep*?): how much longer before the *jackalope*? Or the *manster*?

SHELDRAKE, Rupert (*See* **FORMATIVE CAUSATION**) In *A New Science of Life* (1981) and *The Presence of the Past* (1988), this Cambridge plant physiologist has advanced the controversial theories of formative causation and morphic resonance, suggesting that the form and pattern of things relies primarily on repeated habit transmitted by what he has called 'morphogenetic fields', which operate independently of space and time.

SHIPTON, Mother (*See* **PROPHECY**) This sixteenth-century Yorkshire prophetess is said to have predicted widely for the twentieth century, including global disaster for 1991. Yet study of original editions in the British Museum led writer Alan Vaughan to conclude that she never predicted anything beyond her own lifetime. Prophecies attributed to her by a nineteenth-century writer were, he claims, revamped in the 1960s, amid 'an intricate web of hoaxing for fun and profit'.[1]

1. *Patterns of Prophecy*, Alan Vaughan, Dell, New York 1976, p. 20

SHROUD OF TURIN (*See* **MIRACLES**) Said to be the winding-sheet that once wrapped **Christ**'s crucified body and to which a faint image of Christ himself is said to adhere, this venerated icon in 1989 underwent (via cuttings from the hem) radiocarbon dating that established it as mediaeval. This explains part of the mystery, not all.

Associated with the *Mandylion* (a wrapped cloth bearing the image of Christ's face) of Byzantine Church history, the Shroud is first recorded in Western history as the possession of the French baron Geoffrey de Charny, a descendant of the **Templar** Geoffrey de Charny, burned at the stake in 1314. From the start the Shroud's exhibitors were accused of fraud. When the second Geoffrey de Charny died at Poitiers in 1356, his widow capitalised on it. She and her advisers claimed to possess a fourteen-foot length of linen stained with the blood of Christ and bearing the image of his body, front and back.

Thus the Shroud began its modern career, moving through various owners before coming to rest at Turin, where today it excites controversy again. Though almost certainly manufactured during the fourteenth century, the manner of its creation remains mysterious, while to many it matters not if such icons are proven false scientifically: what they are *believed* to be counts too.[1]

1. *The Turin Shroud*, Ian Wilson, Penguin, London 1979

SIRIUS (*See* **ANCIENT ASTRONAUTS, ISIS**) The Dog-Star Sirius (from Greek for 'sparkling' or 'scorching'), 8.7 light years away in the constellation *Canis Major* (the Great Dog, one of Orion's two hounds), is our close neighbour and brightest star.

Every fifty years Sirius is orbited by its white dwarf Companion Sirius B (magnitude 8.5). It so drowns Sirius B in its brilliance that, even with the two stars at greatest separation, telescopes of 200mm aperture or more are needed to see the Companion – a collapsed star so dense that a matchbox of its matter weighs a ton. Invisible to the eye, Sirius B was discovered in 1862 by American astronomer Alvan Clark's 18–inch refractor. Or was it?

Sirius was always a star of mystery. In Egypt its annual rise presaged Nile-flood and Dog Days. As *Sothis*, they called it the home of **Osiris** and the Winged Isis. Some occultists today claim that Sirius distributes power throughout the local galactic neighbourhood; that it is 'The Sun behind the Sun'. It is said by others to be the home system of supernal **entities** who anciently manifested on Earth to direct human civilisation. Lately this tradition has been explored by Doris Lessing in her *Shikasta* sequence of novels.[1] It seems Sirius B was known about long before 1862.

In 1950 French anthropologists Marcel Griaule and Germaine Dieterlen published their twenty-year investigation of the cosmological lore of the Dogon of Mali. Slowly people noticed. Twenty-six years later Robert Temple's bestseller *The Sirius Mystery* made the matter fully public.[2]

Speaking of a secret star they call *po*, after the tiniest seed they know, Dogon priests describe and draw in sand what appears to be an ancient knowledge of Sirius B, its nature, fifty-year orbit, and eccentricity. They say it is made of a special material, *sagala* ('strong'), not found on earth but heavier than all iron on earth. They speak of a third, supersensible sun in the system, the 'Sun of Women', the *emme ya*, orbiting Sirius A also in fifty years and the same direction as Sirius B, but at right angles to the Dwarf.

As yet unvalidated scientifically, the *emme ya* nurtures a satellite or child, the 'Star of Women'. So the Dogon say.

Also they tell of Earth-landing (on 'the day of the fish') of Nommo, a fish-being from the Sirian system. Like Christ he came to regenerate the outcast, Ogo, the Fox – ourselves. Murdered, he too was resurrected.

The Dogon wandered broadly for two thousand millennia before reaching Mali. Temple traced their cosmology back two thousand years to surviving fragments of the *Babylonian History* by Berossus, a Chaldean priest writing *c.* 300 BC. Berossus tells how the *Annedoti* ('repulsive ones') emerged from the (superphysical?) sea to educate the Sumerians, led by one Oannes, whose 'whole body was like that of a fish . . . and had under a fish's head another head, and also feet below, subjoined to the fish's tail'[2]

Were these 'amphibians' Sirians in Earth-suits, or but Sumerian mythic imagination working overtime? The tale endures. As for Sirius, it's best seen on a winter night, low in the south-west, diamond-bright, sparkling.

1. *Shikasta*, Doris Lessing, Cape, London 1979
2. *The Sirius Mystery*, Robert K. G. Temple, Futura, London 1978

SOCIETY FOR PSYCHICAL RESEARCH (SPR) (*See* **LODGE, MYERS,**

PRICE, SPIRITUALISM) Founded in 1882 by Cambridge scholars F. W. H. Myers, W. F. Barrett, Henry Sidgwick and Edmund Gurney, the English SPR (an American branch formed soon after) represented the first organised group response by the scientific Victorian mind to the Spiritualist upsurge. Attracting Broad, Bergson, Conan **Doyle, Hyslop, James**, Lodge, **Moses** and others to its early ranks, today the SPR still contributes to the field.

Much of its work has been rigorous, sceptical yet fair-minded, adducing considerable evidence for the reality of **psychic** phenomena. Even so, it has made little general impact, perhaps because of its cold, unemotional approach to phenomena by nature *emotional*. Stainton Moses left the SPR in 1886 feeling that science is no way to evaluate *religious* events.

Investigation of mediums like **Palladino**, though rigorous, failed to consider emotional or sexual aspects involved in producing or channelling the phenomena: unsurprising, given the stolid masculine background of many SPR researchers, and the eagerness of the press for scandal. It may also be that sometimes the SPR technique of seeking natural explanations for psychic phenomena wherever possible has obscured genuine mystery. So too the anxiety to prove **fraud** and not be thought naive by a hostile world.

The Borley Rectory scandal may be such a case: the denunciation of Harry Price and the subsequent evidence-bending report by SPR authors to prove him a fake did neither Price nor the SPR any good, though a further report for the Society by R. J. Hastings dismissed the evidence of fraud.

SOLOMON, Paul (1989–) (*See* **POLE SHIFT, PROPHECY**) Son of an Arkansas preacher, in 1972 Baptist minister William B. Dove, dismissed from his church due to a sexual scandal, began experimenting with **trance hypnosis**. A voice (the Source) spoke through him. Impressed, he changed his name to Paul bar Solomon. Later founding a **New Age** church, the Fellowship of the Inner Light, in 1975 Solomon made a dire prediction: 'watch the fifth day of May 2000 for the time when the planets will be aligned one behind the other across the sky, and the strain of **magnetism** will shift the surface of the earth until it takes a new shape and form'.

EEG-tested at Atlanta's Emory University in 1975, he was found during trance-reading to be producing delta brain waves, characteristic of deep sleep. He says his mission is to **heal**, prophesy and spread the word of God in preparation for cataclysm following **Christ's Second Coming**. His biblical language has gained him a following which regards him as a prophet. His predictions are in line with Christian eschatology from St John via **Nostradamus** to Edgar **Cayce**. 'And you will see the earth breaking open as its crust will shift and move. And there will be the noxious gases coming to the surface, and the entire atmosphere will smell of sulphur fumes.'[1]

In many such 1970s predictions Solomon also gave 1984 as the year Japan would submerge, **Atlantis** rise, and North America split in half amid violent earthquakes. Yet in a booklet, *Earth Changes and the New Planet Earth*, he covers himself by pointing out, 'any prophecy that is fulfilled is a prophecy that failed. The only reason for predicting anything is to prepare for it or to change it, to keep it from happening.'

Of these predicted cataclysms he said, 'Mother Earth is pregnant and about to give birth to a New Age. At an imminent birth there is always a birth pain. There are contractions. There are difficulties.'

The Solomon Source must be considered ambiguous.[2]

1. *The Paul Solomon Tapes*, 1974 (1972 reading)
2. *Pole Shift*, John White, W. H. Allen, London 1980, pp. 228ff.

SONGLINES (*See* **ABORIGINES, SACRED GEOMETRY**)

SONG OF THE SPHERES (*See* **SPHERES**)

SORCERY (*See* **BLACK MAGIC, NECROMANCY, WITCHCRAFT**) Sorcery involves the systematic use of **psychic**, extrasensory or **magic** powers, by means of **spells, ritual**, potions and **symbols**, to manipulate the 'hidden powers' for personal ends. **Shamans** nurture power for the good of their tribe, **mystics** have no interest in personal power, true poets, magicians or scientists wield power disinterestedly: sorcerers tap similar forces as a means to self-advantage. The word derives from the Latin *sortiarius*, 'a caster of lots'.

SOUL (*See* **BRAIN MYSTERIES, SPIRIT**) Hypothetical invisible animating principle in human and all other life-forms; a spiritual **entity** evolved via experience in matter; not the **spirit** itself but the spirit's vehicle; said on higher planes to manifest as a sheaf or pillar of light. The physical body itself is said to be but the densest manifestation or layer of soul, incorporating the more refined soul-bodies of higher planes.

The term derives from Danish *sjoel*, or Swedish *sjāl*, is not specific to any particular religious belief or tradition, but finds echoes and parallels in every culture.

Animists ascribe 'soul' to all manifest conditions; thus there is a 'world-soul'; the elements have their soul, as does every tree, mountain or flower. Behind each such individual entity it is understood that there is a primary activating principle, called Pan, or *All*, by the **pagans**.

In general the human soul may be seen as that portion of being found between deathless spirit and mortal physical body. The term being vague, it is sometimes associated with the **astral** and **etheric** bodies.

SPELLS (*See* **CELTIC MAGIC, ILLUSION, MAGIC, SORCERY**) To 'cast a spell' is to seek or gain control over a being or situation by use of mental power so that the other is 'spellbound' – entranced, stopped in their tracks, **hypnotised**, made to act against their conscious will. In all races this **occult** practice is reported of sorcerers, poets and magicians. In Celtic lore, poets and bards were so skilled in weaving spells of words that all feared their power, including kings. The word for *spell* or *taboo* in Gaelic is '*geas*', from *guidh*, 'to entreat', so the association is with prayer, supplication, incantation. Such *geasa* once hedged the kings and heroes of Ireland on every side. Being regarded as reincarnations of gods, these restrictions ensured maintenance of their sacred qualities, so that the people would not suffer. Cuchulin was forbidden to eat the flesh of a dog, to give his name to any other warrior, to decline combat, to swerve from his path in approaching it or to enter any gathering unpermitted. To Llew Llaw Gyffes it was taboo to stand with one foot on the back of a goat and the other on the edge of a bath. Cormac, son of Conchobar, could not yoke his horses to his chariot by an ashwood pole, nor hunt a stag with golden horns, nor listen to the harp of the bard Craptine. All three met their doom by breaking, avoiding or neglecting these spells upon them.[1]

Among all folk the spell arises from the exercise of concentrated will-power, 'the beautiful violent will'. The incantations by which the wizard imposed his intention were usually chanted in verse: the wizard might stand on one foot and close one eye, the better to focus and direct the force. Potent spells like *fith-fáth* (pron. 'fee-fa') were used by Celts to confer invisibility or to **shape-shift** into animal form. The term *fáth* meant 'the poetic art'. 'In the beginning was the Word' – the original spell.

Today the capacity to spell-bind is not lost. Both **Hitler** and Hollywood cast different kinds of spells over millions of people, while many a classical orchestra proves the truth of the Shakespearean prescription that 'music hath charms to soothe the savage breast'. Another kind of musical spell, perhaps not so soothing, has been cast over vast audiences since the 1960s by rock bands like the Rolling Stones. And how many critics have come away from new West End or Broadway plays to insist in their reviews that they were 'spell-bound'?

1. *The Magic Arts in Celtic Britain*, Lewis Spence, Rider, London 1970

SPENCE, Lewis A lifelong student of all aspects of **magic** and **mysticism**, Spence wrote widely and with common-sense erudition. From his *Encyclopedia of Occultism* (1920) to his writings on Atlantis and later books on British mysteries like *The Magic Arts in Celtic Britain* (1946), he remains worth study.

SPERRY, ROGER (*See* **BRAIN MYSTERIES**)

SPHERES (*See* **CYCLES**) Spheres visible and invisible dominate human life. Round Sun, round **Moon**, round Earth, the circling of heavens and seasons, day and night: the sphere is self-evidently holy, complete, rhythmically eternal. So in the Ptolemaic cosmology the Earth lay at the centre of the sublunary sphere, the sphere of imperfection, beyond which rotated the spheres carrying Sun, Moon and planets, and beyond them, the sphere of the fixed stars and *Primum Mobile*. The holiness of circularity was so built into the mediaeval mind that when **Kepler** first confronted evidence that the planetary orbits are elliptical, not spherical, he refused to credit such *ugliness*. This idea of universal spherical harmony was also implicit in the mediaeval image of the *Song* or *Music of the Spheres*. By Ptolemaic interpretation the Earth, Sun, visible planets (Mercury, Venus, Mars, Jupiter, Saturn) the sphere of *fixed stars*, and the *Primum Mobile* beyond, interacted in an ever-shifting yet ever-stable celestial harmony from which all earthly music (and life) is drawn. Today, this image may be seen anew as the intuition or direct perception of ever-shifting cosmic energies and their effect on us: *As above, so below*. For the sphere is not static; but energetic, whirling, vivifying, as we recognise when we speak of *spheres of influence*. The **sephiroth** on the **Tree of Life** are shown as dynamic spheres within spheres; among the orders of **angels**, after the Seraphim and Kerubim come *Wheels*; the tipi of North America or yurt of Asia both reflect the sphere as dynamic domestic centre of rest; the **Templars** built spherical churches (Garway in Herefordshire, the Temple in London), few of which survive; many folk-dances round the world follow a 'round', implicitly restating the course of things from daily round to full circle.

SPIRIT From Latin *spirare*, 'to breathe', the spirit is generally understood to be the immortal element in us, that which was never born and never dies. It is not the same as **soul**, though often loosely called the same, soul being the vehicle or garment of spirit.

SPIRITISM (*See* **ARIGÓ, PSYCHIC SURGERY**) Many Brazilian and Filipino 'psychic surgeons' are Spiritists, a movement founded in 1857 by Hippolyte Leon Denizard Rivail, alias 'Allen Kardec'.

Born in Lyon, France, in 1804 and educated by Pestalozzi, Rivail worked as a teacher then as an accountant. When **Spiritualism** became a craze, he sceptically told a friend he would believe in messages from the dead and so on, 'only when I see it'. In 1855, at a **séance**, he saw it, and concluded, 'there was something serious behind all this apparent triviality . . . like the revelation of a new law, which I decided to investigate thoroughly'.

After intense sittings with a **medium**, Japhet, in 1857, taking the **spirit**-dictated name Allen Kardec, he published *Le Livre des ésprits* (the book of the spirits). Other works followed: he insisted they were not by him but by 'advanced' spirits, communicating through several mediums.

Spiritists claim two worlds exist, visible and invisible, containing material and incorporeal beings respectively. Spirit is a substance formed of 'quintessential' matter, united to the physical body by an intermediate 'perispirit' body. Teaching **reincarnation** and **karmic law** as natural fact, Kardec said Spiritism concerns 'the relation of the material world' with actual **entities**, but claimed his movement to be not a new **religion** but a rational philosophy based on demonstrable fact. Then and later Spiritists and Spiritualists both emphasised differences in their philosophies.

An early **paranormal** researcher, in 1866 Kardec (d. 1869) found his work banned by the Vatican. Yet his books remain influential, especially in Brazil, where today over twenty million people practice Spiritism. Obeying Kardec's injunction on charity as their first duty, they have carried out impressive social welfare projects: there and in the Philippines Spiritism provides the core-belief of many psychic surgeons.[1]

1. *The Indefinite Boundary*, Guy Lyon Playfair, Souvenir Press, London 1976

SPIRIT PHOTOGRAPHY (*See* **RAUDIVE**) Just as ghost-voices can turn up on blank tape, so phenomena that shouldn't be there can turn up on photographs. **Fraud** is easily claimed yet, like the recordings made by Raudive, spirit photographs have often been produced in séances under strict conditions; amateur photographers are dismayed to find their snapshot of friend, pet, or landscape disfigured by the image or images of faces or figures, sometimes recognisably those of dead relatives.

Spirit photography is said to have begun in 1861 when William Mumler of Boston accidentally produced the first such image. Today we still have no clear idea how the phenomenon works. Many researchers claim it involves direct spirit intervention. Journalist W. T. Stead died on the *Titanic* in April 1912 (having ignored Cheiro's **prediction** of doom), but apparently returned in spirit to visit his daughter Estelle. A champion of spirit photography when alive, soon his image began appearing in pictures of her.

As for the 'Lord Combermere's ghost' picture: in 1891 Miss Sybell Corbet photographed the library of Combermere Abbey, Cheshire. On the plate she saw a legless old man in a chair. It emerged that, even as the plate was being exposed, Lord Combermere was being buried a few miles away, having died after a road accident in which his legs had been badly damaged.

Are such images produced by **spirits** seeking a way to 'get through to us'? It remains unclear: the controversy over **Spiritualism** so clouded the issue that no thorough examination has ever been made. In recent times **UFO** images on photographs seem to be a new form of the phenomenon.

The idea that **mediums** and **clairvoyants** unknowingly impose such images on the plate or film – 'thoughtography' – was explored in Japanese tests in 1910, but became prominent only after 1962, via the work of Pauline Oehler, of the Illinois Society for Psychic Research, with psychic Ted Serios.

This ex-bellhop from Chicago, a natural **hypnotic** subject, had in 1955 'met' a spirit claiming to be Jean Lafitte, a French pirate dead for 150 years who took him in search of buried treasure. A few minor finds led only to more downs than ups before he met Pauline Oehler.

Later investigated by Dr Jule Eisenbud of the University of Colorado Medical School of Denver, he proved able to produce pictures of whatever he thought about by staring into the lens of a loaded Polaroid – an old hotel with the name 'Stevens' across it; an image of Westminster Abbey the day after seeing it in a travel magazine, and so on. Drunk before a committee of professors, he grabbed the camera, focussed fiercely, and produced the photograph of a double-decker bus, telling them, 'Put that in your pipe and smoke it'. Another time, trying to 'get' the Chicago Hilton, he muttered, 'Missed, damn it', and got a colour shot of the Denver Hilton instead.[1]

With his errant character and unusual powers Serios has stimulated hostility among scientists unwilling to countenance such phenomena; James 'the Amazing' **Randi** being among those attempting to discredit him. Yet there seems little doubt that his thoughtographs are genuine, and while his contact with 'Jean Lafitte' involves apparent spirit agency, his 'mental pictures' (published by Eisenbud in *The World of Ted Serios* (1967) seem at least to prove the power of the mind to affect photographic film directly.

Can spirits do likewise? The evidence is ambiguous at least: at best it is highly suggestive. In all such issues, predisposition to believe or disbelieve is crucial.

1. *The Occult*, Colin Wilson, Grafton, London 1979, pp. 665–9

SPIRITUALISM (*See* **MEDIUMS, ROBERTS**) The explosively rapid spread of Spiritualism in Europe during the 1850s is paralleled only by that of belief in **UFOs** a century later. In either case orthodoxy was quick to cry **fraud** or illusion, ignoring evidence. Why? To protect the materialist **paradigm** that the only real world is as revealed by the five senses? Who can say? At any rate, the continuing widespread belief today in wider realms of being, and in survival of death, suggests how little scientific method has managed to meet human emotional needs.

Spiritualists hold that life is not a brief biological process but part of something wider. They hold that on death the individual human spirit survives 'on the other side', and that communication with the dead occurs through mediums who, typically in **trance**, may also manifest other effects including **psychokinesis, telepathy** and **precognition.**

Such effects in the cases of mediums and **psychics** like **Garrett, Home, Geller, Manning, Palladino**, Kulagina and others, are so well-established that the chief question now is not as to the *reality* but the *source* of the phenomena. Spirit-activity, or 'hidden psychic powers'? Or both? The problem is as much one of definition and language as of belief.

Spiritualism began in 1848 in a house in Hydesville, New York State. Of John and Margaret Fox's seven children, three were involved in the events – Leah (thirty-four), Margaretta (fourteen) and Kate (twelve). First the whole family was upset by phantom footsteps and knockings on the walls. Mrs Fox's hair went grey in a week. Deciding an unquiet spirit was to blame, they noticed that the knockings pursued Margaretta and Kate, who began to talk to 'Mr Splitfoot'.

When Katie snapped her fingers, the spirit responded. When she snapped her fingers silently, a rap followed. 'Count ten,' Mrs Fox demanded. Ten raps followed. A code of raps was developed: the invisible rapper claimed he had been a pedlar, murdered in the house and buried in the cellar.

Neighbours verified the raps and received answers to questions of their own. It emerged that the previous tenants, named Weekman, (with an eight-year-old daughter) had been similarly upset. Diggings in the cellar flooded and proved inconclusive; committees were set up; the public furore became such that the Fox family moved away. Yet the rappings followed the two girls. Spirit-messages told them they were chosen 'to convince the sceptical of the great truth of immortality'. To the family it seemed 'only' a case of **haunting**. The **poltergeist** aspect (two pubertal girls) is obvious. There the matter might have rested, save for popular demand and need.

In the 1840s **clairvoyance** and **magnetism** were already of huge public interest; the mystic Andrew Jackson Davis had primed expectation with his talk of a '**new age**'. The Fox Sisters endured trial by publicity. Though denounced and physically attacked, in June 1850 (directed by their older sister Leah) they took New York by storm, championed by eminent editor Horace Greeley. During their many sittings no fraud was proved.

New mediums emerged everywhere: the craze spread so fast through the USA and Europe that in 1854 a Parisian journalist reported that hardly a table between the Champs-Elysées and Montmartre remained unturned. A year later, in 1855, E. W. Capron published *Modern Spiritualism: Its Facts and Fanaticism*, suggesting that the term 'Spiritualism' was already widely used just seven years after the phenomena were initially published.

In 1888 Kate and Margaretta publicly admitted their mediumship had been fraudulent. A year later they retracted this admission. Either way, it no longer mattered. Men as eminent as **Crookes, Lodge, James** and **Conan Doyle** openly endorsed their personal experience of the reality of spirit-survival and communication. The Fox sisters catalysed an enduring movement. Even so, 150 years of dispute between materialists and spiritualists has not yet led to resolution of the conflicting claims and beliefs involved.

SPONTANEOUS COMBUSTION (*See* **KUNDALINI YOGA, POLTERGEISTS**) Wholly destructive fires without external source which consume the bodies of the lonely and depressed? Fires so selectively fierce as not only to leave arms, legs and skull intact (an oily residue for the rest), but to no more than scorch or leave untouched piles of newspaper alongside?

No wonder that spontaneous human combustion (SHC) is generally thought no more than a fictional horror, as in *Bleak House* by Dickens. The aura of supernaturalism surrounding this bizarre phenomenon is apparent in its old name, 'Fire from Heaven', as in the biblical destruction Elijah drew down on the priests of Baal. Yet it occurs. A clue to its true nature may lie in the description of it in the USA as *Auto-Oxidation*.

Cases are legion. In Chelmsford, Essex, in 1938, Phyllis Newcombe was out dancing when, suddenly consumed in blue flame, she burned to black ash in minutes. In London nineteen-year-old Maybelle Andrews was dancing 'when flames suddenly burst from her back, chest and shoulders, igniting her hair'. She died on the way to hospital. In Michigan in 1959 Billy Peterson burned up while in his garaged car committing carbon monoxide suicide. He was found smouldering after smoke was seen from the garage. His body was charred, yet body-hair, let alone the scalp-hair, was unsinged: his clothes were not even scorched . . . yet a plastic religious statue on the dashboard had melted.

In Scotland in 1904 Mrs Cochrane, a widow of Falkirk, was found 'burned beyond recognition' in a chair 'stuffed' with pillows, which were not even scorched. There was no fire in the grate. A week later Mrs Clark, a widow of Hull, was found badly burned but alive on an unscorched bed. She had no idea what had happened. That winter in Britain also saw many sightings of 'aerial carriages', inexplicable cattle-maimings and many suicides.[1]

Dancers, suicides, widows? What's the connection? In his survey of the subject Thomas Harrison concludes that SHC is generated in the same way as poltergeists, being a manifestation of 'cosmic force' powered by the will. Like kundalini the 'fire from heaven' sleeps in the body. Cases of SHC suggest rhythmic ecstasy out of control (dancers), huge desire to die (suicides) or old-age weary loneliness (widows). Emotional will triggers the fire when the balance between normal body-energy and the latent power is disturbed beyond a critical point. It may explode within or without. Such frustration, if *thrown out*, manifests as poltergeist activity, or in fire-raising to burn down the hated school or foster-parents' home. This is typical of extrovert adolescents. Yet when inwardly contained by the lonely, repressed, and elderly, this mind-fire destroys what is most hateful to its victims – their continued existence in the flesh.

1. *Fire from Heaven*, Thomas Harrison, Pan Books, London 1977

SPRINGHEEL JACK (*See* **JERSEY DEVIL**) The 'most hideous appearance' of Springheel Jack met Jane Alsop when, in February 1838 at Old Ford, London, she answered the violent doorbell to see a shining **apparition** with a flashing lamp on his chest and eyes of fire. She was grabbed in clawlike fingers as her sister rushed to the rescue: the fiery gas he spat in her face dropped her unconscious as he leapt away.

Springheel Jack had already accosted a Miss Scales of Limehouse in Green Dragon Alley, near a public house. With a 'weird blue flame' about his face, this apparition of a flying man became so commonly seen in London that apparently even 'The old Duke of Wellington himself set holsters at his saddle bow and rode out after dark in search of Springheel Jack'.[1]

1. *Dimensions*, Jacques Vallée, Sphere, London 1990, p. 102

STANDING STONES (*See* **MEGALITHIC MYSTERIES**)

STEINER, Rudolf (1861–1925) Founder of **Anthroposophy**, this 'scientist of the invisible' was born in rural Kraljevec, now in Yugoslavia, the son of an Austrian railway telegraph operator. Early **clairvoyant** experiences increased the stubborn boy's sense of isolation. Once in the station waiting-room, he saw a woman walk in. She said, 'Try to help me if you can – now and later on', then vanished into the stove! He kept quiet about this (his parents were good Catholics) but saw his father was sad. Later he learned a female relative he'd never met had killed herself at that very time. 'From that time onward a **soul** life began to develop into the boy which made him conscious of worlds from which not only external trees or external mountains speak to the human soul, but also the Beings that live behind them,' he wrote years later.

His **visionary** nature was balanced by work on the family smallholding, by his interest in local mores and by a freethinking technical education. This marriage of mystical experience with his love of geometry and Kantian logic led him to seek to describe his inner life with scientific precision.

A proponent of Austrian democracy, as a student in Vienna, his admiration for German philosophy led him in 1890 to Weimar to edit **Goethe**'s scientific writings. Here in this staid town of 'classical mummies' he met Ernst Haeckel, a Darwinian populariser and Friedrich Nietzsche. Both men opened up new vistas. He also met Anna Eunicke, a widow who went with him to Berlin in 1897. They married but later separated. She died in 1911.

Forced by academic outrage to abandon his radical editorship of the *Magazin für Literatur*, he lectured at a Workers' College where, despite a student vote of 348–12 in his favour, he was dismissed as 'unreliable'.[1]

On 22 August 1900 he lectured on Nietzsche to the Berlin **Theosophical** Society, intriguing Countess Brockdorff, Secretary of the Lodge (he spoke of seeing Nietzsche's ***astral body*** three days before the latter's death). Another account says his initial lecture was on Goethe's *Secret Revelation*. Either way, his impact was such that Countess Brockdorff approached Annie **Besant** in London, putting him forward as general secretary of a German Theosophical Society.[2] Though not a Theosophist, in Theosophy Steiner met people responsive to his desire to establish a new perception of practical, *European* spirituality. Emphasising that his function was to *awaken* men, he began his work with the German Theosophists with a course, *Practical Karma Exercises*, using ***karma*** in a Christian context. The results disappointed him: too many of his students sought not personal inner freedom but a **guru**

Chairing an International Theosophical Congress at Munich in 1907, he made it clear that to him the spiritual message was not enough: he wanted to change the world, via 'The Mystery of Golgotha'. He saw the Crucifixion as marking an *objective* alteration in the history of human **consciousness**, wholly changing humanity's relationship with Spirit and the Earth.

Subsequently Annie Besant announced **Krishnamurti** as the reincarnation of Christ. Krishnamurti, later denying such pretension, was not to blame, yet in Besant's attitude Steiner sensed misunderstanding of the meaning of the death and **resurrection** of the Logos, the Holy Word. Now ready to go his own way, later he wrote, 'I have never tried to establish contact with the Theosophical Society, but rather paradoxically as it may seem, the Theosophical Society tried establishing contact with me.'

In February 1913 he founded Anthroposophy. Working with Marija von Sivers, a Russian admiral's daughter (who at their first meeting asked, 'Is it not possible to establish a spiritual teaching as profound as that of the East, but firmly based on European and Christian foundations?'), from his Berlin base Steiner issued three books: *Theosophy, Occult Science* and *Knowledge of the Higher Worlds*.

These describe humankind's spiritual-physical roots, our growth and isolation from these roots, our forgetfulness of them, and the path of development needed to regain and deepen them. They arose out of Marija's concern that people misunderstood and misreported his lectures. He let her (by now they were married) fix his views in print, but made it clear that individual experience of his lectures and their ambience was, to him, more important than any dogmatic literalism.

His practical work now crystallised at Dornach near Basle, where on 20 September 1913 the foundation stone of a centre of anthroposophical art was laid – the *Goetheaneum*. It was built according to the principles of **sacred geometry**, made public by Steiner in a 1911 lecture 'The Temple Is Man'. Like Gaudi and Corbusier after him, he acknowledged ancient principles of harmony and design all but lost today. A twin-domed structure, its domes and their uniting parts fused male and female principle, and the halves of the human cerebrum: left and right lobes; logic and intuition united. Rich in esoteric **symbolism**, this encyclopaedia of symbolic knowledge did not survive. Built of wood amid Europe's worst-ever slaughter, in 1922 the Goetheaneum was fired by unknown hands. Unsurprised, he designed a new building, in pre-stressed concrete.[3]

Meanwhile he had not remained aloof from the War. He saw what it would lead to. Thus in 1916 he bewildered anthroposophists by seemingly turning from spiritual to social questions. From now on he spoke to businessmen, industrialists and politicians. At a cigarette factory a worker told him, 'I see what you are aiming at. But for us it is too late. Could you not do something to give our children a truly human education?'

Thus after the War the first *Waldorfschule* was built. Today there are some 400 such Steiner schools round the world. Along with the Montessori system, they command the grudging respect of conventional educationalists.

Steiner never became an Anthroposophist. He led by telling others to lead themselves, rejecting past techniques while refusing to join present trends. Yet to the end he tried to reinvoke among the Anthroposophists that spiritual self-responsibility which had been his first cause. He travelled and worked so hard that in September 1924 he collapsed in the middle of a lecture, working on from his bed until his death on 30 March 1925.

1. *Rudolf Steiner*, Rudi Lissau, Hawthorn Press, Stroud, 1987
2. *Afterlife*, Colin Wilson, Harrap, London 1985, pp. 184ff.
3. *Sacred Geometry*, Nigel Pennick, Turnstone Press, London 1980, pp. 143–5

STELLA MATUTINA (*See* **GOLDEN DAWN, REGARDIE**)

STELLE GROUP (*See* **POLE SHIFT, SOLOMON**) This Illinois community claims an 80,000-year ancestry originating in the lost continent of **Mu**, drowned, they say, under the Pacific 26,000 years ago. Those joining the Group are carefully screened and subject to rigid qualifications based on what are claimed to be spiritual laws handed down over millennia by secret brotherhoods. The Group says it follows an ancient mandate, directed by higher intelligence on other planes, to establish the Nation of God on **Lemuria** when the coming pole shift brings it above water again. As does Paul Solomon, they say the pole shift will be triggered by the planetary conjunction of 5 May 2000. While emphasising the primacy of values, not events, they predict such a violent cataclysm that, after the 'last war' (1998–9), 'less than a tenth of the world's population will be alive to see the year 2001 AD'[1]

1. *Pole Shift*, John White, W. H. Allen, London 1980, pp. 312–23

STEVENSON, Ian (*See* **GLOSSOLALIA, KÜBLER-ROSS, REINCARNATION**)

STIGMATA (*See* **MIRACULOUS ICONS**) These are wounds appearing on the bodies of Christian believers exactly as if they too have been crucified. The phenomenon is first reported of St Francis of Assisi, stigmatised in 1224 while at prayer. His biographer Thomas Celano, writing in 1229 after his death, described how, 'His hands and feet seemed pierced in the midst by nails, the heads of the nails appearing in the inner part of the hands and in the upper part of the feet . . . Moreover his right side, as if it had been pierced by a lance, was overlaid with a scar, and often shed forth blood.'

Mediaeval exaggeration? In recent years such wounds have often been attested to by doctors and photographed. It is often claimed that they are self-inflicted but there is rarely proof of this. In every case, religious ecstasy and identification with Christ's Passion appears to trigger the onset of the stigmata. Blood from such wounds is invariably arterial, with no trace of disease; the wounds come and go spontaneously, or remain open for long periods without healing or infection; and in most cases reoccur on specific days, typically Fridays (Good Friday), or at Lent or Christmas.

In 1901 a tubercular twenty-three-year-old Italian woman, Gemma Galgani, was found in her room after prayer with her arms and back covered in wounds like whip-marks and her clothes soaked in blood. Weekly until her death two years later these stigmata appeared each Thursday, vanishing next day. Her biographer Father Germano di Stanislao described how, at the onset of her ecstasy, her wounds would redden slowly on the backs and palms of both hands, then burst open, leaving a rent apparently passing right through the hand. The appearance of nails with thick heads could be seen, formed by ridged, darkened flesh and solidified blood.

In 1926 the mysterious illnesses afflicting twenty-eight-year-old Bavarian Teresa Neumann vanished after a vision left her stigmatised. Every Friday for thirty-two years she lost up to a pint of blood from wounds appearing in hands, side, feet and forehead, also losing half a stone in weight each time. Every Sunday she was back to normal. During her **trances** she spoke in Aramaic: she is said to have taken no food for thirty-five years, save for Communion wafer and wine – a fact confirmed by various doctors, who noted that her excreta ceased after 1930 and that her intestinal tact withered up. Nonetheless she remained active until her death in 1962.

Many hundreds of such cases exist. It is notable that a very high proportion of stigmatics are women. An hysterical foundation has been argued, while attempts to produce stigmata by **hypnosis** have led only to slight bleeding. Such wounds do not have to take the form of Christ's stigmata, but do so commonly.

STOKES, Doris (*See* **MEDIUMS**)

STONEHENGE (*See* **MEGALITHIC MYSTERIES, MICHELL, SACRED GEOMETRY**) What legend says of Stonehenge – that before being brought to England from Ireland by **Merlin** the Magician, African **giants** had brought this *Giant's Dance* to Ireland, and that the stones have **healing** properties – is no more amazing than the actuality. For Britain's best-known megalithic structure is not only a precise calendrical and astronomical computer but a model of sacred geometry, its every dimension precise.

Located on Salisbury Plain in Wiltshire, within its circular moat and bank it consists of two concentric stone circles and two inner U-shaped structures. The outer circle, once of thirty pillars of local sarsen stone, each thirteen feet six inches high (seventeen remain), supported a ring of thirty curved lintels (now six) fitted with tongue and groove joints. Within this circle is another, once of sixty bluestones thought to come from the Prescelly Mountains in south-west Wales. Within it, the outer U-shaped cove consists of five detached sarsen trilithons, weighing up to fifty tons and up to twenty-two feet high. The inner cove, once of nineteen bluestones, forms a horseshoe round the recumbent 'Altar Stone'.

Outside this main structure, within the circular outer bank and ditch, is a circle of fifty-six holes once filled with limestone and charcoal, named the Aubrey Holes after antiquarian John Aubrey who discovered them in 1649. Intersecting this ring at a gap in the bank some eighty yards from the Altar Stone is the recumbent Heel or Slaughter Stone. The line between these two recumbent stones extends to the exact point of midsummer sunrise.

Early in the seventeenth century architect Inigo Jones reported Stonehenge to be a ruined Roman temple. Fifty years later Aubrey concluded it had been a **Druid** sanctuary. Only in 1901 was it realised that it predated the Celts' arrival in Britain by over a millennium, when bearings taken by astronomer Sir Norman Lockyer (assuming the line from Altar Stone to Heel Stone to have measured solar altitude on the longest day) gave a construction date of 1680 BC, plus or minus 200 years. In 1935 more precise measurement by Herbert Stone extended this to 1840 BC. Later radiocarbon dating of the Aubrey Holes gave a median date of 1847 BC. This sensational result (and the 1923 discovery that the bluestones had come from distant Wales) brought Boston astronomer Dr Gerald Hawkins to Stonehenge. Drawing 7,140 possible connecting lines between all the stones, he fed the bearings of these lines into a computer, concluding that beyond doubt *c.* 1880 BC Stonehenge had been a solar and lunar observatory. As for the Aubrey Holes, he concluded that, by placing yardsticks in every ninth hole and moving each stick one hole onward clockwise per annum, the priests had been able to predict eclipses. More complex calculations between Aubrey Holes and the trilithons gave more exact predictions. His conclusions were derided – how could prehistoric man have known so much? – but subsequently astro-archaeologist Alexander Thom's thorough survey of some 600 British megalithic structures established their astronomical sophistication. He found not only fifty-eight *certain* sun-alignments and twenty-three **moon**-alignments, but also a large number of megalithic alignments on the stars Capella, Deneb, Arcturus, Castor, Spica and others.[1]

This recognition is important in assessing the claim by John Michell that the units and relationships of measure used at Stonehenge were chosen (as in the **Great Pyramid**) to express geophysical data. The width of the lintel stones (1 sacred rod = 3.4757485 ft.), he claims, represents exactly a six-millionth part of the Earth's polar radius. Other measurements give values for earth's mean radius and circumference, while the dimensions as a whole display the same canonical numbers (108, 216, 432, etc.) as employed in the Jerusalem Temple and the Mexican city of Teotihuacán. He says that the meaning of Stonehenge is revealed in the diameter of the sarsen circle; 316.8 ft. This, a hundredth part of six miles, is the measure round St John's New Jerusalem as given in Revelation xxi, while the number 3168 is prominent in cabalistic numerology, being by **gematria** the Greek for *Lord Jesus Christ*. The New Jerusalem, he concludes,

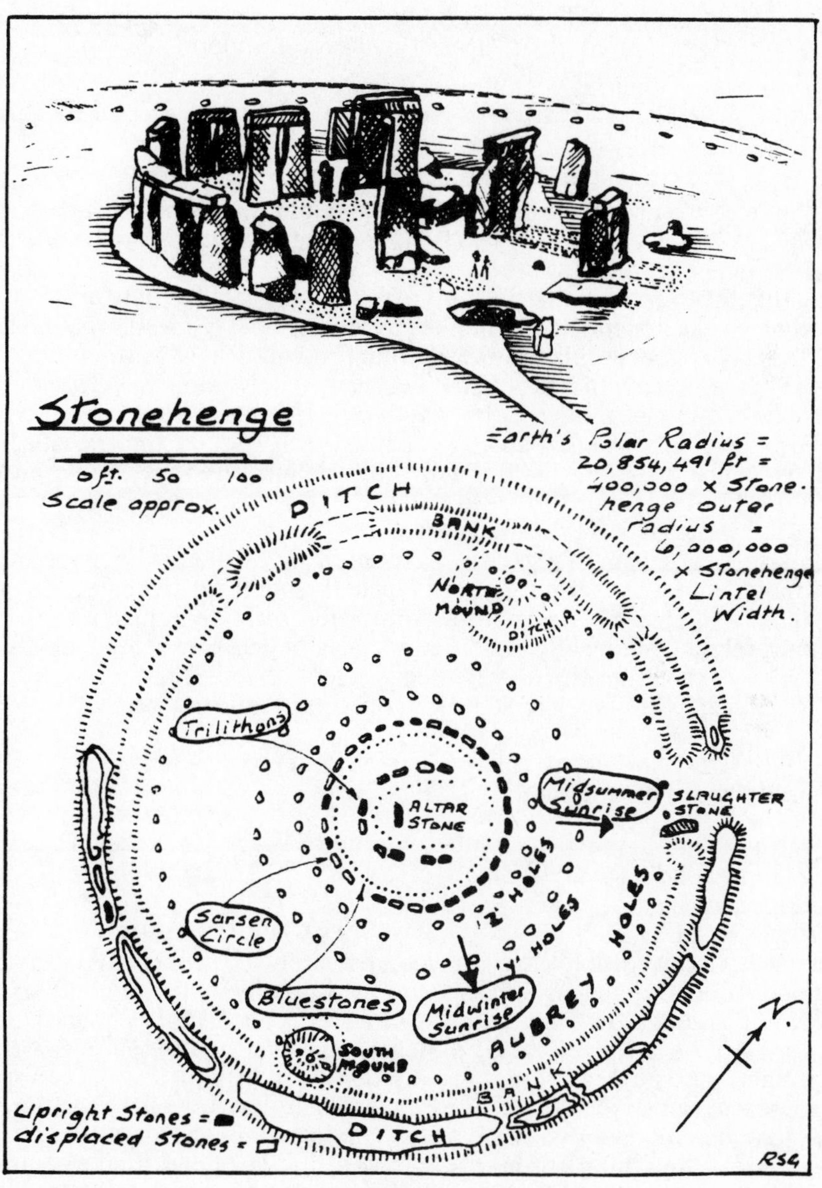
Stonehenge
0 ft. 50 100
Scale approx.
Earth's Polar Radius = 20,854,491 ft = 400,000 x Stonehenge outer radius = 6,000,000 x Stonehenge Lintel Width.
DITCH
BANK
NORTH MOUND
DITCH
Trilithons
ALTAR STONE
Midsummer Sunrise
SLAUGHTER STONE
Sarsen Circle
'Z' HOLES
'Y' HOLES
AUBREY HOLES
Bluestones
Midwinter Sunrise
SOUTH MOUND
BANK
DITCH
Upright Stones =
displaced Stones =
N.
RSG

is Stonehenge with the circle squared – an image of eternal truth, a model of the cosmic order translated to earth via the conscious art of sacred geometry.[2]

Is it far-fetched to assume that the builders of Stonehenge applied a measure and proportion to their work also revealed in other works, whether in stone or in Word, found thousands of miles and years distant?

Perhaps, but only because today we seem to have forgotten so much.

1. *Prehistoric Heritage*, Felix R. Paturi, Book Club Associates, London 1979
2. *City of Revelation*, John Michell, Granstone Press, London 1972, pp. 51–8

STRAIGHT TRACKS (*See* **LEY LINES, MEGALITHIC MYSTERIES**)

STREIBER, WHITLEY (1945–) (*See* **ABDUCTIONS, UFO's**) Previously successful with novels of supernatural horror and ecodoom, this New York-based author's *Communion* (1987) and *Transformation* (1988) present as true his **dream**-like, baffling account of abduction by alien 'visitors'.

Insisting that the events he describes are real and were recalled only under **hypnosis**, and backed up by the appended testimonies of professional witnesses that he is neither insane nor a liar, Streiber seems fully aware that few will believe him. He suggests that our disbelief is precisely the problem. Tested by Polygraph Security Services of London at the request of the BBC, he was asked, 'Are the visitors about whom you write in your book *Communion* a physical reality? Whilst in the presence of your visitors, have you actually felt them touch you?' He answered 'yes' to both questions and 'was found to be telling the truth'. Asked if he had invented the 'visitors' for personal gain, his denial was evaluated as true.

His account is unsettling. As with **Castaneda** or **Daskalos**, bizarre events are described matter-of-factly, striking chords of half-caught far memory. Long known on Earth under many guises, the visitors' connection with the human race seems to be subtle, omnipresent and wholly baffling. Physically real yet rooted in the human unconscious, they can enter the mind, affect perception and 'recycle **souls**'. Drawing on many traditions, Streiber has at least tapped an enduring vein of **supernatural** paranoia.

'We can face the reality of the visitors. The first step is to admit that they exist but that we do not know what they are.'[1,2]

1. *Communion*, Whitley Streiber, Arrow, London 1988
2. *Transformation*, Whitley Streiber, Arrow, London 1989

STRINDBERG, AUGUST (1849–1912) (*See* **DOPPELGÄNGERS**) A second divorce brought this Swedish playwright close to madness. As told in his autobiographical *Inferno* he suffered delusions of persecution amid an emotional crisis stimulating development of unsought **psychic** powers. In *Legends* he describes how, dangerously ill in Paris in 1895, he so longed to be 'in the bosom of my family' that 'I saw the inside of my house and for a moment forgot my surroundings, having lost the consciousness of where I was.' At which instant his distant mother-in-law saw his **apparition** 'behind the piano', took it as a presage of death, and wrote to ask if he were ill.

Another time, stimulating a friend's memory, he described 'that evening in the Augustiner tavern' so thoroughly that again he projected himself. 'Wait a minute,' he told his friend. 'I am now in the Augustiner tavern, but I know very well that I am in some other place. Don't say anything . . . I don't know you anymore, yet I know that I do.' Horrifying his friend, he made an effort and succeeded in relocating himself.[1]

As with Streiber and other imaginative factual writing it is hard to be sure what is true and what is false. Perhaps the true falsity lies in the effort to determine which is which.

1. *The Occult*, Colin Wilson, Grafton, London 1979, pp. 69–70 and 119–23

SUBCONSCIOUS MIND (*See* **BRAIN MYSTERIES, FREUD, JUNG**) A catch-all term referring to layers of **psyche** underlying the conscious level of the mind, often loosely associated with the production of psychic activity and phenomena. Its corollary is the theory that a superconscious overlies the conscious. 'In my experience,' Jung wrote, 'the conscious mind can claim only a relatively central position and must accept the fact that the unconscious psyche transcends and as it were surrounds it on all sides.'[1] If ***consciousness*** is an island, the *subconscious* is the ocean, and the *unconscious* is the entire unknown cosmos, including ultimately both ocean and island.

1. *Dreams*, C. G. Jung, Ark, London 1989, p. 211

SUBTLE BODY (*See* **ASTRAL PLANE, MONROE, OUT-OF-THE-BODY EXPERIENCES**)

SUCCUBI (*See* **INCUBI**)

SUFIS (*See* **DERVISHES, ISLAM**) Believers in **reincarnation**, conscious evolution and human perfectability, the Sufis claim to guard Islam's esoteric philosophy and to have preceded Mohammed, their eastern school deriving from ancient **Zoroastrian** beliefs. As such, Sufism has long bridged gaps between disputing Muslim sects, and has had vast, largely unacknowledged impact on Western thought. According to Idries Shah, **Lully**, Roger **Bacon, Paracelsus**, St Thomas Aquinas and many Popes were all Sufi-inspired; **Freemasonry, Rosicrucianism** and the Franciscan Order likewise bear the stamp of Sufi influence.[1]

The word *Sufi* may derive from *Sophia*, Wisdom, or may denote one wearing wool who pursues simplicity and poverty. Forming many orders including the dervishes, Sufism involves 'the grand idea of one universal creed which could be secretly held under any profession of outward faith.'[2] Hiding their ideas behind the symbolism of 'The Beloved', Sufi poets like Rumi, Hafiz and Saadi still command respect. The *Mathnawi* of Jalaluddin Rumi (1207–73) is thought next in rank to the *Koran*; of him Doctor Johnson said, 'He makes plain to the Pilgrim the secrets of the Way of Unity, and unveils the Mysteries of the Path of Eternal Truth.'

The tales of the Mullah Nasrudin, popular throughout the Middle East, are in origin Sufi teaching devices designed, **Zen**-like, to jolt the mind into lateral thought. Example: one day the Mullah's friend comes down the street to see Nasrudin on hands and knees, peering under the stalls. 'What are you looking for?' he asks. 'My key,' says Nasrudin, 'I've lost it.' So the friend joins him, scrabbling in the dust of the street, but – no key.

'Are you sure you lost it here?' asks his friend.

'Of course not,' says Nasrudin, 'I lost it in my house.'

'Then why are we looking out here if you know it's inside?'

'It's *dark* inside,' Nasrudin explains patiently. 'It's *light* out here.'

1. *The Sufis*, Idries Shah, Doubleday, New York 1964.
2. *Reincarnation*, Head and Cranston, Julian Press/Crown, New York 1977, p. 169

SUMMERS, Montague (d. 1948) (*See* **WITCHCRAFT**) Prominent among post-**Golden Dawn** English **occultists** was Montague Summers, alias the Rev. Montague Summers. What kind of Holy Orders he took, if any, remains unclear. Devoutly Roman Catholic, he brought scholarship to the literature of **witchcraft**, and seemed sinister. Dennis Wheatley, who said Summers inspired him with fear, used him as a model for Canon Copely-Syle in the novel *To the Devil – A Daughter*.

Resident in Oxford, Brighton (a secret **black magic** centre, he claimed) and Richmond, where latterly he met the aging Aleister **Crowley**, Summers usually wore clerical garb, sported long silver hair and had soft, jewel-bedecked hands. Claiming that Satan is real and that witches serve him, he defended the Inquisition's witch-trials, attacking the 'international Satanic conspiracy'. Some claim he was briefed by the Catholic hierarchy to write about the subject in a depth of detail normally discouraged.[1]

Whatever the truth, it seems he devoted his life to attacking in public what privately fascinated him. Among his books are: *History of Witchcraft and Demonology* (1926); *A Popular History of Witchcraft* (1937); *Witchcraft and Black Magic* (1946). He also translated *Malleus Maleficarum* (The Hammer of the Witches), the notorious fifteenth-century bestseller by the Dominicans Axel and Springer.

Colin **Wilson** agrees with Summers that some witches invoked **spirits** and **demons** to perform **magic**, despite dismissal of this proposition by Murray, Cohn and others disposed to rational interpretation alone.

1. *An ABC of Witchcraft Past and Present*, Doreen Valiente, Hale 1973.
2. *Beyond the Occult*, Colin Wilson, Corgi 1989, pp. 349 and 351.

SUPERCONSCIOUS (*See* **SUBCONSCIOUS**)

SUPERNATURAL Refers to the existence, manifestation or activity of any agency or **entity** considered to lie outside the laws of cause and effect as understood by the existing Western material **paradigm**.

SUPERSTITION From the Latin *superstitio*, 'standing over', implying credulity with regard to the **supernatural, occult** or **paranormal**; or irrational fear or dread of the unknown, dark or night; or belief in and undue respect for the supposed activities of supernatural entities; or belief in **omens, charms, spells** and all forms of meaningful but acausal connection.

SWANN, Ingo (*See* **PARAPSYCHOLOGY**) In laboratory tests this New York-based **psychic** (his German grandmother Anna was thought to have the **evil eye** by neighbours in the Rockies where he grew up) has 'disturbed' the **electromagnetic** field of a detector hidden under several feet of concrete, accurately described remote geographical sites with only map coordinates to guide him, and in general run the gamut of **ESP** research. In his autobiographical *To Kiss Earth Goodbye*, he says heavy-handed scientific techniques of **psi** research are 'grinding the diamond into a dust-pile while trying to capture the sparkle.'[1] Mum about his current activity in psi research, he condemns the destructive hostility of most anti-ESP critics: 'Parapsychology lacks many things and one thing it lacks on the whole is an aggressive stance. [It] is filled with those introverted types who can't get their act together enough to go out and do the equivalent of kicking someone in the nuts.'[2]

Rejecting all current terminology he calls **telepathy** and **clairvoyance**, 'buzzwords that caught on somewhere in the history of the research and they stuck. There is no evidence at all . . . that what we're calling telepathy does anything remotely like what the definition says it must be doing.'[3]

A prolific artist, he feels he creates information in his paintings but not yet in his ESP work. 'The goal of the **New Age** artist is to transcend the ego and meld his consciousness into the natural order of **consciousness** that has been assiduously avoided by science.'[4]

1. *Intangible Evidence*, Bernard Gittelson, Simon and Schuster, New York 1987, p.26
2. *Ibid.* p. 92
3. *Ibid.* pp. 101–2
4. *Ibid.* pp. 185–91

SWEDENBORG, Emmanuel (1688–1772) (*See* **BLAKE, SPIRITUALISM**) A skilled mathematician, chemist, anatomist, physicist, psychologist and theologian, fluent in eleven languages, proficient in seven arts, gardener, musician, poet and author translated into thirty languages, metallurgist and mining engineer (assessor of the Swedish Board of Mines at twenty-eight), Swedenborg was also a greatly gifted **seer** who founded a new Christian denomination.

Hurt by rejection in love (a bishop's son, he advocated concubinage) as much as by official rejection of his pioneering ideas on brain science and physics, for years he starved his religious and emotional nature in work.

The dam began to burst in 1736. Deep in **meditation** one day, a 'swoon' 'cleared his brain'. He began recording his **dreams**, anticipating **Jungian symbolism** in his self-analysis. The conflict between his scientific and **mediumistic** sides increased. In 1744 in a dream a roaring wind picked him up and threw him on his face. A hand clutched his own clasped hands. He looked up and saw Christ. Another day, soporific after a large lunch, the room darkened; the floor swarmed with frogs and snakes. A man appeared and cried, 'Eat not so much!' Returning that night, the man said he was the Lord God, and told Swedenborg to tell Mankind the truth of the Scriptures.

His sexual agony declined. Abstemious now, he entered ecstatic **trances**, visiting heaven and hell. In the books that followed (culminating in *True Christian Religion*, 1771), he claimed the afterworld to be much like this, save that it is more rarefied; in it mental states literally create heaven or hell. His reports of conversations with those 'passed over', as well as with **angels** and devils, led most contemporaries to dismiss him as a lunatic or liar. The **spirits** he met called him 'the unaccountable one', as he was the only human able to live at ease in both worlds. Moreover, he entered their world, not they his – not the usual way round as described in later Spiritualist reports.

Modern analysis has tried to lay the Swedenborgian ghost in terms of his repressed sexuality. Maybe *transcended* sexuality is more to the point. His visions, as when in 1760 he woke up believing his hair full of small snakes, better apply to **Kundalini serpent**-fire imagery than to **Freud**. For not only did he express none of the congenital irritation associated with angry repression – contemporaries found him sane, sensible, honest, kind and agreeable, always efficient, always reserved; he met criticism calmly – but the **psychic** talents he developed late in life suggest he found a way to transform and unite his frustrations into **shamanic** energy.

These talents included **precognition** and **prophecy**. In 1759, guest of William Castel at Göteborg and 385 kilometres from Stockholm, at 6 p.m. one evening he left the company. Returning 'greatly agitated', he said he 'knew' that a fire raged in Stockholm; a friend's house was destroyed and his own was threatened. Two hours later he said the fire had been doused three doors from his home. His account was fully confirmed next day by a messenger from Stockholm; a day later the royal courier also confirmed it.

In October 1761 the Queen of Sweden, whose brother Augustus William of Prussia had died in 1758, summoned Swedenborg to contact her dead brother. From her audience with him she tottered as if about to faint, exclaiming, 'That is something which no one else could have told, except my brother!'

At a party in July 1762 Swedenborg went into trance. Emerging from it, he described the assassination in prison of the Russian Tsar Peter III and urged all present to note what he said and compare it with the newspaper reports – which duly confirmed the royal strangulation.

Swedenborg remained a bachelor. His story would not seem so strange to non-Western or 'unscientific' cultures.

SYMBOL The symbol is an abstract instrument of knowledge allowing communication of wordless thought, meaning and knowledge. Striking common chords across the world and through history, it transcends written, spoken or visual language in its communicative power. Shadowing what everywhere is intuitively known but remains inexpressible, the symbol materially captures abstraction and gives it intelligible form. So it reveals (as in *caduceus*) contradictions and possibilities as yet unresolved in the human quest. Perceived as such, the symbol is not only reminder but guide. It is pure expression of truth in that it arises naturally from the universal unformulated sea amid which self-conscious deceit is impossible. It is the primordial image of *what is*.

An effective symbol is not exclusive but reveals many levels of meaning beyond any apparent local religious or social context. The *swastika* is not Nazi alone. *Sun* may shine on *man*, ***moon*** may veil *woman*; neither means a *fig* without the other. In traditional symbolism the heavens are primordial and the earth but a reflection; symbols convey knowledge from former to latter – part of the educational postal service from the un(super)conscious.

You know a symbol when it strikes you. A sight, a sound, a smile, frown or sudden inner vision, trigger-image in painting or stained glass window, enlightening phrase or meaningful **dream**. Ignore it at your peril. Dean Inge said of symbols, 'Indifference to them is not, as many have supposed, a sign of enlightenment and spirituality. It is, in fact, an unhealthy symptom.'

SYNCHRONICITY A term coined in 1952 by C. G. **Jung** to describe 'meaningful coincidence'. It involves the 'simultaneous occurrence of two or more meaningfully but not causally connected events'. In the essay he wrote with the physicist Wolfgang Pauli, Jung describes a case (first recorded by **Flammarion**). It demonstrates the outré humour so often apparent in synchronous events that some call them the work of a **Cosmic Joker** who toys with us for fun.[1]

A certain Monsieur Deschamps, as a boy in Orléans, was fed plum-pudding by a Monsieur de Fortgibu. A decade later, in a Paris restaurant, he saw a plum-pudding and ordered a piece, but found it was already ordered – by a Monsieur de Fortgibu.

Years later, invited at a party to partake of plum-pudding, he joked that the only thing missing was Monsieur de Fortgibu. Just then the door opened and a confused old man walked in. The old man was – need you ask? – de Fortgibu. He had the wrong address and had entered the party by mistake.

Astronomer Archie Roy describes how an unknown man, with an odd name, 'Mr Melchisadec', phoned him at his Glasgow University office to claim the discovery of a new star, perhaps a *nova*. Professor Roy said he should call the Royal Observatory at Edinburgh, then rang a colleague at the university observatory. He said, 'I've just been talking to a Mr Melchisadec on the phone about a nova.' After a bemused silence his colleague replied: 'But you couldn't have. Mr Melchisadec has been here with me for the past half hour talking to me about the nova and he hasn't phoned anyone.'

It transpired that: (a) there were two Mr Melchisadecs; (b) they didn't know each other; (c) one had consulted Roy and the other his colleague about a nova at the same time; and (d) *his* Mr Melchisadec's 'nova' was a star; his colleague's Mr Melchisadec's 'Nova' was a make of computer.[2]

Jung's essay was partly based on *Das Gesetz der Serie* (not in English), published in 1919 by tragic Viennese biologist Paul **Kammerer**. Arguing his concept of 'seriality', Kammerer recorded exactly one hundred examples of synchronous events. Concluding that in such events coincidence rules 'to such an extent that the concept of coincidence itself is negated', he also theorised that, coexistent with normal physical causality, the universe contains an acausal principle loosely described as 'like attracts like'.

This equates with **Sheldrake**'s **morphic resonance** and also with the old magical theory of **Correspondences**. Is anyone in fact *surprised* by such events? 'What a coincidence,' we say if we meet a friend unexpectedly, 'I was just thinking about you.' Our rationality is amazed, but at a deeper level the meeting seems 'just right'. Are we wiser than reason knows?

Physicist Wolfgang Pauli's radical proposal was to extend the notion of meaningful non-causal events from the sub-atomic world (where the principle is fully recognised) to the daily macro- or 'physical' world (where it is not – at least by reason alone). This tantalising Jung-Pauli collaboration nonetheless produced little by way of better understanding of synchronous processes. To date we remain intellectually in the dark, despite the work of **Koestler**, etc. Yet at some level (**collective unconscious**?) we do know what is going on. Any gambler 'running his luck' relies on his *unconscious* understanding of synchronicity. And is it coincidence that the title of Kammerer's book: *Das Gesetz der Serie* is, as Koestler points out, a cliché in German – the equivalent of: 'It never rains but it pours.'[3,4]

1. *Synchronicity*, C. G. Jung (1952) Routledge Kegan Paul, London 1972
2. *A Sense of Something Strange*, Archie E. Roy, Dog and Bone Press, Glasgow 1990, p. 102
3. *Janus*, Arthur Koestler, Pan Books, London 1979, p. 261
4. *The Roots of Coincidence*, Arthur Koestler, Picador, London 1972

T

TABOOS (*See* **CURSES, SPELLS**)

TANTRA (*See* **KUNDALINI, RIGHT-HAND PATH, YOGA**) This ancient body of yoga doctrine derives from a Sanskrit term meaning 'warp', i.e. the written teaching through which is threaded the 'weft' of oral and physical training. The latter involves complex breathing exercises, and profound techniques of **meditation** aim at developing self-control of mind, body and will. This is achieved by uniting the cosmic polarities symbolised by the god Shiva and his consort Shakti who, as Mother Goddess and primal creative force, is seen as the superior of the two.

One route to this unity (the Left-Hand Path) involves **ritual** sexual intercourse. Orgasm is withheld in order to generate kundalini, an energy (symbolised as a sleeping **serpent**, Shakti herself) said to lie dormant near the base of the spine. Kundalini is thus raised through the seven **chakras** to the Shiva-power in the crown of the head. The **alchemical** union of Shiva and Shakti is said to lead to enlightenment, increased longevity and other powers. However, the process may prove dangerous on two counts. Not only can unskilled interference with kundalini lead to physical derangement or madness; the sexual aspect has caused persistent social condemnation.

Existing Tantric texts date back to the tenth century. It is said that older documents were destroyed, often by outraged orthodox **Hindus**. As a result Tantrism has always been practised in secret, though the Left-Hand Path is but one path. Yet it has been highly influential. Many Western magical **rituals** developed out of the broader aspects of Tantric philosophy, while 'sex-**magic**' as practised in the West by **Crowley** and others since the late nineteenth century shows similarities with the Tantric Left-Hand Path.

TAO This ancient Chinese **symbol** of the essential interrelatedness between Man, Earth and Heaven is often translated as 'The Way'. Representing a lateral, allusive, elusive philosophy, its essence lies in the *Tao Te Ching* ('Book of the Way'), a collection of eighty-one poems by the Chinese mystic Lao Tsu, an older contemporary of Confucius (sixth century BC). All his life he taught that 'The Tao that can be told is not the eternal Tao', but, says legend, as he was riding off into the desert to die, being sick at the ways of man, he was persuaded by a gatekeeper to write down his teaching for posterity. So he paused long enough to express the inexpressible. Thus:

> The softest thing in the universe
> Overcomes the hardest thing in the universe.
> That without substance can enter where there is no room.
> Hence I know the value of non-action.
>
> Teaching without words and work without doing
> Are understood by very few.[1]

The goal of Taoism (one branch being esoteric and monastic, the other more populist in its concentration on the magical powers to be attained through harmony with the

Tao), is the achievement of *wu-wei*, a state of positive inaction, creating harmony by integration with the universal flow of Tao.

> The world is ruled by letting things take their course.
> It cannot be ruled by interfering.[2]

1. *Tao Te Ching* (43), Lao Tsu, trans. Gia-Fu Feng, Wildwood House, London 1973
2. *Ibid.*, T. (48)

TAROT (*See* **DIVINATION**) The tarot is a pack of seventy-eight cards used for divination or **fortune-telling** and divided into two sets: *Major* and *Minor Arcana*. The former consists of twenty-two 'trump' cards, each with a specific symbolic design (the Fool, Magician, High Priestess, Hermit, Hanged Man, Death, the Star, etc.). Twenty-one cards are numbered; the additional card, the Fool, is either unnumbered or is given as zero or twenty-two. *The Minor Arcana*, which is basically the playing card pack we know today, consists of fifty-six cards in four suits (Wands, Cups, Pentacles and Swords). Each suit contains not three court cards (as in an ordinary fifty-two card pack) but four – King, Queen, Knight/Jack and *Page*. The fifty-two card pack we know today probably derives from the *Minor Arcana*.

The origin of tarot is unknown. In 1781 Antoine Court de Gebelin, a French linguist, claimed it was based on ancient Egyptian rites associated with worship of the scribe-god Thoth, constituting a 'book' of Egyptian wisdom. Others thought it originated in India, in Morocco as a graphic 'language', or even in **Atlantis**, or that the Gypsies brought it with them on arrival in Europe in 1417 (by which time playing-cards, and thus tarot, were already in use.) In the mid-nineteenth century the French magician Eliphas **Lévi** developed the pack's **occult** connection by associating the cards of the *Major Arcana* with **Qabalah**, assigning each of the twenty-two trumps to letters of the Hebrew alphabet, with corresponding **numerological** significances.

Today about 160 different tarot decks are available, all from different eras and cultures, each with their own graphic **symbolism** and refinements. The three most commonly in use are: (1) the Grimaud 'Marseilles' pack (seventeenth-century design); (2) the Rider-Waite pack, designed by A. E. **Waite** and artist Pamela Coleman-Smith (early twentieth century); and (3) the Thoth pack, designed by Aleister **Crowley** and artist Frieda Harris *c.* 1940. Of these, the somewhat flowery Rider-Waite pack is the most popular, though many question Waite's interpretations. Crowley's striking designs suit those who prefer to focus on more violent, up-to-date imagery; the Marseilles pack suits 'traditionalists'. Others may prefer the Tarot of the Witches, the **Golden Dawn** Tarot, the Aquarian Tarot, or even Salvador Dali's Tarot. The main thing is that the pack selected should 'speak' to the user in the sense that its images stimulate the creative imagination.

The imagery of the twenty-two trumps of the *Major Arcana* (which is often used as a separate pack in itself) has evolved over the centuries, and varies enormously among the many packs available. In effect, anyone can design their own pack: the problem is to design one that is mystically correct, or to choose (for divination or **meditation** purposes) one that suits personal requirements. Yet, despite the variety available, a common sequence is generally apparent, symbolically telling the tale of human evolution.

Taking the Waite derivations, the sequence is as follows:

0. *The Fool*. A brightly dressed youth about to walk over a cliff, his eyes fixed on the heavens. Over his shoulder a bundle containing his past; at his heels a dog (instinct?) barking of danger, which he ignores.
1. *The Magician*. A strong young man standing behind a table which bears sword, **wand**, cup and pentacle. His right hand points a wand up to the heavens, his left

hand points to the Earth. '*As above, so below*'.

2. *The High Priestess*. **Isis** seated between the pillars Boaz and Jachin; waxing crescent **moon** at her feet, the scroll of the Law (Torah) in her lap, the solar cross on her breast, her crown the horned moon.
3. *The Empress*. Venus, fertility, enthroned on Earth amid trees and wheat and flowing water. She is **Gaia**: fertility and abundance.
4. *The Emperor*. A stern old man, crowned, bearded and enthroned. He represents worldly leadership, authority (Jupiter) and its cares.
5. *The Hierophant*. The Pope, seated between two pillars, right hand raised in blessing, left hand holding the papal staff. Two monks kneel before him. He is masculine spiritual rule on Earth.
6. *The Lovers*. Adam and Eve naked in the Garden, backed by the Tree of Knowledge and the Tree of Life, the solar archangel watching over them. Adam (conscious) eyes Eve (unconscious) who eyes the **angel** (superconscious). The Trinity doubled.
7. *The Chariot*. A princely warrior in a chariot drawn by two sphinxes, one black and one white. There are no obvious reins. This is said to represent the relationship between conscious intelligence and instinct.
8. *Strength*. A young woman, the sign of eternity over her head, who holds open the jaws of a lion. The mastery of instinct through love.
9. *The Hermit*. A hooded monk looking down from a mountain, staff in one hand, lantern in the other. The lonely voyage of the **magus**.
10. *Wheel of Fortune*. A wheel in the sky bearing the letters T-A-R-O, alternating with the Hebrew letters for J-H-V-H (Yahweh, Jehovah). The Four Beasts of the **Apocalypse** read books in the corners of the card which expresses the workings of **karma**.
11. *Justice*. Crowned between two pillars she sits, sword raised in right hand, scales depending from left. Her eyes are wide open.
12. *The Hanged Man*. Serenely he hangs upside down, one foot tied to the junction of a Tau cross of living wood, arms bound behind him. He is **spirit** bound in matter, aware of the evolutionary necessity involved.
13. *Death*. Riding a white horse this armoured skeleton bears a black banner carrying a white rose. He looks down on a bishop who prays. The sun sets between two towers. Other decks show Death with a scythe, new life springing up from the bleached bones of dismembered skeletons.
14. *Temperance*. A winged angel, one foot on land, the other in water, pouring water from a cup in the left hand to a cup in its right. Flowering fertility lies about. The message is **tao**; the fruits of harmony.
15. *The Devil*. The horned goat-devil crouching on a pedestal, a naked man and woman (horned and tailed) chained to the pedestal. This is usually taken to mean material bondage; the triumph of desire over spirit.
16. *The Tower*. Two figures plunge from a lightning-struck tower to the rocks below – the consequence (Tower of Babel) of overweening ambition.
17. *The Star*. A naked woman on a shoreline, right foot on water, left knee on land. From pitchers in either hand she pours water both on earth and on water. The star above is surrounded by seven lesser stars. This is **Sirius** surrounded by the Pleiades. The woman is Aquarius.
18. *The Moon*. Between two towers a dog and a wolf howl at the Moon in its several phases. From the foreground sea crawls a crayfish. Shown here is an ideogram of subconscious evolution and instinctual impulses.
19. *The Sun*. A glorious naked child astride a white horse in a garden under the blazing sun. The divination is that of success and attainment.
20. *Judgement*. An archangel blows the Last Trump over a man, woman and child rising from the grave, their arms upraised in transformation.
21. *The World*. Within an oval wreath the naked Gaia dances, surrounded by the Four

Beasts of the Apocalypse – angel, eagle, lion and bull.

From these images (and their variations in other packs) a tarot reader seeks insight to problems personal or general by casting the cards by way of various systems which, like the **I Ching**, rely on **synchronicity**, alias the idea of 'meaningful coincidence', to generate useful information. As much depends upon the **intuition** of the 'fortune-teller' as upon a **symbolic** power in the cards themselves. Yet the images of the tarot cards are not accidental; they have been evolved by centuries, perhaps millennia, of human experience of the world's hidden laws, and so should not be despised.

TATTVA SYMBOLS (*See* **QABALAH, INNER PLANES, SYMBOL**) In Western **magic** the old **alchemical** division of the elements into earth, air, fire and water is still employed. The following **symbols** may be used in **visualisation** or pathworking; a *blue circle* for air; a *yellow square* for earth; a *red triangle* for fire, a *silver crescent* for water. Sometimes, too, the 'fifth element', ***spirit***, is visualised as an indigo egg.

These 'Tattvic' symbols structure what might otherwise become a chaotic journey into **subconscious** imagery, establishing a form of magical 'roadmap' similar to that created by the sephiroth and paths of the **Qabalistic Tree of Life**. By employing them the magician in effect tells his subconscious to focus only on specific paths of entry to the **inner planes**. The symbol is visualised at the crucial stage of the working between sleep and lucid dreaming. The magician imagines himself to be passing through the after-image or complementary colour of the Tattvic symbol.[1]

1. *Don Juan, Mescalito and Modern Magic*, Nevill Drury, Arkana, London 1986

TELEKINESIS (*See* **PSYCHOKINESIS**)

TELEPATHY (*See* **EXTRA-SENSORY PERCEPTION, PSI**) That direct mind-to-mind communication without recourse to the five senses occurs is a matter of common experience, particularly in the relationships between humans and animals, and also in **crisis** situations where an image of or message from a person in danger or dying is telepathically received by a distant relative or loved one.

The term was coined in 1882 by F. W. H. **Myers**. The first major study – the *Census of Hallucinations* – was published in 1890. Later work by Sir William Barrett (1845–1926), Sir Oliver **Lodge**, J. B. **Rhine** and others put the reality of telepathy on a scientific basis, though the *how* and *why* of it remain unclear. In the late 1950s a French press report of successful telepathy between a subject in the submerged submarine USS *Nautilus* and an agent onshore was denied by the US Navy, but the Soviets took it seriously enough to publish their own formerly secret research. Physiologist Dr Leonid Vasiliev in 1962 revealed that he and others, using **hypnotised** subjects to investigate 'mental radio', had made such subjects act by telepathic order. In one case, a woman psychosomatically paralysed down the left side of her body became able to move the paralysed limbs when Vasiliev commanded her to do so telepathically. This was demonstrated before observers, the woman being blindfold, each order being written down and witnessed before Vasiliev or his assistant relayed the mental order.

Russian biophysicist Yuri Kamensky (in Siberia) and actor-journalist Karl Nikolaiev (in Moscow) provided overwhelming evidence of telepathic communication. In one test Nikolaiev correctly described six objects given to Kamensky 2,000 miles away; and also identified twelve out of twenty **Zener** cards shown to Kamensky. With Nikolaiev wired to an EEG machine, the supervising scientists found that, as Kamensky began to transmit images, Nikolaiev's brain-waves altered. Devising a Morse technique, they asked Kamensky to imagine he was fighting Nikolaiev. Each time Kamensky did so, Nikolaiev's brain-waves altered. Imagining 'fights' lasting forty-five seconds (a dash) or fifteen seconds (a dot), Kamensky transmitted the Russian word *mig* ('instant').

One morning in 1980, eighty-one-year-old widow Isabel Casas entered a Barcelona police station, terrified by a **dream** in which she had seen the face of her neighbour Rafael Perez, a fifty-six-year-old chef, 'twisted in fear'. She had heard a voice saying, 'They are going to kill us.' The police found Perez tied up in a rooftop shed on the block of flats where he and Senora Casas lived. Two men had broken in, made him sign twenty-eight cheques making over his life savings to them, bound him, and threatened to return to kill him and Senora Casas once they had cashed all the money. The police duly ambushed and arrested the two men when they returned to the scene of the crime.[1]

Given all the evidence, what is more curious is not the existence of telepathy but our reluctance to credit it.

1. 'Messages in the Mind', Roy Stemman, *The Unexplained*, Orbis partwork, London 1983, pp. 34–7.

TELEPORTATION (*See* **GELLER, PHILADELPHIA EXPERIMENT, POLTERGEISTS**) 'Beam me up, Scotty.' *Star Trek* fans are familiar with the concept that physical bodies may be instantaneously transported through space from one location to another. To date the concept of teleportation remains pure science-fiction – or does it? The weird tale of Project Rainbow and the 'Philadelphia Experiment' is told elsewhere: how in 1943 the USS *Eldridge* was inadvertently teleported from the Philadelphia naval yard to Norfolk, Virginia, and back again. The phenomenon of **apports**, widely described by Victorian **Spiritualists**, at least suggests that the concept is not new. Controversial **psychic** Uri Geller has claimed to be the centre of a number of spontaneous teleportations affecting objects and people close to him. Indian mystic Sai Baba is said to perform materialisations of small objects from thin air, but refuses to operate under 'controlled' conditions. The phenomenon is also frequently reported in poltergeist cases.

In October 1593 a soldier reported for guard-duty at the palace in Mexico City. His uniform being wrong, he was questioned. He claimed to be stationed at Manila in the Philippines – the other side of the Pacific. He had no idea how he had got to Mexico. He was jailed, having told the authorities that the night before he had received his orders to report for duty the Governor of the Philippines had been killed. Two months later the news reached Mexico that the Governor had indeed been murdered. Released, the soldier duly returned to Manila.

No satisfactory theory exists to explain the mechanism of such events. If indeed it is possible to take apart the billions of constituent atoms in any one body, then somehow transport them, or the information as to their organisation, to a distant point, there to reassemble them exactly in their former arrangement, this is a science unknown . . . or forgotten.

Nonetheless, tales of such events persist.

TEMPLE, Robert K. G. (*See* **ANCIENT ASTRONAUTS, SIRIUS**)

TEMPORAL LOBE EPILEPSY (*See* **ABDUCTIONS, STREIBER, UFOs**) One rationalisation of UFO abduction cases is that they are an imaginary product of this illness. It is in the temporal lobe of the brain that sense is made of incoming perceptions. Those suffering temporal lobe epilepsy report *déjà vu*, inexplicable panic, strong smells, **hallucinatory** journeys, and a preoccupation with cosmic and philosophical matters.

American author Whitley Streiber describes in his book *Communion* how, at a loss to explain his own experience as an abductee, he seized on the possibility that temporal lobe epilepsy was responsible – or that his 'visitors' had somehow directly affected the temporal lobe. Subsequent tests established that he was not suffering this disorder.[1]

1. *Communion*, Whitley Streiber, Arrow, London 1988, pp. 128–30.

TESLA, Nikola (1856–1943) (*See* **LIGHTNING CALCULATORS**) Born in Smiljan in what is now Yugoslavia, at school this mathematical and engineering genius was often accused of cheating on the grounds that he gave his answers too fast to be believed. Yet until the end of his life he insisted that all his understanding came in flashes of **intuition**.

Emigrating to New York in 1884, he was soon employed by Edison, for whom he designed twenty-four types of dynamo. Branching out on his own, by 1888 he had been granted thirty patents for his inventions as an electrical engineer. Though now seldom credited as a pioneer, it is clear (as determined by the US Supreme Court the year he died) that he, not Marconi, discovered the tuned circuit on which radio is based. It also seems likely that he was the first to observe cathode rays, X-rays and ultraviolet radiation. He designed the first fluorescent lighting tube; in 1898 demonstrated a radio-controlled boat, and in 1899 built an experimental electrical power station at Colorado Springs. In 1912 he refused the Nobel Prize for physics: it is said he felt he should have received it in 1909 in place of Marconi.

It is also said he had such an accurate control of his imagination that he could mentally design a new dynamo or other device, set it to work in his mind, forget about it, then return to it days or weeks later to learn by mental observation if it was still working in all its parts.

In 1900 he embarked upon his 'World System' – a means of using the Earth's natural 'electrical vibrations' to provide cheap global power. The scheme came to nothing. Increasingly at odds with the scientific community, he went into a long decline, apparently a spent force. Yet, writing in 1934, he described an apparatus which suggests he had discovered the laser.

Described by Lord Kelvin as having 'contributed more to electrical science than any man up to his time, when Tesla died alone in Manhattan's New Yorker Hotel in 1943, FBI agents removed papers from his safe on the grounds that they might contain details of an important secret weapon'.[1]

Today in Belgrade there is a Nikola Tesla Museum. It may be that he was so far ahead of his time that we have yet to catch up with him.

1. *Prodigal Genius*, John J. O'Neill, Spearman, London 1968

THEOSOPHY (*See* **BESANT, BLAVATSKY, KRISHNAMURTI, LEADBETTER**) '**Karma** and **reincarnation**', wrote Helena Petrovna Blavatsky (1831–91), 'are in reality the ABC of theosophy.'

The term theosophy, an old synonym for the mystical quest, derives from the Greek words *theos*, 'god' and *sophia*, 'wisdom'. In New York in 1875 Russian noblewoman Madame Blavatsky and **Spiritualist** lawyer Henry Steel Olcott (1832–1907) adapted it to found the *Theosophical Society*. Since then the movement has spread worldwide. Popularising eastern esoteric teachings, oddly enough it revived interest in the teachings of karma and reincarnation not only in the West but also in the East, particularly among **Hindus** who, affected by Western materialism, had lost faith.

Gandhi was one man who regained interest in his own heritage following introduction to Theosophy. In 1975 the Indian government issued a stamp commemorating the

Society's centenary, reproducing on it the seal as well as the motto of the Society: 'There is No Religion Higher than Truth.'

Blavatsky emphasised that the movement was not confined to the wisdom of the East, but also to the rebirth of esoteric **Christianity** and to the 'revival of the work of Ammonius Saccas' (founder of **Neoplatonism**) who, she claimed, had tried 'to reconcile all religious schools, sects and nations under a common system of ethics, based on eternal verities'.

Purporting to be a modern revival of the most ancient traditions not only of humanity but of the **Earth Spirit** itself, Theosophy's doctrines emanated almost entirely from the writings and teachings of H. P. Blavatsky, though successors like Annie Besant expanded on these.

Blavatsky denied that the complex metaphysics revealed in *Isis Unveiled* (1877) and *The Secret Doctrine* (1888) originated with her. She claimed the information came from **discarnate** spiritual teachers with the initials M. and K. H. (standing for Morya and Koot Hoomi Lal Singh).

In *Isis Unveiled* she outlined an esoteric cosmology drawing on doctrines from all over the world. Today the movement retains the three objectives declared in this book. The first is 'to form the nucleus of a Universal Brotherhood of Humanity, without distinction of race, creed, sex, caste or colour'. The second, initially, 'to promote the study of Aryan and other Eastern literatures, **religions** and sciences', was later expanded to 'the comparative study of ancient and modern religions, philosophies, and sciences'. The third was 'to investigate unexplained laws of nature and the **psychical** powers of man'.

Isis Unveiled was a modest success. Upset by attacks on her by D. D. **Home**, Blavatsky and Olcott removed the fledgling society to India, where further accusations of **fraud** pursued her. Back in Europe, by now dying of Bright's Disease, she wrote *The Secret Doctrine* (1888). In this vast, rambling document she maintains that truth and wisdom are largely lost to modern mankind. The universe and man are older, more complex and elevated than either science or modern religion understands. Yet fragments of a 'Parent doctrine . . . have survived geological and political cataclysms to tell the story; and every survival shows that the now *Secret* Wisdom was once the fountain head.' So she wrote in her introduction. She claims that the main part of the 'secret books' and 'esoteric records' are to be found scattered in thousands of Sanskrit manuscripts, with many aspects preserved in the wisdom literature of the world's sacred traditions.

She retails a history beginning millions of years ago, when the 'Lords of Flame' first impregnated terrene matter with the vital spark of life. Subsequently, five 'Root Races' have emerged on Earth, each perishing in a cataclysm changing the face of the world, and each engendering its successor. Each, save the first, began in the declining years of its predecessor: the cataclysms were the culmination of natural cycles.

The first Root Race were the Chhayas, or 'Shadows': ethereal beings of fire-mist originating near the North Pole in a time before Earth condensed into solid form. The 'continent', the 'Imperishable Sacred Land', cannot be destroyed. The second 'Hyperborean' race inhabited northern Asia and was sufficiently material to split into the two sexes. The third '**Lemurian**' race were anthropoid **telepathic giants** occupying a continent now drowned by the Indian Ocean. Twenty-seven feet tall, they flourished one million years ago. The fourth were Atlanteans, destroyed by their own **black magic** when their continent broke up and sank some 800,000 years ago, though some survived until as recently as 12,000 years ago, when the island remnant of **Atlantis** submerged. We, the 'Aryan' constitute the Fifth Root Race: we came into being about 850,000 years ago, before the First Glacial Period.

She claimed that **pole shift** caused the Ice Ages. In speaking of such global disturbances she drew heavily on the Book of **Enoch** and on Egyptian astronomical records, commenting on the statement made by Egyptian priests to the Greek historian Herodotus (fifth century BC) that the sun has not always risen where it rises now.

The Sixth Root Race, she said, will evolve from us to return to a risen Lemuria, while the seventh will leave Earth to inhabit Mercury.

The sense of her style is given by the following extract, in which she discusses the relationship between modern and **occult** science:

'There can be no possible conflict between the teachings of occult and so-called exact science, where the conclusions of the latter are grounded on a substratum of unassailable fact. It is only when its more ardent exponents, over-stepping the limits of observed phenomena in order to penetrate into the arcana of Being, attempt to wrench the formation of Kosmos and its *living* force from **Spirit**, and attribute all to blind matter, that the Occultists claim the right to dispute and call in question their theories. Science cannot, owing to the very nature of things, unveil the mystery of the universe about us. Science can, it is true, collect, classify and generalise upon phenomena; but the occultist, arguing from admitted metaphysical data, declares that the daring explorer, who would probe the inmost secrets of Nature, must transcend the narrow limitations of sense, and transfer his consciousness into the region of noumena and primal causes. To effect this he must develop faculties which are absolutely dormant – save in a few rare and exceptional cases – in the constitution of our Race.'

Having reviewed this remarkable book Annie Besant met Blavatsky, who chose her as the new leader of the movement. Subsequently, despite many schisms, Theosophy has flourished, and retains many followers today.[2,3]

1. *Collected Writings*, Vols. 1–14, H. P. Blavatsky, Theosophical Publishing House, Wheaton, Illinois, USA 1966–85.
2. *Isis Unveiled*, H. P. Blavatsky, Theosophical Publishing House, 1972.
3. *The Secret Doctrine*, H. P. Blavatsky, Theosophical Publishing House, 1988.

THIRD EYE (*See* **PINEAL GLAND**)

THOUGHT-FORMS (*See* **BEARDEN, DASKALOS, ELEMENTALS, TIBET, UFOs**) It is an **occult** cliché that the material world and its causes and effects proceed from activity of the mind, and thus that *thought* in itself has an effective power not usually granted it by those considering it to be purely *abstract*. According to occultists, thought, whether conscious or not, is so potent that its projected forms literally shape that outer reality which customarily we believe to be thrust upon us by Fate, God or Circumstance.

Thus the world we suffer is one which *we ourselves* create.

TIBET (*See* **DALAI LAMA, DAVID-NEEL**) 'Tibetans do not believe in *miracles*, that is to say, in ***supernatural*** happenings,' wrote Alexandra David-Neel. 'They consider the extraordinary facts which astonish us to be the work of *natural* energies which come into action in exceptional circumstances, or through the skill of someone who *knows* how to release them.' She added, 'Tibetans also tend to believe that everything which one imagines can be realised. They claim that if the imagined facts correspond to no external reality, one could not conceive of their images.'[1]

Today Tibet is enslaved by the Chinese autocracy. The Dalai Lama, the land's spiritual leader (called 'Precious Protector'), said to be the *tulku* or **reincarnation** of many before him, has been in exile since 1959. Condemned Tibetans have their tongues hooked out lest they cry for his return. Yet he says that he forgives the Chinese. He believes that their tyranny harms them more than it harms the Tibetans they murder. From a Western viewpoint this attitude is as extraordinary as the tales of Tibetan magic.

These concern powers of invisibility, mind-generated **entities** (***tulpas***), lamas incarnated or emanated from former bodhisatvas (*tulkus*), men able to generate extra body-heat to survive the Himalayan nights naked (***tumo***), messages 'sent on the wind' (**telepathy**), and doctrines as in the *Bardo Thödol* (***Tibetan Book of the Dead***), instructing the newly-dead on how to deal with phenomena encountered on the after-death plane.

Doubting stories of *tulpas* so energetic as to escape their maker's control, David-Neel visualised and animated such a phantom herself. Choosing for her experiment 'a monk, short and fat, of an innocent and jolly type', after long concentration this *tulpa* 'grew gradually *fixed* and lifelike', and 'became a kind of guest' in her apartment. When she went travelling, 'the monk included himself in the party' and grew independent. 'The fat, chubby-cheeked fellow grew leaner, his face assumed a vaguely mocking, sly, malignant look. He became more troublesome and bold. In short,' she confesses, 'he escaped my control.' Deciding to dissolve him, she succeeded, with difficulty.

'My mind-creature was tenacious of life,' she writes. 'There is nothing strange in the fact that I may have created my own **hallucination**. The interesting point is that in these cases of materialisation, others see the **thought-forms** that have been created.'[2]

She adds that Tibetans disagree in explaining such phenomena. Some think a material form is really brought into being; others consider the **apparition** merely a case of suggestion, the creator's thought impressing others and causing them to see as he sees.

Equally fantastic is her account of *tulkus*, phantom bodies more lasting than *tulpas*. Tibetans hold a *tulku* to be the reincarnation of a saint or sage, or the incarnation of a non-human entity. Such beings may remember their former lives and, at death, select their future parents and place of birth. Many lamas are thought to be the *tulkus* of departed saints, though not every *tulku* is a lama. The *tulku*-manifestation is not necessarily the sole form in which the originating entity resides. So the present Dalai Lama may be but the *tulku* of another being residing elsewhere. He is but the latest of many Dalai Lama *tulkus*. On this basis reincarnations of such beings are sought and found. Lamaists hold that an unspecified period elapses between death and rebirth. Traditionally two years elapse after the death of a high lama before his reincarnation is sought. If he left no specific directions concerning his rebirth, an astrologer seeks signs that reveal the new *tulku*. Once a child fitting the prescribed conditions is found, objects (rosaries, books, etc.) are set before him. Identification of those belonging to the late *tulku* is required. David-Neel drily notes that, where a *tulku*-successor to a wealthy monastery or estate is sought, several plausible contenders may emerge, causing strife among the parents and **clairvoyants** responsible for the decision.

Yet she describes observing a child who, brought as reincarnated *tulku* to an unknown house, told where a certain china cup, its location unknown even to the steward of the house, would be found – as it was.

Such events are not thought odd by Tibetans. David-Neel insists that they employ telepathy as Westerners use radio, to send messages 'on the wind'. Some Tibetans claim telepathy is a science like any other, accessible to those properly taught and able to put theory into practice. She wonders if Tibet's height and silence encourage development of such powers. Tarthang Tulku, a Lama at the Nyingma Institute in Berkeley, California, suggests that they are the result of arduous discipline.[3]

Both points make sense. A high, remote, silent environment also seems to aid **psychism** among Highland Gaels (**second sight**), the **Hopi** of Arizona, etc. Likewise, hard work and self-discipline aids such development.

'I do not care whether you believe or not in these phenomena', a hermit told David-Neel, 'and I have no desire to convince you. I am not a juggler giving theatrical performances.'[4]

Does this explain the Dalai Lama's attitude? If the world is illusory, what matter *who* rules? 'A flag moves. What is it that moves? The flag, or the wind?' The answer to this Tibetan riddle? 'It is the mind that moves.' Which leads to the most important issue: 'Inasmuch as all mankind must relinquish their fleshly bodies and experience death, it is supremely profitable that they should know how rightly to meet death when it comes.'[5]

1. *Magic and Mystery in Tibet*, Alexandra David-Neel, Abacus, London 1977.
2. *Ibid.*, p. 221ff.
3. *The Roots of Consciousness*, Jeffrey Mishlove, Random House, New York 1975, p. 311.
4. *op. cit.* ref. 1, p. 12.
5. *The Tibetan Book of the Dead*, ed. W. Y. Evans-Wentz, Oxford University Press 1927.

TIBETAN BOOK OF THE DEAD (*See* **NEAR-DEATH EXPERIENCES**) Under this title the *Bardo Thödol* (Liberation by Hearing on the After-Death Plane) was published in the West in 1927, edited by W. Y. **Evans-Wentz** from a translation by Lāma Kazi Dawa-Samdup (the guide given by the Dalai Lama to **David-Neel** at the start of her fourteen-year Tibetan journey).

The eighth-century Mahayana **Buddhist** text arises from older oral teaching describing the after-death states. Comprising liturgies read over those dying or newly dead, it explains the after-death **hallucinations** so that rebirth may be avoided. The information is said to have come from lamas recalling their own former deaths. It is recognised that few avoid rebirth, due to continued after-death involvement in ***sangsāric*** delusion. Yet the possibility of liberation exists. The text aims to persuade the deceased that the essence of **consciousness** is divine, and that identification with the divine is the purpose of life. The individual must recognise that he *is* dead, not just dreaming. He must recognise the chief symptoms of death. These are called: (1) 'earth sinking into water'; (2) 'water sinking into fire'; and (3) 'fire sinking into air'. And as he dies he must try to stay conscious, focussed not on fear of death but on compassion and love.

In dying, the departing consciousness preferably leaves the body by means of the '**brahmanic** aperture', or crown of the head. There should be no break in consciousness during this separation from human to the **etheric** 'Bardo' body – which, as western **occultism** also teaches, is a duplicate of the abandoned physical body and subject to the same desires.

Initially the deceased may not realise he is dead. Sight and hearing may persist. Confused, he sees friends and relatives mourning and tries to tell them, 'I'm still here!' – but they can't sense him. He may deny his own passage to the Bardo plane; thus **ghosts** require **exorcism** before they go away – remaining imaginatively bound to bodily life, being ignorant of or denied this teaching to begin with.

The period of *Bardo* existence is symbolically described as lasting forty-nine days between death and rebirth. The first part of the text (*Chikhai Bardo*) describes events at the moment of death. The supreme insight (vision of the Clear Light) is vouchsafed, offering the greatest chance of liberation. This being refused in fear, as is likely, the second part (*Chönyid Bardo*) describes the **dream**-states that follow death, also the onset of the **karmic** illusions marking the start of descent back to rebirth. If liberation is not attained, the mind grows estranged from the illuminative lights in its plunge back to rebirth through terrifying visions. These, consisting of the experience of the 'wrathful' and 'peaceful' deities, are described as projections created by the **psyche**. Yet, while projections, they are *real*. The third part (*Sidpa Bardo*) covers the onset of the birth instinct and subsequent prenatal events.

From a Western viewpoint the main problem is not just that of accepting this metapsychology, nor even the idea of rebirth, but in accepting the assertion that *all* metaphysical beings and manifestations (gods, devils and God the Father Almighty) are (unrecognised) reflections of our own **soul**-activity. Precisely the *central purpose* of the text is to explain this to the dying or newly dead person, thus making it possible for the soul to recover the implicit divinity it lost or forgot upon its (previous) birth, and escape forever the world of illusion, *Maya*.

A true teaching? We shall all find out . . . though maybe we shall forget again . . .

1. *The Tibetan Book of the Dead*, ed. W. Y. Evans-Wentz, Oxford University Press, 1927.

TIGHE, Virginia (*See* **MURPHY**)

TIME (*See* **CYCLES, DUNNE, PRECOGNITION**) '*What is time*?' St Augustine asked nearly 1600 years ago, answering, 'When I do not ask myself the question, I know the answer.' A century earlier Plotinus had declared, 'Time is a measure of movement.'

Tiine's enigma is bound up in our **consciousness** of it. Unconscious, we are unaware of time. Does 'time' even exist without the consciousness that marks its passage via the events, cycles, rhythms, growth and decay that give it substance?

Different cultures experience time differently. The **megalith**-builders (**Stonehenge**, etc.) were concerned not with hours and minutes but with the celestial rhythms that mark seasonal variations in fertility. They sensed time in terms of *process*. The Mayans of Yucatan were obsessed with time, their priests perceiving a cyclic rhythm thought to repeat itself every 260 years, so that new historic events were necessarily the echo of previous events obeying the same rhythm. Likewise the ancient Greek Stoics held that the return of the planets to specific relative positions guaranteed the reenactment of cosmic events as reflected in human history. Once again: As above, so below. The Western notion of time in terms of the *time-clock* (a monastic invention, presaging industrial capitalism and labour by the hour) was unknown in mediaeval times. Folk worked according to sun, moon, hunger and seasonal requirement. The *wristwatch*, ticking off the seconds to tell us *how much time we have* before we have to do *this* or *that*, is perhaps the product of modern labour relations. In the city's artificial environment today, *natural time* is largely ignored.

This abstraction from *natural* (solar, lunar) to *clock* time encouraged the linear Western concept of time as a river rolling inexorably from Past to Future via the eternally experienced Present – a cosmic process reduced to mere material need. Today this seems fatally flawed, dealt a body-blow by Relativity Theory as by the evidence of **Dunne** and other researchers into the mysteries of precognition. For if time is linear, how can future events be 'fixed' so precisely as (in some cases) to be foreseen? How can what is not yet come to pass already exist?

How to explain mental events such as described by historian Arnold Toynbee who, seated above Pharsalus in Greece in 1912, found himself in what later he called a 'time-pocket'. Meditating on the Battle of Pharsalus (197 BC), he found himself not in the sunlight of 1912, but caught in a heavy mist, watching the massacre of the Macedonian army by the Romans. The hallucination was so real that he averted his eyes from the horror of it. He was *there* – or, rather, *then*.

Such experiences of **phantom battles** are not uncommon. They belong to the same 'out of time' process as precognition, incomprehensible only in terms of a mechanistic, historical approach to time. The sensations of *déjà vu* (meaning: *already seen*), of arriving at a place for the first time yet seeming to know it well, or of *presque vu* (*almost seen*), where events on the edge of conscious realisation tantalise the mind with imminent but unfulfilled appearance, seem to belong to this same process.

Likewise the 'time-slip' experience of Anne Moberley and Eleanor Jourdain, two middle-aged English schoolteachers on holiday in France in 1901. Visiting Versailles, they approached the château of the Petit Trianon, immersed in conversation, and only gradually realised that the landscape and people they saw about them did not belong to 1901. Instead, it later appeared, they had somehow found themselves walking in the gardens of the Trianon on 10 August 1792, amid the French Revolution. Though later they returned, the events did not repeat themselves.

Astronomer Fred Hoyle has called the notion of time as an ever-rolling stream, 'a grotesque and absurd illusion'. Hoyle insists that everything that was and will be exists 'all the time', and that the consciousness that gives us the sense of history, of Past and Future, is in fact an illusion.[1]

This scientific endorsement of **Buddhist** thought is startling.

From the **Quantum** viewpoint, in which mu-meson particles can arrive at their destination before they started, our perception of time is purely a function of our own consciousness and its expectations. If our perception is flawed, then no wonder that paradoxes arise. Such paradoxes (beloved by science fiction writers: if you go back in time to murder your own grandfather, could you exist?) arise not from nature but from our own imperfect understanding. We impose a mechanism, a chronology, which falls into paradox as soon as we try to apply it to events that refuse to fit our **paradigm**. So the temptation arises to deny the events as '**paranormal**' or illusory, just to defend the paradigm. So too Galileo's doctors refused to look through the telescope to see the moons of Jupiter. Thus precognition and other events denying orthodox belief are today dismissed purely because they embarrass orthodox belief in linear time by revealing it as false.

Yet still, despite all the revolutionary post-**Einstein** theories with regard to 'space-time'; despite the imagery of theoretical **black holes** in which gravity is so intense that time collapses, we understand time no more than people in the era of Augustine and Plotinus. Time remains a mystery of our consciousness. When we feel energetic and active, time runs fast. When we are depressed, it drags on leaden obscuring wings.

'And have I forgotten forever what I must forget for the time being? Or is it that I should lose so much time? Lose time? What need have I for haste? Is not the whole of eternity mine?'[2]

1. *Timewarps*, John Gribbin, Sphere, London 1979, p. 56.
2. *Education of the Human Race*, G. E. Lessing (1729–81).

TIR NAN OG (*See* **CELTIC MAGIC**) The mythical Celtic paradise, sited over the sea to the west, where **time** stands still and where there is no longer any worldly grief for the heroes who have earned this remission. Like Avalon, Tir nan Og is an enchanted land, outside human spacetime. When Bran and his crew returned from their voyage to the western paradise, they were warned not to set foot on mortal shore again, for a hundred years and a day had passed – in mortal time.

One sailor tried it – and crumbled into dust.

TRANCE (*See* **HYPNOTISM, MEDIUMS**)

TRANSCENDENTALISM (*See* **REINCARNATION**) This nineteenth-century philosophical movement explaining matter and the universe as the products of mental conception rather than material process, was born in the USA in 1836 when a group of Unitarians, believers in the divinity of Nature and the continuity of **soul**-life after death, revolted against the 'corpse-cold Unitarianism' of their Harvard associates. Led by Ripley, Hedge and Ralph Waldo Emerson (1803–82), they formed the Transcendental Club of America to advance ideas anciently taught in India, Persia and Greece, and espoused in Europe by Kant, **Goethe**, Wordsworth, Coleridge and Carlyle. Studying the Platonic philosophers in the original Greek, their vigorous search for spiritual truth influenced many, including poets Walt Whitman and Emily Dickinson, the founders of the British Labour Party, Gandhi and Martin Luther King. Presaging **Theosophical** and modern **New Age** interests (Emerson coined the expression 'do your thing'), their viewpoint was refreshingly original.

Emerson wrote in his final essay, 'It is the secret of the world that all things subsist and do not die, but only retire a little from sight and afterwards return again . . . Nothing is dead; men feign themselves dead, and endure mock funerals and mournful obituaries, and there they stand looking out of the window, sound and well, in some strange new disguise.'[1]

1. 'Nominalist and Realist', from *The Selected Writings of Ralph Waldo Emerson*, ed. Brooks Atkinson, Modern Library, New York 1950, p. 445.

TRANSCENDENTAL MEDITATION (*See* **LEVITATION, MANTRA**) Introduced to the West by Maharishi Mahesh Yogi ('the Giggling Guru') via the celebrated (if brief) interest of the Beatles, transcendental meditation (TM) consists of two twenty-minute sessions of **meditation** daily, during which the devotee repeats a special **mantra**. TM does appear to have beneficial effects, lowering the blood-pressure, slowing the heart-beat and reducing oxygen demand, though some of the claims made by members of the movement have raised eyebrows. In the San Francisco Bay Area during the late 1970s they claimed to have reduced the crime-rate through meditation, while at the Maharishi's Swiss headquarters other students were taught to **levitate**, following a stringent mental training. 'People would rock gently,' said one student, 'then more and more, and then start lifting off into the air. You should really be in a lotus position to do it – you can hurt yourself landing if you've got a dangling undercarriage.'

Drawing on existing techniques of meditation without developing insights or methods not already known in older systems, as a simple digest of existing **yogic** knowledge TM has stimulated wide Western interest in the practices involved. Courses remain widely available.

TRANSMUTATION (*See* **ALCHEMY**)

TREE OF LIFE (*See* **DRUIDS, QABALAH**) The central organisational glyph of Qabalah is an ancient global **symbol** for the junction of the three worlds (heaven, earth and water); also for the *omphalos* (world-navel) and *axis mundi*. It also symbolises the Great Mother or feminine principle in her nourishing, sheltering aspect. As found in Genesis it is both the Tree of Life and Tree of Knowledge in the Garden of Eden: as the former it signifies regeneration; as the latter it signifies knowledge of Good and Evil. As such, in many traditions, not just in the Bible, it is associated with the fall of the first man from paradisal bliss. In the Sumerian Garden the **serpent** represents cosmic fertilisation of Mother Earth, Eve; in Norse mythology the Serpent of Midgard coils about the roots of the World-Tree Yggdrasil.

Likewise the dying god is always killed on a tree; thus the Crucifixion of Christ on the Tree, or Cross, agrees with this old **pagan** tradition. The Celtic **Druids**, or 'Men of the Oak', venerated the oak above other trees not least as the oak, growing above water, is so often lightning-struck – yet again, though obliquely, a connection with the serpent (lightning).

Tree-climbing (as in *Jack and the Beanstalk*, or in the visions of **Black Elk**) symbolises ascent from one plane of reality to another in order to obtain magical knowledge or **shamanic** powers. In this context the **birds** that nest in the Tree are often perceived as **spirit**-guides or messengers.

TRIANON TIME-SLIP (*See* **TIME**)

TULKUS (*See* **TIBET**)

TULPAS (*See* **BUDDHISM, DAVID-NEEL, TIBET**)

TUMO (*See* **TIBET**) By this controlled development of 'inner heat' it is said that Tibetan **yogis** could (or can) survive Himalayan nights at great altitude – naked. The final test for a would-be adept of *tumo* was certainly stringent. Not only was the student required to sit naked all night long on the ice of a frozen river, he was also required to dry, by his body-heat alone, a sheet dipped through a hole in the ice into the freezing river and draped about him – not once but seven times during the course of the night.

TUNGUSKA EVENT Early on 30 June 1908 a fireball shot across the sky 500 miles north-west of Lake Baikal in Siberia and exploded forty miles from the trading post of Vanavara, knocking farmer S. B. Semenov unconscious and off his feet. He came to amid earth tremors that broke his barn door and shattered windows.

The explosion occurred over the remote forest region of Tunguska. For twenty miles around, trees were knocked down and the forest was set ablaze. No living animals were left. The effects were felt for 600 miles round about, there were reports of a mysterious 'black rain' and microbarograph records indicated that atmospheric shock waves had circled the Earth twice.

Bright crimson hues in the sky were reported faraway in Europe: in England the night grew so radiant that soon after midnight on 1 July it was possible to read large print indoors.

The event remained unexplored until 1921. Soviet mineralogist Leonard Kulik, convinced that it must have been caused by a huge iron meteorite, began planning the expedition he undertook in 1927. On struggling through the devastated region and finally reaching the centre of the blast area he found not the expected crater, but a frozen swamp and a stand of trees which, though at the blast-centre, had survived. Whatever had caused the explosion, it had never reached the ground. Local Tungus tribespeople, claiming that the area had been visited by the god of fire, also reported that, after the blast, many of their reindeer had broken out in scabs. Kulik found no evidence of his meteorite.

In 1930 English meteorologist F. J. W. Whipple suggested that the event had been caused by the entry into the Earth's atmosphere of a small comet which had shattered explosively in mid-air. Yet no comet had been seen in the sky before the sudden appearance of the fireball followed by the blast.

Since then many bizarre theories have been proposed to explain this still-inexplicable event. One is that a tiny **black hole** blasted into the Earth and continued through. If so, it should have re-emerged in the North Atlantic, departing as violently as it arrived. Another, proposed in 1946 by Soviet science fiction writer Alexander Kazantsev, is that the event involved the explosion of a nuclear-powered spaceship, plummeting out of control into the atmosphere and overheating until the engine blew up. The report of reindeer breaking out in scabs has been taken by modern writers like John Baxter to indicate radiation burns.[1]

Between 1958 and 1962 Soviet geochemist Kirill Florensky led three expeditions to the area. His team traced a line of cosmic dust stretching 150 miles north-west of the site, composed of **magnetite**, vitrified droplets of rock, and metal and silicate particles fused together. He concluded that these were the vapourised remains of a comet's head. Even so, the 'nuclear blast' theory persisted, fuelled by findings of excess radiocarbon in tree rings worldwide in the year following the event. However these findings lay within the range of normal fluctuation and were localised.

The evidence suggests that the cometary theory is correct – not that this is reassuring. What happens once can happen again.[2]

1. *The Fire Came By*, John Baxter and Thomas Atkins, Macdonald and Jane's, London 1976.
2. 'The Great Siberian Fireball', Ian Ridpath, *The Unexplained*, Orbis partwork, London 1983, pp. 1030–33 and pp. 1058–60.

U

UFOs (*See* **ABDUCTIONS, ADAMSKI, ANCIENT ASTRONAUTS**) Reports of UFOs (Unidentified Flying Objects) are ancient. A mediaeval Irish account (also recorded in the thirteenth-century Norse *Speculum Regale*) described how, 'One day the monks of Clonmacnoise were holding a meeting on the floor of the church, and as they were at their deliberations there they saw a ship sailing over them in the air, going as if it were on the sea. When the crew of the ship saw the meeting and the inhabited place below them, they dropped anchor, and the anchor came right down on to the floor of the church, and the priests seized it. A man came down out of the ship after the anchor, and he was swimming as if he were in the water, till he reached the anchor; and they were dragging him down then. "For God's sake let me go!" said he, "For you are drowning me." Then he left them, swimming in the air as before, taking his anchor with him.'[1]

The modern UFO cult began on 24 June 1947. Businessman Kenneth Arnold, flying his private plane, saw nine shining discs flying near Mount Rainier, Washington State, USA. Later he told a reporter that these discs moved as a saucer would 'if you skipped it across the water'.

This initial 'flying saucer' report gained credibility in January 1948 when USAF Captain Thomas Mantell, flying a P–51 Mustang fighter, between Georgia and Kentucky, chased a round white object. Climbing too high too fast, he blacked out. His plane went into a fatal dive. UFO sightings so multiplied that in 1952 a USAF investigation into the Mantell event was expanded into **Project Blue Book**'. This led to the 1968 Condon Report, which explained away or denied all UFO sightings as hoax, illusion or error. Astrophysicist J. Allen **Hynek**, who developed the **Close Encounter** system of definition while a Blue Book consultant, later asserted that the Project had been a cover-up.[2]

But for what? And why? There are four main possibilities. One, those in authority cover up information to avoid social turmoil. Two, they are as confused as everyone else, but won't admit it. Three, they have to deny evidence that offends or shocks their own belief-systems. Four, they are right: UFOs are purely the product of imagination or hysteria.

Whatever the truth, by the mid–1950s accounts of UFO sightings, like that by George Adamski, who claimed he had met Venusians in the California desert and visited UFO lunar bases, became bestsellers. Hollywood movies like *Invasion of the Bodysnatchers* and *Red Planet Mars* exploited paranoia about Communism. Meanwhile sightings not only of flying saucers but flying cigars (the parent ships of scouting saucer ships) abounded. And not only sightings, but physical contact, and even abductions.

Cases of the latter typically involve individuals driving or isolated at night prior to the encounter; the failure of electrical equipment; an experiential time-lapse, and later recollection (under **hypnosis**) of buried memory involving medical and sexual experiments imposed by the abducting aliens. Brazilian farmer Antonio Villas-Boas claimed to have been taken into a saucer where two 'little men' took blood samples before introducing him to a lovely naked lipless girl who seduced him. His case, as with that of Barney and Betty Hill, or (more recently) Whitley **Streiber**, is as **archetypal** as those in which contactees (like Adamski) are told to warn the world against nuclear energy.

The phenomenon seemed entirely modern. Yet soon it was noted that it persists in every era, all over Earth. The Clonmacnoise account is matched by many reports in the USA in 1897 of slow-flying 'airships' from which, in one case, a man was seen descending a rope. The term 'flying saucer' was used in 1878. Japanese records from 1180 mention a flying 'earthenware vessel'. Changing course in mid-air, it left a luminous trail. Mediaeval French chronicles tell of men on 'cloudships'. In 1491 seven men 'made of air' with 'shining shoes' visited Facius Cardan in Italy. Tales of flying craft (*vimanas*) in the Hindu ***Mahabharata***, and the visions of **prophets** like Ezekiel and **Enoch** are quoted by Blumrich, Downing, Drake, and **Von Däniken** as 'evidence' of alien intervention in human affairs since early times.

Typically such aliens are said to come from Mars or Venus, or from the hypothetical planets of nearby stars like **Sirius**. It is darkly claimed that they have not only persistently interfered in human affairs, but (as **angels, demons, elementals, fairies**, etc.) have bred with or genetically altered humanity. In *Secret Places of the Lion* Dr George Hunt Williamson (a friend of Adamski) said 'spacemen' told him, via **automatic writing**, how they came to Earth eighteen million years ago (as **Blavatsky** dates the arrival of the 'Lords of Flame') and built the **Great Pyramid** a mere 24,000 years ago.

Such claims only cloud an already obscure picture. The data is so various that it serves any particular theory simply by selectivity.

Some writers assert that UFOs are hostile, and that the sightings are of reconnaissance vehicles preparing invasion. Others, like Brinsley Le Poer Trench, hypothesise the presence of two kinds of 'sky people', one ancient and friendly, the other recent and sinister.

Carl **Jung** speculated that UFOs are a symbolic manifestation of human unconscious content 'projected' into the sky, the disc or 'saucer' being a **mandala**, expressing our common anxiety about the Bomb and modern science in general. Yet he admitted his unease at the notion of a 'materialised **psychism**' – a literal, physical manifestation in the skies of unconscious human mental content (as with the **Fatima** visions in Portugal in 1917).[3]

Latterly he accepted that *some* UFOs cannot be explained by psychic means alone. His theory survives in revised form in the '**psychotronic**' speculations of **Bearden**, etc., embracing mysteries like **corn circles** and **cattle mutilations**.

Hollow Earth theorists like Richard S. Shaver claimed that UFOs came from an advanced civilisation living inside the Earth. **Bermuda Triangle** fans thought the phenomena originated in other **dimensions**, or via time-slip from **Atlantis**. Others like John A. **Keel**, intrigued by the bizarre reports of '**Men in Black**', pointed out the similarity of UFO-behaviour to old reports of fairy activity, asserting that not only has the UFO enigma always been with us, but that it is associated with specific 'window areas' on Earth where geomagnetic conditions encourage it. Jacques **Vallée** and John **Michell** also point out this similarity between UFO behaviour and the folklore of fairy faith. Magical flying craft, beautiful alien beings, abduction of humans by aliens/fairies into other worlds where other laws prevail, the distortion of space and time – there is nothing new about it.

French researcher Aimé Michel's theory of 'orthotenies' linked UFOs with the **ley-lines** interconnecting old **megalithic** sites. Ideas that leys were lines of telluric force used by ancient people and visiting spacecraft were developed by **Lethbridge**, etc. Such notions, emerging during the 1960s, were later revised by Paul Devereux and others (*see below*).

To summarise, before continuing:

Thinkers confronted by the new UFO phenomena first publicised in 1947 (two years after Hiroshima) quickly divided into two camps.

The first camp insists on the objective external reality of UFOs as visitation by beings from 'outer space', with all the corollaries of threat and salvation. Those belonging to this camp maintain the 'Extraterrestrial Hypothesis' (ETH), explaining such phenomena as intervention by superior (God-like) beings, whose purpose is justified in comprehensible human terms – e.g. conquest, education, genetic experimentation, interstellar war requiring convenient planetary outpost and so on.

The second camp insists on the 'psychic' aspect. UFO phenomena arise from forgotten **archetypes** buried deep in the **collective unconscious**.

What if (as Keel and Vallée claim) both camps purvey aspects of a wider truth that lies beyond our current understanding?

Since the 1960s, those advocating the psychic-geophysical approach have linked UFOs with seismic-related sources and human perception of resulting phenomena. Canadian scientists Michael Persinger and Gyslaine Lafrèniere, studying 1242 UFO and **Fortean** events, concluded, 'the data consistently point towards seismic-related sources'.

Such theorists connect production of electric fields through pressure on rock **crystals** with perception of phenomena visible not only as columns of light, or as anomalous electrical systems such as 'ball lightning', but with the direct stimulation of the electrical systems of the percipient brain, leading to dreamlike states and complex visual imagery.

Is this why UFO events are perceived in the cultural terminology of the contactee – space visitors to modern American or European, Virgin Mary to a Catholic, demons to a mediaeval **Qabalist**, or **Isis** to an ancient Egyptian?

In 1982 English UFO researcher Paul Devereux published a closely argued thesis connecting UFOs not only with geological faults and intrusions, but with megalithic circles, barrows, etc., sited on precisely such fault zones (holy places) where UFO manifestations are, even today, most common.

Like **acupuncture** meridians, these sites represent specific zones where geomagnetic energies manifest. Here 'UFO phenomena' erupt to interact not only with the atmosphere but with the electrical fields of the human brain. Plastic, like 'planetary ectoplasm', they take any form willed upon them by the preconception, unconscious or otherwise, of the observer. Objective forms are thus produced, though the viewer may not realise his involvement in their production. Such forms take the shape of pre-existing or expected archetypes (Virgin Mary or flying saucer) as projected by the viewer. The energies involved, arising equally from the depths of the planet and the human mind, are of a potency which reason alone cannot comprehend. The UFO experience, Devereux argues, is thus essentially psychic. This is not so terrible given the will to identify with the forces involved, but given our modern rejection of the 'primitive' or '**pagan**', the consequences of such experience may well result in terror.[4]

Devereux thus relates UFO phenomena to the 'geophysical knowledge and psychic expertise' of our ancestors who built the megalithic and ley-line system. This is an interesting theory. It may even provide a piece of the jigsaw. Yet still we remain in the dark. UFO phenomena still stretch our imagination to the breaking-point. Theories claiming to explain the UFO mystery are useful, if only in that they provide interim rationalisations of a set of phenomena which seem to mock all rationalisation.

Perhaps the openly acknowledged bemusement of long-term researchers like Jacques Vallée is more valuable. The fact is nobody knows what UFOs are, which is why they are called UFOs. It is as easy to advance a spurious explanation as it is to deny the reality of the phenomenon. What is much harder is to live with the continuing uncertainty.[5]

1. *A Celtic Miscellany*, K. H. Jackson, Penguin, London 1971, p. 165.
2. *The UFO Experience: A Scientific Enquiry*, J. Allen Hynek, Regnery, Chicago 1972
3. *Flying Saucers: A Modern Myth of Things seen in the Sky*, C. G. Jung, Harcourt Brace, New York 1959
4. *Earthlights*, Paul Devereux, Turnstone, London 1982
5. *Dimensions*, Jacques Vallée, Sphere, London 1990

UNIVERSAL MEMORY (*See* **COLLECTIVE UNCONSCIOUS, KIRLIAN, MAP DOWSING**) The notion of a Universal Memory called by **occultists** the Akashic Record is ancient. Everything that ever has, does, or will happen, however trivial, is said to be imprinted in the basic structure of the phenomenal universe. No event is ultimately separate from any other. Examination of any one event (however mundane) reveals meaningful information about all others. Through this universal library, study of worm, petal or cloud can reveal as much about the universe and our place in it as any radio telescope.

The notion is reaffirmed by the insights of contemporary British physicist David **Bohm**, Californian neurologist Karl **Pribram** and Swiss psychologist Carl **Jung**. Proposing his theory of the 'Implicate Order', Bohm (a devotee of **Krishnamurti**) emphasises that the apartness of things is illusory, just as Pribram insists that reality is hologrammatic, meaning that any one part or perception of things reflects and includes in itself the essence of all other parts and perceptions. This echoes the evidence of Kirlian research in, for example, the finding that the electrophotograph of a cut leaf shows the '**aura**' of the *whole* leaf, not just the part cut off.

Likewise Jung developed the notion of the collective unconscious by which, the deeper one penetrates the ancient, instinctual depths of the mind, the more one arrives at an inherited **archetypal** level of perception.

On this level, with individually conscious linear perception of **time** and space redundant, access to the universal memory may be possible.

It is at this level, it may be, that the faculties of **precognition, prophecy** and **map-dowsing** operate.

To date there is no rational proof of such assertions. Nevertheless it is interesting how the notion of universal memory persists at an intuitive level from one age and culture to another. Despite all rational denial, the idea not only persists but continually re-emerges in new form.

V

VALENTINE, Manson J. (*See* **ATLANTIS, BERMUDA TRIANGLE**) Indications of ancient constructions on the shallow sea-bed of the Bahama Banks off the Florida coast – rectangular forms marked by variations in vegetation and what appear to be long stone walls or 'roads' off the coast of Bimini – have been found by this Miami palaeontologist, geologist and underwater archaeologist. Convinced of the reality of pre-Flood societies from his earlier investigation of giant rocks carved in animal form found in caverns in Yucatan, Valentine began work on the Bahama Banks in 1958, and since then has located over thirty areas which, he claims, show 'probably man-made remains' either on the sea bed or below it. Diving near Paradise Cay off Bimini in 1968 on the sea bed he found a regular pattern of huge stones. Cut, closely fitted, running for hundreds of yards and terminating in cornerstones, these became known as the Bimini Road or Wall. Many are of flint-hard micrite, not beach-rock. He concluded that it was part of the Sacbé, the ceremonial 'white road' of the Maya, and that the builders belonged to the same ancient **megalithic** society responsible for Baalbek, Carnac, **Stonehenge**, the walls of Sacsahuamán, etc.

He insists that at the time of his discovery he was unaware of the Edgar **Cayce** prophecy, dating from 1940, that evidence of Atlantis would be found in 1968 or 1969 near Bimini. He refutes archaeologists who say the Road is a natural formation: 'Such thinkers don't want to find anything that has to do with sudden change.'[1]

1. *Atlantis*, Charles Berlitz, Fontana, London 1985, pp. 94–8

VALLÉE, Jacques (*See* **FAIRIES, INCUBI, UFOs**) Astrophysicist by training and computer scientist by profession, Jacques Vallée's interest in UFOs began in the 1950s when at a French observatory he witnessed the destruction of tracking tapes of unknown objects. Moving to the USA in 1962, he provided the model for the French scientist played by Truffaut in Spielberg's *Close Encounters of the Third Kind* (1978).

His researches into and theories about the UFO mystery are described in books like *Passport to Magonia*, *Messengers of Deception* and *Dimensions*. Like **Keel** he highlights the similarities between modern UFO reports and the ambiguous, tricksy behaviour of **fairies, incubi**, sylphs and other 'supernatural' beings as recorded in global folklore and myth.

He concludes that UFOs are real physical objects, but not necessarily extraterrestrial in origin. They and their crews more probably originate in a *multiverse* about us, remaining incomprehensible so long as we ignore their **psychic**, **symbolic** component. How else to explain an intelligence 'that can masquerade as a Martian invader, as the Blessed Virgin, as a fleet of airships'. He adds, 'What we see here is not an alien invasion. It is a spiritual system that acts on humans and uses humans.' There is no reason to doubt the integrity of UFO witnesses, but their recollections need not be taken literally. UFOs and associated events are natural aspects of human consciousness. 'The phenomena function like an operational system of symbolic communication at a global level. There is something about the human race with which (UFOs) interact, and we do not yet know what it is.'[1]

1. *Dimensions*, Jacques Vallée, Sphere, London 1990, pp. 284–91

VAMPIRISM (*See* **ELEMENTALS, INCUBI**) The **archetypal** fear of 'undead' beings who by night rise from their graves to sustain their unnatural existence by drinking the blood of the living is the stuff not only of Transylvanian legend but of many modern horror tales and movies. Vampire-myth as we have it today consists of several different strands. One is the old belief that to drink fresh blood is to absorb life-force. Another lies in the psychological capacity of some people to drain the vitality of others and thus wax stronger themselves – mental vampirism.

Dracula, the most famous vampire of all, was created in 1897 by Irish novelist Bram Stoker (1847–1912). Stoker based his tale on the fifteenth-century Transylvanian Count, Vlad the Impaler, the son of Dracul (Latin *draco*, or '**dragon**') – thus 'Count Dracula'. Vlad's favourite pastime was to impale prisoners on high, pointed poles, feasting as they writhed to death. It is said that once he impaled 30,000 Turks in one day.

The combination of such horrific sadism (as also in the cases of Gilles de Retz – Bluebeard – and the Hungarian Countess Elizabeth Bathory), with an older body of **superstition**, provides modern vampire-myth with a head-start simply in terms of human murderousness and the fear it provokes.

What of the **supernatural** aspect? Eastern European reports suggest that in the eighteenth century vampirism reached epidemic proportions. It is hard to judge the truth, such reports being compounded by superstitious terror, but Wallachia, Moldavia and Transylvania (in modern Austria, Hungary and Romania respectively) chiefly provide the myth of the blood-drinking undead who walk at night, hate light, garlic, running water, iron and the cross, and who can be set at rest only by driving a stake of iron or wood through the heart.

Typically, the 'undead' were the restless spirits of suicides, until recent times in eastern Europe (and elsewhere), buried at crossroads, their graves spiked with crosses to prevent them 'walking'. Crossroads and cross in this context are pre-Christian: the cross is the same as a knot: tying up the fearful restless spirit thus bound.

Reacting to the many reports of vampirism, the eighteenth-century philosopher Jean-Jacques Rousseau wrote, 'If ever there was in the world a warranted and proven history, it is that of vampires. Nothing is lacking: official reports, testimonials of persons of standing, of surgeons, of clergymen, of judges; the judicial evidence is all-embracing.'

Today our rational dismissal of vampires is undercut by their survival in fictional form. From Thomas Prest's 1847 bestseller *Varney the Vampire* to *Nosferatu*, from Dracula as played by Christopher Lee to recent vampire movies like *The Lost Boys*, the subject still fascinates us. Why? It adds up to an uneasy, persistent sense that life is not quite as reason would have it. Like **poltergeists**, **UFO**s and other phenomena, vampires remain part of the underside of life. However secure our house, it seems we still wish to open our windows to the old terrors . . . and who can say for sure that these are not based on a residue or distortion of fact?

Cypriot healer **Daskalos** describes a case in southern Greece where an unmarried twenty-five-year-old girl fell in love with a fifty-year-old shepherd, Loizo. Her parents forbade the marriage. Loizo died in a car crash. Over five years later he visited the girl by night. She said he came 'through the walls'. When examined, she was found to be no longer a virgin. The doctor insisted that she was deflowered by her own fingers. On her neck Daskalos found two reddish spots. 'He kisses me there but his kisses are strange,' she said. 'They are like sucking and I like them.' Daskalos sought out Loizo, to tell him he was dead. 'Should you continue bothering this girl you will remain in this narcotized state like a vampire,' he told Loizo, who then departed and left the girl alone.

'I never found out whether it was the dead shepherd who deflowered the girl or whether he made her break the hymen with her fingers,' Daskalos told his biographer. 'People get possessed by elementals which they themselves create as a result of their weaknesses. Only in rare cases do I encounter **possession** by beings who reside in the **etheric** world.'[1]

1. *The Magus of Strovolos*, Kyriacos C. Markides, Routledge Kegan Paul, London 1985, pp. 162–4

VASILIEV, Dr Leonid (*See* **TELEPATHY**)

VAUGHAN, Thomas (*See* **ALCHEMY**)

VELIKOVSKY, Immanuel (1895–1979) (*See* **POLE SHIFT**) Born in Vitebsk, Russia, Velikovsky studied at the universities of Moscow, Berlin,Vienna and Edinburgh, then practised psychoanalysis in Europe and at Haifa before in 1939 emigrating to the USA. At Princeton in New Jersey he formulated the mythic-anthropological theory that brought him notoriety with the publication of *Worlds in Collision* (1950), in which he argued that Biblical history (and other global folklore) form a distorted memory of an event so cataclysmic as to cause racial amnesia. His training suggested that if individuals can blot out painful events, so can entire species. So he tried to reconstruct Earth-history on the basis that our global past is so painful that we literally forgot it, save as **myth**.

His thesis is that 4,000 years ago Jupiter ejected a planet-sized mass that became the planet Venus. Wandering the solar system, *c*. 1500 BC this proto-planet nearly collided with Earth. The passage of the Earth through the comet's trailing edge of dust and gases led, among other catastrophes, to the Ten Plagues of Egypt. Red dust filled the air. There was 'a great inundation,' said the Mayan *Popul-Vuh*. 'People were drowned in a sticky substance raining from the sky.' This, claimed Velikovsky, was raw petroleum. Some rained down unignited, some caught fire. 'Then the heavens burst, and fragments rained down and killed everything and everybody,' says the tradition of the Sashinaua of Brazil. The Persians watched in awe as one day lasted for three. The Chinese wrote of a time when the sun did not set for several days while the entire land burned. There were hurricanes, the planet tilted, the **poles shifted**. Populations vanished: the Israelites fled Egypt. The hydrocarbons drenching the Earth in petroleum turned into an edible substance – *manna* or *ambrosia*, or the honey-like *madhu* of the Hindus. Darkness shrouded Earth for many years. 800 years later Venus pulled Mars out of orbit: Mars drew near Earth, causing fresh catastrophe. Earth's axis again shifted; the year lengthened from 360 to 365 days.

In a sequel, *Earth in Upheaval* (1955), Velikovsky surveyed geological evidence for sudden cataclysm. What brought glaciers to Madagascar and Brazil; corals to Spitzbergen; coals to Alaska; seashells to the top of the Himalayas and fig trees to Greenland? What explained the sudden death by quick-freezing of Siberian mammoths?

'Do not accept my work as ultimate truth,' he warned in 1972 – but the scientific community denied it altogether. When *Worlds in Collision* came out, its would-be publisher, Macmillan, was threatened with a boycott of all its books. The editor who had bought the manuscript was fired; the book was turned over to Doubleday, which had no textbook division, and could not be intimidated. A concerted effort was made to suppress Velikovsky's ideas. His data was distorted, the presentation of his views blocked, his books boycotted or scurrilously reviewed, his supporters fired, his integrity impugned – all because his ideas challenged an existing dogma. This alone commends them to serious attention. Whether they are correct is another matter . . . but the response to them was shameful.[1,2]

1. *Worlds in Collision*, Immanuel Velikovsky, Abacus, London 1972

2. *Earth in Upheaval*, Immanuel Velikovsky, Gollancz, London 1956

VIRGIN BIRTH (*See* **ANNUNCIATION**)

VISION From the Latin *visio* 'faculty of seeing', *videre*, 'to see', the word's derivations include the mental representation of a visual object not actually external present; thus a form of 'meaningful **hallucination**' that may involve **prophetic** perception or **supernatural apparition**. Vision as such typically occurs in a state of **dream** or **trance**, or in a state of **sensory deprivation**.

VISUALISATION (*See* **MAGIC, MEDITATION**) The act of summoning up a mental picture or image, controlled visualisation is a skill essential to active meditation and magical working.

VITALISM (*See* **KIRLIAN**) The doctrine that life originates in a principle distinct from chemical or other physical forces. Following the work of Luigi Galvani (1737–98) and the biologist Hans Driesch (1867–1941), who argued that organisms can be understood only as living *wholes*, the Yale anatomist Harold Saxton Burr concluded that all living organisms are influenced by their electric fields – which he called L-fields (life-fields). The later work of Semyon **Kirlian** suggests that Driesch's holism and Burr's L-fields are not, as geneticist Theodosius Dobzhansky has put it, 'a sham solution of biological riddles'. Indeed, mechanistic reductionism increasingly seems to be the real sham.

VITRIFIED FORTS (*See* **EARTHWORKS**)

VOICE PHENOMENA (*See* **RAUDIVE**)

VON DÄNIKEN, Erich (1935–) (*See* **ANCIENT ASTRONAUTS**) Famed for his bestselling *Chariots of the Gods* (1968) and its sequels, this German autodidact exemplifies the pitfalls involved in trying to elucidate ancient mysteries. Claiming 'religious uncertainty' as the major reason for the success of his books, and 'religious doubt' as his reason for writing them, this ex-hotelier so zealously insisted that 'gods' from outer space have visited Earth that today many remain convinced that Peru's **Nazca** lines, Easter Island's statues, and other ancient artefacts are the product of alien intelligence. That he dealt in 'Third World' mysteries alone largely escaped critical attention: the implication being that 'primitive' cultures could not have been responsible for such marvels.

Popularising and debasing ideas researched by others, he skimmed the cream and claimed it as his own. Yet he stimulated millions of people to look deeper into the mysteries he advertised.

VOODOO (*See* **SORCERY, ZOMBIE**) According to one account this Haitian **spirit-religion** derives its name from a twelfth-century **Gnostic** sect, the Waldensians or Vaudois. Accused of cannibalism and orgiastic **devil**-worship, they acquired such notoriety that sorcery became known in France as *vauderie* and witches as *vaudoises* – hence *voodoo*.[1] Another possible derivation is from the word *vodun*, which in the Fon language of West Africa means 'god', 'spirit', 'sacred object'.

Founded in African spirit-religions brought to Haiti by slaves imported by French plantation-owners, voodoo also draws elements from Catholicism and European magical *grimoires*. Pictures of Catholic saints are found in most voodoo temples, being identified with the individual voodoo gods and goddesses. St Patrick, driving the snakes from Ireland, is said to be *Damballah*, the **serpent**-god; John the Baptist is *Shango*, a thunder-god.

Associated with **trance**-inducing dance and rhythmic chanting leading to ecstastic states and **possession** by the *loa* (the gods and goddesses of the voodoo pantheon), voodoo is best known for its darker side, as in the use of **black magic** to cause death or illness in enemies, and particularly for the macabre creation of the walking dead, or **zombies**. Closely associated with the voodoo 'cult of the dead' is the sinister Baron Samedi, lord of cemeteries and black magic: the chief ceremony of this cult occurs on All Souls' Day, supposedly providing protection from the evil creatures of Haitian folklore. Apart from the zombie, these include the *loup-garou* (a kind of red-haired female **vampire** which makes its incisions between the victim's toes), and the *baka* – the spirits of black magicians who **shape-shift** into animal form and prowl by night, seeking victims to devour.

In earlier life the late Haitian dictator, François Duvalier ('Papa Doc') wrote a serious study of voodoo; he was reputed to use black magic against his enemies, and certainly had it used against him, his father's skeleton once being stolen from its grave by his enemies.

But the black element is but one aspect of voodoo. In 1947 American film-maker Maya Deren, on an assignment for *Life* magazine, took part in a voodoo dance. Amid it she involuntarily entered trance and was seemingly possessed by the goddess Erzulie (a cross between Aphrodite and the Virgin Mary). As she danced she felt a numbness creeping up her legs, a feeling she called 'a white darkness – its whiteness a glory and its darkness a terror'. This force flooded her body, threatening (**kundalini**-like?) to explode her skull. Inwardly begging for mercy, she heard a shrill chorus crying 'Erzulie' in her mind. Passing out for several hours, later she was told by the *hungan* (priest) that she had been 'mounted by Erzulie'. This experience changed her attitude. She came to see voodoo as an authentic religion with its own ethical values and life-style. In *Divine Horsemen: the Living Gods of Haiti* (1953), she points out that voodoo differs from other religions like **Christianity** or **Islam** in that, in trance, the voodoo devotee actually *becomes* a god or goddess.

The Catholic Church has failed to persuade voodoo devotees that voodoo and Catholicism are not complementary. 'The things of the Church are always affairs of magic,' one devotee told an anthropologist.[2]

1. *The Magical Arts*, Richard Cavendish, Arkana, London 1984, p. 296
2. 'Possessed by the gods', Francis King, *The Unexplained*, Orbis partwork, London 1983, pp. 2490–93

W

WAITE, Arthur Edward (b. 1857) (*See* **ALCHEMY, GOLDEN DAWN, ROSICRUCIANS, TAROT**) Born in Brooklyn, brought to England as a baby, remembered today for the popular Rider-Waite tarot pack he designed in collaboration with artist Pamela Coleman Smith, this noted **occult** scholar was an early member both of the **Theosophical Society** and the Order of the Golden Dawn. He 'hated' **Blavatsky**'s *Isis Unveiled* for what he saw as its 'anti-Christian bias', but was impressed by Annie **Besant**. Unable to accept the doctrine of the Secret Masters, he left the society. Joining the Golden Dawn, he loathed the arrogance of **Mathers**, but hoped the Order might offer the basis of a genuine spiritual revelation. Leaving the Order, he rejoined it and led it after the **Crowley/Yeats** split, rewriting its **rituals** in Christian terms.

Thought tedious by contemporaries, including Crowley, his suspicion of occult claims to antiquity led him to deny, in his *The Real History of the Rosicrucians*, that the movement reached into ages past. In *The Secret Tradition of Alchemy* he rejected any idea that the **Greek Mysteries** contain secret teaching about **trance** states. Yet he persisted in hoping that a spiritual reality exists beyond the framework of the Christian Church: 'I believe to this day that it is a pregnant illustration of truth in the Spiritual world; that there is a Church behind the Church on a more inward plane of being, and that it is formed of those who have opened the iridescent shell of external doctrine and found that which abides in it. It is a Church of more worlds than one, for some of the Community are among us here and now and some are in a stage beyond the threshold of the physical senses.'[1]

1. *Shadows of Life and Thought*, A. E. Waite, Selwyn and Blount, London 1938

WAND (*See* **MAGIC**) The 'magic wand' is more than a prop used by stage magicians. Held up in the right hand of *The Magician* in the Rider-**Waite tarot** it is a symbolic 'lightning rod', conducting cosmic energy down to Earth. As such it has affinity with the ancient image of the **serpent**, and with the rod or staff of Moses that turns into a serpent. Connection with the male imagery of phallus, tower, mace, sceptre, trident and crozier is likewise apparent.

An attribute of all **shamans**, magicians and medicine men, in mediaeval **fairy** literature the wand is used to grant divine insight. The wand of Hypnos had the power of granting forgetfulness and sleep; the **angel** in the Book of Revelation strikes the Elect thrice between the eyes, causing them great suffering. The point touched is the 'third eye', associated with the **pineal**. In *Communion*, Whitley **Streiber** describes one of his 'visitors' touching the centre of his forehead with a *ruler* (wand) with a silver tip, whereupon he sees pictures of the world blowing up.[1]

1. *Communion*, Whitley Streiber, Arrow, London 1988, pp. 64, 67, 75

WATCHERS (*See* **ANCIENT ASTRONAUTS, ENOCH**)

WATKINS, Alfred (*See* **LEY LINES**)

WATSON, Lyall (1939–) (*See* **PLANT CONSCIOUSNESS, PSYCHIC SURGERY**) This globetrotting naturalist took his Ph.D at London University in 1963 and worked with Desmond Morris at London Zoo before embarking on a nomadic career as anthropologist, palaentologist, marine biologist, botanist and **paranormal** researcher. Author of several books before *Supernature* (1973) catapulted him to fame, his subsequent 'Position Papers' (as he calls them) such as *The Romeo Error, Gifts of Unknown Things, Lifetide, Lightning Bird, Dreams of Dragons, Heaven's Breath*, etc. have maintained his reputation as an informed thinker who challenges scientific sacred cows, uniting diverse strands from many disciplines into summaries (and speculative extensions) of existing knowledge across a wide front. A modern 'Renaissance Man', all fields of enquiry are grist for his mill. In addition to his scientific expeditions and work as an author, he has also been a BBC TV producer, zoo director, and representative of the Seychelles on the International Whaling Commission. When not on his travels he lives in the west of Ireland.

WEREWOLVES (*See* **SHAMANISM, SHAPE-SHIFTING**) As with the **vampire** legend, the idea that men can turn into animals – particularly wolves, and particularly when the **Moon** is full – retains its emotional potency. No amount of evidence that such shape-shifting is impossible eradicates the basic image. It is **archetypal**, as in *Little Red Riding Hood*, or as in the Lascaux cave-paintings showing ancient hunters in animal guise, or as in shamanic tradition the world over. Echoes of it are found today in existing **astrological** zodiacs with their divisions of human types into goat, bull, crab, etc., or as in the way we refer to people as being *bird-like, bovine, catty* . . . or, if sexually predatory, as *wolves*.

The origin of the belief is hard to pin down. In the fifth century BC the Greek historian Herodotus mentions how Greeks and Scythians settled on the Black Sea shores regarded the native Neurians as magicians able to take wolf-form whenever they wanted. Such beings were seen as humans so obsessed by cannibalistic appetite that lycanthropy provided them with a source of gratification. Roman writers like Virgil and Petronius were not averse to telling such tales, which did not always involve wolves: in *The Golden Ass* (second century AD) Apuleius describes the transformation of his unlucky hero into a donkey. But the werewolf transformation always carried more weight.

Sometimes the change was thought spontaneous and uncontrollable. In other cases it was deliberately sought by donning the skin of a real wolf – just as Celtic **Druids**, in the rite called *taghairm*, would put on the skin of a newly flayed bull, in order to take on the animal's power, and **prophesy**. In many cases, the use of a **charm** was thought sufficient: no actual change would take place, but observers would really imagine that they saw a wolf.

Belief in this shape-shifting power was so common that, during the fifteenth and sixteenth centuries, anyone suspected of being a werewolf was destroyed with the same cruelty that greeted suspected witches. In France between 1520 and 1630 over 30,000 cases of lycanthropy (*lycos*, 'wolf'; *anthropos*, 'man') were recorded. Cannibal appetite among poor, half-starved peasants might explain part of the phenomenon, yet it is sure that many so accused really thought themselves wolves, killing and eating people under the influence of this delusion.

Cases continue to be reported into modern times. In 1975 a youth from Eccleshall in Staffordshire, sure he was turning into a werewolf, plunged a flick-knife into his own heart. Just before his death, a workmate told the inquest, the youth had telephoned to say 'that his face and hands were changing colour – and that he was changing into a werewolf. He would go quiet and then start growling.'

Traditionally, there are three types of werewolf – the *hereditary*, the *voluntary* and the *benevolent*. The first is passed down from generation to generation by a **curse**. The second arises from deliberate depravity. The third is one who, though so bound (as by heredity) feels nothing but human shame for his bestial affliction.

All this argues a *genetic* source, or maybe a form of **astral projection** that overwhelms the **consciousness**, and thus the body, leading the afflicted individual to wander abroad, literally out of his human mind, taken over by the primeval 'wolf-image'. Civilisation is not, after all, so easily won: we human beings are not that far from the animal.

It is also possible that ergotised grain (ergot is a fungus from which is produced lysergic acid, LSD) as baked into bread produced werewolf **hallucinations**. As recently as 1951 the mediaeval terror of *St Anthony's Fire* (madness caused by ergotised grain) erupted in the southern French village of Pont-Saint-Esprit. The entire community was affected by a batch of poisoned bread. Five died. Of the survivors, some saw great balls of fire falling on them, others felt a huge urge to jump from windows or saw monstrous animals intent on eating them. Collectively, the villagers went insane.

Was such insanity, born of ergot-poisoned bread, a relatively frequent event in mediaeval times? If so, lycanthropy would have been the least of it.[1]

1. *The Day of St Anthony's Fire*, John G. Fuller, Hutchinson, London 1969

WHALES (*See* **DOLPHINS, SERPENTS**) The largest animal ever evolved on Earth, mythically the whale represents the power of the cosmic waters, hence both regeneration and the grave. So in the Old Testament Jonah, swallowed by the whale, enters the darkness of death, yet is **resurrected** (cast out on to dry land) after the traditional three days (of the dark of the **moon**). Yet when misidentified as Leviathan, serpent of the cosmic sea, the whale becomes a disparaged monster, slain by Yahweh (Jehovah). In **Christianity** the whale represents the **Devil**, its jaws the gates of hell and its belly hell itself.

Such **symbolism** scarcely justifies how today the very survival of the many species of whale is as endangered as that of the dolphin. While the dolphin usually dies 'accidentally' by asphyxiation in nets meant for squid or tuna (the total length of nets used by Japan's squid fisheries is some *750,000 miles*), the systematic slaughter of whales has been conducted for centuries for the sake of its blubber, flesh and perfumed ambergris.

Soon the whale may be extinct, though now it appears that these giants (an adult blue whale may be thirty metres long and weigh up to 150 tons) are as intelligent, or more so, than the violently destructive human being.

The successors of carnivorous mammals that returned to the sea some seventy million years ago, most whales are placid browsers. Sight and smell being useless in the ocean, whales rely on a highly developed sense of sound to communicate over distances of up to 10,000 miles. Ranging over a wide band of frequencies, whale 'songs' may last for ten minutes to an hour, often to be repeated beat for beat and identically by other whales. Whales may leave their winter waters in the middle of a song and, returning six months later, pick it up at just the right note. Specific songs may change by collaboration between the population. One whale may pick up another's song and return it note-perfect, but with individual embellishments suggesting not only a highly developed memory but individual creativity. The song of the humpback whale contains about 200 notes, from high-pitched squeaks to low resonant rumbles lasting ten minutes or more. Seen as a tonal language, the number of 'bits' of information in such songs is about 10^6 – a similar information content to that in the *Iliad* or *Odyssey*.[1] Yet humans not only slaughter whales but pollute their aural environment. There is so much noise in the oceans today that songs once heard 10,000 miles away are now inaudible at a hundredth of that distance. Yet not only do we not know what the whales (and dolphins) are talking about, it seems soon the chance to learn will be lost forever.

Perhaps a clue lies in the mass suicide of whales that cast themselves up on beaches to die. Do they know us better than we know ourselves?

1. *Cosmos*, Carl Sagan, Macdonald, London 1981, pp. 270–72

WICCA (*See* **WITCHCRAFT**)

WILHELM, Richard (1873–1930) (*See* ***I CHING***) While working as a missionary in China this German theologian encountered a number of texts including the *I Ching* and the **Taoist alchemical** text now known in the West as *The Secret of the Golden Flower*. His translation and interpretation of these texts, particularly the former, made them available *in comprehensible form* to a wide Western audience for the first time. His version of the *I Ching* (recast into English from his German translation by Cary F. Baynes) remains unrivalled, not least because, unsatisfied with the purely academic approach espoused by earlier translators (Legge, 1882; de Harlez, 1889), he made every effort to understand its **symbolism**, studying its philosophy under the tutelage of the Chinese sage Lao Nai-hsuan, and putting the **oracle**'s techniques into practice in his everyday life.

A friend of C. G. **Jung** (who wrote commentaries to both texts), Wilhelm never readapted to European life following his return from China, and died relatively young within a year of the German publication of *The Secret of the Golden Flower*.[1,2]

1. *I Ching*, Wilhelm/Baynes, Routledge Kegan Paul, London 1951
2. *The Secret of the Golden Flower*, Richard Wilhelm, Arkana, London 1984

WILSON, Colin (1931–) Born in Leicester, Wilson worked at various jobs after leaving school at sixteen. In 1956, publication of *The Outsider* gained him the reputation of an 'Angry Young Man'. The critical and popular success of this romantic analysis of a specific personality type (from the beginning he suggested that artist and criminal are similar in that both are 'outsiders') led to a range of works on philosophy, music, **religion**, crime and history. Yet increasingly his mind moved in an unorthodox direction. *The Occult* (1971), a massive survey of the history of magical thought and phenomena, was the first of many later works in which he has examined every aspect of the **paranormal**.

He argues that each human being houses a hierarchy of selves, but that for the most part we deny our real potential. Following **Gurdjieff** and **Maslow**, he asks how human beings fall prey to boredom and to the 'robot' of habitual, unconscious activity. He postulates the existence of 'Factor X' – a faculty of higher consciousness which, consciously triggered and released, re-establishes (via Maslow's theory of 'peak experiences') the world as implicitly meaningful. Synthesising scientific, psychological and **occult** research, his enthusiastic approach inevitably renders him suspect in English academic circles. Yet his 'Outsider' status does not affect his output, nor the way in which he continues to seize on new data contributing to his central thesis. Offering an opinion or theory about every subject, it matters little if he is right or wrong concerning particulars. What is more important is that he rejects the academic timidity of those who dare not express a thought without first assessing its acceptability. Such exuberance has led to a massive body of valuable work.[1,2,3]

1. *The Occult*, Colin Wilson, Grafton, London 1979 (1971)
2. *Mysteries*, Colin Wilson, Grafton, London 1979
3. *Beyond the Occult*, Colin Wilson, Corgi, London, 1989

WILSON, Robert Anton (*See* **LEARY**) This always-entertaining and original

American writer became known in the 1970s for the *Illuminatus* trilogy (co-written with Robert Shea), a cult science-fiction extravaganza that simultaneously satirised and shed light on a wide range of **occult**, scientific and '**New Age**' thought. This he has followed up with a number of highly provocative novels (*Shrödinger's Cat*, etc.) and encyclopaedic surveys and syntheses of borderline evolutionary theory. Books like *The Cosmic Trigger* (1978) and *Prometheus Rising* (1983) are invaluable not only for the extraordinary range of their intellectual roving but for their effervescent humour. It is perhaps no surprise that Wilson is better appreciated in the USA than in Europe or Britain: where the European theorist typically adopts a sombre tone, Wilson laughs, plays and makes jokes out of the most complex and profound notions. Yet in so doing he renders otherwise arcane material more accessible by bringing it down to earth. Like his British namesake Colin **Wilson**, his main thesis is that 'We are all giants, raised by pygmies, who have learned to walk with a perpetual mental crouch.'

It is his serious purpose, like that of the laughing **Zen** master, to stimulate, infuriate, and encourage us to reject the nonsense we are taught by academic pygmies masquerading as giants, and stand up straight.

Thus, speaking of specific neurological principles by which brainwashing is accomplished, he writes, 'In one of my Immortal Novels I describe a religious cult called Loonies, founded by one Neon Bal Loon, in which members pray in pig-Latin while standing on one leg like storks. This is considered satire, but any would-be messiah who understands the above principles could create such a cult easily; and the members would soon have a quite sincere sense of superiority to those outside that reality-tunnel.'[1]

1. *Prometheus Rising*, Robert Anton Wilson, Falcon Press, USA 1983, p. 145

WITCHCRAFT (*See* **BLACK MADONNA, ISIS, MOON**) From the fourteenth to eighteenth centuries in Europe thousands of women were burned alive at the stake as witches. The persecution began at the behest of the Dominican Inquisition, established in the 1220s to deal with the **Cathars**: dualists who accorded women equal status with men. Once they were broken it was the turn (in 1307) of the **Knights Templar**. Nineteen years later in 1326 Pope John XXII, a paranoid convinced that his enemies wished to kill him by **magic**, accepted the Dominican demand for a crusade against witches, making '**sorcery**' (as distinct from 'heresy') a crime.

Few at the time thought sorcery or witchcraft criminal. Practice of the 'cunning arts' was widespread, and as likely to cure as to curse. The old **pagan** fertility **religion** was still deeply rooted. Folk did not easily accept that there was anything *wrong* (*Satanic* or *anti-Christian*) about it.

The first secular witchcraft trial occurred in Paris in 1390. Jehane de Brigue, accused by a man she had cured when on the edge of death, was tortured, 'confessed' to having a demonic familiar and was burned at the stake. The time was ripe. It was just forty years since the first assault of the Black Death. Scared, no longer sure of the old ways, people were easily persuaded that God was angry with them. The **Jews** had already been blamed for the Plague, and exterminated throughout Europe: the Cathars and Templars were gone; now it was Woman's turn. It was said Eve had caused the Fall by heeding Satan; it was simple enough to argue that the devilish female Craft endangered Christian society's survival. So the Dominicans claimed, exploiting an ancient and increasing misogyny. Yet it was another century before the hysteria truly took hold. In 1486 the publication of *Malleus Maleficorum* ('The Hammer of the Witches') by the German Dominicans, Kramer and Sprengler, set it in motion. It was maintained in the following century by Jean Bodin's *Démonologie* and by Calvinist texts like John Knox's *First Blast of the Trumpet Against the Monstrous Regiment of Women*. White or black, witchcraft was the work of Satan. The witches' horned god was the **Devil**. In effect, femininity itself was satanic. Any woman thought 'odd' was at risk. The epidemic of panic spread. In parts of Germany the female population of entire areas was all but wiped out. At Bamberg between 1609 and 1633 over 900 women were tortured in the 'witches' chair' – made of iron, it was covered with studs and heated over a fire. Confessions thus wrung out of those set in it led invariably to the stake.

The horror of these events and the hatred of female sexuality that they imply runs so deep that even now it remains hard to comprehend. The plague was exclusively a Western European phenomenon, most marked in France and in the German and Swiss states. In England the craze for incinerating women, old or young, was not so pronounced as in Puritan Scotland. King James VI (later James I of England) was convinced that a storm which nearly drowned him at sea was caused by the **spells** of the witches of Berwick: some burned. In the 1660s at Auldearn in Moray, Isobel Gowdie admitted to intercourse with Satan: she and other women were executed. To those weaklings who felt appalled by such cruelty, a French writer explained consolingly, 'the witches are so bent on [Satan's] devilish service that there is no torture or punishment that can frighten them; and they say that they go to a true martyrdom and to death, for love of him, as gaily as they go to a festival of pleasure and public rejoicing.'[1]

The insanity was so great, and died away so slowly (the last execution for witchcraft in Britain occurred in the 1750s, the last Witchcraft Act was not repealed until 1951), that until recently it was as if a collective amnesia prevailed. Then in 1921 anthropologist Margaret Murray published her argument that witchcraft was a relic of a pre-Christian fertility religion, dating back to prehistoric times.[2]

Her thesis was widely accepted. Yet its implications upset many. Some historians, like Norman Cohn, today claim *there never were* any witches, but that the madness arose from sexual neurosis caused by the impossibly high moral standards demanded by the Church.[3] This may well be so. Yet that there was an 'old religion' is no more in doubt than that its classical and mediaeval adherents, from **Gnostics** and Manichees to Cathars, Templars and 'witches', were systematically persecuted and finally all but exterminated. The process was intermittent, enduring over a thousand-year period after the rise to power of patriarchal Western Christendom. Seen as a whole, it was an assault against a set of philosophies in conflict with the assumed masculine right to rule, as epitomised by the Church. It is no coincidence that 'scientific method' became prominent precisely during the era when witchcraft – female religion – was most under attack. It was, after all, only a millennium or so since Isis and the other manifestations of the Great Goddess of the Ancient World had been subsumed into the decorous, safe image of the Blessed Virgin Mary. In short, it was a matter of sexual politics – the demonisation of Eve and all female ways.

Today the lunar, intuitive principles that underlie witchcraft make a tentative return. The negative effects of several centuries of masculine (scientific) dominance suggest to many that the balance of nature has been warped, and that it is time to consider a more sympathetic approach.

In the 1950s witchcraft (*wicca*) began to show its face again. At first its new examplars were men. Gerald **Gardner** overruled the doubts of women in surviving covens who, remembering past horrors, had no desire for public exposure, by going public.[4] Soon it became clear that, though the movement was laughed at or pilloried in the press, the old hysteria had largely died. Many women *and* men came forward, expressing a new interest in the old wisdom. Now popular post-feminist movies like *The Witches of Eastwick* openly satirise male attitudes formerly held literally sacred.

Today witches may still be thought strange, but they are not arrested or burned at the stake for practising their religion. Their festivals are those of the old nature religion – the Beltane (*Beallteinn*, when the need-fire was lit) on the eve of May Day; the summer solstice; Lammastide (the Celtic *Lugnasad*) on 1 August; Hallowe'en (Celtic *Samhain* or Saturnalia) on 31 October; the winter solstice (Christmas) and Candlemas on 2 February (the Celtic *Imbolc*, or lambing festival). Their working unit remains the coven of thirteen, just as there are thirteen months in the year ($13 \times 28 = 364$).

The principal deity is the Mother Goddess (Isis, Bridget, the Triple or White Goddess of poets as espoused by Robert **Graves**). Her consort is the Horned God (Cernunnos, Herne the Hunter, the Green Man). The High Priestess and High Priest of each coven personify these profound natural forces and their various faces. Some covens work robed, others naked, or 'sky-clad', the latter doing so to let the natural energies flow freely. These may or may not include the sexual energies, which are no more nor less than part of the natural equation of things.

1. *Bothwell and the Witches*, Godfrey Watson, Hale, London 1975, p. 73
2. *The Witch-Cult in Western Europe*, Margaret Murray, Oxford University Press, 1921
3. *Europe's Inner Demons*, Norman Cohn, Paladin, London 1976
4. *Witchcraft Today*, Gerald B. Gardner, Arrow, London 1975 (1954)

WOLVES (*See* **WEREWOLVES**)

X

XENOLALIA (*See* **GLOSSOLALIA**) While *glossolalia* means speaking in *unidentified* tongues, *xenolalia* means speaking in real languages knowledge of which is accessible to the speaker only by **paranormal** means. Thus 'speaking in tongues' as practised by those taken by ecstasy at Pentecostalist church services is more properly defined as glossolalia, not xenolalia. Before they could be recorded on tape, the unintelligible stream of words pouring from such ecstatics were widely thought to be genuine 'tongues' or languages, ancient or modern, or even the 'tongues of **angels**'. But computer-analysis of the tape-recorded sounds typically produced at Pentecostal services indicates that invariably they belong not to languages, but languge-types, lacking any vocabulary or identifiable syntax.

Such analysis does not however prove that true xenolalia never occurs in these circumstances. In addition, xenolalia, or xenoglossy, has been established in at least one case of **hypnotic regression** involving apparent memory of former incarnation. This, the experience of American housewife 'Lydia Johnson', is discussed in the entry on glossolalia.

Y

YEATS, William Butler (1865–1939) (*See* **CROWLEY, GOLDEN DAWN**) Widely acknowledged as one of the great modern poets, this Anglo-Irishman was all his life involved with the **occult**. Carrying a boyhood fascination with **fairy** lore into adulthood, in Dublin with the mystic George (A.E.) Russell he founded a group (the Hermetic Society) to study **paranormal** phenomena. He soon mastered a basic principle of **magic** – the capacity to ***visualise*** and focus his dream world clearly before forging it into poetry.

Meeting Macgregor **Mathers** in the Reading Room of the British Museum, in summer 1887 he was initiated into the Order of the Golden Dawn, taking the secret name *Diabolus est Deus Inversus* ('The Devil is God Reversed'). Though not entirely convinced by Mathers, he was sufficiently impressed to help in writing the Golden Dawn **rituals**. Less impressed by Crowley ('an unspeakable mad person'), he led the movement to expel the Beast from the Order. The Golden Dawn never recovered from the resulting schism: Yeats himself resigned in 1905. Thereafter he had no formal occult contacts, yet esoteric **symbolism** pervades his later poetry to such a degree that, though most of his admirers and critics either ignore or remain unaware of this aspect, it remains hard to assess him without taking it into account.

Shortly after his marriage to Hyde Lees in 1917, she tried **automatic writing**. The results so excited him that he persuaded her to continue. After eight years' study of the work she produced, in 1925 he published *A Vision*. This widely ignored thesis had been called by **Colin Wilson**: 'arguably the most important **hermetic** book since **Bruno**'s *Art of Memory*'.[1]

Consisting of an interpretation of human character in accord with the twenty-eight daily phases of the **moon**, *A Vision* is literally hermetic in that it is based on the fundamental proposition of **Hermes Trismegistus**: 'As Above, So Below'. Like **Jung**, Yeats sees man as a balance of four basic forces or aspects. These he designates: *Will* (a man's basic purpose or aim), *Mask (persona*: how he appears to the world), *Creative Mind* (his means of self-expression) and *body of Fate* (what the 'stars' intend for him).

Interaction of these four forces (their marriage is needed for health) with the twenty-eight phases produces a continual shift of psychological balance. Of the twenty-eight phases, those ruled by phases One to Fourteen are 'expanding' (Jung's *extrovert* character); those under Fifteen to Twenty-eight are 'contracting' (Jung's *introvert*). Phase One is a dark and formless chaos, from which anything might emerge. Phase Two is animal energy, symbolised by Pan. Phase Seven rules men (Carlyle, Dumas) whose basic drive is to assert individuality. Phase Fourteen is the 'Obsessive Man': he mentions Keats, Giorgione and 'many beautiful women'. Those born under subsequent phases include Shelley, **Swedenborg** and Luther as examples of developing civilisation.

Appealing to intuition, not intellect, *A Vision* is usually regarded as a perverse intellectual game. Yet it reasserts universal coherence in an age when materialism has reduced the world to 'a bundle of fragments'. It is too easy to assume that the world-weary Yeats was simply playing games, and that his perceptions were purely arbitrary. His own warnings deny it. Of the 'lunar knowledge' with which he worked he said, 'It is perhaps well that so few believe in it, for if many did many would go out of parliaments and libraries and run into the wilderness to so waste the body, and so hush the unquiet mind that, still living, they might pass the doors the dead pass daily;

for who among the wise would trouble himself with making laws or in history or in weighing the earth if the things of eternity seemed ready to hand?'

More than any other modern poet working in the English language, Yeats walked and talked with the two minds, right and left brain, human and fey. And this too he understood, as in his late poem 'Under Ben Bulben':

> Know that when all words are said
> And a man is fighting mad,
> Something drops from eyes long blind,
> He completes his partial mind.
> For an instant stands at ease
> Laughs aloud, his heart at peace . . .

Like any *true* poet, Yeats was an occult **visionary**, hopelessly enthralled by the White Goddess of whom **Graves** also spoke so tantalisingly.

1. *Mysteries*, Colin Wilson, Grafton, London 1979, pp. 290–99

YETI (*See* **ABOMINABLE SNOWMAN**)

YIN AND YANG (*See* **ACUPUNCTURE, *I CHING*, TAOISM**) In Chinese philosophy these eternally interacting principles of female and male, dark and light, moon and sun, passive and active, earth and sky, water and fire (etc.), operate within the circle of manifestation to produce all the phenomena of life. Entirely interrelated, unable to exist one without the other, their infinite argument is the ultimate marriage.

YOGA (*See* **BUDDHISM, HINDU MYSTERIES, MEDITATION**) From the Sanskrit root *jog*, meaning *'yoke'*, *'union'*, *'conjunction'* (as in the English 'con*jug*al'), in India the technical term for one of the six Dársanas or Schools of Philosophy, its foundation ascribed to the ancient sage Patanjali. The term itself describes the objective of the school, this being the attainment of union or at-one-ness (*atonement*) with the divine or spiritual essence inspiring humanity. As known in the West, *yoga* implies a system of meditation associated with various exercises leading to the calm, clear mind: in India ten different forms of yoga are acknowledged as leading to the goal of ***samādhi***.

Bhakti Yoga is the way of Love, involving devotion to humanity and all other living creatures as the route to God. *Dhyana Yoga* (the root of **Zen**) is a mental, meditative practice. *Hatha Yoga* is well known in the West via its *asanas*, physical disciplines yoking body to mind. *Jnana Yoga* requires understanding of the Hindu *Vedas* and *Upanishads*, being an intellectual Way. *Karma Yoga* is the path of charity and good deeds, as expressed by Mother Teresa of Calcutta. *Kriya Yoga* is the path for those drawn to **ritual** and **religious** observance. ***Kundalini Yoga*** is for those so impatient to attain *samādhi* rapidly that they willingly risk the wreck of their physical body: some **tantrics** take this path. *Laya Yoga* attempts activation of ***chakras*** via chant and **mantra**. Likewise, *Mantra Yoga* activates the higher body via the vibration of chant and mantra. Last and first, *Raja Yoga* ('The King of Yogas') encompasses all the others in the search for enlightenment.

YOGIN (YOGI) A devotee of one or another of the various **Yogic** systems described above. Typically one devoting his or her life to the conquest of bodily demand and physical temptation. The term denotes not mastery, but search.

YUGA (*See* **KALI YUGA**)

Z

ZEN (*See* **BUDDHISM, KOAN, TAO**) The obscurity (to the Western mind) of this Eastern philosophy lies in that it expresses the 'everyday mind', as involved only in 'sleeping when tired, eating when hungry'. Intellectual analysis is deliberately discouraged.

Reaching Japan via the spread of Dhyana Buddhism in China, Zen rejects ritualised or habitual thought-patterns. It is the 'artless art', occupying empty ground where what is consciously known is that nothing is consciously known, where activity occurs irrespective of conscious desire.

Despite popular Western interpretations like *Zen Flesh, Zen Bones* (by English-born Californian Alan Watts, influential in **New Age** circles since the 1960s), Zen defies intellectual or bookish analysis. Those seeking its heart go not to books but to Zen masters who teach without speaking, so as not to betray what cannot be spoken or written about. They use the **koan** to shock the logical mind out of its presuppositions and to banish the ego. They may answer deep questions by hitting the questioner with a stick.[1]

Among the best Western expositions on the subject is *Zen in the Art of Archery*, by German philosopher Eugen Herrigel. Living in Japan during the 1930s he undertook the study of archery as a way to penetrate a philosophy which, he was told, was impossible for a European to understand. He took up archery on, as he puts it, the 'completely erroneous assumption that my experiences in rifle and pistol shooting would be to my advantage'.

Approached, the Master Zenzo Awa at first refused the request to train him. Only when Herrigel said he wished to learn the art not for pleasure but for the sake of the 'Great Doctrine' did the Master relent.

Over five years Herrigel struggled with the concept that, in order to shoot straight, the art required him to forget about shooting straight.

'Put the thought of hitting straight right out of your mind,' said the Master. Herrigel, still wrestling with unmastered concepts, answered the criticism as to his approach by insisting that, if all the Master said were so, 'Then you ought to be able to hit (the target) blindfolded.'

Taking up the challenge, in darkness the Master not only shot his first arrow into the heart of the bull's-eye, but his second arrow splintered the shaft of the first. Said the Master: 'I . . . know that it is not "I" who must be given credit for this shot. "It" shot and "It" made the hit. Let us bow to the goal as before the **Buddha**!'[2]

In his popular 1970s book *Zen and the Art of Motorcycle Maintenance*, American author Robert M. Pirsig tried to convey to Western readers a sense of this 'artless art' by autobiographical description of a motorbike tour of discovery of North America with his son: a tour which was also a voyage of unrelenting self-discovery, turmoil and agony derived from recovered memory *en route* of the errors and psychiatric problems of his former life.[3]

Yet there is a vast difference between the self-conscious exposition of the art as given by Pirsig and the lack of egoism in Herrigel's archery Master.

'The mind has first to be attuned to the Unconscious,' writes Daisetz Teitaro Suzuki in the foreword to Herrigel's book, explaining that all Zen arts are meant not for utilitarian purposes of aesthetic pleasure but 'to train the mind; indeed, to bring it into contact with the ultimate reality. . . . One has to transcend technique so that the art becomes an "artless art" growing out of the Unconscious."[4]

1. *Zen Flesh, Zen Bones*, Alan Watts, Penguin Books, London
2. *Zen in the Art of Archery*, Eugen Herrigel, Routledge Kegan Paul, London 1953
3. *Zen and the Art of Motorcycle Maintenance*, Robert M. Pirsig, Corgi, London 1975
4. *op. cit.*, ref. 2, p. 5

ZENER CARDS (*See* **EXTRA-SENSORY PERCEPTION**) Employed in ESP testing by J. B. **Rhine** and his successors, Zener cards are a set of easily-visualised symbols (wavy lines, square, cross, star, circle and triangle) designed to make a distinct impression on the **telepathically** transmitting mind, so as to be easily recorded by the test receiver.

ZODIAC (*See* **ASTROLOGY**)

ZOMBIES (*See* **VOODOO**) It is said of Haiti's voodoo sorcerers that they can partially reanimate newly dead corpses, turning them into witless, shambling slaves known as 'zombies'. The term derives from the word *zumbi*, as found in many African languages. In the Congo it means a fetish; in Dahomey it refers to the Python-god; in modern voodoo usage in Haiti a snake-god is supposedly called on to animate the corpse.

Zombies are neither a **myth** nor the reanimated dead, despite reports of zombies 'reanimated' after having been 'dragged from the actual graves in which they lay in their coffins, buried by their mourning families'.[1] The victims are not dead but in a coma caused by a drug, tetradoxin. In small doses, tetradoxin causes external anaesthesia. Large doses trigger '**out-of-the-body**' experiences. Greater quantities cause apparent death – even the brain ceases detectable function. The drug is usually absorbed through the feet, being scattered by the sorcerer in the dirt at the door of the victim's cabin. In deep coma, the victim is buried, then later disinterred and 'reanimated' by applying an antidote. The reanimation is never total: brain damage is the usual result – ideal from the sorcerer's viewpoint: the victim cannot testify to the horrible trick played on him.

Tetradoxin, the '*fugu*' poison of Japan, is found in the tissues of the blowfish. Esteemed as a dangerous aphrodisiac, trained chefs prepare this deadly fish to be eaten raw by connoisseurs. Get it wrong and they risk killing or paralysing their clients – literally turning them into zombies.

1. *The Magic Island*, William Seabrook, Harrap, London 1936

ZOROASTRIANISM A **dualistic** religion founded in the seventh century BC by the Persian **prophet** Zoroaster, or Zarathustra, who taught that Ahura Mazda, the Wise Lord, had revealed to him that God the Creator is One. However this unity manifests in diversity: Ahura Mazda being eternally opposed by the fiend Ahriman, the personification of lies, destruction and darkness. Surviving today among the Parsees of India, Zoroastrianism was influential in the development of European **Gnostic** and **dualist** movements like Manichaeanism and **Catharism**, speaking as it did of the never-ending war between Good and Evil, **spirit** and matter.

Select Bibliography

(Bracketed dates refer to first edition of text cited, where known. Not every text referenced to encyclopaedia entries is listed here: some listed here are not referenced in the encyclopaedia.)

Arguelles, José and Miriam, *Mandala*, Shambala, London 1972

Ashcroft-Nowicki, D., *The Ritual Magic Handbook*, Aquarian, Wellingborough 1986

Baba Ram Dass, *Be Here Now*, Lama Foundation, USA 1970

Baigent, Michael; Leigh, Richard; and Lincoln, Henry, *The Holy Blood and the Holy Grail*, Corgi, London 1983

The Messianic Legacy, Corgi, London 1987

Baigent, Michael, and Leigh, Richard, *The Temple and the Lodge*, Corgi, London 1990

Begg, Ean, *Myth and Today's Consciousness*, Coventure, London 1984

The Cult of the Black Virgin, Arkana, London 1985

Berlitz, Charles, *The Bermuda Triangle*, Granada, London 1975

Atlantis, Fontana, London 1985

The Philadelphia Mystery (with William Moore), Granada, London 1980

Bernstein, Morey, *The Search for Bridey Murphy*, Hutchinson, London 1956

Blair, Lawrence, *Rhythms of Vision*, Warner Books, New York 1977

Blake, William, *Poems and Prophecies*, Dent Everyman, London 1972 (1927)

Blavatsky, H. P., *Isis Unveiled*, Theosophical University Press, Pasadena, California 1972 (1877)

Boddington, *The University of Spiritualism*, Psychic Press, London 1947

Bord, Janet and Colin, *Mysterious Britain*, Paladin, London 1974

Alien Animals, Granada, London 1980

Sacred Waters, Granada, London 1985

Modern Mysteries of the World, Grafton, London 1989

Brown, Joseph Epes, *The Sacred Pipe*, Penguin, London 1981 (1953)

Brunton, Paul, *A Search in Secret Egypt*, Rider, London 1969

Bucke, Richard M., *Cosmic Consciousness*, University Press, New York 1961

Budge, Wallis (trans.), *The Egyptian Book of the Dead*, Routledge Kegan Paul, London 1969

Butler, W. E., *The Magician: His Training and Work*, Aquarian, London 1959

How to Read the Aura, Aquarian, London 1971

Campbell, Joseph, *The Hero with a Thousand Faces*, Abacus, London 1975 (1949)

The Masks of God, (4 vols.), Penguin, London 1976

Capra, Fritjof, *The Tao of Physics*, Fontana, London 1976

The Turning Point, Fontana Flamingo, London 1983

Carter, Mary Ellen, *Edgar Cayce on Prophecy*, Warner, New York 1988 (1968)

Castaneda, Carlos, *The Teachings of Don Juan*, Penguin, London 1970

A Separate Reality, Penguin, London 1973

Cavendish, Richard, *The Magical Arts*, Arkana, London 1984 (1967)

The Powers of Evil, Routledge Kegan Paul, London 1975

King Arthur and the Grail, Paladin, London 1980

(ed.) *The Unexplained: Mysteries of Mind, Space and Time*, Orbis partwork, London 1983

Chardin, Teilhard de, *The Phenomenon of Man*, Fontana, London 1968
Charpentier, Louis, *The Mysteries of Chartres Cathedral*, Avon, New York 1975 (1966)
Chatwin, Bruce, *The Songlines*, Picador, London 1988
Cheetham, Erika, *The Prophecies of Nostradamus*, Corgi, London 1975
Churchward, James, *The Lost Continent of Mu*, Paperback Library, New York 1969
Cohen, Daniel, *Myths of the Space Age*, Tower, New York 1967
Cohn, Norman, *The Pursuit of the Millennium*, Paladin, London 1970 (1957)
Europe's Inner Demons, Paladin, London 1976
Conway, David, *Magic: An Occult Primer*, Aquarian, Wellingborough 1988 (1976)
Cooper, J. C., *An Illustrated Encyclopaedia of Traditional Symbols*, Thames and Hudson, London 1978
Couttie, Bob, *Forbidden Knowledge*, Lutterworth Press, Cambridge 1988
Cranston, S. L. and Head, Joseph, *Reincarnation: The Phoenix Fire Mystery*, Julian Press, New York 1977
Crowley, Aleister, *Magic in Theory and Practice*, Routledge Kegan Paul, London 1973
The Book of Thoth, Weiser, New York 1984 (1944)

David-Neel, Alexandra, *Magic and Mystery in Tibet*, Abacus, London 1977 (1931)
Davidson, Hilda Ellis, ed., *The Seer in Celtic and Other Traditions*, John Donald, Edinburgh 1989
Davis, Michael, *William Blake: A New Kind of Man*, University of California Press, Berkeley 1977
Dee, Dr John, *The Rosie Crucian Secrets*, Aquarian, Wellingborough 1985
Devereux, Paul, *Earthlights*, Turnstone Press, London 1982
Dick, Philip K., *Valis*, Bantam, New York 1981
The Transmigration of Timothy Archer, Pocket Books, New York 1983
Radio Free Albemuth, Grafton/Collins, London 1987
Donnelly, Ignatius, *Atlantis, the Antediluvian World*, Sidgwick and Jackson, London 1970
Downing, Barry H., *The Bible and Flying Saucers*, Avon, New York 1970
Drake, W. Raymond, *Gods and Spacemen in the Ancient East*, Sphere, London 1973
Drury, Nevill, *Don Juan, Mescalito and Modern Magic*, Arkana, London 1986
Dunne, J. W., *An Experiment with Time*, Faber and Faber, London 1927

Eco, Umberto, *Foucault's Pendulum*, Picador, London 1990
Evans-Wentz, W. Y., *The Tibetan Book of the Dead*, Oxford University Press 1927
The Fairy Faith in Celtic Countries, 1909

Feng, Gia-Fu, and English, Jane, *Tao Te Ching*, Wildwood House, London 1973
Ferguson, Marilyn, *The Aquarian Conspiracy*, Routledge Kegan Paul, London 1981
Fisher, Joe, *Hungry Ghosts*, Grafton, London 1990
The Case for Reincarnation, Grafton, London 1984
Fontbrune, Jean-Charles de, *Nostradamus: Countdown to Apocalypse*, Pan, London 1983
Fort, Charles, *The Complete Books of Charles Fort*, Dover, New York 1974
Fortune, Dion, *The Mystical Qabalah*, Benn, London 1966
Psychic Self-Defence, Aquarian Wellingborough, 1977
Fox, Oliver, *Astral Projection*, Citadel Press, New Jersey 1962
Francis, David Pitt, *Nostradamus: Prophecies of Present Times?* Aquarian, Wellingborough 1985
Fraser, James, *The Golden Bough*, Macmillan, London 1963 (1922)
Fuller, John G., *The Day of St Anthony's Fire*, Hutchinson, London 1969

Gale-Kumar, Kristina, *The Phoenix Returns*, Cardinal, Hawaii 1983
Gardner, Gerald, *Witchcraft Today*, Rider, London 1954
Garrett, Eileen, *My Life*, Psychic Book Club, London 1939
Gauquelin, Michel, *The Cosmic Clocks*, Peter Owen, London 1969

Gittelson, Bernard, *Intangible Evidence*, Simon and Schuster, London 1987
Gleick, James, *Chaos*, Sphere Cardinal, London 1987
Gooch, Stan, *Total Man*, Allen Lane (Penguin), London 1972
The Neanderthal Question, Wildwood House, London 1977
The Paranormal, Wildwood House, London 1978
The Secret Life of Humans, Dent, London 1981
Creatures from Inner Space, Rider, London 1984
Goodman, Jeffrey, *Psychic Archaeology*, Berkley, New York 1977
We Are The Earthquake Generation, Seaview, New York 1978
Goss, Michael, *The Evidence for Phantom Hitch-Hikers*, Aquarian, Wellingborough 1984
Gribbin, John, *Timewarps*, Dent, London 1979
Graves, Robert, *The White Goddess*, Faber and Faber, London 1961 (1946)
Graves, Tom, *Needles of Stone Revisited*, Gothic Image, Glastonbury 1986
Guirdham, Arthur, *The Cathars and Reincarnation*, Turnstone, London 1982 (1970)
The Great Heresy, Spearman, Sudbury 1977
The Psyche in Medicine, Spearman, Sudbury 1978
Gurdjieff, G. I., *Meetings with Remarkable Men*, Routledge Kegan Paul, London 1963

Harding, M. Esther, *Woman's Mysteries*, Rider, London 1982 (1955)
Harrison, Michael, *Fire From Heaven*, Pan, London 1977
Harvey, David, *The Power to Heal*, Aquarian, Wellingborough 1983
Hawken, Paul, *The Magic of Findhorn*, Fontana, London 1976
Hendry, Allan, *The UFO Handbook*, Sphere, London 1980
Herrigel, Eugen, *Zen in the Art of Archery*, Routledge Kegan Paul, London 1972 (1953)
Heywood, Rosalind, *The Infinite Hive*, Pan, London 1966
Hippesley Coxe, Anthony D., *Haunted Britain*, Hutchinson, London 1973
Hitching, Francis, *Earth Magic*, Picador, London 1977
Pendulum: the Psi Connection, Fontana, London 1977
Hoeller, Stephan A., *The Gnostic Jung*, Quest, Wheaton, Illinois 1982
Holiday, F. W., *The Great Orm of Loch Ness*, Faber and Faber, London 1968
The Dragon and the Disc, Sidgwick and Jackson, London 1973
Holmyard, E. J., *Alchemy*, Penguin, London 1968
Holroyd, Stuart, *Alien Intelligence*, Abacus, London 1980
Howe, Ellic, *The Magicians of the Golden Dawn*, Routledge Kegan Paul, London 1972
Huxley, Aldous, *The Doors of Perception/Heaven & Hell*, Granada 1984 (1954/1956)

Inglis, Brian, *The Unknown Guest*, Chatto and Windus, London 1987
The Hidden Power, Jonathan Cape, London 1986

James, William, *The Varieties of Religious Experience*, Fontana, London 1960
Jaynes, Julian, *The Origin of Consciousness in the Breakdown of the Bicameral Mind*, Houghton Mifflin, Boston 1976
Jochmans, J. R., *Rolling Thunder*, Sun Books, Santa Fé 1980
Jones, G. and T. J. , (trans.), *The Mabinogion*, Dent, London 1984 (1949)
Jung, C. G., *Dreams*, Ark Books, London 1985
Memories, Dreams and Reflections, Fontana, London 1967
Man and his Symbols (ed), Aldus Books, London 1964
Synchronicity: An Acausal Connecting Principle, Routledge Kegan Paul, London 1972

Kardec, Allen, *The Mediums' Book*, Psychic Press, London 1971
Keel, John A., *Our Haunted Planet*, Spearman, London 1971
Operation Trojan Horse, Abacus, London 1973
The Mothman Prophecies, Dutton, New York 1975
Knight, Damon, *Charles Fort: Prophet of the Unexplained*, Gollancz, London 1971

Knight, Gareth, *A Practical Guide to Qabalistic Symbolism*, (2 vols.), Helios, Cheltenham 1965
The Rose Cross and the Goddess, Aquarian, Wellingborough 1985
Koestler, Arthur, *The Act of Creation*, Hutchinson, London 1964
The Roots of Coincidence, Pan Picador, London 1972
Janus, Pan Picador, London 1979
The Sleepwalkers, Penguin, London 1988
Krippner, Stanley, and Daniel, Rubin, *Galaxies of Life: the Human Aura in Acupuncture and Kirlian Photography*, Gordon and Breach, New York 1973
Kübler-Ross, Elizabeth, *On Death and Dying*, Macmillan, London 1969
Kuhn, Thomas, *The Structure of Scientific Revolutions*, University of Chicago Press, 1970

Larsen, Stephen, *The Shaman's Doorway*, Harper Colophon, New York 1977
Larson, Bob, *Larson's Book of Cults*, Tyndale, Illinois, 1989
Lemesurier, Peter, *The Great Pyramid Decoded*, Element, Shaftesbury 1977
The Armageddon Script, Element, Shaftesbury, 1981
LeShan, Lawrence, *The Science of the Paranormal*, Aquarian, Wellingborough 1987
Lethbridge, T. C., *A Step in the Dark*, Routledge Kegan Paul, London 1967
The Power of the Pendulum, Arkana, London 1984 (1976)
The Legend of the Sons of God, Arkana, London 1990 (1972)
Lévi, Éliphas, *The History of Magic*, Rider, London 1959
Lewis, C. S., *Out of the Silent Planet*, Pan, London 1952 (1938)
Voyage to Venus (Perelandra), Pan, London 1953 (1943)
That Hideous Strength, Pan, London 1955 (1945)
Lilly, John C., *The Centre of the Cyclone*, Paladin, London 1973
Lindsay, David, *A Voyage to Arcturus*, Gollancz, London 1963 (1920)
Lindsay, Hal, *The Late Great Planet Earth*, Zondervan, Michigan, 1970
Lissau, Rudi, *Rudolf Steiner*, Hawthorn Press, Stroud 1987
Long, Max Freedom, *The Secret Science Behind Miracles*, DeVorss, USA 1981
Lorimer, David, *Survival?*, Routledge Kegan Paul, London 1984
Lovelock, James, *Gaia: A New Look at Life on Earth*, Oxford University Press, 1979

Mackenzie, Alexander, *The Prophecies of the Brahan Seer*, Constable, London 1977 (1877)
Markides, Kyriacos C., *The Magus of Strovolos*, Arkana, London 1985
Homage to the Sun, Arkana, London 1987
Mathers, S. L., *The Kabbalah Unveiled*, Routledge Kegan Paul, London 1951
Michell, John, *The Flying Saucer Vision*, Sidgwick and Jackson, London 1967
City of Revelation, Abacus, London 1973
The Earth Spirit, Avon, New York 1975
The New View Over Atlantis, Thames and Hudson, London 1983
The Dimensions of Paradise, Thames and Hudson, London 1989
Mishlove, Jeffrey, *The Roots of Consciousness*, Random House, New York 1975
Monroe, Robert A., *Journeys out of the Body*, Souvenir Press, London 1972
Far Journeys, Souvenir Press, London 1986
Moody, Raymond M., *Life After Life*, Bantam, New York 1977
Moses, Stainton, *Spirit Teachings*, Spiritualist Press, London 1949
Muldoon, Sylvan, and Carrington, Hereward, *The Projection of the Astral Body*, Rider, London 1968
The Phenomena of Astral Projection, Rider, London 1969
Myers, F. W. H., *Human Personality and its Survival of Bodily Death*, University Books, New York 1961 (1903)

Noone, Richard, *Ice: The Ultimate Disaster*, Genesis, Georgia 1982

O'Brien, Christian, *The Megalithic Odyssey*, Turnstone, London 1983

The Genius of the Few, Turnstone, London 1985
Oldfield, Harry and Coghill, Roger, *The Dark Side of the Brain*, Element, Shaftesbury 1988
O'Neill, John J., *Prodigal Genius*, Spearman, London 1969
Ostrander, Shiela, and Shroeder, Lynn, *Psychic Discoveries Behind the Iron Curtain*, Sphere, London 1973
Ouspensky, P. D., *A New Model of the Universe*, Routledge Kegan Paul, London 1969
In Search of the Miraculous, Routledge Kegan Paul, London 1969

Pagels, Elaine, *The Gnostic Gospels*, Pelican, London 1982
Pálos, Stephan, *The Chinese Art of Healing*, Bantam, New York 1972
Pearsall, Ronald, *The Alchemists*, Weidenfeld and Nicolson, London 1976
Pennick, Nigel, *Sacred Geometry*, Turnstone, London 1980
Plato, *Timaeus and Critias* (trans. Desmond Lee), Penguin, London 1971
Playfair, Guy, *The Flying Cow*, Souvenir Press, London 1975
The Indefinite Boundary, Souvenir Press, London 1976
Post, Laurens van der, *Jung and the Story of Our Time*, Penguin, London 1978
Prophet, Elizabeth Clare, *Forbidden Mysteries of Enoch*, Summit University Press, USA 1983
Puharich, Andrija, *Uri*, Futura, London 1974
Purucker, G. de, *An Occult Glossary*, Theosophical University Press, California 1969 (1933)

Randles, Jenny, and Fuller, Paul, *Crop Circles*, Hale, London 1990
Regardie, Israel, *The Tree of Life*, Rider, London 1937
The Art and Meaning of Magic, Helios, Cheltenham 1964
The Art of True Healing, Helios, Cheltenham 1966
The Philosopher's Stone, Llewellyn, USA 1970
The Golden Dawn, Llewellyn, USA 1972
The Eye in the Triangle: An Interpretation of Aleister Crowley, Falcon Press, Las Vegas 1989
Reich, Wilhelm, *Selected Writings*, Farrar, Strauss and Giroux, New York 1979
Reichenbach, Karl von, *The Odic Force*, University Books, New York 1968
Robinson, James M. (ed.), *The Nag Hammadi Library*, Harper and Row, New York 1981
Rogo, D. Scott, *Life After Death*, Aquarian, Wellingborough 1986
The Infinite Boundary, Aquarian, Wellingborough 1988
Roy, Archie E., *A Sense of Something Strange*, Dog and Bone, Glasgow 1990
Runciman, Steven, *The Medieval Manichee*, Cambridge University Press 1982 (1947)
Rush, Anne Kent, *Moon, Moon*, Random House, New York 1976
Rycroft, Charles, *Reich*, Fontana, London 1971

Sabom, Michael, *Recollections of Death*, Corgi, London 1982
Sagan, Carl, *Cosmos*, Macdonald, London 1981
Santesson, Hans Stefan, *Understanding Mu*, Paperback Library, New York 1970
Schuré, Edouard, *The Great Initiates*, Harper and Row, New York 1980 (1889)
Seymour, Percy, *Astrology: The Evidence of Science*, Arkana, London 1990
Seymour-Smith, Martin, *The New Astrologer*, Sidgwick and Jackson, London 1981
Shah, Idries, *The Secret Lore of Magic*, Muller, London 1957
The Sufis, Doubleday, New York 1964
Sheldrake, Rupert, *A New Science of Life*, Blond and Briggs, London 1981
The Presence of the Past, Vintage/Random House, New York 1989
Spence, Lewis, *Encyclopaedia of Occultism*, University Books, New York 1960 (1920)
The Magic Arts in Celtic Britain, Rider, London 1970 (1946)
Steiner, Rudolf, *An Outline of Occult Science*, Rand McNally, New York 1914
Reincarnation and Immortality, Rudolf Steiner Publications, New York 1970
Stevenson, Ian, *Twenty Cases Suggestive of Reincarnation*, American Society for Psychical Research, New York 1966
Stewart, R. J., *The Prophetic Vision of Merlin*, Arkana, London 1986

Prophecy, Element, Shaftesbury 1990
Stirling, William, *The Canon*, Garnstone Press, London 1974 (1897)
Story, Ronald, *Guardians of the Universe?* New English Library, London 1980
Streiber, Whitley, *Communion*, Arrow/Hutchinson, London 1988
Transformation, Arrow/Hutchinson, London 1989
Summers, Montague, *History of Witchcraft*, University Books, New York 1956
Sutherland, Elizabeth, *Ravens and Black Rain*, Corgi, London 1987
Suzuki, D. T., *An Introduction to Zen Buddhism*, Rider, London 1969
Swann, Ingo, *To Kiss Earth Goodbye*, Hawthorn Books, New York 1975

Tansley, David, *Omens of Awareness*, Spearman, Sudbury 1977
Targ, Russell, and Puthoff, Harold, *Mind-Reach*, Paladin, London 1978
Tart, Charles, *Altered States of Consciousness*, Doubleday, New York 1969
Taylor, Gordon Rattray, *The Natural History of the Mind*, Paladin, London 1981
Temple, Robert K. G., *The Sirius Mystery*, Sidgwick and Jackson, London 1976
Thom, Alexander, *Megalithic Sites in Britain*, Oxford University Press 1967
Megalithic Lunar Observatories, Oxford University Press, UK 1971
Thomas, Keith, *Religiion and the Decline of Magic*, Peregrine, London 1978
Tolstoy, Nikolai, *The Quest for Merlin*, Sceptre, London 1988
Tompkins, Peter, *The Secrets of the Great Pyramid*, Allen Lane, London 1973
The Secret Life of Plants, (with Bird, C.), Harper and Row, New York 1973
Trevelyan, Sir George, and Matchett, Edward, *Twelve Seats at the Round Table*, Spearman, Sudbury 1976

Valiente, Doreen, *An ABC of Witchcraft Past and Present*, Hale, London 1971, revised 1984
Vallée, Jacques, *Messengers of Deception*, And/Or Press, Berkeley, California 1979
Dimensions, Sphere, London 1990
Vaughan, Alan, *Patterns of Prophecy*, Dell, New York 1976
Velikovsky, Immanuel, *Worlds in Collision*, Abacus, London 1972 (1950)
Earth in Upheaval, Gollancz, London 1956
Mankind in Amnesia, Abacus, London 1983
Vogh, James, *The Thirteenth Zodiac*, Granada/Mayflower, London 1979

Waite, A. E., *The Pictorial Key to the Tarot*, Weiser, New York 1977 (1910)
The Book of Ceremonial Magic, University Books, New York 1961
Waters, Frank, *Book of the Hopi*, Penguin, London 1977 (1963)
Watson, Godfrey, *Bothwell and the Witches*, Hale, London 1975
Watson, Lyall, *Supernature*, Hodder and Stoughton, London 1973
The Romeo Error, Coronet/Hodder and Stoughton, London 1976
Lifetide, Coronet/Hodder and Stoughton, London 1980
Dreams of Dragons, Sceptre/Hodder and Stoughton, London 1987
Beyond Supernature, Hodder and Stoughton, London 1986
Watts, Alan, *The Way of Zen*, Penguin, London 1957
White, John, *Pole Shift*, W. H. Allen, London 1980
Wilhelm, Richard (trans.), *I Ching*, Routledge Kegan Paul, London 1951
The Secret of the Golden Flower, Arkana, London 1984 (1931)
Wilson, Colin, *The Occult*, Grafton/Collins, London 1979 (1971)
Order of Assassins, Panther Granada, London 1975
Mysteries, Grafton/Collins, London 1979
Starseekers, Hodder and Stoughton, London 1980
Frankenstein's Castle, Ashgrove Press, Bath 1980
Poltergeist, New English Library, London 1981
Afterlife, Grafton/Collins, London 1987
Beyond the Occult, Corgi, London 1989

Wilson, Ian, *The Turin Shroud*, Penguin, London 1979
The After-Death Experience, Corgi, London 1989
Superself, Sidgwick and Jackson, London 1989
Wilson, Peter Lamborn, *Angels*, Thames and Hudson, London 1980
Wilson, Robert Anton, *Prometheus Rising*, Falcon Press, Las Vegas 1983
Wood, David, *Genisis*, Baton Press, Tunbridge Wells, 1985

Yates, Frances A., *Giordano Bruno and the Hermetic Tradition*, Routledge Kegan Paul, London 1964
The Art of Memory, Routledge Kegan Paul, London 1966
The Rosicrucian Enlightenment, Routledge Kegan Paul, London 1972
The Occult Philosophy, Routledge Kegan Paul, London 1979